ELIZABETH BISHOP IN CONTEXT

Elizabeth Bishop is increasingly recognised as one of the twentieth century's most original writers. Consisting of thirty-five groundbreaking essays by an international team of authors, including biographers, literary critics, poets, and translators, this volume addresses the biographical and literary inception of Bishop's originality, from her formative upbringing in New England and Nova Scotia to long residences in New York, France, Florida, and Brazil. Her poetry, prose, letters, translations, and visual art are analyzed in turn, followed by detailed studies of literary movements such as surrealism and modernism that influenced her artistic development. Bishop's encounters with nature, music, psychoanalysis, and religion receive extended treatment, likewise her interest in dreams and humour. Essays also investigate the impact of twentieth-century history and politics on Bishop's life writing, and what it means to read Bishop via eco-criticism, postcolonial theory, and queer studies.

ANGUS CLEGHORN is editor of *Elizabeth Bishop in the 21st Century: Reading the New Editions* (2012), *The Cambridge Companion to Elizabeth Bishop* (2014), and *Elizabeth Bishop and the Music of Literature* (2019). He co-organized an "Elizabeth Bishop in Paris" conference at the Sorbonne in 2018.

JONATHAN ELLIS is the author or editor of *Art and Memory in the Work of Elizabeth Bishop* (2006), *The Cambridge Companion to Elizabeth Bishop* (2014), *Letter Writing Among Poets* (2015), and *Reading Elizabeth Bishop: An Edinburgh Companion* (2019). He is also the author of a map of Elizabeth Bishop's Paris (2018).

ELIZABETH BISHOP IN CONTEXT

EDITED BY

ANGUS CLEGHORN

Seneca College, Canada

JONATHAN ELLIS

University of Sheffield

CAMBRIDGE
UNIVERSITY PRESS

CAMBRIDGE
UNIVERSITY PRESS

University Printing House, Cambridge CB2 8BS, United Kingdom

One Liberty Plaza, 20th Floor, New York, NY 10006, USA

477 Williamstown Road, Port Melbourne, VIC 3207, Australia

314–321, 3rd Floor, Plot 3, Splendor Forum, Jasola District Centre, New Delhi – 110025, India

79 Anson Road, #06–04/06, Singapore 079906

Cambridge University Press is part of the University of Cambridge.

It furthers the University's mission by disseminating knowledge in the pursuit of education, learning, and research at the highest international levels of excellence.

www.cambridge.org
Information on this title: www.cambridge.org/9781108495974
DOI: 10.1017/9781108856492

First published 2021

A catalogue record for this publication is available from the British Library.

Library of Congress Cataloging-in-Publication Data
NAMES: Cleghorn, Angus J., editor. | Ellis, Jonathan, 1975– editor.
TITLE: Elizabeth Bishop in context / edited by Angus Cleghorn, Seneca College, Canada, Jonathan Ellis, University of Sheffield.
DESCRIPTION: Cambridge ; New York : Cambridge University Press, 2021. | Series: Literature in context | Includes bibliographical references and index.
IDENTIFIERS: LCCN 2020058018 (print) | LCCN 2020058019 (ebook) | ISBN 9781108495974 (hardback) | ISBN 9781108856492 (ebook)
SUBJECTS: LCSH: Bishop, Elizabeth, 1911–1979 – Criticism and interpretation. | BISAC: LITERARY CRITICISM / American / General | LITERARY CRITICISM / American / General
CLASSIFICATION: LCC PS3503.I785 Z654 2021 (print) | LCC PS3503.I785 (ebook) | DDC 811/.54–dc23
LC record available at https://lccn.loc.gov/2020058018
LC ebook record available at https://lccn.loc.gov/2020058019

ISBN 978-1-108-49597-4 Hardback

Contents

Figure

Contributors

LINDA ANDERSON is Professor of Modern English and American Literature at Newcastle University and the author of *Elizabeth Bishop: Lines of Connection* (2013) and numerous essays on Bishop. Recently she has edited, with Mark Byers and Ahren Warner, *The Contemporary Poetry Archive: Essays and Interventions* (2019) and has published her first poetry collection, *The Station Before* (2020).

STEVEN GOULD AXELROD is Distinguished Professor of English at the University of California, Riverside. He is the author of *Robert Lowell: Life and Art*, *Sylvia Plath: The Wound and the Cure of Words* (1990) and articles on Elizabeth Bishop in *American Literature*, *Arizona Quarterly*, and elsewhere. He is co-editor of *The New Anthology of American Poetry*, Volumes 1–3 (2012). His most recent co-edited volume, *The Memoirs of Robert Lowell*, will be published by Farrar, Straus and Giroux in 2021.

SANDRA BARRY is a poet and an independent scholar. She is a co-founder of the Elizabeth Bishop Society of Nova Scotia. She co-owned and administered (2004–15) the Elizabeth Bishop House Artists' Retreat in Great Village, Nova Scotia. She co-edited *Divisions of the Heart: Elizabeth Bishop and the Art of Memory and Place* (2001). Her biography, *Elizabeth Bishop: Nova Scotia's "Home-Made" Poet*, was published in 2011.

CHARLES BERGER is the author of *Forms of Farewell: The Late Poetry of Wallace Stevens* (1985). Recipient of a Guggenheim Fellowship, he has written many essays on modern and contemporary American and British poetry. He is Professor of English Language and Literature at Southern Illinois University Edwardsville.

NEIL BESNER was born in Montréal and grew up in Brazil, where he has traveled and taught widely, mainly on Canadian literature. He taught at the University of Winnipeg for thirty years, retiring in 2017 as Vice-

President, Academic. His prize-winning translation from Portuguese into English of *Rare and Commonplace Flowers: The Story of Elizabeth Bishop and Lota de Macedo Soares* (2002), written by Carmen Oliveira in Brazil, was a major source for the 2013 feature film *Reaching for the Moon*.

STEPHANIE BURT is Professor of English at Harvard. Her recent books include *After Callimachus* (2020), *Don't Read Poetry: A Book About How to Read Poems* (2019), and *Advice from the Lights* (2017). Her poems, reviews, and essays on poetry, comic books, gender, and other matters appear semi-regularly in *The London Review of Books*, *The New York Times Book Review*, and other journals in the USA, UK, and New Zealand. With Carmen Gimenez Smith, she is co-poetry editor for *The Nation*.

ANGUS CLEGHORN is Professor of English & Liberal Studies at Seneca College in Toronto. He is the author of *Wallace Stevens' Poetics: The Neglected Rhetoric* (2000), twice guest editor of *The Wallace Stevens Journal*, co-editor of *Elizabeth Bishop in the 21st Century: Reading the New Editions* (2012) and *The Cambridge Companion to Elizabeth Bishop* (2014), as well as editor of *Elizabeth Bishop and the Music of Literature* (2019). His essays on Bishop and Stevens appear in various critical collections and journals.

BONNIE COSTELLO is William Fairfield Warren Distinguished Professor and Professor of English Emerita at Boston University. Best known for her work on Marianne Moore, Elizabeth Bishop, and Wallace Stevens, her most recent books are *Shifting Ground: Reinventing Landscape in Modern American Poetry* (2003), *Planets on Tables: Poetry, Still Life and the Turning World* (2008), and *The Plural of Us: Poetry and Community in Auden and Others* (2017). She has also published creative nonfiction and is working on a collection of essays entitled *Changing Places*. Professor Costello was elected to the American Academy of Arts and Sciences in 2004.

JONATHAN ELLIS is Reader in American Literature at the University of Sheffield. He is the author of *Art and Memory in the Work of Elizabeth Bishop* (2006), co-editor of *The Cambridge Companion to Elizabeth Bishop* (2014), and editor of *Letter Writing Among Poets: From William Wordsworth to Elizabeth Bishop* (2015) and *Reading Elizabeth Bishop: An Edinburgh Companion* (2019). His nonfiction work has appeared in *The Letters Page*, *The Manchester Review*, and *The*

Tangerine. He is currently writing a book on letter writing for Oxford University Press.

ANDREW EPSTEIN is a Professor of English at Florida State University. He is the author of *Attention Equals Life: The Pursuit of the Everyday in Contemporary Poetry and Culture* (2016) and *Beautiful Enemies: Friendship and Postwar American Poetry* (2006). His essays have appeared in *Contemporary Literature*, *The Wallace Stevens Journal*, *The Cambridge Companion to American Poets*, *Wallace Stevens in Context*, and many other publications.

JO GILL is Pro-Vice-Chancellor of the College of Humanities and Professor of Twentieth-Century and American Literature at the University of Exeter, UK. She is the author of *The Poetics of the American Suburbs* (2013) and *Anne Sexton's Confessional Poetics* (2007), and the editor of *The Cambridge Companion to Sylvia Plath* (2006). She is a recent holder of a Leverhulme Trust Research Fellowship for the forthcoming book, *Modern American Poetry and the Architectural Imagination*, which includes a chapter on Bishop's engagement with architecture.

LORRIE GOLDENSOHN's poems have appeared over decades in journals like *Salmagundi*, *American Poetry Review*, and *The New Republic*. Her books on poetry include *Elizabeth Bishop: The Biography of a Poetry* (1992), *Dismantling Glory: 20th Century American and English Soldier Poets* (2003), and *American War Poetry: An Anthology* (2006). She has published many essays on literary subjects (*Ploughshares*, *Parnassus*, and *The Yale Review*) and in critical volumes from 1993 (*Elizabeth Bishop: The Geography of Gender*) to 2014 (*The Cambridge Companion to Elizabeth Bishop*).

LISA GOLDFARB is Professor at New York University's Gallatin School, President of *The Wallace Stevens Society*, and Associate Editor of *The Wallace Stevens Journal*. She is the author of *The Figure Concealed: Wallace Stevens, Music, and Valéryan Echoes* (2010) and *Unexpected Affinities: Modern American Poetry and Symbolist Poetics* (2018), and co-editor of several edited collections on Stevens. She has recently contributed a chapter to *Elizabeth Bishop and the Music of Literature* (2019).

JEFFREY GRAY is the author of numerous articles on American poetry and of the book *Mastery's End: Travel and Postwar American Poetry* (2005).

He is co-editor, with Ann Keniston, of *The News from Poems: Essays on the New American Poetry of Engagement* (2016). His poetry has appeared in *The American Poetry Review*, *The Atlantic*, *Yale Review*, *PN Review*, and other journals. He is a professor of English at Seton Hall University and lives in Ocean Grove, New Jersey, and Alghero, Sardinia.

LANGDON HAMMER is Niel Gray Jr. Professor of English at Yale University. He is the author of *James Merrill: Life and Art* (2015) and the editor of the Library of America's *Hart Crane: Complete Poetry and Selected Letters* (2006) and *May Swenson: Collected Poems* (2013). He writes about poetry for *The New York Review of Books*, *The Yale Review*, and *The American Scholar*, where he has been poetry editor since 2004. He is currently writing a critical biography of Elizabeth Bishop.

BETHANY HICOK is Lecturer in English at Williams College. She is the author of *Degrees of Freedom: American Women Poets and the Women's College, 1905–1955* (2008) and *Elizabeth Bishop's Brazil* (2016), editor of *Elizabeth Bishop and the Literary Archive* (2020), and co-editor of *Elizabeth Bishop in the 21st Century: Reading the New Editions* (2012). Hicok is also the recipient of a 2017 NEH grant.

KAMRAN JAVADIZADEH is Associate Professor of English at Villanova University, where he works on the history of poetry and poetics. He is the author of *Institutionalized Lyric* (forthcoming from Oxford University Press). His essays appear or are forthcoming in *PMLA*, *Modernism/modernity*, *Arizona Quarterly*, *The Yale Review*, *The New Yorker*, *The New York Review of Books*, and *The Point*.

SARAH KENNEDY has published on a variety of topics in modern and contemporary poetry. She is the author of *T. S. Eliot and the Dynamic Imagination* (2018) and is currently working on a study of twentieth century poetry, landscape, and literary selfhood. Her essay on Eliot and Stevens published in the *Wallace Stevens Journal* won the 2019 John Serio Award. She is a Fellow of Downing College, Cambridge.

MARIANA MACHOVÁ is a translator and Associate Professor of American literature at Charles University, Prague, and at the University of South Bohemia. She translated Elizabeth Bishop's poetry and prose into Czech and is the author of *Elizabeth Bishop and Translation* (2017), in which she examines the role of translation in Bishop's works.

MARIANNE MACRAE is a freelance writer and academic based in Edinburgh. She holds a PhD in Creative Writing from the University of Edinburgh. Her primary research interests are contemporary poetry, animal poetry, and the poetics of grief and loss. She is a 2020 Scottish Book Trust New Writers Awardee. Her debut poetry pamphlet, *Recital*, is forthcoming from Tapsalteerie.

PHILIP MCGOWAN is Professor of American Literature at Queen's University Belfast and President of the European Association for American Studies (2016–24). He has published articles on the poetry of John Berryman, Elizabeth Bishop, and Anne Sexton, and the fiction of Nelson Algren, Saul Bellow, and most recently F. Scott Fitzgerald. He edited the centenary edition of Fitzgerald's *This Side of Paradise* (Oxford World's Classics, 2020).

MARIA LÚCIA MILLÉO MARTINS is a retired volunteer professor in the Graduate Program in English at Universidade Federal de Santa Catarina. She has published *Antologia de Poesia Norte-Americana Contemporânea* (as translator in 1997), *Duas Artes: Carlos Drummond de Andrade e Elizabeth Bishop* (2006, the first critical study on Bishop in book form published in Brazil), and *Poesia Canadense Contemporânea e Multiculturalismo* (2018). Currently, she is working on a translation project of Charles Simic's poetry, memoir, and critical essays.

BARBARA PAGE is retired Helen D. Lockwood Professor of English at Vassar College. Among her essays on Elizabeth Bishop are "Off-Beat Claves, Oblique Realities: The Key West Notebooks of Elizabeth Bishop" from *The Geography of Gender* (1993) and "Home, Wherever That May Be: Poems and Prose of Brazil" from *The Cambridge Companion to Elizabeth Bishop* (2014).

SANDEEP PARMAR is a poet, critic, and Professor of English Literature at the University of Liverpool, where she also co-directs the Centre for New and International Writing. She edited *The Selected Poems of Nancy Cunard* (2016), *The Collected Poems of Hope Mirrlees* (2011), and is the author of *Reading Mina Loy's Autobiographies: Myth of the Modern Woman* (2013). She currently writes on contemporary British and American poetry and race. Her poetry collections include *The Marble Orchard* (2012) and *Eidolon* (2015).

VIDYAN RAVINTHIRAN is an Associate Professor at Harvard University. *Elizabeth Bishop's Prosaic* (2015) won both the University English Prize and the Warren-Brooks Award for Outstanding Literary Criticism. He is also the author of two books of poetry: *The Million-Petalled Flower of*

Being Here (2019) won a Northern Writers Award, was a PBS Recommendation, and was shortlisted for the Forward and the T. S. Eliot Prizes.

DERYN REES-JONES is a poet and critic. She teaches at the University of Liverpool where she is Professor of Poetry and editor of the Pavilion Poetry series for Liverpool University Press. Her latest poetry collection, *Erato* (2019), was shortlisted for the T. S. Eliot Prize in 2019 and Wales Book of the Year in 2020. Her most recent critical book is *Paula Rego: The Art of Story* (2019). EIRA MURPHY is an undergraduate at the University of Oxford.

LLOYD SCHWARTZ has been writing about Elizabeth Bishop and editing her work for forty years. His books include *Elizabeth Bishop and Her Art* (1983), the Library of America's *Bishop: Poems, Prose, and Letters* (2008), and Bishop's *Prose* (2011). He's been awarded Guggenheim and NEA fellowships in poetry and the Pulitzer Prize in criticism. He's the classical music critic for NPR's *Fresh Air* and Poet Laureate of Somerville, Massachusetts. His latest poetry collection is *Little Kisses* (2017).

MICHAEL D. SNEDIKER is the author of *Contingent Figure: Chronic Pain & the Queerness of Embodiment* (forthcoming) and *Queer Optimism: Lyric Personhood & Other Felicitous Persuasions* (2009), a finalist for the MLA First Book Prize and the Phi Beta Kappa Christian Gauss Prize. His most recent book of poems, *The New York Editions* (2018), won the Poets Out Loud Prize. He is Associate Professor of American Literature & Poetics at the University of Houston.

CHRISTOPHER SPAIDE is a Junior Fellow in the Society of Fellows at Harvard University. His book project, "Lyric Togetherness," examines the plural pronouns and collective voices of American poetry from 1945 to today. His essays, reviews, and poems have appeared or are forthcoming in *College Literature*, *Contemporary Literature*, *Harvard Review*, *Poetry*, and *The Yale Review*.

PETER SWAAB is Professor of English Literature at University College London. He is the editor of the *Selected Nonsense and Travel Writings of Edward Lear* (2005) and of the first editions of poetry and prose by Sara Coleridge. His other publications include a BFI Film Classic book on *Bringing Up Baby* (2010) and a co-edited book about the British film director Thorold Dickinson. He edits the *Sylvia Townsend Warner Journal* and his next project is a book on Warner.

HEATHER TRESELER'S *Parturition* (2020) received the Munster Literature Centre's international chapbook prize, and her sequence of poems, "The Lucie Odes," won *Missouri Review*'s Editors' Prize (2019). Her poems appear in *Boston Review*, *Harvard Review*, *Cincinnati Review*, and *PN Review*, and her essays appear in *The Los Angeles Review of Books* and in seven books of criticism. She is Associate Professor of English at Worcester State University and a visiting scholar at the Brandeis Women's Studies Research Center.

THOMAS TRAVISANO is Founding President of the Elizabeth Bishop Society, author of *Love Unknown: The Life and Worlds of Elizabeth Bishop* (2019), as well as *Midcentury Quartet: Bishop, Lowell, Jarrell, Berryman* (1999), and *Elizabeth Bishop: Her Artistic Development* (1988). He is principal editor of *Words in Air: The Complete Correspondence between Elizabeth Bishop and Robert Lowell* (2008), and co-editor of *Gendered Modernisms: American Women Poets and Their Readers* (1996) and *Elizabeth Bishop in the 21st Century* (2012). He is Emeritus Professor of English at Hartwick College.

RACHEL TROUSDALE is Associate Professor of English at Framingham State University. Her scholarly work includes *Nabokov, Rushdie, and the Transnational Imagination* (2010), *Humor in Modern American Poetry* (2017), and, forthcoming, *The Joking Voice: Humor and Empathy in Twentieth-Century American Poetry*. She also writes poetry. More information is available at www.racheltrousdale.com.

CHERYL LAWSON WALKER is Professor of English at Scripps College and the author of six books including four about American women poets. *God and Elizabeth Bishop: Meditations on Religion and Poetry* was published in 2005.

GILLIAN WHITE teaches English at the University of Michigan in Ann Arbor. She is the author of *Lyric Shame: The 'Lyric' Subject of Contemporary American Poetry* (2014). Her essays on Elizabeth Bishop have appeared in the *London Review of Books*, *Twentieth-Century Literature*, and *Elizabeth Bishop in the Twenty-First Century*. She is working on a book about contemporary writing and genre theory.

Acknowledgements

A book this big incurs many debts (and at last count at least 1,489 emails). We've attempted to remember all of them.

Ray Ryan approached us to edit the book ("I'd like to do a book called *Elizabeth Bishop in Context*," the email began) and has been a constant and reassuring presence as we moved from book proposal to manuscript submission. Edgar Mendez has also assisted us regularly, particularly regarding the preparation of the manuscript.

At a very early stage of the project, even before contacting possible contributors, Tracy Brain very kindly shared her experience of editing *Sylvia Plath in Context*. In her acknowledgements to her collection, she credits the wise counsel of Terry Gifford, who edited *Ted Hughes in Context*. No doubt his advice is present in this volume too.

As we brainstormed chapter titles, we were in the middle of co-organising a conference on Elizabeth Bishop and Paris with Juliette Utard, Associate Professor at Université Paris-Sorbonne. In addition to giving us the chance to follow Bishop's footsteps around Paris, especially in and around the Jardin du Luxembourg near where Bishop and her friend Louise Crane stayed in an apartment, the conference also brought together several generations of Bishop scholars, many of whom were able to deliver the first drafts of chapters you will find here.

Shortly after this, the anonymous reviewers of the book proposal endorsed the project and offered us many insightful suggestions on how to improve it. We have acted on all of them. The main activity of editing the book has necessarily involved a continual transatlantic correspondence between the two co-editors and nearly forty contributors, all of whom have responded to our feedback with good humour and patience. We hope our contributors won't mind our singling out Marianne MacRae who stepped in at the very last minute to write her chapter when she was about to give birth. She completed the final changes as her daughter, Bonnie, was just a few weeks old.

Several of the contributors looked over the Chronology for us. It's not easy to get the facts right, particularly in relation to an author who travelled so much and had so many friends all over the world. Thanks to Sandra Barry, Neil Besner, Langdon Hammer, and Thomas Travisano, each of whom read several drafts of a constantly shifting document. Bishop famously admitted to having what she described as a "George-Washington-handicap. I can't tell a lie even for art, apparently; it takes an awful effort or a sudden jolt to make me alter facts" (*WIA* 402). Fingers crossed readers experience no sudden jolts on reading our account of her life and works. Mistakes, alas, are our own.

The Introduction has benefited from Steven Gould Axelrod and Heather Treseler's attentive reading. Catherine Greenwood, who arranged the works cited and index, has been an effective and unfussy research assistant. At the copy-editing stage, we have both enjoyed working with Ursula Acton.

Angus is grateful for the American Literature Association and Elizabeth Bishop Society that have brought many of the people in this book together, as well as subsequent conferences and good times with Jonathan Ellis in particular, who is a pleasure to work with. When I say that we rarely disagree on any editorial point, it sounds like a lie but is honestly the case. Thanks to my Seneca College students who continually show me how relevant and perceptive Bishop continues to be in so many ways, especially regarding the environment, animals, and people. My family – especially Julie, Andrew, Simon, Amanda, Gavin, Laura, Paul, and Janet – consistently enlarge the windows of my scholarly obsessions. I'd like to give a shout out to everyone determined to address the full realities of our difficult times rather than sequestering themselves among factions who fraction the truth and bury their heads in the sands of denial. My best friends Dale, Rob, Suzanne, Krys, Duncan, Duane, Dave and Cathy keep the pleasure principle going strong with good times in a beautiful northern Ontario environment that makes life enjoyable. Thanks also to my father for instilling passion for people, nature, learning, and seizing the day.

Jonathan is grateful to literally hundreds of undergraduate and postgraduate students whose sharp and subtle readings of Bishop's work continue to inspire and provoke his own writing. Angus Cleghorn is a calm and unflappable co-editor. Making the difficult "second" album has been just as fun as the first. The School of English at the University of Sheffield remains a friendly and inspiring institutional home. My best friends have thoughtfully not asked me about this book! I appear to have developed a habit of finishing books in "interesting" times. Even I couldn't have predicted a twenty-two-day strike *and* a global pandemic. In lockdown I have enjoyed sharing breakfasts with Amber Regis and Amy Ryall and Saturday night cocktails with James and Mel Healy Dufosse-Belton. Joe Bray and Hamish Mathison are great golf partners. Maddy Callaghan remains the quickest and most sympathetic respondent to my grouchy texts. Deryn Rees-Jones sends me the best postcards. Last but not least, my love and thanks to Ana María and Pablo, with whom I have shared a bittersweet lockdown and of course Friday film nights. Finally, we got to see *Groundhog Day* together.

On behalf of all the contributors to this book, we would like to pay particular thanks to Dean Rogers for assisting many of us with archival queries and Victoria Fox at Farrar, Straus and Giroux for generous help in arranging permissions.

Rollie McKenna's glorious but rarely seen 1961 photograph of Elizabeth Bishop graces the book's cover. Sincere thanks to Yale University Art Gallery for giving us permission to reproduce it. The original print was a gift of the artist and purchased with the A. Conger Goodyear B.A. 1899 Fund.

Note on Referencing and Abbreviations

Unless otherwise indicated, poems discussed in this volume are from Elizabeth Bishop, *Poems* (London: Chatto & Windus; New York: Farrar, Straus and Giroux, 2011).

EAP	Elizabeth Bishop, *Edgar Allan Poe & The Juke-Box: Uncollected Poems, Drafts, and Fragments*, ed. Alice Quinn (Manchester: Carcanet; New York: Farrar, Straus and Giroux, 2006).
EH	Elizabeth Bishop, *Exchanging Hats: Elizabeth Bishop Paintings*, ed. William Benton (Manchester: Carcanet; New York: Farrar, Straus and Giroux, 1996).
OA	Elizabeth Bishop, *One Art: Letters*, ed. Robert Giroux (London: Chatto & Windus; New York: Farrar, Straus and Giroux, 1994).
NYr	Elizabeth Bishop, *Elizabeth Bishop and The New Yorker: The Complete Correspondence*, ed. Joelle Biele (New York: Farrar, Straus and Giroux, 2011).
P	Elizabeth Bishop, *Poems* (London: Chatto & Windus; New York: Farrar, Straus and Giroux, 2011).
Pr	Elizabeth Bishop, *Prose*, ed. Lloyd Schwartz (London: Chatto & Windus; New York: Farrar, Straus and Giroux, 2011).
PPL	Elizabeth Bishop, *Poems, Prose, and Letters*, eds. Robert Giroux and Lloyd Schwartz (New York: Library of America, 2008).
VC	Elizabeth Bishop Collection, Vassar College Library, Poughkeepsie, New York.
WIA	Elizabeth Bishop and Robert Lowell, *Words in Air: The Complete Correspondence between Elizabeth Bishop and Robert Lowell*, ed. Thomas Travisano with Saskia Hamilton (London: Faber and Faber; New York: Farrar, Straus and Giroux, 2008).

Chronology

(*Italics* denote historical events)

1872 William Thomas Bishop (Bishop's father) is born in Worcester, Massachusetts, where he grows up and attends high school. Becomes vice president and manager of the John W. Bishop Co., a leading construction firm founded by his father.

1879 Gertrude May Bulmer (Bishop's mother) is born in Great Village, Nova Scotia, where she grows up and attends the village school. Gains her teaching licence and teaches school in Nova Scotia. Later trains and serves as a nurse in Boston, Massachusetts (1903–4 and 1905–7): sometime during this period, she meets William Bishop.

1908 June 22: William and Gertrude marry privately in New York City. They honeymoon in Jamaica and sail to Panama before setting up house at 875 Main Street in Worcester.

1911 February 8: Elizabeth Bishop born in Worcester, Massachusetts; the only child of William and Gertrude.

October 13: Bishop's father dies from Bright's disease and is buried in Hope Cemetery, Worcester.

1914 Spring: Gertrude is hospitalized in Brookline, and then in Norwood, Massachusetts, for a period of three months, during which Bishop lives with her aunt Maude Bulmer Shepherdson and uncle George Shepherdson in Revere, Massachusetts.

June 25: The Great Salem Fire destroys over one thousand buildings. Bishop watches the fire with her mother from the Bishops' summer home in Marblehead (see the posthumously published poem, "A Drunkard").

1914–18 *World War I. As a self-governing dominion of the British Empire but with no control of its foreign affairs, Canada is involved from the moment Great Britain declares war on Germany on August 4, 1914. The USA enters the war on April 6, 1917.*

1915 Spring: Bishop relocates with her mother from Revere to Great Village, Nova Scotia.

1916 June: Bishop's mother admits herself to the Nova Scotia Hospital in Dartmouth as a result of severe mental illness. Biographers differ about the causes of Gertrude's illness and her major symptoms.

Bishop stays with her maternal grandparents in Great Village where she attends Primer Class from fall 1916 to spring 1917.

1917 Winter: Bishop suffers severe bronchitis.

October: Bishop is taken by her paternal grandparents to live with them in Worcester. In her story "The Country Mouse" (1961), she recalls feeling very ill. "First came eczema, and then asthma."

December 6: The Halifax Harbour Explosion. Nearly two thousand people die following a collision between two ships, one laden with wartime explosives, in Halifax Harbour. The Nova Scotia Hospital, where Bishop's mother is confined, is damaged but functional enough to become a place for the injured to go to be operated on.

1918 February: Shortly before her seventh birthday she accompanies her aunt Florence Bishop to a dentist's appointment. She recalls what happens there twice in her work, first in her story "The Country Mouse," later in her poem "In the Waiting Room" (1970).

May: Moves in with her aunt Maude Bulmer Shepherdson and uncle George Shepherdson in Revere, Massachusetts. In letters to Dr. Ruth Foster written in 1947, Bishop revealed that she was sexually and physically abused by George Shepherdson from the age of eight until she was fourteen or fifteen.

1918–20 *Outbreak of Spanish flu, also known as the 1918 flu pandemic. It is estimated the pandemic infected around 500 million people, approximately a third of the world's population at the time. Around 500,000 Canadians and over 679,000 Americans die during the pandemic.*

1919 August: Returns to Nova Scotia with her aunt, Grace Bulmer (she changes her name to Grace Bulmer Bowers on marriage to

William Bowers in 1923). The journey was a dramatic one. The steamer on which they were travelling, the *North Star*, ran aground off Yarmouth. Although Bishop never lives for an extended period in Great Village again, she continues to make yearly summer trips throughout her adolescence and at other times of the year.

1923 Bishop's paternal grandparents, John W. Bishop and Sarah Bishop, die within a few days of each other. Bishop is left $10,000 in John W. Bishop's will, a sum of money which, combined with an inheritance from her father, allowed her to pursue a literary career as a poet.

1924–29 Summer: Bishop attends Camp Chequesset on Cape Cod, a sailing camp for girls, for the first time. At Boston South Station, she meets and subsequently begins a decade-long friendship with Louise Bradley. In the Dr. Foster letters, Bishop remembers this as the time when she makes "my first real friends."

1925–26 Attends Saugus High School in Saugus, Massachusetts.

1926–27 Attends North Shore Country Day School in Swampscott, Massachusetts, where she publishes her first poems and stories in *The Owl.*

1927–30 Attends Walnut Hill School in Natick, Massachusetts. Publishes poems and other writings in school magazine, *The Blue Pencil.* Begins lifelong friendships with Frani Blough Muser and Rhoda Wheeler Sheehan.

1929–30 Bishop spends Christmas and New Year's Eve in Great Village.

February 1930: Her beloved maternal grandfather, William Bulmer ("Pa"), dies. Her maternal grandmother, Elizabeth Bulmer ("Gammie"), moves to live with her daughter Mary in Montréal. Gammie dies there in April 1931.

Summer: Works in a bookshop in Hyannis for a month. Later she travels with uncle George to Great Village, then drives with him from Great Village to Montréal where she sees Gammie for the last time. Bishop does not visit Nova Scotia again until 1946.

Meets Robert Seaver when visiting her Walnut Hill friend, Barbara Chesney in Pittsfield, Massachusetts. The courtship starts in 1932. Bishop and Seaver spend time together, alone, on Nantucket and Cuttyhunk Island as late as 1934. Seaver proposes marriage and is refused, probably in 1935.

1930 Fall: Enters Vassar College. Intends to major in music but switches to English. Contemporaries at Vassar include Mary McCarthy and Muriel Rukeyser. Her closest friendships are with Louise Crane and Margaret Miller.

1932 Summer: Goes on a three-week walking tour of Newfoundland with Vassar classmate Evelyn Huntington.

1933 Frustrated at being shut out of the college's established literary journal, Bishop and her friends found a new magazine they name *Con Spirito*. The first issue is published in February. In Bishop's senior year, she also edits *The Vassarion* with Margaret Miller.

May: Interviews T. S. Eliot for Vassar's *Miscellany News*.

1934 March 16: The Vassar librarian Fanny Borden introduces Bishop to Marianne Moore. They meet for the first time at the New York Public Library.

May 29: Bishop's mother dies at the Nova Scotia Hospital from a variety of medical causes. Grace Bulmer Bowers accompanies Gertrude's body back to Worcester where she also meets Bishop. Gertrude is buried beside her husband in Hope Cemetery.

After graduation, Bishop moves into the Hotel Brevoort and later a small apartment in Greenwich Village, New York, and works briefly at a correspondence school for aspiring authors that she later writes about in "The U.S.A. School of Writing."

Summer: Begins an autobiographical story about her childhood in Nova Scotia.

November 10: Bishop attends a lecture by Gertrude Stein entitled "Portraits I Have Written and What I Think of Repetition, Whether It Exists or No."

Shortly before Christmas, she completes "The Map." Years later, she would claim that the poem was written home alone with a cold on New Year's Eve.

1935 Marianne Moore chooses "The Map," "Three Valentines," and "The Reprimand" for the anthology *Trial Balances*. Moore's brief introduction to the poems is the first published criticism of Bishop's work.

Makes first trip to Europe and North Africa with Louise Crane. They reside for several months in a large apartment at 58 rue de Vaugirard in Paris, next to the Jardin du Luxembourg. Bishop meets several artists and writers in passing, including James Joyce and Pablo Picasso. She attends a further lecture by Gertrude Stein (on "entity vs. identity") but is too shy to accept an invitation to have tea. When in Paris, Bishop has shipped from England a custom-made clavichord from Arnold Dolmetsch. The clavichord travels with Bishop for most of her life until she sells it to Howard Moss in 1975 for $1,000 with "a lot of early keyboard music."

1936–39 *Spanish Civil War.*

1936 Spends summer and fall at Chelsea Hotel in New York.

November: Robert Seaver, who had wanted to marry Bishop, commits suicide. Before killing himself, he mails Bishop a postcard which arrives a few days after his death. It says: "Go to hell, Elizabeth."

First trip to Florida with Louise Crane. Becomes friends with Red and Charlotte Russell. Bishop likened Red to Tarzan. He wrestled alligators and hunted with a bow and arrow. She visited the Russells' home in Brevard, North Carolina, many times over the years.

1937 Returns to Europe with Crane. Travel from Ireland to France where they are joined by another Vassar friend, Margaret Miller. In July, while they are travelling in Burgundy, Crane's car is forced off the road. Miller's right arm is amputated between the wrist and elbow, a blow to her career as a painter. Crane's insurance company agrees to pay Miller a financial settlement if Crane is convicted of negligence. Crane pleads guilty at the subsequent trial. Bishop and Crane travel to southern France and Italy before returning to the USA via Genoa in December.

1938 Buys 624 White Street in Key West, Florida, with Louise Crane.

1939 *Outbreak of World War II.*

1940 Spends spring and summer in Key West. Becomes close friends with Pauline Pfeiffer, Ernest Hemingway's estranged second wife.

August: Visits North Carolina. On her arrival she is sent a telegram informing her of Maude Shepherdson's death on a visit to Great Village. See Bishop's unfinished elegy for Maude, "For M.B.S., buried in Nova Scotia."

October: Disagreement with Marianne Moore over Bishop's poem "Roosters."

1941 Begins six-year-long relationship with Marjorie Stevens in Key West. In Key West, she befriends the philosopher John Dewey and his daughter Jane Dewey.

December 7: Pearl Harbor attack. USA enters World War II.

1942 April–October: Travels to Mexico with Stevens. By chance meets Pablo Neruda who helps her find a Spanish tutor. Years later Bishop admits Neruda's poetry "had more influence on me than I knew at the time."

Fall: Meets Lota de Macedo Soares and Mary Morse in New York. Macedo Soares and Morse later invite Bishop to visit them in Brazil.

1943 Bishop works for five days grinding binocular lenses in a US Navy optical shop in Key West. Eyestrain and eczema force her to quit.

1945 June: Wins the Houghton Mifflin Poetry Prize Fellowship for the publication of her first book, *North & South*, which appears the year later.

August: Atomic bombs detonated at Hiroshima and Nagasaki. End of World War II.

1946 Spring: Begins treatment with Dr. Anny Baumann for depression, asthma, and alcoholism. Following Baumann's advice, she also begins analysis with Dr. Ruth Foster.

Summer: Returns to Nova Scotia for the first time since 1930. Spends time in Halifax, Lockeport, and Great Village. On the return bus journey from Great Village to Boston, the bus driver has to stop suddenly for a moose wandering down the road. Twenty-six years later she completes a poem ("The Moose") about this experience.

August: Publication of Bishop's first book of poems, *North & South*.

1947 Winter: Meets Robert Lowell at a dinner party hosted by Randall Jarrell. Lowell reviews *North & South* in *Sewanee Review*.

April: Awarded Guggenheim Fellowship.

Travels to Cape Breton with Marjorie Stevens, a trip remembered in the eponymous poem.

1947–48 Her last extended stay in Key West. Relationship with Stevens ends.

1948 November: Attends poetry conference at Bard College. Other attendees include Robert Lowell, William Carlos Williams, Richard Wilbur, Jean Garrigue, and Kenneth Rexroth. She also meets James Merrill for the first time. Merrill becomes a lifelong friend and advocate for her work.

1949–50 September: Begins year-long appointment as Consultant in Poetry (now Poet Laureate) at the Library of Congress. Hosts Robert Frost, Dylan Thomas, and William Carlos Williams. Pays regular visits to Ezra Pound at St. Elizabeths Hospital. Visits Jane Dewey at her farm in Havre de Grace, Maryland, and writes "A Cold Spring."

1950–53 *Korean War.*

1950 Stays at Yaddo writer's colony. Meets May Swenson and Kit and Ilse Barker, who became lifelong friends.

1951 Receives fellowships from Bryn Mawr College and the American Academy of Arts and Letters.

August: Travels to Sable Island, Nova Scotia, where, according to family tradition, her great-grandfather had been lost at sea. A projected prose piece ("The Deadly Sandpile") about Sable Island for *The New Yorker* is never finished.

November: Travels to South America on Norwegian freighter *S.S. Bowplate*, intending (so she later said) to stop in Brazil for only a few weeks. While in Brazil has an allergic reaction to the fruit of a cashew tree and is nursed back to health by Lota de Macedo Soares.

1952 Bishop and Macedo Soares fall in love and Bishop accepts Macedo Soares's offer to build her a studio behind Macedo Soares's modernist house then being constructed at Samambaia in the mountains above Petrópolis. Samambaia remains Bishop's primary residence in Brazil until 1961, when she and Macedo Soares begin to spend more time in Rio de Janeiro.

February 8: On her forty-first birthday Bishop is given a toucan by one of Macedo Soares' neighbours. She names him Uncle Sam ("Sammy" for short).

March 16: Bishop gives Macedo Soares a still life of an oil lamp for her birthday inscribed with a short love poem: "Longer than Aladdin's burns, / Love, & many Happy Returns."

Bishop returns to Key West and New York to have her books and other possessions shipped to Brazil.
Wins Shelley Memorial Award.

1953 April: Bishop visits Ouro Preto in the mountains of Minas Gerais for the first time. Founded at the end of the seventeenth century, Ouro Preto (Black Gold) was the focal point of the gold rush. Ouro Preto is now known for its baroque architecture, numerous churches and chapels, and steep, winding cobbled streets.

July: *The New Yorker* rejects "The Shampoo," Bishop's love poem for Macedo Soares.
Publication of stories "Gwendolyn" (June 27) and "In the Village" (December 19) in *The New Yorker.*

November 9: Dylan Thomas dies in New York.

December: On a trip to Rio with Macedo Soares, meets Manuel Bandeira. Bandeira buys Bishop a hammock for Christmas. Bishop sends Bandeira a letter-poem with a pot of jam ("To Manuel Bandeira, With Jam and Jelly").

1954 *August 24: Suicide of President Getúlio Vargas.* See Bishop's posthumously published poem, "Suicide of a Moderate Dictator."

1955 July: Publication of *Poems* (a reissue of *North & South* with her new collection *A Cold Spring*).

3 October: Election of President Juscelino Kubitschek.

Edits and translates Henrique Mindlin's *Modern Architecture in Brazil.*

1956 April: Visits Diamantina, setting of *The Diary of "Helena Morley,"* which she was then translating.
Receives a *Partisan Review* fellowship and Pulitzer Prize for Poetry for *Poems: North & South – A Cold Spring.* She celebrates the latter by eating "some awful chocolate cookies – Oreos, I think."

1957 January: Receives Amy Lowell Traveling Fellowship.

March–October: Long trip to New York with Macedo Soares.

December: Publication of her translation of *The Diary of "Helena Morley."*

1958 Aldous and Laura Huxley visit Bishop and Macedo Soares in Petrópolis. Bishop travels with them to Brasília, including a day excursion to see the Uialapiti tribe living on a tributary of the Xingu River.

1959 *First American servicemen die in Vietnam.*

November: Receives a pair of binoculars from May Swenson. Bishop describes this gift in a thank-you note as "the nicest & most overwhelming present I've received in years and years."

1960 February: Travels down the Amazon, visiting Manaus, Santarém, Vigia, and Belém.

May: Bishop and Macedo Soares stay with Lilli Correia de Araújo, owner of the Pouso do Chico Rei, in Ouro Preto. Bishop leaves the following poem in the guestbook: "Let Shakespeare & Milton / Stay at a Hilton – / I shall stay / At Chico Rei."

October: Jânio Quadros is elected President of Brazil. Quadros' political rival, João Goulart, is elected Vice-President. Carlos Lacerda, Macedo Soares's friend and Petrópolis neighbour, is elected governor of the state of Guanabara (Rio).

Christmas: Lacerda invites Macedo Soares to begin work on Aterro do Flamengo on the Rio waterfront. When finished in 1965, it becomes the largest public park within the city of Rio.

1961 *January 31: Quadros takes office. On August 25 he resigns.*

September 8: Goulart becomes President, his powers constrained by parliament and the newly created post of prime minister.

November: Bishop and Macedo Soares spend five weeks in New York.

1962 February: Publication of *Brazil*, written by Bishop but considerably altered by the book's editors, for *Life*'s World Library series.

Summer: Robert Lowell, Elizabeth Hardwick, and their five-year-old daughter Harriet visit Brazil for two months. Lowell has a breakdown toward the end of the trip and is hospitalized on his return to the USA.

October: The Cuban Missile Crisis.

1963 Begins correspondence with poet Anne Stevenson. Bishop's letters to Stevenson include some of her most memorable statements about poetry and her fullest account of her own biography.

November 22: Assassination of U.S. President John F. Kennedy.

1964 *April 1: The Brazilian military stages a coup to overthrow President João Goulart. Carlos Lacerda, supports the coup.*

Visits Northern Italy with Macedo Soares, then England on her own, staying with her friends Kit and Ilse Barker.

Summer: *The Kenyon Review* publishes Bishop's translations of three Clarice Lispector stories, "The Smallest Woman in the World," "A Hen," and "Marmosets."

Becomes a fellow of the Academy of American Poets.

1965 *Beginning of US ground war in Vietnam, which lasts until 1973.*

January: Begins affair with Lilli Correia de Araújo.

April 3: Opening of Aterro do Flamengo.

Purchases and begins restoring a colonial house in Ouro Preto, across town from Lilli Correia de Araújo's home. Bishop names it Casa Mariana in honour of Marianne Moore and because of its position on the road from Ouro Preto to Mariana.

November: Publication of *Questions of Travel*, dedicated to Macedo Soares.

1966 Spring: Teaches at the University of Washington in Seattle where she begins a relationship with Roxanne Cumming.

Fall: Macedo Soares, already depressed about Bishop's decision to teach in Seattle, learns of Bishop's affair with Cumming.

November: Travels with Macedo Soares to England and Holland but cuts trip short when Macedo Soares's health deteriorates. Macedo Soares is hospitalized on her return to Rio.

Anne Stevenson publishes *Elizabeth Bishop* in the Twayne United States Author Series. It is the first critical book on Bishop's poetry.

1967 January: Macedo Soares's doctor recommends a temporary separation. In February, Bishop is treated for alcoholism at the same clinic where Macedo Soares is hospitalized. Bishop and Macedo Soares are reunited in March but in June the doctor recommends another break.

July: Bishop flies to New York. Stays at 61 Perry Street, the apartment of her friends Loren MacIver and Lloyd Frankenberg.

September: Against the advice of her doctor, Macedo Soares travels to New York to see Bishop, arriving (according to a letter to U.T. and Joseph Summers) on 17 September. Overnight she takes an overdose of Nembutal and goes into a coma. She dies at St. Vincent's Hospital on September 25. Anny Baumann advises Bishop not to accompany the body back to Rio.

November: Returns to Brazil. She is unable to return to Samambaia while Macedo Soares's will is being contested by her sister. Many of Bishop's letters to Macedo Soares are destroyed by Mary Morse. When the will is finally settled, Morse inherits Samambaia and Bishop the apartment in Rio.

December: Stays with Lilli Correia de Araújo in Ouro Preto.

1968 Lives for a year in San Francisco with Roxanne Cumming and her one-year-old son. Meets Thom Gunn and Robert Duncan. Travels with Cumming in Canada and visits New York. Awarded a grant from the Ingram-Merrill Foundation. Publication of *The Ballad of the Burglar of Babylon* in a children's edition illustrated by Ann Grifalconi.

1969 February: Interviews Black Panther member Kathleen Cleaver, wife of party leader Eldridge Cleaver. The interview has never been published.

April: Publication of *The Complete Poems.*

May: Gives readings at the Library of Congress and the Guggenheim Museum where Robert Lowell introduces her as "the famous eye." Bishop begins her reading by saying "The 'famous eye' will now put on her glasses."

June 28: Beginning of Stonewall Riots in Greenwich Village. Spends summer and fall in Ouro Preto with Cumming and her son.

1970 March: Wins National Book Award for *The Complete Poems.*

Spring: Bishop's relationship with Cumming collapses. Cumming has a breakdown and returns to the USA to recover.

July: James Merrill visits Bishop in Ouro Preto.

September: Moves to Cambridge, Massachusetts, to teach at Harvard, initially as a temporary replacement for Robert Lowell. Meets Alice Methfessel. Makes the first of several visits to Nova Scotia.

1971 Spends several months in Ouro Preto. Brazilian government awards her the Order of Rio Branco.

August: Meets Alice Methfessel in Quito for a long-planned trip to the Galápagos Islands and Machu Picchu.

Returns to Harvard for the fall term where she teaches a seminar on letter writing "as an art form or something." Meets Octavio Paz.

November: Hospitalized for asthma.

1972 February 5: Marianne Moore dies.

March: Bishop and Lowell disagree over his decision to publish versions of Elizabeth Hardwick's letters in his book-length poem, *The Dolphin.*

April: Publication of *An Anthology of Twentieth-Century Brazilian Poetry*, edited with Emanuel Brasil.

June 13: Reads "The Moose" at Harvard's Phi Beta Kappa ceremony. The poem is dedicated to Grace Bulmer Bowers, Bishop's "favorite relative."

Summer: Flies to Ouro Preto followed by trip to Scandinavia and Soviet Union with Methfessel.

1973 March: Purchases a condominium at Lewis Wharf on the Boston waterfront.

Spring: Teaches at the University of Washington.

Fall: Four-year appointment as lecturer at Harvard begins. Introduces Gwendolyn Brooks at a reading.

1974 Bishop spends her first summer on Sabine Farm on the island of North Haven, Maine. She returns there every summer until her death.

1974 Winter: Falls and breaks shoulder. Weekend visits in winter and spring to Duxbury, Massachusetts, where she and Methfessel stay in John Malcolm Brinnin's house. Duxbury is the setting for Bishop's poem "The End of March," dedicated to Brinnin and his partner Bill Read.

Spring: Bishop visits Ouro Preto to arrange for her belongings to be shipped to Boston. This is her final visit to Brazil.

August: *President Nixon resigns.*

August: Moves into Lewis Wharf.

1975 Winter: Separation from Methfessel and medical leave from Harvard, during which she writes "One Art."

1976 February: Awarded Neustadt International Prize for Literature.

Summer: Travels to England where she visits Kit and Ilse Barker and Robert Lowell. Attends International Poetry Conference in Rotterdam, and travels to Lisbon, where she meets Methfessel. Hospitalized for asthma at Harvard on her return.

December: Publication of *Geography III*; receives National Book Critics Circle Award.

1977 Spring. The end of her teaching contract at Harvard as Bishop passes Harvard's mandatory retirement age of sixty-five years old.

August 22: Bishop's aunt Grace Bulmer Bowers dies.

September 12: Robert Lowell dies.

Fall: Teaches at New York University. Revises will, making Alice Methfessel executor, and Methfessel and Frank Bidart literary executors.

1978 Receives Guggenheim Fellowship.

Spring: Travels with Methfessel to the Outer Banks of North Carolina and then to Quebec.

August: Completes "North Haven," her elegy for Robert Lowell.

1979 May: Bishop makes her last visit to Nova Scotia, to receive an honorary degree from Dalhousie University, then travels with Methfessel to England and Greece.

September: Begins teaching at Massachusetts Institute of Technology.

October 6: Dies suddenly of a cerebral aneurysm at Lewis Wharf. She is buried in Hope Cemetery, Worcester, beside her father and mother.

1981 Vassar College purchases Bishop's archive from her executor, Alice Methfessel.

1983 Publication of *The Complete Poems: 1927–1979*.

1984 Publication of *Collected Prose*, edited by Robert Giroux.

1991 Elizabeth Bishop Society is formed.

1993 First exhibition of Bishop's paintings is held at the East Martello Tower in Key West.

1994 Publication of *One Art: Letters*, edited by Robert Giroux. Elizabeth Bishop Society of Nova Scotia is formed.

1996 Government of Nova Scotia purchases the Bulmer family archive, which is deposited at Acadia University.

Publication of *Exchanging Hats: Paintings*, edited by William Benton.

2004 Purchase of Bishop's childhood home in Great Village by a group of private owners.

2006 Publication of *Edgar Allan Poe & The Juke-Box: Uncollected Poems, Drafts, and Fragments*, edited by Alice Quinn.

2008 Publication of the Library of America edition of Bishop's writing, *Poems, Prose, and Letters*, edited by Robert Giroux and Lloyd Schwartz.

Publication of *Words in Air: The Complete Correspondence between Elizabeth Bishop and Robert Lowell*, edited by Thomas Travisano with Saskia Hamilton.

2009 Bishop's literary executor, Alice Methfessel, dies. After her death, a large collection of documents, letters, and photographs is sold to Vassar College. The collection includes letters to her psychoanalyst Ruth Foster in 1947, letters from Bishop to Macedo Soares in 1963–4, letters from Macedo Soares to Bishop in summer 1967, and letters from Bishop to Methfessel in the 1970s.

2011 The centenary of Bishop's birth is celebrated by two new editions of her work, *Poems* and *Prose*, the latter edited by Lloyd Schwartz.

Publication of *Elizabeth Bishop and The New Yorker: The Complete Correspondence*, edited by Joelle Biele.

An exhibition of artworks by Bishop and paintings from her personal collection is held at the Tibor de Nagy Gallery in New York.

2015 Publication of *The North Haven Journal, 1974–1979*, edited by Eleanor McPeck, working from transcriptions by Alice Quinn.

2017 Elizabeth Bishop House in Great Village is given to the St. James Church of Great Village Preservation Society, which operates it as a retreat for artists and writers.

2019 Purchase of Bishop's Key West house at 624 White Street by Key West Literary Seminar.

2020 Bishop is chosen (and then rejected) as the honouree for the eighteenth edition of Brazil's biggest annual literary festival, FLIP (Festa Literária Internacional de Paraty). Bishop would have been the first foreign writer chosen for this honour, but a press campaign in Brazil drawing attention to statements Bishop made about Brazil in the 1960s and a change in festival director led to the dissociation of FLIP from the online events held in the summer of 2020 that celebrated Bishop's writing.

Introduction

Angus Cleghorn and Jonathan Ellis

In 1966, Elizabeth Bishop arrived in Seattle to teach for the first time. She was a month short of her fifty-fifth birthday. In a letter to Howard Moss, her editor at *The New Yorker*, Bishop explained her pay and conditions as follows:

> *The Poet* can come for one, two (like me), or three "quarters" and the pay is $7,000 a quarter—which seems very good by my humble standards. That is $7,000 each ten weeks, more or less. There are only 2 small classes—15 to 20—and they meet for 50 minutes, supposedly 4 times a week but I have cut the writing class to 3 times a week. This part of the world, and the breezy western manner, and teaching, rather staggered me at first – but now I am beginning to enjoy most of it except the classes. (*NYr* 285)

A day later, writing to Robert Lowell, she complained about the students' poetic influences, in particular the influence of the poet she replaced, Theodore Roethke: "They are so wrapped up in Roethke, still, and he also left an anti-Pound, anti-Eliot heritage, but I go blithely on giving them things they look blasé about – even Tennyson and Keats. The eastern influence! – only here it's west. One boy gave me *100* haikus – or haikai, as I believe the plural is" (*WIA* 599). One of Bishop's students, the artist Wesley Wehr, made notes he later published on what Bishop talked about in the classroom. In her very first class, as if to dispel Roethke's influence directly, she read Eliot aloud and told them to look up e.e. cummings and the rain poems of Apollinaire. For their first assignment, they were given A. E. Housman to read. "Some of you have good ears," she told them. "But your sense of rhyme and form is atrocious."[1]

Contexts like these are drawn from various biographical and epistolary sources, all published after Bishop's death. They give us a very vivid sense of what Bishop was like as a person, a poet, and a rookie teacher. We learn that she liked to give advice and had strong opinions; that she was funny, often hilariously so, particularly when drawing attention to people's bad writing habits. They also tell us which poets she valued, and what she thought of free verse and haikus. In reading this book, we presume you are more familiar with Elizabeth Bishop's writing than writing about her. The Library of America edition of Bishop's writing is sub-titled "Poems, Prose and Letters." In our estimation, that is the best order in which to first read Bishop, supplemented by a fourth category: her drawings and paintings. Bishop had little truck with what normally comes next on a reading list, literary criticism. In the same class in which she encouraged her students to read Housman, she also told them not to read any criticism: "I would suggest you read one poet – *all* of his poems, his letters, his biographies, everything *but* the criticisms on him."[2] There are several objections one might make to this statement. Is biography not a form of criticism? What about criticism *by* rather than *about* the particular poet? Surely not all criticism is bad? And why does Bishop gender the poet male?

Contexts do not provide all of the answers to the many questions her poems and stories ask. In some cases, it feels as if they make things messier. Are we hearing too many allusions in her work, or not enough? What happens when one context contradicts the other? Which context matters more? Why these contexts and not others?

The idea that context can be separated from text is, as Bishop would admit, false. As her career progressed, her employment of dedications, endnotes, and other italicized extra-textual information increased. The idea of a pure, unmediated poetic text disappears. The evidence is there in many of her poems. In "Over 2,000 Illustrations and a Complete Concordance," her famous statement – "Everything only connected by 'and' and 'and'" (*P* 58) – is in part a recognition that nothing we see or do, and certainly nothing we read, is ever really free of other people's interpretations, memories, or touch. "The gilt rubs off the edges / of the pages and pollinates the fingertips" (*P* 58). We are changed by other people's interpretations of what we have ourselves just read. We can't forget or unread somebody else's marginalia.

Context functions in a similar way. Like the gilt that rubs off on us as we read an old book, pollinating the fingertips, our reading experience is also mediated by somebody else's look, somebody else's politics. "Gilt" encompasses the homonym "guilt": the embarrassment of not having thought of that before, or of somebody else having written it down before you. At the same time, aligning text and context can be a giddy pleasure, even if the edges don't quite match.

*

What does it mean to read an author in context? Primarily, it reveals the author's formative living environments – geographical, familial, historical, artistic, intellectual, social, cultural and political influences – and how those forces play out in creative literary transformation. Readerly reception then determines the ways in which a writer is perceived through time. Elizabeth Bishop's "famous eye" for earthly detail was the initial quality that sparked admiration from fellow poets and continues to amaze just about every person who reads one of her poems. From microscopic attention to patterned fish skin to conceptions of geological morphology over millennia, "that sense of constant re-adjustment" (*P* 12) enables readers to quickly observe the instant amidst the gradation of slow time. Bishop registers the flux of daily light, as well as the historical and cultural forces that change how we see light. Synchrony and diachrony reverberate in everyday perceptions through the voices of her poems, stories, and letters.

The collected contexts in this book provide points of entry, interest, and overview for readers and scholars at all levels. Whether it might be fundamental places such as Nova Scotia, New England, New York, Paris, Florida, or Brazil; the mind-shaping contexts of literary movements, twentieth-century history, music, psychoanalysis, religion, anthropology, and travel; or the way these vectors play out in Bishop's dreams, sense of humour, or her negotiation of gender, race, and sexuality, readers will find what they are looking for. This includes scholarly traces of Bishop studies, and the way her work has been received through time, and as an influence on contemporary poets.

Bishop's publishing history from her late teens to her death in 1979 at the age of sixty-eight demonstrates an early accomplished gift with words that evolves and simmers into seemingly effortless skill in her late, flowing, and sometimes prosaic language. And yet her vast archives, left behind for executors to manage, show that Bishop endlessly revised her seemingly natural work. The trickle of posthumous writing unearthed in the 1980s and 90s gained major attention and impact in 2006 with Alice Quinn's *Edgar Allan Poe & The Juke-Box*, an edition of previously uncollected fragments and poems. Since then, more of Bishop's unpublished writings, especially her letters to psychoanalyst Dr. Ruth Foster have revealed personal history that enables better understanding of Bishop and her work. Newly acquired archival materials have given us crucial information about the final stages of her relationship with Lota de Macedo Soares in 1967 and allowed us to know more about her relationship with Alice Methfessel in the 1970s. Early friendships with Louise Bradley and Rhoda Wheeler Sheehan have also been fleshed out by letters. Quinn's edition of Bishop's notebooks promises further revelations, as do future editions of her correspondence with Marianne Moore and May Swenson.

While last century's reputation of Bishop as a nearly perfect poet with a modest output has changed to that of a more experimental and prolific author working in and across various genres, this century's new knowledge about Bishop allows deeper insights into the contextual forces that inform her "untidy activity" (*P* 59) and the hard work an apparent genius undergoes to produce what her friend Robert Lowell in a poem memorably called her "casual perfection." The publication of three major volumes of Bishop's correspondence – her selected letters in 1994, an edition of her correspondence with Robert Lowell in 2008, and an edition of her correspondence with *The New Yorker* in 2011 – has enabled us to understand more about her views on cultural politics such as race, class, and gender, as well as her myriad tastes in poetry, visual art, and music. Bishop taught a class on correspondence and in a typically offhand manner, called letters "an art form or something" (*OA* 544). Langdon Hammer's chapter in this book asks what type of "something."

The ways in which Bishop transforms traditional literary musicality into contemporaneous rhythms and voices is perhaps her most subtle yet tremendous accomplishment. The colloquial utterances come to rest in our ears almost without our notice. Yet her words register diverse cultural tones that teach us about what it was like to live in her time and place. Her epigraph for Brazilian gardener "Manuelzinho" states "*A friend of the writer is speaking*" (*P* 94). But who is the writer and who is the writer's friend? Bishop's relationship to the speakers of her poems (and by implication her readers) changes throughout her career. The first person plural that begins the early poem "The Imaginary Iceberg" – "We'd rather have the iceberg than the ship" (*P* 6) – is gradually but not entirely replaced by the first person singular of her final collection, *Geography III* (1976). Successive generations of readers have felt befriended by her. As a welcoming, provocative, and insidious companion, Bishop ingratiates herself upon readers, and then seemingly casually gets us to reconsider just about every conception we ever learned.

In an unfinished talk Bishop titled "Writing poetry is an unnatural act ...," she cited Coleridge's famous discussion of Wordsworth from *Biographia Literaria* approvingly: "the characteristic fault of our elder poets is the reverse of that which distinguishes too many of our recent versifiers; the one conveying the most fantastic thoughts in the most correct and natural language, the other in the most fantastic language conveying the most trivial thoughts" (*EAP* 207). Bishop, like Coleridge, preferred the former method though she was not above including the odd "fantastic" word like "divagation" or "dialectic" (*P* 191, 207). In the same essay, she pinpointed "the three qualities" she admired in the poetry she liked best: "*Accuracy, Spontaneity, Mystery*. My three 'favorite' poets – not the best poets, whom we all admire, but favorite in the sense of one's 'best' friends,' etc. are Herbert, Hopkins, and Baudelaire" (*EAP* 208). Bishop's choice of poetic friends is audacious. She doesn't identify any of her actual poet friends such as Marianne Moore, Robert Lowell, May Swenson, or James Merrill, or indeed any other twentieth-century poet. At Vassar, her English tutor Barbara Swain described her as "an enormously cagey girl who looked at authorities with a suspicious eye and was quite capable of attending to her own education anyway."[3] Perhaps her independence is one of the reasons why she was so respected among her peers? She didn't take sides in any of the poetry wars, at least not publicly. Privately, though, she always had an opinion.

Across various forms, Bishop can make readers feel as if they are in on her jokes, often with a smirking sense of humour. This compelling and at times spiky companion is someone that is enjoyable to spend time with, an effect often owing to her many parenthetical remarks that undercut and revise her statements, showing multiple perspectives, often unfinished or in the formative process of becoming, as at the end of "The Monument." Bishop's love of questions is another factor in this; so too her use of ellipses. The speaker of her poems frequently knows more about animals or botany or geography than the reader does, but we are never made to feel ignorant or stupid for not possessing these facts. Her authority is expressed without ceremony. Indeed, the speaker sometimes knows less at the end of the poem than at the beginning. It is a process of unknowing. Such an experience can be positive. Readers feel they are completing a friend's thoughts, as if we know her well enough to finish the next sentence. At other times, we are left frightened. A calm world is replaced by a spinning one and we have no idea if or when it will stop.

What about Bishop as a philosopher? Bishop does not go as transcendentally far as her mentor Blake, but students of her work do gravitate to newfound understandings of where the finite and infinite overlap. Like Blake, she is not afraid to stare at grains of sand and wonder at their connection to our experience of scale, size, and time. A parenthetical phrase from her poem "Sandpiper" – "no detail too small" (*P* 129) – is a motto of her entire aesthetic. People growing up in the twenty-first century might rightly observe that the habits and practices of older generations largely lead to ruin, yet find themselves at the same time skeptical of the limited knowledge capacity of peers who look up every fact rather than remembering anything in this age of information overload. So when contemporary students read a twentieth-century writer who can deconstruct the epistemologies of her era while also appreciating the world's natural beauty and diversity of life, young eyebrows may be raised. Bishop anticipates many of the concerns of twenty-first-century life, not least the anxiety that humans are making the planet uninhabitable for ourselves and others. She mourns the death of local cultures and customs and is sensitive to the effects of capitalism and globalization, particularly on countries she knew well like Brazil. She writes about animals as fellow creatures not as humans-in-disguise. Bishop offers such concepts undogmatically with casual rhetorical persuasion. Her questions of mastery, as Bonnie Costello terms them in her book title,[4] are not those of a pedantic parent or didact; yet she quietly provides an ecological model for an enduring planet. In "Brazil, January 1, 1502," the imperial tourist in the early 1950s is not much better than the rapacious Portuguese conquistadores who conquered the country and its indigenous people. In "Cape Breton" the mist that eternally flows through the landscape to unite sky, sea, fish, and birds exhibits more enduring power than the Christian missionaries dotting the landscape with churches on top of the arrowheads that could not adequately defend against them.

In this age of the Anthropocene, Bishop devotes significant energy to animal–human relations. She did her best to present foreign cultures and peoples as accurately as she wrote about Nova Scotia, Florida, or New York, even if she can be criticized for both appropriation and superiority at times, especially with regards to race. Yet her imaginative reach into animal existences such as fish, birds, moose, and insects without hierarchical reason (as one finds in the enlightenment's version of the great chain of being) impresses those of us who think that human dominance has nearly doomed us. Look, for example, at her prose poems, "Rainy Season; Sub-Tropics," in which her creatures are used to reflect themselves, the author, and humanity in the first person. "*Giant Snail*" is fittingly "ghost-like" and thinks "Withdrawal is always best" (*P* 164), admiring the waterfalls over black rock that it cannot climb. A model of empathy in its environment, the snail nonetheless has a healthy ego with a beautiful shell it cannot see: "I fill it to perfection."

> My wide wake shines, now it is growing dark. I leave a lovely opalescent ribbon: I know this.
>
> But O! I am too big. I feel it. Pity me.

> If and when I reach the rock, I shall go into a certain crack there for the night. The waterfall below will vibrate through my shell and body all night long. In that steady pulsing I can rest. All night I shall be like a sleeping ear. (*P* 165)

Rarely quoted, this prose poem is signature Bishop: snail slime is a glowing tribute of its perfect debased beauty. At once pushing its own bodily boundaries, the snail meanwhile hides peacefully so it will feel the waterfall's vibrations while it rests. Amazingly oxymoronic, the snail "like a sleeping ear" slumbers attentively. This type of "perfectly useless concentration" is what Bishop admired in the dreams of Darwin (*Pr* 414). Unconscious and conscious at once, this is the waking life we all experience; Bishop posits it in the body of a snail, or another time in the hybrid "Man-Moth." As with her mentor Marianne Moore, Bishop led humans out of themselves into the animal world to reflect back the foibles of human reason. From *North & South* on, Bishop often exposed "The Irrational Element of Poetry," the title of an essay by fellow twentieth-century poet Wallace Stevens.

Bishop's approach to genre continues this story of undoing master narratives. When Robert Giroux in 1994 chose one of her most accomplished poems as the title for her selected letters *One Art*, he suggested that the letter form bleeds into the poem and vice versa as it had with Emily Dickinson, a poet Bishop admired but never felt close to as she did with Herbert or Hopkins. As Bishop's career progressed, her lyric poetry increasingly drew on prose styles. In addition, she is perhaps one of the most painterly of poets. In *Exchanging Hats*, a book of her selected paintings, editor William Benton followed Giroux's example by employing a title from a gender-bending Bishop poem. Just as the letter, prose, lyric, and visual art contribute to Bishop's implosion of genres in her one art, so does her use of translation as a formative poetics enable her to register other languages, ethnicities, and cultures. Fluid and adaptive, these are skills admired and needed for survival today.

*

The more one learns about Bishop's life and writing, the more contexts present themselves. Although the beginning and end of her life suggest a certain circularity, or return to origins – she was born in Worcester, Massachusetts, and died just fifty miles away in Boston – a map of her homes, residences and travels tells a different story. While we have represented the main points on her compass, a compass that always pointed "north" to Nova Scotia as an unpublished poem has it (*P* 313), we could easily have commissioned a whole book on place.

Bishop is celebrated primarily as a poet. We are glad to include chapters on her prose and translations too. At the same time, we note and miss the genres and sub-genres of poetry and prose that might have been given chapters of their own. Our first draft of this book contained a chapter on Renaissance literature. Donne, Herbert, and Shakespeare were constant reference points in her writing. At the beginning of her career, influenced by Ben Jonson, she drafted a couple of masques, one intriguingly titled "The Proper Tears." Peter Swaab adeptly condenses the contexts of Romantic and Victorian literature into just one chapter. A book double the length might have had space for individual chapters on her debt to Blake, Coleridge, Wordsworth, Keats, and Shelley. She knew Victorian poetry by heart, and not just Tennyson and Browning. We hope somebody is writing an article or thesis on Bishop and Clare, or Bishop and Rossetti. Her lifelong love of the blues was reflected in her teaching of the line, "I hate to see that evenin' sun go down," to creative writing students at Harvard. In Brazil she translated many sambas, drawing on the form in several poems, not least "The Burglar of Babylon" and "Pink Dog." In terms of poetic form, Bishop's innovative and influential employment of the sestina and villanelle are important turning points in mid-century poetics. For a while it seemed as if every new collection of poetry contained one or other or sometimes both of these forms. Bishop wrote relatively few dramatic monologues and just a few sonnets but when she chose these forms she made them her own. Rachel Trousdale provides a wonderful chapter on humour here. If we had considered humour as a poetic form, we might have included further chapters on her comic verse or her love of nonsense writing. At the other end of the tonal scale, Bishop's elegies are increasingly praised by readers and scholars and not just for the elegies she finished. A cursory glance at the contents page of *Edgar Allan Poe* suggests Bishop had at least half a collection of unfinished or unpublished elegies. Charles Berger discussed "Bishop's Buried Elegies" in *Elizabeth Bishop in the 21st Century*.[5] May Swenson admired the love poems *The New Yorker* refused to publish, John Ashbery her triplets. Other critics have noted her employment of parentheses and question marks, or her use of pronouns. In the introduction to the *Companion*, we hoped somebody would write an article or book on Bishop's prose poetry. We are glad Vidyan Ravinthiran, a contributor to this book, took up the challenge. Eleanor Cook's *Elizabeth Bishop at Work* is particularly sharp on what she calls Bishop's "ordinary diction."[6] She also pinpoints Bishop's mastery of poetic genre. About

North & South, she notes, "Bishop displays her virtuosity with forms by shaping every poem differently."[7] In addition to being a painter herself, Bishop also wrote about visual art. Unlike many other twentieth-century poets, her ekphrastic poetry does not often depend upon our knowledge of a famous antecedent. Indeed, she often makes jokes out of forgetting or misremembering other artists. In the case of two poems, both inspired by paintings by a relatively unknown uncle, the magic of the poem depends on our not knowing the object she is looking at. When her prose was first collected in 1984, Robert Giroux divided it into two categories: "fiction" and "memoir." As Lloyd Schwartz observes in his editor's note to the 2011 edition of Bishop's *Prose*, the distinction between "fiction and memoir" is often blurred:

> In such pieces as "In the Village," "Gwendolyn," "The Country Mouse," "The U.S.A. School of Writing," and "Memories of Uncle Neddy," she treats what are clearly autobiographical narratives as if they were fiction. Other stories, some bordering on the surrealistic, are more obviously "made up," while such pieces as "Gregorio Valdes, 1979–1939" and her extended remembrance of her mentor and friend, Marianne Moore, "Efforts of Affection," land more firmly on the memoir end of this polarity. (*Pr* vii)

When collecting her prose pieces for a possible collection, Bishop couldn't decide on a title, hovering between *In the Village & Other Stories* and *In the Village: Stories & Essays*. Did she always write with more than one genre in mind?

Bishop's reputation continues to evolve and grow. Her poetry has featured prominently in two Hollywood films, *In Her Shoes* in 2005 and *Still Alice* in 2014, and in the twelve-part TV series *Normal People* (2020), an acclaimed adaption of Sally Rooney's novel. In 2013, *Flores Raras e Banalíssimas/Reaching for the Moon*, a feature film based on Bishop's relationship with Brazilian architect Lota de Macedo Soares, was released. Directed by Bruno Barreto and loosely based on the biography by Brazilian writer Carmen Oliveira (1995 in Portuguese; 2002 in English translation by Neil Besner), the film stars Miranda Otto as Bishop and Gloria Pires as Macedo Soares. In 2015, the feminist filmmaker Barbara Hammer created *Welcome to this House*, a documentary film on Bishop's homes and travels. Whereas both Hollywood films emphasise Bishop's status as poet, *Flores Raras* and *Welcome to this House* focus on Bishop as a queer icon. We have yet to see a film that does both.

We can observe Bishop's changing reputation in other places too, not least in poetry anthologies. In Bishop's lifetime, her most anthologized poem was "The Fish." Its repeated inclusion in similar-sounding anthologies eventually frustrated her. In a letter to Robert Lowell in 1970, she threatened "to turn that damned FISH into a sonnet, or something very short and quite different. (I seem to get requests for it every day for anthologies with titles like READING AS EXPERIENCE, or EXPERIENCE AS READING, each anthologizer insisting that he is doing something completely different from every other anthologizer … But I'm sure this is an old story to you.)" (*WIA* 663). What did anthologists like about the poem? If we are to believe Bishop's account to Lowell, they liked its account of an experience. But what type of experience? Read in the context of Bishop's career and eighty years of subsequent literary history, it does showcase many of Bishop's most characteristic gestures and mannerisms, in particular a slow and remarkably tender examination of an animal that the poem's speaker relates to but can never know or see completely. "Half out of water," the fish looks a lot like some of the things she has seen on land. She compares his skin to wallpaper, the torn fishline in his jaw to military medals. For all her effort at comparison, at finding likeness, the fish never becomes fully human in the poem. He remains half out, half in the water, half seen but also half invisible. Half-looks and hybrid creatures are everywhere in Bishop's first book, *North & South*. Do we ever see round or through any object fully in these poems? Can any body be known well, even one's own reflection? Read in such terms, "The Fish" remains a strange and unusual poem about our being in the world, in particular animal–human relations. Bishop's fish isn't transformed, as in many animal poems, into a myth or symbol. It stays, one might say, fish-like. The poem acknowledges a debt to but marks a swerve away from Wordsworth's *The Prelude*, replacing young William's rowing through the water ("I struck and struck") with an equally active but less transcendent focus on sight ("I stared and stared"). Whereas Wordsworth looks at things to see through them, Bishop looks and looks to see what's actually there. He is on the move to translate present feelings and sights into future memories, future words; she is content to find a poem here, in the messy moment of the poem's coming-into-being. At the same time, Bishop does include a Romantic-sounding epiphany in the poem ("everything / was rainbow, rainbow, rainbow!"), one based on the coming together of oil and water, before letting the fish go. Many poets would end on the miracle of that rainbow, celebrated three times and underlined with an exclamation mark. Bishop ends on a diminuendo ("And I let the fish go"), a release of the fish literally down into the water that sounds like a simultaneous release of the reader back into the world.

Bishop's endings frequently send the reader back to the beginning again. She is an expert in leaving us with questions unanswered. Why does she let the fish go? Did she always plan to release him, or has she suddenly changed her mind? If the latter, when did she decide? We begin the poem again to see if we missed something. Much of our reading of "The Fish" now is indebted to critics doing the same. There are other contexts we might add. This is a poem written in Key West, just a couple of months before she finished "Roosters." That same winter, Bishop became close friends with Pauline Pfeiffer, Ernest Hemingway's estranged second wife. How much of the poem is a response to Hemingway's writing? The poetic "I" is used relatively rarely by Bishop, particularly in her early poems, but here we find it seven times: "I caught . . . I thought . . . I looked . . . I admired . . . I saw . . . I stared . . . I let the fish go" (*P* 43–44). How important is this pronoun to this poem? Eco-critics have long explored Bishop's examination of the natural world. What type of nature poet is she? There's a curious moment in the poem when the speaker thinks of "the course white flesh / packed in like feathers, the big bones and the little bones" and "the pink swim-bladder / like a big peony" (*P* 43). Follow the leap from fish flesh to bird feathers to flower petal and we find ourselves not just exchanging species from fish to bird but also moving in and out of the body to end on a flower that is neither fish nor fowl but still connected to each if only by the poet's imagination. How do eco-systems work in Bishop's writing? Such questions are another way of saying that "The Fish" remains a significant poem. Anthologists were not wrong to like it, or to think about it as representative of Bishop's writing.

If you type the words "Elizabeth Bishop" and "Anthologies" into any good search engine today, you will soon come across Bishop's famous and frequently stated refusal to be part of all-women anthologies. In a letter to May Swenson in 1971, she elaborated on the reasons for her refusal.

> Literature is literature, no matter who produces it. Probably it's true that some of the earlier women poets have not been brought to people's attention enough – men's & women's attention. [. . .] I like black & white, yellow & red, young & old, rich and poor, and male & female, all mixed up, socially – and see no reason for segregating them, for any reason at all, artistically, either. (*PPL* 884)

Adrienne Rich tried to persuade Bishop to contribute to a different anthology devoted to American women poets a couple of years later and was met, at least publicly, with the same response. In *Remembering Elizabeth Bishop*, Lloyd Schwartz recalls a tense conversation between Bishop and Rich:

> One evening, near the end of a pleasant party at Elizabeth's apartment, Adrienne Rich asked her about this policy of hers. One of the things she said was something like, "But Elizabeth, don't you want to have a bigger audience?" Elizabeth responded by saying that she thought her audience was large enough. She obviously felt a little wounded.[8]

After Rich's visit, Bishop told poet Richard Howard that she preferred "closets, closets, and more closets,"[9] a phrase that has become almost as well known as some of the lines from her poems. The context of her friendship and rivalry with Rich is perhaps as important as the issue of gender and sexuality.

Bishop's most anthologized poem nowadays is undoubtedly "One Art," the villanelle she first published in *The New Yorker* in 1976. "One Art" is not just popular; it is also seen as her signature poem. Bishop biographers to date (Brett Millier, Sandra Barry, Colm Tóibín, Megan Marshall, and Thomas Travisano) have made it central to her life story, in particular her relationship with Alice Methfessel. The fact Alice Quinn decided to publish the drafts of the poem in the Appendix to *Edgar Allan Poe* is also crucial. Readers can quite literally see what Robert Lowell was talking about when he celebrated her drafts and her ability to wait months, even years, for the "unimaginable phrase." Reading *Edgar Allan Poe*, the drafts for "One Art" come poignantly after her drafts for an elegy for Lota de Macedo Soares, a poem she was never able to finish. Perhaps "One Art" is an elegy too, but one with a happy ending? Bishop was able to "*Write* it" both ways (*P* 198). She and Methfessel were reconciled and she lived to see the poem in print in both *The New Yorker* and *Geography III*.

"One Art" is a perfect example of Bishop's art and the usefulness (or uselessness) of context. While it is possible to read and teach the poem "blind" without any extra-textual information, context adds to our understanding of what was happening in Bishop's life as she was writing the poem and where the poem sits in late-twentieth-century culture. In the first draft of the poem, the speaker is aware this might be a career-defining poem. "This is by way of introduction," she writes in the first draft of stanza one:

> I really
> want to introduce myself – I am such a
> fantastic lly good at losing things
> I think everyone shd. profit from my experiences (*EAP* 225)

By the final draft, these introductory remarks have gone but the poem can still be read as a mini-autobiography, a *Prelude* not in two, thirteen, or fourteen books, but in nineteen lines. Arguably, every chapter in the book addresses this poem in some way, from the places Bishop lived in and lost to the political and social upheavals the poem addresses directly and sideways. The detail of the mother's watch has added poignancy when we learn about Gertrude May Bulmer, Bishop's mother. The counting of "three loved houses," "two cities," "two rivers," and "a continent" makes sense when we know more about Bishop's long stays in Key West and particularly in Brazil (*P* 198). Her control of form, of grammar, and of tone build on a lifetime's love of literature in English, French, Portuguese, and Spanish, not to mention her devotion to music. The poem's repetitions read like a psychological trauma. Do poetic devices like repetition and rhyme aid us to forget or force us to remember? How does a lyric poem's focus on *my* loss of *you* – "the joking voice, a gesture / I love" (*P* 198) – relate to historical and political losses at the time of the poem's composition, not least America's "loss" in Vietnam and Nixon's resignation from the US Presidency?

The last letter Bishop ever wrote was on the subject of context, specifically whether to include footnotes when anthologizing her poetry. Her answer was typically forthright:

> I'm going to take issue with you – rather violently – about the idea of footnotes. With one or two exceptions [. . .] I don't think there should be ANY footnotes. You say the book is for college students, and I think anyone who gets as far as college should be able to use a dictionary. If a poem catches a student's interest at all, he or she should damned well be able to look up an unfamilar word in the dictionary. (*OA* 638)

Can you still remember Bishop's advice to her first class? Begin with the poems, then letters, then biographies. Perhaps the dictionary needs to come after the poems? Or after the letters? It's up to you when you decide to read *this.*

Notes

1. Elizabeth Bishop, "Elizabeth Bishop: Conversations and Class Notes," in *Conversations with Elizabeth Bishop*, ed. George Monteiro (Jackson: University Press of Mississippi, 1996), 40.
2. Ibid.
3. Cited by Brett C. Millier, *Elizabeth Bishop: Life and the Memory of It* (Berkeley: University of California Press, 1993), 42.

4. Bonnie Costello. *Elizabeth Bishop: Questions of Mastery* (Cambridge, MA: Harvard University Press, 1991).
5. Charles Berger, "Bishop's Buried Elegies," in *Elizabeth Bishop in the 21st Century*, eds. Angus Cleghorn, Bethany Hicok, and Thomas Travisano (Charlottesville and London: University of Virginia Press, 2012), 41–53.
6. Eleanor Cook, *Elizabeth Bishop at Work* (Cambridge, MA: Harvard University Press, 2016), 36–55.
7. Ibid., 198.
8. Cited by Gary Fountain and Peter Brazeau, *Remembering Elizabeth Bishop: An Oral Biography* (Amherst: University of Massachusetts Press, 1994), 330.
9. Ibid.

PART I

Places

CHAPTER 1

Nova Scotia

Sandra Barry

How far back do you go to find the sources of a writer's life and work? To ancestry and community? To family and childhood? To education and experience? At one end of the spectrum, some literary critics argue that art exists more or less independently of external context, to be seen, explored and interpreted based on what exists within it, usually founded on a theory. At the other end, some biographers argue that the work of art is an expression of the self, understandable primarily by knowing a good deal about the creator. Both ends are, perhaps, dubious. Art is, probably, created somewhere in the messy middle of this gamut – at least one can argue it was so for Elizabeth Bishop, who described life as an "untidy activity" (*P* 59).

One way to look at Bishop's life and art is through a frame of duality: geographical (e.g., *North & South*), aesthetic (e.g., literal/surreal), historical (e.g., memory/dream), relational (family/orphanhood), experiential (familiar/strange); but nothing about these dualities is rigid. Her view (which she offered, in one version, in her late poem "Santarém" as "life/death, right/wrong, male/female") was that such binaries ultimately "resolved, dissolved straight off / in that watery, dazzling dialectic" (*P* 207). Bishop often opted for a littoral, a dynamic (creative) place where land and sea meet.

This essay looks at a foundational context for Elizabeth Bishop and her art: her childhood – a good deal of which was spent in Great Village, Nova Scotia, with her mother's family, the Bulmer-Hutchinsons. It offers a glimpse of Bishop's Nova Scotia, but keep in mind Bishop's image of "The Imaginary Iceberg." Most of the context remains nine-tenths below the surface (and rather beyond these pages). This essay is divided into three sections: People: that is, family, which includes parents, relatives and ancestors; Place: that is, Great Village, NS, which includes the ideas of home and travel; and Past: that is, childhood, which includes the phenomena of memory, dream and imagination. These people, this place and her past overlap in intricate ways; all were deep influences on Bishop's life and art.

In an April 1978 letter to literary critic Jerome Mazzaro, Bishop wrote: "Well, it takes an infinite number of things coming together, forgotten, or almost forgotten, books, last night's dream, experiences past and present – to make a poem" (*OA* 621). The impossibility of knowing the "infinite" does not, nor should it, deter biographers and critics from their explorations. There is something to be gained by respectful contextualizing. Bishop continued in the letter to Mazzaro: "The settings, or descriptions, of my poems are almost invariably just plain facts[1] – or as close to facts as I can write them. But, as I said, it is fascinating that my poem should arouse in you all those literary references!" Now to turn to some of these experiences and facts.

People

Elizabeth Bishop was no genealogist, yet for her entire life she was interested in her ancestors and immediate family. At times she actively sought information about the former and remained in steady contact with the latter until her death. Yet she did so while also declaring, especially in adolescence and early adulthood, that she was an orphan, and claimed that her friends were her family.

The facts about her childhood are known, but are often so rigidly condensed that they have become a source of misinformation. This summary is also inadequate, but more or less accurate based on what is known from the records.[2] Bishop was born in Worcester, MA, on 8 February 1911, to Gertrude May Bulmer and William Thomas Bishop. Gertrude was from Great Village, NS, and William from Worcester. On 8 October 1911, William died of Bright's disease and for the next few years Gertrude struggled to carry on and care for her child. She suffered a breakdown in early 1914 from which she recovered, and then, in early 1915, she returned to Great Village, with her daughter, to live with her parents William and Elizabeth Bulmer (Pa and Gammie to Bishop). Gertrude's ill health (she had hyperthyroidism) and tensions with her in-laws triggered another breakdown in the winter of 1916. Seeking the kind of help she had received in 1914, Gertrude voluntarily admitted herself to the Nova Scotia Hospital, Dartmouth, NS, in June 1916. Sadly, Gertrude never left this institution, dying there on 25 May 1934.[3] Elizabeth Bishop remained in Great Village for the next year, but in October 1917 she was removed by her paternal grandparents, John and Sarah Bishop. She lived with them in Worcester for less than a year and became seriously ill. She was taken to Revere, MA, in May 1918 to live with her maternal Aunt Maude and her husband George Shepherdson. When Bishop recovered, she began to visit Nova Scotia again, first returning in 1919 and then nearly yearly throughout the 1920s.

While it is a fact that Bishop never saw her mother after June 1916 and that she was in the strictest sense an orphan (a state of being that *did* have a profound effect on her), it is also a fact that Bishop grew up amid a complex array of relatives (on both sides): grandparents, aunts, uncles and cousins, each of whom brought all manner of positive and negative influences. Members from both sides of her family appear directly or obliquely in some of her poetry and prose, the latter being predominantly memoir and often directly related to her family relationships.[4]

I have argued at length elsewhere[5] that Bishop's relationship with her mother was the most important of her life, even as this central person disappeared from that life when the poet was so young. One of the most important works of art Bishop wrote, "In the Village," is about her mother and the impact of their relationship, of her loss and absence. "In the Village," which Bishop described as "prose-poetry" (*OA* 272) and "completely autobiographical . . . poetic prose" (*OA* 291), is a complex, nuanced word portrait that takes a deeply intimate and fraught relationship, puts it through the powerful compression of the creative process, and transforms the actual, the lived, the individual, into something universal and timeless. How many of us can say we have experienced and achieved that with our mother?

Bishop chose to include "In the Village" between the "Brazil" and "Elsewhere" sections of *Questions of Travel*, the only substantial "prose" piece given this kind of placement in her books (a littoral placement, one might say). She knew it was a significant work, describing it only half-jokingly to Ilse and Kit Barker as a "masterpiece" (*OA* 268). She had sent it first to *The New Yorker*, even though she felt it was "too poetic" for their consideration (*NYr* 90). After a lengthy, sometimes frustrating correspondence with Katherine White, her editor, the magazine finally accepted it, White assuring Bishop, "We all of us like its poetic quality," even as she tried to get Bishop to "strengthen the thread of the narrative" (*NYr* 94–95).

While her mother was the central existential force in Bishop's childhood, her beloved maternal grandparents were, arguably, the anchoring, stabilizing influence. William Brown Bulmer was a tanner, currier and shoemaker, an artisan who could take an animal hide and create sturdy footwear. Elizabeth Hutchinson Bulmer was a homemaker who kept her family fed, clothed and tended. These gentle, devout, caring but not sentimental people taught Bishop hymns, Robert Burns' poems, Bible passages, courtesy, patience, and an idiom – think of "that peculiar / affirmative, 'Yes . . . '," the "sharp, indrawn breath" immortalized in "The Moose" (*P* 192). They embodied and expressed the rich oral tradition of the community, singing, reciting and "uninterruptedly / talking," "peacefully, on and on," (*P* 191–2) to their granddaughter.

Bishop's maternal family also included Aunt Maude, a gifted painter who introduced her niece to art and tried to shield her, not always successfully, from the darker forces of life[6]; Uncle Arthur Bulmer, a tinsmith and alcoholic, who was the only immediate relative to warrant an extensive memoir, "Memories of Uncle Neddy"; Mary Bulmer Ross, the youngest of Bishop's aunts (only eleven years older), a pert, smart, self-confident woman who taught her niece about punctuality and the sharp edges of relationships. And, finally, Grace Bulmer Bowers, who Bishop referred to as her favourite relative. Aunt Grace was a gifted, capable, stoic obstetrics and, later, geriatric nurse with the same "literal imagination" (*OA* 291) and sense of humour as Bishop. She was the longest-surviving Bulmer, dying in 1977 (at nearly ninety), only two years before Bishop herself. Grace and Bishop corresponded continuously during her Brazil years.[7] Grace's importance is seen in Bishop's dedication of her late masterpiece "The Moose" to this beloved aunt.

Relatives were plentiful, but there were also ancestors. Her grandfather's people, Yorkshire immigrants who arrived in Nova Scotia in the 1770s, settled in places such as River Phillip and Williamsdale, deep in the wooded heart of the Cobequid Mountains of Cumberland County. During Bishop's childhood they would emerge, as she vividly remembered, on their wagons bringing gifts of venison and bear meat. For her whole life she was fascinated by people who stayed close to the land, their own land. She admired the resilience, creativity and courage needed to "live off the grid," as we say today.

Her grandmother's people, the Hutchinsons, were more recent arrivals (mid-nineteenth century) from the suburbs of London and were from seafaring stock. Of all her ancestors Bishop was most fascinated by Great-Grandfather Robert Hutchinson, a master mariner who sailed the Atlantic, went "around the Horn" and was shipwrecked in 1866 somewhere off Sable Island. So intrigued was Bishop about this ancestor that she went to Sable Island (a forty-kilometre-long crescent of sand, over 155 kilometres off the coast of Nova Scotia "cheerfully known as 'the graveyard of the Atlantic'") in 1951, to see the nesting Ipswich Sparrow or "get wrecked, too," as she wrote to Robert Lowell (*OA* 221).[8]

Elizabeth Hutchinson Bulmer had three brothers, all of whom had fascinating lives and careers. The youngest, William Bernard Hutchinson, was a Baptist minister, translator and educator who was the first graduate of Acadia University, Wolfville, NS, to become its president.[9] The middle brother, John Robert Hutchinson, was a missionary in India who translated into English *Fortune's Wheel*, the first novel written in Telegu. He married three times, had a large progeny and wrote at least a half-dozen more books. The oldest brother was the most important to Bishop: George Wylie Hutchinson. He was a well-known painter and illustrator in *fin de siécle* London. A good deal of his artwork hung in the Bulmer family home. Bishop wrote two poems based on his paintings: "Large Bad Picture" and "Poem," which span her career, the first in *North & South* (1946), the second in *Geography III* (1976). These poems deal with the role of the artist and art in the world, questions of "commerce and contemplation" (*P* 14) and "life and the memory of it" (*P* 197). Bishop knew about all these ancestors and identified her own creative abilities with her mother's family.

Place

That Bishop loved Great Village and her grandparents' house is evident throughout her writing and in interviews. Bishop resided in Great Village continuously from April 1915 to October 1917, though she likely first visited *in utero*. From 1919 to 1930, she returned nearly every year, mostly for long stretches during the summer, though her favourite time to be in Nova Scotia was autumn to see the colours.

Great Village in the 1910s was a bustling community, bigger in population then than it is now.[10] It had a remarkable outward-looking perspective, being part of a vast web of marine commerce and history. Beyond her own family and the inhabitants, Bishop's most vivid memories of the village were of its landscape (set as it is beside a tidal river not far from the Bay of Fundy with its massive tides – the highest in the world – extensive red mud flats and cliffs) and of its architecture (the imposing St. James Presbyterian Church with its 112-foot steeple; the elegant homes built during the heyday of shipbuilding and Age of Sail; and the impressive civic and commercial buildings, especially the charming school built in 1914, which was the site of Bishop's first formal pedagogical experience and immortalized in "Primer Class").[11]

Bishop is regarded as a poet of geography – place mattered to her. She said she liked to know where she was on the map and often carried a compass. All her ancestors emigrated from England to North America at different times and many of them travelled the world. Her mother was the first Bulmer to go to New England to train as a nurse (followed quickly by her sisters and two nieces), part of a historical pattern of migration between the Maritimes and the "Boston States," which had existed since the eighteenth century. Moving through space-time was a powerful, active force in Bishop's family, thus in Bishop's own life. She understood this "wanderlust," as she called it, as well as its opposite urge: a desire for a rooted connection to one spot, something called "home."

Though Bishop never permanently lived in Great Village, that place was her "home," a fact she declared in her Vassar College yearbook in 1934. Below her photo is written:

Elizabeth Bishop
Great Village, Nova Scotia

– the only non-American listed in over 120 young women.

If Great Village was a template for a decent place to live, her grandparents' small, ordinary, cosy farm house, situated in the very centre of the village beside the river, was the exemplar of what a home should be: old, wooden, busy with comings and goings, a menagerie of pets, lots of artwork on the walls, places to gather, places to hide and be alone and overhear adult conversations. Bishop searched her whole life for another such home and after a number of attempts found it in Brazil, in two quite different contexts: Lota de Macedo Soares's modern house at Samambaia, with her own *estudio* tucked under a mountain, and an eighteenth-century house she restored in Ouro Preto, which she called "Casa Mariana." Of the latter she wrote to Lowell that she was "re-creating a sort of de luxe Nova Scotia all over again, in Brazil. And now I'm my own grandmother" (*WIA* 676).[12]

Past

In her late poem "Crusoe in England," Bishop has her castaway declare, in her classic equivocation of a question, "Home-made, home-made! But aren't we all?" (*P* 184).[13] In 1978, Bishop told Alexandra Johnson, "I've never felt particularly homeless, but, then, I've never felt particularly at home. I guess that's a pretty good description of a poet's sense of home. He [*sic*] carries it within him" (Johnson 102).

The composition of this home "within" is a sum of everything the poet has absorbed, accepted and rejected. Bishop began pondering "home" in her childhood. To say that she was a precocious child is a truism abundantly supported by her art, which is filled with vivid memories from her earliest years. All children are sponges. Indeed, Bishop referred to herself, in the parlance of 1910s Great Village, as "a little pitcher with big ears" (*Pr* 151). Because of the familial and logistical complexity of her childhood, she was, it can be argued, hyper-vigilant, which was both a burden and a blessing. For example, her poems, stories, journals and letters are loaded with sensory images – and not only the conventional kind: sound, sight, smell, taste and touch, but also a sixth sense (call it mystery) that most of us experience but usually ignore, deny or miss entirely.

Is an artist born or made? Probably a combination. Bishop's childhood in Great Village (and in Worcester for that matter) brought to her, a child born into an artistic, expressive, peripatetic maternal family, a vast array of people, places and experiences, all of which affected and stayed with her for her entire life.

Bishop was no historian. She privileged geography over history in "The Map," the first poem in her first book. She regarded "knowledge as historical," but described it as "flowing, and flown" (*P* 64). Yet she cared about facts, the truck of historians. She told Anne Stevenson that she "use[d] dream-material whenever I am lucky enough to have any" (*PPL* 844), revealing her fascination with the subconscious. Yet she prized her "total recall" memory and filled her work with layers of vivid description, often taking years to find the right word for an object, event, person or experience. The literary critic Randall Jarrell sensed that "All of her poems have written underneath, *I have seen it*" (Schwartz and Estess 181). Bishop wrote about what she knew – and what she knew began not only in the moment of creation but had accreted continually through space and time, even from the realm of before she was born.

Arguably, if you take any image in a Bishop poem or story, you can trace a line back to Great Village, maternal family and childhood. This idea is not meant to reduce Bishop's art to a single source, but to show the genesis of the vast, diverse universe that is Bishop's *oeuvre*. Bishop took all that came to her in the first decade of her life, stored it and drew on it in many obvious and not so obvious ways to create her art. She did it over and over again. Bishop was a master recycler. For Bishop, creativity was a kind of alchemy, like the tanning that her grandfather did in the ponds behind his tannery, turning one thing into something else.

"The Moose" is one of Bishop's most important poems. It is also one of her longest – literally, in length, but also in how long it took her to write. Its origin was a visit to Great Village in 1946, but the poem travels both forward and backward in time and crosses a great space (literal geography, family history, creative aspiration). Think about it: this crucial poem, which evokes so much of Bishop's childhood gestalt and *Zeitgeist*, begins in a most unremarkable way, with one simple word: "From." Prepositions (those little helping words so many of us have trouble with) were vital to Bishop. A whole study of them could be done. The "From" in "The Moose" is a profound beginning; its sound echoes throughout the poem – a cosmic vibration; its meaning is far more complex than is initially apparent: What does it mean to be "from" a place, to go "from" a place? Bishop spent a lifetime exploring just such questions, questions she first asked in childhood.

Great Village, her maternal family and childhood memories were not just subjects in her poetry and prose. These forces helped to condition her; they affected her world view and shaped her aesthetic sensibility. She went away from the village and her family – quite far in space and time – as she grew up. But even when she ended up living in Brazil for nearly eighteen years, she wrote often about how things she saw and experienced there reminded her of Nova Scotia. Not surprisingly, it was in Brazil where a flood of new writing about Great Village, family and childhood occurred.

There is little wonder that Bishop, who described herself as "naturally curious" (*PPL* 840),[14] took in so much of the world around her. She was primed to do so by the example of her mother's family, by the vibrancy of Great Village and by her own innate precociousness. Bishop's childhood held more loss and pain than many people experience in a lifetime. She could easily have succumbed to despair – she did struggle with depression, alcoholism and bouts of ill health, which must always be acknowledged. Yet she kept writing through it all and wrote some of the most memorable poems of the twentieth century. For Bishop, the "constant re-adjustment" (*P* 12) and "coincident conundrum" (*P* 71) of life and creativity were, as her favourite phrase from all her poems declares, "awful but cheerful" (*P* 59).[15]

Notes

1. In today's world, the word "fact" is fraught, but Bishop regarded and used this word in a basic way, to indicate something that, for her, was based in reality, existed in a realm of actuality, even truth. Coming, as many of the facts did, from her memory, they could be wrong or askew, but she still held that there was an external, knowable solidity to space and time, even if it was difficult to pin it down.

2. I have written three books about Bishop's Nova Scotia connections: *Elizabeth Bishop: An Archival Guide to Her Life in Nova Scotia*, published in 1997; *Elizabeth Bishop: Nova Scotia's 'Home-Made' Poet*, published in 2011, and "Lifting Yesterday: Elizabeth Bishop and Nova Scotia," which remains unpublished. The latter is a 400-page monograph that offers extensive details and analysis of all the elements of this essay, drawing on documents and records held in numerous public and private archives.
3. "Lifting Yesterday" contains a full chapter on Gertrude's life, illness and hospitalization, revealing, as Bishop herself came to understand as an adult, that her mother had been a victim of her time and the vagaries of early institutional mental health care.
4. Some of the published poems: "For C.W.B.," "The Prodigal," "Manners," "Sestina," "First Death in Nova Scotia" and "The Moose." Some of the prose stories: "Primer Class," "Gwendolyn," "Memories of Uncle Neddy" and "In the Village." Some of Bishop's unpublished poetry and prose devoted to family members can be found in various posthumously published volumes, for example: "For Grandfather," "The Grandmothers," "Homesickness," "For M.B.S. buried in Nova Scotia," "Salem Willows," "A Drunkard" and "Mrs. Sullivan Downstairs."
5. Not only in "Lifting Yesterday" and *'Home-Made' Poet*, but also in a half-dozen published essays, including "In the Village: Bishop and Nova Scotia," *The Cambridge Companion to Elizabeth Bishop* (97–110).
6. Maude Bulmer Shepherdson essentially raised Bishop, who lived with her aunt and uncle from 1918 to 1930, the year she entered Vassar College. George Shepherdson was a domineering, abusive man, to both his wife and Bishop. She never forgot this abuse, but managed to exorcise it, to some degree, with the help of Dr. Ruth Foster, her therapist in 1946–47. Recently discovered letters that Bishop wrote to Foster (now at Vassar) provide new information about this difficult time in her life.
7. Only a handful of Bishop's 200+ letters to Grace were published in *One Art*. I have written a series about this correspondence, "Letters to Aunt Grace," on the Elizabeth Bishop Centenary blog. Sadly, Grace's letters to Bishop have been lost.
8. Bishop spent several years trying to write a piece about Sable Island, tentatively entitled "The Deadly Sandpile," for *The New Yorker*. She never finished it.
9. Acadia University Archives is a repository for a large collection of Bulmer-Hutchinson family material, a collection that helps place Bishop in her Nova Scotia context.
10. The long, slow decline of Nova Scotia's rural population, the "out migration" that depleted so many villages and small towns, began in earnest after World War II.
11. The school in Great Village still operates. In 2014 it was designated a Provincial Heritage Property.

12. Bishop's grandparents' house in Great Village, NS, has operated as an artist retreat for over a decade. It is currently owned by the St. James Church of Great Village Preservation Society and welcomes dozens of artists each year. In 1997 it was designated a Provincial Heritage Property and in 2018 received municipal heritage status.
13. In 1992 the residents of Great Village placed a bronze plaque, bearing this quotation, in memory of Bishop, on St. James Presbyterian (now United) Church.
14. I have taken this phrase, in a letter to Anne Stevenson, out of context. Bishop was referring to a specific thing, that is, Stevenson's literary criticism about Bishop's work; even so, it is no stretch to apply it to Bishop's *modus vivendi*. And perhaps it is a forerunner to that tender moment in "The Moose" (started over a decade before this letter to Stevenson, and finished over a decade after), when the "quiet [bus] driver" says of the "otherworldly" animal, "Curious creatures."
15. Bishop taught this phrase to her pet mynah bird when she lived in San Francisco in 1968. The last lines of "The Bight" are engraved on her gravestone.

CHAPTER 2

New England

Heather Treseler

Addressing her "Darling Alice" Methfessel in March of 1971 from her house in Ouro Preto, Brazil, Elizabeth Bishop confessed in a letter to her twenty-eight-year-old lover that she felt "homesick" for the United States, her "own poor rich bad country," for the first time in her life (VC 114. 36). Several months into her love affair with Methfessel, Bishop acknowledges that in her sixtieth year, habitable geography is as much a matter of intimate companionship as climate or local sensibility. Indeed, she confides to Methfessel that in the years that had elapsed since Lota de Macedo Soares' death, Brazil had ceased, in her words, to feel "like mine," an admission that anticipates the lost "continent" she includes in "One Art," her sardonic catalog of survivable griefs (VC 114. 36; *P* 198).

The New England region and, more specifically, the state of Massachusetts was Bishop's birthplace and burial ground. It was also the locale that informed a consequential portion of her childhood and adolescence and served, in later years, as the backdrop of her canonization as a poet, as she taught in the hallowed echelon of Harvard University and befriended critics and younger poets, several of whom became stewards of her literary reputation. In Boston, Bishop acquired a seaside condominium on Lewis Wharf, which she decorated with emblems from her travels. And in Alice Methfessel, the secretary at Harvard's Kirkland House, Bishop found a late love's "saving grace," a person whose warmth and élan seemed to enable Bishop to achieve some of her best work as well as a measure of contentment and stability (*P* 327).

"I love the things you mean to me about the north and Massachusetts and Gloucester and all those old things I used to know," Bishop opined to Methfessel, pairing geography with love's compass and its recent northerly turn (VC 114.36). Technically, Methfessel was not a native New Englander: born in New York City; raised in Summit, New Jersey; and educated at Queens University in North Carolina, she came latterly to Cambridge for her job at Harvard.[1] Biographer Megan Marshall reports, moreover, that Methfessel's parents were "conservative Pennsylvania country-club Republicans."[2] If not strictly a Yankee, Methfessel nonetheless served as Bishop's practical helpmate and affective axis as the poet reconstituted her life in New England, worked in an elite academic setting, and completed the poems for her last book, *Geography III* (1976).

The epigraph of that collection, borrowed from a children's geography textbook, includes the question, "*What is the Earth*?" and the suggestive answer, "The planet or body on which we live" (*P* 178). For Bishop, in her last decade, earth included a beloved body for whom she lived and loved; a pair of "early & instant blue" eyes she was loath to exchange for "ugly death"; and a person who evinced Yankee common sense, cheer in all four seasons, and doughty countenance of difficulty (*P* 327). Methfessel's appearance in her life – her "joking voice, a gesture / I love" – must have seemed, to Bishop, in her sixth decade, an astonishing if tenuous gift of fortune (*P* 198).

Indeed, an individual's "earthly trust" or the "little we get for free" is sharply delimited in the poems of *Geography III*, which locate speakers in a variety of environs that become, in defining moments, unfamiliar, uninhabitable, or unknowable (*P* 197). These poems record moments of self-estrangement and the desire, in some ultimate sense, to return to a state of being without a "sense of shame," without "objects putting the laws / of identity through hoops," and with "home-made" tools that, in their purposeful necessity, "reek [. . .] of meaning" (*P* 203, 201, 184, 186).

Thus Bishop's speakers include a bewildered child grappling with the complexities of gender, race, and empire in a dentist's waiting room in Worcester, Massachusetts; Robinson Crusoe, restored to an England that resembles New England in its acquisitive curation of a colonial past; and a narrator waking in an apartment building, akin to Bishop's fifth-floor studio in Cambridge, who observes a backyard drama unfolding below.[3] Fittingly, the collection begins and concludes with poems aligned with the poet's experiences at either end of her life. "In the Waiting Room," in fact, features a child who does not want to look *up* from her magazine, who "scarcely dare[s] to look / to see what it was I was," whereas in "Five Flights Up," the concluding poem of *Geography III*, the adult speaker finds "yesterday [. . .] almost impossible to lift" and cannot help but look *down* at the scene below, where a "little black dog" frolics in fallen leaves, oblivious to reprimand (*P* 180, 203). New England, in many respects, was the diameter line in Bishop's life's circle.

Geography III, as a title, hints at this experience of physical space across temporal dimensions of past, present, and future and across the three countries – Canada, the United States, and Brazil – in which she constructed a sense of home. But there is a recognizable turn toward New England, and toward the cry "from inside," which marks the collection as a whole (*P* 180). It situates, with new candor, selfhood in the psychic spaces of traumatic memory, internalized exile, aesthetic contemplation, and interpolating worldly events. Indeed, the New England scenes that appear in such magisterial poems as "In the Waiting Room" and "The End of March" revisit Bishop's sense of her identity as she described it to Robert Lowell in 1960. Writing from Brazil, she confided: "I don't want to become a poet who can only write about South America, etc. It is one of my greatest worries now, how to use everything and keep on living here, most of the time, probably, and yet be a New-Englander-herring-choker-bluenoser at the same time" (*WIA* 317). Her anxiety about putting to "use" her exposure to the cultural richness of Brazil while remaining a "bluenoser," which denotes someone from Nova Scotia, hardy in cold weather or fond of blue potatoes, is both humorous and revealing: Bishop was aware of her life's triangulation between countries.[4] Yet she was eager to retain her "New Englander" heartiness even if she was enjoying, in South America, a much warmer climate and some distance from the American literary scene.

Writing to Anne Stevenson in 1963, Bishop characterized her family background as "3/4ths Canadian, and one 4th New Englander – I had ancestors on both sides of the Revolutionary war" (*Pr* 392). She added that she spent "a few months" in Worcester with her father's parents and lived with "a devoted aunt, in or near Boston, until I went away to school at 16. I also went to summer camp on Cape Cod for 6 summers" (*Pr* 392). In this condensed list, Bishop glosses over two auto-immune illnesses that appeared during her unhappy stay in Worcester, which kept her from regular school attendance until she was fourteen. Nor does she mention the uncle by marriage, George Shepherdson, who abused Bishop emotionally and sexually while she lived with her "devoted aunt" between the ages of eight and sixteen.[5] She also does not detail her formative experiences at Walnut Hill School in Natick, where she made life-long friends, or at Camp Chequesset in Wellfleet, a girls' sailing camp, where she discovered children as "clever, or cleverer" as she was (*Pr* 429). Yet, as William Logan relates in "Elizabeth Bishop at Summer Camp," Chequesset's emphasis on describing nature – in individual, carefully kept notebooks – likely informed the observational style that emerged in Bishop's early letters, including letters addressed to fellow camper Louise Bradley, with whom she maintained an avid and often passionate correspondence for over ten years (Travisano 65). Bishop's first published poem, "The Call," also appeared in the *Camp Chequesset Log*, and it celebrates Wellfleet Bay and the "tang" of sea air, a harbinger of many poems about the Atlantic coast in the poet's New England imaginary (Logan).[6]

A proficient sailor and swimmer and a frequent habitué of seaside towns in Massachusetts, New Hampshire, and Maine, Bishop brings her familiarity with New England's shoreline to bear in "Wading at Wellfleet." This signature poem from *North & South* (1946) offers a surreal take on the surf's approach to shore along the southern tip of Massachusetts. As in Bishop's late poem "In the Waiting Room," a New England scene hinges into a metaphysical dimension: ocean waves are compared to an Assyrian chariot with bladed wheels, menacing a field of warriors as they speed toward shore. Yet the waves' bellicosity is cleverly undercut in the poem's concluding tercet.

> The war rests wholly with the waves:
> they try revolving, but the wheels
> give way; they will not bear the weight. (*P* 9)

As in Marianne Moore's "What Are Years?" (1940) in which "the sea [is] in a chasm, struggling to be / free and unable to be," Bishop's ocean brims with power.[7] Yet superficies surrender to their own façade: controlled by moon and wind, the ocean succumbs to invisible forces that direct its "case of knives'" and limit its capacity for "war" (*P* 9). What appears to be a memorable description of the Atlantic also intimates tensions between appearance and reality, human projection and nature's frail theater of volition. Meditating on the sea, Bishop enlivens a facet of human reality, a brandished power that cannot exert itself beyond its own materiality.

Three other poems, "Sandpiper," "The End of March," and "North Haven," engage with the New England shoreline to explore "inscape," as Gerard Manley Hopkins termed psychic topography. In "Sandpiper," the small feathered creature "runs to the south, finical, awkward, / in a state of controlled panic, a student of Blake" (*P* 129). He is too intent in his search for "something, something, something" under his speeding feet to notice the tides or volume of the waves. Instead he watches, somewhat morbidly, as "the Atlantic drains / rapidly backwards and downwards" from the strand he travels (*P* 129). Here tides, and their independence from human cycles of circadian and clock time, nod to the broader cycles of nature, to planetary forces beyond immediate observation, and to a literalized undertow of loss. The bird himself is helplessly driven, myopic by instinct. Yet the poem concludes with two lines about the varied colors of sand, suggesting that Bishop's "poor bird" is governed, in his hunt, as much by aesthetic as gustatory appetite (*P* 9).

In "The End of March," a human narrator similarly studies the shore as if she could divine – and achieve – her "impossible" wishes there (*P* 200). The poem is dedicated to the poet and travel writer John Malcolm Brinnin and his partner Bill Read, whose "casual but elegant beach house" Bishop and Methfessel frequently visited.[8] In many ways, Bishop's poem functions as a Yankee qualification to the Romantic ode. Indeed, Bishop told Howard Moss, poetry editor of the *New Yorker*, that this was her response to W. B. Yeats's "The Lake Isle of Innisfree," which idealizes a speaker's retreat to a lakeside cabin where he "live[s] alone in the bee-loud glade," allowing nature to feed his "deep heart's core."[9]

Bishop's poem begins less auspiciously with a hint of self-scolding: "It was cold and windy, scarcely the day / to take a walk on that long beach" (*P* 199). Instead of the "glimmer" and "glow" in Yeats's rhapsody, Bishop recounts a bitterly cold stroll at low tide when "Everything was withdrawn as far as possible, / indrawn: the tide far out, the ocean shrunken" (*P* 199). In place of abundant succor, she chronicles absence, chill, and misdirection: a stern wind blows Canadian geese out of formation and pulverizes waves into a "steely mist." Walking the liminal shelf between land and water, between the extremity of low tide and its return, the speaker notes that "The sky was darker than the water – / *it* was the color of mutton-fat jade" (*P* 199). Yeats's Celtic twilight has gone the way of postmodernism, albeit with a distinctly Yankee inflection: Bishop's idiolect mixes the bleak concreteness of New England sensibility with her characteristic playfulness.

"The End of March," as a title, intimates the conclusion of earthly travel, and the poem is wrought with the evocative "surrealism of everyday life" and an unmistakable thread of Thanatos, or a desire for rest and death (*Pr* 414). In "rubber boots" familiar to New Englanders, the speaker and her companion track large dog-prints in the sand; "more like lion-prints," these markings inaugurate the poem's childlike metaphors. Similarly, sea foam at the tide-line is described as a "kite string" that forms a "snarl" and a "man-size [. . .] / sodden ghost," riding the waves (*P* 199). Charmingly jejune and subtly morbid, Bishop's imagery continues in this disarming vein as the speaker in the third stanza yearns to reach her "proto-dream-house," a shack on pilings in the distance, "a sort of artichoke of a house," which may be a figment of her desiring imagination (*P* 199). There, she fantasizes, she could spend the rest of her life alone, doing "nothing much, forever, in two bare rooms" (*P* 199). But unlike Yeats's speaker, Bishop's narrator goes unrewarded. With resignation, she relates that the wind is far too cold to reach her "crypto-dream-house" and "of course the house was boarded up" (*P* 199–200).

At its conclusion, "The End of March" expresses a profound yearning for solitude. It bypasses the spiritual restoration of Yeats's isle to consider the annihilating rest that is death: Bishop's speaker yearns for an otherworldly state of leisure, removed from the labor of human connection, in dialogue with "boring books" and water droplets "heavy with light" (*P* 199–200). Instead of idealizing solitude in nature in the mode of the Romantics, Bishop considers the natural world in its cold caprice. In the final stanza, the speaker and her nameless companion turn back and, in a mock Christological gesture of turning the other cheek, they feel their faces freeze "on the other side" (*P* 200). Briefly, the sun emerges, glazing "drab, damp, scattered stones" (*P* 200). The poem, like the speaker, approaches the inevitable: she makes the end of *her* march among lengthening shadows that dwarf a sense of human agency or time. Bishop's Atlantic imaginary, invoking mortality and the conditions of "giving up the ghost," differs considerably from the violent moil of Robert Lowell's Quaker graveyard (*P* 199). Yet "The End of March" is no less wrought with chthonic drives, human ambivalence, and an aggregation of wishes.

Given their attraction to the New England shore and maritime lore, it is fitting that Bishop set "North Haven," her poignant elegy for Lowell, on an island off the coast of Maine where he spent youthful summer days and she vacationed in her later years. In a letter to Anne Stevenson, Bishop noted "Cal (Lowell) and I in our very different ways are both descendants from the Transcendentalists" (*Pr* 396). In her elegy, she gestures toward this shared ideological bedrock while also distinguishing herself, as a poet and person, from her dear friend (*Pr* 396).

As in "The End of March," Bishop's elegy features a speaker who looks outward in a manner that also looks recursively inward. She sees with almost supernatural clarity "*the rigging of a schooner / a mile off*" and can "*count / the new cones on the spruce*" (*P* 210). Whether using binoculars or relying on imaginative projection, born of years' familiarity, she details the scene in a manner that lends it to extrapolation. Departing from the concrete, she observes:

> The islands haven't shifted since last summer,
> even if I like to pretend they have
> – drifting, in a dreamy sort of way,
> a little north, a little south or sidewise,
> and that they're free within the blue frontiers of bay. (*P* 210)

Seascape provides the setting, again, for a meditation on fixity and flux, stasis and release. Against the images of a traveling schooner, new cones on the spruce, and islands seeming to shift inside the bay, Bishop's speaker notes seasonal arrivals and departures as the backdrop of Lowell's earthly exit. In the tradition of a formal elegy, she memorializes the deceased in a beloved place, a *locus amoenus*: North Haven was the locale, she recalls, where Lowell said he "first 'discovered *girls*' / and learned to sail, and learned to kiss" (*P* 210).

Bishop positions Lowell, in all his fame and foibles, as part of nature, subject to its perennial urges. Thus she names, in the third stanza's allusion to Shakespeare, seasonal flora that "paint the meadows with delight" (*P* 210). Repetition, which marked Lowell's creativity and bipolar cycles, also appears in sparrows' song.

> The Goldfinches are back, or others like them,
> and the White-throated Sparrow's five-note song,
> pleading and pleading, brings tears to the eyes.
> Nature repeats herself, or almost does:
> *repeat, repeat, repeat; revise, revise, revise.* (*P* 210)

The sparrow's "pleading" song, and nature's annual patterns, evoke nostalgia in the etymological sense of the pain of returning home. Completing this poem while on North Haven the summer after Lowell's death in 1977, Bishop uses the theme of perennial returns to signal what cannot come back, what she has wholly lost, as well as her own homecoming to the region of her birth.

During Bishop's career, Lowell's correspondence, professional aegis, and artistic drive often spurred or sponsored her own. But at the time of his decease, there were strains in their friendship: Bishop had refused a visit from Lowell and novelist Mary McCarthy on North Haven months before his death. And her disagreement with Lowell about the publication of *The Dolphin* (1973), which distorted his ex-wife's letters, had induced lingering tension. In the poem, Nature's instinct to "*repeat, repeat, repeat; revise, revise, revise*" intimates Lowell's obsessive revision of his poems, not always to salutary effect, as he sought to improve them and, at times, to redress the distress he had caused himself and others. Bishop's line also hints at Freud's repetition compulsion: unconscious urges that compel behavior in defiance of the pleasure principle, a condition that often seemed true of Lowell's life.

Bishop might have had Freud's paradigm in mind as she writes, of Lowell, in the next stanza: "You had 'such fun,' you said, that classic summer. / ('Fun' – it always seemed to leave you at a loss . . .)" (*P* 210). Lowell's life often eluded the self-forgetful pleasure implied by "fun" and defied tactics of self-preservation. He died of cardiac arrest in a taxicab, shuttling between his third and second wives, his allegiances unclear. Yet Bishop's metaphors situate Lowell, a New England native, among the habitual alterations of its flora and fauna; restoring him to "nature," she reminds us that a poet's death marks the cessation of new songs in a familiar voice. Unlike species of birds and flowers, Lowell has permanently "left North Haven [. . .] / afloat in mystic blue" (*P* 211). He can no longer metamorphose, "derange, or re-arrange," his poems or his person (*P* 211). "Sad friend," she addresses him directly, "you cannot change," and her words have the force of both an edict and epitaph (*P* 211). Eulogizing Lowell as a poet whose revisionary process and personality sharply differed from her own, Bishop nonetheless celebrates the storied landscape that birthed – and would bury – them among their Transcendental forebears for whom the natural world was a secular place of worship and reprieve.

Bishop's return to New England in 1970 coincided with her completion of the poem "In the Waiting Room," which draws upon her autobiographical prose story, "The Country Mouse" (1962). Both pieces situate Bishop's strong ties to New England as a portal for her identity and as a point of relation to the larger world. In the story, for instance, Bishop states that Beppo, her grandparents' Boston bull terrier, "adopted" her (*Pr* 91). Poignantly, she felt allied with him, "being on the same terms in the house": both were benignly ignored by elderly guardians who seemingly did not understand children or pets (*Pr* 91). Beppo, she reports, suffered from nervous ailments, hyperthyroidism, and a "peculiar Bostonian sense of guilt," punishing himself preemptively for an attack of gastritis (*Pr* 91). As lonely and distressed as Beppo in her grandparents' household, Bishop suffered from asthma and eczema while acquiring, in that domestic interval, a distaste for sentimentality, an understanding of class distinctions, and bewilderment at her own existence as "a human being" (*Pr* 99).

Two unfinished poems, "Salem Willows" and "A Drunkard," unpublished at the time of Bishop's death, also revisit her early memories of New England. In the former, a child narrator rides a "golden lion" on a carousel in an amusement park in Salem, a town on the North Shore of Massachusetts, while her aunt Maud knits, waiting patiently for her. Studying the carousel's gilt figures, the child wonders, "Were we all touched by Midas? / Were we a ring of Saturn, / a dizzy, [blank space] nimbus?" (*P* 333). "A Drunkard" is more sinister, as it animates Bishop's memory of the Great Salem Fire of 1914, which she observed from her crib in the town of Marblehead, across the bay from Salem. The fire displaced twenty thousand people and damaged more than a thousand buildings

(Marshall 11). Bishop recalls her "amazement" at the spectacle of the blaze, and she characterizes such "amazement" as her "infancy's main emotion" (*P* 317). Revealingly, she also reports anxiety when her mother, tending to survivors, failed to respond to her cry of thirst (*P* 317). In the last stanza, Bishop wonders whether her alcoholism might be linked to that experience of "abnormal thirst" and her inability to "get enough" (*P* 318). Both of these auspicious poem drafts show the poet's recursive turn to New England memories as she sought to understand – and narrativize – the trajectory of her life.

Bodily shame and abjection are also constitutive features of the published poem "In the Waiting Room" in which the child-narrator reads a *National Geographic* in the early dark of a February afternoon. Studying photographs of adventurers Osa and Martin Johnson, "A dead man slung on a pole," infants with "pointed heads," and bare-breasted women, the narrator reports: "I read it right straight through. / I was too shy to stop" (*P* 179). Fixated by images, she reads compulsively, driven by "shyness" that seems to stem from concomitant interest and discomfort as she partakes of the magazine's commercial objectification of a non-Western culture.

Her aunt's cry of pain in the dental chair spurs the narrator's ontological swoon in which she wonders at the particularity of her identity, "you are an *Elizabeth*," as well as her somatic connection to others, "you are one of *them*" (*P* 180). It is in Worcester, "waiting" for her life to commence as an almost seven-year-old, that the narrator puzzles over the accidents of fate that result in personhood. "How had I come to be here, / like them, and overhear / a cry of pain that could have / got loud and worse but hadn't?" (*P* 181). As the poem concludes, she roots herself in historical time, demarcated by violence.

> Then I was back in it.
> The War was on. Outside,
> in Worcester, Massachusetts,
> were night and slush and cold,
> and it was still the fifth
> of February, 1918. (*P* 181)

Subtly, the narrator links a cataclysmic foreign war to sounds and images of bodily pain closer to hand and to the constricting conscriptions of race, gender, age, and geography. Bishop revisits a version of this recognition – a consideration of how person, place, and historicity inform subjectivity – in *Geography III*'s final poem, "Five Flights Up," which offers a mordant Yankee version of an aubade.

From the outset, Bishop's poem defies the conventions of an alba: instead of daybreak, it begins with the two-word line, "Still dark," and the "quavering" sounds of an "unknown bird" and "little dog" in their slumbers. Seemingly alone, the speaker does not mourn the morning's interruption of intimacy. She soberly observes sunlight illuminating a tree's bare branches and watches a dog running in his yard. As in "In the Waiting Room," an urgent voice interrupts her reverie: "You ought to be ashamed!" The dog owner chastises his pet for an unknown wrong. Oblivious – and utterly unlike Beppo of "The Country Mouse" – the little black dog "bounces cheerfully up and down," unperturbed by his owner's displeasure (*P* 203). "Obviously," the speaker comments in the last stanza: "he has no sense of shame." Envying the canine for its utter lack of guilt, she counterpoints its freedom with the weight of human remembrance, the gravity of subjectivity. Her last lines are subtly devastating, " – Yesterday brought to today so lightly! / (A yesterday I find almost impossible to lift.)" (*P* 203).

Bishop's final decade in New England brought her back to the mortmain of her early life and to "all those old things I used to know," to include the Atlantic coastline, New England's seasons, and signature events from her childhood (VC. 114.36). Whether living provisionally with wealthy grandparents in Worcester, with her aunt and uncle in working-class Revere, or alongside Harvard University's campus, where she styled herself a teaching poet, she was aware of identity's multiple geographies and the particular gifts and conscriptions of her New England home.[10]

Notes

1. Alice Methfessel's obituary, *San Francisco Chronicle* (July 12, 2009).
2. Megan Marshall, *Elizabeth Bishop: A Miracle for Breakfast* (Boston: Houghton Mifflin, 2017), 242.
3. Thomas Travisano, *Love Unknown: The Life and Worlds of Elizabeth Bishop* (New York: Viking, 2019), 330.
4. According to the *Oxford English Dictionary*, "bluenose" denotes a native of Nova Scotia or New Brunswick, a purple potato grown in Nova Scotia, a Nova Scotian schooner, a Presbyterian, or a softshell mud clam.
5. Travisano, *Love Unknown*, 8.
6. See Fiona Sheehan 's presentation of correspondence between Bishop and her schoolmate Rhoda Sheehan in "'Affectionately Yours, Bishop': The Early Correspondence of Elizabeth Bishop and Rhoda Wheeler Sheehan," *Resources for American Literary Study* (2018).
7. Marianne Moore, *The Complete Poems of Marianne Moore* (New York: Macmillan Company, 1969), 95.

8. Qtd. in Travisano, *Love Unknown*, 353.
9. Travisano, *Love Unknown*, 354; W. B. Yeats, *The Collected Poems of W. B. Yeats* (New York: Macmillan Company, 1971), 39.
10. See Priscilla Paton 's chapter on Bishop in *Abandoned New England: Landscape in the Works of Homer, Frost, Hopper, Wyeth, and Bishop* (Lebanon, NH: University Press of New England, 2003).

CHAPTER 3

New York

Jo Gill

Elizabeth Bishop's preoccupation with place has often been noted. The importance to her poetics of her childhood memories of Nova Scotia and Worcester, Massachusetts; of her stay in Paris in the mid-1930s; of her early adulthood in Florida, and the years in Brazil that brought her to maturity as a poet, have been amply traced in the criticism to date.[1] So, too, her fascination with the processes and technologies of travel – with freighter journeys, trips up river, bus journeys and airplane flights, and with maps, gazetteers and compasses – has attracted widespread scholarly attention. In an unpublished letter of 26 April 1948, Bishop observes: "I always like to *feel* exactly where I am geographically, all the time, on the map" (VC 43.17). The titles of three of her collections, *North & South* (1946), *Questions of Travel* (1965), and *Geography III* (1976) are visible emblems of this deep and sustained fascination with location and dislocation and with literal and emotional geographies. Surprisingly, in this richly suggestive context, Bishop's time in New York City has received little critical attention. And while I concur with the view that Nova Scotia, Paris, Florida, and Brazil were formative places, I will argue that New York, too, was a crucial site which informed her work over a sustained period of time, even if not always in ways that are explicit to see. The city offered new perspectives – both metaphorical and literal – and it provided stimulation and provocation in turn.

Bishop visited New York from time to time in the early 1930s while a student at Vassar College in upstate New York, sometimes to visit friends such as Mary McCarthy (*OA* 14) and on other occasions to see plays or exhibitions. Newly graduated, she lived from July 1934 on Charles Street in the West Village before departing for Europe the following summer. It was here, while ill on New Year's Eve, that she wrote the first poem, "The Map," of her first collection.[2] She was back in New York in July 1936, living on W. 20th Street (*OA* 81), and again in October when she stayed "at the old Hotel Chelsea for a few months" (*Pr* 429). An unpublished prose fragment in her archive, "Foggy Night at the Chelsea," shows her beginning to develop the subdued tone, the monochrome colour palette, and the disturbing images (flickering lights, noxious chemicals, depopulated spaces) that were to figure in New York poems of the period such as "Love Lies Sleeping" and "The Man-Moth":

> Rain over tenements and roof-lines a swamp [. . .], gaseous, full of poison [. . .] Lights going off and on – not all at once – peculiar effect – like a slow flicker. Odors of oils, gasses, chemicals, all goods. [Blue]-day bright lamps, col[or]s of no blue sky over earth.
>
> Lone shirts flapping on roof-top clothes lines – distress signals, rafts in a fog. (VC 68.3)[3]

Soon after, Bishop settled in Florida. She visited the city again, though, in January 1947, this time taking a "garret" on King Street, just off Varick Street (see my later discussion of the poem of the same name) (*Pr* 444; *NYr* 27). She was back once more in spring of 1951, staying for a while at the Vassar Club (*OA* 217). By the end of April 1951, she had secured a sublet on E. 69th Street – a "railroad, five flights up" as she describes it in a letter to Joseph and UT Summers (*OA* 219). In spring 1957, she had a short period at E. 67th Street (*OA* 337) but for most of the rest of the 1950s and early 1960s, was resident in Brazil at the modern home her partner, Lota de Macedo Soares, had built. On occasion, she and Lota visited New York together; an undated draft letter to a friend in Brazil from a Madison Avenue hotel describes with glee the sight of the two women "bending over the bathtubs doing our laundry, N.Y. peasant-style" (VC 113.8). In 1967, she returned to New York, staying from August to October in her friend Loren MacIver's studio on Perry Street (*OA* 465–80) – the late poem, "Trouvée" (*P* 172) about the incongruous sight of a dead hen on a local street belongs to this period – before departing for San Francisco, Brazil, and finally making a home in Boston. It is important to note how peripatetic her experience was and yet to observe that New York seemed to exert a strong pull. Bishop is on record as saying that she "could NOT" (her emphasis) have lived permanently there (*Pr* 431). At other moments, though, she identifies strongly as a "New Yorker" (*Pr* 444).

New York is where, just prior to graduating from Vassar, Bishop met Marianne Moore (see her prose memoir, "Efforts of Affection" [*PPL* 471–99]); a decade later, it is where she first got to know Robert Lowell (*Pr* 430). It was the place where, over the years, she visited exhibitions, attended readings, and otherwise engaged – albeit sometimes with misgivings – with contemporary cultural life (see "Letter to

New York," soon discussed). It is where she established her vital, long-term relationship with *The New Yorker* and the place where, for a long time, she accessed support from her doctors, Ruth Foster and Anny Baumann. The city is also, and conversely, where she experienced Lota's traumatic death in September 1967 (*OA* 468). New York provides the backdrop to, inspiration for, or subject of, a number of key poems, from "The Map," "Love Lies Sleeping," "Three Poems" and "The Man-Moth" to "Varick Street," "Letter to N.Y.," "Invitation to Miss Marianne Moore," and "Trouvée." The city also, as I will argue in closing, inflects the late Massachusetts poem, "Five Flights Up." New York, then, is often present imaginatively, if not in actuality.

With this in mind, I begin my discussion in a perhaps unexpected place, with the early poem, "The Imaginary Iceberg," the second in *North & South* after "The Map" (*P* 6). The association with New York is not immediately apparent. The poem has been read as revealing Bishop's "emerging preoccupation with imaginative travel" or, in Bonnie Costello's terms, as "a metaphor for the mind's longing for the absolute."[4] I concur with both. But I also want to suggest, before turning to more explicitly New York poems, that "The Imaginary Iceberg" tells us something about Bishop's journey to get there – both metaphorically and literally. It shows us how it feels to long for something and simultaneously to dread fulfilment, or to set sail while hoping that, somehow, the journey will be curtailed. It is a poem of profound ambivalence which is replete with possibility (the ship) yet also drawn to stasis (the iceberg); her speaker's "good-bye [...] good-bye" in the final stanza is a wave of delighted relief. There is also a more literal subtext, though, which further helps us to understand the poem and its place in Bishop's (journey to) New York. To travel to the city from Vassar in the early 1930s, as today, one takes the train from Poughkeepsie down the bank of the Hudson River. In the winter months, the Hudson often freezes and the view from the train – as I saw for myself in the early months of 2015 while a visiting Professor at Vassar College – is of vast expanses of ice, lying like a " breathing plain of snow" as though "all the sea were moving marble," in the words of stanza one. The Hudson is tidal for much of its length and floes from the north meet ice from the south and are pressed into jagged icebergs, and "glassy pinnacles" (stanza two) which, some seasons, can be seen as far as Manhattan. This would likely have been the case in March of 1934 (one of the coldest springs on record) when Bishop first went to meet Moore.[5] Thus the poem evokes an "imaginary iceberg." But it also recalls the real ones that Bishop would have seen for miles on end as the train from Poughkeepsie travelled south to the city.

Other early poems have a more explicit – perhaps even over-determined – New York setting. As Wanda Corn has argued, in the early decades of the century, responses to the modern city among artists, photographers, and writers, tended to emphasise certain features (light, shade, height, speed), producing "a schematic definition of 'New Yorkness'."[6] This tendency is apparent in Bishop's early draft "Three Poems" (1935) and in "Love Lies Sleeping" from 1937 where, as a newcomer to the city, Bishop is visibly trying to formulate a response to the strange, and often alienating, environment. In both poems, Bishop gives us a speaker gazing from an elevated window during the darkness of night or the dim light of dawn on the frenzy of urban life below. The view from on high was common to contemporary artistic representations of the city (see, for example, Edward Hopper's 1921 painting, *Night Shadow*, or Alfred Sticglitz's 1930–1 photograph, *From my Window at An American Place, North*) and a feature of what Adnan Morshed calls a new "aesthetics of ascension."[7]

In "Three Poems," Bishop begins to get the measure of New York.[8] In Part I, she captures the frantic energy of the city through the use of a perpetually shifting, unstable viewpoint. The emphatic rhyme scheme of the opening lines adds pace and urgency. The poem starts with a view "From the eighth floor" but, after a slight caesura, takes us up to "the twenty-eighth floor" and then plummets to leave us: "Face to on the sidewalk." The vertiginous trajectory emphasises the height of the new skyscrapers, their novelty, and the risks that attended their rise (at the time, the observation platform on the Singer Building was referred to as the "suicide pinnacle").[9] There is a debt here to Hart Crane's image of the falling bedlamite in the prologue to his great poem of New York, *The Bridge*, published in 1930 just a few years before Bishop arrived in the city.[10] In Bishop's impressionistic account, the city is characterised by movement (the "speeding car" and "machines"), by technological innovation ("wires," "headlamps," the "agile camera," and the "cinema") but also, as the poem proceeds, by a sense of disorientation and waste, hence the image of the dilapidated, burned out Coney Island Dreamland in Part II and the solitary figure in the closing section.

These impressions recur in "Love Lies Sleeping" (*P* 18–19). Again, we open with a view from on high, or "from the window," but this time the descent to ground-level, which culminates in the close-up of the dead man in his bed in the final stanza, is more controlled and the tone more subdued. Again, the "New Yorkness" of the city is made apparent through references to transport (the train "switching all the tracks" in stanza one) and to new technologies such as the neon signs of stanza two, all seen through the dim light of a crepuscular dawn. The sound of the city is also a feature, hence the implied noise of the trains changing tracks in stanza one, the "Boom!" of the wrecking ball in stanza seven, the factories in stanza eight (see also "Varick Street") and, closer to home, the sound of bed springs in stanza eleven. New York at this time – the recent Great Depression notwithstanding – was still in a state of constant and noisy development; the Rockefeller Centre, for example, was constructed between 1932 and 1940.

Central to the poem (stanzas four, five and six) is the brilliantly evocative and gradual portrayal of the "immense" city's distinctive new architecture which is "carefully revealed" to us. Bishop guides our attention so that we see the intricacy of the detail and the layering of architectural effect, as "cornice upon façade" the new buildings rise. The "over-workmanship" that she describes is evident, too, in her own careful handling of the material; her judicious adjectives, her subtle repetitions, the alliteration ("weak," "white," "waver"), the enjambment and the superb crafting of the line which takes us in stanza five past successive commas and the extended stanza break to an elevated point where both the building she describes and the reader's own attention appear "to waver there," suspended for a moment at the end of the line. In the parenthetical section which follows, Bishop shows us the "immense city" in microcosm, captured in a glass jar so that we can better grasp its beauty. Set in "skies of water-glass" – a reminder, perhaps, that Manhattan is an island set between rivers and the sea – the "chemical 'garden'" of iron and copper crystals is indistinguishable from the urban skyline of "pale blue, blue-green, and brick" which invokes the iron, copper, and brick used in the skeletal structure, roofing, and curtain walls of the iconic buildings of the day, including the General Electric Building (1929–31), the Chrysler Building (1930), and one of New York's then tallest buildings, the Bank of the Manhattan Company (1930). What the poem goes on to concede, though, is the vulnerability of this exquisite architecture to New York's perpetual process of change; in stanza seven, the sound of the wrecking ball reminds us that nothing lasts in the city that never sleeps.

As the "cloud of smoke" dissipates (stanza nine), the perspective shifts once more. Bishop takes us down to ground level and to a street scene which, again, we might read both as a sign of the poem's conscious "New Yorkness" and of the influence of contemporary visual representations of urban life. Of particular relevance here is the work of Bishop's contemporary, the photographer Berenice Abbott, whose exhibition, *Changing New York*, was shown at the Museum of the City of New York in 1935. Abbott lived in Greenwich Village at the same time as Bishop and photographed the latter's front door at 16 Charles Street, albeit three years after Bishop had vacated it.[11] In stanzas nine and ten of "Love Lies Sleeping," like in several Abbott photographs, and like in the later poem, "Letter to N.Y.," it is the human uses to which the streetscape has been put (the "threadlike clothes-line" and the "water-wagon" seen "throwing its hissing, snowy fan across / peelings and newspapers") that attract her attention. In Abbott's work, as in Bishop's New York poems, the focus is on the tiny but distinctive details that animate the scene and that provide a sense of scale, perspective, and proportion.

There is a similar effect in "The Man-Moth" where instead of the "bird's eye" view that was characteristic of contemporary renderings of New York we have what architect Denise Scott Brown was later to identify as a "worm's eye view."[12] And although the poem's curtailed opening line, "Here, above" invites us momentarily to look upwards, the rest of the poem focuses our gaze downwards, first on the man-moth's "hat" and then on his "feet" (stanza one) and then, lower still, on the "pale subways of cement" that he "calls his home" (stanza four). The vision is disorientating. The "Man" to whom we are fleetingly introduced in line three is, it transpires, smaller than a man (he is the size of a moth, or a "doll") and yet, at the same time, he represents something bigger than both – the "mammoth" to which a note to the title refers (Bishop later recalls that the "newspaper misprint for 'mammoth' [. . .] kindly explain[ed] New York to me, at least for a moment" (*PPL* 715)). This is an emphatically urban and modern vision, framed by high-rises, and sparsely illuminated by "battered moonlight." Successive references to the moon and, specifically, to its strangely distorted appearance (in stanza two, it looks "different to him," and appears as "a small hole") help us to date and locate the poem. On 15 July 1935, shortly before Bishop left America for Paris, there was a partial eclipse of the moon. The *New York Times* reports that this was visible to half of the world's population "including everyone in the United States" and describes rooftop parties, including "atop the Empire State Building and the RCA Building" which were "crowded with 'moonstruck' men and women."[13] The image suggest a source both for stanza one's image of the man-moth being "magnetized" by the moon and for his sense of exclusion. The man-moth, after all, fails in his ascent. He cuts a strange, lonely figure – a representation in insect form of the isolated observers of the prose draft "Foggy Night at the Chelsea Hotel," "Love Lies Sleeping," and "Three Poems," and a manifestation of the fearful outcome of venturing out and away that we saw in "The Imaginary Iceberg." This is a perspective that Bishop was also to develop in "Sleeping on the Ceiling" (1938), a meditation on a solitary night in a Paris hotel.[14] In her New York and Paris poems alike, her tendency is to defamiliarize and thereby to expose the uncanny features of the urban environment.

The slightly later poem, "Varick Street" (*P* 73), from January 1947 when Bishop had returned from Florida and was staying just off Varick Street, reverts to the same tone of unease. The poem features another despondent speaker, alone in an alien and alienating urban environment. It returns, too, to the metaphor of the iceberg (in stanza two, the light on the factory floor is likened to "some captured iceberg / being prevented from melting"); we might note the winter date of drafting, and that Varick Street is just a few blocks from the Hudson River. "Varick Street" is also (and here again "The Imaginary Iceberg" is an interesting model) both highly allusive and very literal. Bishop was later to recall in a letter to her friends Joseph and UT Summers that the poem emerged from a dream even as its rhythms and metaphors depict a real place – the print factory around the corner from her apartment (*OA* 308). As in "Love Lies Sleeping" and "The Man-Moth," the urban environment is anthropomorphized – or, worse still, pathologized. The pipework's "elongated nostrils" exude "stenches" while the "mechanical moons" (the factory lights, recalling the cold moon of "The Man-Moth") are "sick." The colour palette is the same subdued monochrome as in the earlier poems, as though the return to New York after several years among the softer and more compelling colours of Key West (see the greens, blues and golds of the 1939 poem, "Florida" (*P* 33)), offers little by way of comfort.[15] "Varick Street" is a poem of disenchantment, bleakly laid out in curtailed lines with the rather threatening couplet at the end of each stanza ("*I shall sell you, sell you*") adding "a dislocating effect, as intended."[16] The Varick Street dream-factory provides Bishop with a suitably troubling metaphor for her own work as a poet (this is, after all, a print shop) and for her possible misgivings about laying herself bare, or selling herself, through this medium.

On a different note, though, two other poems from the early 1940s, collected in her second book, *A Cold Spring*, in 1955, offer a more affirmative vision of New York life. The first of these, interestingly, offers a perspective from afar. "Letter to N.Y." (*P* 78), written "For Louise Crane," as the dedication explains, encodes the geographical and cultural distance that separates speaker and addressee. In this poem, as in others such as "The Monument" or "Arrival at Santos" (*P* 25; 87), it is the relationship between here and there, near and far, that matters to Bishop. She exploits the clarifying power of the long view – especially when coupled with remembered or imagined detail – and steps free of the schematic approach of some of the earlier poems. According to Howard Moss, her editor at *The New Yorker*, the poem "says more" about the city than "a lot of people who go on and on about pushcarts and Rolls Royces" (*NYr* 153). The poem's intimacy and warmth, coupled with its buoyant form, capture her fondness for the city, deployed as a metonym for Crane.

"Letter to N.Y." opens in the midst of a conversation. Not quite a question, the tone is slightly plaintive ("I wish you'd say") as the speaker imagines the busy whirl (first "plays" and then the drive "round and round" Central Park) of Crane's social life. There is a volta or turn in stanza three, though. The excitement and energy of the opening stanzas begins to recede to reveal the speaker alone and disorientated "in a different place" where things appear "to happen in waves." The image anticipates that moment of horrified self-realisation in the later poem, "In the Waiting Room" (*P* 179). As we saw in "Love Lies Sleeping" and "Three Poems," the city provides anonymity and, with it, freedom. But this comes at some cost. "Letter to N.Y." shows us the other side of New York; one of late, drunken nights and furtive early mornings (stanza five uses the same metaphor as "Love Lies Sleeping," of the "watered streets" which have been swept clean overnight). The poem closes with a return to the appeal of the opening line, this time more emphatic: "I'd like to know." It's an urgent request from the fringes of Florida, where Bishop was then living, for news from the centre.

Bishop's most celebratory New York poem is her warm "Invitation to Miss Marianne Moore" (1948). Moore herself seems to have treasured the gesture, writing to Bishop on 24 August 1948: "Your magic poem – every word a living wonder – with an enfoldment that does not ever go back on itself."[17] New York in this poem (or, more accurately, the boroughs of Brooklyn and Manhattan which Bishop, unusually, names) represents, and even invites, community. "Invitation" is also unusual in Bishop's New York poems in its evocation of the city's vibrant colours. In place of the austere tones of "Love Lies Sleeping" or "The Man-Moth," we have "blue drums" and a "mackerel sky" (stanza one), a "sapphire highlight" and "butterfly wings" (stanza three). Opening with a view of John Roebling's magnificent Brooklyn Bridge (again, invoking Crane's *The Bridge*), Bishop lifts Moore – and thus herself, clinging imaginatively to her coat tails – across the still-industrial tip of Manhattan, through a "cloud of fiery pale chemicals" (recalling the "chemical 'garden' in a jar" of "Love Lies Sleeping"), past the harbour and piers and over the skyscrapers that "glint in the tide." The metaphor evokes the light limestone, glass, and steel that characterized modern skyscraper architecture. As Moore, pictured as butterfly, bird, angel, or fairy godmother, begins her descent, we gain a successively closer view of city life – of movie theatres and taxi cabs (stanza five), museums and finally the "steps" and "doors" of the New York Public Library where the two poets first met. This is a poem of celebration, but it is also a poem that shows Bishop taking control of the relationship. She is the one who issues the invitation and lays claim to the New York that she sets beneath Moore's feet as an enticement and promise.

I suggested in my introductory discussion of the early poem "The Imaginary Iceberg" that New York inflects Bishop's work in ways that are not always explicit. In closing, I want to propose that this influence is sustained through to one of her late poems, "Five Flights Up," the last in her final collection, *Geography III* (*P* 203). Although the poem was probably written from her Brattle Street apartment in Cambridge in 1973, its title and theme return to the New York of the 1950s when Bishop, as I noted earlier, was delighted to have found a sublet "five flights up" (*OA* 219). In the poem, "Five Flights Up," something about the view from the window and the nocturnal setting ("Still dark," the poem begins) conjure for Bishop the New York of memory, or of "a yesterday I find almost impossible to lift," as the poem concludes. This is, in many ways, a poem of disenchantment. But what it shows is the persistent call of New York on Bishop's imagination, long after she had left the city behind.

Notes

1. See Marilyn May Lombardi, ed., *The Geography of Gender* (Charlottesville: University of Virginia Press, 1993); Bethany Hicok, *Elizabeth Bishop's Brazil* (Charlottesville: University of Virginia Press, 2016); Sandra Barry, Gwendolyn Davies and Peter Sanger, eds., *Divisions of the Heart: Elizabeth Bishop and the Art of Memory and Place* (Kentville: Gaspereau Press, 2001).
2. Alexandra Johnson, "Geography of the Imagination," in *Conversations with Elizabeth Bishop*, ed. George Monteiro (Jackson: University of Mississippi Press, 1996), 101.
3. Manuscript fragment, 8 lines, on lined paper (recto) torn from the top half of a notebook page. No date but presumed October 1936. The handwritten text is difficult to decipher; square brackets indicates my conjecture about the word used.
4. Bethany Hicok, "Becoming a Poet: From North to South," in *The Cambridge Companion to Elizabeth Bishop*, ed. Angus Cleghorn and Jonathan Ellis (Cambridge: Cambridge University Press, 2014), 112; Bonnie Costello, "Bishop and the Poetic Tradition," *Cambridge Companion*, 81.
5. "The City That Never Stops Slows in a Freeze," *New York Times*, 17 January, 1994, 1, 23.

6. Wanda Corn, "The Artist's New York: 1900–1930," in *Budapest and New York: Studies in Metropolitan Transformation, 1870–1930*, ed. Thomas Bender and Carl E. Schorske (New York: Russell Sage Foundation, 1994), 277.
7. Adnan Morshed, *Impossible Heights: Skyscrapers, Flight, and the Master Builder* (Minneapolis: University of Minnesota Press, 2015), ix.
8. "Three Poems" is an incomplete draft and was unpublished until collected in Alice Quinn, ed., *Edgar Allan Poe & the Jukebox: Uncollected Poems, Drafts, and Fragments* (New York: Farrar, Straus, and Giroux, 2006), 18.
9. Rem Koolhaas, *Delirious New York: A Retroactive Manifesto for Manhattan* (New York: Monacelli Press, 1994), 93.
10. Hart Crane, *Hart Crane's The Bridge: An Annotated Edition*, ed. Lawrence Kramer (New York: Fordham University Press, 2011), 2–3.
11. Bonnie Yochelson, *Berenice Abbott: Changing New York* (New York: Museum of the City of New York, 1997), 173.
12. Corn, "Artist's New York," 282–83; Denise Scott Brown, *Having Words* (London: Architectural Association, 2009), 98.
13. "Millions Watch Eclipse of Moon, the Longest Here in Fifty Years," *New York Times*, 16 Jul. 1935, 1, 3.
14. For more on this and other Paris poems, see Jonathan Ellis, *Art and Memory in the Work of Elizabeth Bishop* (Aldershot: Ashgate, 2006).
15. For a reading of the aesthetic of Bishop's Florida poems, see Angus Cleghorn, "Bishop's 'Wiring Fused': 'Bone Key' and 'Pleasure Seas'," in *Elizabeth Bishop in the Twenty-First Century: Reading the New Editions*, ed. Angus Cleghorn, Bethany Hicok and Thomas Travisano (Charlottesville: University of Virginia Press, 2012), 69–87.
16. Eleanor Cook, *Elizabeth Bishop at Work* (Cambridge: Harvard University Press, 2016), 52.
17. Marianne Moore, *The Selected Letters of Marianne Moore*, ed. Bonnie Costello, Celeste Goodridge, and Cristanne Miller (London: Faber and Faber, 1998), 467.

CHAPTER 4

Paris

Lisa Goldfarb

In a 1935 letter to Frani Blough, a few months after she arrived in France, Elizabeth Bishop began to lay out her plans for her first stay in Paris, among various activities, to take a "French literature course 16th to 18th centuries and maybe something in Art" at the Sorbonne. She concedes in the same letter to her college friend that "This sounds as if I was settling down here for life," and proclaims, "I am not, never, never, an EXPATRIATE" (*OA* 37). While Bishop remained true to her word, her travels are key to understanding her poetry and poetics. That Bishop identified Europe, and France, in particular, as a place where she wished to travel, and French as important to her poetic development, is clear from her letters a few years before she ever landed there. Her poems, both those written in Paris and over the course of her life, bear the mark of her time in the city.

Already in the summer of 1933, Bishop writes to Blough from Wellfleet to express her intense desire to go to Europe. Although she enjoys the beaches, she writes: "I wish to hell I did have enough money to get over there [Europe] somehow" (*OA* 8). In New York following her graduation, she looked to study French with a tutor at Columbia University. When she writes to Marianne Moore of her poor skills in French, she highlights how much she wished to expand her command of the language, but, even more, to achieve a better grasp of modern French poetry, which she maintains she has only the broadest knowledge: "I have a general idea of the poets' names, at least up to about 1920," she writes, "but that's about all" (*OA* 32).

She would, however, have the opportunity to hone her French language skills soon after she sailed to Antwerp on August 2, 1935. Before heading to Paris, she awaited her friend Louise Crane in a small fishing village, Douarnenez, in the province of Brittany where she enjoyed the beauty of the countryside, its scenery, and local customs. Looking back at this period in a 1964 letter to Anne Stevenson, she fondly recalls that during her time in Brittany, she spent the entire month reading Rimbaud. Brett Millier informs us that during her time in Douarnenez, "Elizabeth began translating poetry, especially Rimbaud, as a way of disciplining her own verse.“ Millier contends that her reading and translating of Rimbaud also left its mark on her poetry, for “This was her first intimate acquaintance with the French surrealists, an important influence on her early poems, especially those she wrote in France.”[1] Bishop's travels, as her stay in Brittany demonstrates, help us to trace both her personal story and the evolution of her poetic tastes and ideas.

Bishop's time in Paris falls roughly into two periods: the first, from the fall of 1935 to February 1936; the second in 1937 after a month of travel in Ireland. Her first extended stay was especially fruitful, both in her activities and in the work the city inspired. Bishop lived with Louise Crane in a luxurious apartment in the heart of the sixth arrondissement, near the Sorbonne and Sylvia Beach's famous bookstore, Shakespeare and Company, then located at 12 rue de l'Odéon. Letters, poems, and sketches reveal her delight with her accommodations. Her poem, “Luxembourg Gardens,” memorializes her time there and shows her familiarity with the area, for she writes of the statues that ring the pond and the nearby carousel where children play: “The Queens of France, / Female-diplomats and flirts, / Their long legs quiet in marble skirts, / Smile, and ponies on the carousel dance” (*EAP* 27).

Letters, too, reveal her ease in moving about Paris and her engagement with the literary and art scenes. Determined to improve her language skills, Bishop enrolled for two hours of French class a day at the Alliance Française. Her recognition of her need for more work on language, however, did not keep her from exploring the city and its cultural resources: she studied the clavichord at the Schola Cantorum, visited galleries, such as André Breton's, and, among the lectures she attended, one by Gertrude Stein. Drawn to the galleries and Beach's bookstore, Bishop's shyness nonetheless prevented her from talking with those artists and writers she met there. When Beach invited her to a party to meet various prominent writers, years later Bishop could not remember whether it was one or several occasions that her timidity got in the way of her taking advantage of such introductions: “In Paris I did meet a lot of famous people, I suppose – even Picasso for a moment – [. . .] G Stein and Alice B – I was invited to tea, with a friend – and the friend went without me, finally. What an idiot!” (*Pr* 430).

Bishop's stays in Paris also gave her opportunities to travel within France and beyond its borders, so that between 1935 and 1937 she had visited not only Brittany, Burgundy, and Provence, but also London, Morocco, Spain, Ireland, and Italy. It was during a trip to Burgundy, at the time of her second trip to Europe with Louise Crane and Margaret Miller that Bishop was in a car accident with her friends. The accident left Crane and Bishop uninjured, but Margaret Miller with a severed arm. The episode was a pivotal moment in Bishop's life that would mark her memories of Paris and France. Her poetic fragment "Villanelle" chronicles feelings of guilt in the aftermath of the accident, as Bishop recounts a dream that Louise had days before her trial: "She was to be executed at a certain hour – but / not formally=anyone could do it / when the right minute came – " (*EAP* 35). That the accident had a bearing on her memories of Paris is clear from a letter she wrote to Marianne Moore in November of 1937: "Paris (and the Îsle Saint-Louis, in particular) does not suit me very well" (*OA* 64). After a trip to Arles in the south of France, and then to Paris for hospitalization for asthma, she returned to the USA the following month.

Still, Bishop's sojourns in Paris proved fruitful, for there she worked on poems and stories that would help launch her poetic career: "Paris, 7 A.M.," "Quai d'Orléans," and "Sleeping on the Ceiling" were composed in the city and published shortly after her stay. Together with her unpublished work – "Song – for the Clavichord," "Luxembourg Gardens" and "Villanelle" – these poems present a vivid picture of the Paris she inhabited. (She also began work on her story, "The Sea and Its Shore" and her two other sleeping poems, "Love Lies Sleeping" and "Sleeping Standing Up," in Paris, though these do not make explicit reference to the city.) In "Paris, 7 A.M.," Bishop first anchors us in the domestic space of the apartment she and Crane shared on rue de Vaugirard: "I make a trip to each clock in the apartment: / some hands point histrionically one way / and some point others" (*P* 28). Just as soon as she speaks from the interior space of the apartment, she then quickly broadens our view to the wider city: "Time is an Etoile; the hours diverge/ so much that days are journeys round the suburbs,/ circles surrounding stars, overlapping circles" (*P 28*). With her reference to Place de l'Étoile (now Place Charles de Gaulle), Bishop portrays the central point of Paris, from which the twelve boulevards spread out in star-like fashion. In the second stanza, she again shifts our lens from the overall design of the city to the immediate neighborhood, specifically to the courtyard into which she gazes. In so doing, she creates a visual portrait of the Parisian rooftops and their courtyards, visible only from the interior space.

Bishop does more than depict the Parisian physical setting. Eleanor Cook offers a detailed reading of the poem in her book *Against Coercion: Games Poets Play*, and emphasizes the poem as reflective of the geography of the city as well as the temporal moment in which it was composed.[2] To grasp the significance of "Paris, 7 A.M.," it is helpful, too, to consider the poem in the light of her thinking about poetry a couple of years before she traveled there. In a letter to Donald E. Stanford in November 1933, Bishop lays out aspects of her poetic thinking that she brings to life in "Paris, 7 A.M." Responding to Stanford's comments about some earlier poems she had sent to him, she explains what she aims to accomplish in terms of rhythm, thought, and structure. First, she writes, "This is a very hard thing to explain, but for me there are two kinds of poetry, that [. . .] *at rest*, and that which is in action, within itself." She suggests that hers is the latter, and wishing to "get this feeling of action within the poem," she allows her rhythm and meter to "find their way through" (*OA* 11). Another aspect of her emerging poetic is variation: "What you say of variation holds true for me," she continues, and "I become very intent upon what I *must* say, the series of ideas being built up in my head" (*OA* 13).

In the three stanzas of "Paris, A.M." Bishop perfectly realizes her aim to "get this feeling of action" in the poem. "Paris, 7 A.M." is at once a travel poem in its presentation of Paris itself, and a poem that emotionally travels from the physical setting to "a mind thinking" (*OA* 12) in that setting. Although the stanzas vary in length, there is a structure to the poem that mirrors the speaker's emotional journey. The first stanza is declarative and situates the speaker "in the apartment" and in the city, yet the "clocks" which point in divergent directions declare "Time" and its confusions as the central focus of the poem. These disparate clocks call to mind the various clocks in Apollinaire's iconic poem, "Zone," which, rather than stabilize time, surrealistically reflect the speaker's leaps from one location to another, Paris to Prague and back again.[3] In the second stanza, Bishop turns inward, not only in terms of the view of the courtyard, but with respect to her thinking; her view of Paris carries the speaker to another time and place. As the speaker notes how "houses are built" toward the courtyard, she, too, turns inward: "It is like introspection / to stare inside, or retrospection." With an em dash in the middle of stanza one (after line seventeen, exactly in the center of this 1934 poem of thirty-four lines), Bishop shows us "a mind thinking" (*OA* 12). It is as if the sight of the inner courtyard sparks for the speaker a Proustian recollection of earlier winters in Nova Scotia, "this hollow square could easily have been there. / – The childish snow-forts, built in flashier winters, / could have reached these proportions and been houses" (*P* 28).

If the architecture of Paris prompts Bishop to feel the proximity of her childhood winters in her native landscape, she does not dwell there long. Bishop returns to Paris in the third stanza, and evokes still another time, the post WWI city: "Where is the ammunition, the piled-up balls / with the star-splintered hearts of ice?" Yet in this poem that traces "the act of experiencing" (*OA* 12) Bishop resists closure, and the poem ends with insistent questions: "When did the star dissolve, or was it captured / by the sequence of squares and squares, circles, circles? / Can the clocks say; is it there below, / about to tumble in the snow?" (*P* 28). With repetitions of words and images from earlier in the poem – "circles," "snow," and "clocks" – Bishop bends us back to the beginning of the poem, not to find resolution, but to re-experience both her physical and interior journey.

In "Quai d'Orléans," Bishop provides another visual rendering of Paris, this time from her second stay, near her quarters on the Îsle Saint Louis alongside the Seine. From the quay, the speaker portrays the steady movement of the barges as they move up the river and the imprint on the water they leave behind: "Each barge on the river easily tows / a mighty wake, / a giant oak-leaf of gray lights" (*P* 29). Bishop presents a moving portrait of the boats on the Seine, conveying their characteristic gray and the leafy color of the water. She also exquisitely creates the "feeling of action in the poem" (*OA* 11) by advancing its twenty-four lines as though she were covering the barges' movements over the course of a single day. The alternating lines create a regular rocking rhythm akin to the movement of the boats along the river. It is hard for me to read this poem without recalling Baudelaire's "L'Invitation au voyage," a poem in which the French poet addresses a lover summoning her to take a voyage to an idyllic land, for the lilt of Bishop's language recalls the earlier poet's musical verses, in which he also creates the sense of the rhythmic motion of a ship over waves.[4] It is less Baudelaire's yearning for an ideal that Bishop echoes than the way his rhythmic verses and refrains convey the river's lapping motion, inducing a kind of reverie.

Key to the development of "Quai d'Orléans" is the concept of variation that she alludes to in her letter to Stanford. Bishop intently focuses on description in this poem: of the barge, of the water behind it ("a giant oak leaf"), and the "real leaves" that float with the current. Yet, she questions whether what we see is real or imagined, the "real leaves" or the imagined ones that the speaker detects in leaf-like shapes she sees in the water, by repeating the words "giant," "leaves," "real" intermittently in the poem. With each repetition and variation, Bishop conveys a sense of the movement of the water and the images that play upon its surface. Are we looking at the reflections of the leaves in the water, the shape of leaves in the wake of the barges' movement," or actual, "real" leaves"? Variations of what we see as leaves appear repeatedly in the poem, and in the repetition and variation, Bishop not only probes the images we see, but the way we remember them.

As much as Bishop explores the view from the quay in this poem, what the last lines powerfully demonstrate is that "Quai d'Orléans" is as much a poem about memory – what we remember about what we see – as it is about how we see. Cook names this poem a "memory poem [. . .] personal memory this time and unspecified."[5] Bishop takes a personal turn with the use of first-person pronouns: "'If what we see could forget us half as easily,' / I want to tell you, / 'as it does itself – but for life we'll not be rid / of the leaves' fossils'" (*P* 29). Given the dedication to Margaret Miller, it is especially moving that the last lines not in quotes read, "I want to tell you," as if Bishop must gesture to what is still powerfully unspoken.

When I suggest that Bishop's "Paris 7 A.M." calls to mind Proust and Apollinaire, or that her rhythms in "Quai d'Orléans" are reminiscent of Baudelaire's in "L'Invitation au voyage," it is not to argue for direct influence, but rather to speculate on how her interest in and reading of French writers and poets – specifically of the symbolist tradition – might have impacted her work. For Bishop's prose demonstrates her extensive reading in French literature, especially from the late nineteenth century onward. That Bishop looked to Proust as a model for thinking about time and memory before she arrived in Paris is clear from a 1933 essay, "Time's Andromedas," in which she considers the treatment of time primarily in novels. Of Proust, she contends that he comes nearest to "the perfect acquiescence of the past with our own time-pattern." A problem she identifies with Proust is, however, that "the moment of acquiescence, to the reader of PROUST, comes in that after-realization of the whole book, not as we read along" (*PPL* 644). In her 1934 essay, "Dimensions for a Novel," she returns to her criticism of Proust and explicitly relates her complaint to her own poetic ambitions: "the thing I should like to get at, is the ever-changing expression" (*Pr* 483). It seems that in the way she addresses time and memory in both "Paris, 7 A.M." and "Quai d'Orléans," she was already attempting to rectify that problem by showing the act of experiencing time in the very structure and method of these poems.

That modern French poetry had a strong hold on Bishop's imagination is clear also from her prose, not only as we have seen in anticipation of her trips to Paris, but throughout her writing life. Reviewing an edition of *Selected Writings of Jules Laforgue* in 1956, Bishop praises his visual aesthetic: "His poetry is filled with the same visual excitement as the impressionists', and the eight and a half pages of *Landscapes and Impressions* often sound the way the impressionists look" (*Pr* 269). Bonnie Costello notes that Bishop's library demonstrates her interest in surrealists as well as symbolists, for it "contained volumes of Apollinaire, Baudelaire, Char, Corbière, Jacob, Proust, Reverdy, and Rimbaud."[6] In 1963, nearly thirty years after her first stay in France, Bishop recalls her reading of Rimbaud: "I've always thought one of the most extraordinary insights into the 'sea' is Rimbaud's L'eternite [*sic*]" (*Pr 414*). In light of Bishop's penchant for poems of the sea, it is not surprising that Rimbaud's highly compressed image would exercise such a fascination for her. Surely, his prose poems, especially *Illuminations*, with their rhythmic prose and startling surreal images would have been alluring for Bishop as well.[7] It must be said, too, that Bishop's translations of several of Jacob's verse poems ("Rainbow" and "Banks") and prose poems ("Patience of an Angel" and "Hell is Graduated") likewise reflect how compelling she found his prose rhythms and his often jarring surrealist images.

Of all modern French poets, however, Bishop reserves her highest praise for Baudelaire. Just after she discusses Rimbaud in her letter to Anne Stevenson, she writes of Baudelaire: "Two of my favorite poets (not best poets) are Herbert (I've read him steadily almost all my life), and Baudelaire" (*Pr* 415). She elaborates in her essay, "Writing poetry is an unnatural act," tying Baudelaire closely to her own poetic aims. Of poetry broadly, she writes that it "takes great skill to make it seem natural" (*Pr* 327). Bishop then goes on to suggest Baudelaire as one of the poets who most accomplishes this task, identifying the poetic features that she most values: "The three qualities I admire in poetry I like best are: *Accuracy, Spontaneity, Mystery*" (*Pr* 328). Referring to the French poet's poem, "Le Balcon," Bishop clarifies her point about mystery, and cites the image of 'Les soirs illuminés par l'ardeur du . . .' where *charbon* is the telling word – surprising, accurate, *dating* the poem, yet making it real, yet making it mysterious – " (*Pr* 330). Referring to Bishop's discussion of the word "charbon," Cook contends, "she read him closely enough to hear a surprising word for modern ears and how it works."[8] Costello finds such mysterious "Baudelairean effects" in poems across Bishop's oeuvre: "The iridescent flies in 'At the Fishhouses,' the rainbow in the oil spill in 'The Fish,' the image of 'gooey tarts' as 'red and sore' eyes in 'Going to the Bakery.'"[9] Angus Cleghorn, too, sees a strong Baudelairean impact on Bishop: "Like Stevens," he writes, "Bishop found that Baudelaire's violent tone, color, and line, and especially word choice, allowed for precise sensual assaults in spontaneous rhythms."[10] As Cleghorn notes, this is evident in "The Bight," a poem in which she explicitly names

Baudelaire. Frances Leviston, as well, asserts that this poem not only engages directly with Baudelaire, but also "with the seven-hundred-year old tradition of the *danse macabre* that Baudelaire reimagined."[11]

Bishop's structure in "The Bight" is as "untidy" as the coastline it describes: it is composed of one long stanza with no discernible rhyme scheme. She opens in painterly fashion: "At low tide like this how sheer the water is. / White, crumbling ribs of marl protrude and glare" (*P* 59). The irregular rhythms of her lines, and the poem's jagged structure initially seem distant from the tighter forms of Baudelaire's sea poems ("L'Homme et la Mer," L'Invitation du Voyage," "Le Voyage").[12] Bishop's poem, however, draws from Baudelaire in several key ways. First, her language here is as precise as Baudelaire's: she describes the scene in meticulous detail: the "sheer" water; "the crumbling bits of marl," etc. "The Bight," too, recalls Baudelaire, and the symbolists more broadly, in the way she works through the senses. She alerts our visual sense to the complexity of the terrain she describes, which is at once translucent and opaque. She then asks us to imagine the texture of the objects strewn about: "the boats are dry," "pilings as dry as matches" and even registers the absence of "wetness" in the water itself ("the water in the bight does not wet anything"). It is when she tries to render the scene sonically that she names Baudelaire, as if to conjure his synesthetic powers: "One can smell it turning to gas; if one were Baudelaire / one could probably hear it turning to marimba music" (*P* 59). Even in Bishop's dense descriptive language and her looser structure, we can sense her knowledge of symbolist experimentation. Baudelaire, Mallarmé, Rimbaud, and Valéry composed verse in traditional forms, yet they also often blurred the boundaries of verse and prose in their innovation of the prose poem. Bishop, too, as Vidyan Ravinthiran has demonstrated in *Elizabeth Bishop's Prosaic*, challenges the distinctions between verse and prose. In poems such as "The Bight," "At the Fishhouses," and "Cape Breton," one can hear the resonance of the symbolists' experimental spirit as they worked to renew what constitutes form and musicality in poetry.[13]

Along with the destinations Bishop travelled to and lived in for a time – Key West, New York, Brazil, Mexico – Paris holds a key place. Her extended periods of time there in the mid-1930s, where she studied the French language, met fellow artists, and immersed herself in the culture, became a wellspring for her poetic development, for it was at this time that she began to publish her poems, pen her stories, and shape her poetics. While it is her earlier poems – most notably, "Paris, 7 A.M." and "Quai d'Orléans" – where she incorporates her experience of Paris most directly, even her later work reflects her continuous interest in those French poets whom she most admired. As we have seen, Bishop frequently refers to those writers: Baudelaire, especially, and the symbolists and surrealists who follow him. There is still more work to be done to fully explore Bishop's French connections, including her translations and correspondence with other poets (Lowell and Moore) about theirs; certainly, too, the impact of surrealist and other schools of French poetry on her own. Bishop did not adhere to any one poetic school; however, her poems and stories reflect her engagement with many traditions, including her reading and grasp of modern French poetry and poetics.

Notes

1. Brett C. Millier, *Elizabeth Bishop: Life and the Memory of It* (Berkeley: University of California Press, 1993), 89.
2. Eleanor Cook, *Against Coercion: Games Poets Play* (Stanford, CA: Stanford University Press, 1998), 44–50.
3. Guillaume Apollinaire, *Alcools* (Hanover, NH: Wesleyan University Press, 1995), 2–11.
4. Charles Baudelaire, *Flowers of Evil and Other Works*, ed. Wallace Fowlie (New York: Dover, 1992), 56.
5. Eleanor Cook, *Elizabeth Bishop at Work* (Cambridge University Press, 2016), 74–75.
6. Bonnie Costello, *Elizabeth Bishop: Questions of Mastery* (Cambridge: Harvard University Press, 1991), 26.
7. *Rimbaud, Complete Works, Selected Letters*, ed. Wallace Fowlie (Chicago: University of Chicago Press, 1966), 138, 213.
8. Cook, *Elizabeth Bishop at Work*, 50–51.
9. Bonnie Costello, "Bishop and the Poetic Tradition," in *The Cambridge Companion to Elizabeth Bishop*, ed. Angus Cleghorn and Jonathan Ellis (New York: Cambridge University Press, 2014), 89.
10. Angus Cleghorn, "Bad Boy for Good: Baudelaire in Stevens and Bishop," in *Wallace Stevens, Poetry, and France: "Au pays de la métaphore,"* ed. Juliette Utard, Bart Eeckhout, and Lisa Goldfarb (Paris: Éditions rue d'Ulm ENS, 2017), 123–37.
11. Frances Leviston, "Mothers and Marimba in 'The Bight': Bishop's Danse Macabre," *Twentieth-Century Literature*, 61.4 (2015), 437.
12. Baudelaire, *Flowers of Evil and Other Works*, 32, 56, 94.
13. Vidyan Ravinthiran, *Elizabeth Bishop's Prosaic* (Lewisburg, PA: Bucknell University Press, 2015).

CHAPTER 5

Florida

Sarah Kennedy

Of all the places Elizabeth Bishop lived in her achingly peripatetic life, Florida might be the most liminal. From the tropical wetlands of the Everglades, to the mangroves of the Ten Thousand Islands and the coral reefs of the Keys, Florida is a state in flow, a slow-moving river of swamp, hardwood, and grassland melting into sea. In Florida, as Bishop wrote in her poem of that name, the sky becomes liquid: a wake of buzzards drift down towards the swamp "in circles like stirred-up flakes of sediment / sinking through water" (*P* 33). The Florida Keys, where Bishop spent most of her time, are a series of islets extending outwards into the Florida Straits: an archipelago stranded between land, sea, and sky. Alligators, sea turtles, manatees, and dolphins suggest the permeability and deliquescence of the natural world.

The string of islands ends with Key West, an outcrop of land only four miles long and two miles across. From Key West, you can watch the sun rise out of the Atlantic, and set into the Gulf of Mexico. Its ecosystems born of the admixture of saline and fresh waters, the Keys are a place of hybridity; of silt, shadows, and shifting histories. As the southernmost point of the continental United States, Key West is closer to Havana than to Miami. Cuban, Seminole, and Caribbean cultures touch, run together, and transform. If Bishop had been searching for somewhere that mirrored her ambivalence – her sense of the self as profoundly contingent – she could not have alighted on a better place.

As global temperatures increase, the archipelago at the bottom of Florida will change. Rising sea levels will bring an influx of saltwater, and in Key West, the flooding that periodically submerges the Old Town will become a regular event. In the future, we will be faced with the prospect of king floods and hurricanes that wipe out the pretty "conch houses" with their white fences, genteel porches, swaying palms, and slatted windows. Yet even in Bishop's time – in the heyday of literary-bohemian Key West – the threat of environmental devastation was never far away. Bishop first visited

Florida in early 1937, a mere year and a half after the Labor Day Hurricane of 1935 had killed hundreds of people in the Upper Keys, collapsed buildings and bridges, and destroyed thirty-five miles of the railway line connecting Key West with the Florida mainland.[1]

In January 1937, when she was twenty-five years old, Bishop embarked on a fishing trip along the Gulf Coast with her partner and former Vassar classmate Louise Crane. After fishing on Keewaydin, one of the barrier islands off the coast of Naples in Southwest Florida, they travelled to Key West by boat, staying for two months. Bishop returned to Key West in January 1938, staying in a boarding house close to the home of her Aunt Maude and Uncle George. Louise Crane joined her, and the pair bought a traditional "eyebrow"-style house together at 624 White Street, moving in on 24 May 1938.[2]

Key West became a proving ground for much of the poetry that made up Bishop's first collection, *North & South* (1946). It gave shape to the imagined South that forms one of the volume's poles. Bishop wrote to Marianne Moore from Keewaydin:

> From the few states I have seen I should now immediately select Florida as my favorite. [. . .] it is so wild, and what there is of cultivation seems rather dilapidated and about to become wild again. [. . .] we took a very slow train from Jacksonville here. All day long it went through swamps and turpentine camps and palm forests and in a beautiful pink evening it began stopping at several little stations. The stations were all off at a tangent from the main track and it necessitated first going by, then stopping, backing up, stopping, starting again. (*PPL* 742)

The train's unhurried motion, its tangential stops and back-tracking inefficiencies likely appealed to Bishop's revisionary impulses and desire to adopt a leisurely pace of living. Even at this early stage, Bishop clearly felt a kinship with the "careless, corrupt state" (*P* 34) where life attained "a natural pace," and "drunkenness is an excuse as correct as any other" (*OA* 76).

Responding to the sensuality of the Everglades, Bishop remarked upon seeing "the strangest and most beautiful birds" (*PPL* 743). Her Key West correspondence with Moore is full of the gastronomic pleasures of mangoes, guavas, sugar apples, and Spanish lime; of rich Cuban coffee and conch chowder. Years later, recalling her decision to settle in Key West, Bishop spoke longingly of the "light and blaze of colors," and of her love of swimming.[3] Yet there was something in the florid plenitude of the Gulf that Bishop mistrusted. Her first Key West poem "Late Air" celebrates the seductive late-night music that arcs its magic over "dew-wet lawns" (*P* 45) only, finally, to refuse its inducements. The poem finds a more apt and austere complement for "love on summer nights" in the lights of a navy aerial, burning red and remote in the darkness.

Key West looms large in the American literary imagination as the city of Ernest Hemingway, of Wallace Stevens, and Robert Frost. The tiny coral island hosted John Dos Passos, Tennessee Williams, and Charles Olson in the years preceding WWII. The balmy climate, exotic landscape, relative isolation, and possibility of living cheaply made Key West an immediately attractive prospect for artists and writers during the first half of the twentieth century. Bishop quickly adopted this community. As Barbara Page observes, "in the desuetude of Key West, at the geographical periphery of the country, Bishop found a place corresponding to her own disposition for the margins."[4]

David Kalstone suggests that the Key West Bishop encountered after 1938 was a village that recalled for her the Great Village, Nova Scotia, of her early childhood, reminiscent "of the intimacies and improvisations of village life."[5] This view is supported by Dana Gioia's recollection of Bishop's musing on her Key West neighbour Wallace Stevens, during her modern poetry class at Harvard:

> To Miss Bishop, Stevens' greatest subject was not poetry, the supreme fiction. It was Florida, the supreme landscape. She [. . .] returned to the subject repeatedly. [. . .] Her comments on Key West were always prefaced with disclaimers like "Back in the thirties, there used to be . . . " She spoke of it as if she were Eve remembering Eden.[6]

The Gulf is a littoral zone, with all the embodied provisionality of land borrowed from the sea. The shifting geography of the Florida Keys encodes the violence of loss – historic, ongoing, and future – in ways that must have deeply resonated with Bishop. In a string of islets, everything is "only connected by 'and' and 'and'" (*P* 58). It is not surprising, then, that Bishop would later speak of Florida in ways that link it with the inescapability of losing. Florida's literal metonymies were to be encoded in Bishop's rhythmic rehearsals of loss, each grief islanded from and yet looking toward the next, as in "One Art." Key West is, moreover, a place of bones. The modern English place-name is a corruption of the Spanish "Cayo Hueso," "bone cay." A "cay" (from Taino) is a small island or reef. Nineteenth-century accounts suggest either that conquistadors encountered the bones of native people (possibly Tequesta or Calusa), as the island had been used as a communal graveyard, or that in the eighteenth century the island was the site of a massacre of native people by their mainland counterparts.[7]

Bishop was aware of this local history, it seems, and of Key West as a place of death and reanimation, submersion and salvage. One of her Key West notebooks refers to "Bone Key" and "A Key of Bone" as alternative titles for her sequence of poems written in and about Key West.[8] In a notebook entry from October 1939 Bishop remarked on "something inherent about the soil here – so shallow" (*EAP* 265). Something in the psychic life of the ever-metaphysical Bishop was forever seeking for the skull beneath the skin. "The Bight" finds death in the revelations of low tide. The receding waters expose glaring mudstone "ribs" that crumble in the air (*P* 59). The poem "Florida" is similarly saturated with terminal beauty: the giant turtles, "helpless and mild," are bleached to white skulls, staring blindly from "round eye-sockets / twice the size of a man's" (*P* 33). Bishop's evocations of barnacled turtle-shells strewn on beaches and dead oysters that turn the swamps bone-white connect her portraits of place explicitly with Key West's founding legend. This pelagic environment is unstable, perilously perched on osseous fragments and tethered only loosely to itself. The "state that floats in brackish water, / held together by mangrove roots" (*P* 33) is reliant on a shifting, subterranean network, forever under threat of dissolution. Alive but unseen, these networks contain and conceal histories of violence and death that threaten to rupture the delicate ornamentation of Key West's day-lit surfaces. "The island starts to hum / like music in a dream," Bishop writes in "Full Moon, Key West," "a zither laid / upon the flood / of the glittering Gulf" (*EAP* 59–60).

But, as with so many moments in Bishop's work which link an experience of shock or trauma with attenuated self-realisation, the space opened up by loss also creates a space for becoming. The genesis of "The Monument" (1939) appears in the first of Bishop's Key West notebooks (from 1937), as a pen-and-ink figure situated on the seashore, framed by a poetic statement of intent:

> this is the beginning of a painting
> a piece of statuary, or a poem,
> or the beginning of a monument.
> Suddenly it will become something.
> Suddenly it will become everything.[9]

The monument is constructed from found items on the beach (Bishop links it to surrealist aleatory techniques, referring to a "frottage" of the sea and evoking *objet trouvé* in the forms of her sketch). The process of movement from something to everything follows the logic of the scavenger.

The short story "The Sea and Its Shore" (published in 1937) suggests Bishop's ambiguous view of scavenging as the underlying model for the "literary life" (*Pr* 12), as both mode of reading and process of creative accretion, although it does so in uncomfortably autobiographical terms. The protagonist is an alcoholic named Edwin Boomer, who cleans the beach by night. Boomer uses his lonely and menial employment to scavenge for fragments of writing that he collects and meditates upon in a state of mystical semi-drunken bewilderment. Bishop's story intersperses descriptive narrative with extracts from newspaper clippings, letters, and poetry, its construction mimicking the method of Boomer's accretive practice as well as its effects of disruption and deferral. Although the story is full of literary references, its deeper interest is in the materiality and degradability of written matter. Fascinated by the processes of breakdown he witnesses through the papers' "stages of soddenness," Boomer sculpts animal and human figures from the pulp before burning them (*Pr* 12). There is an unresolved tension between the natural world and the world of letters whose "presses turn out too much paper" (*Pr* 12). Yet the metamorphic flights of waste paper into wheeling flocks form the basis of Boomer's visionary imagination, "headlines and sentences streaming around him, like a man shooing a flock of pigeons" (*Pr* 13). Text spills out into the world, which it reshapes in its own image. A sandpiper appears "like a point of punctuation," leaving its own print in the sand (*Pr* 16).

Boomer is a poignant figure, trapped by inebriated fears, isolated and confused. Yet he shares a sly likeness with Bishop's other troubled but gifted secret-keepers, "The Man-Moth" and "The Gentleman of Shalott." Boomer observes of the airborne papers that their manner is "an oblique one, slipping sidewise" (*Pr* 13). It is in the aleatory motions of fragmentary papers caught by the sea-wind that the matter of art lies, a wild dance of shifting waste and lost particles. Would such a story have been possible if not for its grounding in the shifting seascape of Key West? Jani Scandura observes that in Key West "it dawns on you finally that the disorder, the mismanaged fragments, the half-baked scraps of speech are really, actually, precisely the point."[10] It is a place that "built itself by acknowledging wreckage, by embracing dead things, tossed fragments and scraps."[11]

In the nineteenth century, Key West was for a time the richest city in the United States. The island prospered from wrecking and salvaging the cargoes of ships that foundered on the Florida reefs. Scavenging can be a healthy practice, a recycling and repurposing of things whose value would otherwise be unrealied. But it also has darker associations. In seeking out the disorderly, and in cultivating the creative possibilities of dilapidation,

Bishop engaged in artistic practices that we look upon now with a sense of unease. Scavenging is, after all, an ambiguous method of appropriation.

Bishop was drawn to Key West's shabbiness. When Bishop arrived, the city was broke. The advent of the machine-rolled cigarette that destroyed the local cigar industry coincided with the broader economic pressures of the Great Depression. After a decade of serious economic decline, the Key West government declared bankruptcy on 2 July 1934, and handed over administration of the city to state – and eventually federal – control. The city became a model site for New Deal economic recovery policy, overseen by Julius Stone, a lawyer and Roosevelt protegé, who ran the Federal Emergency Relief Administration. Stone assembled a volunteer labour force to clear the putrid garbage left on the streets by unpaid city workers and embarked on an ambitious construction programme to revive Key West's dilapidated housing with a view to improving the city's tourist amenity. The refurbishment of the city was still very much underway three years later when Bishop arrived. As she put it, "I seemed to have a taste for impoverished places in those days."[12]

Bishop's "taste for impoverishment" is unsettling, entangled as it is with issues of race and class. During the late nineteenth and early twentieth century, large numbers of immigrant workers had been attracted to Key West by the booming cigar industry, including thousands of Cubans, as well as Spanish, Italian, and Bahamian migrants. For a while, the city had been a site of relative interracial integration, particularly within the community of Cuban émigrés where the crude racial binary of the American South was not enforced. By the 1930s, however, Key West, like the rest of Florida, was in thrall to American nativism and Jim Crow. The Instituto San Carlos, which had once housed an interracial school catering to Black and white Cubans, now offered education to whites only.[13] African Americans and communities of colour from Cuba, the Bahamas, and the wider Afro-Caribbean diaspora were corralled by Jim Crow in the Key West district known as Jungle Town or *La Africa* (now Bahama Village).[14]

Bishop's boarding house at 529 Whitehead Street was on the edge of Jungle Town. During the autumn and winter of 1938, Bishop produced several poems about her African American and Black Cuban neighbours. "Jerónimo's House" combines Bishop's natural self-positioning as an outsider with close, almost ethnographic observation in its cataloguing of the contents of the Cuban's modest clapboard house: "a little dish / of hominy grits," "tissue-paper roses" and the "old French Horn" hung on the wall, played in the José Martí day parade (*P* 35).[15] The poem's surprising willingness to ventriloquise Jerónimo is an instance of what Margaret

Dickie terms Bishop's "poetic possession of the dispossessed" and her apparent need "to project onto [people of colour] an exuberant variety of her own artistic endeavours."[16] "Cootchie," from *North & South*, is similarly discomforting. The poem is framed as a subdued lament for the eponymous maidservant. Yet the dead woman is offered up as an occasion for feeling, rather than being the primary object of the poem's grief. The funereal landscape is permeated by a blanched and waxen whiteness repeatedly figured as deathly, suggesting an ambivalence towards whiteness and a melancholic fantasy of succour from Black others. Whiteness is represented as a state of enervation, but it is precisely in this neurasthenic sensitivity that we can locate the unexamined white exceptionalism of Bishop's racialised poetics. This is a poem in mourning for its life; "a line to mark Miss Lula's losses" (*P* 46). Despite its elegiac potential, the poem's self-regarding sympathies fail to overcome the fastidiousness of the racialised mistress/servant relationship, leaving only a lost grave and "wave after wave" of the sea.

Tyler T. Schmidt describes Bishop in Key West in critical terms as a "guide for her fellow cultural tourists into sexually and racially transgressive spaces."[17] In the wide-ranging later poem "Over 2,000 Illustrations and a Complete Concordance" (1948) the speaker regards "the little pockmarked prostitutes" of the brothels of Marrakesh dispassionately as they serve themselves up as entertainment (*P* 58). Although the moment draws on Bishop's experiences during her 1936 trip to North Africa with Louise Crane, it also echoes accounts of Bishop and Crane's excursions "slumming" with Black prostitutes at the Square Roof, a brothel in Key West at the corner of Emma and Petronia Streets that catered to a white male clientele. Bishop took Tennessee Williams and James Laughlin to Sunday tea at the Square Roof in 1940, where (as James Laughlin recalls), the women were in their "church" dresses: "They were not talkative, though Elizabeth and Louise tried to draw them out."[18] These accounts suggest in Bishop a sustained and fascinated sympathy, but a sympathy so tentative that it is largely mute.

Silent as they are on questions of race and class, Bishop's Key West love poems provide striking exceptions to her self-protective rule of demurral from passionate self- expression. Poems such as "'It is marvellous to wake up together,'' "The walls went on for years & years . . ., " and "Pleasure Seas" provide a belated window into what Angus Cleghorn calls "Bishop's developing sexual-geographic poetics."[19] These poems were likely written for Marjorie Stevens while she and Bishop were living together at 623 Margaret Street in the early 1940s,[20] yet remained unpublished until many decades later. "Pleasure Seas" (1939), Bishop's self-delighting paean to embodied lesbian eroticism, remained unpublished until 1983. The poem offers a vision of sensual amplitude "out among the keys / Where the water goes its own way, the shallow pleasure seas / Drift this way and that mingling currents and tides." The poem's palate builds from the delicate pink, lavender, and pistachio of a pastel eroticism into the chromatic intensity of "violent" reds, "neon," and purple. The tender opacity of "Mermaid Milk" becomes a sea of burning glass from which "pleasure strikes off humming"; a crackling *jouissance* both "poisonous and fabulous" (*P* 279). Relieved of its human scale, Key West is refigured as an erogenous zone; a shuddering landscape "whose bells vibrate" and "shock after shock" turns the sea to "delight." In this thrilling psycho-sexual playground for Bishop's supreme abstractions, Grief spreads and Love shatters, burning itself out in bright focus. What remains animates the empty, inhuman sea, "Dancing happily by itself" (*P* 281).

Key West became, as John Lowney observes, an "increasingly complex site of social – as well as geographical – marginality" in Bishop's writing,[21] as is apparent in her "Bone Key" poems. Relinquishing the abstractions of the sea for the social striations of Key West's urban grid, "The Street by the Cemetery" (*EAP* 43) probes the dynamics of racial inequality and dislocation. Shadowy, moonlit figures gaze, hypnotised, at the moonlit gravestones from their modest verandahs. Although confined by the domestic boundaries of their neighbourhood, these night watchers momentarily slip the constraints of class and colour. Something ineffable and unexplained in the "warm & brilliant night" has gifted these "steerage passengers" with "deck-chairs" as they contemplate in silence the "long row of white oleanders" that border the cemetery. Jonathan Ellis sensitively reads this poem as a meditation on the sterilising effects of whiteness, but it retains a racialising diffidence in its concluding depiction of flotsam as "dark accumulations [. . .] in the dirty harbour" (*EAP* 43). As Ellis concludes, "there is a political point being made here, but only if one wants to locate it."[22] Here, as often in her depictions of racialised others, Bishop frustratingly avoids what she elsewhere calls "the acuteness of the question" (*P* 72). And yet there is, unmistakeably, a critical consciousness of violence, alterity, and historical indifference in her portrayals, such that Jani Scandura can argue that Bishop's work appears "aware of the dynamics of race in Key West in a way that almost no other Anglo-American writer is."[23]

"Songs for a Colored Singer" goes furthest of all Bishop's published poems about race in its immersion in a Black female subject position, constructing a series of blues-poem monologues in the voice of a jazz singer. Critics disagree as to the extent to which the poem successfully manages its multiple subjectivities,[24] although most would, I think, accept Adrienne Rich's description of the intention (however misguided) underlying "Songs for a Colored Singer" as "respectful" but "risky."[25] The final poem (Song IV) clearly displays Bishop's racial ambivalence, fascination, and confusion. The poem is structured by a series of questions, weak attempts to arrive at a settled understanding of the fluid that flows through the poem's leafy environment like manna. This substance appears at first as dew or tears, but coalesces into blood – unacknowledged and decoloured by the moonlight. It forms "black seeds" that "take root like weeds" and grow into a sea of dark faces "like an army in a dream" (*P* 50–51). The poem's surreal metamorphoses press upon white fears of contamination and subsumption, while drawing out a burgeoning sense of guilt.

Bishop's "curious flower or fruit" (*P* 50) self-consciously takes up the image of "Strange Fruit" from the well-known song recorded by Billie Holiday in 1939. Bishop wrote "Songs for a Colored Singer" with Billie Holiday (whom she knew) in mind.[26] Originally titled "Bitter Fruit," and written as a poem by Abel Meeropol published in 1937,[27] Holiday's "Strange Fruit" is a haunting and visceral protest against lynching: "Southern trees / Bear a strange fruit / Blood on the leaves / And blood at the roots." Its "strange and bitter crop" help us to reframe Bishop's Song IV as contributing to this anti-lynching discourse, and with good cause. During the decade in which Bishop spent substantial time in Florida, the Ku Klux Klan was an active presence and lynchings were extremely common. Contrary to its later self-mythologisation as a place of interracial harmony, the state had the second-highest rate of lynchings per capita. Florida maintained its rate of lynching at the peak levels reached in the 1880s right up to 1950, defying a nationwide declining trend over the course of the early twentieth century.[28] One of the most notorious Klan incidents in Florida history occurred in Tampa in 1937, with the lynching murder of labour organiser Joseph Shoemaker.

Bishop must have been aware of these events. Indeed, in a letter to her Aunt Grace many years later, Bishop wrote: "Don't forget I did live in the south. – My dear old laundress's (black) son was murdered by the Key West police because one of them wanted his wife. – Everyone knew this and nothing was done about it."[29]

Through what Camille Roman terms "quasi-visible" and "multiple codings,"[30] Bishop's Key West poems diffidently attempt to unearth the oft-submerged but ever-present reality of racist violence. The landscapes of her "Bone Key" poems cough back up the words of the unquiet dead:

"from a graveyard's thin gray soil / springs the stubble of sound: / A voice calls out, / 'Where is he at?'" (*EAP* 42). "Cootchie" makes explicit Bishop's understanding of Florida as a place of savagery and salvage, loss and survival. The servant woman "lies in marl, / black into white she went / below the surface of the coral-reef" (*P* 46).

As the years passed, Key West became increasingly militarised, and Bishop found fewer and fewer reasons to return. Her gaze had shifted further south, first to Mexico and then Brazil. But Florida, with its thousands of islands, would always embody for her the weeping archipelago, with the violent beauty of a world in flux. Her Key West notebook contains a page headed simply "The world's obsessive imagery – " that records the Gulf Coast as:

> The ground that would dry their tears like
> blotting paper – in the cemetery –
> or let it through, scarcely detaining
> it, to join the sea below. (*EAP* 266–67)

Notes

1. Maureen Ogle, *Key West: History of an Island of Dreams* (Gainesville: University Press of Florida, 2003), 179.
2. See Brett C. Millier, *Elizabeth Bishop: Life and the Memory of It* (Berkeley: University of California Press, 1992), 133–165; and Gary Fountain and Peter Brazeau, *Remembering Elizabeth Bishop* (Amherst: University of Massachusetts Press, 1994), 70–74. In 2019, Key West Literary Seminar purchased Bishop's house in order to restore and preserve it. See www.kwls.org/bishop/
3. Ashley Brown, "An Interview with Elizabeth Bishop," in *Conversations with Elizabeth Bishop*, ed. George Monteiro (Jackson: University Press of Mississippi, 1996), 27.
4. Barbara Page, "Off-Beat Claves, Oblique Realities: The Key West Notebooks of Elizabeth Bishop," in *Elizabeth Bishop: The Geography of Gender*, ed. Marilyn May Lombardi (Charlottesville: University Press of Virginia, 1993), 197.
5. David Kalstone, *Becoming a Poet: Elizabeth Bishop with Marianne Moore and Robert Lowell* (New York: Farrar, Straus and Giroux, 1989), 24.
6. Dana Gioia, "Studying with Miss Bishop," in *Conversations with Elizabeth Bishop*, ed. George Monteiro (Jackson: University Press of Mississippi, 1996), 146.
7. See Jefferson B. Browne, *The Old and the New* (St Augustine, FL: The Record Company, 1912), 7–9; and James W. Covington, *The Seminoles of Florida* (Gainesville, FL: LibraryPress@UF, 1993, 2017), 4.
8. These poems include "From the shallow night-long graves . . ., " "The Street by the Cemetery," "Florida Deserta," and "Full Moon, Key West."

9. Quoted in Page, "Off-Beat Claves, Oblique Realities," 202.
10. Jani Scandura, *Down in the Dumps: Place, Modernity, American Depression* (Durham NC: Duke University Press, 2008), 76. I am highly indebted to Scandura's compelling account of Key West during the 1930s and 1940s.
11. Ibid., 84.
12. Brown, *The Old and the New*, 27.
13. See Andrew Gomez, "Jim Crow and the Caribbean South: Cubans and Race in South Florida, 1885–1930s," *Journal of American Ethnic History* 36.4 (2017), 25–48.
14. The area was also known by more savage racial epithets. See Scandura, *Down in the Dumps*, 111.
15. José Martí was a prominent leader of the nineteenth-century Cuban independence movement of the 1880s.
16. Margaret Dickie, "Race and Class in Elizabeth Bishop's Poetry," *The Yearbook of English Studies* 24 (1994), 46. See also Sandeep Parmar's chapter in this volume, which argues persuasively that Bishop's self-obliquity in these poems functions as a racialising enactment of her own interior dividedness externalised onto African American and Latin American subjects.
17. Tyler T. Schmidt, *Desegregating Desire: Race and Sexuality in Cold War American Literature* (Jackson: University of Mississippi Press, 2013), 48.
18. *Remembering Elizabeth Bishop*, 78–82.
19. Angus Cleghorn, "Bishop's 'Wiring Fused': 'Bone Key' and 'Pleasure Seas,'" in *Elizabeth Bishop in the Twenty-First Century*, ed. Angus Cleghorn, Bethany Hicok, and Thomas Travisano (Charlottesville: University of Virginia Press, 2012), 69–87, 69.
20. Alice Quinn notes the difficulty of ascribing a chronology to Bishop's Key West notebooks, and suggests that "It is marvellous to wake up together . . . " may have been written in the late 1930s. Its presiding presence would then be Louise Crane, rather than Stevens (*EAP* 267).
21. John Lowney, *History, Memory, and the Literary Left: Modern American Poetry, 1935–1968* (Iowa City: University of Iowa Press, 2006), 90.
22. Jonathan Ellis, "Elizabeth Bishop's Bone Key Poems," *PN Review* 34.3 (2008), 37–40.
23. Scandura, 111.
24. See, for example, Zhou Xiaojing, "Subject Positions in Elizabeth Bishop's Representations of Whiteness and the Other," in *White Women in Racialized Spaces: Imaginative Transformation and Ethical Action in Literature*, ed. Samina Najmi and Rajini Srikanth (Albany, NY: SUNY press, 2002), 167–89; and C. K. Doreski, *Elizabeth Bishop: The Restraints of Language* (Oxford: Oxford University Press, 1993), 122–23. For a discussion of the racial elements of "Faustina," see Marilyn May Lombardi, *The Body and the Song: Elizabeth Bishop's Poetics* (Carbondale and Edwardsville: Southern Illinois University Press, 1995), and Sandeep Parmar's chapter in this volume.
25. Adrienne Rich, "The Eye of the Outsider: Elizabeth Bishop's Complete Poems, 1927–1979," *Boston Review* (April 1983), 15–17. As Parmar argues, Bishop's attitudes to racial others could not always be characterised as respectful.

26. *Remembering Elizabeth Bishop*, 328.
27. Dorian Lynskey, *33 Revolutions Per Minute: A History of Protest Songs* (London: Faber & Faber, 2011), 9.
28. Equal Justice Initiative, *Lynching in America: Confronting the Legacy of Racial Terror*, 3rd ed. (Montgomery, AL: Equal Justice Initiative, 2017), 4, 39.
29. Quoted in Jonathan Ellis, *Art and Memory in the Work of Elizabeth Bishop* (Farnham, Surrey: Ashgate, 2006), 137–38.
30. Camille Roman, *Elizabeth Bishop's World War II–Cold War View* (Basingstoke: Palgrave Macmillan, 2001), 19.

CHAPTER 6

Brazil

Neil Besner

Beginning with her arrival in Brazil in 1951, the tensions that Bishop quickly recognized in her conflicted perceptions of the country resonated throughout her work over the next twenty years. The history of Brazil's colonization, the sharp and stark divides between its social classes, the deep poverty of many Brazilians, the volatility of Brazilian politics during her years in the country, Bishop's difficult relationship with the Portuguese language, and what often appeared to her eye as Brazil's startlingly outsized landscapes – all of these productive tensions at once informed, troubled, and enriched her years in the country. Her recreations of her conflicted experience of the Brazil of her time were further complicated by Brazilian and American critiques of these representations in her art – superintended, under many Brazilian eyes, by critiques of her foreigner status.

Bishop's Brazilian sojourn was layered with interrogations that began with her own explorations and discoveries of her motives for her travels in Brazil, of her settling in Samambaia with Lota de Macedo Soares and later in the house that Bishop named Casa Mariana in Ouro Preto. Although she became an informed and astute commentator on many aspects of Brazilian culture, politics, society, history, and geography, Bishop and her work, early and late – and as recently as November 2019 – have provoked strong Brazilian responses. In the foundational perspective of Brazilian scholar Regina Przybycien, for example – in 1993, Przybycien was the first Brazilian to complete a PhD on Bishop's work in Brazil – Bishop inevitably saw Brazil under a colonial gaze:

> Éinégavel que Bishop viu o Brasil, como do resto toda a América Latina, com o olhar de superioridade de quem pertence a uma cultura dominante, respaldada pelas imagens que foram construídas sobre essa região ao longo da história, desde a época da colonização.
>
> It is undeniable that Bishop looked at Brazil, like the rest of Latin America, with the gaze of superiority of one who belongs to a dominant

> culture, based on the images constructed of this region over the sweep of history since the era of colonization.[1]

This tone and tenor inflect much Brazilian scholarship on Bishop's work, and Brazilians' perceptions of Bishop, to this day. In a 2015 article, for example, Maria Clara Paro and Evelyn Mello, in an excellent Derridean analysis of Bishop's "Arrival at Santos," open by discussing Bishop's "olhar estrangeiro que procura decifrar as novidades das paisagem" – her "foreigner's gaze that seeks to decipher a new landscape."[2] The most comprehensive North American overview that we have to date of the extent and the depth of Bishop's perceptions of Brazil, meanwhile, is American scholar Bethany Hicok's fine recent study, *Elizabeth Bishop's Brazil*.[3]

What all Bishop scholars agree on is that the two decades that Bishop lived and worked in Brazil (1951–70, with annual returns until 1974) constitute a vitally important period in the development of her career as a poet and prose writer, in her personal life, and in her lifelong engagement with the meanings of travel and of home. In November 1951, Bishop boarded the freighter HMS Bowplate in New York in search of the new beginning that travel had always promised her. Her original plan was to stop only briefly in Brazil and then carry on around South America, but several events changed her mind, chief among them her relationship with Lota de Macedo Soares, a brilliant Brazilian aristocrat, architect, and intellectual whom Bishop had met once in New York years earlier. Upon her arrival in Brazil, Bishop soon found herself falling in love with Lota, who was drawn equally strongly to this talented but diffident foreigner. Lota modified her plans for the modernist house she was building in Samambaia, just outside of Petrópolis, an hour and a half's drive from Rio into the mountains, deciding to include an attractive two-room writing studio for Bishop with a beautiful view of the close by mountain and waterfall; the studio, like the house itself, is still standing. Neighbours of Lota at Samambaia presented Bishop, who loved animals, with an irresistible toucan, whom Bishop immediately christened Sam, marvelling at his gorgeous plumage and his insatiable appetite. And an intense allergic reaction to the Brazilian caju fruit laid up Bishop for weeks and provided Lota and her circle the opportunity to lavish on Bishop the warmth and care that had so often eluded her; distinguished Brazilian novelist Rachel de Queiroz (1910–2003), who became friends with Bishop, described her in a 1997 interview as "carente," in English "needy."[4] Drawn to Lota and to the exotic surroundings native to Lota, intriguingly foreign to her, Bishop decided to change her plans and stay in Samambaia.

The poems, stories, and translations Bishop produced in Brazil – as well as the innumerable letters she wrote[5] – trace the rich trajectory of her art's development in this vital period. And her several trips throughout Brazil gave her the landscapes and occasions – linguistic, geographical, social, and political – for many major poems, beginning with "Arrival at Santos," published in 1951, and ending with "Santarém," – finally published in 1978, a year before Bishop's death, after she had left Brazil definitively and was living in Boston and teaching at Harvard – and "Pink Dog," published in 1979.

Bishop's sharp traveller's eye, her talent for what readers often first perceive as exacting description, and the searching questions about travel that so often permeate her poems are all in evidence in "Arrival at Santos," first published in *The New Yorker* in September 1952. Bishop opens by naming a series of land- and seascapes: "Here is a coast; here is a harbor; / here, after a meager diet of horizon, is some scenery: / impractically shaped and – who knows? – self-pitying mountains, / sad and harsh beneath their frivolous greenery" (*P* 87), as if she were a tentative geographer seeking elementary information about a new place, but a geographer who quickly begins to ascribe human characteristics (self-pitying, sad, and harsh mountains) to this new vista. The perspective, the tone, and the style of this first poem set in Brazil will recur with variations throughout Bishop's twenty years in the country, widening and deepening her reach as her experience of Brazil is enlarged. By the time readers arrive at the poem's closing – "We leave Santos at once; / we are driving to the interior" (*P* 88) – we have entered the landscape of Bishop's poem and her sensibility deeply enough to perceive that her drive to the country's "interior" is mediated as much by her internal compass as it is by her literal travel; she is headed to Rio de Janeiro and her meeting with Lota de Macedo Soares, which will constitute her port of entry into an unexpected new life.

Since the mid 1980s, several leading Bishop scholars have provided careful and thorough analyses, often varying richly in their readings, of "Arrival at Santos" as well as of other Bishop poems written during her years in Brazil – beginning with discussions by Thomas Travisano, Lorrie Goldensohn, and Lloyd Schwartz, among the many others that have followed. Bishop's readers will of course differ as to which of Bishop's poems set in Brazil are the most important; but no reader would contest the vital importance of at the very least the following poems, in chronological order of their first book publication, all of them discussed at length over the years, and all of them deserving of continuing attention: "Arrival at Santos," "Brazil, January 1, 1502," "Questions of Travel," "Manuelzinho," "The Riverman," "The Burglar of

Babylon," "Santarém," and "Pink Dog." And of course the fragments, drafts, and poems that Alice Quinn collected and annotated in *Edgar Allan Poe & The Juke-Box* (2006) include a trove of material related to Bishop's years in Brazil.[6]

Not only have all the major Bishop scholars and biographers commented on the immediate impact of Brazil on Bishop's poetry; as well, most have noted that during Bishop's early years in Brazil, she discovered she was now able to shape memories from her early years in Nova Scotia into compelling stories – narratives such as "In The Village," in which Bishop represents her haunting experience at the age of five of her mother's mental breakdown. She never saw her mother after that, but the effects of this loss troubled her for the rest of her life. Most scholars also agree that what freed Bishop in Brazil to write of these traumatic experiences from her childhood in Nova Scotia were the similarities between the two environments: in Samambaia Bishop rediscovered herself in a rural landscape with its familiar intimacies and relatively primitive amenities, and that recognition may well have allowed her memories to re-emerge in these powerful stories.

Bishop's discovery of and attraction to elements of Brazilian life that awoke intimate memories was often troubled and tempered by her corollary discovery of the abiding strangeness that surrounded her – not only of landscape, but of a new language and of long-ingrained social custom and class divisions. Her poems always reflect her own awareness of the conflicts engendered by these Brazilian realities; one of the finest poems set in Brazil to first explicitly embody and work through the social contradictions she encountered is Bishop's early Brazilian poem, "Manuelzinho." As Vidyan Ravinthiran has shown in an excellent recent essay on the poem, "'Manuelzinho,' Brazil and Identity Politics,"[7] this dramatic monologue moves beyond describing and then interrogating many of the distinctively Brazilian qualities of the charged relationship between landowner and her squatter (Lota and Manuelzinho), as well as the relationship between Lota and Bishop; the poem also opens out the possibility of an incipient change or growth in these relationships. That potential moment provides one local, experiential, and dynamic incarnation of Bishop's perennial conflict in Brazil: is she only another privileged outsider, a spectator reporting on the age-old but charged intimacies of the enduring but corrosive Brazilian relationships between classes? Is Bishop's rendering of the tonal complexities of Lota's voice addressing Manuelzinho simply an act of inspired ventriloquism that condescendingly reinscribes the old colonial conditions, as some have read the poem; or, as Ravinthiran suggests, does

Bishop move beyond ventriloquism to open up the new interiors hinted at in "Arrival at Santos"? Ravinthiran argues persuasively that "Manuelzinho" broaches the possibility that Bishop's relationship with Lota, like Lota's with Manuelzinho, might open out and grow as both Lota and Bishop arrive at new perceptions of their relationship with each other and with Manuelzinho, their (tellingly silent) Brazilian interlocutor. Ravinthiran's perspective on "Manuelzinho" points one way towards further contemporary re-readings of Bishop's major Brazilian poems.

Over her years in Brazil, Bishop became familiar enough with Portuguese to become an accomplished translator, not only of major Brazilian poets such as Carlos Drummond de Andrade and João Cabral de Melo Neto, but also, early in her sojourn, of the Brazilian classic of small town life, *Minha Vida de Menina* ("My Life as a Girl"), which she translated in 1956 as *The Diary of "Helena Morley,"* and of several stories by renowned Brazilian writer Clarice Lispector. Throughout her years in Brazil, however, Bishop remained reticent about speaking the language. As Barbara Page reminds us in her excellent essay on Bishop's Brazilian years, "Home, Wherever That May Be: Poems and Prose of Brazil," Bishop told her friend Ashley Brown in a 1966 interview that she understood Portuguese "like a dog: I understand everything that's said to me, but I don't speak it very well."[8] As Page notes, Bishop's difficulties with Portuguese were apprehended unsympathetically by Bishop's most talented Brazilian translator, Paulo Henriques Britto – further evidence of the conflicted Brazilian reception and perception of Bishop's work.

For some Brazilian commentators, no North American's perspective, in English or in Portuguese, no matter how much she might claim to sympathize with Brazil, to speak the language, to know Brazilian culture, history, or geography, could be accepted at face value. Bishop's perspective, however deeply informed, would always be suspect because it was North American, and because Brazilians have, understandably, long harboured deeply ambivalent and conflicted feelings about the USA.

An exemplar of this Brazilian perspective emerged spontaneously twenty years ago at the first Elizabeth Bishop conference in Brazil, in May 1999, in Ouro Preto, Minas Gerais. At the beginning of that conference, distinguished Brazilian critic, poet, and novelist Silviano Santiago gave a keynote address on Bishop, widely praising her poetry. However, in the question period directly following, he surprised his audience by suddenly changing course and lashing out at this foreigner whose scandalous exploitation of and contempt for Brazil were evident to him. Both of Santiago's appraisals were deeply felt; but the second, angry one was more impassioned. His visceral condemnation of this audacious foreigner was not idiosyncratic; rather, in its way it was representative. Santiago did not lash out at Bishop because in his estimation she was a bad person. He resented Bishop because of what he understood as her essential and unalterable foreignness, and resented it all the more deeply, perhaps, because she represented Brazil in her art so powerfully, pungently, and knowledgeably. As Francesco Rognoni, an Italian scholar who attended this 1999 conference, noted in *The Elizabeth Bishop Bulletin*, describing Santiago's "eloquent, if controversial, lecture":

> The debate that followed was perhaps the most animated of the conference, dismissing such favorites as "Manuelzinho" and "The Burglar of Babylon," dividing up the audience in the ancient struggle of militancy *vs.* academia. Something exquisitely *retro* – to my Italian ears, at least – was going on then, and I felt privileged that I did not have to take sides. But even those most baffled by Santiago's ideological bias must have been fascinated by his offhand suggestion that Bishop's significance for Brazilian literature may be found not in her openly 'Brazilian' texts, but in the way her poetry of intimacy filled a gap in the necessarily more politicized Brazilian poetry of the fifties and sixties.[9]

This Brazilian current of resentment continued (and continues) to carry similar cargo over Bishop's years in the country. A notorious example occurred in the 1960s, when Bishop published a piece in *The New York Times Magazine* in May 1965 entitled "On the Railroad Named Delight," which quoted from Rio's Carnaval (the Portuguese word for "Carnival") lyrics of the time, and in which Bishop famously commented that Rio de Janeiro was not a beautiful city, but instead the world's most beautiful setting for a city. The response in the Brazilian press was vehement: one journalist, Fernando de Castro, writing in the newspaper *Correio da Manha*, cribbed a well-known lyric from a popular Carnaval song to admonish Bishop: "Macaco, olha o seu rabo" – "Monkey, look at your own tail" – in an angry retort to Bishop's perceived blasphemy.

This story of Bishop's original piece and the Brazilian response is well known. Like Santiago's outburst in 1999, the Brazilian columnist's comments were in one sense unsurprising. They exemplified, and were nourished by, a distinctively Brazilian complex of feelings, beliefs, and convictions that Brazilian culture, for all its celebrated, outsized, and erotic exoticism under North American eyes, has always been misapprehended. These misapprehensions have been perceived by Brazilians as confirmation that foreigners can never really understand Brazil; and these Brazilian attitudes towards foreign readings of their culture persist to this day.

Under Brazilian eyes, Bishop's poems might be both beautiful and powerful, their trenchant social and political commentary revelatory; but the poetic licence granted to this talented foreigner was not accompanied by a corollary permission to write critically, in English, in an important publication like *The New York Times Magazine,* about Rio de Janeiro as if Bishop knew something true about the city.

While Bishop was buffeted from time to time by Brazilian responses to her work and to her presence in Brazil, some insidious American responses undercut Bishop's work in Brazil from another perspective: that of the allegedly progressive, if uninformed, neoliberal benevolence of American editors of the 1960's, determined to have their own shallow views of Brazilian culture sustained for them and for their American audience. This attitude is incarnated in the unhappy but revelatory saga of Bishop's writing of *Brazil* under contract for the Time Life series as part of its Life World Library (1962). Bishop was so irritated by the editors' bowdlerized whitewash of her more informed and sharp-eyed account of the country that she was loathe to allow her name to stand as the book's author; her grudging compromise was to insist that authorship be ascribed on the title page to "Elizabeth Bishop and the Editors of LIFE." In his biting essay on the interventions of Bishop's editors at *Life*, Angus Cleghorn shows in detail how their superimposed American worldview vitiated and corrupted Bishop's own far more clear-eyed writing. As Cleghorn reminds us, Lloyd Schwartz's 2011 edition of Bishop's *Prose* restores the original text of *Brazil* and in the process shows us just how differently the two versions read, and to what effect.[10] This unhappy episode stands as a corollary to the Brazilian views of Bishop and her work as outlined here. On the one hand, some Brazilians perceived Bishop as a condescending foreigner. On the other, some Americans – like the editors at Time Life – insisted on presenting a sanitized "Brazil" to their readers. Their "Brazil" rendered the country through the same rose-coloured glasses that construed the "Alliance for Progress" of the Kennedy years purely as pioneering work that would bring along a backward Brazilian into the American twentieth century.

It is in representations of Bishop's long and loving relationship with Lota Macedo de Soares, however, that we can see most clearly how the narratives of Bishop's Brazilian sojourn are most deeply inflected. This relationship – the longest of Bishop's life – was the subject of a Brazilian novelized biography, Carmen Oliveira's *Flores Raras e Banalíssimas: A História de Lota de Macedo Soares e Elizabeth Bishop* (1995), drawn on in its translation into English (Besner, 2002) as the main source for the award-winning feature film *Flores Raras* (2012; the English title is *Reaching for the Moon*). Oliveira's dramatized account of the rise and decline of Bishop and de Macedo Soares' relationship is the most comprehensive and detailed Brazilian treatment of the subject. It is ably complemented by another Brazilian approach to Bishop and de Macedo Soares by Nadia Nogueira in her intriguing 2008 study in Portuguese, *Invenções de Si em Histórias de Amor: Lota Macedo Soares e Elizabeth Bishop* (*Self-inventions in Love Stories: Lota Macedo Soares and Elizabeth Bishop*). The book is founded on Nogueira's PhD dissertation, undertaken to address the revealing sparsity of accounts in Brazil – statistical, scholarly, or creative – of women's love stories. Oliveira's fictionalized biography culminates in her account of Lota's suicide in New York in 1967; Oliveira perceives, correctly, that Brazilian responses to Lota's death placed the blame largely on Bishop, while Bishop in the book's closing sentence, perceives Brazil to have killed Lota. The constellation of Brazilian responses to Lota's death, particularly the widely shared sentiments of Lota's circle, crystallized in the perception that Bishop bore the major responsibility for Lota's suicide. Rachel de Queiroz remembers Bishop calling her from New York and "saying two words to her in a choked voice: "Lota morreu' (Lota died)"; when Bishop came back to Brazil some weeks after Lota's death, de Queiroz remembers, she "cried and cried".[11]

American biographers, beginning with Brett Millier's *Elizabeth Bishop: Life and the Memory of It* (1993) and ending at present with Thomas Travisano's *Love Unknown: The Life and Worlds of Elizabeth Bishop* (2019) tend to treat the suicide more dispassionately, as does Nogueira in her account.

The distinctive divide in approaches to their relationship and its tragic decline can be understood as reinscribed in another vein in the readings of what many perceive to be Bishop's final great poem to be set in Brazil, "Santarém" (1978) – most tellingly, in readings of the much-discussed closing lines of the poem, invoking a Mr. Swan – "Dutch, the retiring head of Philips Electric, / really a very nice old man, / who wanted to see the Amazon before he died," who asks in the poem's last words, 'What's that ugly thing?'" (*P* 209). Literally, the "ugly thing" is a wasp's nest that the poem's speaker had admired in a pharmacy; it was "small, exquisite, clean matte white, / and hard as stucco. I admired it / so much he gave it to me." The pharmacist's gift of the nest could stand, in the 1960s as now, as a typically spontaneous Brazilian gesture of generosity. In Brazil, under the eyes of one discerning Brazilian reader in 1999 – twenty years after the poem was published, and twenty years from our contemporary readings of

Bishop's Brazilian years – the line and our reading of it take on a freighted significance. In the *Elizabeth Bishop Bulletin*, Maria Clara Bonetti Paro, in her admirably succinct and suggestive overview of the Ouro Preto conference at which Silviano Santiago spoke so passionately about Bishop's foreignness, comments:

> Among the many issues raised, the one that provoked most interest, debate and controversy – and proved crucial for anyone who wanted to engage her work critically – was the quest to determine how much of Mr. Swan's blindness, or colonial gaze, depicted in the poem "Santarém," was present both in Bishop's view of Brazil and in her texts related to her experience there.[12]

Beginning in late November 2019, Brazilian social media lit up with outrage over the announcement that Bishop was the writer chosen as the 2020 honouree for the eighteenth edition of Brazil's biggest annual literary festival, FLIP – the acronym stands for Festival Literária Internacional de Paraty – the International Literary Festival of Paraty (Paraty is a small town in the state of Rio de Janeiro).[13] A large majority of commentators were emphatically opposed to the choice, quoting from Bishop's letters to friends in support of the 1964 military coup in Brazil as evidence that she was an elitist, right-wing foreigner whose circle of aristocratic friends shielded her from Brazilian social and political realities. A few voices defend her as a writer who did in fact understand Brazil, citing her poems "Pink Dog" and "The Burglar of Babylon." One suggestion was that Paulo Henriques Britto, her finest Brazilian translator, be honoured along with her. But the predominant tone was angry denunciation of what was seen as another confirmation of the country's veering, once again, to the right under its current President, retired General Jair Bolsonaro.

Since FLIP was founded in 2003, no foreign writer has been chosen as the year's honouree; the writers chosen before Bishop in 2020 include prominent Brazilian novelists, poets, and academics – including two whose works Bishop admired and translated, poet Carlos Drummond de Andrade (2012 honouree) and novelist and short story writer, Clarice Lispector (2005). In the official announcement of Bishop's selection, Artistic Director Mauro Munhoz commented:

> Although it was written in English, Bishop's poetry was no less steeped in Brazil than the work of Drummond or João de Cabral de Melo Neto. For Mauro, [Bishop] fulfilled to perfection the original intention of this honor, more real than ever in 2020 – 'to make the rich experience of Brazilian art better known in any other place in the world.'

Curator of FLIP Fernanda Diamant added that Bishop was

> above all, one of the most important poets of the twentieth century [. . .]. [Bishop] lived more than fifteen years in Brazil and created part of her work here, clearly influenced by both her Brazilian and her foreign experience. You only have to read her letters to understand this. [. . .] She was also an important source of diffusion for Brazilian literature to English speaking countries, having translated our major poets.[14]

As of late March, due to Coronavirus, the 2020 FLIP festival was postponed to September. In the summer of 2020, the continuing controversy over Bishop's selection led to the resignation of the festival director and the dissociation of FLIP from the online events held then in Bishop's honour. It appears that the richly conflicted Brazilian view of Bishop and her work in Brazil will endure for much longer.

Notes

1. "Nas Trilhas de Elizabeth Bishop," in *Feijao-Preto e Diamantes: O Brasil na obra de Elizabeth Bishop*, ed. Regina Przybycien (Belo Horizonte: Editora UFMG, 2015), 13. All translations in this chapter are my own.
2. Maria Clara Paro and Evelyn Mello, "Olhos de Elizabeth Bishop e Ana Cristina César: Paisagens em Deconstrução" ("The Gazes of Elizabeth Bishop and Ana Cristina César: Deconstructed Landscapes"), *Fólio: Revista de Letras* 7.2 (2015), 611–23.
3. Bethany Hicok, *Elizabeth Bishop's Brazil* (Charlottesville: University of Virginia Press, 2016).
4. Neil Besner, "Bishop in Brazil: A Review, Interview, and Memoir," *Elizabeth Bishop Bulletin* (hereafter *EBB*) 6.1 (Summer 1997), 3.
5. For the fullest and most recent evidence of the importance of Bishop's letters, see Thomas Travisano, *Love Unknown: The Life and Worlds of Elizabeth Bishop* (New York: Viking, 2019).
6. See, for one example among many, the poem "Gypsophilia" (*EAP* 128–29), which should be read alongside "Manuelzinho" (*P* 94–97).
7. Vidyan Ravinthiran, "'Manuelzinho,' Brazil and Identity Politics," in *Reading Elizabeth Bishop: An Edinburgh Companion*, ed. Jonathan Ellis (Edinburgh: Edinburgh University Press, 2019), 33–47.
8. Barbara Page, "Home, Wherever That May Be: Poems and Prose of Brazil," in *The Cambridge Companion to Elizabeth Bishop*, ed. Angus Cleghorn and Jonathan Ellis (New York: Cambridge University Press, 2014), 124–40.
9. Rognoni, *EBB*, 8.1 (Summer 1999), 2. Santiago's essay, "The Status of Elizabeth Bishop's Descriptive Poem," translated by Julio Pinto, is collected in *The Art of Elizabeth Bishop*, ed. Sandra Regina Goulart Almeida, Glaucia Renate Gonçalves, and Eliana Lourenço de Lima Reis (Belo Horizonte: Editora Universidade Federal de Minas Gerais, 2002), 15–24.

10. Angus Cleghorn, "The Politics of Editing Elizabeth Bishop's 'Brazil,' Circa 1962," *Global Studies Journal*, 4.3 (2011), 47–58.
11. *EBB* 6.1 (Summer 1997), 3.
12. Maria Clara Bonetti Paro, "The Bishop Celebration [in] Ouro Preto, Brazil May 1991," *EBB* 8.1 (Summer 1999), 1–2.
13. See FLIP discussion, "Escolha de Elizabeth Bishop como homenageada da Flip é recebida com revolta" ("The choice of Elizabeth Bishop as FLIP's honoree attracts indignation") https://cultura.estadao.com.br/noticias/literatura,escolha-de-elizabeth-bishop-como-homenageada-da-flip-e-recebida-com-revolta,70003103615?utm_source=estadao:mail&utm_medium=link (primarily in Portuguese but some material in English).
14. See *18a Festa Literaria Internacional de Paraty 29 Julho-02 Agosto 2020*, "Elizabeth Bishop" n.p.

PART II

Forms

CHAPTER 7

Lyric Poetry

Gillian White

Did Elizabeth Bishop write lyric poems? Given that "poetry has, in the minds of many, become synonymous with definitions of the lyric," as Marion Thain writes in her introduction to *The Lyric Poem* (2016), the question might seem immaterial.[1] Ellen Bryant Voigt presumes in her introduction to *The Flexible Lyric* (1999) that "lyric is what most of us are writing these days when we write in lines," but it is worth asking whether Bishop, writing from the 1930s through the 1970s, would have shared the same presumption.[2]

Though today's critics might call Bishop's poems "lyric," it is doubtful that Bishop herself would have used that word for them, and certainly not in the same spirit. Concerns about the status and politics of lyric have greatly preoccupied readers of the late-twentieth century and after, though Bishop's era of productivity predates and only somewhat overlaps with the establishment of "lyric reading" as a pedagogical and poetic norm.[3] She frequently uses the words "poem" and "poetry" in her published correspondence but there are no uses of the word "lyric." In her decades-long correspondence with Robert Lowell, the word appears only once, and Bishop uses "lyrical" to describe poetry fewer than five times (see *WIA*). This may tell us little more – and no less – than that *concern* about lyric was not much in the air in her day. Yet Bishop lived through an era when, critics have shown, the idea of lyric became so broad as to encompass the reading of all poetry, and an era in which forms of lyric reading became normative, so as to seem natural, and, later, oppressive. One step in thinking about Bishop in the context of lyric, then, entails exploring the shifting ideas of lyric that Bishop inherited as she was studying and producing poems, and distinguishing these from claims made for and against her poems by later critics steeped in late-twentieth-century lyric discourses. What aspects of Bishop's poetry emerge or change when we test the terms of Voigt's late-twentieth-century presumption that lyric is all there is to read?

It is safe to say Bishop's college reading exposed her to a small and mixed set of uses of "lyric" as a term or idea. In her significant reading in pre-eighteenth-century poetics, for instance – Plato, Aristotle, Horace, John Dryden, Philip Sidney, and Samuel Daniel (to name just a few) – "lyric" tends to refer to song, or is used adjectivally to invoke musical or metrical qualities in individual poems or in verse genres such as elegies and odes. In later-eighteenth- and early-nineteenth-century poetics texts, such as Percy Bysshe Shelley's "A Defence of Poetry," "lyric" could still refer to a metrical form, along with "epic" and "dramatic," taken to be the three ancient rhythmic poetic orders Plato eschewed for philosophy.[4] In her extensive notes on William Wordsworth's "Preface" to his *Poems* (1815), Bishop copies out Wordsworth's idiosyncratic formal-generic logic for his own work: six major "moulds" ("narrative, dramatic, lyrical, idyllium, didactic and satire") into which "Poetry" might be shaped by "Imagination, Fancy, and Observation"; and the "forms" occurring within these "moulds." His "Lyrical mould" umbrellas the "forms" of "ode, elegy, song, ballad," all forms that Bishop practiced (VC Box 69B, folder 11, 116–17).

But already, we may be struggling. For a twenty-first-century reader, part of the challenge to place Bishop's work in the context of lyric involves the difficulty in deciding what Voigt and we mean by "lyric," *other* than writing in lines, or prose's opposite, and how that has changed. Is lyric, for instance, a super-form (as Wordsworth imagines) for many types of short poems? Must those then be metrical or have song-like elements? Is it a verse genre, determined in part by its occasions and social situations? Is it a quality of writing found in various kinds and forms, including in prose? Others yet may think of lyric as a set of tropes, as here implied by Dan Chiasson (writing about Claudia Rankine): "lyric poets [get into] this business partly to talk about rain, trees, moons, skies, dejection, and joy."[5] Complicating our answer further, the idea of lyric has not been stable across the eighty years since the 1930s start of Bishop's career. And its meaning changed in her own lifetime, and continues to function variously.

Indeed, this chapter's presumption, following from recent arguments in historical poetics, is that "lyric" is a potent, culturally loaded abstraction used variously across the period of Bishop's productivity as a poet and into our own moment. As Virginia Jackson argues in her entry on "lyric" in the *Princeton Encyclopedia of Poetry and Poetics*, "a persistent confusion [...] may be the best way to define our current sense of the lyric. It is a confusion that has proven enormously generative for both poets and critics."[6] The confusion persists because lyric is not a genre, contrary to what many introductory textbooks report, but an ideal that, over the nineteenth and twentieth centuries, abstracted particular verse genres into one broad category, serving during Bishop's lifetime (and after) as the default category and interpretive norm for all kinds of poetry (odes, songs, epistles, elegies) that had before been read in light of specific verse cultures and social settings.

*

Returning to Bishop's college notes on literary theory, we can consider the continuity and discontinuity between her and Wordsworth's practices. Bishop was fascinated by Wordsworth's point, hardly a lyric expectation of the 1930s, that in all of these genres or forms in the "lyrical mode" (he collapses these two terms), "accompaniment of music is indispensable [. . .] for the production of their *full* effect" (VC Box 69B, folder 11, 116). While Bishop would not have assumed lyric poems needed musical accompaniment, her notes emphasize points and questions about poetry's relationship to music, and she read poetry and poetics through studies of sound, prosody, music, and (to a lesser degree) the art and "science" of scoring and measuring these. In notes on Wordsworth's "Preface to Lyrical Ballads" (1802–3), perhaps shoring up her defense against early-modernist animus toward metrical poetry, Bishop wonders over his claim that meter regulates emotion, dismissing as "feeble" the idea that meter "divest[s] language. . . of its reality" by throwing a "half-consciousness of unsubstantial existence over the whole composition," and objecting to his claim that metered, rhymed poetry mollifies readers' experiences of painful subjects (VC Box 69B, folder 11, 113–14).

Such intensity of focus on claims about meter characterizes her concerns of the period, attesting to her interest in music (she entered Vassar in 1930 as a music major), and evidences her not-uncommon investment in the prosodic verse culture of the Victorian period. Her notes on literary theory and poetry emphasize connections between musical and verse composition, including perhaps a "study of the interval" in poetry (VC 51). Bishop was reading late-nineteenth- and early-twentieth-century poetics texts in which the primary mode of analysis was metrical and prosodic: George Saintsbury's *Historical Manual of English Prosody* (1910), Edmund Gurney's *The Power of Sound* (1880), and Sidney Lanier's *The Science of English Verse* (1880), from which she took notes on such topics as the "imagination of the ear" and the importance of "tune" to both poetry and music (VC 47–48). She read normative theories of prosodic composition – J. J. Sylvester's *The Laws of Verse* (1870) – and more "modern" rhythmic analyses of poetry, such as by William Morrison Patterson – *The Rhythm of Prose* (1916) – and

George David Birkhoff's broad-ranging *Aesthetic Measure* (1933), which advocated a rigorous "scientific" formalist accounting of aesthetic experience. For contemporary readers, it may be hard to imagine the centrality of metrical questions and assumptions for Bishop, who singled out such claims as in Birkhoff's chapter on "The Musical Quality of Poetry," that while "significance [. . .] is perhaps the most important single element in poetry [. . .] poetry without musical quality and meter is not properly poetry at all" (VC Box 69B, folder 11, 52). Bishop directed her note-taking on such issues toward developing her own craft.

The aforementioned poetics texts were thinking with what Sylvester interchangeably calls "lyrical poetry" and "lyric verse," meaning poetry that, in large part for its meter, has a musical aspect drawn in part from emotions, or is expressive of an author's feelings. In a footnote in a chapter theorizing laws of accentual meters, he writes, "At the base of and giving nourishment to our poetical plant, lies Emotion, at once the root and crown of lyric verse."[7] Notably, this is Sylvester's one (adjectival) use of the term "lyric" in nearly 200 pages. Lanier only uses the word "lyric" twice in his study of over 300 pages, once to call the sonnet English lyric poetry's "primordial form."[8] Lanier's use reminds us that lyric, mentioned or not, was understood in the nineteenth century as poetry's heart – its earliest and most essential form, or, as John Stuart Mill put it, lyric is "more eminently and peculiarly poetry than any other" and "most natural to a really poetic temperament."[9]

This means that Bishop was absorbing lyric both as an object of prosodic analysis and as offered in Romantic theories of art. In these texts and in Bishop's notes, lyric's supposed essentiality is assumed – not a point to prove or a subject in itself, as is true in the work of later twentieth-century defenders and detractors of the idea of lyric. If the Romantic and Victorian prosodic theorists Bishop was reading presume by lyric passionate and subjective metrical poetry, they *engaged* the topic less as an abstract cause than through the prosodic analysis of specific verse genres, by contrast with more contemporary lyric theory's tendency to attempt to bring into view or respond to (mis)characterizations of the abstract super-genre. Voigt, for instance, works to articulate "the lyric project" and "the lyric point of view" to better judge the politics of first-person poetics or the weight and value of particular poems as they engage personality or impersonality, or to respond to charges of subjectivism by recasting our understanding of "lyric" *as* a "point of view" that universalizes emotion.[10] Lanier and Sylvester, by contrast, debate prosodic effects and "laws" across verse genres – odes, epistles, hymns, songs – that had varying investments in the person, the subject, personality and impersonality and so on. They are working primarily to codify "lyric" effects, not shoring up an ideal of the personal and expressive.

Bishop is not fully in either Lanier and Sylvester's worlds, nor in Voigt's. As Eleanor Cook reminds us, Bishop *was* trained to think through compositional conventions of genres, and foregrounded verse genres in titled drafts and published work and in discussions of poetry in her letters. That is, she wrote "songs," "ballads," and "sonnets," and worked at imitating or thinking about other writers' efforts at elegy, aubade, riddles, charm-poetry, mock-elegy, hymn, ode, epistle, eclogue, parody, monologue, masques, and nursery rhymes, to name a few.[11] And Bishop was also part of a verse culture that lyricized those forms in various ways. Her poems, written for publication in print journals and collections, abstract the situations of address and the verse cultures in which, historically, odes or elegies and so on were written. So it would seem Bishop had one foot (pun intended) in a verse culture defined by its investment in prosodic conventions and debates about them, and one foot in the culture of lyric reading that had been developing alongside it, and which was finding increasing status and normative power through the institutional success of New Critical ideas in the mid-twentieth century.

If for Bishop, lyric was not understood to be a "project" or a defensible "point of view" in the sense that it is for Voigt or for poets of her own and later generations, nevertheless Bishop did struggle to keep her own sense of poetry separate from associations "lyric" had begun to accrue in the first third of the twentieth century. Bishop loved many poets who wrote poems we would call lyric – George Herbert, Gerard Manley Hopkins, Thomas Hardy, Edgar Allan Poe. Nevertheless, as I have argued elsewhere, she also expressed the "lyric shame" of her day, straining against an image of the poet as a self-centered male, Romantic rake and egotist; in a posthumously published, unfinished review of W. H. Auden from the 1930s, she lampoons the "Byronic man" entranced by his own image, and in college notes, argues with William Wordsworth's idealization of peasants' desires as "simple" and "beautiful," and critiques his belief, stated in "Preface to Lyrical Ballads," that the poet (above the biographer or historian) speaks in an unmediated fashion to a common, abstracted "Man." Next to her notes, she writes, "This is all wrong and a typical Romantic idea of Man. Wordsworth reached few people even in his day."[12]

James Longenbach and Betsy Erkkila have further argued that in the 1930s, moving in leftist circles, Bishop worried about writing what many would have construed to be apolitical poetry.[13] Though Bishop does not use the term "lyric" in articulating these critiques and concerns, there is evidence that she wanted to distance herself from poetry construed as "lyric" – understood as apolitical and too subjective. Many of her peers writing during the Depression felt the inadequacy of poetry-writing to the aims of radical politics, and may have shared Malcolm Cowley's sense that poetry fostered a "desperate feeling of solitude and uniqueness," a tendency strongest in "lyric," and that he argues leftist literature should work against.[14] He was not alone in wondering if, as scholar Milton Cohen puts it, "'lyricism' [. . .] was becoming irrelevant to the times."[15] Leftist poets such as Josephine Herbst, Genevieve Taggard, and Laura Riding argued in the 1930s that ethical poetry had to resist subjectivism (long associated with 'lyrical' tendencies,) attention to the self, and (for Riding especially) traditional forms. "Lyric" would become synonymous with the object of these critiques across the century, especially in avant-garde anti-lyricism in the USA. In other words, leftist poets and critics in part produced the modern (anti)ideal of lyric that Bishop came to understand as shameful.

We have slight but compelling evidence that Bishop retained this negative construction of lyric in 1948, when, writing to Robert Lowell, she laments her inability to produce a poem, "not even a little lyric as Miss [Louise] Bogan would approve of from me" (*WIA* 75). This remark suggests that Bishop aspired to write something other than (and 'bigger' than) "a little lyric"; lyric was not a default category for her. Furthermore, the slight putdown of Bogan is revealing. Thirty years the chief poetry reviewer for *The New Yorker* (starting in 1930), Bogan argued strenuously (and unpopularly) for "lyric purity" in the 1930s and 1940s.[16] Such purity meant apoliticism, universalism, and abstractness; lyric's cultivation of these Bogan took as a sign of maturity, as contrasted with political poetry: "The true artist," Bogan wrote in response to a 1939 *Partisan Review* questionnaire concerning "The Situation in American Writing," "will instinctively reject 'burning questions' and all 'crude oppositions' which can cloud his vision or block his ability to deal with the world."[17] By 1948, Bogan stood for a conservative, hierarchical sense of 'lyric' that Bishop was not alone in resisting.

*

Indeed, Bishop's comment needs placing in a moment when a lyricized ideal of poetry as autonomous and formally whole was being advanced in widespread methods of lyric reading canonized by the success of New Critical ideas in the post-war US classroom.[18] It's a shift in lyric reading cultures that registers in the slight but important difference between definitions of "lyric" from the 1950s and those we might encounter today.[19] Both might take "lyric" poems to be short and expressive of "personal feelings," but later definitions tend to assume the poem's words belong to a fictional voice or "speaker," rather than their author. The New Critical technology of "speakers" marks a significant shift from poetic reading conventions Bishop inherited in college, where *genre* dictated the use (or not) of a dramatic speaker or persona for poems; if the dramatic monologue had a fictionalized speaker, for example, ballads had quite different sorts of ones. This shift in reading culture, articulated most explicitly by Reuben Brower (the critic who trained Helen Vendler and Paul DeMan), imagined both poetry's "speaker[s]" and "audience[s]" as abstracted from their "time and place in history," as Brower famously argued: "the voice we hear in a lyric, however piercingly real," he wrote, "is not Keats's or Shakespeare's; or, if it seems to be [. . .] we are embarrassed and thrown off as if an actor had stopped and spoken to the audience in his own person."[20] It's a model of lyric reading that privileges poems approaching the autonomous "purity" – timeless monuments, "well-wrought urns" of New Critical lyric theory – that Bogan championed and Bishop put down.[21]

I offer the preceding because, though this modern ideal of lyric as personal expression spoken as if from no place or time is now and has long been normative, Bishop's poems rarely match it. Only eight of thirty poems in Bishop's first collection, *North & South* (1946), for instance, contain a first-person pronoun, and very few of these seem primarily expressive of feeling, and then only indirectly: the function of the 'I' of "Chemin de Fer," for instance, is to describe someone else expressing a feeling; other poems similarly deflect or mute or don't contain "personal feelings." Some poems imply the presence of a person through deictic gestures or the specificity of their description. However, that first-person presence is manifested by situated description rather than expression, as in "Wading at Wellfleet," which is located specifically in place and time (Wellfleet, MA, "this morning") but whose descriptive conceit (rolling waves and sunshine as war vehicles) is the focus, rather than its person (*P* 9). Approximately ten other poems in that collection are in the first-person plural ('we'), explicitly dislocating thoughts and feelings from either an author's or a single persona's perspective. In short, *North & South* doesn't represent the passion, personal expression, or explicit subjectivism definitive of lyric in the twentieth and twenty-first centuries.

Some critics might reply that at the early stage of her career, Bishop was writing lyric under the sign of Eliotic impersonality, deflecting feeling, "digest[ing]" and "transmut[ing]" emotion – Eliot's verbs for an artistic process that transforms the merely personal into something with broader relevance.[22] Late poems such as "Sonnet" or "The Shampoo," it would follow, reveal a more authentically expressive lyric Bishop. Yet even Bishop's first-person work of the 1970s, written at the height of confessional poetics and late in her career, and dominated by the figure of voice, seem ill-served by the lyric descriptor, if by that we mean an expression of universalized personal feeling. The late poem "In the Waiting Room," for instance, goes to great lengths to specify that its words belong to the author, to emphasize orthography (thus undermining the idea of it as spoken), and seems rather to theorize a state of mind and affect, than to serve as a dramatized expression of personal feeling. It narrates an experience that reveals the contingency and indeterminacy of the first-person subject position: "But I felt: you are an *I* / You are an *Elizabeth*" (*P* 180). At its crux, the poet recounts the associated nausea in thinking, "why should I be my aunt, or me, or anyone?", a realization that wonders over, and even undermines, Western emphasis on individuality and "personal feelings" as the marks of personhood.

I could read almost any poem in the Centenary Edition of Bishop's *Poems* to show how it fails to satisfy the terms of definitions of lyric as these have been animated (variously) by different critics. Yet finally, to cast Bishop's progress across her career, on the one hand, as a throwing off of the mantle of Eliotic impersonality toward an implicitly liberated, autobiographical lyric practice, or to argue, on the other, that Bishop's first-person poems of the 1970s are not expressive, but rather dramatize and theorize modern identity, won't decide the question of Bishop and lyric. Rather, we discover in such debates that lyric has been a lively discursive site for thinking about modern conceptions of identity, subjectivity, art's address, forms of readerly identification, and forms of cultural visibility and expressive power. The questions that arise in the attempt to clarify the lyric abstraction through individual poems sustains a significant part of the critical public's interest in Bishop studies.

*

What's at stake in asserting Bishop's work as lyric or not, especially given the fact that the meaning of "lyric" is itself so vague? The lion's share of Bishop's published poems feel less to be generalized vatic expressions of fictionalized speakers than descriptions we don't really doubt to be Bishop's, given their descriptive and narrative specificities, their addresses to real people, or their marked occasions – "([On my birthday])" in "The Bight," the dating of the *National Geographic* issue in "In the Waiting

Room"). Dedications, historical markers, dramatic characters, allusions to real people ("Invitation to Miss Marianne Moore"); the mediating presence of other artworks or generic markers ("song," "air," "Letter to N.Y."); flagrant literalizations of the expectation that poems "speak" (as in "Arrival at Santos," "The Filling Station," and "One Art"): in these and other aspects, Bishop's poems strain against lyric readings of them. While there are a few exceptions – small love poems that feel generalized, such as "The Shampoo," "Varick Street," or "Argument" – Bishop's body of work largely points to how inadequately "lyric" models how they should be read.

I offer this to suggest that readers might usefully test Bishop's lyric reputation in light of both shifts in lyric reading cultures in Bishop's lifetime, and also in light of her work's failure to accord to most available definitions of "lyric." Nevertheless, perhaps this leads to the recognition that very few to no poems could realize the multiple, sometimes conflicting, or very abstract ambitions that critics invest in the idea of lyric across Bishop's lifetime and today.

One even gets the sense that Bishop herself wrote self-consciously about the odd shift in ideas about poetic address that her era's models of lyric reading demanded. Among these is the very early poem "The Monument" (1939), which imagines the art object as precipitating not one right, enduring reading stabilized in the object's autonomous formal properties (the ultimate fantasy of New Critical interpretation) but conflicting discourses that admit that art's meaning depends on modes of reception that activate it, which are multiple and can change over time.

It stages a scene of interpretation in two voices, each offering a competing interpretation of an obscure wooden object – maybe a two-dimensional depiction of a seaside statue in wood, maybe a crude sculpture – that the first voice would like to claim is a "monument." The work is apparently difficult to make out, or to interpret as monumental, as the opening lines suggest:

> Now can you see the monument? It is of wood
> Built somewhat like a box. No. Built
> Like several boxes in descending sizes
> One above the other. (*P* 25)

The first voice goes into significant detail in describing the monument's formal features, but the second voice finds the object unimpressive:

> "It's piled up boxes,
> outlined with shoddy fretwork, half-fallen off,
> cracked and unpainted. It looks old." (*P* 26)

Overall, the poem highlights the object's exceeding any single stable interpretive use to which it might be put, highlighting multiple, evolving, contingent uses and readings (aesthetic, formalist, historical, sentimental) it might serve. As Penelope Laurans has argued, Bishop's shifts from lines and passages of iambic pentameter in the poem ("the crudest scroll-work says 'commemorate,'" or, with slight variation, "The bones of the artist-prince may be inside / or far away on even drier soil") to quite prose-like lines and passages "keep the reader from losing himself in the first speaker's magical description," a characteristic move that Laurens argues allows Bishop to deflect "lyrical intensity" here and elsewhere.[23]

But such moves also remind us of cultural specificities of production (such as Victorian verse cultures) that persist, though their site-specific meanings have become tattered, lost. Bishop's interest in the fate of such vestigial cultural specificities, and in the contingency of historical objects' receptions, could be read as a critique, *avant la lettre*, of the ideal of lyric as a non-contingent object of interpretation. And this is what the lyric-reading culture of her moment would increasingly insist upon. Nineteen-thirty-nine is the year after Cleanth Brooks and Robert Penn Warren (later called New Critics) published their first edition of *Understanding Poetry*, a textbook that over the next sixty years would install "lyric" as the monumental sign of "human" feeling and drama, often at the expense of multiplicity, history, and at the expense of our complex relations with others – indeed, with everything external in our worlds.

Notes

1. Marion Thain, "Introduction." *The Lyric Poem*, ed. Marion Thain (Cambridge, UK: Cambridge University Press, 2013), 3. The most famous critics to assume or argue so are Helen Vendler and Marjorie Perloff – Vendler as a term of praise, and Perloff, a term of derision. See Vendler, "Life Studies: The Collected Prose of Elizabeth Bishop," *New York Review of Books*, February 16, 1984, www.nybooks.com/articles/archives/1984/feb/16/life-studies/. 18. See Perloff, *21st-Century Modernism: The 'New' Poetics* (Malden, MA: Blackwell, 2002), 10. Perloff, "A Conversation with Marjorie Perloff," interview by Hélène Aji and Antoine Cazé, May 26, 2007, on Marjorie Perloff's website, marjorieperloff.com/interviews/aji-caze-interview.
2. Ellen Bryant Voigt, *The Flexible Lyric* (Athens: University of Georgia Press, 1999), ix.
3. See Virginia Jackson, "Lyric," in *Princeton Encyclopedia of Poetry and Poetics*, ed. Roland Greene and Stephen Cushman (Princeton, NJ: Princeton University Press, 2012), 826–34.

4. Broad comments on Bishop's college reading refer to material in *Elizabeth Bishop Papers*, Vassar College Library Special Collections, Series VII, Box 69B, folder 11, [Literary Critical Theory, 1933–34], hereafter VC.
5. Dan Chiasson, "Color Codes: a poet examines race in America," *The New Yorker*, October 27, 2014. www.newyorker.com/magazine/2014/10/27/color-codes. Last accessed July 9, 2019.
6. Jackson, "Lyric," 826.
7. J. J. Sylvester, *The Laws of Verse, or Principles of Versification* (London: Longmans, Green, and Co., 1870), 65.
8. Sydney Lanier, *The Science of English Verse* (New York: C. Scribner's Sons, 1880), 245.
9. John Stuart Mill, "Thoughts on Poetry and Its Varieties (1833)," in *Collected Works of John Stuart Mill, Vol 1. Autobiography and Literary Essays*, ed. John M. Robson and Jack Stillinger (Toronto: University of Toronto Press, 1981), 359.
10. Voigt, 175–78.
11. Eleanor Cook, *Elizabeth Bishop at Work* (Cambridge, MA: Harvard University Press, 2016), 194.
12. "Byronic man" is a phrase Bishop uses in "The Mechanics of Pretense" (*EAP* 183). Her critique of Wordsworth critique can be found in Bishop's papers, referenced previously.
13. James Longenbach, "Elizabeth Bishop's Social Conscience," *ELH* 62.2 (Summer 1995), 467–86; Betsey Erkkila, "Elizabeth Bishop, Modernism, and the Left," *ALH* 8.2 (1996), 284–310.
14. Malcolm Cowley, "The Last of the Lyric Poets," *The New Republic*, January 27, 1932, 299. Qtd. in Milton Cohen, *Beleaguered Poets and Leftist Critics: Stevens, Cummings, Frost, and Williams in the 1930s* (Tuscaloosa: University of Alabama Press), 2010, 93.
15. Cohen, 93.
16. Wendy Hirsch, "Bogan, Louise (1897–1970), poet and critic." *American National Biography*. 1 Feb. 2000.
17. See "The Situation in American Writing, 1939," *Partisan Review* 6.5 (Fall 1939): 105–08. Reprinted in *The Partisan Reader 1934–44: An Anthology*. See also Alan Filreis, *The Counter-revolution of the Word: The Conservative Attack on Modern Poetry, 1945–1960* (Chapel Hill: University of North Carolina Press, 2012), 70.
18. See Cleanth Brooks and Robert Penn Warren, "Preface," in *Understanding Poetry: An Anthology for College Students* (New York: Holt, 1938), especially vi.
19. For 1950s *Oxford English Dictionary* definition of "lyric," see T. S. Eliot, *The Three Voices of Poetry* (1953), 2nd ed. (London: Cambridge University Press, 1955), 15. For 2019 definition, see "lyric," *Glossary of Poetic Terms*, Poetry Foundation website. www.poetryfoundation.org/learn/glossary-terms/lyric.
20. Reuben Arthur Brower, *The Fields of Light: An Experiment in Critical Reading* (1951) (Philadelphia, PA: Paul Dry Books, 2013), 19. My view of this is informed directly by Yopie Prins and Virginia Jackson's critical introduction to "Section 3: Anglo-American New Criticism," *The Lyric Theory Reader*, 159–65.

21. From Cleanth Brooks's *The Well Wrought Urn: Studies in the Structure of Poetry* (1947).
22. T. S. Eliot, "Tradition and the Individual Talent" [1919], reprinted in *Selected Prose of T.S. Eliot*, ed. Frank Kermode (New York: Harcourt, 1975), 37–44, 41. For Bishop's use of impersonality, see Bonnie Costello "Elizabeth Bishop's Impersonal Personal," *American Literary History*, 15.2 (Summer 2003), 334–66.
23. Penelope Laurans, "'Old Correspondences': Prosodic Transformations in Elizabeth Bishop," in *Elizabeth Bishop and Her Art*, ed. Lloyd Schwartz and Sybil P. Estess (Ann Arbor: University of Michigan Press, 1983), 75–95, 87–88.

CHAPTER 8

Prose

Vidyan Ravinthiran

Bishop's book on Brazil was mauled by the editors at Time-Life, and what we have of it in the collected *Prose* is mostly dryly factual. There are moments, however, when her expressiveness shines through. She cherishes, for example, Brazilian idioms, and what they reveal; the convenor of a class at Harvard on reading letters as art-works, Bishop explains that Pero Vaz de Caminha's "wonderfully vivid letter" has been called the first page of both Brazilian history, and Brazilian literature. She creates a kind of appreciative art-language to give value to all sorts of things – "*capoeira*, a form of combined wrestling and jujitsu, using the feet, lightning quick, graceful" – and draws out, as in her poems, the multifariousness of a hybrid culture (with its "racial mixtures" among the population, its zebu cattle imported from India, the *azulejos* "revised in contemporary Brazilian architecture"). We sense her unease with US values, as when she says that Brazil is "still one country where human-man, poor as he may be, is still more important than producing-man or consuming-man or political-man," and that in it "culture and the arts are more respected than in our own industrialized and middle-class country" (*Pr* 175, 197, 231, 222, 250, 229). She doesn't idealise Brazil, though she admires qualities in it known to be fleeting, specific to one stage of economic and social development.

Prose was both a fascination and a bugbear for Bishop. Lloyd Schwartz editorially divides her output into "stories and memoirs," "essays, reviews and tributes," translations (*The Diary of "Helena Morley"*, which I'll examine, and stories by Clarice Lispector); and the "early prose," which includes her undergraduate essays, in which, looking for a poetics, she finds it in Morris Croll's analysis of baroque prose, which sought – in his phrase – to portray "not a thought, but a mind thinking."[1] There are also her letters, which are genuinely creative, stylishly humane. Yet Bishop wasn't comfortable as a literary critic, and she'd have liked to write more fiction, but worried she wasn't good enough at entering other people's minds.

Let's consider two tales from the late Thirties, in which the problem of other people leads Bishop to picture isolatoes. The narrator of "In Prison" voices her anxieties about the form; he wishes to voluntarily confine himself, to learn freedom within constraint:

> I should rather face the east than the west since I much prefer sunrises to sunsets. Then, too, it is by looking towards the east that one obtains the most theatrical effects from a sunset, in my opinion. I refer to that fifteen minutes or half an hour of heavy gold in which any object can be made to look magically significant. If the reader can tell me of anything more beautiful than a stone court-yard lit obliquely in this way so that the shallowly rounded stones each cast a small shadow but the general surface is thickly sanded with gold, and a pole casts a long, long shadow and a limp wire an unearthly one, – I beg him to tell me what it is. (*Pr* 22)

This mannered prickliness feels unstably ironised: Bishop's using the narratorial voice to think with; she isn't at a safe distance from this strange man and his compulsions. She'd revisit this imagery (sunset, shadows, wires) in one of her masterpiece-poems, "The End of March"; and with it the idea that the writer shouldn't posit significance declaratively, but be alert to effects of change, flux, shifts in the light, which permit – if we're looking closely – the nondescript to shimmer into life. The narrator talks pedantically, but the final long sentence has in it unpredictable energies. The sound of *gold*, *stone*, and *shadow* is passed on to *pole*, just as alliteration takes us from the "long, long shadow" to the "limp wire": punctilious elucidation is replaced by experiential poignancy. In "The Sea and Its Shore," Edwin Boomer, collecting beach-drifted scraps of print, which appear enlivened with an eerily drifting life of their own, would seem to contemplate the point or non-point of literary endeavour – "he made no distinction between the bewilderments of prose and those of poetry" (*Pr* 15) – the pleasures, and disturbances, we get out of reading and writing. Bishop's not-quite-stories aren't always satisfying: they don't please, or disturb, as we'd like them to. They've the dreamy quality of someone thinking out loud, rather than speaking to us with a clear motive.

Is it because Bishop's an acknowledged genius in verse that – from our angle of approach – her prose prompts caveats? In the verse, her presiding dilemmas glitter more overtly, we know what to do with them. A self-questioning formalist, Bishop masterminded firm structures, but also invented a style of straggling longish poem which Mary Kinzie, for one, compared insultingly to prose, though in fact Bishop worried she remained too iambic deep down.[2] Prose fascinated her as a concept aligned with a wished-for sane worldliness, powers of empathy rather than self-expression, and an outward gaze inclusive of modern materials that could outpace the narcissism encoded (it might seem) within the structures of old-style metrical verse. But she was also intrigued by it as a literary form which we still don't know how to analyse. The Victorians and Edwardians had a go, but George Saintsbury's procedure, for example, involves scanning prose as if it were in fact verse.[3] So Bishop's uncertainty about prose, and how to write fiction, overlaps with an area of literary-critical neglect. Having written about this elsewhere, I'd like to explore how her thinking about prose (and her worrying about it) emerges in *Brazil* – in the shape of its sentences, as they negotiate issues of authority and cultural distance.

Reading through *Brazil*, I was struck by a passage about soccer where that expressiveness I mentioned is unusually sustained. The prose moves towards artistic appreciation, in which a subculture is both admired and probed:

> In the country on Sundays, the population of every small village will be out watching the local *futebol* teams. The big pale-green fields will be edged with people in their Sunday best, carrying babies, carrying umbrellas against the sun. The *Kibon* ("Eskimo pie") man with his yellow wagon, a spun-sugar wagon (home-made, mounted on a bicycle); buzzards and delicate tissue paper kites hang overhead, and the players in their brilliantly striped jerseys and brief shorts are running, running. (*Pr* 236)

Bishop's theorising about prose occurs in her letters, and undergraduate essays – one of which, "Time's Andromedas," analyses the work of Dorothy Richardson and Gertrude Stein:

> In [*The Making of Americans*] there seems to be a group of movements prolonged to numbness, then repeated; the whole producing a static, a frieze, certainly with more of time in it than other novels, but time that is frozen and expanded.
>
> But within these long stretches, however lacking in the sense of present time they may be, are many curious tricks which perhaps further the sense of present time defeated in the book as a whole. One of these, seemingly very simple but in reality, I think, very important, is the use of the present participle. Whenever we stop in the midst of doing something to contemplate and inform ourselves what it is we are doing, we announce it with the help of an i-n-g word. That very ending has a peculiar ringing effect, carrying the word on from the actual sense of the verb into the realm of present time, into action. (*PPL* 656–57)

It's Bishop's memoir-fictions, "Primer Class," "In the Village" and (I'll move on to consider it) "Memories of Uncle Neddy," which move back and forth in time – but the effect she describes is never so precisely replicated as in this passage on Brazilian football.

The future tense creates such a "frieze," or, to follow Bishop's perhaps unconscious wordplay, "time that is frozen and expanded." The people "will be out," the fields "will be edged" with them – where "edged" suggests an illustration ("Seascape" has its "bright green leaves edged neatly with bird-droppings"). The picture leaps with colour and detail. But the next sentence breaks with this, to create "the sense of present time" – suggesting, in a tourist book, the impossible dream of plunging without mediation into foreign life. Bishop combines the picturesque (the repeated word "wagon," and another parenthesis which ruffles the rhythm; the buzzards, kites, and kits) with a moment where imaginative effort is required, a faintly disturbing visual comparison of the floating kites with predatory birds. So after the initial "frieze," there isn't a rush but a regulated movement towards the wonderful feeling of "present time" at the end, where those footballers aren't frozen in the past, but "running, running," as we watch. They resemble Bishop's famous sandpiper – "he runs, he runs" – but Bishop's prose (the stories, the letters, fragments like this) challenges us to read it not in a subsidiary relation to her verse, but as an achievement in itself.

I don't mean by this to suggest that *Brazil* is an undiscovered masterpiece of Modernism, but that Bishop's tormented relationship with prose was never put aside: she's always fascinated with what it can do, and wonders if she's up to the challenge. If she worried that in fiction she was incapable of authorial empathy, then writing this book must have activated similar concerns. Her sentences balance a closeness to Brazil against the recognition that she doesn't truly belong there, a worry no doubt amplified by her commission: to write for Time-Life not an impressionistic memoir, but a factual account for the US reader. Why, then, does she end this chapter on "Groups and Individuals" with this long description – whose final one-sentence paragraph, is surely a little mysterious?

> It is also a common sight to see the local washerwoman's line hung with the jerseys of one team, sweaters striped like wasps, a cheerful display, sometimes against the background of a city dump, with buzzards and paper kites hovering above. (*Pr* 236)

The commas space out the elements in the sentence, insinuating a significance which can't be strictly paraphrased. Bishop refuses to sell Brazil to the foreign tourist as a delightful commodity: she praises the country which has taken her in, but without neglecting the ugly "city dump." "It is also a common sight" is the dull, bloodless tone required of her, like "it is interesting to note" earlier on: but the sentence comes to life with an assonance connecting *line, striped, sometimes*, and *kites*; "hang," now "hung," returns, along with the kits, the kites and buzzards. In her unpublished essay on the "unnatural act" of writing poetry, Bishop admires this verb in Robert Lowell – "Salem fishermen / Once hung their nimble fleets on the Great Banks" – and how it "suggests the immensity, the depths of the cold stormy water and the tininess, the activity of the small 'nimble' ships – and yet it's the simplest sort of natural verb to use" (*Pr* 330). As she describes Brazilian city-life, details persist, or return, and the US reader is asked not to skim-read but to actively imagine what may remain strange to them.

Bishop both respects and fears prose, as a form expressive of social, rather than personal, matters. She writes unlineated sentences with a feeling for the effort it takes to move beyond the perimeters of a conscientiously observing, maybe slightly fussy and neurotic, self, whose streams of noticing strain to acknowledge the other while also erecting defensive fortifications. Her translation of *The Diary of "Helena Morley"* allows her to write, as it were, Brazilian prose, hurdling the problem by inhabiting from the start a voice which isn't hers. In her introduction, she quotes from "Helena's soliloquy on November 5th, 1893, on the meaning of Time (her style improves in the later years)":

> She goes on to tell about "mama's" waking her and Luizinha up to go to four o'clock Mass, because the rooster has already crowed twice. They drink their coffee and start out. "I kept looking at the moon and the stars and saying to mama, 'This time the Senhora's going to see whether the rooster can tell time or not.' The street was deserted. The two of us walked holding onto mama's arms. When we passed by the barracks the soldier on duty looked at mama and asked, 'What's the Senhora doing in the street with these little girls at this hour?' Mama said, 'We're going to Mass at the Cathedral.' The soldier said, 'Mass at midnight? It isn't Christmas eve. What's this all about?'
>
> "I was afraid of the soldier. Mama said, 'Midnight? I thought it was four o'clock. Thank you very much for the information.'
>
> "We went home and lay down in our clothes. But even so we missed Mass. When we got to church later Father Neves was already in the Hail Marys."
>
> I like to think of the two tall, thin little girls hanging onto their mother's arms, the three figures stumbling up the steep streets of the rocky, lightless little town beneath the cold bright moon and stars; and I can hear the surprised young soldier's voice, mama's polite reply, and then three pairs of footsteps scuttling home again over the cobblestones. (*Pr* 287–88)

Bishop's prose merges into Helena's, and because the girl writes with spoken verve – it's like listening to her talk – there's the feeling of speech-acts nested within each other: Helena tries to convince her mother; the soldier enquires what they're up to; Mama decorously responds. But following this, Bishop reinstates a distance between herself (and the reader), and Helena Morley and her family. Their existence must be imagined to be made real to the foreigner, although Bishop positions this glide into another life as happily compulsive: "I like to think of the two tall, thin little girls hanging onto their mother's arms." It resembles "Manuelzinho", when the speaker of the poem, a Brazilian landowner, half-sees, half-imagines, her tenant and his family descending the hill: "I see you all up there [. . .] / coming down at night, / in silence, except for hoofs, / in dim moonlight, the horse / or Formoso stumbling after" (*P* 96). As in that poem, we sense uncrossable distances – Bishop tries to imagine Helena's life without exoticising it – and, as in the earlier passage of prose, the verb "hang" is pivotal. It captures a harried essence, the failure of the children to persuade the mother, and her hustling them along. It's not surprising that Bishop was drawn to this passage, given the mother she, in Adrienne Rich's suggestively brusque phrasing, "lost … into a mental institution" when still a child.[4]

Bishop writes prose fastidiously (the alliteration, the adjectives), and the effect can be of overcaution. Sounds twin and circumspectly recombine, as if she's ill-at-ease writing without the armatures of poetic form, either open or closed. She knowingly uses an unusual word, "lightless," to stress the contrary brightness of the moon, and to urge the reader to pay attention – but this, too, might seem fussy. In the memoir to which I'm about to turn, "Memories of Uncle Neddy," Bishop observes of her relative's portrait his eye, in which "the painter has carefully placed a highlight of dry white paint, like a crumb"; she remembers, too, that Neddy used to wear "a stickpin with a small, dead diamond in it, much like the white highlight in his left eye that I am contemplating right now" (*Pr* 148, 149). We have here another surprising shift into the present tense, the now of writing, but also Bishop's attraction to brilliantly static details, which she's always trying to redeem with motion, to reassert within an overall vision of (going back to Bonnie Costello's book on her, still the best) uncertainty and flux.[5] Her prose seems to will itself into motion, and for some, flourishes like "lightless" will seem small dead diamonds, rather than entry-points into a living past.

Returning to *The Diary of "Helena Morley,"* we find an arc familiar from her verse: details flare, collect, and then – this is what's extraordinary, and how she tries to reintroduce spirit into crystallised matter – they generate a suggestiveness which isn't simply a technical achievement, a feat of fine writing, for what is renovated is our awareness both of the structures of perception, and the tensions of a specific culture. Following the semi-colon, the sentence ceases its careful exact listing, and states an immediacy of feeling which Bishop, an outsider on the scene, can only tentatively assume. We move from the debonairly self-amusing "I like to think" to a direct inhabiting of the scene, a kind of transnational time-travel: "I can hear." Bishop's prose considers the limits of empathy, the risks involved in translation, and of speaking in another person's voice, on behalf of another culture. She had need of a style of intelligent hesitance in both it and her verse, partly to express her temperament, but also – and this is more important – due to her feeling for how imperilled our utterances become when they move beyond a narrowly autobiographical frame of reference.

This is why she worries that "In the Village" is "completely autobiographical," that mastering the "Art of story writing" – this in a letter to the Barkers – will involve more "thinking about *people*, balancing this with that, time, etc" (*OA* 271–72). Here she connects empathy with issues of thematic and narrative structure. The passages I've examined are designed, following Bishop's thoughts on Richardson, to enhance the reader's sense of "time." So we might say that Bishop worried about being a writer of the individual sentence, or paragraph: she made smaller units within the prose-work innovatively exploratory (mentioning at one point a theory of the "proliferal sentence," drawn from Edgar Allan Poe) but felt unable to do this on a larger scale, in terms of plot as well as characterisation. Her memoir-fictions "In the Village" and "Primer Class" are rightly admired, but in terms of macrostructure, they're obtrusively circular, beginning and ending with reference to an act of strenuous memory which carries Bishop out of the present into the past, and back again. This reveals both the failure to break definitively with an autobiographical approach – everything comes out of the perceiving authorial self, into which the storyline then vanishes – and also an obsession as to "balancing this with that": in a sense, Bishop has turned her would-be stories into closed couplets. There's an effort at self-justification through the accomplishment of narrative shaping.

The effect deepens, however, in "Memories of Uncle Neddy," a text which hasn't received much attention. Writing to Robert Lowell, Bishop raised her envy of the assurance with which he assumed not just his own life, but that of his family, to be of interest; a point relating to confessionalism, but also a style of confidence, related to gender as well as Lowell's illustrious background, that she craved to siphon. Only years later would she author – discussing her uncle – her own version of "91 Revere Street." She begins in Rio de Janeiro, where it's "raining, raining, raining," taking us directly into the scene of composition – "I'm writing in a penthouse apartment, eleven floors up, facing southeast over the sea" – and establishing this atmosphere of rain, spray, mildew, damp, and mould in terms of a rising tide of decay, a possible obliteration of domestic comforts. A type of leisured observation thus grows unsafe, a shade jittery:

> And Uncle Neddy, that is, my Uncle Edward, is *here*. Into this wildly foreign and, to him, exotic setting, Uncle Neddy has just come back, from the framer's. He leans slightly, silently backwards against the damp-stained pale-yellow wall, looking quite cheerfully into the eyes of whoever happens to look at him – including the cat's, who investigated him just now. Only of course it isn't really Uncle Neddy, not as he was, or not as I knew him. This is "little Edward," before he became an uncle, before he became a lover, husband, father or grandfather, a tinsmith, a drunkard, or a famous fly-fisherman – any of the various things he turned out to be. (*Pr* 146)

It's like a trick of lineation, or a poem with a conceit: the portrait stands for the man himself ("he leans slightly, silently backwards" makes him weirdly present) and when Bishop admits it's not "really Uncle Neddy," there's another little surprise, another idea introduced, for she explains that it's a painting of him as a child. The central sentence, beginning "only of course," thus looks in two directions; and the sentence following it, long and ending the paragraph, gives in summary much of what's to follow, suggesting the futility of trying to summarise in a portrait (as this memoir, too, is supposed to be) the variegations of a life. Or, it's as if Bishop sat down to write another of her ekphrastic poems, only to find it morphing into something different, and in prose.

Bishop establishes a parallel between the black mould on the walls, and her one-time view of Neddy as a sort of "gentle black" devil – "he had looked, too, then, like a dried-out wick, in the smoke-blackened chimney of an oil lamp" – contrasted with the "red, real one," his wife Aunt Hat: "redheaded, freckled, red-knuckled, strong, all fierce fire and flame." His work, as a tinsmith, is amid darkness and grime ("he was like a black snail . . . leaving a silvery, shiny trail of solder"; or, "instead of being like a dark snail, he was a thin, dark salamander, enjoying, for a moment, his wife's fieriness"); during the infamous "Black Christmas," he dresses up as

Santa, but frightens Bishop, as a child, by resembling a "Negro" (*Pr* 147, 152, 153, 155, 157). The colour-patterning here resembles the racialised imagery of "In the Waiting Room," and suggests, like that poem, Bishop's uncertainties, nearing fear, regarding people of colour; but the effort of this memoir is to render Neddy, both within and outside his unhappy marriage, as a creaturely, tender, loveable figure. The prose changes pace, lingering where it feels possible to (the "night sky" of Neddy's shop – Bishop shifts into the present tense, uses her favourite verb again, "is hung with the things he makes himself: milk pails, their bottoms shining like moons; flashing tin mugs in different sizes; watering pots like comets"); and, in contrast, sliding over the complexities which give rise to a person's character when neither they, nor we, are watching:

> Well, Uncle Neddy grew up; he skated a great deal, winters (without bundling up), went through all the grades of the village school, and very early (I heard much later) began to fall in love and to – alas for Neddy – "chase women." I even heard, overheard, rather, that there had been prolonged family worry about a "widow." He must have begun drinking about this time, too, although that was never mentioned until years later when he became, on occasion, a public disgrace. (*Pr* 150)

Bishop's verse is praised for its tricks with epanorthosis, or self-correction, which creates Croll's effect of a mind thinking; here, we might consider this constant nuancing in terms of a buoyant, ever-varying rhythm suggestive of the complexities of inheritance, and the muddled textures of the past. The parentheses, the interjection between two dashes, the correction of "heard" to "overheard, rather," and the minor addition "on occasion," which, assonating with "public disgrace," seem to ameliorate that dreadful idiom, to try to in some way let Neddy off the hook (Bishop was, of course, an alcoholic too) – it amounts to nothing less than the noise of life, the tortuousness of simply existing at all. It is a fine achievement in prose, by a poet who never fully realised (in either sense) her gift for it.

Notes

1. Morris Croll, "The Baroque Style in Prose" (1929); repr. in *Style, Rhetoric and Rhythm: Essays*, ed. Morris W. Croll, J. Max Patrick, and Robert O. Evans, with John M. Wallace and R. J. Schoeck (Princeton, NJ: Princeton University Press, 1966), 210.
2. See *The Cure of Poetry in an Age of Prose: Moral Essays on the Poet's Calling* (Chicago: University of Chicago Press, 1993), 96–97.

3. See *A History of English Prose Rhythm* (London and Bloomington: Indiana University Press, 1965).
4. *Culture, Politics, and the Art of Poetry: Essential Essays*, ed. Sandra M. Gilbert (New York: Norton, 2018), 220.
5. This is the central thesis of *Elizabeth Bishop: Questions of Mastery* (Cambridge, MA and London: Harvard University Press, 1991).

CHAPTER 9

Letters

Langdon Hammer

Announcing, in a letter from 1971, that she planned to teach a seminar at Harvard "on 'Letters'!," Bishop described the subject matter as "Just *letters* – as an art form or something" (*OA* 544). A course "on 'Letters'!" that will be about . . . "Just *letters*"? The phrase "an art form or something" barely saves Bishop's course description from tautology. But what it adds is not obvious. It asserts that the letter is a genre worthy of independent investigation and academic study, like poetry, plays, or the novel. But then "or something" blurs the point, and half takes it back. Letters have a claim to the status of art, and yet they remain an unspecified something else.[1]

Rather than generalize further, Bishop sketches a syllabus, demonstrating her idea for this course by examples: "I'm hoping to select a nicely incongruous assortment of people – Mrs. Carlyle, Chekhov, my Aunt Grace, Keats, a letter found in the street, etc. etc." (*OA* 544–55). The list's "nicely incongruous" quality points out that the letter is a genre used not only by literary artists like Keats and Chekhov, but by ordinary people like Bishop's Aunt Grace, and by women who were brilliant writers in the genre but not published in their lifetimes, like Jane Carlyle, as well as by celebrated public figures like her husband, the Victorian polymath Thomas Carlyle who declared that "the History of the world is but the Biography of great men." When Bishop plans a course on letters beginning with Mrs. Carlyle, she suggests an alternative history of the world in which women and ordinary people will participate alongside Mr. Carlyle's great men.[2]

Our letters are, by convention, the key to our hearts. But it follows from this that the subjectivity of a letter is to some degree formulaic, a property of the genre, rather than the indelible expression of a unique individual. Add to this the fact that the letter-writer is never quite the same person she was when she wrote a given letter. The present tense in a letter is specific and historical, and therefore categorically different from the present tense in a lyric poem, which is reactivated across time with every reading.[3] Once detached from the moment and circumstances of its composition, there is something impersonal and strange about any piece of correspondence. On that level, every letter is "a letter found in the street."

That Bishop is writing about her letters course *in* a letter points up other aspects of the form. The informality of her prose in letters is essential: its playfulness, apparent spontaneity, and nonchalance (sometimes even sloppiness, as in that double "etc. etc.") simulate a voice in conversation, with the aid of writerly tools like dashes, italics, and scare quotes, which make her tones and emphases audible. The premise of that informality is the intimacy of her address: typically, Bishop's correspondent is familiar, indeed a friend, or a friend in the making, rather than the anonymous reader of a book or magazine. The relationship is based on trust, even affection; and the casualness of the communication keeps whatever she has to say fluid, unpretentious, keyed to the particular occasion, and embedded in the performance of a personal style for a select audience.

In this case, she is writing to Arthur Gold and Robert Fizdale – duo pianists, authors, and domestic partners with whom she had been exchanging gossipy letters since Lota de Macedo Soares, her partner in Brazil, introduced her to them in the early 1950s. Because manners and style are paramount in letters, and much goes without saying in them, letters were a vehicle for gay sociability in an era when there were strong constraints on speech about sex and sexual identity. Writing to Gold and Fizdale, Bishop does not have to hide *or* declare the nature of her relationship with Lota; she can simply hand the pen to her, as when she and Lota take turns writing a letter Gold and Fizdale in 1952, a letter-writing practice something like playing four-hand piano, as Gold and Fizdale would have appreciated (*OA* 262–64).

Letters are collaborative and dialogic. They introduce chains of interaction, soliciting response, as Bishop does when she breaks off her list of letter-writers and asks Gold and Fizdale to help her plan: "But I need some ideas from you both – just on the subject of letters, the dying 'form of communication'" (*OA* 545). There is here, as in many Bishop letters, a mood of mild, amused conspiracy. She is pleased to smuggle into the Harvard College curriculum a subject as personal, pleasurable, and therefore trivial-seeming as correspondence; and she is pleased to share the plan with these particular friends. The "dying 'form of communication'" may be out of sync with the times and its informal norms of behavior,[4] but Bishop and her friends can smirk at the style-less sociological idiom in which this idea is expressed. In their case, they know, letter-writing is alive and well.

*

Just how important letters were to Bishop, and what a central place they have in the body of her work, has become clear in stages after her death, as her correspondence has been mined for works of criticism and biography, and edited for publication in books and journals. David Kalstone's *Becoming a Poet: Elizabeth Bishop with Marianne Moore and Robert Lowell* (1989) was the first book to draw heavily on Bishop's correspondence with Moore and Lowell in order to narrate her evolving sense of poetic vocation. Bishop's letters were a primary source for Brett C. Millier's *Elizabeth Bishop: Life and the Memory of It* (1993), the first biography of Bishop. *One Art*, the first and still the most comprehensive selection of her letters, appeared in 1994, reinforcing the biographical approach that had begun to dominate readings of her poetry by that time. *Words in Air: The Complete Correspondence Between Elizabeth Bishop and Robert Lowell* (2008) presented both sides of her long dialogue with Lowell. *Elizabeth Bishop and 'The New Yorker': The Complete Correspondence* (2011), collected her back-and-forth with Katherine White and Howard Moss, who published the majority of her poems over four decades in their roles as editors at *The New Yorker*.

Bishop's *New Yorker* correspondence shows her making friends with her editors, discovering shared points of reference, personalizing their professional dealings, and ultimately creating deep friendships. Something similar happens in the 1960s in her correspondence with Anne Stevenson, who had written to Bishop to gather information for the first critical book about her work (both sides of that correspondence were included in Bishop's collected *Prose* in 2011).[5] Bishop's address to her evolves over twelve months from "Dear Mrs. Stevenson" to "Dear Mrs. Elvin" (her married name) to "Dear Anne." Bishop comes to trust Stevenson as they exchange personal information and establish a common idiom, a way of talking easily with each other. In the process, Bishop's letters get longer and longer, more confiding and at ease, until she has used their correspondence to give a detailed account of her family history, described the development of her poetic career, and meditated on her preferences in music, art, and literature.

A passage from the longest of her letters to Stevenson, from 1964, known as "The 'Darwin' Letter," was one of the first pieces of her correspondence to gain attention when it was excerpted in *Elizabeth Bishop and Her Art* (1983). The passage begins: "There is no 'split.' Dreams, works of art (some), glimpses of the always-more-successful surrealism of everyday life, unexpected moments of empathy (is it?), catch a peripheral vision of whatever it is one can never really see full-face but that seems enormously important." Bishop goes on to talk about her admiration for Darwin, whom she pictures as a "lonely young man, his eyes fixed on facts and minute details, sinking or sliding giddily off into the unknown." That image directly leads to a summary statement about the nature of art. For Bishop, artist and audience have a parallel and equivalent experience of it: "What one seems to want in art, in experiencing it, is the same thing that is necessary for its creation, a self-forgetful, perfectly useless concentration" (*Pr* 414). The whole passage can be pored over. Rich in imagery that links up to Bishop's poetry, and rhythmically complex, it is like a poem itself.

But in its excerpted form, which critics have often quoted, the fact that it is part of a letter, written in response to Stevenson's comments on Bishop's work, gets lost. Shorn from the excerpt was the beginning of it – "Dear Anne, Yes, I agree with you" – and the question Bishop posed at the end of it: "Dearest Anne, (In this sense it [the experience of art] is always 'escape,' don't you think?)" (*Pr* 414).[6] That question complicates her otherwise final-sounding statement, leaving the idea open-ended, in need of further discussion. Once it is restored to its context, we recognize the passage's dense, probing, speculative prose as dialogic and specifically epistolary. Bishop's careful second-guessing and self-questioning are ways of engaging and acknowledging her correspondent. This is not trivial politeness on her part, but an effort to get at an idea by sharing it, even while the letter's conversational form keeps Bishop's thinking unsettled and incomplete. Her letter gives a "peripheral" rather than "full-face" view of her "enormously important" subject.

There is a purposefully sketchy, offhand quality to Bishop's thinking in letters, as in her definition of the letter itself as "an art form or something." We might see the style as imprecise, and find it curious in a poet particularly noted for her precision of observation. But imprecision of this sort in her letters appealed to Bishop because it prevented her ideas from becoming prematurely or permanently fixed, as they would be in print. Letters allowed her to speculate, muse, joke, hesitate, qualify, and change her mind, all in the course of a letter, or sometimes in the course of a sentence. In letters, Bishop could try out sharp, avowedly partial opinions, rather than patiently build up arguments and take reasoned positions for which she would be held publicly accountable, as demanded by the book reviews she struggled to complete.[7] Letters allowed her to mix topics in meandering association, or with less connection than that, shaped only by the flow of thought and the chance nature of experience.

Each of Bishop's important correspondences has its own character and dynamics. But the series of letters she wrote to her psychoanalyst, Dr. Ruth

Foster, over a period of days in 1947, is unique in its intensity. These letters detail Bishop's sexual history and its connections to her creativity in an extended reverie, presumably written at Dr. Foster's request or suggestion. Although unpublished, they have been discussed in essays and papers, and used as evidence by Bishop's latest biographers.[8] They include personal revelations that are shocking in view of the poet's celebrated reticence. It is tempting to see those revelations as simple facts that can be extracted from their context and plugged into Bishop's life story. But that would be to ignore the way they are embedded in Bishop's tangled, drunken address to her analyst. Statements in a letter always demand interpretation and contextualization, and all the more when the letter takes the form of a quasi-analytic monologue in which dreams and hallucinations are discussed, and conscious and unconscious role-playing prevails. When Bishop describes for Dr. Foster being sexually abused as a child by her uncle, is she dramatizing or underplaying the force of the abuse and its effect on her? What is Bishop really saying when she announces to Dr. Foster, "I have no clitoris at all"[9]?

Less sensational but no less revelatory than the Foster Letters are Bishop's letters to Louise Bradley, another unpublished correspondence.[10] Fourteen years old at the time, Bishop met Bradley in 1924 on the train platform in Boston when they were both on their way to camp on Cape Cod. Bradley, three years older and in her last year of camp, found Bishop, a first-time camper, standing among the girls she was greeting. "I don't know *you*," she said to Bishop, "but I'll kiss you, too," as Bishop later repeated the introduction back to her in a letter.[11] They became close friends at camp, and, although – or because – they met only infrequently after that, they exchanged letters (over sixty by Bishop) through Bishop's high school and college years. There are only a few pieces of correspondence dated after 1934, and Bradley's side of it is almost entirely lost, save for a witty valentine and drafts of a letter she may not have sent.

The gaps in this correspondence and the many questions they raise are typical of the biographical problems posed by letters. How did Bradley think of Bishop? Were her letters to "Bishie," as Elizabeth signs herself in hers, equally devoted and passionate? To make sense of a correspondence, however complete or incomplete, is to constellate fragmentary evidence, and make surmises about what is missing (including what may not have been apparent to the letter-writers themselves). Even so, a clear picture of the teenage Bishop emerges here. In her letters to Bradley, she is revelling in the excitement of a same-sex intimacy, gaining the confidence to declare her likes and dislikes, accepting her felt difference from her schoolmates and the adults around her, boldly claiming her ambition to write poetry, and discovering that letters allow her to connect all these developments, and push forward in life.

Bishop's letters to Bradley sometimes include poems that she has written, or her comments on Bradley's poems. They are full of intimations of the poet Bishop would become, as well as, crucially, ideas about the style of life she imagined for herself as a poet. These are suggested by a persistent fantasy of travel to an exotic, isolated, usually island locale with her "Dearest Kindred Spirit."[12] Here are two elaborations of it, from 1926 and 1927 respectively:

> Louise–is it right for a young woman to trail off to the ends of the earth–Norway–India–alone? And live in strange places and do strange things–or two young women. You come with me. When my – – – education is finished. Lets. And then retire to Ireland and raise bees–and live by the ocean in a stone cottage–and write poetry for a living. Oh!! Will you![13]

> I'm going to live in Tahti [*sic*] or one of those islands with a piano and stacks of books–and the sea and sun–and stars. So you must come with me and bring the Irish harp and we'll play together–not just music. Wouldn't you like to live on a South Sea Island–and forget calendars, and church and subways, and doctors, and Logarithms? Say yes or rather, write it to me.[14]

Fifty years later, Bishop published "Crusoe in England," in which Crusoe remembers his life on the island with Friday. Bishop had by then lived out versions of the idea behind the poem with Louise Crane and then Marjorie Stevens in Key West, Lota in Brazil, and Alice Methfessel on the island of North Haven. Her letters to Bradley demonstrate that the idea was coeval with her wish to be a poet and her discovery of romantic feeling for girls, and that it was fully formed as early as her adolescence. The future life that these letters project will include strangeness and domesticity, escape and adventure, solitude and companionship, books and the senses, the sea and the stars. Meanwhile, short of actually setting out for Tahiti, Bishop invites Bradley to join her on the private island constituted by their letters, where love and poetry already flourish. "Say yes," Bishie begs her friend, "or rather, write it to me."

*

Bishop stopped regularly writing letters to Bradley after she graduated from Vassar and began to correspond with Marianne Moore. Bishop's letters to Moore start out as a courtship in which Bishop adopts a deferential tone, produces distinctive gifts calculated to please Moore's eccentric sensibility (e.g., swan feathers [*OA* 33]), and gallantly proposes to take her mentor to the circus (*OA* 31) and Coney Island (*OA* 33, 45). These topics – swan feathers and the circus – sit in the letters beside discussion of Moore's strenuous efforts to improve Bishop's writing and to help Bishop publish it. But there is no sense of discontinuity in the juxtaposition. In seeking to join in Moore's interests in life, Bishop is cultivating her own sensibility, which is the basis of her writing; she is taking lessons from Moore in both. The focus in their correspondence on the articulation of personal taste in all things identifies writing poetry with a way of living, rather than advancement in a profession, which would associate poetry with the utilitarian and self-promotion. What could be further from the purpose of art as Bishop later defined it for Stevenson: "a self-forgetful, perfectly useless concentration"?

The Bishop–Moore correspondence in the 1930s has the quality of an elaborate game conducted with rigorous formality. It is four years after they begin writing to each other that Bishop addresses Moore as "Marianne" for the first time, and when she does, Bishop writes her friend's first name in capital letters lit up as on a marquee with dots for electric lights (*OA* 76), making it clear that proper deportment is a bit of a joke between them. Yet the question of what Bishop can and can't say to Moore remains. It comes to a head in 1940 when Moore (and her mother) aggressively rewrote a draft of Bishop's "Roosters," effectively censoring the poem's feminist anger and hints of eroticism. In reply, Bishop stood up for the poem and held to her intentions. But her mock-prim manner in response – "What I'm about to say, I'm afraid, will sound like ELIZABETH KNOWS BEST" (*OA* 96) – turned Moore's fussiness back on her, rather than rejecting it. As a peace offering, Bishop ends her letter by asking Moore to go to Museum of Modern Art with her (*OA* 96). Their game would go on.

In 1947, Lowell effectively replaced Moore as Bishop's most important poet-correspondent. A pattern is established in the second letter Bishop writes to him. She begins by thanking Lowell for his insightful review of her first book, *North & South*. While mentioning a "silly piece" by another critic, she interrupts herself in the middle of a sentence, then starts a new paragraph: "Heavens – it is an hour later – I was called out to see a calf being born in the pasture beside the house" (*WIA* 5). A description of the birth follows, before she turns back to poetry, praising a recently published Lowell poem. Next comes a paragraph on Cape Breton, Nova Scotia, where she is visiting. This leads to a paragraph about Lowell's appointment as a consultant in poetry to the Library of Congress, a second paragraph on the newborn calf, and a last paragraph about Yaddo, the writer's retreat, where Lowell is currently working and she is writing to him.

The zig-zag movement between topics and locations charts Bishop's effort to position herself not only in relation to Lowell but to the poetry world he inhabits. Lowell is in the United States, thoroughly engaged in the business of poetry: publishing poems, writing reviews, taking an official government job in poetry, enjoying a fellowship opportunity. Bishop will benefit from his professional wherewithal: he will help her win prizes and fellowships, and see that she replaces him at the Library of Congress, and much later, that she replaces him on the faculty at Harvard. She looks to him to advise her about how to get on professionally. She admires his poetry (as she puts it in this letter) "extremely" (*OA* 5). But she is perfectly ready to interrupt her discussion of it – and to foreground the interruption, not conceal it, as would have been easy, or even easier, to do in her letter – in order to go outside and see a calf being born. She insists on fidelity to her experience, and differentiates her experience from Lowell's. Indeed, she is at best ambivalent about the life of the poet as Lowell is leading it. About Yaddo, she remarks: "I almost went there once but changed my mind" (*WIA* 6). Instead of Yaddo, she is writing from a remote village on Cape Breton where she is spending the summer by the sea with her lover Marjorie Stevens (whom she doesn't mention to Lowell) in a northern version of her teenage Tahiti dream.

Bishop's letter constitutes an intermediary space between Nova Scotia and the United States, the everyday doings outside her room in Breton Cove and what is going on in the literary culture Lowell is absorbed in. We might think, when Bishop goes out to see the calf being born, she is avoiding poetry, or the discussion of it; and often in her correspondence, Bishop speaks of her interest in travel and daily life, or even the writing of letters, as an evasion of work (*OA* 219). In one letter, she refers to correspondence as "like working without really doing it" (*OA* 271). But that is not necessarily the case. The topics in this letter to Lowell that might seem like a distraction, digression, or even an escape from the literary, show her discovering its materials in ordinary life, while allowing those materials to shape the literary form of the letter itself. In fact, the letter looks forward to several poems in Bishop's future. The birth of the calf is revisited in "A Cold Spring," the title poem of Bishop's second collection. The rough mountainous landscape and other details mentioned in the letter reappear in "Cape Breton," another poem in *A Cold Spring*. And that exclamation used as a transition, "Heavens," turns up again in "Poem," a late poem (also about Nova Scotia) that adapts the stylistic features of Bishop's epistolary prose in colloquial free verse.[15]

Bishop and Lowell's thirty-years-long correspondence entailed a debate about the power and privilege of the poet. On one side was Lowell, who, inheriting the prophetic stance of modernist poets like Eliot, Pound, and Yeats, tried to write like one of Thomas Carlyle's great men; on the other was Bishop, who was committed to a skeptical, secular poetry rooted in particulars and a "delicate" (her word in "The Map") poetics of description. Letters hosted this debate, but they did more than that: they were part of it. This was so not only because letters helped Bishop to establish and refine her poetics and sensibility, and to find phrases, images, anecdotes, and perspectives that she could put to use in her poetry, but because questions about the relation between letters and poetry (what these forms have in common, how they are different, and how they should be valued differently) were a focus for broader questions about the relation between art and life that Lowell and Bishop were both preoccupied with, individually and in conversation with each other.

The climax of the debate is Bishop's response to Lowell's book *The Dolphin*, a work in which he quoted, or appeared to quote, his former wife Elizabeth Hardwick's letters, which she addressed to him in states of rage and grief after he had left her. Bishop reproved her friend fiercely:

> One can use one's life as material – one does, anyway – but these letters – aren't you violating a trust? IF you were given permission – IF you hadn't changed them . . . etc. But *art just isn't worth that much.* I keep remembering Hopkins' marvelous letter to Bridges about the idea of a "gentleman" being the highest thing ever conceived – higher than a "Christian" even, certainly than a poet. It is not being "gentle" to use personal, tragic, anguished letters that way – it's cruel. (*WIA* 708)

Lowell's betrayal of Hardwick's "trust" by using her private letters in his poem, without her approval, while failing to indicate what was hers and what was his – for Bishop (and others), this was indefensible.[16] That she found her moral authority on this subject in a poet's letters was apt. She believed Hopkins had his priorities straight. A "gentle" person is a higher thing "certainly than a poet." If letters are "an art form or something," the addition of that "or something" does not mean any less important. Art was not worth what Lowell had done. Letters were worth more.

Notes

1. On Bishop's ideas about letters, her letter-writing practice, and the relation between letters and poetry in her body of work, see the essays by Jonathan Ellis, Paul Muldoon, and Thomas Travisano in *Letter-Writing Among Poets*, ed. Jonathan Ellis (Edinburgh: Edinburgh University Press, 2015); Langdon Hammer, "Useless Concentration: Life and Work in Elizabeth Bishop's Letters and Poems," *American Literary History* 9.1 (1997), 162–80; Siobhan Phillips, "Bishop's Correspondence," in *Cambridge Companion to Elizabeth Bishop*, ed. Angus Cleghorn and Jonathan Ellis (Cambridge: Cambridge University Press, 2014), 155–68; and Vidyan Ravinthiran, *Elizabeth Bishop's Prosaic* (Lewisburg, PA: Bucknell University Press, 2015), 83–124.
2. Thomas Carlyle, *On Heroes, Hero-Worship, and the Heroic in History* (New York: Appleton, 1841), 34.
3. On the present tense in letters, see Janet Gurkin Altman, *Epistolarity: Approaches to a Form* (Columbus: Ohio State University Press, 1982), 122–29, and on the "iterable" present tense of the lyric, see Jonathan Culler, *Theory of the Lyric* (Cambridge: Harvard University Press, 2015), 226 and 289.
4. Bishop comments: "Writing letters, not telephoning, is . . . a bit like getting dressed up and going to the symphony concert instead of sitting at home in pajamas and listening to it on the radio." Quoted by Jonathan Ellis, *Art and Memory in the Work of Elizabeth Bishop* (Aldershot: Ashgate, 2006), 14.
5. See Jonathan Ellis, "'Between Us': Letters and Poems of Stevenson and Bishop," in *Voyages Over Voices: Critical Essays on Anne Stevenson*, ed. Angela Leighton (Liverpool: Liverpool University Press, 2010), 28–54.
6. Compare the text in *Elizabeth Bishop and Her Art*, ed. Lloyd Schwartz and Sybil P. Estess (Ann Arbor: University of Michigan Press, 1983), 288.
7. For instance, see the brief account of Bishop's failure in the role of *The New Yorker*'s poetry critic, *Elizabeth Bishop: Life and the Memory of It* (Berkeley: University of California Press, 1993), 424–25.
8. See Lorrie Goldensohn, "Approaching Elizabeth Bishop's Letters to Dr. Ruth Foster," *Yale Review* 103.1 (2015), 1–19; Megan Marshall, *Elizabeth Bishop: A Miracle for Breakfast* (Boston: Houghton Mifflin, 2017); and Thomas Travisano, *Love Unknown: The Life and Worlds of Elizabeth Bishop* (New York: Viking, 2019).
9. Bishop makes this remark in the third of the letters to Dr. Foster dated "Feb. 1947." Elizabeth Bishop to Dr. Ruth Foster, Elizabeth Bishop Papers, Special Collections, Vassar College Library.
10. See the discussions of the Bishop-Bradley letters by William Logan, *Guilty Knowledge, Guilty Pleasure: The Dirty Art of Poetry* (New York: Columbia University Press, 2014), and Travisano, *Love Unknown*.
11. Elizabeth Bishop to Louise Bradley, October 26, 1926, Louise Bradley and Elizabeth Bishop Correspondence Collection, Wylie House Museum, Indiana University Libraries, Bloomington.

12. Elizabeth Bishop to Louise Bradley, July 26, 1926, Wylie House Museum, Indiana University.
13. Elizabeth Bishop to Louise Bradley, August 29, 1926, Wylie House Museum, Indiana University.
14. Elizabeth Bishop to Louise Bradley, April 19, 1927, Wylie House Museum, Indiana University.
15. See Hammer, "Useless Concentration," and Ravinthiran, *Bishop's Prosaic*, for commentary on Bishop's use of a prose style, adapted from her correspondence, in "The End of March" and other poems.
16. See *The Dolphin Letters, 1970–1979: Elizabeth Hardwick, Robert Lowell, and Their Circle*, ed. Saskia Hamilton (New York: Farrar, Straus and Giroux, 2019).

CHAPTER 10

Translation

Mariana Machová

Elizabeth Bishop never considered herself a translator. "I wish you'd skip the translations. They amount to next to nothing, no real work, and no real interest," she wrote to Anne Stevenson, who was working on a book on Bishop, in 1965 (*Pr* 444), and in another letter she insists: "I don't think much of poetry translations and rarely attempt them" (*Pr* 411). She was deeply skeptical about the possibilities of translation, especially the translation of poetry, and was aware of the difficulty, even impossibility, of the job: "Translating poetry is like trying to put your feet into gloves," she wrote in her notebook (*EAP* 314). Despite her repeated disparaging claims about it, translation was very much present in Bishop's career, from her college years on. In terms of quantity, her translation production was not large, but for someone who was not a translator, she created a surprisingly varied body of translations. She translated from four different languages: Portuguese, French, Spanish, and Ancient Greek, and she covered an unusual variety of genres: there is not only lyric poetry, but short stories, prose poems, a diary, a comedy, a dramatic poem, even some popular songs among her translations. She published her translations in the same literary journals and with the same publishers as her own poetry, sometimes as parts of her books of poems. The longest work she ever published in her lifetime was a book-length translation of a young girl's diary. She wrote reviews of poetry translations and discussed details of translations in her correspondence, both with the authors she translated and with the translators of her own poems. One of the major clashes she had with her lifelong friend Robert Lowell was over translations. Clearly, she was not a professional translator, but translating formed a part of her creative effort that cannot be ignored. More than that, translation in a broader sense – as a way of meeting the foreign and trying to understand it in its foreignness – can be seen as a creative approach not limited to her translating of texts from one language to another. Rather, it is a poetic principle that lies at the heart of Bishop's own poetics, which is characterized by the "continuing vibration of her work between two frequencies – the domestic and the strange," as Helen Vendler noted in an early and still insightful assessment of Bishop's poetry.[1]

This chapter will discuss not only Bishop's work as a translator of other authors' works into English, but also the inherent presence of translation in her own work.[2] As an English-speaking poet living for many years in Brazil, surrounded by a language she never fully mastered, she was constantly faced with the problem of translating between two different languages and cultures. In Brazil, she was very sensitive to the strangeness of the language around her, aware of the literal meanings a native speaker of Portuguese would not probably even notice. This is well documented in her poems, stories, and letters, which often work with literal translations of Portuguese names, words, phrases, and idioms that sound unusual and surprising in English. In this broad sense, translation relates closely to questions of understanding and misunderstanding the other, and to the complex relationship between the familiar and the foreign. All these are crucial to Elizabeth Bishop's poetics, even in her work outside the exotic context of Brazil.

Bishop first started practicing translation at high school – translating classic prose and poetry was an essential part of her Latin classes, which were part of her curriculum at Walnut Hill. She continued her training in Latin at Vassar College, where she also started studying Ancient Greek. In retrospect, she valued the close work with classic texts as the best preparation for her career as a poet, suggesting to the students of her creative writing courses that "instead of learning to write poetry, they would do better to study Latin and Greek."[3] For the independent study project in her senior year at Vassar, 1933–4, she decided to translate Aristophanes' comedy *The Birds* from Ancient Greek, hoping that the play might be performed on campus. The translation was never finished, but the parts that can be found in the archive at Vassar clearly show that Bishop did not approach the task as a mere philological exercise. She tried to create a full-blooded comedy that would work for a contemporary audience. The dialogues are in verse, but they flow very naturally; the language is colloquial, sometimes rough, while the rhyme is often used to add comic effect. The quick and witty comic parts are balanced with the more solemn and formal passages of the parabasis. It is not difficult to imagine a successful staging of the play; Bishop's frequent stage notes help to visualize the scenes and the action.

Bishop's first big translation project was a comedy, which is not as surprising as it might seem at first sight. While she would hardly be considered a comic poet herself, there is a clear penchant for humour and the comic that can be found throughout her work.[4] Bishop is often seen as a very polite, restrained, serious poet, which she certainly is, but there is always the comic, subversive, even grotesque line in her poetics. This dimension of her poetics stands out even more clearly when we put her works in the context of her translations, which started with a wild ancient comedy.

Aristophanes was the only translation Bishop did that involved a dead language and a long-dead author. All her other translations were much closer to her own writings, in terms of genre, period, and language: most of them are poems, sometimes prose, written by her contemporaries. The three modern languages she translated from were French, Portuguese, and Spanish. She learnt French at school and she continued studying it after graduating from Vassar in 1934, when she moved to New York and took French classes which involved reading and translating French poetry.[5] A year later, she immersed herself in the language during her trip to France, where, apart from her stay in Paris, she spent several weeks alone in the village of Douarnenez in Brittany reading and translating French poetry (particularly Rimbaud) with a dictionary. It was an intense experience for her, and she mentioned it years later in connection with poetry translation: in a draft of a lecture on poetry translation she was supposed to give at Boston University in the late 1970s,[6] and also in the letter she wrote to Robert Lowell about his translations of French (and other) poets in 1961.

The famous controversy between Bishop and Lowell about *Imitations* (1961), a book of his free versions of poems by famous poets ranging from Sappho to Boris Pasternak which he dedicated to Bishop, well illustrates not only Bishop's views of translation, but also the difference between the two poets' approach to poetic creation in general. As David Kalstone pointed out, "their disagreement about tone, about the autonomy of the original texts, is almost a parody of their temperamental differences about poetry."[7] In her response to Lowell's manuscript, Bishop is concerned with the liberties her friend took with the poems he translated. She says the changes he made "*sound* like *mistakes*, and are open to misinterpretations," and could make Lowell liable to "charges of carelessness or ignorance or willful perversity" (*WIA* 356). She is worried about Lowell's lack of respect toward the originals and about his dominance over the texts, which makes them sound more like Lowell than the original poet. For Bishop, such an attitude was unacceptable. In translation, as in her own poetry, she wanted to remain true to the original source. In a letter to Anne Stevenson from 1964 she distances herself from Lowell's approach to translation once again: "I wouldn't attempt the kind of 'imitation' Robert Lowell does, although he makes brilliant Lowell-poems that way, frequently" (*Pr* 411). Bishop insists on the necessity of keeping as close to the original text, its author, and their intentions as possible; doing justice to the original is crucial for her. Typically, one of her requirements for a good translation is "politeness" toward the original, as she mentions in her unpublished notes for the lecture on poetry translation (VC 54.12), and it is the lack of politeness that bothers her in Lowell's imitations.

Elizabeth Bishop's views on poetry translation can be connected to her views on poetry more generally. The accuracy, the respect, and the politeness she required from translations in their relationship to the originals were also relevant for her when it came to her own poems. Bishop did not see poetry as free, self-contained, or willful creation, but as a way to convey things that exist autonomously outside the world of poetry. As Marilyn May Lombardi points out, Bishop defined "poetic creation as an act of translation" and for her, "the task of 'translating everything into words' is ethical before it is ludic."[8] Bishop always insisted on the truthfulness of her poetry, its reliance on fact, repeatedly claiming that what she writes about has "really happened" (like catching the fish in "The Fish" or meeting the moose in "The Moose"). While such claims do not mean that she is to be trusted as a reporter or that her poetry could be read as a kind of documentary, they suggest that a translator-like respect to the original other (be it an experience, a landscape, an animal, or a memory), which keeps existing independently of the translated text or of the written poem, is one of the key elements of her poetics.

Bishop's first published translations were four short texts by Max Jacob (1876–1944), which appeared in *Poetry* magazine in 1950 – two verse poems ("Rainbow" and "Banks") and two prose poems ("Patience of an Angel" and "Hell Is Graduated").[9] She translated them a year earlier, during her stay at the Yaddo writer's colony, together with some more poems by Jacob which remain unpublished. The Jacob texts that Bishop chose for translations are all rather different from her own poetry, ranging from meditative poems questioning the role of the poet to playful compositions close to Dadaism. However, at a closer look, the features of Jacob's poetics are present in Bishop's own works, too, only in a much more oblique and implicit way. Reading her poems next to her translations of Jacob, these features of her poetry – such as the playfulness reminiscent of European avant-garde movements, the spiritual dimension, the concern with the situation of the poet – stand out more clearly and the works of the two different poets create a revelatory dialogue. Some fascinating connections can be found between Max Jacob's poem "Establishment of a Community in Brazil," which Bishop translated only as a draft and never published, and her own "Brazil, January 1, 1502."[10] Both poems create parallels between the utopian colonial project and the poets' contemporary creative approach; each of them offers a different and unique take on the issue. Together they create a rich web of echoes and of multiple perspectives of utopia, creation, and translation.

While most of Bishop's translations were of individual poems or stories, she undertook two book-length translation projects. Both are translations from Portuguese and both are connected to her life in Brazil: the first one was her translation of *The Diary of "Helena Morley,"* which she started working on very shortly after she moved to Brazil in 1952; the second one was her co-editing of and translating poems for *An Anthology of Twentieth-Century Brazilian Poetry*, which came out in 1972, when Bishop's time in Brazil was virtually over. Her translations of Brazilian poets, all of them her contemporaries, include Manuel Bandeira, Vinícius de Moraes, Joaquim Cardozo, Carlos Drummond de Andrade, and João Cabral de Melo Neto.[11] She was friends with Manuel Bandeira (to whose memory the *Anthology* is dedicated) and Vinícius de Moraes, but her favorite Brazilian poets were João Cabral de Melo Neto, and particularly Carlos Drummond de Andrade. Four poems by Drummond and three fragments of *The Death and Life of a Severino* by Cabral also form a separate section (*Translations from the Portuguese*) of her *Complete Poems* published in 1969. Bishop was always wary about being too closely connected to Brazil in the minds of her English-speaking readers, and she explicitly refused to be perceived as "a cultural go-between" (*Pr* 444). However, when her future co-editor asked her to participate in the anthology project, after some initial reluctance she accepted, seeing it almost as a kind of duty: "I never wanted to get involved in *any* anthology, but couldn't seem to avoid this one" (*OA* 494), she wrote to her friend Ashley Brown, one of the co-translators. Despite her refusal to be seen as a cultural mediator, it was Bishop, who, through her translations and her editorial work, introduced modern Brazilian poetry to an English readership.

If the *Anthology* can be seen as an elegiac farewell to Bishop's time in Brazil (she started working on it shortly after Lota de Macedo Soares's death, and by the time it was published her time in Brazil was limited to scarce visits), and a work of duty, her other big translation project, *The Diary of "Helena Morley,"* a labour of love, marks the happy beginning of her love affair with Brazil. When she moved to Brazil in 1952, Bishop started learning Portuguese and she was looking for books she could read to get to know Brazilian culture better. One of the books recommended to her was *Minha Vida de Menina* (literally "My Life as a Young Girl"), a diary written by a teenage girl living in a small mining town of Diamantina in the 1890s. The diary was published in Brazil in 1942 and it quickly became very popular. Bishop enjoyed the book very much and she soon decided to translate it and have it published in the USA. When her publisher, Houghton Mifflin, was not interested in the translation of an unknown Brazilian author, Bishop decided to leave them and signed a publishing contract with a new publisher, Farrar, Straus and Cudahy. The translation came out in 1957 and remains the longest finished and published work by Bishop. She wrote a long introduction for it describing her own trip to Diamantina and her meeting with the author of the book, Mrs. Alice Dayrell Caldeira Brant, who published the diary under the pen name of Helena Morley.

Reading the diary, it is not difficult to understand its attraction to Bishop: it is written in a lively style, full of energy, spontaneity, humour and exact observations of everyday life – qualities Bishop valued in people and in art. Despite its apparent exoticism and its distance in time and space, the diary felt strangely familiar to Bishop, who was sure it would have the same effect on other readers, too. "So many of those remarks took me right back to Nova Scotia; I'm sure I've heard most of them before," she wrote to Marianne Moore (*OA* 357), and she encouraged May Swenson to read the book saying: "It will take you back to your early family life with a bang" (*OA* 353). The connection of the book to her Nova Scotia childhood was relevant for Bishop with respect to her own work. After she moved to Brazil, she had "total recall about Nova Scotia" (*OA* 249) and quickly wrote two autobiographical stories about her childhood, "Gwendolyn" and "In the Village." The discovery of the diary and the decision to translate it coincided with this sudden return to childhood themes. But while Bishop's childhood experience and childhood vision had to be remembered and recreated in the stories (and later in poems like "First Death in Nova Scotia," "Sestina," or "Manners"), Helena Morley's diary was direct and authentic; its speaker was no artist reinventing the voice of the child, but the child herself speaking in her authentic voice. The diary had the qualities of primitive art Bishop admired in the Key West primitive painter Gregorio Valdes (and also in the Brazilian carnival sambas, some of which she also translated): the spontaneity, immediacy, and authenticity, which are difficult, even impossible to achieve by "high" art and are therefore a kind of mystery. "But surely anything that is impossible for others to achieve by effort, that is dangerous to imitate, and yet, like natural virtue, must be both admired and imitated, always remains mysterious," she says in her memoir of Valdes (*Pr* 31), and the same could be applied to the diary. The diary, an essentially non-literary genre, offered the authenticity and immediateness in its relationship to the world outside literature Bishop strove for in her poetics, knowing that they are ultimately unattainable in art.

Among the authors Bishop met in Brazil was Clarice Lispector (1920–77), who is now seen as one of the greatest modern Brazilian writers and whom Bishop considered "better than Borges."[12] Bishop translated three of her short stories, which came out in the *Kenyon Review* in 1964 and were the first English translations of Lispector's work. With respect to what has been said about Bishop's admiration of primitive art, it is interesting to notice that she saw the "primitive" aspect in Lispector, too: "She's never read anything I can discover – I think she's a 'self-taught' writer, like a primitive painter," she wrote to Lowell (*WIA* 479). Of the three translations of Lispector Bishop did, the story "The Smallest Woman in the World" has received most critical attention in connection to Bishop's works. The story of a European anthropologist in the African jungle, who discovers an unknown tribe of the smallest people, offers many links to Bishop's own poems and poetics. The main theme of the story is the meeting with "the other"; but what starts as a rather straightforward encounter of two cultures – the "civilized" one of the scientist and the "barbaric" one of the jungle tribe – gets more disturbing as we realize that the similarities between the two may be as disconcerting and dangerous as the differences. The story has been successfully compared to Bishop's poem "Brazil, January 1, 1502,"[13] which was written shortly before Bishop's translation. The two texts bear interesting resemblances, including some verbal echoes,[14] shed revealing light at each other, and form another dialogue, parallel to the one between Max Jacob's "Establishment of a Community in Brazil" and "Brazil, January 1, 1502."

Elizabeth Bishop's translations were also, necessarily, relationships to other poets and writers. In some cases, these relationships were not restricted to their texts, but were personal; some of them were friendships. This is certainly true about Bishop's last translation relationship, that with the Mexican poet and essayist Octavio Paz (1914–98). Bishop and Paz met in Boston in the early 1970s when both of them were already famous poets and both were teaching at Harvard. They immediately struck up a friendship, which involved translating each other's poems and exchanging letters about the translations. These letters, which present a unique example of creative communication, clearly show that, for these two poets, translation was a creative act related to their own poetic work. Despite the obvious differences between their respective poetics, in both poets there is a shared awareness of the plurality of languages and the reflection of the possibilities and limits of language expression, which accounts for the importance translation had for them.

Some of the original poems they translated were still unpublished manuscripts at the time of translation and in some cases the process of translation influenced the final version of the poem. In other cases, changes were made to the original after the translation was done (even published) and it had to be revised accordingly. As a result, different versions of the same poem by Paz exist in Bishop's translation (this is the case of "The Grove," which Paz revised significantly after Bishop's translation was published in the *Harvard Advocate* in 1972, and Bishop changed the translation for the book of Paz's poetry in English, *Draft of Shadows*). One poem by Paz has a special position in the body of Bishop's poetry: "Objects & Apparitions," which she decided to include among her own poems in her last book of poems *Geography III* (1976). It is a poem dedicated to the visual artist Joseph Cornell (1903–72), whose works both Bishop and Paz admired. In this poem, Paz explicitly relates his own poetics to the poetics of Cornell's works. Bishop's translation and her decision to make it a part of her book can be seen as a gesture analogous to the gesture of Paz's original poem – not only as an homage to another artist, but as a linking of his poetics to her own work. Through her translation, she relates her poetry not only to Paz's work, but at the same time to Cornell's art. In this way, the translation displays a complex set of creative relationships crossing borders between languages, genres, and media. It seems appropriate that "Objects & Apparitions" was the one translation by Bishop that was read at her memorial service in 1979 (by Frank Bidart, while the Spanish original was read by Octavio Paz).

Shortly before he met Elizabeth Bishop, Octavio Paz published a long essay on poetry translation and its relationship to the original creation called "Translation: Literature and Letters" (*Traducción: Literatura y literalidad*, 1971). In the final part of the essay, he says:

> Throughout the ages, European poets – and now those of both halves of the American continent as well – have been writing the same poem in different languages. And each version is an original and distinct poem. [. . .]. If we take a step backward, we can understand that we are hearing a concert, and that the musicians, playing different instruments, following neither conductor nor score, are in the process of collectively composing a symphony in which improvisation is inseparable from translation and creation is indistinguishable from imitation.[15]

Reading Bishop's translations alongside her poetry allows us to hear this rich polyphony and admire a complex web of poetic relationships, exchanges, and dialogues, which is so characteristic of modern western poetry. It also makes us aware of the implicit, but fundamental presence of translation at the core of Elizabeth Bishop's poetics, which is marked by the openness toward the other, the use of different languages and voices, and the awareness of the many possible ways of seeing the world around us.

Notes

1. Helen Vendler, "Domestication, Domesticity, and the Otherworldly" [1977], in *Elizabeth Bishop and Her Art*, ed. Lloyd Schwartz and Sybil P. Estess (Ann Arbor: University of Michigan Press, 1983), 32.
2. For a detailed examination of Elizabeth Bishop's translations and their relationship to her own poetics, see Mariana Machova, *Elizabeth Bishop and Translation* (Lanham, MD: Lexington Books, 2017).
3. George Monteiro, ed., *Conversations with Elizabeth Bishop* (Jackson: University Press of Mississippi, 1996), 80.
4. For a detailed discussion of humor in Bishop's works, see Rachel Trousdale's chapter on "Humor" in this book.
5. Gary Fountain and Peter Brazeau, eds., *Remembering Elizabeth Bishop. An Oral Biography* (Amherst: University of Massachusetts Press, 1994), 62.
6. The lecture never happened; the fragmentary notes called "Remarks on Translation – of poetry, mostly," can be found in the Vassar College archive (VC 54.12).
7. David Kalstone, *Becoming a Poet: Elizabeth Bishop with Marianne Moore and Robert Lowell* (New York: Farrar, Straus and Giroux, 1989), 207. Other critics discuss the controversy in similar terms. See, for example, Lorrie Goldensohn's *Elizabeth Bishop: The Biography of a Poetry* (New York: Columbia University Press, 1992), 223–25; or Peter Robinson's *Poetry and Translation: The Art of the Impossible* (Liverpool: Liverpool University Press, 2010), 158–62.
8. Marilyn May Lombardi, *The Body and the Song: Elizabeth Bishop's Poetics* (Carbondale: Southern Illinois University Press, 1995), 140.
9. All of Bishop's published translations of prose and poetry can be found in the Farrar, Straus and Giroux Centenary editions of Elizabeth Bishop's *Prose* and *Poetry*.
10. See Sylvia Henneberg, "Elizabeth Bishop's 'Brazil, January 1, 1502' and Max Jacob's 'Etablissement d'une communauté au Brésil': A Study of Transformative Interpretation and Influence," *Texas Studies in Literature and Language* 45.4 (2003), 37–51.
11. Bishop's translations of these poets and her relationship to them is discussed in more detail in Maria Lúcia Milléo Martins's chapter on "Brazilian Literature" in this book.

12. Quoted by Benjamin Moser in *Why This World: A Biography of Clarice Lispector* (Oxford: Oxford University Press, 2009), 257.
13. Among the critics who note the revealing parallels between the two texts are Marilyn May Lombardi, *The Body and the Song*, 142–44; Lorrie Goldensohn, *The Biography of a Poetry*, 204–05; Victoria Harrison, *Elizabeth Bishop's Poetics of Intimacy* (Cambridge: Cambridge University Press, 1993), 181–82; Robert Dale Parker, *The Unbeliever: The Poetry of Elizabeth Bishop* (Urbana: University of Illinois Press, 1988), 95–97; and Bethany Hicok, *Elizabeth Bishop's Brazil* (Charlottesville: University of Virginia Press, 2016), 64–96.
14. See Maria Lúcia Milléo Martins's discussion of the verbal relationship between the two texts in her chapter in this book, 206.
15. Octavio Paz, "Translation: Literature and Letters," in *Theories of Translation*, ed. Rainer Schulte and John Biguenet (Chicago: University of Chicago Press, 1992), 160–61.

CHAPTER 11

Visual Art

Linda Anderson

Elizabeth Bishop had a lifelong interest in art and painting, acknowledging in 1966 that she was "more visual than most poets" and that she had been flattered when the art critic Meyer Schapiro was reported as saying about her that "she writes poems with a painter's eye." In this same interview Bishop suggested that the roots of her interest went back to her family, some of whom painted, and to her memories of being "dragged round the Boston Museum of Fine Art and Mrs Gardner's Museum and the Fogg" as a child.[1] All these collections in Boston contain very fine historical European collections but it was later and less reluctantly that she began to explore modern European art in both New York, and on two trips to Europe in 1935 and 1937, she found ways of connecting its innovations with her own writing.

Modernism as a movement, as Glen McLeod has suggested, was spearheaded by visual art and new artistic practices: "Painters were the first to explore the revolutionary possibilities of Modernism [. . .] Modernist writers often patterned their literary experimentation on parallels drawn from the visual arts."[2] This was the view shared by many American poets at the beginning of the twentieth century. The Armory exhibition of 1913, where works by Picasso, Duchamp, and Gauguin were exhibited in New York for the first time – to the dismay and consternation of many – was a crucial moment for Modernism, and according to William Carlos Williams, reminiscing fifty years later in his autobiography, it shook New Yorkers out of their complacency. The "revolutionary canvasses" displayed in the exhibition were a challenge and an inspiration for painting, but for poetry too. "I felt as if an enormous weight had been lifted from my spirit for which I was infinitely grateful," Williams confessed.[3] Wallace Stevens was equally clear about the significance of the exhibition on his own poetic development, writing in 1948: "In recent years, poetry began to change character about the time when painting began to change character." With Stevens, the influence of cubism on his early work has been frequently cited, and whatever influence there was would have been greatly enhanced by his friendship with Walter Conrad Arensberg, the art collector, who underwent a dramatic "conversion to modern art" and reported himself "transfixed" by the exhibition.[4]

For Elizabeth Bishop's early mentor, Marianne Moore, the Armory exhibition was also an important threshold into an era of experimentation, and she keenly followed the controversy the exhibition provoked.[5] However, by the time Bishop met Moore in 1934, the first shock of the exhibition had worn off and, after the First World War, the issues had moved on from a purely "analytic" cubism – and its particular use of a stripped down abstraction – to dada and surrealism, as represented in another groundbreaking exhibition, "Fantastic Art, Dada, Surrealism," this time in the Museum of Modern Art, in 1936. This exhibition, curated by Alfred Barr, featured work by Max Ernst, Man Ray, Joan Miró and Salvador Dalí. Barr himself drew a comparison between the "aesthetic of form and colour and of distorted and disintegrated objects" that people had encountered in the Armory exhibition, and the evocation of the irrational and subconscious featured in the later exhibition. Whilst cubist objects, he argued, "appealed largely to a sense of design or form [. . .] Dadaist and Surrealist objects have primarily a psychological interest – bizarre, dreamlike, absurd, uncanny, enigmatic [. . .] objects of 'concrete irrationality.'"[6]

Marianne Moore's appreciation of the visual in writing was linked to the fact that she generally wanted to evade categories and minimize the distinctions between the different art forms: "It is all one, isn't it?" she wrote to an artist friend, Robert Motherwell.[7] Consequently it was also easy for her to "see" how the appearance of the page itself contributed to a poem and she experimented with trying to make the shape and architecture of poems more prominent. Early work, such as "Those Various Scalpels," shows her dissecting, possibly in self-conscious parody, the "subject" of poetry, and arriving at a poem which splits lines and even words, substituting hard-edges for what is both linear and fluid, to produce what Linda Leavell has called "her most 'cubist' poem."[8] This is perhaps the furthest Moore went in finding abstract poetic equivalents for cubism's play with surface and deconstruction of referential meaning. By the time she met Elizabeth Bishop, Moore was still exploring spatial patterning within her poetry but linking it more, though never exclusively, to organic forms she found in nature – a shell or a tree, for instance – and to the shaping qualities of the images themselves. Bishop and Moore, once their friendship was established, found a common interest in sharing "specimens" from nature, the leaves or seeds or even alligator teeth, that Bishop had collected on her travels and enclosed in her letters to Moore. Moore's role was to describe the objects back to Bishop in minute and forensic detail. Bishop was later to describe Moore as "The World's Greatest Living Observer" and wonder "why had no-one ever written about things in this clear and dazzling way before?" (*Pr* 253, 118)

Yet, as Peggy Samuels has pointed out, what the poets agreed about in terms of the importance of the visual, did not mean that they shared a poetics, and their correspondence was soon revealing latent differences about how the surface of writing related to its "meaning."[9] In 1938, Moore wrote to Bishop, wanting her to risk, as she said, "some unprotected profundity of experience." While Moore accepted that form and content are indivisible – that "treatment really is substance" – still she believed Bishop's tendency to "tentativeness and interiorizing" was, in terms of her writing, "your danger as well as your strength."[10] If Moore's version of "substance" at this stage involved her promoting Reinhold Niebuhr's Christian morality and mysticism as a model, Bishop had already framed her difference from Moore in terms of the formal positioning of the writing subject. In her notebook she explored her own ideas about surface and depth:

> It's a question of using the poet's proper material, with which he's equipped by nature, i.e., immediate intense physical reactions, a sense of metaphor and decoration in everything – to express something not of them – something I suppose, *spiritual*. But it proceeds from the material, the material eaten out with acid, pulled down from underneath, made to perform and always kept in order, in its place [. . .] Miss Moore does this – but occasionally I think, the super-material content in her poems is too easy for the material involved – it could have meant more.[11]

The words "proper" and "spiritual" seem derived from Moore's lexicon; however, Bishop's reference to the power of what is "underneath" (or unconscious), and criticism of Moore's controlling response to her material, suggests her greater allegiance to poetry as exploration – and a greater openness, at this stage at least, to the "psychological interest" of surrealism. Later she would write of Wallace Stevens in similar terms: "Poetry so aware lacks depth. Poetry should have more of the unconscious spots left in."[12] While Moore saw herself as constructor, collector, and synthesizer, Bishop, with no settled place to be, seems to have assumed uncertainty as a condition for both her life and her writing.

In his book on the relation between painting and modern American poetry, Charles Altieri, in discussing Georges Braque, draws attention to an important physical dimension of the "eye," commonly lost in the assumption that knowledge is both transcendent and universal: "We see the life created by seeing," he writes. This different, embodied positioning involves both multiplicity and movement and the intersection of different points of view. "We see what the eye frames, and we see the eye as a frame, itself contained within the play of visual forces."[13] In a resonant passage from her diary in 1935, on board SS Königstein bound for Europe, and already experiencing severe seasickness which easily transformed itself into feelings of displacement or "homesickness," Bishop dreamt about paintings:

> I dreamt last night of paintings that wouldn't stay still – the colors moved inside the frames, the objects moved up closer then further back, the whole thing changed from portrait to scenery and back again – keeping the same "lines" all the time.[14]

Here, as in other places in her notebooks, paintings fuse with dreams, becoming resonant figures for the unconscious. The movement *within* the painting becomes synonymous with the movement of the observer – from which the act of seeing cannot be separated – as the perspective changes from close-up to far away. This also seems to follow Bishop's own physical experience of visual disturbance on this Atlantic crossing, with her eyes painfully drawn into the unfathomable distance.

Bishop, herself, was the first to point to the fact that her dream might have been influenced by her reading of the art critic Heinrich Wölfflin, whose book, *The Principles of Modern Art*, first published in 1915, had been translated and republished in New York in 1932.[15] In thinking about the relationship between art and poetry, the mediating effect of art theory is important, and the verbal bridges and interpretive possibilities between the different art forms it helps to create. In Bishop's case this is almost certainly relevant since one of her closest friends from Vassar, Margaret Miller, was an art historian and in her job as curator for the Museum of Modern Art helped to prepare the exhibition, "Fantastic Art, Dada, Surrealism," already referred to, as well as a later exhibition in 1941 on Paul Klee, one of Bishop's favourite painters, and on collage in 1948, which involved a survey of work by Braque, Picasso, Gris, and Ernst. In 1934–5, with Miller, Bishop attended lectures on art history given by Meyer Schapiro, who was also the early supervisor for Miller's doctoral study; she also mentions reading in 1934, R. H. Wilenski's, *The Modern Movement in Art* – perhaps at Miller's suggestion – and later, in 1947, quoted from John

Rewald's *The History of Impressionism*;[16] later still, in 1960, she is reading another magisterial work of art history, E. H. Gombrich's, *Art and Illusion* (*OA* 388).

Wölfflin, however, is of particular interest because of the way he found parallels between Baroque and Modern art, referring to their shared use of unsettled or plural perspectives. In his book, *The Principles of Modern Art*, Wölfflin cites the idea of mobility as significant: as opposed to Renaissance art and its celebration of the "solid" and "enduring" figure, the Baroque, he argues, turns to the "changing appearance" and "movement." For him the Baroque is an art of flux and momentary effects, which are not containable within the frame of the picture.[17] Bishop, as a student of literature, was seeking out similar parallels with the Baroque and famously turned to M. W. Croll's essay on "The Baroque Style in Prose" to help her describe the way Gerard Manley Hopkins, one of her touchstones for writing, was influenced by seventeenth century poetry and prose. Bishop introduces this quotation from Croll about "Baroque" writers into her essay: "Their purpose was to portray, not a thought, but a mind thinking [. . .] They knew that an idea separated from the act of experiencing is not the same idea that we experienced" (*Pr* 473). Again, as with the Baroque in Wölfflin's writing, there is no fixity and no transcendent position: everything is embodied, in process or in movement.

Bishop's earliest poems drew on seventeenth-century models, and there are obvious correspondences between Richard Crashaw's poem, "The Weeper" – a poem we know she admired – and her own "Three Sonnets for the Eyes," which stage – in Baroque fashion – the drama of vision. Behind or beyond the multiplying effects of vision is the fear of an abyss. The changeable tidal water, in the first sonnet, offers the image of the empty eyes of graveyard statuary for the "vacancy" the outgoing tide reveals, an image that also returns in the third sonnet:

> "How blind
> Are eyes!" says it, (dragging its slippery feet)
> "Now they're left vacant truths, like angel eyes on
> The old gravestones; seeing into the graves. (*P* 221)

That vision is always embodied vision – that vision and knowledge cannot be totally aligned – preoccupied Bishop throughout her career and is perhaps captured in the putative title for a poem she never completed and wanted to name "Grandmother's Glass Eye." This physical disability fascinated her as a child, and seemed to provide an analogy in adulthood for the problem of combining the real and the unreal in poetry, a poem too being "as normal as sight and yet as synthetic, as artificial, as a glass eye" (*EAP* 212). If the idea of the Baroque was used in the twentieth century as a way of defining a modern instability, a decentreed subject, and the difficulty of distinguishing reality from illusion, it also crucially staged this drama in the field of the visual. The visual therefore exceeds its own domain within visual art, forming a powerful theme and strategy within poetry too. For Bishop, the visual allowed her to develop a language for what is uncertain, multiple, misty; the changing relation of bodies to spaces, and the indeterminacy of boundaries and lines.

Bishop often incorporated ideas of bodily movement and encounter into the early poems she wrote in the 1930s and 1940s, where there is no one, unified point of view or way to stabilize reality. In her poem, "Paris, 7 A.M.," having visited the clocks in the apartment, which fail to offer a secure or stable version of time, she pictures the view down into a courtyard where angles and shapes proliferate, and inside and outside overlap:

> Look down into the courtyard. All the houses
> are built that way, with ornamental urns
> set on the mansard roof-tops where the pigeons
> take their walks. It is like introspection
> to stare inside, or retrospection,
> a star inside a rectangle, a recollection. (*P* 28)

The strongly marked lines define a hollow space, where time and matter dissolve. In other, related poems, such as "Love Lies Sleeping" or "The Weed," there is again a complicated rhetoric of seeing, where excessively described objects are brought close in precise detail – for instance the representation of the miniature "'garden' in a jar" (*P* 18) – or alternately captured within a "black space" which threatens uncertainty or dissolution (*P* 23).

Later, Bishop's scepticism about the influence of surrealism – and particularly Max Ernst's work – on her poetry was recorded in her famous and much quoted letter to Anne Stevenson in 1964, where she talked about preferring "the always-more-successful-surrealism of everyday life" (*Pr* 413–14). Yet even this letter, for all its vigour of denial, includes concessions since she acknowledges at the same time, that she liked Ernst's *Histoire Naturelle* and still found his photo-collages "brilliant" (*Pr* 414). As Susan Rosenbaum argues, while Bishop might have eschewed the more flamboyant gestures and imagery of surrealism, its persistent influence can be detected throughout her career, particularly in the way she expanded the category of the "natural" to include the "unconscious, irrational and perverse."[18] It is also interesting to note, as Mary Ann Caws has suggested, the continuity between what was being sought in the ideas of Baroque art at this time – by Bishop herself and others – and Surrealism: "The baroque sensibility and techniques have an urgent application in the world of surrealism and its reversal of words, thoughts and concepts and its exuberant ways of thinking and expressing in general."[19] Moreover, there is in surrealism an emphasis on the look, the look "through" or the gaze that is returned from somewhere else, a non-human gaze which surprises with its unexpected, disorientating, and unassimilable perspective.

Bishop's poem, "The Monument," written in 1938, takes its inspiration from Max Ernst, and, if Bonnie Costello is correct, from a particular "frottage" in the *Histoire Naturelle*, "False Positions."[20] The poem, one of several in her career where Bishop makes art the subject, plays with notions of representation, since the "monument" she is writing about is also a piece of *trompe l'oeil*, created by taking a rubbing from wood. It requires the viewer's imagination to give it meaning and substance: "Now can you see the monument? It is of wood / built somewhat like a box." In the poem, two voices, are in dialogue, one which "sees through" the illusion to the flat surface – "It's like a stage-set; it is all so flat!" – and the other which validates the shifting views, and attempts to make something, "roughly but adequately" – just as the poem does – from the viewer's repeated acts of observation and assembly (*P* 25–27).

In "The Man-Moth" too, a poem dating from a few years earlier, and one of her most "surreal" poems, Bishop also employs different perspectives for disorientating effect. The idea of this poem, stemming from a newspaper misprint, illustrates the way Bishop was open to the intervention of chance or serendipity into her writing – much as the surrealists were – and also attests to her interest in the technique of *papier collé*, employed by artists such as Picasso, Braques, and Gris, who pasted printed matter on to their canvasses in order to encourage attention to – in the words of Alfred Barr, carefully copied by Bishop into her notebook – the "sensuous tactile reality of the surface itself" rather than what the paintings might represent.[21] Bishop was generally interested in collage techniques, how different materials and registers and objects, could be juxtaposed or superimposed on each other. However, as Peggy Samuels points out, of the artists who practised collage, it was Kurt Schwitters who most interested both Bishop and Margaret Miller, probably because Schwitters was less committed to sharp discontinuities than how different materials could modulate across a work, breaking down boundaries.[22] Bishop gives us an imaginative version of herself as collage artist in her notebooks and there she is rather like Schwitters, collecting objects and detritus randomly – "Everything and Anything" – which she can place together in "a junk-room, store-room or attic," so that she can later experience how "it decayed and fell together and took on a general odor."[23] Like Schwitters' Merzbild series of pictures, the word "Merz" itself coming from a found fragment of print, Bishop seems to be imagining rooms where a kind of merging and unification could be achieved, almost independent of any artistic volition.[24]

Going back to "The Man-Moth," we can see in this poem Bishop's interest in surfaces – "the faces" of buildings – and the way she works into her description references to visual art, both a "photographer's cloth," and the tube of paint, which the Man-Moth imagines erroneously he may be able to force himself through, "in black scrolls on the light" (*P* 16). The imagined encounter at the end of the poem concentrates on the eye as detachable physical object, in the way, for instance, Magritte did in his famous painting, "The False Mirror." The eye of the Man-Moth is "all dark pupil [. . .] whose haired horizon tightens / as he stares back." The tear he sheds, however, while it seems to veil sight, as the eye closes up, seems to well up from elsewhere, from the unconscious "underground" or memory. Looking could, for Bishop, as it did in her poem, "Paris, 7 A.M.," move inwards, slide easily into "introspection" or "retrospection."

If "The Man-Moth" is a poem where the fantastic and the real seem to meet each other, in other poems too, where description takes precedence, Bishop summons a phantasmal eye or gaze, which looks back, questioning the omniscient stance of the viewer. That look seems implicit in "The Fish," where the intense description of the eye of the fish also reflects an opaqueness (*P* 43–44), or in the "conundrum" of the face of Faustina, in "Faustina, or Rock Roses" where the eyes provide no one answer but say equivocally "only either" (*P* 72), or even in the late poem, "The Moose," where the moose's seemingly benign gaze is nevertheless "grand, other-worldly," carrying intimations of the "woods" beyond the frame of the poem which are both "dark" and "impenetrable" (*P* 192–93). Perhaps the most disturbing of all the gazes in Bishop's work is in her poem, "In the Waiting Room," where vertigo overcomes the child, who feels exposed to the eyes of others, and who resists the signifiers of adult femininity she is looking at in *The National Geographic* that will "place" her as a body, in the world. That vertiginous sense of being neither inside nor outside herself is also the mark of the dangerous contiguity of interior and exterior worlds which destabilizes both. Looking and being looked at cannot be reconciled for the child, and the usual contexts which make for adjustment and balance, are replaced by a void, the "cold, blue-black space" so powerfully evoked in the poem (*P* 180). Something is felt to elude our knowledge – there is a breach – and representational and visual connection with the world is temporarily lost. Bishop experienced this too, as we have seen, when seasickness – another experience of vertigo – seemed to merge with the feeling of the homesickness of her childhood, that loss of belonging which always shadowed her relation to place.

In his essay "On Modern Art," published in 1924, Paul Klee wrote that "the objects in pictures looks out at us serene or severe, tense or relaxed, comforting or forbidding, suffering or smiling."[25] Klee is a painter Bishop often referred to in her letters and notebooks and whose exhibitions she visited in 1940, and then again in 1950, in New York.[26] Bishop would also have known Klee's writing from the catalogue her friend Margaret Miller prepared for the 1940 exhibition at the Museum of Modern Art and referred to his famous dictum about how a line in painting or drawing "goes for a walk." The continuation of this passage from his notebooks is also included in the catalogue where Klee goes on to bring subjectivity and landscape (interior and exterior worlds) together in some detail in the intermediate space of abstraction.[27]

Bishop followed her family tradition, referred to at the beginning of this essay, by producing small watercolours intermittently throughout her life of places she had temporarily inhabited on her travels. People are notably absent from these sketches, though traces of them exist in the luggage, and carefully positioned plant and book and pen in the painting entitled "Cabin with Porthole," or the hastily propped bicycle in "Harris School," suggesting a held moment in a continuing sense of flux and movement (*EH* 45, 21). She also experimented with collage in "Anjinhos" and "Feather Box" (*EH* 51, 49), perhaps taking her inspiration from Joseph Cornell, whose "minimal, incoherent fragments" she commemorated in the poem she translated from Octavio Paz, "Objects and Apparitions" (*P* 201). However, it is in her attentiveness to lines, whether they be the kite strings in "Harris School," jauntily disappearing behind the straight lines of the building, or the electrical cable in "Interior with Extension Cord," or the criss-crossing lines of wires and cables in "County Courthouse," carrying energy across distances into an indecipherable future that suggest Klee's influence,[28] and introduce a kind of muted, abstract commentary into the paintings on representation itself (*EH* 21, 43, 23). In her poems, Bishop also depicted lines, as in the ravelling kite string in "The End of

March," doodling its way across the beach, or in the same poem the electrical cable, its end point – and unknown source of power – somewhere out of sight, "off behind the dunes" (*P* 199–200). Lines in her paintings and her poems, both join and separate; they trace the wavering, indeterminate boundary between one thing and other, the encounter between inside and outside; they also mark the shared process of bringing both art and writing into being.

In one of her later poems, simply called "Poem," and published in *Geography III*, Bishop revisited her family inheritance, both as memory and as a modest sketch inherited from the same great uncle who was also responsible for the large, bad picture, the subject of another, much earlier poem. The multiple perspectives that Bishop had explored in other poems, often with disorientating effect, are here transferred into a complex temporality, which can hold both past and future in the contemplation of the painting's landscape. It is as if Bishop had summed up her aesthetic – deeply thought for all its seeming "modesty" – and found a way through that "tentativeness and interiority" distrusted by Moore, to create a discursive and linear set of relations between inside and outside, space and representation, "life and the memory of it." That she does so through contemplating a painting – a painting linked to her childhood – is a fitting tribute not only to art's enduring place in her life, but to the journey that thinking about art had taken her on. Perhaps the last challenge was to also find a form to embody that journey – holding together a complex set of relations between poetry and painting – in a poem.

Notes

1. Elizabeth Bishop, "An Interview with Elizabeth Bishop [1966]," in *Conversations with Elizabeth Bishop*, ed. George Monteiro (Jackson: University Press of Mississippi, 1996), 24.
2. *The Cambridge Companion to Modernism*, ed. Michael Levenson (Cambridge: Cambridge University Press, 2011), 194.
3. Quoted in Bram Dijkstra, *Cubism, Stieglitz, and the Early Poetry of William Carlos Williams* (Princeton, NJ: Princeton University Press, 1969), 9.
4. Quoted in Glen MacLeod, *Wallace Stevens and Modern Art: From the Armory Show to Abstract Expressionism* (New Haven and London: Yale University Press, 1993), 6.
5. See Linda Leavell, *Marianne Moore and the Visual Arts* (Baton Rouge: Louisiana State University Press, 1995), 64.
6. Quoted in Sybil Gordon Kantor, *Alfred H. Barr, Jr. and the Intellectual Origins of the Museum of Modern Art* (Cambridge, MA: MIT Press, 2003), 338–40.

7. Leavell, *Marianne Moore and the Visual Arts*, 57.
8. Ibid., 7.
9. Peggy Samuels, *Deep Skin: Elizabeth Bishop and Visual Art* (Ithaca: Cornell University Press, 2010), 29–31.
10. Marianne Moore, *Selected Letters*, ed. Bonnie Costello (Harmondsworth: Penguin Books, 1998), 391.
11. Quoted in Linda Anderson, *Elizabeth Bishop: Lines of Connection* (Edinburgh: Edinburgh University Press, 2013), 16.
12. Quoted in Barbara Page, "Off -Beat Claves, Oblique Realities: The Key-West Notebooks of Elizabeth Bishop," in *Elizabeth Bishop: The Geography of Gender*, ed. Marilyn May Lombardi (Charlottesville and London: University Press of Virginia, 1993), 201.
13. Charles Altieri, *Painterly Abstraction in Modernist American Poetry: The Contemporaneity of Modernism* (Cambridge: Cambridge University Press, 1989), 197.
14. See Anderson, *Elizabeth Bishop*, 37.
15. From her notebook at the time. See Anderson, *Elizabeth Bishop*, 37.
16. See quotation from Bishop's letters to her psychoanalyst quoted in my essay, "Disturbances of the Archive: Repetition and Memory in Elizabeth Bishop's Poetry," *Reading Elizabeth Bishop: An Edinburgh Companion*, ed. Jonathan Ellis (Edinburgh: Edinburgh University Press, 2019), 24.
17. Heinrich Wölfflin, *Principles of Art History: The Problem of the Development of Style in Later Art*, trans. M. D. Hottinger (New York: Dover Publications, 1932), 10.
18. Susan Rosenbaum, "Bishop and the Natural World," in *The Cambridge Companion to Elizabeth Bishop*, ed. Angus Cleghorn and Jonathan Ellis (Cambridge: Cambridge University Press, 2014), 70.
19. Mary Ann Caws, *The Surrealist Look* (Cambridge, MA: The MIT Press, 1999), 8.
20. Bonnie Costello, *Elizabeth Bishop: Questions of Mastery* (Cambridge Massachusetts: Harvard University Press, 1991), 220.
21. The quotation from Alfred Barr is from *Picasso: Forty Years of Art* (1946). See *Elizabeth Bishop: Lines of Connection*, 75.
22. Samuels, *Deep Skin*, 102–103.
23. See *Elizabeth Bishop: Lines of Connection*, 83.
24. https://hattongallery.org.uk/collections/kurt-schwitters-merz-barn-wall. Accessed 15 January 2020.
25. Paul Klee, *On Modern Art* (London: Faber and Faber, 1966), 33.
26. Samuels, *Deep Skin*, 56–63.
27. *Paul Klee*, ed. Margaret Miller (New York: Museum of Modern Art, 1941), 11.
28. See Angus Cleghorn's extended discussion of Bishop's use of wire imagery in her writing in his essay, "Bishop's 'Wiring Fused,'" *Elizabeth Bishop in the 21st Century: Reading the New Editions*, ed. Angus Cleghorn, Bethany Hicok, and Thomas Travisano (Charlottesville and London: University of Virginia Press, 2012), 69–87.

CHAPTER 12

Archives

Bethany Hicok

In her 1971 poem "Crusoe in England," written at a time in her life when she contemplated where her own papers and effects would be placed, Elizabeth Bishop's avatar, Crusoe, safe in England after having been rescued from his island, notes that the local museum has asked him to "leave everything to them" – all the products of his island industry, such as a flute, his knife, "shrivelled shoes," and "shedding goatskin trousers" (*P* 186). These objects, made by Crusoe on his island and used for his very survival, will now be placed in a museum as things torn from their original use and value. "How can anyone want such things?" Crusoe asks (*P* 186). Bishop herself was preoccupied with how objects separated from their original use might be interpreted. In a 1947 letter to her psychoanalyst Ruth Foster, Bishop wrote: "I am writing a poem about a litter of objects in a museum whose uses the spectator can't make out" (VC 118.33). In a life full of chaos and travel, Bishop managed to preserve and even partially catalogue, a large collection.[1]

We find the largest share of that collection at Vassar College in more than 120 boxes filled with some 3,500 pages of drafts of poems, stories, and essays, notebooks, postcards, mementos, travelogues, photographs, artwork, and hundreds of letters, including those to major poets and writers of the twentieth century. And the archive continues to expand on a regular basis. Vassar recently catalogued, for example, more than 2,000 volumes from Bishop's library and made it available to scholars (the rest of her library is at Harvard). A number of these books contain Bishop's under-linings and annotations, so that scholars may trace her reading activity across her life.

Such "things" were important to Bishop; she was, in fact, a major curator of her own effects, which is why we have so many of them. The result is that Bishop's collection has become one of the great literary archives for the study of mid-century poetry and poetics, providing important documentary evidence of her creative process and the various social forces that help to shape a career. In addition, Bishop's archival practice – her curatorial poetics – provides an excellent case study for understanding the value of archival research for teaching and scholarship in the humanities. In short, Bishop's career, reputation as a poet, and poetic craft cannot be fully understood unless we consider it in the context of her expanding archives and how that has influenced how we read her. The poet and her archives, then, is the subject of this chapter, which will offer a brief history of Bishop's archives and a discussion of how the expanding archives and changes in literary scholarship have influenced our reading of Bishop. More broadly, we can ask: How do institutional archives contribute to our understanding of literary careers? What part do they play in the historical, cultural, and social forces that shape writers and readers?

But, first of all, what do we mean when we refer to Bishop's Archive? Because the largest share of Bishop's collected papers can be found at Vassar, we might say that Vassar houses Bishop's archives, yet Bishop's documents and those relating to her can also be found in other collections in the United States, Canada, and Brazil,[2] and some have not been "arrested" yet, to use Jacques Derrida's terms.[3] When I was traveling in Brazil in 2011, I was pleasantly surprised to walk into the sitting room of Pousada do Chico Rei, the bed and breakfast where Bishop stayed in Ouro Preto, Brazil, only to find a letter signed by Bishop in a glass case. The letter is addressed to Lilli Correia de Araújo, who was the hotel's owner and with whom Bishop may have had an affair, as letters to Correia de Araújo in the Vassar archives suggest. The present owner of the bed and breakfast, a Correia de Araújo relative, referred provocatively during my stay to other Bishop papers that might reside in a box in the basement somewhere. Perhaps, as with other documents of or relating to Bishop, these will eventually find their way into institutional repositories in the United States or Brazil, or "elsewhere," to use a favored Bishop term.[4] In 2004, for instance, a significant series of letters that Bishop wrote to Louise Bradley, a friend from summer camp and Bishop's first known correspondent and love interest, was acquired by Indiana University.[5]

Carolyn Steedman provides a definition of the archive that is useful when thinking about Bishop's case. "The Archive," Steedman writes,

> is made from selected and consciously chosen documentation from the past and also from the mad fragmentations that no one intended to preserve and that just ended up there [. . .]. [It is] a name for the many places in which the past (which does not now exist, but which once did actually happen; which cannot be retrieved, but which may be represented) has deposited some traces and fragments.[6]

More poetically, Steedman notes, it is "also a place of dreams" – a place "where the past lives, where ink on parchment can be made to *speak*."[7]

Whether we are explicitly aware of it or not, the identities of literary figures, as many archivists agree, "are constructed and reconstructed through the experience of archival documents."[8] Archives themselves are shifting "sites of knowledge" that are "incomplete," "fragmentary," and subject to additions and deletions.[9] The history of Bishop's archive at Vassar is a testament to these statements. Vassar purchased the bulk of Bishop's papers in 1981 from Bishop's final partner, Alice Methfessel, as part of the college's larger liberal arts mission to support the use of primary documents in undergraduate research.[10] Bishop graduated from Vassar, and the college was a significant influence on her poetic development.[11] Institutional context is important when we think about the archive, and Bishop's close connection to Vassar makes her archive there a particularly symbolic space for thinking about the literary archive's role in the liberal arts. Since Vassar's initial purchase, the college has made forty-eight additional acquisitions. We can map some significant shifts in our reading of Bishop across these acquisitions as they track with changes in literary scholarship.

Let us take as one example our comparatively recent reading of Bishop as a queer poet. We can mark the beginning of that reading with Adrienne Rich's reassessment of Bishop in 1983 when she began to reread Bishop's well-known poetry in terms of outsider-hood and lesbian identity. Rich's initial reading of Bishop found her sometimes "coy" and mannered, like the poet she was so often compared to, Marianne Moore.[12] Then, in 1988, Lorrie Goldensohn published a hitherto unknown poem by Bishop, the openly lesbian love poem "It is marvellous to wake up together" in *American Poetry Review*. At the time, the poem was in private hands – part of Bishop's "unarrested archive" to use Linda Morra's term.[13] Goldensohn was one of the first scholars to describe the moment when a major new discovery is made and the critical sands shift to accommodate a really new work of art, one that had a major impact on the criticism that followed. In *Elizabeth Bishop: The Biography of a Poetry*, where the poem was reprinted in 1992, Goldensohn describes how during her time in Brazil, the then-owner of Bishop's house in Ouro Preto, Linda Nemer, handed over "a sheaf of papers ... [and] a shoebox full of small notebooks"[14] – all in Bishop's hand. Goldensohn writes how she "unfolded a sheet of brittle onionskin and read through a typed, completed poem [she had] never seen before."[15] Vassar acquired the poem along with other Bishop papers from the Portinari family in Brazil in 2002, and it has now been reprinted in several new editions of Bishop's previously unpublished work, including *Edgar Allan Poe & The Juke-Box* (2006), the Library of America edition of Bishop's *Poems, Prose, and Letters* (2008), and in *Poems* (2011), making it very much a part of the Bishop canon. By the early 1990s, following Goldensohn's discovery and under the influence of feminist, psychoanalytic, gender, and queer criticism, scholars began exploring in more depth the psychosexual tensions in Bishop's work and her lesbian identity, which culminated in a groundbreaking book of essays edited by Marilyn May Lombardi, *Elizabeth Bishop: The Geography of Gender*.

More recently discovered materials acquired by Vassar, as well as the aforementioned letters to Louise Bradley at Indiana University, also deepen our understanding of Bishop as a queer poet. In 2011, Vassar College purchased a trove of new materials that add significantly to Bishop's queer archive, including Bishop's 1947 letters to her psychoanalyst, Ruth Foster, as well as 243 exuberant love letters exchanged between Bishop and her final partner and literary executor, Alice Methfessel, from November 1970 to June 1976. In the Foster letters, Bishop documents her alcoholism, the sexual abuse she suffered as a child, her candid exploration of her sexual identity as a lesbian, from her teens onward, at a time of extreme homophobia and persecution, and many facets of her traumatic childhood – each of which Bishop links explicitly to her own poetry. These pages constitute one of the most detailed psychosexual memoirs we have of any twentieth-century writer, and provide insight into the relationship between trauma, sexual identity, and the creative process.

Recent scholarship on Bishop and the archives notes the impact of this new material on queer readings of Bishop. Heather Treseler discusses these letters alongside Bishop's drafts of "In the Waiting Room" and a number of other archival documents to explore queer scenes of reading in Bishop's work across the archives and the published work. Alyse Knorr focuses on the intimate love letters between Bishop and Methfessel and argues that they constitute one of the most important series of queer love letters of the twentieth century, providing a rich material presence for this exuberant final love in Bishop's life and its influence on this final phase of her career.[16] But it is not just new archival material that can generate queer readings of Bishop, but changes in both scholarly approaches and the Bishop archives that can send Bishop's readers back into the archive to sift through the sedimentary layers of older archival documents in order to make more visible and legible the traces, erasures, and reading and writing practices of the queer poet across her unpublished and published work.[17]

In my emphasis on new approaches to the Bishop archive, I do not want to suggest that important readings have not already been done by Bishop's readers in and around the archives. Goldensohn's discovery, mentioned earlier, is a prime example of how attention to previously unknown material can have a tremendous impact on the field. Bishop's archive at Vassar has been an important source for scholars and readers at least since Vassar made its initial acquisition in 1981, a practice that has led to insightful new readings of the poet. Work by Victoria Harrison, Barbara Page, Thomas Travisano, Lorrie Goldensohn, Eleanor Cook, Jonathan Ellis, Peggy Samuels, Camille Roman, Linda Anderson, myself, and many others have provided us with a strong critical foundation for thinking about the relationship between the poet and her archives, as have Bishop's biographers: Brett Millier, Megan Marshall, and Travisano.[18]

New editions of archival materials published in the last decade, including *Edgar Allan Poe & The Juke-Box*, a collection of Bishop's "uncollected poems, drafts, and fragments" (edited and annotated by Alice Quinn in 2006), and *Words in Air: The Complete Correspondence Between Elizabeth Bishop and Robert Lowell* (edited by Thomas Travisano with Saskia Hamilton, 2008), have added well over one thousand pages of previously unpublished or long-out-of-print poetry, prose, drafts, and letters to Bishop's previously published work, a phenomenon that her readers began to address in the essay collection *Elizabeth Bishop in the 21st Century: Reading the New Editions* (edited by Angus Cleghorn, Bethany Hicok, and Thomas Travisano). These editions have also sparked fresh approaches to Bishop's work. But they cannot serve as a substitute for careful archival study, nor can they be treated as totally reliable in the case of Quinn's *Edgar Allan Poe*, which scholars have found to be somewhat inconsistent in its editorial choices and at times inaccurate in its transcriptions.[19] Quinn is currently working on an edition of Bishop's notebooks for Farrar, Straus and Giroux, which will make more accessible to Bishop's readers these extraordinary working notebooks; Bishop's handwriting is notoriously difficult to read, so published transcriptions will contribute a great deal to scholarship, but it is hoped the publisher will include facsimiles of these collage-like notebooks with this edition, as they sometimes did in *Edgar Allan Poe & The Juke-Box*, in order to give readers some sense of how image and text work together to inform Bishop's creative process, which a mere transcription of text could not possibly represent. Such an edition would also benefit from a digital component. Marianne Moore scholars have been working collaboratively for a number of years to develop a digital and searchable version of Moore's extraordinary notebooks that serve as an example of what could be done in Bishop Studies (if copyright restrictions can be renegotiated or lifted).

What I *am* suggesting, then, is that despite all this activity in and around the archives, Bishop's archive has been treated more as a source to be mined for information (and new editions) rather than as a subject of inquiry in its own right, even while scholarship on Sylvia Plath and other mid-century writers has moved more intentionally into interdisciplinary approaches at the intersection of literary and archival study. Returning to the archive and describing original documents is crucial to understanding and accurately representing the powerful currents of this poet's career. As a writer's reputation changes dramatically (as it has for Bishop), so does our reading of the archives, and, indeed, of the poet's work. We see here with Bishop what Anita Helle has called, in reference to Sylvia Plath's legacy, "an absorbing instance of archive formation as a cultural process, occurring through a variety of means (historical, popular, biographical, fictional) and engaging a range of public interests."[20] As with Bishop, new primary materials made available to Plath scholars at the beginning of this century led to a reassessment of Plath and the subsequent publication of an important and widely cited volume of essays in 2007, edited by Helle and titled *The Unraveling Archive: Essays on Sylvia Plath*. Since then, new archival research on Plath has presented readers with a poet "who is more historically located and multiple."[21]

I want to call attention to a second issue influencing approaches to Bishop's material archive, and that is reformatting. Not long after the collection was acquired in the early 1980s, the Vassar Library created a duplicate set of preservation photocopies to ensure long-term access to this fragile, valuable, and soon-to-be heavily used collection (digital technologies had not yet been developed).[22] A policy was established whereby researchers were first offered copies of the papers, though anyone could view originals upon request. While this approach has helped to preserve the collection, in recent years scholarly trends have emerged which highlight the material aspects of originals and the importance of examining them closely. For instance, let us take the badly water-damaged and frayed original of Bishop's baby book as an example of the importance of accurately describing original documents. Titled *A Biography of Our Baby*, it was acquired from Brazil by Vassar in 2002 among the Portinari family papers. For Thomas Travisano, Bishop's current biographer, the original of this document is important as the first account of Bishop's life, a book that despite its damage reveals a great deal about a much-cherished and loved child (this was a deluxe version of a popular baby book) whose early days were documented with photographs and careful notations of weight and growth.[23] Yet the pages also reveal the crisis that began to unfold with the death of Bishop's father and the mental deterioration of her mother. Though in this case some color photocopies are available, by their very nature these cannot convey all aspects of the original, nor can they replicate the overpowering experience of holding and examining the baby book directly. High-quality, digital reproductions (rather than photocopies), like the images used in *Elizabeth Bishop and the Literary Archive*, provide insight into aspects of the collection that might be otherwise invisible to scholars working from photocopies. Or consider the Foster letters. Photocopies of these letters reveal very little beyond content, while the original documents tell us a more complete story. For instance, Bishop's letters to Foster are originals, not carbons.[24] The letters have been folded in half, rather than trifolded to fit in an envelope, so Bishop may not have sent them. In short, if we are going to use the archives, we must be attentive to the materiality of the archive and the stories these artifacts can tell.

Carolyn Steedman reminds us that archives and the stories we tell about them are necessarily incomplete. Iain Bailey notes that we should consider the archive "as a place of work, rather than as a cache from which to draw certainties."[25] It could be argued that no poet knew this better than Bishop, for Bishop's poetic practice encourages a return to the archive. As Linda Anderson has noted, Bishop's recursive writing process, which involved "returning to drafts, [and] using ideas and images from notebooks written years before," meant that Bishop actually gathered into her work "archival traces and memories which could also provide connections and echoes across time."[26] Bishop's poetry is full of archival documents that act as indexical signs to the business of recapturing and re-finding long-buried memories of family, nation, and history. Consider the "buried Indian Princess's skirt" that turns up on the beach in Bishop's "Florida" poem, suddenly revealing the trace of colonial oppression in the history of "the state with the prettiest name" (*P* 33); or, there is the "little painting" described in "Poem," "a minor family relic," which has been "handed along collaterally to owners" for seventy years. In the poet's hands now, this family artifact prompts her musings on art and memory (*P* 33, 196). These signs point a way to understanding human suffering and loss and constructing one's own identity from the shards unearthed from the past and placed in the larger context of family and nation: "Every text," Claire Colebrook has argued in "The Anthropocene and the Archive," "is a time capsule and a time machine, containing the present, but sending the present into a future that the present cannot control."[27]

Bishop's archival practice also involved using "archival" evidence in her own writing to explore family ties, identity, or to provide important details of character, such as in her memoir of her mentor Marianne Moore, "Efforts of Affection." Bishop recounts the story of Moore and her mother's famous rewriting of Bishop's poem "Roosters." Bishop writes: "The revised poem had been typed out on very thin paper and folded into a small square, sealed with a gold star sticker and signed on the outside 'Lovingly, Rose Peebles'" (*Pr* 133). Rose Peebles was a favorite teacher of Bishop's at Vassar. However, a search of Bishop's own archive reveals slightly different material "evidence." The first part of the description is accurate – the onion skin paper, the folds, the gold star sticker, but it is not signed "Lovingly, Rose Peebles," but rather the handwriting, which appears to be Moore's, instructs (in black ink outlined by someone in red pencil): "Do not read at mealtime or ~~before~~ [the word on is inserted above ~~before~~] going to bed. D.D." Moore is most likely referring to Dorothy Dix, a popular advice columnist of the 1890s through the early twentieth century. Why does Bishop change the inscription? Dorothy Dix makes more sense in terms of Moore's "advice" about "Roosters," and it seems more light-hearted. Bishop took Moore and her mother's rewriting of "Roosters" very hard and never sent Moore anything that was unfinished again. It would seem that appropriating the voice of one of Bishop's favorite teachers is potentially more menacing than Moore's perhaps more playful intent. Ultimately, the point is that we cannot be sure, and so, if we took Bishop's statement at face value, her misreading of her own archive might potentially be ours, as well. Finally, Bishop's poetic practice, like our work in the archives, requires her readers to understand "that sense of constant re-adjustment" that Bishop herself called our attention to very early in her career when she wrote "The Gentleman of Shalott" (*P* 12).

Notes

1. Parts of this essay appeared in Bethany Hicok, "Introduction to *Elizabeth Bishop and the Literary Archive*" (Lever Press, 2020). Lever Press is an open-access, peer-reviewed, scholarly, all-digital publication platform: www.fulcrum.org/leverpress.
2. For a thorough guide to Bishop-related materials held in institutions and private collections in Nova Scotia, see Sandra Barry, *Elizabeth Bishop: An Archival Guide to Her Life in Nova Scotia* (Hantsport, NS: Lancelot Press, 1996).

3. In "Archive Fever," Jacques Derrida notes that the word archive itself derives from the Greek *arkheion* – house of the archons – where the law is determined in Ancient Greece. Because of their recognized authority, official documents were kept in the house of the archons; hence, they are placed under house arrest. See "Archive Fever: A Freudian Impression," *Diacritics* 25.2 (Summer 1995), 9.
4. Bishop divided her 1965 volume *Questions of Travel* into two parts: "Brazil" and "Elsewhere," and the term, elsewhere, in its openness to possibility, can be considered one of the defining terms of Bishop's art.
5. William Logan writes on the correspondence between Bishop and Louise Bradley and the importance of Bishop's years at Camp Chequesset in "Elizabeth Bishop at Summer Camp," in *Guilty Knowledge, Guilty Pleasure: The Dirty Art of Poetry* (New York: Columbia University Press, 2014), 250–302. Thomas Travisano discusses these letters in detail in chapter four of his biography *Love Unknown: The Life and Worlds of Elizabeth Bishop* (New York: Viking, 2019).
6. Carolyn Steedman, *Dust: The Archive and Cultural Memory* (New Brunswick, NJ: Rutgers University Press, 2002), 68–69.
7. Ibid., 69–70.
8. Louise Craven, "From the Archivist's Cardigan to the Very Dead Sheep: What are Archives? What are Archivists? What do they do?" in *What Are Archives? Cultural and Theoretical Perspectives: A Reader*, ed. Louise Craven (New York: Routledge, 2008), 17.
9. Lisa Stead, "Introduction," in *The Boundaries of the Literary Archive: Reclamation and Representation* (New York: Routledge, 2016), 2.
10. The papers can be found in Vassar's Archives & Special Collections Library, which holds the college's extensive rare book, manuscript, and archival collections. The Library has an active teaching and outreach program, and each year responds to more than one thousand research requests. The Bishop collection is one among several heavily used collections.
11. See my discussion of Bishop at Vassar in *Degrees of Freedom: American Women Poets and the Women's College, 1905–1955* (Lewisburg: Bucknell University Press, 2008), 84–130.
12. See Adrienne Rich, "The Eye of the Outsider: Elizabeth Bishop's Complete Poems, 1927–1979," rpt. in *Blood, Bread, and Poetry: Selected Prose, 1979–1985* (New York: Norton, 1986), 125.
13. See Linda Morra, *Unarrested Archives: Case Studies in Twentieth-Century Canadian Women's Authorship* (Toronto: University of Toronto Press, 2014).
14. Lorrie Goldensohn, *Elizabeth Bishop: The Biography of a Poetry* (New York: Columbia University Press, 1992), 27.
15. Ibid.
16. Heather Treseler's "'Too Shy to Stop': Elizabeth Bishop and the Scene of Reading" is one of six essays to address Bishop's Queer Archive in *Elizabeth Bishop and the Literary Archive,* ed. Bethany Hicok (Lever Press, 2020). Alyse Knorr's "'Keeping Up a Silent Conversation:' Recovering a Queer Bishop

through Her Intimate Correspondence with Alice Methfessel," is published in the same volume.

17. In "Odd Job: Bishop's 'The Fairy Toll-Taker,'" John Emil Vincent returns to the archival drafts of this late prose poem as a case study in queer archival reading in *Elizabeth Bishop and the Literary Archive*, ed. Bethany Hicok (Lever Press, 2020).
18. Ron Patkus, Head of Special Collections at Vassar College, documented some of this scholarly activity in a special exhibition in 2011 commemorating the 100th anniversary of Bishop's birth. See the exhibition booklet, *From the Archive: Discovering Elizabeth Bishop* (Vassar College Libraries, 2011).
19. In "Postcards and Sunsets: Bishop's Revisions and the Problem of Excess," Jeffrey Gray questions why Quinn chose some drafts over others to include in *Edgar Allan Poe & The Juke-Box, in Elizabeth Bishop in the 21st Century: Reading the New Editions*, ed. Angus Cleghorn, Bethany Hicok, and Thomas Travisano (Charlottesville and London: University of Virginia Press, 2012), 26–40. John Emil Vincent notes transcription errors in the version of the "The Fairy Toll-Taker" published in *Edgar Allan Poe*, in *Elizabeth Bishop and the Literary Archive*, ed. Bethany Hicok (Lever Press, 2020).
20. Anita Helle, "Lessons from the Archive: Sylvia Plath and the Politics of Memory," *Feminist Studies* 31.3 (Fall 2005), 634.
21. Ibid., 641.
22. This has long been an accepted practice used by research libraries; for more seewww.nedcc.org/preservation101/session-7/7paper-reproductions.
23. See Travisano, *Love Unknown.*
24. Lorrie Goldensohn misidentifies them as carbon copies in "Approaching Elizabeth Bishop's Letters to Ruth Foster," *The Yale Review* 103.1 (January 2015), 2.
25. Iain Bailey, "Allusion and Exogenesis: The Labouring Heart of Samuel Beckett's III Seen III Said," in *The Boundaries of the Literary Archive: Reclamation and Representation*, ed. Carrie Smith and Lisa Stead (New York: Routledge, 2016), 41.
26. Linda Anderson, *Elizabeth Bishop: Lines of Connection* (Edinburgh: Edinburgh University Press, 2015), 7.
27. Claire Colbrook, "The Anthropocene and the Archive," *Durham University Memory Network*, thememorynetwork.net/the-anthropocene-and-the-archive/. Accessed October 17, 2018, n.p.

PART III

Literary Contexts

CHAPTER 13

Romantic and Victorian Poetry

Peter Swaab

Elizabeth Bishop grew up in an atmosphere of nineteenth-century poetry. "As for the books in our house, we had Emerson, Carlyle, all the old poets," she recalled in 1966. In a later interview she elaborated: "My aunt, like so many Victorians, belonged to the village's poetry society and she recited a great deal to me – Longfellow, Browning, Tennyson."[1] She started reading poetry, she remembered, when she was eight.[2]

She advised her students at the University of Washington: "You should have your head filled with poems all the time, until they almost get in your way."[3] Her primary focus here is on poems as against poets. A head full of poems is the way to make more poems; tradition should almost but not quite impede the individual talent. In her own writing, Bishop sees poems as a series of possibilities to be revisited gratefully, shrewdly, critically, neither agonistically as precursors to battle or displace, nor polemically in the spirit of a literary politics championing a school or movement. The primary importance of poets, for her, was as a help in making new poems.

While Bishop admired a number of British nineteenth-century poets, above all Wordsworth and Hopkins, she had little interest in an overall conception either of Romanticism or Victorianism. Nonetheless, she occasionally seemed to espouse an anti-Romantic position. An early journal entry made in 1934, for instance, discusses the relation between the material and spiritual in the creative process:

> It's a question of using the poet's proper materials, with which he is equipped by nature, i.e., immediate, intense physical reactions, a sense of metaphor and decoration in everything – to express something not of them – something, I suppose, *spiritual.* [. . .] The other way – of using the supposedly "spiritual" – the beautiful, the nostalgic, the ideal and *poetic*, to produce the *material* – is the way of the Romantic, I think – and a great perversity.[4]

She had been reading T. S. Eliot's *The Use of Poetry and the Use of Criticism* shortly after its 1933 publication,[5] and her phrasing echoes Eliot's polemically classical position of this time, including his idea that "a wilful perversity had taken hold of literary men, a new literary disease called Romanticism."[6] More than a generation later, in a 1966 interview, she would call the Beats "Romantic and self-pitying … I hate self-pity poems."[7] The word "Romantic" here comes at the start of a sentence, so we can't quite tell if it should have a capital "R," nor whether she means the word in its colloquial or its historical sense. But in recruiting the "Romantic" as an anti-Beats category she is again clearly influenced by the cultural politics of a particular moment. Within her poetry, however, the story is different. Bishop's dealings with Romantic writers and the Romantic period in her poetry are, as we might expect, more considered and measured.

When in 1976 Bishop was awarded the Neustadt International Prize for Literature, her poem "Sandpiper" was printed in the programme. She wryly noted in her acceptance speech that all her life she had "lived and behaved very much like that sandpiper" (*PPL* 731). The bird in her poem is "awkward, / in a state of controlled panic" (*P* 129), so this was partly a joke about awards ceremonies. The sandpiper was also "a student of Blake," perhaps doomed to be so because he started his famous "Auguries of Innocence" with the line "To see a World in a Grain of Sand." How far was Bishop herself, in fact, a student of Blake? The question is complicated because the purport of Blake's famous lines, to which the sandpiper can't help alluding, is not entirely clear:

> To see a World in a Grain of Sand
> And a Heaven in a Wild Flower
> Hold Infinity in the palm of your hand
> And Eternity in an hour[8]

These opening lines stand apart, partly as a quatrain in a poem composed almost entirely of couplets, and partly because they make a freestanding unpunctuated non-sentence, a series of infinitives but neither a grammatical sentence nor manifestly a proposition. They are not in the imperative voice of (for instance) Blake's "Hear the voice of the Bard," though we are likely to take them at first as an injunction. Seeing the world in a grain of sand like this could indeed be a visionary aspiration, but the following lines suggest that it may involve agonies of sensitivity, and they beg difficult questions around hyperbole:

> A dog starvd at his Masters Gate
> Predicts the ruin of the State
> A Horse misusd upon the Road
> Calls to Heaven for Human blood[9]

Bishop's sandpiper doesn't follow Blake far into the world-shaping grandeur of his auguries. He is indeed more of a follower of the later poets of Romantic quest, Keats and Shelley. They too imagine searches for something that can never be a stable point of arrival. The protagonist of Shelley's "Alastor," for example, journeys through the world and finds only an empty self-reflection at the end of his travels; Keats's protagonist in *Endymion* searches endlessly for something that exists only in dreams or visions. We know that Bishop had a Shelley phase, and she told Howard Moss "I adore Keats anyway – even *all* the poetry" (*NYr* 228). Her sandpiper may be "a student of Blake," but that doesn't make him altogether a follower of Blake.[10]

He may for instance be a student with more than one teacher. "Sandpiper" implies more than a single poetic heritage, a complication of influence and allusion characteristic of Bishop. Even in "Casabianca" and "The Gentleman of Shalott," her two published poems the titles of which openly allude to previous poems, the focus is not entirely on their apparent precursors Hemans and Tennyson. Bishop's very enigmatic "Casabianca" is a poem about the absurd and sacrificial nature of love, as against duty in Hemans's original; her Gentleman of Shalott sees himself in a Stevens-like mirror of doubled identity, a differently problematic situation from Tennyson's narrative of the Lady of Shalott. Each poem, too, uses a metrical form markedly different from its precursor. The point of her choices is partly their famous afterlives. She often responds poetically to an anthology warhorse like these two; she is sceptically interested in moments when the cultural heritage is sliding towards cliché. Sceptically, however, and not cynically, because the very fame of such moments implies a continuing and engaging history in which they have merited attention.

Bishop's sandpiper ends with a vista of continuing quest:

> His beak is focussed; he is preoccupied,
> looking for something, something, something.
> Poor bird, he is obsessed!
> The millions of grains are black, white, tan, and gray
> mixed with quartz grains, rose and amethyst. (*P* 129)

"Poor bird," perhaps, but we could hear in these lines not only a sorry plight but also an absorbing and rewarded vocation. To see the world in these grains of sand, for instance, enables the painterly sequence in which "tan" richly interrupts and complicates the monochrome tones of black, white and gray. And the final line, opening into the metaphorical as part of the sensory, is reminiscent of the end of Hopkins's "Windhover," with its visionary evocation of a transcendent world beneath the observer's feet:

blue-bleak embers, ah my dear,
Fall, gall themselves, and gash gold-vermillion.[11]

The sandpiper's search for "something" might further put us in mind of the poet for whom more than any other the word "something" is often crucial, and this is not Blake but Wordsworth. Several of Wordsworth's greatest poems and lines surround "something" with mystery and grandeur: "a sense sublime / Of something far more deeply interfused"; "O joy! that in our embers / Is something that doth live" ; "twas a sound / Of something without place or bound"; "whether it were by peculiar grace, / A leading from above, a something given."[12] The Wordsworthian "something" combines elusive intimations with a sense of solid confidence. For Bishop's sandpiper, too, the quest for "something" is driven by belief in the existence of a desirable object alongside the experience of its recurrent or perpetual slippage. Whether it is recurrent or perpetual depends on whether we take the line to refer to three somethings or just one – a record of the bird repeatedly finding its object and then moving on, or a record of its always missing the object and being compelled to continue the search.

Such ambiguous possibilities in "something" contribute to another beautiful and uncanny moment in Bishop, when she evokes the bus passengers' talk in "The Moose":

deaths, deaths and sicknesses;
the year he remarried;
the year (something) happened. (*P* 192)

Had she written "the year something happened" the line would already impart a doubleness to "something," its substantiality as the subject of the verb lessened by its lack of definition and its location in the past. But Bishop has enclosed the word in brackets, with a further estrangement. This is partly an estrangement from ordinary grammar in a sentence that already lacks the proper component of a main verb (it extends dreamily from line 90 to line 105). For it is a principle of a parenthesis that "it may be taken out without injuring the sense of that which encloses it" (Samuel Johnson's definition)[13]; but to exclude Bishop's parenthesis is to transform the sentence: "the year (something) happened" becomes "the year happened." This makes sense, and it has the placidity of a truism; but it is a very different sense from the one conjured by "the year (something) happened." Bishop creates an evocation of time that includes the effacement of human damage; she makes this unspecified event of the past spectral. The line quiets the grievousness of the surrounding stanzas, with their visitings of death, sickness, and even (since it implies termination as well as inception) of remarrying. In the "Preface" to *Lyrical Ballads*, Wordsworth speaks of the poet as having "a disposition to be affected more than other men by absent things as if they were present."[14] In these lines the absent "something" is at once parenthetically present in the sentence and strangely absent from it. The effect resembles what Wordsworth describes as one of the effects of poetic meter, namely "to throw a sort of half consciousness of unsubstantial existence over the whole composition" with the result that "more pathetic situations and sentiments, that is, those which have a greater proportion of pain connected with them, may be endured in metrical composition, especially in rhyme, than in prose."[15] Bishop's stoicism, her art of coping, owes a good deal to Wordsworth.

She was rueful but not only rueful when she told Robert Lowell that "I find I'm really a minor female Wordsworth" (*WIA* 122). You can be quite a major writer by being a minor Wordsworth, so this is not just a lament; moreover, to be a female Wordsworth gives you advantages and differences, not just a lower place in the pecking order. Dorothy Wordsworth, after all, might be described that way. Bishop was talking about a preponderance of "Nature poems" in her recent work when she referred to herself this way. But there are several other ways in which Wordsworth is her crucial precursor among the English Romantic poets – in for instance such phrasings as "small leaves, real leaves" in "Quai d'Orléans" (*P* 29) (recalling Wordsworth's "the Sea, the real Sea"), or "I liked the place" in "Santarém" (*P* 207) (recalling "I liked the greeting" in "Stepping Westward").[16] The sensation of "falling off / the round, turning world" in "In the Waiting Room" (*P* 180) might remind us of Wordsworth's "Fallings from us, vanishings,"[17] both expressing the intuition that crucial moments may combine negativity and revelation. Above all, in terms of what he meant to Bishop, he is the poet with the most central insistence on the provisionality of vision. "Tintern Abbey" pays tribute to "the mighty world / Of eye and ear, both what they half-create, / And what perceive:"[18] eye and ear are mighty and creative, not just unreliable. Wordsworth figures the relationship between inner and outer at its happiest as an "ennobling interchange."[19] At other times, the interchange becomes an overbalance either of the external or the internal, in which the world may appear only as "a soulless image on the eye"[20] or else may be overcome by the power of visionary perception. Such a sense that perception is fallible and changeable leads to many instances in Wordsworth, on both a large and small scale, of revised and reframed details. The sequence in "Tintern Abbey" describing "hedge-rows, hardly hedge-rows, little lines / Of sportive wood run wild"[21] is a forerunner of numerous such alternations and alterations of phrase in Bishop. The "big leaves, little leaves, and giant leaves" in "Brazil, January 1, 1502" (*P*, 89) are one such moment; "little, big, giant" would describe a more lucid progression, but it is characteristic of Bishop to complicate the sequence. The disruption helps us see the variety of leaves with a little surprise, a provocation to the reader more sharply to register the magnifying term "giant" leaves, which may seem at first a harmless botanical word but comes into focus as the poem continues as an instance of paranoid imperialist vision. The earlier settlers in Brazil, "the Christians" as Bishop disconcertingly calls them, perceive or half-create monstrous and wicked figures in the Brazilian jungle, and they bring violence and conquest. Such a sequence doesn't insist that the arrivers of 1502 and 1952 are identical, but suggests that it is very hard to know where the continuities begin and end. Bishop's evocation of the cultural density of perception carries with it a politics and an ethics that we could reasonably call Wordsworthian. It centres on the imperfect authority of the poet's point of view, and a consequent need "to be reserved in speech."[22]

Bishop valued Wordsworth as a poet of depression as well as its management. Her most direct reference to his work comes in obtrusively anachronistic lines from "Crusoe in England":[23]

> the poems–well, I tried
> reciting to my iris-beds,
> "They flash upon that inward eye,
> which is the bliss . . . " The bliss of what? (*P* 184)

In Wordsworth's "I wandered lonely as a Cloud," another anthology piece, the daffodils help him change from being "lonely as a Cloud" to experiencing "the bliss of solitude."[24] What worked for Wordsworth doesn't here work for Crusoe. The iris-beds don't give him anything back, and these irises, actually snail-shells, aren't even flowers, never mind eyes. Insofar as the poem is a critique of Wordsworth, its plot implies that imaginative vision is crucially to be supplied not by nature but by human company and love: in this it follows on early critiques of Wordsworth by, for instance, William Hazlitt and Sara Coleridge.[25] But Crusoe's unreceptiveness is partly his own failure of vision; he is not offered as an exemplary perceiver. Wordsworth's poem, moreover, isn't as simple as it has often been taken to be. Its final stanza begins: "For oft when on my couch I lie / In vacant or in pensive mood / They flash upon that inward eye / Which is the bliss of solitude."[26] Does "oft" imply that the magic sometimes doesn't work? The moods may return, the recovery is provisional and has to be made and remade. As the creator of the dejected figure of "The Solitary" (in *The Excursion* Books II and III) Wordsworth was familiar with the unblissful sides of solitude. He was familiar, too, with the kind of blank unredeemed vision that ends Bishop's poem. Crusoe's knife, which used to "reek of meaning," has become blank:

> Now it won't look at me at all.
> The living soul has dribbled away. (*P* 186)

In Wordsworth's great "Elegiac Stanzas," he imagines how once he had beheld an idyllic peaceful vision of Peele Castle, "And seen the soul of truth in every part." But after the death of his brother John no longer: "A power is gone, which nothing can restore; / A deep distress hath humanized my Soul."[27] Bishop combines Wordsworth's bereft and stoic vision with a remembrance of one of Hopkins's finest maxims: "What you look hard at seems to look hard at you."[28] Both Wordsworth and Hopkins offer Bishop examples of the vicissitudes of poetic illumination, its bafflement as well as its arrival.

Bishop does not conceive the Victorian period monolithically. As she was born in 1911, the nineteenth century was perhaps far enough away for its poetry not to be felt as a strongly oppressive influence; modernist poetics were well-established when she began writing. Indeed, Gerard Manley Hopkins, the Victorian poet by whom she was most strongly influenced, was often thought of as a proto-modernist after the first publication of his *Poems* in 1918. Bishop named Hopkins along with Herbert and Baudelaire as one of her three favourite poets (*PPL* 703). His influence on her writing is pervasive. She was also at times influenced by two poetic genres, the dramatic monologue and nonsense poetry, that reached their creative zenith in the Victorian period.

When asked by an interviewer in 1966 what she thought about the dramatic monologue as a form, Bishop replied: "I haven't given it much thought. Robert Lowell and others have done brilliant things in this form. I suppose it should act as a sort of release. You can say all kinds of things you couldn't in a lyric. If you have scenery and costumes, you can get away with a lot. I'm writing one right now."[29] She sounds a little guarded, perhaps protective of the one she was writing "right now" – which would probably have been an early version of "Crusoe in England." But within her reply lies a large claim for what the form can afford: "a sort of release," saying "all sorts of things you couldn't in a lyric," being able to "get away with a lot." Bishop didn't write many dramatic monologues, but they include three of her longest poems, "Manuelzinho," "The Riverman" and "Crusoe in England." What did the permissiveness of the form allow her to get away with? One answer would be that it released her from what she called her "George-Washington-handicap" of not being able to tell a lie (*WIA* 402).[30] The speakers of dramatic monologues are *expected* to stand in a dubious relation to truth, to be unreliable, excessive. "The Riverman" and "Crusoe in England," in particular, allow Bishop to explore speakers at a distance not just from reliability but from humanity. The creatures in the three prose monologues titled "Rainy Season; Sub-Tropics," again, are all egotists, reluctant to acknowledge ties to one another. They don't know they are all gathered under the umbrella of the title that makes them less unique than they each feel. The dramatic monologue is a form that finds comedy or grotesquerie in the problems of the overweening self. As such, it may be cautionary about excesses of self-attention such as Bishop sometimes associated with English Romanticism.

How far has the speaker of "The Riverman" left the world behind? In a normal dramatic monologue there would be a listener to whom the speaker speaks – the "silent interlocutor" – for reasons that are integral to the poem. Here there isn't one, in particular not his wife, but the speaker hasn't entirely left behind the wish to be heard, looked at, and perhaps thanked.

> Godfathers and cousins,
> your canoes are over my head;
> I hear your voices talking.
> [. . .] I will go to work
> to get you health and money.
> The Dolphin singled me out;
> Luandinha seconded it. (*P* 106–7)

He hears them, but can they hear him? If the poem is a dream of entry to a new magical element, what is the price in terms of distance from human contact? Such questions about communication might occur to a poet drawn to the complexities of surrealism and symbolism; here the monologue gives them a dramatic context. The ending proffers more than one version of his motives: first the altruistic option – "to get you health and money" – but then one that turns on the egoism of being "singled out," and turns away from the human even; the privacy and fantasy of the waterworld comes at a price. As a dramatic monologue testing the limits of an isolated subjectivity, "The Riverman" draws on the heritage of the two great inaugurators of the genre, Browning and Tennyson, perhaps especially Browning's necromancers and Tennyson's recluses.

At other points "The Riverman" seems to draw into its life of fantasy two further nineteenth-century poets much admired by Bishop, namely Baudelaire and Lear. When the Riverman says that

all is sweetness there
in the deep, enchanted silt

we could hear an echo and variation of Baudelaire's "L'Invitation au Voyage":[31]

Là, tout n'est qu'ordre et beauté,
Luxe, calme et volupté.[32]

The complexity of Baudelaire's sequence, combining classicism and romance, sexuality and calm, becomes a simpler enchantment for Bishop's speaker. His recourse to the river is perhaps more childlike as well, akin to Edward Lear's figures who take leave of the human world for fellowship with other creatures, most often birds and insects, but sometimes fish too.

There was an old person of Ems, who casually fell in the Thames;
And when he was found they said he was drowned,
That unlucky old person of Ems.[33]

Despite the words of the verse, the old person of Ems looks neither unlucky nor drowned in Lear's drawing. As another riverman he seems to be flourishing in the company of a support group of variously shaped fish, having changed his human world for a water-world.

Thanking her *New Yorker* editor Howard Moss for his 1969 book *Writing Against Time: Critical Essays and Reviews*, Bishop noted how

Figure 13.1 Edward Lear's "There was an old person of Ems" (1846)

much they both loved Edward Lear; she included "Chekhov, Keats, Lear" among "our favorite writers" (*NYr* 308).[34] Nonsense writing was important to her, and in particular that of Lear, like her a connoisseur of the "awful but cheerful" (*P* 59). Mildred J. Nash remembered that in Bishop's bookshelves "Lewis Carroll had two biographies, as did Edward Lear. How she adored that man! She paused to leaf through his *Nonsense Book*, talking of his sad life."[35] She made connections between nineteenth- and twentieth-century nonsensicality; teaching Stevens, for instance, she became "most animated in discussing pieces that bordered on inspired nonsense verse."[36]

Many of Bishop's poems, especially the early ones, have titles suggestive of the nonsensical, for instance "Sleeping on the Ceiling," "Sleeping Standing Up" and "The Man-Moth." Nonsense for Bishop is often a resource for dreams of felicity, of worlds unbound by the rules of the sensical. In "Insomnia," for instance, the portal to love is through the looking-glass "world inverted / where left is always right, / where the shadows are really the body" (*P* 68). Brett Millier suggests that Lewis Carroll is the "truest antecedent" for the mad-hatting deviant world of "Exchanging Hats."[37] When the early poem "Seascape" uses the phrase "beautiful pea-green back-pasture," we are likely to hear an echo of the "beautiful pea-green boat" in which Edward Lear's Owl and Pussy-cat went to sea.[38] Bishop's back-pasture is part of a heavenly fluid scene.

> and the beautiful pea-green back-pasture
> where occasionally a fish jumps, like a wild-flower
> in an ornamental spray of spray (*P* 41)

The jumping fish seems an amphibious creature here, as untethered to its home element as the cow that jumps over the moon in the nursery rhyme. A "spray of spray" is a phrase at once tautological and nonsensical. Language cooperates here in uniting the floral spray and the sea spray, and the poet in charge of such a language game is acting like Lewis Carroll's Humpty Dumpty, able to make language mean what she wants it to.[39] The lighthouse later in "Seascape" takes and gives a contrasting view, in which "heaven is not like this," but for most of the poem it has been.

Gerard Manley Hopkins mattered to Bishop both formatively and abidingly. She admired Hopkins ethically, and championed his idea of the gentleman as "still applicable and very moving" in the context of both of her crucial poetic colleagues, Marianne Moore and Robert Lowell.[40] In details of prosody, too, Hopkins was a precursor for some of Bishop's more audacious effects. Her 1934 essay follows G. F. Lahey's 1930 book on

Hopkins in noting that he "occasionally uses quasi-apocope" (*PPL* 667), a term Lahey uses to describe the elision of a syllable in such enjambments as "does set danc- / Ing blood" and "I wéar- / Y of idle a being."[41] Lahey had deprecated such moments (he lists seven) as a tendency to "degenerate into a quasi-apocope,"[42] but Bishop defends them: "by these difficult devices his poetry comes up from the pages like sudden storms" (*PPL* 667). Such Hopkins metrical audacities as these inform her own poetry, for instance the vertiginous mention in "Arrival at Santos" that Miss Breen's "home, when she is at home, is in Glens Fall // s, New York" (*P* 87–8). Hopkins's stressed and strained rhymes, too, are precursors to Bishop's rhyming in such poems as "Exchanging Hats" and "Pink Dog," with its tercet contriving an excruciating rhyme of "*fantasía*" with "to be a-" and "ever see a" (*P* 213).

In a 1966 interview, Bishop recalls being impressed as a student by Hopkins's phrase "Fancy, come faster" in *The Wreck of the Deutschland*: "He breaks off and addresses himself [. . .] the present tense helps to convey this sense of the mind in action."[43] Like Wordsworth and Baudelaire, Hopkins exemplified for Bishop a poet dynamically observing his own process of observation (Baudelaire called such a process "dédoublement").[44] Moreover, Hopkins's descriptions dramatise an observer urgently seeking God's plan and presence in the details of the created world; his intensity is religious. That Bishop once expressed (to Marianne Moore) a reservation about "that emotional *rushing* effect he sometimes produces" (*OA* 335) points to the ways in which her own poetics characteristically calm Hopkins's tempo as well as drawing on his example. Her quest for the transcendent is relatively muted. The affinities and contrasts emerge in a comparison of lines from Hopkins's "Hurrahing in Harvest" and Bishop's "A Cold Spring" (with its epigraph from Hopkins, "Nothing is so beautiful as spring"). Here is Hopkins:

> Summer ends now; now, barbarous in beauty, the stooks rise
> Around; up above, what wind-walks! what lovely behaviour
> Of silk-sack clouds! has wilder, wilful-wavier
> Meal-drift moulded ever and melted across skies?[45]

And Bishop:

> Now, from the thick grass, the fireflies
> begin to rise:
> up, then down, then up again:
> lit on the ascending flight,
> drifting simultaneously to the same height,
> – exactly like the bubbles in champagne. (*P* 56)

In both poets "now" registers an alignment of the time in the poem and in the world; both respond to a process of "rising" dynamically registered by prepositions ("Around; up, above" in Hopkins, "up, then down, then up again" in Bishop). Hopkins's exclamations and question are absorbed into the less demonstrative implications of Bishop's description. He sees the sensuousness of the world more erotically than Bishop, in phrases at once alluring and troubling ("barbarous," "wilful-wavier"), and the direction of his poem is religious: "Í lift úp heart, éyes, / Down all that glory in the heavens to glean our Saviour." Lifting "up" eyes turns into "Down all that glory," where "down" has become not a preposition but a verb, as if he were downing a pint, but eucharistically. Bishop's "drifting" is less luxurious than Hopkins's "meal-drift," her rhythms gently rise and fall with less of a "rush" than Hopkins's dense compacted lines, her final champagne simile is celebratory but a little rueful, moving us from the cosmic to the oenophile. The contrast is one of temperaments, periods and methods; but the influence is clear and important.

Notes

1. *Conversations with Elizabeth Bishop*, ed. George Monteiro (Jackson: University of Mississippi Press, 1996), citing a 1966 interview with Ashley Brown (20) and a 1978 interview with Alexandra Johnson (98). See also *WIA* 399–400.
2. Ibid., 20.
3. Ibid., 40.
4. Brett C. Millier, *Elizabeth Bishop: Life and the Memory of It* (Berkeley: University of California Press, 1993), 64; citing a journal entry for 1934.
5. She writes about *The Use of Poetry and the Use of Criticism* in a letter of 12 December 1933 ("Very dry, but there are some pretty good spots") (*OA* 15); and she cites a passage from the book in her 1934 essay on Hopkins (*Pr* 471).
6. *The Use of Poetry and the Use of Criticism* (London: Faber and Faber, 1933), 128.
7. *Conversations*, 35.
8. William Blake, *The Complete Poems*, ed. Alicia Ostriker (Harmondsworth: Penguin, 1977), 506; lines 1–4.
9. Ibid., 507; lines 9–12.
10. For other valuable discussions of Bishop and Romanticism see Michael O'Neill's *The All-Sustaining Air: Romantic Legacies and Renewals in British, American, and Irish Poetry since 1900* (Oxford University Press, 2007), and Bonnie Costello's "Bishop and the Poetic Tradition," in *The Cambridge Companion to Elizabeth Bishop*, ed. Angus Cleghorn and Jonathan Ellis (Cambridge University Press, 2013), 79–96.

11. *Gerard Manley Hopkins: The Major Works*, ed. Catherine Phillips (Oxford: Oxford University Press, 2002), 132, omitting diacritical marks. Bishop cites and scans these lines (without diacritical marks) in her 1934 essay "Gerard Manley Hopkins: Notes on Timing in His Poetry" (*PPL* 662).
12. *William Wordsworth: The Major Works*, ed. Stephen Gill (Oxford: Oxford Major Authors, 1984), 134, 300, 314, 262; quotations from "Tintern Abbey", "Ode (There was a time)," "Stepping Westward" and "Resolution and Independence".
13. I am indebted here to Christopher Ricks's discussion of parenthesis in *Eliot and Prejudice* (London: Faber and Faber, 1988), 153.
14. *Wordsworth: The Major Works*, 603.
15. Ibid., 609–10.
16. *The Major Works*, 579 and 314; from *The Prelude* (1805), xiii. 49, and "Stepping Westward," line 13.
17. *The Major Works*, 301.
18. Ibid., 134; "Lines written a few miles above Tintern Abbey," lines 106–08.
19. *The Prelude* (1805), xii. 376.
20. Ibid., vi. 454.
21. *The Major Works*, 132; "Tintern Abbey," lines 16–17.
22. *Wordsworth: The Major Works*, 205; "Poems on the Naming of Places. IV," line 78.
23. It is interesting that Bishop does *not* make Wordsworth her model, metrically or otherwise, in her major effort at a ballad, "The Burglar of Babylon" (*P* 110–15).
24. *Wordsworth: The Major Works*, 303–04.
25. See for instance Hazlitt's remarks on *Romeo and Juliet* in his *Characters of Shakespear's Plays* (1817), and Sara Coleridge's poem "The Pair that will not meet" in her *Collected Poems*, ed. Peter Swaab (Manchester: Carcanet Press, 2007), 100.
26. *Wordsworth: The Major Works*, 304.
27. Ibid., 326–28; "Elegiac Stanzas, Suggested by a Picture of Peele Castle in a Storm, Painted by Sir George Beaumont," lines 31, 35–36.
28. *The Journals and Papers of Gerard Manley Hopkins*, edited by Humphrey House and Graham Storey (Oxford: Oxford University Press, 1959), 204.
29. *Conversations*, 26.
30. Lee Edelman's essay "Elizabeth Bishop's 'In the Waiting Room'" shows that there were sometimes limits to Bishop's stringency with truth-telling; see *The Geography of Gender*, edited by Marilyn May Lombardi (Charlottesville: University Press of Virginia, 1993), 91–110.
31. Bishop lists Baudelaire as one of her three favourite poets in "Poetry is an Unnatural Act", along with Herbert and Hopkins. The essay, which is unfinished, includes a note to herself to include "B here," but unfortunately she didn't (*PPL* 703). Baudelaire is cited directly in "The Bight": "if one were Baudelaire / one could probably hear it turning to marimba music" (*P* 59).

32. Charles Baudelaire, *Oeuvres complètes* (Paris: Editions de la Pléiade, 2 vols., 1975–6), i. 51.
33. *A Book of Nonsense* (London: T. McLean (1846); eighteenth edition, 1866), 100.
34. Moss's book includes his article "Edward Lear: An Introduction."
35. *Conversations*, 137.
36. Ibid., 145.
37. *Life and the Memory of It*, 279.
38. Edward Lear, *The Complete Verse and Other Nonsense*, ed. Vivien Noakes (London: Penguin, 2001), 238.
39. Compare the reference to Lewis Carroll at the end of "Efforts of Affection" (*Pr* 140).
40. In a letter to Lowell, 21 March 1972 (*WIA* 708), and in relation to Moore in "Efforts of Affection" (*PPL* 498–99).
41. *Hopkins: The Major Works*, 167, 166.
42. G. F. Lahey, S. J., *Gerard Manley Hopkins* (New York: Haskell House, 1969; first published 1930), 98.
43. *Conversations*, 26.
44. In his essay "De l'"essence du rire," Baudelaire commends "la force de se dédoubler rapidement et d'assister comme spectateur désintéressé aux phénomènes de son *moi*" (*Oeuvres completes*, ii. 532); "the power of getting outside himself quickly and watching, as a disinterested spectator, the phenomenon of his ego," in *Baudelaire: Selected Writings on Art and Artists*, translated by P.E. Charvet (Cambridge: Cambridge University Press, 1972), 148.
45. *Hopkins: The Major Works*, 134.

CHAPTER 14

Surrealism and the Avant-Garde

Andrew Epstein

Elizabeth Bishop is perhaps best known as a clear-eyed, realist poet who masterfully renders experiences and objects through vivid, precise description. But how can it be that she was also so powerfully drawn to surrealism, the avant-garde movement devoted to the unconscious, the irrational, the fantastic, and the power of dreams? This apparent contradiction is just one of the many paradoxes that make Bishop's work and life so fascinating, but it is also one of the most significant and generative.

While Bishop scholars have long acknowledged her formative, early encounter with surrealism, the question of how to interpret surrealism's importance to her poetry remains a vexing one.[1] According to the standard critical narrative, Bishop had a brief, somewhat misguided flirtation with surrealism while in Paris in the 1930s, an encounter which fueled a number of poems in her first book; however, she soon began to distance herself from the movement and her interest in it waned. Although she would continue to draw on some surrealist devices, she moved towards a more mature aesthetic, one committed to the daylight world of "real," everyday life. Although this narrative arc is a helpful starting point in understanding Bishop's work, it underestimates the complexity and duration of her links to surrealism, and downplays her ambivalent fascination with the possibilities and dangers it embodies.

This chapter will argue that Bishop's interest in surrealism is not merely a youthful enthusiasm, not just a passing indulgence in a fashionable trend that she definitively leaves behind. Indeed, surrealism, and the range of ideas and practices it represents for Bishop, struck a deep chord within her and remained a significant element of her poetic toolkit from beginning to end. Bishop's experiments with surrealistic techniques stretch from poems like "The Man-Moth," written in 1936, to "12 O'Clock News," a late tour de force of surrealist estrangement published four decades later in 1973. As Susan Rosenbaum notes, surrealism provided "essential grounding for her career-long exploration of the unconscious, irrational, and perverse; the experience of sleep, dream, and imagination; and the ubiquity of mixed feelings and ambiguity."[2]

This is not to say we should label Bishop a surrealist, far from it, but rather to acknowledge that, for Bishop, "the surrealist's way of looking got in the bone," as Thomas Travisano observes.[3] Furthermore, Bishop's poems are not just influenced by surrealism, but in some ways are *about* it, thematically. She carries on a lifelong debate with surrealism and its implications, composing poems which probe fraught tensions between the unconscious and the conscious mind, between dream and waking, freedom and control. Even Bishop's disavowals of surrealism are revealing, as they tell us a good deal about her work as a whole. "Some surrealist poetry terrifies me," she once wrote in a letter, "because of the sense of irresponsibility & *danger* it gives of the mind being 'broken down' – I want to produce the opposite effect."[4] For Bishop, then, surrealism seems to represent the enigmatic power of dreams and the wildness of the imagination, but it also triggers her deep fear of psychological breakdown, madness, and chaos; it thereby serves as a catalyst for the desperate thirst for order or stability one finds throughout her poetry. Like the third rail which the Man-Moth "does not dare" look at because it is an "unbroken draught of poison," "a disease / he has inherited the susceptibility to," surrealism stands as a seductive yet dangerous possibility haunting Bishop's entire body of work (*P* 17).

Highlighting Bishop's long-standing fascination with surrealism also allows for a reconfiguration of her place within the development of twentieth-century poetry, connecting her more firmly to avant-garde traditions both before and after her. Rather than assuming, as conventional wisdom often seems to hold, that she belongs on the "cooked" side of the infamous "raw versus cooked" divide that structures the period, foregrounding her ties to surrealism enables us to see a wilder, more experimental Bishop, a weirder and more adventurous poet than she is sometimes taken to be. It also allows her affinities with a range of avant-garde figures, from visual artists like Paul Klee, Kurt Schwitters, and Joseph Cornell, to writers like Gertrude Stein and John Ashbery, to come into sharper focus.[5]

Surrealism, one of the most influential avant-garde movements of the modernist period, was founded out of the ashes of Dada by André Breton and other French writers and artists in the early 1920s. Inspired by Freud and Marx, the surrealists called for writers and artists to free the mind from the chains of rationality and bourgeois consciousness through radical experimental techniques, such as the use of chance, automatic (spontaneous, uncensored) writing, free association, collaboration, the collaging together of unlike images or objects to create startling juxtapositions, and other methods. By circumventing the repressive force of logic and reason, they hoped they could foment a revolution, both aesthetic and political, against the status quo.

Bishop's attraction to surrealism can be traced back to her early fascination with dreams and her belief in the link between dreaming and poetry. In an interview with the *Paris Review*, Bishop recalls one of her "eccentricities" from her college days:

> I had a theory at that time that one should write down all one's dreams. That that was the way to write poetry. So I kept a notebook of my dreams and thought if you ate a lot of awful cheese at bedtime you'd have interesting dreams. I went to Vassar with a pot about this big – it did have a cover! – of Roquefort cheese that I kept in the bottom of my bookcase.[6]

In 1935, just after graduating from Vassar, Bishop travelled to France, where she "began translating French poetry, especially Rimbaud, as a way of disciplining her own verse."[7] As Brett Millier notes, "this was her first intimate acquaintance with the French surrealists, an important influence on her early poems, especially those she wrote in France."[8] In Paris that winter, "surrealism was much on her mind," as she "acquainted herself with the French avant-garde" and, as she told an interviewer, "read a lot of surrealist poetry and prose."[9] But she also saw some of the key players in the flesh, even if her inveterate shyness and social awkwardness kept her at a remove. She later recalled in a letter to Anne Stevenson that "In Paris I did meet a lot of famous people, I suppose, – even Picasso for a moment – and many more to look at, a good many painters, etc. – but that doesn't mean I ever exchanged any words with them except 'Enchantée' [. . .]. What was going on in Paris then was mostly surrealism, that I remember – André Breton & his gallery; I met Ernst, Giacometti, etc. – but – I just looked at them" (*Pr* 430).[10]

While in Paris, Bishop wrote a series of poems that represent her most direct attempt to incorporate surrealist themes and techniques, including "Paris, 7 A.M.," "Sleeping on the Ceiling," "Sleeping Standing Up," and "Cirque d'Hiver." During this period, Bishop was particularly taken with the artist Max Ernst and his work *Natural History* – a surrealist take on Darwin which Ernst created by means of "frottage," a method he developed in which images are created by chance by rubbing a pencil over a rough, textured surface. Bishop began making frottages herself, and was inspired to write at least two important early poems about Ernst's work,

"The Weed" and "The Monument." Poems such as these, which pay tribute to the powers of the imagination and probe the mysteries of sleep and dream, abound in her first book, *North & South*, which appeared in 1946.

Despite this fruitful early attraction to surrealism, Bishop was hardly a card-carrying member of the movement, and in fact rejected some of its more radical practices and ideas. As Richard Mullen argues in one of the first sustained critical examinations of this topic, Bishop actually "draws very little from the surrealists' extreme experiments in technique."[11] For example, Bishop is no devotee of automatic writing, chance procedures, disjunctive, fragmented form, collage, or other experiments with form that were so dear to the avant-garde. While "Bishop shares the surrealists' interest in the unconscious," Mullen argues, "she does not seek to subvert logical control, and she refuses to accept the 'split' between the roles of conscious and unconscious forces in our perception of the world. Unlike the surrealists, she does not endow the unconscious with a revolutionary power to remake experience."[12] But even while she views their formal, linguistic experimentation and heady political aspirations with suspicion, her poems, on the level of content and theme especially, return again and again to the intertwining of reality and dream so dear to the surrealist project.

Nonetheless, as her career began to take off, Bishop took pains to distance herself from the movement. In 1946, she asked her publisher not to use a comment Moore had made about Bishop's enthusiasm for Max Ernst on the back cover of her first book, *North & South*. "Although many years ago I once admired one of Ernst's albums," she wrote, "I believe that Miss Moore is mistaken about his ever having been an influence, and since I have disliked all of his painting intensely and am not a surrealist, I think it would be misleading to mention my name in connection with his" (*OA* 135). One could argue that, thanks to the anxiety of influence, Bishop doth protest too much (especially in light of such Ernst-inspired masterpieces as "The Monument"). Nevertheless, it is clearly important for her to let the world know she is "not a surrealist." At times, Bishop even uses "surrealist" as a negative critical term, especially as shorthand for poetry that lacks formal control or is overly playful and bizarre in imagery. For example, in 1942 Bishop tells Moore that she has begun reading the poetry of Pablo Neruda, who she had recently met in Mexico: "but I'm afraid it's not the kind I – nor you – like, very very loose, surrealist imagery, etc." (*OA* 108). Years later, in a 1959 letter to Robert Lowell, she writes that "there is one other poet I have found occasionally good – mostly bad in the surrealist way – but I think he's improving, and is very, very clever: Frank O'Hara" (*OA* 371).

In an often-discussed 1964 letter, Bishop responds to Anne Stevenson's questions about her use of "hallucinatory and dream material" by explaining her preference for "the always-more-successful surrealism of everyday life."[13] Much has been made of this rich phrase, with some reading it as a pithy explanation of her move away from the more orthodox surrealism of her early work ("I can't believe we are wholly irrational") towards a "postsurrealist" poetry devoted to uncovering strangeness within the quotidian.[14] For instance, Thomas Travisano takes this statement to mean that "for one kind of surrealist search she substitutes another [. . .] hers would be a casual, consciously controlled revision of surrealism based on freshly seeing the unlikely features of ordinary things."[15]

However, rather than a rejection or revision of surrealism itself, Bishop's comment seems more of an attempt to distinguish what interests her about surrealism from a version of it that traffics solely in fantastical or wholly imaginary realms. Surrealism itself was actually "a vital source of inspiration for thinking about everyday life," as Michael Sheringham argues in his study of everyday life theory and aesthetics. Even though "Surrealism can look like pure surrender to the world of dream," it "always sought to break down the barriers between waking life and dream life, the ordinary and the extraordinary."[16] As Sheringham observes, surrealism aims to expose "what is latent but elusive within the everyday co-ordinates of existence rather than what lies outside them."[17]

Like Wallace Stevens, one of her chief influences, Bishop worries that surrealism, in its more extreme form, can become too easy, a game in which the artist simply has to conjure up the weird and dream-like. As Stevens argued: "The essential fault of surrealism is that it invents without discovering. To make a clam play an accordion is to invent not to discover."[18] For both Stevens and Bishop, the key – actually inherent in the surrealist project itself – is to uncover what philosopher Stanley Cavell calls "the uncanniness of the ordinary," to discover the strangeness at the heart of the quotidian, a goal Bishop would relentlessly pursue for the rest of her career.[19]

One reason Bishop may have found surrealism so inspiring is that it gave her an opportunity to forge her own path as a poet, allowing her to diverge from the powerful, at times overbearing, example of her primary mentor, Marianne Moore. As Lynn Keller has argued, by exploring "the enigmatic internal realms of dream and consciousness," Bishop was "clearly distinguishing her poetics from Marianne Moore's."[20] Where Moore "associates clear poetic vision with the objective and rational methods of scientific observation" and dislikes "the element of unreason" prized by the movement, Bishop more enthusiastically embraces "the surrealists' desire to penetrate the unconscious by articulating fantasies and dreams."[21]

Perhaps for this reason, surrealism seemed to help Bishop jump-start her poetic career and hone her distinctive voice. Take, for example, "The Man-Moth," the much-loved 1936 work that Travisano calls her "first great poem."[22] Even the story of its origins betrays Bishop's debt to surrealist and avant-garde aesthetics: as her note informs us, the idea for the creature named in the title came from a "newspaper misprint for 'mammoth'" (*P* 16). This suggests that Bishop, like many avant-garde artists and writers before and after her, believes art can be inspired by chance and accident, that error and randomness can be fruitful for creativity. From this serendipitous spark of inspiration, Bishop weaves one of her many enigmatic parables, where weird and eerie events are relayed in a controlled and calm manner that recalls Kafka, as Lowell noted in his 1947 review of her first book.

In this case, Bishop invents a magical creature, half-man, half-insect, and places him in "a bizarre yet familiar world."[23] The hybrid nature of this impossible figure echoes surrealism's fascination with odd mixtures and juxtapositions, and its fondness for blurring the human and non-human. With the precision of the natural historian, Bishop tracks the Man-Moth's nighttime quest through the dreamlike city, as he "emerges / from an opening under the edge of one of the sidewalks / and nervously begins to scale the faces of the buildings," strives and fails to reach the moon, and sadly rides the subway "facing the wrong way" (*P* 16–17). The final stanza depicts a moving moment of contact between this bizarre visitor – an outcast who has often been read as a stand-in for the poet herself – and the everyday, urban world: "if you catch him," she instructs the reader, "hold a flashlight up to his eye." If you do so, a single tear will slip from the Man-Moth's dark pupil. "If you watch, he'll hand it over, / cool as from underground springs and pure enough to drink" (*P* 17). By staging this chilling encounter, Bishop forces us to reflect on the relationship between the uncanny and the "real," which collide here, in the dark space of the subway, in mysterious, endlessly rich ways.

Other early poems suggest different facets of Bishop's "surrealist inheritance."[24] For instance, "The Weed" closely mirrors surrealism's obsession with liberating the repressed erotic content and sexual desires latent in dreams and daily life alike. Inspired by the work of Max Ernst, Bishop's poem uses a plain-spoken and matter-of-fact voice to chronicle a disturbing, sensual dream in which a phallic weed bursts through the chest of the speaker and splits her heart in two: "I dreamed that dead, and meditating, / I lay upon a grave or bed [. . .] A slight young weed / had pushed up through the heart and its / green head was nodding on the breast" (*P* 22–23). This dream poem's intense and weird eroticism – after "the stem grew thick," liquid gushes forth, "drops fell upon my face / and in my eyes," and so on – owes a great deal to surrealism's preoccupation with sex and Freudian motifs (*P* 22–23).

Such poems are hardly confined to Bishop's first book, however, and recur repeatedly throughout her entire career, suggesting that surrealism was not merely a trendy stylistic quirk she had cast aside by the 1940s. Her second collection, *A Cold Spring* (1955), features the dream poem "Varick Street" (which she told Anne Stevenson is "almost all dream – just re-arranged a bit"), the topsy-turvy internal landscape of "Insomnia" ("that world inverted / where left is always right, / where the shadows are really the body"), and the whimsical, odd poem "Invitation to Miss Marianne Moore" (*P* 73; 68; 80).[25] In the latter, Bishop imagines Moore, her dear friend and modernist mentor, dressed all in black and adorned with a broad black hat, soaring over the city-scape of Manhattan like a figure in a painting by the surrealist artist Marc Chagall, who frequently depicted peasants flying over rooftops and city squares: "From Brooklyn, over the Brooklyn Bridge, on this fine morning, please come flying. / In a cloud of fiery pale chemicals, / please come flying, / to the rapid rolling of thousands of small blue drums / descending out of the mackerel sky" (*P* 80). The echo of Chagall is perhaps not incidental, as Bishop later made clear that this poem's roots lie in surrealism: it was inspired by Pablo Neruda's "Alberto Rojas Jiménez Comes Flying," a poem for a drowned poet which uses the phrase "you come flying" as a recurring refrain.[26]

Bishop adapts Neruda's poem for a surreal invocation of her own, casting Marianne Moore as a spirit, a muse, and figure she calls to for inspiration. Much like the Neruda poem that she took for a model, Bishop's is replete with fanciful, surreal imagery: Moore has "a black capeful of butterfly wings and bon-mots," she is "a daytime comet / with a long unnebulous train of words," and even the stone statues of "agreeable lions" on the steps outside the New York Public Library are "eager to rise and follow through the doors / up into the reading rooms" (*P* 80–81). As many have noted, the poem sustains a complex tone, part homage, part gentle criticism, as Bishop celebrates Moore's work and outlook even while tweaking her friend's prim and moralistic outlook. (For example, Moore wears "a slight censorious frown" and "Manhattan / is all awash with morals this fine morning" (*P* 80)).[27]

While some critics have rightly noted that Bishop at times echoes Moore's own style in the poem, the overall form and focus of the piece seem completely un-Moore-like.[28] Why would Bishop draw on the surrealist playbook – and turn to Neruda's work as a model – for this particular poem? Why would she depict her mentor, the master of precision and exactitude, the poet who had criticized "the element of unreason" in surrealism, as a kind of charming Mary Poppins of poetry surreally fluttering over the Brooklyn Bridge? Bishop seems to quite deliberately use surrealist methods to write a tribute to Moore as part of a subtle conversation or argument with her friend, and perhaps even a quarrel with herself. She again stages a tense dialogue between different facets of her own sensibility – on the one hand, the drive for accuracy and the careful observation of "facts and skyscrapers" (embodied in Moore herself), while on the other, the surrealistic flights of fancy and imagination, the "element of unreason," towards which she always found herself so forcefully drawn (*P* 80).

As I have suggested, the allure of surrealism never wanes for Bishop, and continues to drive her work to the very end. As late as her final book, *Geography III*, which appeared three years before her death, Bishop publishes one of her most unusual and experimental surrealism-inflected pieces, the prose poem "12 O'Clock News" (*P* 194–95). Like the surrealist French poet Francis Ponge, whose own prose poems describe everyday objects like a candle, a cigarette, and a piece of bread as if they are being viewed for the first time by an alien, Bishop creates a delightful, weird exercise in surrealist defamiliarization.[29] Turning the writer's own desk into what Paul Muldoon calls "a dreamscape," she takes up ordinary items one by one – a lamp, a typewriter, a stack of papers, an ashtray – and imaginatively magnifies and transforms them, so that the lamp becomes the moon that "seems to hang motionless in the sky," and a typed sheet of paper becomes "a large rectangular 'field,' hitherto unknown to us, obviously man-made [. . .] An airstrip? A cemetery?" (*P* 194).[30]

From Bishop's earliest poems to her last, the strange, irrational, dreamworld of surrealism is never far away, even when at first glance it may seem absent or distant. It always seems to lurk at the margins of even her most studiously empirical texts. As Susan Rosenbaum notes, "even a late, apparently realist narrative poem such as 'The Moose' can be read as 'a dreamy divagation [. . .] a gentle, auditory, / slow hallucination.'"[31] The threat of surrealism's "element of unreason" makes its presence felt in the blood-curdling scream of the mentally ill mother in Bishop's story "In the Village," in the "wretched" insane inmates who reside in "the house of Bedlam" in "Visits to St. Elizabeths," and in the terrifying, surreal visions that plague poor Crusoe ("dreams were the worst [. . .] I'd have / nightmares of other islands / stretching away from mine, infinities / of islands, islands spawning islands") (*P* 133; 185). And it reverberates in the primal moment recounted in her famous late masterpiece "In the Waiting Room," which depicts young Elizabeth experiencing an utterly destabilizing existential crisis: "the sensation of falling off / the round, turning world / into cold, blue-black space" (*P* 180). The poem deftly evokes a fleeting, quotidian moment in a dentist's office in which the world suddenly opens up to reveal a profound uncanniness at the heart of the ordinary: "I knew that nothing stranger / had ever happened, that nothing stranger could ever happen" (*P* 180). But it also narrates a turn away from that horrifying recognition of strangeness and instability: "Then I was back in it. / The War was on. Outside, / in Worcester, Massachusetts, / were night and slush and cold, / and it was still the fifth / of February, 1918" (*P* 181). The crucial, disorienting movement this poem tracks, from the stability of the daylight world to the surreal abyss and back again to a now-altered version of "reality," echoes across Bishop's entire body of work.

Without surrealism as an alluring but disturbing possibility, Bishop's poetry would lack a good deal of its tension. She seems to have needed its magnetic pull, and the terror of what it represented to her imagination, to balance and complicate her attentiveness to the ordinary and concrete. This mixture of qualities helps explain why her work has found admirers from across the gamut of American poetry, from avant-gardists to staunch upholders of tradition. One of her most distinguished, and most experimental, heirs, John Ashbery once noted:

> the extraordinarily intense loyalty her work inspires in writers of every sort – from poets like myself, sometimes considered a harebrained, homegrown surrealist whose poetry defies even the rules and logic of surrealism, and from a whole generation of young experimental poets to experimenters of a different sort and perhaps of a steadier eye, such as Robert Duncan and James Tate, and to poet-critics of undeniable authority like Marianne Moore, Randall Jarrell, Richard Wilbur and Robert Lowell. It shouldn't be a criticism leveled at Miss Bishop that her mind is capable of inspiring and delighting minds of so many different formations. We must see it as her strength, a strength whose singularity almost prevents us from seeing it.[32]

As Ashbery suggests, these paradoxes at the heart of Bishop's work – the irresolvable tension between avant-garde playfulness and technical mastery, between surrealist logic and rational clarity – are a major source of its power, its far-flung influence, and its enduring fascination.

Notes

1. Zachariah Pickard notes that "Bishop's relationship to surrealism is difficult and somewhat tangled" and refers to this issue as "the surrealist question" ("The Attack on Surrealism in Elizabeth Bishop's Darwin Letter," *Studies in the Humanities* 31.2 (2004), 121, 125). Among the many discussions of Bishop's relationship to surrealism, some of the most important and helpful include Richard Mullen, "Elizabeth Bishop's Surrealist Inheritance," *American Literature* 54.1 (1982), 63–80; Pickard's "The Attack on Surrealism"; Ernesto Suárez-Toste, "Une Machine À Coudre Manuelle: Elizabeth Bishop's 'Everyday Surrealism,'" *Mosaic* 33.2 (2000), 143–60; Susan McCabe, "Stevens, Bishop, and Ashbery: A Surrealist Lineage," *Wallace Stevens Journal* 22.2 (1998), 148–68; Thomas Travisano, *Elizabeth Bishop: Her Artistic Development* (Charlottesville: University of Virginia Press, 1988), 42–51; Bonnie Costello, *Elizabeth Bishop: Questions of Mastery* (Cambridge: Harvard University Press, 1991), 26–35; and Lorrie Goldensohn, *Elizabeth Bishop: The Biography of a Poetry* (New York: Columbia University Press, 1992), 118–34.
2. Susan Rosenbaum, "Bishop and the Natural World," in *The Cambridge Companion to Elizabeth Bishop*, ed. Angus Cleghorn and Jonathan Ellis (New York: Cambridge University Press, 2014), 70.
3. Travisano, *Elizabeth Bishop*, 45.
4. Quoted in Megan Marshall, *Elizabeth Bishop: A Miracle for Breakfast* (Boston: Mariner Books, 2017), 59.
5. For more on Bishop in relation to these figures, see Peggy Samuels, *Deep Skin: Elizabeth Bishop and Visual Art* (Ithaca, NY: Cornell University Press, 2010). On Bishop and Cornell, see Costello, *Elizabeth Bishop: Questions of Mastery*, 223–226. For more on Ashbery and Bishop, see Susan McCabe, "Stevens, Bishop, and Ashbery: A Surrealist Lineage," and Luke Carson, "John Ashbery's Elizabeth Bishop," *Twentieth Century Literature* 54.4 (2008), 448–471.
6. Elizabeth Spires, "Elizabeth Bishop: The Art of Poetry," *Paris Review* 80 (1981). Web.
7. Brett Millier, *Elizabeth Bishop: Life and the Memory of It* (Berkeley: University of California Press, 1993), 89.
8. Ibid., 89.
9. Ibid., 89; Travisano, *Elizabeth Bishop*, 42; Ashley Brown, "An Interview with Elizabeth Bishop," *Shenandoah* 17.2 (1966), 13.
10. For more on Bishop's formative experience in Paris, see Jonathan Ellis, *Art and Memory in the Work of Elizabeth Bishop* (Burlington, VT: Ashgate, 2006), 37.
11. Mullen, "Elizabeth Bishop's Surrealist Inheritance," 63.

12. Ibid., 64. See also Pickard, who argues it is a mistake to associate Bishop with surrealism at all, and insists that she fiercely "attacks it" from the start, and then "leaves it behind" (122).
13. Quoted in Mullen, "Elizabeth Bishop's Surrealist Inheritance," 64.
14. Ibid., 64; Travisano, *Elizabeth Bishop*, 11.
15. Travisano, *Elizabeth Bishop*, 45.
16. Michael Sheringham, *Everyday Life: Theories and Practices from Surrealism to the Present* (Oxford; New York: Oxford University Press, 2006), 66.
17. Ibid., 68.
18. Wallace Stevens, *Collected Poetry and Prose* (New York: Library of America, 1997), 919.
19. Stanley Cavell, *In Quest of the Ordinary: Lines of Skepticism and Romanticism* (Chicago: University of Chicago, 1988), 153–178.
20. Lynn Keller, *Remaking It New: Contemporary American Poetry and the Modernist Tradition* (Cambridge; New York: Cambridge University Press, 1987), 114.
21. Ibid., 114, 115.
22. Travisano, *Elizabeth Bishop* 30.
23. Ibid., 30.
24. Mullen, "Elizabeth Bishop's Surrealist Inheritance," 63.
25. Quoted in Costello, *Elizabeth Bishop: Questions of Mastery*, 27.
26. See Goldensohn, *Elizabeth Bishop: The Biography of a Poetry*, 136; and Laurel Kornhiser, "North and South: The Bishop-Neruda Connection," in *Jarrell, Bishop, Lowell, & Co.*, ed. Suzanne Ferguson (Knoxville: University of Tennessee Press, 2003), 217–38.
27. For example, see Joanne Diehl, who notes that Bishop was chagrined to learn that others felt that this "deeply ambivalent poem" was "mean" towards Moore, seemingly unable to see "the aggression so clearly manifested in the poem," *Elizabeth Bishop and Marianne Moore: The Psychodynamics of Creativity* (Princeton, NJ: Princeton University Press, 1993), 50. Bonnie Costello writes that "some have read Bishop's tribute to Moore, 'Invitation to Miss Marianne Moore' as ambivalent or even subversive, but we might rather say that it is a tribute aware of their different temperaments and perspectives," "Bishop and the Poetic Tradition," in *The Cambridge Companion to Elizabeth Bishop*, 92.
28. Keller, *Remaking It New*, 106–07.
29. On Bishop and Ponge, see Mullen, "Elizabeth Bishop's Surrealist Inheritance," 71–72.
30. Paul Muldoon, *The End of the Poem* (New York: Farrar, Straus and Giroux, 2006), 106.
31. Rosenbaum, "Bishop and the Natural World," 70.
32. John Ashbery, "Second Presentation of Elizabeth Bishop," *World Literature Today* 51.1 (1977), 8.

CHAPTER 15

Modernism

Philip McGowan

"I've never studied 'Imagism' or 'Transcendentalism' or any isms consciously. I just read all the poetry that came my way, old and new" (*PPL* 858). Resisting the idea that her reading occurred in tandem with formal categorizations of a writer's work, Bishop neatly sidesteps classifications, including the modish movements that defined modernism. "The three qualities I admire in the poetry I like best are: *Accuracy, Spontaneity, Mystery*" (*PPL* 703), she writes in "Writing Poetry is an unnatural act . . ." before listing Herbert, Hopkins, and Baudelaire as her three "favorite" poets. Regarding modernism: for Bishop it existed as both an aesthetic inheritance and a personal reality, marked as much by her relationships with particular figures such as Marianne Moore, T. S. Eliot, and Ezra Pound as it was by her own carefully charted course between the contours of modernist, and later, aesthetic movements. Add to this the heteronormative gender politics central to Pound and Eliot's ideas about modernist aesthetics in particular and modernism becomes a considerably more complicated legacy, if that is the right term, for a poet such as Bishop to inherit.

Indeed, to identify this writer who was born in 1911 in Worcester, Massachusetts[1] with one or other aspect of modern or postmodern poetry is not immediately straightforward for two related if parallel sets of facts: Bishop's own transitive life, and modernism's refusal to be an easily defined, monolithic entity that had precise start and end dates. According to Marjorie Perloff, "modernism remains unfinished, a project aborted first by World War I and the two great Totalitarianisms of the 1930s, and then by World War II and the ensuing Cold War."[2] Elsewhere, she rejects the "tired dichotomy that has governed our discussion of twentieth-century poetry for much too long"[3]: the split between modernism and postmodernism. It's particularly clear that such a dichotomy neither appealed to nor instructed Bishop's personal or professional interests. Reading the various strains of twentieth-century American poetry as a modulating continuum, Bishop navigates the spaces between each poetic offshoot as they rose, then fell. That said, Bishop's engagement with modernism, particularly some of its main exponents, was at times forensic even if she held their more theoretical aspects at arm's length.

The correspondence with Anne Stevenson (January 1963–November 1965) outlines Bishop's thoughts on individual writers and the broader fields of twentieth-century literature. She name-checks a series of modernist authors, whether poets or fiction writers, navigating for herself a route that would set her just apart from "Miss Moore's generation from about 1928 on" (*PPL* 845) but, equally, from considerable swathes of her own generation. Assembling the map of Bishop's favoured writers while also including space for the acknowledged literary titans and primary aesthetic influences of the period produces an archipelagic miscellany reminiscent of the variegated terrains mapped in "Crusoe in England" (1971). In his invaluable *Modern Poetry After Modernism*, James Longenbach highlights Bishop's "complicated relationship to the political and intellectual climate of the thirties" as a contributing factor to her "formal idiosyncrasy (her desire to bend traditional poetic forms without breaking them)." Having entered Vassar as a student in 1930, Bishop would interview Eliot in May 1933 for the *Vassar Miscellany* with the result that, for Longenbach, "her sense of her own relationship to modernism was consequently not so clearly or comfortably antagonistic."[4] What is clear from reading Bishop on other authors and artists is that she retained an admiration for, even a sense of loyalty to, individual writers and practitioners from across different time periods irrespective of any association they might have with a specific aesthetic movement. Whatever inheritance Bishop recognized, it was as much inflected by Romantics (Wordsworth) or Victorians (Hopkins) or the mid-nineteenth-century Transcendentalists[5] as it was by advocates for different strains of modernist experimentation.

Bishop's wish not to be identified with particular groups or individuals comes through in the Stevenson letters, whether as exasperation or as strategically placed commentary. "I am rather weary of always being compared to, or coupled with, Marianne" (*PPL* 842) she tells Stevenson on 18 March 1963, "proof that reviewers really very rarely pay much attention to what they're reading & just repeat each other" (*PPL* 843). Her next letter, begun two days later, goes into considerably more detail about the writers she admires and from whom she "undoubtedly learned enormously": "I think of Marianne, Cummings (we shared the same maid in N.Y. for several years), Dr Williams, Crane, Frost, as Heroes" (*PPL* 845). Remarking on those writers considered to be her peers – "my 'contemporary' poets," she writes, pointedly including quotation marks around "contemporary" to question quite how contemporaneous they might actually be with her, or she with them – Bishop questions her inclusion in any sequential ordering of the poetic generations: "it is odd how I often feel myself to be a late-late Post World War I generation-member, rather than a member of the Post World War II generation" (*PPL* 846). The difference she indicates is intriguing: not part of a postmodern generation, but also not firmly identified with high modernism either, Bishop carves out a space for herself between categories, moving fluently from one to another but never defined wholly within the critical parameters or formal constraints of any single group.

Alongside Moore, Wallace Stevens was the significant figure in Bishop's early development, and his poetry and essays feature as regular discussion topics in her correspondence with Moore.[6] He was "more of an influence" than William Carlos Williams, she readily acknowledges to Stevenson – "[a]t college I knew 'Harmonium' almost by heart. ('Wading at Wellfleet' I believe is the only poem that shows this influence much.) But I got tired of him and now find him romantic and thin" (*PPL* 862) – though Barbara Page, for example, reads Bishop's "The Monument" (1939) as her version of Stevens' *Owl's Clover* (1936).[7] Moore had more direct opportunities to be an influence, encouraging Bishop to be more experimental with her first collection, *North & South* (1946), by including prose sections[8]: it would take Bishop almost two decades to do this with her story "In The Village" bisecting the "Brazil" and "Elsewhere" poems in the first edition of *Questions of Travel* (1965). The Moore–Bishop relationship was "playful and provocative, as well as careful and reticent,"[9] as Linda Anderson notes, but it adapted as Bishop's writing career retained an independent course between the multiple nodes of modernist writing. In Moore, Bishop recognized aspects of Hopkins' prose rhythms but would afford herself freer methods of structure and organization: Longenbach astutely characterizes Bishop's modulation of Moore's poems, which "transform description into a structural principle," into Bishop's own works which "turn the process of describing into a structural principle."[10]

Bishop adopted a more circumspect position when it came to Williams. Like Pound's work, she was uncomfortable with Williams' "diffuseness" believing that "both he & Pound, and their followers, would be vastly improved if one could lean on a sense of 'system' in their work somewhere" (*PPL* 862). From Bishop's comments on other writers in her essays, letters, and reviews, she was not a fan of poetic experiment just for poetic experiment's sake. In 1970 she noted that "[a]s for concrete poetry, I like only

Cummings – a brilliant and good humored poet, one who really had something to say. Concrete poetry that other poets make, I find uninteresting."[11] Even so, despite this late praise for cummings, her review of his collection *Xaipe* (1950) two decades previously is mixed to say the least: while acknowledging "he is still playing his game and winning it" she laments several of the more forced moments of cummings' "obscene and epigrammatic" (*PPL* 688) humour in the volume. To Bishop, cummings' circumscribed and self-regulated domain demonstrates the confines of adhering to one mode of writing which, while demarcating the realm of his success, simultaneously highlights its limits.

In terms of her own work, and with *North & South* appearing in August 1946, one might assume that Bishop, along with her "contemporary" peers, would by dint of timing be direct inheritors of modernism or be the ones tasked to write "the sort of poetry that replaces modernism," as Randall Jarrell formulated it.[12] However, whether it is in the 1930s or the 1970s, Bishop pulls towards earlier exemplars of writers that interest her: "read a lot of poetry – all the time – and *not* 20th-century poetry" she advises a Miss Pierson in May 1975; "read Campion, Herbert, Pope, Tennyson, Coleridge – anything at all almost that's any good, from the past [. . .]. Then the great poets of our own century – Marianne Moore, Auden, Wallace Stevens" (*OA* 596). With advice that mentions poets from different time periods and that makes no mention of defined schools or styles of writing, Bishop embodies Thomas Travisano's argument that she, Jarrell, Robert Lowell, and John Berryman (Travisano's mid-century quartet) were "particularly reluctant to make master statements of aesthetic doctrine" and held an "abiding suspicion of and resistance to 'totalizing' ideologies of every stripe." The "shared determination" of this loosely aligned quartet "to bypass or unmake modernism's impersonal aesthetic" developed out of "acutely felt differences with their galaxy of modernist mentors, whose often avowedly 'reactionary' critical and political dictums"[13] proved a barrier to their own articulations of independent and new poetic positions. For Bishop, the pervasive sense is of a writer preferring not to be part of any school or to be identified with any one poet, remaining apart in her own perfectly useful seclusion. Accepting the Neustadt International Prize for Literature in 1976, she invokes the figure of the sandpiper from her 1962 poem of that name to articulate this very sense: "all my life I have lived and behaved very much like that sandpiper – just running along the edges of different countries and continents, 'looking for something'" (*PPL* 731–32).

Rather than searching among the various modernist grains offered by others, it would be to her own theories that Bishop would return.

Longenbach notes that her career "demonstrates not so much a linear development as a continual unfolding of the possibilities inherent in positions she articulated early on"[14] in the essays she wrote while at Vassar, each one as crafted and engaging as her poetry. Of particular interest here are "Time's Andromedas" (1933), "Gerard Manley Hopkins: Notes on Timing in His Poetry" (1934), and "Dimensions for a Novel" (1934), the last of which highlights how Bishop's first theoretical consideration of modernism focussed on prose, not poetry.[15] Return and revision define Bishop's writing, as "North Haven" (1978) notably summarizes: "Nature repeats herself, or almost does: / *repeat, repeat, repeat; revise, revise, revise*" (*P* 210). Nature almost repeats itself, daily: each successive day brings new phenomena for the sandpiper poet to discover within a wider cycle of repeated order. Stevens similarly concludes his 1941 Princeton lecture "The Noble Rider and the Sound of Words": "a wave is a force and not of the water of which it is composed, which is never the same."[16] For Bishop, the creative process mirrors this: like modernism, it is the latest instantiation of what it means to produce poetry in the world today.

Taking its title from Hopkins' "Andromeda" (1879) – a poem that, according to Paul Mariani, Hopkins used to resist the "new moral anarchy"[17] of Whitman, Swinburne, and the New Aestheticism of the 1870s – Bishop's essay "Time's Andromedas" comprehensively analyses the use of time in modernist writers such as Woolf, Joyce, and Proust, though her main critical focus falls on Gertrude Stein and Dorothy Richardson, "two women novelists, widely different yet both 'modern,' 'experimenters,' [who are] both excessively time-conscious" (*PPL* 645). Bishop's essays are a mine of astutely positioned and persuasively argued observations on literature, and "Time's Andromedas" develops important ideas on modernist techniques, particularly in relation to time. Yet, even before the essay's critical work proper begins, Bishop describes the evening migrations of birds in a simply stunning passage, first through the auditory experience of their flight and then in a detailed description of their regular, if arbitrary, formation. Their "multitude of small sounds" provides "a faintly rhythmic irregularity [. . .] resembling the retreat of innumerable small waves, lake-waves, rustling on sand" (*PPL* 642), and she detects in their flight an analogy for her discussion of time and modernist literary techniques:

> [B]y watching one bird, then another, I saw that some flew a little slower than others, some were trying to get ahead and some flew at an individual

> rubato; each seemed a variation, and yet altogether my eyes were deceived into thinking them perfectly precise and regular. I watched closely the spaces between the birds. It was as if there was an invisible thread joining all the outside birds and within this fragile net-work they possessed the sky [. . .]. It came to me that the flying birds were setting up, far over my head, a sort of time-pattern, or rather patterns, all closely related, all minutely varied, and yet all together forming the *migration*[.] (*PPL* 642; emphasis in original)

The flight and formations of the migrating birds both arrest *and* create time, variously and collectively within the one overall movement: as analogy for the modulations within literary movements, and within modernism in particular, this perfectly introduces an essay that measures Stein and Richardson against predecessors like Dickens, Turgenev, and Andersen. Flying birds, time, and motion become recurring emblems in Bishop's work: they are notably connected to Moore in Bishop's 1948 poem "For M. M." (later retitled "Invitation to Miss Marianne Moore" when published in *A Cold Spring* in 1955): the request to the most direct modernist influence on her early work to migrate, however briefly, from Brooklyn to Manhattan, while humorous, contains within its structure the motif of birds flying, most notably Bishop's description of Moore's "grammar that suddenly turns and shines / like flocks of sandpipers flying" (*P* 81). Mention of sandpipers sparks simultaneous forward and backward associations across Bishop's corpus: back to a 1933 poem "The Flood" in which the footprints of "two sand-pipers" (*P* 217) signal the poem's only specified life form; and forward to "Sandpiper" in which the titular bird experiences a combination of Stevens' wave of water "which is never the same" and John Ashbery's "recurring wave / Of Arrival"[18] breaking on a shoreline, the bird identified as "a student of Blake" (*P* 129) attuning its romantic sensibilities to the ever-changing yet ever-constant task of sifting meaning and beauty from rhythmic chaos.

For a gay female poet, with a transnational upbringing, who would live in Brazil for sixteen years of her life, the multiplicities of modernism's incarnations would, potentially, have offered numerous avenues of investigation and possibility, be that the gendered modernisms of Stein or H. D., the more form-based literary innovations of James Joyce, Eliot, and Pound, or the prevalent examples in Surrealism, Expressionism, Cubism, or Dadaism across the art world. Bishop regularly references Paul Klee, whom she admired, or Pablo Neruda, for whom she demonstrated a more selective regard, in her letters to Moore and Stevenson, though she is careful to note that she was "interested in surrealism long before I met [Neruda]" (*PPL* 857). Indeed, a postscript on the subject of the "surrealism of everyday life" being "always more successful, – or more amazing – than any they can think up" (*PPL* 864) completes the Darwin letter as Bishop recounts seeing Orson Welles' "absolutely *dreadful*" *O Processo* (*The Trial*, 1962).

Whichever variant is under discussion, modernism offers itself as a home for certain aspects of Bishop's work but not for others. Steven Gould Axelrod is not alone in characterizing her as disruptive, both in terms of her poetic subjects and her sexuality. Axelrod's Bishop is a writer who epitomizes his Cold War–era poets, sharing with Lowell and Allen Ginsberg a particular space of "ruptures and resistances."[19] His classification of Cold War poetry as part of, yet apart from, the wider currents of modernist and postmodernist debates of poetic practice rethinks the very categories that it both reinforces and revises, disrupting standard distillations of the twentieth century into a linear progression from modernism into postmodernism. Axelrod carefully plots this distinct category, but whether it helpfully accommodates Elizabeth Bishop is another question entirely. As the schools and groups proliferated in the twentieth century, the Venn diagram of allegiances and associations between poets and their forms of poetry became an increasingly convoluted map of cross-currents and poetic narratives and counter narratives. Following Perloff's argument that modernism is better understood as a returning cycle of change within an overall drive towards order aligns its movement with that of the oceans and the tides, constantly repeating themselves in new, individual waves that make their mark upon the waiting shore. Bishop, the sandpiper/student on the shoreline, focuses intently on "the spaces [. . .] between them" (*P* 129), navigating a path for herself between and through each new wave.

In 1950, the trajectories of American poetry (whether in the wake of modernism or as a continuation of its strategies of innovation – it was the year, after all, that Olson's "Projective Verse" essay was published) are written into Bishop's own comments on the contemporary poetry scene and on theories circulating within critical circles. In the short commentary "It All Depends" she offers both latitude for the airing of her own opinions and also perspective on the necessity of applying theoretical models to poetry. "To all but two of the questions raised here my answer is *it all depends*": so begins her response to the questionnaire in *Mid-Century American Poets* (1950), edited by John Ciardi, a volume that featured the work of thirteen poets including, among others, Lowell, Muriel Rukeyser, Delmore Schwartz, John Holmes, Karl Shapiro, and Bishop herself. Typically provisional, and astutely contingent, Bishop queries the relevance of theories in the interpretation of any poem – "no matter what theories one may have, I doubt very much that they are in one's mind at the moment of writing a poem or that there is even a physical possibility that they could be" – and she resists the "pretentious and deadly" "highbrow" debates about poetry that are "reminiscent of those places along the coast where warnings are posted telling one not to walk too near the edge of the cliffs because they have been undermined by the sea and may collapse at any minute."[20] Such interpretative drives produce a continual categorizing of poetry that destabilizes the original, independent, creative endeavour of any individual poem. The cliff-edge warning signs prove more deterrent than incentive, and Bishop's analogy is both instructive and well-chosen: we walk the cliff edges *because* of the view provided of the sea even though, over time, the sea's eroding force will alter the solid ground on which we believed we stood.

Ciardi's volume is a curious document: the prefatory note to Bishop's contribution, for example, claims she was "born and brought up in Maine,"[21] while modernism as a term is almost wholly absented from the book. Schwartz cuts through Ciardi's forced editorial positioning by noting that "any modern poet exists in an inescapable relationship to all modern *and* modernist poetry written since Baudelaire."[22] In "Two Problems in Writing of Poetry," Schwartz warns that the poet who ignores the "complicated" legacy of modernism "is depriving himself of what is an important part of his inheritance as a poet, and also a powerful presence in the minds of everyone who is capable of reading poetry."[23] He is surely correct. Whether for better or worse, modernism is a fact of the twentieth-century poetry landscape: to argue otherwise is fallacy. When considering Bishop in relation to modernism – what her aesthetic or critical allegiances may or may not have been, how her own poetry was either influenced by, or exhibited the influence of, so-called modernist poets – she herself pinpoints a central truth: it really does all depend on which Bishop one is discussing. Whether it is the young Bishop who attended Vassar and interviewed Eliot or the Bishop who, in the same period, would acknowledge Stevens as the major influence on her earliest writing; whether it is the Bishop who, while the Poetry Consultant at the Library of Congress between September 1949 and the summer of 1950, arranged recordings of Frost and also visited the incarcerated Pound at St. Elizabeths Hospital in Washington, DC, or the Bishop who would live in Brazil between 1951 and 1967 immersing herself in the aesthetic and literary currents of a radically different cultural environment. Just as there are multiple modernisms, there are multiple Bishops, "contradictory, complex, incompatible, but gloriously so,"[24] as Jonathan Ellis reminds us.

In her 1966 interview with Ashley Brown, while discussing the influence living in Brazil might have upon her work and her engagement with an intellectual milieu away from New York in particular, Bishop notes how English poetry and the Portuguese poetry of Brazil are divergent entities and she roots this division – "our poetry went off in a different direction much earlier" – in specifically American experiments with modernism:

> what happened with Eliot and Pound as early as 1910 – modernism. The Brazilians' poetry is still much more formal than ours – it's farther from the demotic. It is true, of course, that they had a *modernismo* movement in 1922, led by Mario de Andrade and others. But they still don't write how they speak. And I suppose they have still never quite escaped from romanticism.[25]

Bishop pinpoints modernism, and particularly the variants espoused by Eliot and Pound, as the catalyst for a new poetic methodology and a possible fracturing of the previous orthodoxies in poetry in English. Her introduction to *An Anthology of Twentieth-Century Brazilian Poetry* (1972), co-written with Emanuel Brasil, highlights some of the moves made towards a modernist poetry in Brazil from the 1920s forward, shifting from the more formal and old-fashioned attitudes of the nineteenth century towards a more colloquial poetic that attempted "a complete honesty, bringing the anguish and conflicts of the period into poetry for the first time" (*PPL* 726). Bishop's immersion in the literary scenes of Latin America expands the transnational perspectives of her wider literary portfolio. In terms of the geopolitics of the period, it disrupts Axelrod's category of Cold War poetry, and further layers of complexity are added when her translations of modernist poets such as Octavio Paz, Manuel Bandeira, Carlos Drummond de Andrade, and Joaquim Cardozo are brought into the discussion of Bishop's relationship with modernism. Whichever Bishop is under discussion, what is crystal clear is Bishop's own detailed understanding of the nuances and variations across multiple national, poetic environments.

Bishop's well-established engagement with contemporary visual cultures is brought to the fore in her translation of Paz's "Objects & Apparitions" (1974), a poem positioned at the intersection of modern artistic theories and praxis, including artist and filmmaker Joseph Cornell's avant-garde assemblage techniques, Paz's Mexican distillation of the currents of Anglo-American forms of modernism (the early influence of Eliot on his work was key here), and Bishop's own engagement with each of these components in a poem that assembles "Monuments to every moment" (*P* 201). When Bishop notes that "out of your ruins you have made creations," echoes of

Eliot's "fragments I have shored against my ruins"[26] sound briefly in an aesthetic environment that ensures, for Paz and also for Bishop, that "inside your boxes / my words became visible for a moment." The correspondences with Bishop's "The Monument" amplify that poem's cross-cutting of poetry, sculpture, and modernist conceptualizations of meaning and the impersonality of the artist in relation to the artwork. The monument's instability within Bishop's poem, continually in the act of becoming itself while keeping what "cannot have been intended to be seen" (*P* 27) within its interior, is a performance of form and simultaneously of meaning, neither of which remain constant, either within the poem or the monument itself. Centrally, both poem and monument engage the motions of time within their dual acts of becoming and their paralleled modes of interpretation.

Bishop's awareness of the shifts and divides within and between poetic generations and literary movements is a facet of much of her writing, particularly her letters; that said, there persists within her discussions of other writers either a reticence to be identified, or a clear determination not to be associated, with any particular brand of 'modern' poetry. For Bishop, the questions of allegiance to a specific or rigidly conformist idea of poetry were not the first ones that concerned her, whether she was in New York, Brazil, or elsewhere. Like her sandpiper, "The roaring alongside" that characterized the debates about modernism she took for granted; instead it was "the spaces [. . .] between them" (*P* 129) that drew her attention in precisely the same way that the Bishop of "Time's Andromedas" "watched closely the spaces between the birds" (*PPL* 642) to chart the modulations inherent within each successive wave of timely arrivals.

Notes

1. With numerous variations across forms, genres, and cultural and social practices, modernism had multiple catalysing impulses. The influence that psychoanalysis's emergence had on the shaping of personal and public consciousness in the early 1900s falls outside this chapter's immediate remit. However, in September 1909, seventeen months before Bishop was born, Sigmund Freud delivered five lectures on "The Origin and Development of Psychoanalysis" and Carl Jung three on "The Association Method" (including a case of female child psychology) as part of Clark University's twentieth-anniversary celebrations as the second graduate school in the USA. Clark University is located in Worcester, Massachusetts.
2. Marjorie Perloff, "'Pound/Stevens: Whose Era?' Revisited," *Wallace Stevens Journal* 26.2 (Fall 2002), 139.

3. Marjorie Perloff, *21st Century Modernism: The "New Poetic"* (Oxford: Blackwell, 2002), 2.
4. James Longenbach, *Modern Poetry after Modernism* (New York and Oxford: Oxford University Press, 1995), 38, 47, 9.
5. "I also feel that Cal (Lowell) and I in our very different ways are both descendents from the Transcendentalists – but you may not agree" (*PPL* 846), she writes to Stevenson in March 1963.
6. Angus Cleghorn, "Bishop's 'Wiring Fused': 'Bone Key' and 'Pleasure Seas,'" in *Elizabeth Bishop in the 21st Century*, ed. Angus Cleghorn, Bethany Hicok, and Thomas Travisano (Charlottesville and London: University Press of Virginia, 2012), 71.
7. See Barbara Page, "Off-Beat Claves, Oblique Realities: The Key West Notebooks of Elizabeth Bishop," in *Elizabeth Bishop: The Geography of Gender*, ed. Marilyn May Lombardi (Charlottesville and London: University Press of Virginia, 1993), 196–211.
8. Moore makes this suggestion in a letter to Bishop on 1 March 1937, as noted by David Kalstone, *Becoming a Poet: Elizabeth Bishop with Marianne Moore and Robert Lowell* (New York: Farrar, Straus and Giroux, 1989), 77.
9. Linda Anderson, *Elizabeth Bishop: Lines of Connection* (Edinburgh: Edinburgh University Press, 2013), 17.
10. Longenbach, *Modern Poetry after Modernism*, 25.
11. Regina Colônia, "Poetry as a Way of Life," in *Conversations with Elizabeth Bishop*, ed. George Monteiro (Jackson: University Press of Mississippi, 1996), 52.
12. Randall Jarrell, "A Note on Poetry," in *Kipling, Auden & Co.: Essays and Reviews 1935–1964* (New York: Farrar, Straus and Giroux, 1980), 51.
13. Thomas Travisano, *Midcentury Quartet: Bishop, Lowell, Jarrell, Berryman, and the Making of a Postmodern Aesthetic* (Charlottesville and London: University Press of Virginia, 1999), 26, 9, 15.
14. Longenbach, *Modern Poetry after Modernism*, 27.
15. Ibid., 24.
16. Wallace Stevens, "The Noble Rider and The Sound of Words," in *The Necessary Angel* (New York: Vintage Books, 1951), 35. Stevens here is discussing the force of nobility, "a violence from within that protects us from a violence without. It is the imagination pressing back against reality" (36).
17. Paul L. Mariani, "Hopkins' 'Andromeda' and the New Aestheticism," *Victorian Poetry* 11.1 (1973), 39.
18. John Ashbery, "Self-Portrait in a Convex Mirror," in *Self-Portrait in a Convex Mirror: Poems* (Harmondsworth: Penguin, 1976), 68.
19. Steven Gould Axelrod, "Between Modernism and Postmodernism: The Cold War Poetics of Bishop, Lowell, and Ginsberg," *Pacific Coast Philology* 42.1 (2007), 2.

20. Elizabeth Bishop, "It All Depends," in *Mid-Century American Poets*, ed. John Ciardi (New York: Twayne, 1950), 267; emphasis in original. (This short commentary is also published in *PPL*, 686–87.)
21. Ibid.
22. Delmore Schwartz, "Two Problems in Writing of Poetry," *Mid-Century American Poets*, 284; emphasis in original.
23. Ibid., 284.
24. Jonathan Ellis, "Introduction: Incompatible Bishops?", in *Reading Elizabeth Bishop* (Edinburgh: Edinburgh University Press, 2019), 14.
25. Ashley Brown, "An Interview with Elizabeth Bishop" in *Conversations with Elizabeth Bishop*, ed. George Monteiro (Jackson: University of Mississippi Press, 1996), 19.
26. T. S. Eliot, "The Waste Land," in *The Complete Poems and Plays* (London: Faber and Faber, 1989), 75.

CHAPTER 16

Mid-Century Poetics

Kamran Javadizadeh

I believe in swimming, flying, and crawling, and burrowing.
(Elizabeth Bishop to Robert Lowell, July 27, 1960, *WIA* 335)

When Elizabeth Bishop died in 1979, James Merrill fondly remembered his late friend's aversion to shoptalk: "Why talk *letters* with one's gifted colleagues? They too would want, surely, to put aside work in favor of a new baby to examine, a dinner to shop for and cook, sambas, vignettes."[1] Merrill recalls both Bishop's geniality and her reluctance to allow work to displace, in conversation, the position properly accorded to life. In his account, Bishop's reticence on matters of poetics was of a piece with her famous modesty and extended to her professional persona. In an era in which most poets held academic positions from which they could be expected to make critical pronouncements, Bishop spent nearly two decades in Brazil – far from the North American academic poetry world.

The thousands of miles that Bishop put between herself and the capitals of mid-century US poetry – a geographic distance that literalized a temperamental one – should not be taken, however, to signal a lack of interest in the questions of poetics raised within them. Rather, Bishop's choice to observe, from a distance, developments in the literary scene that she had left behind aligned with her preference to develop her own poetics in shifting, idiosyncratic, and provisional relation to the schools of poetry that were consolidating back home. The archive we should consult when we want to give an overview of Bishop's relation to mid-century poetics is not, therefore, a collection of essays or lectures, interviews or manifestos. Instead, Bishop thought through the questions raised by mid-century poetics in the more informal genre of correspondence, which routinely thematized the remoteness of its writer.

"Living this far away," Bishop wrote, "I often feel there were two of me, one who stayed in the U.S.A. and one who came to Brazil, and that the one who stayed in the U.S. may well have died without my knowing it."[2] She wrote that sentence on a sheet of canary-yellow onionskin in Rio de Janeiro on October 18, 1962, folded it in half and again in thirds, and sealed it in an envelope. Over the next several days, that envelope flew north, all the way to Newton Lower Falls, Massachusetts, where it was opened and read by Anne Sexton. Letters made it possible for Bishop's feeling – of existing in two places at once, both in touch with and at a remove from a fractious poetry world back home – to enjoy its own kind of occasional truth.

The mid-century arguments about poetry that were most meaningful for Bishop plotted their positions along two axes: Was poetry essentially impersonal or was it the genre of introspective meditation? Was metrical form a precondition for poetry or did formal constraint deaden the creative impulse and reduce *poetry* to mere *verse*? What emerges from Bishop's correspondence is a belief in a kind of art that could be sufficiently flexible and intricate, diverting and personal, to resemble the forms of life – the sambas, the vignettes – in favor of which it might otherwise have been set aside.

*

Letters made it possible for Bishop's thinking about poetry to move in and out of technical and literary questions, both evading the need to make her commitments more than provisional and allowing her to imply that questions of poetics might be raised and answered by daily life. Nowhere is this clearer than in Bishop's response to a letter in which Robert Lowell had confessed, "By the way, meter is a puzzle to me now," describing how he was attracted, on the one hand, to the pleasures of writing and reading metrical verse and yet aware, on the other, of how little such pleasures had to do with "experience or intuition," which he took to be the domain of free verse (*WIA* 331). Bishop's response came at the end of her letter:

> What you say about meter: well, I have loads of thoughts on the subject and think I'll have to write again tomorrow. I have a theory now that all the arts are growing more and more "literary"; that it is a late stage, perhaps a decadent stage, and that un-metrical verse is more "literary" and necessarily self-conscious than metrical – If I were Shapiro I'd write a book about it. (And have you read *Art & Illusion*? by one Gombrich? – it is fascinating.) I find it is time to go to market. What kind of plan do you have for your opera or is it an opera? Now you must teach Harriet to swim – or have you – it is just the age to learn. I believe in swimming, flying, and crawling, and burrowing. (*WIA* 335)

The poet who Bishop wasn't, by her own account, was Karl Shapiro, whose recent *In Defense of Ignorance* (1960) had offered no shortage of strident opinions about the state of poetry. "Isn't poor Karl's a dull roar of bombast," Lowell would reply (*WIA* 338).

Bishop avoided Shapiro's bombast – and his dullness – by thinking through Lowell's quandary in epistolary form, which allowed her to defer a proper exposition of her thoughts until "tomorrow," an occasion for writing at greater length that both she and Lowell must have known was unlikely to come, and thereby gave her the freedom to try out a theory about meter and literary history without committing to it or following it to its conclusion. Bishop implies that Lowell's understanding of the relative cultural meanings of metrical and free verse was out of date.[3] No longer was it the case, in 1960, that literariness was signaled by the ornament of verse. Whereas Pound had once instructed modernist poets to abjure the "sequence of a metronome"[4] and took credit for "break[ing] the pentameter,"[5] nearly half a century later, free verse had become its own kind of literary convention, just as tightly allied with what it meant to be "literary" as elaborate meters had once been for, say, Swinburne. Bishop's sense that she and Lowell were working in "a late stage" implied a cyclical view of literary history, which meant that a poet who aspired, in 1960, once again to "make it new" would have to negotiate the competing attractions of meter and colloquiality not as modernists had done but in correspondingly novel ways.

Having offered this insight, however, Bishop doesn't prescribe an updated constellation of metrical and free verse. Instead, she offers: first, a digression into an adjacent field ("have you read *Art & Illusion*?"); second, the interruption of daily commerce ("I find it is time to go to market"); third, a follow-up question about one of Lowell's new projects ("What kind of plan do you have for your opera or is it an opera?"); and, finally, parenting advice for the father of a young child ("I believe in swimming, flying, and crawling, and burrowing"). At first glance, these seem like non sequiturs, ways of changing – or of dropping – the subject.[6] But Bishop's serial beliefs, which punctuate her speculative paragraph on meter, suggest not only pastimes for young children but also ways of moving through the world – or through a poem. Swimming, flying, crawling, burrowing: each conjures a mode of poetic progress. Swimming requires a regular stroke to propel oneself through an immersive environment; the most common strokes suggest analogues in traditional, accentual-syllabic English meters. Flying promises freedom from gravity, the ability to move omnidirectionally, constrained only by the limits of one's fancy; its analogue is the open promise of *vers libre*. Crawling suggests unbroken contiguity between origin and destination; what crawling sacrifices in speed and freedom it gains in contact with the world; crawling resembles the minutely descriptive mode for which

Bishop was celebrated. If crawling slows movement, burrowing sacrifices any progress *out* for contraction *in*; if crawling suggests objective description, burrowing describes the work of introspection and memory. Bishop doesn't herself lay out these analogues; I doubt she intends them. They simply hang from the bottom of her paragraph on meter as a series of parallel commitments that collectively, like so much ballast, put her abstract theory within hailing distance of the ground below.

Bishop's commitment to idiosyncratic constellations of regularity and freedom, description and introspection, also surfaces in the poems she was writing at the time. Her letters to Lowell make clear that she was keeping tabs on their peers:

> I get so depressed with every number of POETRY, *The New Yorker*, etc. [. . .] so much adequate poetry all sounding just alike and *so* boring – or am I growing frizzled small and stale or however you put it? There seems to be too much of everything – too much painting, too much poetry, too many novels – and much too much money, I suppose. (Although I certainly welcomed mine.) And no one really feeling anything much . . . (*WIA* 344)

The kind of poetry that Bishop bemoans – "adequate" but "boring" because lacking any "feeling" – is what Lowell had described, when accepting the National Book Award earlier that spring for *Life Studies*, as "cooked."[7] While Bishop and Lowell may themselves have seemed like establishment poets, both defined themselves against what they understood as the academic magazine verse of the day.[8] But just as Lowell's indictment of "cooked" poetry expressed enough sympathy to make room for the allure of meter in his own writing, so too did Bishop's criticism of *The New Yorker* implicitly acknowledge her security in its pages.[9]

Lowell may have shared his friend's dismal appraisal of the poetry appearing in *The New Yorker*, but he thought differently of *her* poems there, which managed to give him the pleasures he associated with craft without sacrificing vitality. Just a couple of months after their exchange about meter, Lowell wrote to Bishop: "A beautiful poem of yours is in *The New Yorker*, rising wonderfully in the last stanza and perfect" (*WIA* 343). That poem, "Song for the Rainy Season" (*P* 99–100), exemplifies how Bishop calibrated the demands of meter and freedom, description and introspection, and did so in a negotiation of the modernist inheritance that had made those demands feel urgent. Like Lowell, Bishop felt drawn to accentual-syllabic meters; Bishop understood that tendency as one that distinguished her tastes from those of modernism. Writing to Anne Stevenson in 1963, Bishop complained about always being grouped with her friend and mentor Marianne Moore; with Moore's sui-generic preference for pure syllabics in mind, Bishop protested: "For one thing – I've always been an umpty-umpty poet with a traditional 'ear'" (*PPL* 842). The story is in fact a bit more complicated than this; while Bishop may have claimed a preference for iambic verse, and while the rhythms of traditional English prosody can be heard throughout her oeuvre, relatively few of her mature poems maintain for their duration a traditional accentual-syllabic meter. Instead, a characteristic Bishop poem glides into and out of recognizable meters, the way a conversation between friends might drift into and out of the rhythms of a familiar song.

"Song for the Rainy Season" does just this, braiding the spontaneity of Bishop's lived experience into metrical regularity (six rhyming stanzas, each of ten short lines). No two stanzas rhyme according to precisely the same scheme, and the lines, while all short, vary in number of accented beats and syllables. The effect, according to Bishop, was not quite "umpty-umpty" but rather something more like Latin American music. "Thank you for the kind words about the Rain poem –", she wrote to Lowell, "there are some words that *must* be changed, somehow – and it seems to me now it is in *rumba* rhythm" (*WIA* 346). While she made minor revisions between the poem's magazine and book publications, its rhythm survived.[10] The poem's short lines, coupled with its peculiarly insistent rhyme, create the rumba-like effect that Bishop describes. "Song for the Rainy Season" advances in a rhythm that manages both to burrow and, if not quite to fly, then to float, to tread the air as one might water:

Hidden, oh hidden
in the high fog
the house we live in,
beneath the magnetic rock,
rain-, rainbow-ridden,
where blood-black
bromelias, lichens,
owls, and the lint
of the waterfalls cling,
familiar, unbidden.

The first line's terminal "hidden" finds a full rhyme at mid-stanza in "rainbow-ridden" and at its closing in "unbidden" – but also slant rhymes, along the way, in "live in" and "lichens." "Rock" finds a slant rhyme in "blood-black" and assonance in "fog"; "lint" and "cling" nearly rhyme and also echo the "-in" sound throughout the stanza. Cumulatively, the aural atmosphere of this first stanza is one in which the sounds associated in the first line with shelter and interiority ("Hidden, oh hidden") are interlaced with the description of Bishop's elevated perch, so that the stanza itself, which stacks image upon image into its narrow shape, becomes, without ever reaching a main verb, an architectural space like the one it describes, situated in relation to a natural world whose existence can feel both intimate ("familiar") and strange ("unbidden").

The poetics that guide this effort, like the house they describe, provide shelter for the familiar even as they remain open to the intrusions of the strange. The poem is thus representative of Bishop's inclination to find a middle ground not only between metrical and free verse but also between interiority and objectivity. The poem's first line, "Hidden, oh hidden," is echoed and inverted by the first line of its fourth stanza, "House, open house." Just as the house upon which this poem was based – Samambaia, the glass, concrete, and verdant example of international modernism in which Bishop lived with Lota de Macedo Soares – provided a place for two women to share a domestic life in an era largely hostile to lesbians, so, too, do the poem's formal arrangements allow Bishop to publish a domestic scene without exposing herself to public scandal. And yet, just as the house's architecture remains "open," the poem's formality avoids what to Bishop seemed the perils of modernist impersonality. "Song for the Rainy Season" concludes by conjuring a future in which the salutary intrusions of extramural vitality have dried up:

> Without water
> the great rock will stare,
> unmagnetized, bare,
> no longer wearing
> rainbows or rain,
> the forgiving air
> and the high fog gone;
> the owls will move on
> and the several
> waterfalls shrivel
> in the steady sun.

The allusion to *The Waste Land* ("Here is no water but only rock") is clear, but that quintessential modernist landscape is presented not as dismal reality but as dystopic negative image of the poem's present fecundity.[11] The implication is that the house, whose openness lets in "the white dew / and the milk-white sunrise," and yet also encourages onto its walls "the mildew's / ignorant map," can nevertheless secure a habitat for the forms of life – swimming, flying, crawling, burrowing – prized by its poet in residence.

*

Bishop did not have to look far for a mid-century innovation that rejected modernist claims for impersonality. Confessional poetry had been popularized by Lowell's *Life Studies* (1959) and by the first books of two of his former students: Snodgrass's *Heart's Needle* (1959) and Sexton's *To Bedlam and Part Way Back* (1960). Bishop's correspondence in the period makes clear that she was reading these books, that her response to confessionalism was more ambivalent than her most famous reactions to it suggest, and that she derived from its example a provocation to find her own way to tell the truth.

Unsurprisingly, given her admiration for Lowell, Bishop's criticisms of the mode of poetry that he was credited with inaugurating involved distinguishing what made *Life Studies* appealing from what she found distasteful in the work of those who were his unlucky imitators. Chief among them, according to Bishop, was Sexton, about whom she wrote to Lowell:

> She *is* good, in spots, – but there is all the difference in the world, I'm afraid, between her kind of simplicity and that of *Life Studies*, her kind of egocentricity that is simply that, and yours that has been – what would be the reverse of *sub*limated, I wonder – anyway, made intensely *interesting*, and painfully applicable to every reader. (*WIA* 327)

Bishop senses a great difference between Lowell and Sexton but struggles to account for it.[12] Two months later, writing again to Lowell, Bishop was still thinking about what she didn't like in Sexton: "That Anne Sexton I think still has a bit too much romanticism and what I think of as the 'our beautiful old silver' school of female writing which is really boasting about how 'nice' *we* were" (*WIA* 333). Bishop went on to explain that such writers "have to make quite sure that the reader is not going to misplace them socially, first – and that nervousness interferes constantly with what they think they'd like to say" (*WIA* 333). For Bishop, Sexton fails because she succumbs to a pressure that is unduly exerted upon women and indeed upon all those – though Bishop doesn't say this – who lack the obvious social capital that preceded Lowell wherever he went, whether in life or in print.

One implication of Bishop's criticism was that confessional poetry depended for its drama upon putting its disclosures of *badness* (infidelity, breakdown, dysfunction) in tension with an expectation of the poet's *niceness* (social respectability, literary decorum). Lowell could rely on his family name and literary reputation to provide the backdrop of respectability and authority against which the shock of disclosure in *Life Studies* played, which meant that he didn't have to do as much of that shoring up explicitly within the poems.[13] Sexton, who lacked Lowell's social standing, seemed to have to work too hard to establish the reputation that her confessional disclosures punctured. When Bishop read Donald Davie's "rather unkind" review of *Heart's Needle* in *The Spectator*, she found that it had given her the language to make a similar critique of Snodgrass (again in a letter to Lowell):

> The point made is that Snodgrass is really saying, "I do all these awful things – but don't you really think I'm awfully *nice*?" This is the masculine version of that "our old silver" feminine-thing I wrote you about, too, I think, and it is the vast vast difference between you and one of your better imitators. You *tell* things – but never wind up with your own darling gestures, the way he does (he'd be giving Lepke home-made cookies or something). (*WIA* 359–60)

Bishop is referring to Lowell's "Memories of West Street and Lepke," which describes his view, during his year-long imprisonment as a conscientious objector, of a fellow inmate, Murder Incorporated's once fearsome Czar Lepke, now "[f]labby, bald, lobotomized."[14] Bishop prefers *Life Studies* because, unlike Snodgrass and Sexton, who tend to soften their own waywardness by anxiously reassuring the reader of the decorum they generally observe, Lowell doesn't, in this case, familiarize Lepke's unnerving image. Though confessionalism purports to tell the truth, even or especially when that truth is shocking, Bishop's complaint in these letters to Lowell about Sexton and Snodgrass is that all too often its practitioners domesticate the truth with their own "darling gestures."

But if Bishop was wary of the temptation felt by confessional poets to soften the edges of truth in order to preserve literary decorum and their social standing, she also understood her own tendency to write a kind of poetry that could make life seem more placid than it actually was. Two years after she had complained to Lowell about Sexton's membership in "the 'our beautiful old silver' school of female writing," Bishop wrote to Sexton herself with praise for her second book, *All My Pretty Ones* (1962). Sexton responded by writing twice on the same day, thanking Bishop for her encouragement and extolling her example: "I keep looking to your poems for a kind of sanity and beauty . . . you stretch out like a straight and good road showing me where to head for."[15] Bishop's response was full of gratitude for Sexton's praise, but also self-conscious about its terms:

> This business about "sanity" and "serenity" etc, always takes me by surprise. I'm not sure that it is a good sign – to be able, apparently, to write poems

> that give the impression of a writer quite different from the real one – to give an effect of serenity when one is just as distraught as everyone else, if not more so. [. . .] [Y]our letter has made me decide again I must tell more of the truth, if possible . . . not that I don't try to, but never hard enough.[16]

Here, Bishop again testifies to feeling as though there are two of her, a serene one whom Sexton recognizes in the poems and one who, Bishop assures her, "is just as distraught as everyone else." The obligation Bishop feels to tell the truth is a desire to align those two selves – even as her characterization of that decision as a matter of effort ("not that I don't try to, but never hard enough"), and of the "truth" itself as a relative matter ("more of the truth") – suggests that such an alignment will ultimately prove unstable for her, that the distance between her two selves may never be more than provisionally closed.

In the wake of confessional poetry's emergence and her resolution to "tell more of the truth," Bishop felt increasingly interested in the possibility of making her writing a site of contact between the self who'd left and the one who'd stayed behind. From Brazil and feeling, in her words, a "wave of nostalgia for the NORTH," Bishop wrote to her Aunt Grace and described a gift that she had received from another of her late mother's sisters:

> Mary sent me a little painting by Uncle George (I'm sure. – It isn't signed; but it must be) – tiny, a long shape – adorable. – Do you remember it? I am crazy about it – it is really awfully good – just a little sketch. I think it must be Nova Scotia – there's a brown house, the other ones white, and it looks like N S – I never saw that kind of brown house anywhere else! Do you know anything about it? I am awfully glad to have it.[17]

"It must be Nova Scotia." Readers of Bishop's poetry will recognize that declaration, quiet but certain, from "Poem" (*P* 196–97), though it would take another nine years before those words from the letter found their way into the manuscript that she sent to Howard Moss, poetry editor of *The New Yorker*. "Here," wrote Bishop to Moss in 1972, "is an old-fashioned umpty-umpty nostalgic poem that perhaps you'll be able to use" (*NYr* 339). Old-fashioned as Bishop felt it to be, the poem's rhythm in fact moves flexibly into and out of the "umpty-umpty" of blank verse.[18] Here, for instance, is how the line from the letter to Aunt Grace appears in the poem Bishop wrote about her Uncle George's painting:

> It must be Nova Scotia; only there
> does one see gabled wooden houses
> painted that awful shade of brown. (*P* 196)

One line of iambic pentameter moves seamlessly into two lines of a more conversational tetrameter; the certainty and precision of the first line drift into colloquial and ironic local color. This kind of accommodating approach to meter and colloquiality is characteristic of the poem as a whole – and indeed of Bishop's oeuvre writ large. Her self-deprecating claims to be the author of "umpty-umpty" poems springs from a recognition that a preference, however provisional or flexible, for meter puts her out of step with the more "literary" poetry of her day.

Although iambic prosody ran the risk of making Bishop seem old-fashioned, what it afforded her, especially when allowed to emerge as though organically from within the rhythms of colloquial speech, was a way of connecting her two selves in a third space, the space of the poem.[19] "I wish I could read a poem like that every day for the rest of my life," wrote Moss, immediately upon receiving the manuscript of "Poem" (*NYr* 339). Bishop wrote the poem out of a commensurate wish: to gain a view in daily life of a world she'd left behind. Helen Vendler notes that the poem, which first minutely describes a painting and then vividly recalls the landscape represented within it, thus performs acts of "domestication" only so as to dismantle the familiar visions it conjures.[20] Following Vendler's lead, we might note that Bishop's prosody at the end of "Poem" puts the desire for a familiar world in contact with the poet's knowledge that such a world has gone away. The perfectly regular pentameter of the poem's final line makes a world in the space of the poem precisely by acknowledging that such a world exists nowhere but in the words the poet has chosen. What does a desire to tell "more of the truth," to try "hard enough," get us, when, at the same time, we cannot but acknowledge the gap between who we were and who we have become? Not much, Bishop thinks. But perhaps enough:

> – the little that we get for free,
> the little of our earthly trust. Not much.
> About the size of our abidance
> along with theirs: the munching cows,
> the iris, crisp and shivering, the water
> still standing from spring freshets,
> the yet-to-be-dismantled elms, the geese. (*P* 197)

Notes

1. James Merrill, "Elizabeth Bishop (1911–1979)," in *Collected Prose*, ed. J. D. McClatchy and Stephen Yenser (New York: Knopf, 2004), 232.

2. Elizabeth Bishop to Anne Sexton, October 18, 1962. Anne Sexton Papers, Harry Ransom Center, Box 18, Folder 1.
3. See also Gillian White, *Lyric Shame: The "Lyric" Subject of Contemporary American Poetry* (Cambridge: Harvard University Press, 2014). 88.
4. Ezra Pound, "A Retrospect," in *Pavannes and Divisions* (New York: Knopf, 1918), 95.
5. Ezra Pound, "Canto LXXXI," in *The Cantos* (New York: New Directions, 1996), 538. See Meredith Martin, *The Rise and Fall of Meter: Poetry and English National Culture, 1860–1930* (Princeton: Princeton University Press, 2012), 181–206.
6. See Siobhan Phillips, "Bishop's Correspondence," in *The Cambridge Companion to Elizabeth Bishop*, ed. Angus Cleghorn and Jonathan Ellis (Cambridge: Cambridge University Press, 2014), 158.
7. Robert Lowell, "Robert Lowell accepts the 1960 National Book Award in Poetry for *Life Studies*." www.nationalbook.org/robert-lowells-accepts-the-1960-national-book-awards-in-poetry-for-life-studies/.
8. See White (78–80). John Ashbery, in a 1969 review, wrote, "Miss Bishop is somehow an establishment poet herself, and the establishment ought to give thanks; she is proof that it can't be all bad." John Ashbery, "*The Complete Poems*," *The New York Times Book Review* (June 1, 1969), 8.
9. See Fiona Green, "Elizabeth Bishop in Brazil and the 'New Yorker,'" *Journal of American Studies* 46.4 (November 2012), 804–11.
10. Elizabeth Bishop, "Song for a Rainy Season," *The New Yorker* (October 8, 1960): 40. The changes Bishop made between magazine and book publication are listed in *Words in Air* (*WIA* 346n1). See also Green (820–25) and Bishop's correspondence with the magazine (*NYr* 230–36).
11. T. S. Eliot, "The Waste Land," in *The Poems of T. S. Eliot: Volume I: Collected and Uncollected Poems*, ed. Christopher Ricks and Jim McCue (London: Faber & Faber, 2015), 68.
12. See Christopher Grobe, *The Art of Confession: The Performance of Self from Robert Lowell to Reality TV* (New York: New York University Press, 2017), 38.
13. When Bishop first read the autobiographical sequence in *Life Studies* in manuscript, she made precisely this point, remarking that he was "the luckiest poet I know," since his famous relations meant that all he had to do to command public attention and cultural significance when telling a family story was to "put down the names" (*WIA* 247).
14. Robert Lowell, "Memories of West Street and Lepke," in *Collected Poems*, ed. Frank Bidart and David Gewanter (New York: Farrar, Straus and Giroux, 2003), 188.
15. Anne Sexton to Elizabeth Bishop, September 26, 1962 (VC).
16. Elizabeth Bishop to Anne Sexton, October 18, 1962. Anne Sexton Papers, Harry Ransom Center, Box 18, Folder 1.
17. Quoted in Brett C. Millier, *Elizabeth Bishop: Life and the Memory of It* (Berkley: University of California Press, 1993), 347–48.
18. See Eric Lindstrom, "Money, Painting, and the Generic Abidance of Elizabeth Bishop's 'Poem,'" *Modernism/modernity* 25.2 (April 2018): 351.

19. By "third space" I mean something like the "third area" – between subject and object, child and mother – as defined by D. W. Winnicott, *Playing and Reality* (Abingdon: Routledge, 1971), 10–13. See Langdon Hammer, "Useless Concentration: Life and Work in Elizabeth Bishop's Letters and Poems," *American Literary History* 9.1 (Spring, 1997), 162–80.
20. Helen Vendler, "Domestication, Domesticity, and the Otherworldly," in *Elizabeth Bishop and Her Art*, ed. Lloyd Schwartz and Sybil P. Estess (Ann Arbor: U of Michigan P, 1983), 41.

CHAPTER 17

Brazilian Literature

Maria Lúcia Milléo Martins

During her time in Brazil, Elizabeth Bishop not only had the opportunity to read and translate Brazilian literature, but also to be in contact with a select group of writers. Letters from the early 1950s detail this contact, mostly when Bishop was involved in her translations for *An Anthology of Twentieth-Century Brazilian Poetry*, co-edited with Emanuel Brasil. Four poets in this anthology had singular relevance in Bishop's translations and her own poetic production: Manuel Bandeira, Carlos Drummond de Andrade, João Cabral de Melo Neto, and Vinicius de Moraes. In prose, Bishop's translation of Clarice Lispector also found resonance in her poetry. Considering a network of epistolary texts, translations, and poetry, this chapter offers a contextual reading of Bishop's relation with these Brazilian writers. The critical perspective includes a historicity of individual, personalistic[1] experiences and sociocultural records. As a result, this fruitful literary exchange has left curious correspondences in Bishop's own poetry.

Bandeira was the first poet Bishop met in a visit to his apartment in the company of Lota de Macedo Soares, as she tells Marianne Moore in a letter.[2] Bishop comments on Bandeira's translations and the apartment that resembles Moore's, and finally tells an anecdote. When leaving late at night, Bishop and Lota are locked inside the building and do not remember the number of Bandeira's apartment. When Lota eventually finds the poet, he comes down "in green stripped pajamas and a bright red dressing gown and flapping slippers" to open the door. (One can imagine the impact of this exuberant exposure of intimacy to Bishop.) Years later, Bishop sends Bandeira a letter-poem with a jar of jam. First, she humorously tells of the dilemma of reserve and desire for closeness and, then, praises the poet as translator and celebrity. To conclude, she writes: "accept and spread / these compliments upon your bread, / And, Manuel, may this silent jelly / speak sweetly to your poet's belly, / and once more let me say I am / devoted with a jar of jam" (*PPL* 238). As Flora Süssekind notes, "the epistolary form always keeps a tension between intimacy and disclosure, between closeness in tone and actual distance."[3] Transferring the authorship of admiration to the jar of jam emblematically shows this tension, allowing the poet to present her compliment with the detachment of humor.

In response, Bandeira sends Bishop a poem thanking her for the jam and a book by e. e. cummings he had also received from her. Written in a typographic play imitating cummings's style, the poem ends with an invitation: "An / d now – / Get into this brazilian hammock / and / let me sing for you: / 'Lullaby. / Sleep on and on.'"[4] Here Bandeira appropriates Bishop's lines in "Songs for a Colored Singer" to lull her to sleep, a rather ambiguous invitation considering the dark tone evoked in the lullaby section of Bishop's poem. Years later, he would include his translation of the third part of Bishop's poem in *Poemas Traduzidos* under the title of "Lullaby" ("Acalanto"). The exchange of poems clearly reveals distinct personalistic traits – Bishop's sense of reserve, and Bandeira's liberation from a restrained lyricism – recurrent in their poetic production. Bishop translated two poems by Bandeira: "My Last Poem" and "Brazilian Tragedy." The desire for the last poem "to be gentle saying the simplest and least intended things," and the interest in ordinary urban dramas are features that Bishop incorporates in her own poetry. "Going to the Bakery" and "Under the Window: Ouro Prêto" confirm this.

While Bishop's relation with Bandeira can be summed up in this brief story, her connection with Drummond is far more reaching. It involves not only letters and translations but writings about experiences in common – memories of origins and childhood surprisingly similar and coincidental depictions of Brazilian daily life.[5] The long story starts in the early 1960s with Bishop's letter to Drummond asking for his appreciation of her translation of "Travelling in the Family." At the end of the letter, she writes:

> I have heard that you are "shy" with strangers – well, unfortunately, so am I, and I also speak Portuguese badly. So I thought that rather than telephoning or calling in person, it might be a good idea to confine our relationship to writing, for the time being.[6]

The provisional proposal ends up becoming the only means of communication, rather ironic considering their geographical proximity in Rio. But, as Bishop remembers in an interview with George Starbuck, they met once by chance on the sidewalk at night: "We had just come out of the same restaurant, and he kissed my hand politely when we were introduced."[7]

In the letters that follow, it is possible to observe, on the one hand, the anxiety of a meticulous translator; on the other, total confidence in the mastery of the interpreter. Bishop's translations of seven poems by Drummond are published both in the anthology she co-edited with Brasil, and later in her *Complete Poems*. "Seven-Sided Poem," one of the first, marks Drummond's poetic initiation: "When I was born, one of the crooked / angels who live in shadow, said / Carlos, go on! Be *gauche* in life" (*P* 137). Affonso Romano de Sant'Anna defines the *gauche* type as an "ex-centric" in both connotations of the word, in the sense of spatial displacement (removed from the center, or decentered) and incompatibility with the world.[8] Both notions apply to Drummond and Bishop who turn their *gaucherie* into a personalistic trait in their art. It is possible to trace this in their writings from the sense of displacement in childhood and in adult life (Drummond, "The air farmer"; Bishop, "a stranger in the strangest of theatres") to various poetic masks throughout their works to their last poems.[9] The *gauche* trait can also be extended to the two poets' positioning as translator and translated on the margin of the text; Bishop reluctant to interfere in an alien text, Drummond de-authorizing himself as consultant. There is yet a certain proneness "to love crookedly"[10]; Drummond in his affair with Lygia Fernandes, Bishop in her relationship with Lota de Macedo Soares. Disguised in poetic masks, kept in dusk, Bishop's muse makes her ultimate appearance as Friday in "Crusoe in England," Drummond's in "The Ill-fated," in the brief reference to having loved the wrong woman. Coincidentally, these poems are a kind of inventory of the two poets' *gauche* trajectories.

Another important detail in Bishop's translations of Drummond is that four poems are about memories of childhood. By this time, Lowell's elegies in *Life Studies* are a great motivation for Bishop to brood over her own family portraits. Thus, it is not accidental that Bishop felt particularly attracted by the elegiac side of Drummond. Two poems by Bishop from her archives, only published in more recent collections, reveal similarities with poems by Drummond she has translated. Victoria Harrison calls attention to curious resemblances between Drummond's poem "Travelling in the Family" and Bishop's "For Grandfather."[11] She points out the coincidence of the imaginary trip – Drummond's father leading him through the desert of Itabira, Bishop's grandfather taking her through the snows of the North Pole (*P* 329). The initial lines of "Infancy" by Drummond – "My father got on his horse and went to the field. / My mother stayed sitting and sewing. / My little brother slept" (*P* 246) – also resemble lines by Bishop in the poem "For T. C. B." – "Father's in the studio / Painting hill and dale. / Mother's in the sitting-room / Typing up a tale, / Hepple's in the pasture / Looking at the rabbits!" (*PPL* 250).

Correspondences between the two poets' memories of childhood do not involve only textual resonance but a larger range of intertextuality showing common features of the provincial life of Great Village, New England, and Itabira such as patriarchy, religious practices, social relations, and even echoes of the distant War (WWII) in Europe. Bishop's choice in translating "Family Portrait," "The Table," and "The Dead in Overcoats" (unfinished) by Drummond, certainly account for her interest in the motif of loss, present in poems like "Sestina" and "First Death in Nova Scotia." Rituals of dressing children/infants as angels in church, processions, and funerals, present both in Drummond's writings and in Joaquim Cardozo's "Cemetery of Childhood" (translated by Bishop) is a cultural trait that Bishop assimilates in her shadow box "Anjinhos" about infant mortality in Brazil.

In Rio, at the same time Bishop and Drummond were writing about their origins, they were also sensitive to urban conflicts. Coincidentally, the two poets lived near the hills and this results in depictions of the social reality of the slums: Drummond in "Hill of Babylon," and Bishop in "The Burglar of Babylon." More than thematic and contextual coincidence, these poems reveal a similar gaze at the hills' "horror and delicacy." In her drafts for the *Brazil* book, Bishop mentions this contrast, associating the architecture of the slums with birds' nests. She keeps the same association in the poem moving from architecture to human beings. It is in this sensitivity to nuances of human delicacy amidst the frightening violence of the slums that Bishop approaches Drummond's view.

> In "Hill of Babylon":
> voices come down creating terror
> (urban terror, fifty per cent cinema,
> and the rest that came from Luanda or got lost in the general language).
>
> When there was revolution, the soldiers spread out on the hill,
> the headquarters caught fire, they didn't come back.
> Some, shot, died.
> The hill became more enchanted. [12] (60–61)

Here the poet narrates the cliché of the repeated story of the armed conflicts in the slums – but breaks it with the lines: "Some, shot, died. / The hill became more enchanted." The magic of the line functions as a kind of transition to the magic of the hill that, despite its horrors, enchants with its music. In the final lines, a well-tuned *cavaquinho*[13] "comes down to us, modest and amusing, / as if a delicacy from the hill." John Gledson notes that those were the "golden" years of popular music in Brazil, a time that favored an "artistic link between rich and poor, black and white, popular and intellectual."[14] In the poem, the link is made by the sound of the *cavaquinho* that "comes down to us," "us" suggesting the urban middle class to which the poet belonged. The "delicacy," however, does not come as an apology for the effacement of boundaries, but rather as an invitation to hear a few human notes that cross those limits.

Bishop's poem "The Burglar of Babylon" articulates the social conflicts of the slums in a more detailed way, starting with an account of their origins:

On the fair green hill of Rio
    There grows a fearful stain:
The poor who come to Rio
    And can't go home again.

On the hills a million people,
    A million sparrows, nest,
Like a confused migration
    That's had no light and rest . . . (*P* 110)

In a foreword to the 1968 publication of this poem, Bishop identifies "the poor who come to Rio" as migrants from the north and northeast, the *retirantes.* Comparing them to sparrows that build their nests and then "cling and spread like lichen," the poet observes their vulnerability and dramatic permanence. The list of slums' names that follows historically contextualizes the extent of that reality and prepares the scenario for Micuçu's tragedy. Micuçu is a kind of anti-hero who, despite his crimes, has some remnant of humanity. This is evident in the talk with his aunt, and in the aunt's final discourse affirming human values that survive the stigma of the slums – a kind of human version of the "horror and delicacy" first observed in the slums' architecture. Lloyd Schwartz acknowledges this when he says that violence is humanized "in the nonjudgemental sympathy for the innocence and helplessness of both the criminal and his captors – all of them equally caught up in Brazil's self-contradictions."[15]

Bishop's use of the lyrical ballad, a form familiar to both *samba* and *cordel* literature,[16] shows her interest in popular culture and, as Cleber Teixeira notes, interest also in a poetic tradition at the time in singing the saga of popular heroes or anti-heroes.[17] In regard to *samba*, Bishop manifests her admiration for the sagacity of lyrics; moreover, those criticizing politicians and urban problems, some of which she translated, and are included in the 2011 edition of her *Poems.* As for sagas proper to *cordel* literature, there is Bishop's translation of "The Death and Life of a Severino," by João Cabral de Melo Neto. Two decades after "The Burglar of Babylon," Drummond would write "National *Favelário*," an inventory of the proliferation of the slums in the country. Echoes of Bishop are everywhere in the poem.

Other coincidental gazes at Rio's landscape, provincial life in Ouro Preto, and features of Brazilian history and culture allow a variety of comparative readings. To conclude this sample, there is the dialogical relation between Bishop's last portrait of Rio, "Pink Dog," and Drummond's poem "Carnival 1970." "Pink Dog" begins with a scenario of Rio's contrasts: the blazing sun, the crowded beach, and the sick dog on the avenue. The dramatic monologue that follows surprises by the ironic tone, assimilating the ambiguity of carnival. The urge to "dress up and dance" sums up the tension between mask/masquerade, at the same time, simulation imposed by a repressive order, and transgression disguised as playfulness.

> Now look, the practical, the sensible
>
> solution is to wear a *fantasia**
> Tonight you simply can't afford to be a-
> n eye sore. But no one will ever see a
>
> dog in *máscara* this time of year.
> Ash Wednesday'll come but Carnival is here.
> What sambas can you dance? What will you wear?
>
> *Carnival costume (*P* 212–13)

Regarding the poem's corrosive humor, Schwartz notes that, unusual for Bishop, bravado is "characteristically Brazilian – not only bravado in the face of crisis and catastrophe but the deeper irony of bravado in the aftermath, of crisis and catastrophe."[18]

In "Carnival 1970," Drummond also depicts this irony, criticizing the artificiality of "plastic dolls, laths / in procession over the heads,"

> playing in the place of those who do not play
> or demanding to play, tourist's order.
> And my Rio, clown-embroidered,
> played on the stave, played outside the stave.
> Playing is its fate, even when
> there are unreasons* to be happy,
> or because of that, who knows? (943)
>
> * A neologism corresponding to no reasons.

The two poems criticize the degeneration of carnival, evils of commercialism or tourism. In the *Brazil* book, Bishop criticizes the American movie industry for turning carnival into a "cinematic nightmare," and the Government for prohibiting costumes and floats "[making] sports of politicians, the Church or the military." "Some of the cleverest displays of wit," she says, "were formerly inspired by these traditional objects of satire."[19] In Drummond's poem, criticism includes the judgment of carnival and the contrast between the splendor on the avenue and the poverty in the suburbs. Yet in completely different tones – Drummond, nostalgic; Bishop, in her own definition, "ghastly" – they translate the essence of carnival's contradictions.

Brazilian popular culture appears in many of Bishop's writings. Her translation of *The Death and Life of a Severino* is one of the most relevant examples. Bishop's first contact with Cabral dates from the mid-fifties when he was working as a diplomat in Seville. First, in a short note, he congratulates her on the Pulitzer Prize. In a second more detailed letter, Cabral comments on the draft of her preface to the *Diary of "Helena Morley"* (by then entitled *Black Beans and Diamonds*). He praises her precision and objectivity in contrast with some Brazilian writers' limitations in this respect. Later, by the time of Bishop's translation of his poem, Cabral again praises the quality of her work, this time for having elevated "an insignificant poet from Pernambuco" to the level of an Elizabeth Bishop.[20]

A Christmas play, Cabral's text is a lyrical ballad that follows the tradition of *cordel* poetry. It tells the saga of Severino, a *retirante*, who leaves the interior to escape drought. A very common name in the Northeast, Severino stands for a plurality of other migrants:

> We are many Severinos
> and our destiny's the same:
> to soften up these stones
> by sweating over them,
> to try to bring to life
> a dead and deader land,
> to try to wrest a farm
> out of burnt-over land.
> But, so that Your Excellencies
> can recognize me better
> and be able to follow better
> the story of my life,
> I'll be the Severino
> you'll now see emigrate. (*P* 153)

The rest of the poem then details his harsh experience as wanderer. Correspondences between Cabral's poem and "The Burglar of Babylon" start with the identification of "the poor who come to Rio" with the *retirantes*, and the similarity of telling an individual's saga representative of many. Also, like Cabral, there is Bishop's choice of a lyrical ballad resembling *cordel* to approach the poetic language of popular culture. Paulo Henriques Britto notes that, although as translator of Cabral Bishop has limitations, "The Burglar of Babylon" shows that she could write in her own language a poem "in loud voice" at the level of the master of Pernambuco.[21] As for other affinities between the two poets, Regina Przybycien points out the economy of language (chiseled to its essence and deprived of artifice), precision of form, and concreteness of imagery.[22] This certainly explains Cabral's own admiration for Bishop expressed in his letters.

Differently from the other poets discussed here, Vinicius is the closest to Bishop. Przybycien writes about the two poets having first met in the late 1960s in Ouro Preto, Bishop's retreat to escape the tensions in Rio. They stayed at a small hotel, Pouso do Chico Rei, where they engaged in long conversations, sipping whisky. She adds that "with his habitual irreverence, Vinicius amused Bishop, telling stories of his love affairs and frustrated marriages."[23] Vinicius's letters to Bishop keep this tone of intimacy. In one of them, he tells Bishop of Cabral having criticized him for becoming more a composer than a poet, throwing in his face names like Eliot, Auden, Mallarmé, Moore, and Bishop. In a letter to Robert Lowell, Bishop recognizes the quality of Vinicius's poetry but criticizes some of his lines in *Black Orpheus*: "They lack that surprise, the mis-used words, the big words, etc., that sambas always have." Still, she mentions as a favorite line one about "how Woman drags down Man – with all his 'beauty and nobility'" (*WIA* 314).

Bishop translated only "Sonnet of Intimacy" by Vinicius, about his memories of farm afternoons. "Chewing a blade of sticky grass, chest bare, / In threadbare pajamas of three summers back," the poet contemplates the cattle:

> The smell of cow manure is delicious.
> The cattle look at me unenviously
> And when there comes a sudden stream and hiss
>
> Accompanied by a look not unmalicious,
> All of us, animals, unemotionally
> Partake together of a pleasant piss. (*P* 250)

Schwartz remembers that Bishop "was always tickled to think that she had become the first poet to get away with a 'four-letter' word in the pages of *The New Yorker*" (93). Schwartz also notes the relation of the landscape evoked in the poem with Bishop's Nova Scotia. In a final letter to Bishop, Vinicius continues the long story of marriages and, when touching the issue of *saudade*,[24] says: "I consider you – even without entering the merit of the poet – *uma mulherzinha muito amorável.*"[25] Old streets of Ouro Preto keep other memorable stories like the one of the two poets, late at night, singing together.

In Rio, streets of neighborhoods are also sites for remembrance. As with Drummond, Bishop met Clarice Lispector for the first time on the street, the same where both lived in Leme. Bishop admired Lispector as a person and a writer and was particularly interested in the writer's short stories. Bishop translated three of them for publication by *Kenyon Review*: "The Smallest Woman in the World," "A Hen," and "Marmosets." The former is a story about a French explorer who meets a native woman pigmy in Africa. The importance of his finding is due not only to her belonging to a rare race but to her vulnerability: "The tiny race, retreating, always retreating, has finished hiding away in the heart of Africa, where the lucky explorer discovered it."[26] A similar context of colonialism and vulnerability is present in Bishop's appropriation of Lispector's lines in the poem "Brazil, January 1, 1502." The final scene depicts the Portuguese colonizers (the "Christians") in pursuit:

> Directly after Mass, humming perhaps
> *L'Homme armé* or some such tune,
> they ripped away into the hanging fabric,
> each out to catch an Indian for himself –
> those maddening little women who kept calling,
> calling to each other (or had the birds waked up?)
> and retreating, always retreating, behind it. (*P* 90)

Like the explorer in Lispector's story, the Portuguese colonizers are surrounded by an exuberant and primitive nature, the "tapestried landscape," ready to be "ripped away" by exploration or conquest.

To know more about Bishop's connections with Brazilian writers it is necessary to leave behind concepts such as the anxiety of influence and instead search for new paths of contextual readings, potentially infinite. This involves a pleasurable task of opening tin trunks and finding unpredictable relics, old letters, poem's drafts, newspapers' clippings. Also, there is the privilege of oral tradition in listening to stories from those who were contemporaries of these writers, and that are passed on to new generations. These are precious sources.

One of these sources, a note by Drummond published by *Jornal do Brasil* on the occasion of Bishop's death, is perfect to conclude this brief story of poetic ties:

> Now I am feeling that we could have known and loved better Elizabeth Bishop, who passed away recently in the United States. She knew how to love Brazil, living long years in Petrópolis and Ouro Preto, extracting from our everyday themes for her poetry. Who has so far written the most touching poem about the social condition of the *carioca* slums if not the author of the Micuçu ballad . . . ?[27]

This poem, he says, according to Lowell, reveals much more about Brazil than the *Brazil* book written for Time-Life. Drummond mentions Bishop's translations and the fact of her being so little known in Brazil outside a small circle of friends. "In the Samambaia Farm, in Petrópolis, or in the house of Ouro Preto," he concludes, "something – bird, leaf, shadow corner – must have kept, for a few devoted, the discreet *saudade* of Elizabeth Bishop."

Notes

1. I use this term here in the Bakhtinian sense. In the essay "Toward a Methodology for the Human Sciences," Bakhtin argues for the recognition of the personalistic element in contextual readings. *Speech Genres and Other Late Essays*, translated by Vern W. McGee, ed. Caryl Emerson and Michael Holquist (Austin: University of Texas Press, 1986).
2. Bishop's letter to Moore, December 08, 1953, *One Art*, ed. Robert Giroux (New York: Farrar, Straus and Giroux, 1994), 281.
3. I translate here this and other citations in Portuguese, keeping the original references. Flora Süssekind, "A Geleia & o Engenho: em torno de uma carta poema de Elizabeth Bishop a Manuel Bandeira," in *Papéis Colados* (Rio de Janeiro: Editora UFRJ, 1993), 349.
4. The poem is included in Bandeira's *Poesia Completa e Prosa, Poesia Completa e Prosa* (Rio de Janeiro: Editora Nova Aguilar S. A., 1996), 436.
5. I discuss this in detail in *Duas Artes: Carlos Drummond de Andrade e Elizabeth Bishop*, a shorter version of my doctoral dissertation, originally written in English and entitled *Elizabeth Bishop and Carlos Drummond de Andrade: verse / universe in four acts* (https://scholarworks.umass.edu/dissertations/AAI9920628/).
6. Arquivo Carlos Drummond de Andrade, Arquivo Museu de Literatura Brasileira, Fundação Casa de Rui Barbosa, Rio de Janeiro.
7. Elizabeth Bishop, *Conversations with Elizabeth Bishop*, ed. George Monteiro (Jackson: University Press of Mississippi, 1996), 96.
8. Affonso Romano Sant'Anna, *Drummond: o gauche no tempo* (Rio de Janeiro: Lia, Editor S. A., 1972) 27–28.
9. The expression "air farmer," title of a collection of poems by Drummond, evokes his childhood in Itabira as a farmer's son, and the sense of dissolution of this time, "air" also suggestive of living in an apartment in Rio. Bishop's lines, "a stranger in the strangest of theatres," from the poem "Questions of Travel," refers to her initial sense of displacement as a foreigner in Brazil.

10. The expression is from Drummond's poem "The Ill-fated" ("O Malvindo"), *Farewell*, 74.
11. Victoria Harrison, *Elizabeth Bishop's Poetics of Intimacy* (Cambridge: Cambridge University Press, 1993).
12. Drummond's poems are published in *Carlos Drummond de Andrade: Poesia e Prosa.* I translate here this and other lines by Drummond not translated by Bishop.
13. A small four-string guitar known as soprano guitar, typical of *samba* ensembles.
14. John Gledson, *Poesia e Poética de Carlos Drummond de Andrade* (São Paulo: Livraria Duas Cidades, 1981), 120.
15. Lloyd Schwartz, "Elizabeth Bishop and Brazil," *The New Yorker* 30 September (1991), 91.
16. *Cordel,* "string literature" from the Northeast of Brazil is one of the best-known expressions of popular culture. Originally sold in pamphlets hanging from strings, it still circulates in oral tradition and literature.
17. Oral comment by poet Cleber Teixeira comparing "The Burglar of Babylon" to Drummond's poem "Clorindo Gato."
18. Lloyd Schwartz, "Elizabeth Bishop and Brazil," *The New Yorker*, 30 September (1991), 95.
19. Elizabeth Bishop, *Brazil* (New York: Time & Life, 1962), 88.
20. Cabral's letters to Bishop belong to Elizabeth Bishop Collection, Vassar College Library. The note dates May 17, 1956, and the letters respectively April 02, 1957, and February 15, 1966.
21. Paulo Henriques Britto, "Bishop no Brasil," in *Elizabeth Bishop: Poemas do Brasil* (São Paulo: Companhia das Letras, 1999), 40.
22. Regina Przybycien, *Feijão preto e diamantes: O Brasil na obra de Elizabeth Bishop* (Belo Horizonte: Editora UFMG, 2015), 163.
23. Ibid., 173.
24. *Saudade* is a profound nostalgic longing for someone or something.
25. Vinicius's letter to Bishop, November 11, 1971. Elizabeth Bishop Collection, Vassar College. In the expression "*uma mulherzinha muito amorável*" ("a very lovable little woman"), the diminutive "*mulherzinha*" implies affection.
26. Clarice Lispector, "The Smallest Woman in the World," trans. Elizabeth Bishop, *Kenyon Review* 26.3 (Summer 1964), 501. Reprinted in *PPL* 302–07.
27. Drummond, *Jornal do Brasil*, October 13, 1979, Arquivo Carlos Drummond de Andrade, Arquivo Museu de Literatura Brasileira, Fundação Casa de Rui Barbosa, Rio de Janeiro.

PART IV

Politics, Society and Culture

CHAPTER 18

War

Charles Berger

The last verse-paragraph of Elizabeth Bishop's late poem, "In the Waiting Room," contains lines that might serve as a fitting epigraph for an essay devoted to the question of how she responded, through her poetry, to war and the threat of war that she, along with every other member of her generation, faced continually throughout her life: "The War was on. Outside, / in Worcester, Massachusetts" (*P* 181). The suffix "-cester" can be traced back to the Latin *castrum,* a military camp or fort; intriguingly, the word was also at the root of "castrate." "Massachusetts" derives from the language of an extinct Native American tribe and means "great hill," another way of looking at a fort. The poet, looking back on her life, acknowledges that although the War was always on, it also remained somehow "Outside," even as she was aware of living in a War camp, erected on the site of an extinguished people. Life-long readers of Bishop understand how the profound, insinuative workings of her layered language allow them at times to focus on how she was able to keep war at a distance, while also opening her poetic consciousness to its inexorable presence. She lived and wrote both inside and outside the camp.

While many critics have noted ways in which Bishop writes indirectly and obliquely about war, it should also be noted that when her first volume, *North & South*, appeared in 1946, Louise Bogan, reviewing the book in *The New Yorker*, had no difficulty registering the presence of war in Bishop's poetry, declaring that it "contains all manner of references to war and warriors." Susan Schweick, in *A Gulf So Deeply Cut: American Women Poets and the Second World War*, puts it this way: "Bishop's first book might be read, in fact, as a war book *in-directed.* In it the matters of war literature – naval engagements, border crossings, skirmishes, search missions, even a monument of sorts – appear, but only as covert operations."[1] This method of circling about war and the build-up to war that marked the 1930s was a technique employed as well by male poets such as Auden and Stevens. In certain ways, the anxiety of war and voices prophesying war registers more harrowingly for Bishop in poems that were written prior to America's formal entry into the war in December 1941. Once war actually breaks out for the USA, Bishop seems to choose silence as a weapon of response, as Camille Roman points out in *Elizabeth Bishop's World War II–Cold War View*.

The opening poem of *North & South*, "The Map," though published in 1935, is eerily predictive of war maps that will come to predominate newspapers after 1 September 1939, just as they did in the so-called Great War of the previous generation. The poem's whimsical tone does not dispel the chill of weaponized cartography, of dominance in the drawing of boundaries, the aggressive crossing of national borders: "Are they assigned, or can the countries pick their colors? / – What suits the character or the native waters best? (*P* 5). And how did Bishop "know" that in a mere four years "Norway's hare" indeed "runs south in agitation" (*P* 5). The second poem in *North & South*, "The Imaginary Iceberg," opens with apocalyptic apprehension: "We'd rather have the iceberg than the ship, / although it meant the end of travel" (*P* 6). Here Bishop confesses to a semi-conscious instinct, a death-drive, that "we" seem to share as human beings propelling us to destroy what beauty we have created.

The trope of "sleep" runs throughout *North & South*, carrying with it a self-accusatory charge of closing one's eyes to a sense of growing dread at the political situation of Europe in the 1930s. Bishop does not shirk from leveling this claim against herself, largely for the reason that some of her strongest poems from this period stage a disruption of this somnolent cocoon, dramatize moments in which the poet's room is invaded by instinctive, semi-conscious realization that the beast in the jungle cannot be locked out. No poem better illustrates this than "Sleeping on the Ceiling," a poem of placid horror, Bishop's own yellow wallpaper. The poet lies in a Parisian hotel room whose walls and ceiling are layered with kitschy drawings and wallpaper, all designed to mollify the touristic appetite. "It is so peaceful on the ceiling! / It is the Place de la Concorde" (*P* 30). Of course there is nothing peaceful about the historical Place, as even a cursory browse through a Baedeker would have revealed. Inevitably, the poet's eyes stray from ceiling to the peeling wallpaper, with its depiction of the Jardin des Plantes, and the imagination then supplies the true theme, that which cannot be seen, but can be apprehended: "The mighty flowers and foliage rustle; / under the leaves the insects tunnel" (*P* 30). Bishop ends this brief, macabre poem with an effort to flip perspective, to miniaturize the threat, but the chill is not dispelled, even as the wish to stay above it all remains: "We must go under the wallpaper / to meet the insect-gladiator, /

to battle with a net and trident, / and leave the fountain and the square. / But oh, that we could sleep up there. . ." (*P* 30).

There is general agreement that Bishop's most overt war poem – of necessity, an anti-war poem – is "Roosters," written in Key West and published in *The New Republic* in March 1941, although the poem was essentially completed by October 1940. As Bishop put it in a famous letter to Marianne Moore, the poem expresses her detestation of "militarism" (*OA* 96). The poem is fueled by outrage at masculinist aggressivity, but it is also richly oblique in its search for the roots of war; nor does it fail to implicate civilian observers in practices of betrayal that go some way toward erasing clear demarcations between active and "passive" participants in violence. Like Moore, Bishop employs Aesopian fable buttressed by brilliantly accurate natural description in order to generalize her polemic and provide a genealogy of violence, along with a litany of recuperative cultural pivots that prove capable of converting betrayal into benediction. As the poem widens its focus from barnyard to basilica it becomes something of a modernist, miniaturist cultural epyllion, along the lines of Moore's "Marriage," investigating the cultural origins and outgrowths of peremptory male dominance.

"Roosters" is written in rhymed tercets and it is divided into three parts, unnumbered but separated by extra spacing. The opening movement in this triptych is also the longest, consisting of twenty-six stanzas which have been characterized by Susan Schweik as "the most fiercely vivid critique of male power and of militarism by an American woman poet during the Second World War," providing "a ready fund of barbed indictments of masculine aggression and pretension."[2] The poem's opening section gives us tableau after tableau of semi-comic but deadly cock-strutting (akin to goose-stepping) ending in the destruction of combatant and non-combatant alike. From the beginning, the poet alerts us to how the news of war, even before Pearl Harbor (but after the fall of France and subsequent Nazi moves against Denmark and Norway) has contaminated the dawn, turning daybreak into reveille: "At four o'clock / in the gun-metal blue dark / we hear the first crow of the first cock // just below / the gun-metal blue window" (*P* 36). In her October 17, 1940, letter to Moore, Bishop could not be more explicit about the triggering events behind the writing of the poem: "In the first part I was thinking of Key West, and also of those aerial views of dismal little towns in Finland and Norway, when the Germans took over, and their atmosphere of poverty. [. . .] (I also had in mind the violent roosters Picasso did in connection with his *Guernica* picture)" (*OA* 96). War-cries emanating from the roosters as each asserts its territorial imperative are met by approval from their "rustling wives" (*P* 36). One of the more striking and depressing *aperçus* derived from this barnyard battle comes with the realization that the instinctual drive toward war appears to be governed by forces that are both "uncontrolled" and "traditional": "from their beaks there rise / the uncontrolled, traditional cries" (*P* 36). A little further on this is reiterated: "deep from raw throats / a senseless order floats / all over town" (*P* 36). No degree of skillful poetic parodying and dismantling of the myth of martial heroism and its culpable devotees, female as well as male, can dispel the profound realization that species after species, human and non-human, seems to have lodged at its core an irrational (uncontrolled) but instinctual (traditional) drive toward aggression.

Although Bishop can adopt a wide-lens view when she investigates the genealogy of warfare, she also does not shy away from assigning more immediate, more topical blame for brutal militarism, as when she singles out the Germans in the letter to Moore, and their Spanish Fascist allies through the reference to Picasso. In the poem, Bishop employs a barely disguised pun to indict the Nazis: "what right have you to give / commands and tell us how to live, // cry 'Here!' and 'Here!' / and wake us here where are / unwanted love, conceit and war?" (*P* 37). "Here" glides all too easily into "Herr!" and then, with only a bit of further stretching, into "Heil!" But one should also note that even at this point, Bishop cannot resist problematizing the topical allusion by also punning on "man" in "command," as if to warn her American readers not to rest too easy in their self-righteousness. But perhaps the most profound and unexpected expansion of the sphere of complicity comes when Bishop jolts the reader by deploying enjambment to strip the embedded lovers of any claim to redemptive innocence. They, too, belong to a here and now, "where are / unwanted love, conceit and war" (*P* 37). *Et in Arcadia ego* holds true as well in the purlieu of the lesbian aubade. Not only must the American reader not become too complacent but, more specifically, the American woman reader, the American lesbian reader, while bristling at the "virile presence" (*P* 38) that would pre-empt and police them, should not regard themselves as being immune from the aggressive strain. This does not mean that Bishop is constructing facile equivalences, only that she is loathe to believe in the *cordon sanitaire* of the privileged and protected room.

The long first part of "Roosters" ends with a bang and a whimper, as cock and hen alike are flung on the local "ash-heap" (*P* 38) which is not, unfortunately, the ash-heap of history, since the Thanatos principle is not so easily discarded. The double-spaced separation that ensues marks an extraordinary turn in the poem, a daring pivot (to use one of the poem's key terms) to another arena where virile presence is on display, though in a far subtler, and perhaps therefore more dangerous, avatar. Focusing on the figure of the rooster, Bishop performs an utterly unanticipated pirouette to the Gospel story of Peter's predicted denial of Jesus: "I tell you, this very night, before the rooster crows, you will deny me three times" (Matthew 26: 34). The immediate connection to the poem's first section comes by way of the reference to "unwanted love," thus opening the door to a variety of betrayals, and continuing the theme of complicity in wider structures of aggressive actions.[3]

But the truly daring nature of Bishop's dialectical turn comes when the poem addresses what is termed by religious tradition as the Repentance of Peter. For, as we know, tradition has exercised a control over this act of betrayal, insisting that Peter's Fall becomes Fortunate in that it leads to repentance, grace, and the monumental established power of the basilisk-like Basilica. "*Gallus canit; / flet Petrus*" reads the inscription on "Old holy sculpture" (*P* 38–9), which "could set it all together" (*P* 38) as in the setting of broken bones. This ability to heal might be seen by some as a sign of forgiveness and "inescapable hope" (*P* 39). On its most overt level, this is how the poem reads. But undercutting that sanguine interpretation is also a creeping and perhaps creepy sense that this monumentalizing of forgiveness is also an act of monumental masculine hubris, the all-too-easy ability of men in power to commit crimes and then accord themselves the perquisites of forgiveness. Indeed, this is what Bishop terms the "pivot": "There is inescapable hope, the pivot" (*P* 39). Etymologically (and thematically, in this poem), "pivot" is an Old French word with many phallic overtones; indeed, it was a slang term for penis – which also happens to be the case for "peter," a vulgarism that somehow slipped by the censorious Moore in her critique of Bishop's language. Some critics have seen the second section of "Roosters" as an abandonment of female rage against militarism,[4] but I read it as more of a tonal transition on the scale of outrage. The subject-positioned lesbian poet seems almost "dazed," like Peter himself, agog with admiration, at the ability of these historical actors (almost always men) to absolve and re-christen themselves. She, and all those who identity with her counter-perspective, can scrawl graffiti on the monuments – "Poor Peter," "those cock-a-doodles," etc. (*P* 39) – but this is no mere barnyard brawl that she beholds. It is a battle for the keys to the kingdom in which only at the most obvious level is it clear who is "enemy, or friend" (*P* 40).

No later poem of Bishop's, with the exception of "Brazil, January 1, 1502," will so clearly express the revulsion against militarism of all sorts that we find in "Roosters." But this does not mean that she remains impervious to the War that is always "on" and which stays securely "outside." Just as Bishop testified to the anxiety penetrating her privileged room in the build-up to WWII, a sense of angst shared by many non-combatant witnesses removed from the immediate damage of the war zone, but threatened nonetheless by the possible spread of the infection, so we can find similar attestations in the aftermath of that war and the glide into the Cold War (a label that conveniently ignores the blood-bath on the Korean Peninsula). For an American poet, male or female, writing about the vulnerability of civilians who live in eras of constant threat, the danger no longer comes from old-style invasion or, indeed, from old-style bombing raids, but from the development of weapons of mass destruction which threaten every one and every thing. "The Armadillo" is an example of the former; "At the Fishhouses" a chilling embodiment of the latter.

"The Armadillo" was submitted to *The New Yorker* in the summer of 1956 and published the following summer. Thus, the poem was completed in the interval between the Suez Crisis and the Hungarian Revolution. Howard Moss, poetry editor of *The New Yorker*, wrote to Bishop: "We love THE ARMADILLO, which is charming and much more" (*NYr* 180). I will focus on the much more, namely the sense of danger emanating from the poem's lines as the poet beholds the beautiful fire balloons of carnivalesque ritual "suddenly turning dangerous," getting caught "in the downdraft from a peak" (*P* 101). Robert Lowell, to whom the poem was eventually dedicated, and who was himself a conscientious objector during WWII on the basis of his opposition to the indiscriminate bombing of civilians, wrote to Bishop: "I see the bomb in it in a delicate way" (*WIA* 591). As always with Bishop, the poem is achingly exact in its depiction of the actual scene, even as it expands the sphere of the actual to include that which cannot be seen but demands imagining – namely, the repercussions involved when the "innocent" fire balloons turn incendiary. The "real" damage is limited but pathos-ridden. When the fire balloon falls to earth, instead of soaring away from us, it rouses *the* pair of owls (not an impersonal "a") that the poet has come to know, leading her to mournfully observe that "The ancient owls' nest must have burned" (*P* 102). *Multum in parvo:* so much depends upon keeping beautiful small things safe from destruction. And yet, inevitably, our toys and our weapons – it is sometimes difficult to keep the two apart – threaten to turn, or be turned against us and the world we inhabit. The owl, the armadillo, we ourselves are in danger of becoming collateral (or targeted) damage when we aestheticize instruments of destruction, finding a certain apocalyptic beauty in firepower. But to Bishop's mind, what is most crucial is that we never succumb to a fascination with instruments of destruction, never believe that a terrible beauty is being born. Terror is not absolved by beauty. Bishop reinforces this point in the italicized opening line of the final stanza: "*Too pretty, dreamlike mimicry!*" (*P* 102). "The Armadillo" is constructed in a deliberately small-scale, localized setting, but it compels the reader to extrapolate the larger argument without naming it directly, much as Wallace Stevens does in "The Auroras of Autumn," where flashing lights from horizon to horizon simulate the atomic bomb in a not-so-delicate fashion.[5] Whether festive fire balloons or extravaganzas such as the celestial light show put on by Stevens, the point is that these displays cannot avoid serving as auguries of experience.

Interestingly, the poem of Bishop's which presents perhaps the most vivid sense of apocalyptic threat comes in the aftermath of World War II. "At the Fishhouses" was submitted to *The New Yorker* in 1947. "Cold dark deep" (*P* 63), as the poem's refrain runs, is a good description of its deliberate plunge into exploratory depths. The poem is a modern *katabasis*, a poem of descent: "Down at the water's edge, at the place / where they haul up the boats, up the long ramp / descending into the water" (*P* 63). There are many strata to this great poem, but the one I wish to explore has not been fully recognized, for the nightmare at the core of this sounding of the depths involves imagining what can only be described as an annihilating Flood of biblical proportions:

> The water seems suspended
> above the rounded gray and blue-gray stones.
> I have seen it over and over, the same sea, the same,
> slightly, indifferently swinging above the stones,
> icily free above the stones,
> above the stones and then the world. (*P* 63)

Here is a scenario of "total immersion," as the poem frames it in a different context, a dream-vision of the world sliding into extinction almost as an inevitable development, while the universe looks on indifferently. This is how the world ends, according to Bishop – not with a bang or a whimper but under a deluge. We are free to imagine our version of what might trigger such a wave, but the totality of the war and its conclusion in the unveiling of a weapon of mass destruction offers example enough. It is deeply significant that the end of the war seems to fill Bishop with a sense of apocalyptic foreboding. Bishop imagines dipping her hand into the icy water, "element bearable to no mortal" (*P* 63), and then immediately summons the image of fire: fire and ice, the apocalyptic duo. The water is so unbearably cold that "your bones would begin to ache and your hand would burn / as if the water were a transmutation of fire" (*P* 63). She imagines tasting the water: "If you tasted it, it would first taste bitter, / then briny, then surely burn your tongue" (*P* 63–4). The burning tongue is Pentecostal, which is to say, apocalyptic, but also cognitive, for the poet imagines that the destruction of the world might bring with it a taste of "what we imagine knowledge to be" (*P* 64). If, surely, some Revelation is at hand, the price to pay is too enormous and this is why "At the Fishhouses" ends with the poet declaring that "our knowledge is historical" (*P* 64) not apocalyptic. If we need to be reminded of the cost to be paid by the innocent for such "absolute" knowledge, Bishop provides it with a startling image of total destruction. Looking at the hillside above the frigid waters, she observes how "a million Christmas trees stand / waiting for Christmas" (*P* 63). Is there a more shockingly powerful instance of enjambment anywhere else in English language poetry? The slash marks the cutting down of the trees, an emblem of total death under the aegis of messianic birth. This is a grim reaping prefigured by the image of the old man at the beginning of the poem who has "scraped the scales, the principal beauty, / from unnumbered fish with that black old knife" (*P* 63), in another image of mass death.

"Roosters" may be Bishop's most "overt" anti-war or anti-militarist poem, but the most graphic moment of militaristic, masculinist violence comes in the 1959 poem, "Brazil, January 1, 1502" *The New Yorker* accepted the poem in November of 1959 (*NYr* 220). It is worth recalling that Castro came to power on January 1, 1959, so Bishop sets her poem against the backdrop of the Cold War crisis in Latin America brought on by the success of the Cuban Revolution. The way Bishop weaves the current crisis into the tapestry of the past is extraordinarily subtle. The American government was alarmed, to put it mildly, by the "invasion" of the southern portion of the Western Hemisphere by the Soviet Union acting through its Cuban proxy government, or so ran the narrative. The complexity of deliberate pronominal confusion created in the opening lines of the poem signifies Bishop's intention to complicate the question of who is invading whom. By staging the poem at an original moment of historical invasion – the date in the title marks the first time European conquistadores entered the harbor that would be named, by them, Rio de Janeiro – and then erasing the boundaries between "their" eyes and "ours" (the latter referencing the touristic gaze of the twentieth-century traveler), Bishop erases easy distinctions between the USA and THEM: "Januaries, Nature greets our eyes / exactly as she must have greeted theirs" (*P* 89). The last word of the poem is "it," and if there is one thing that unites us and them it is the shared sensation that the fabric of jungle landscape beheld from a touristic distance is an *it*, an other. All of the warring parties at the time – Russian, American, Cuban – can be said to derive from these original invaders and all share, in one form or another, a desire to plunder the land and its original peoples, to tear into the "hanging fabric" (*P* 90) of the tapestry that is the fabric of the very land itself. But Bishop takes the carnage even deeper as she associates the land with the native women of the land and, thus, the hanging fabric with the hymen. The true course and source of the plunder, in her historical vision, lodges in the manic desire of each conquistador "to catch an Indian for himself" (*P* 90). "Brazil, January 1, 1502" makes brutally clear what "Roosters" implied: despite different degrees of shared complicity, war at its most primal core is not far removed from rape, and rape is overwhelmingly a violent masculinist Sin. I use that word because Bishop uses it. Gazing at the veil of jungle, the eye of the tourist beholds a frozen tableau of terror, an ur-rape scene: "Still in the foreground there is Sin: / five sooty dragons near some massy rocks. [. . .] / The lizards scarcely breathe; all eyes / are on the smaller, female one, back-to" (*P* 89). The male attackers, whether "Christians, hard as nails" (*P* 90), or these sooty dragons, are the progenitors of all our wars, hot and cold, as Bishop sees it.

Perhaps the most mysterious, and richly elliptical, of Bishop's war poetry is the haunting prose poem, if that is the best term to use, "12 O' Clock News" (*P* 194–95), which employs the trope of the poet's desk as a microcosm for the world at large. But rather than celebrating her power to survey that world from "a superior vantage point," like some latter-day Penseroso, Bishop mocks the arrogance of the distanced observer, whether poet or official broadcaster, who would presume to gain interpretive clarity over distant wars. The poem has been brilliantly interpreted by Steven Gould Axelrod who describes it as "a parody newscast," an example of "televisual imperialism" (39).[6] What gives the poem its peculiarly sharp edge is the fact that the poet does not spare herself from satire, since the way in which objects on her writing table are described gibe nicely with the newscaster's glib description of "this small, backward country" (Vietnam, surely) with "its inscrutable people." One is tempted to say that "12 O' Clock News" is as much about news reportage – think Walter Cronkite – and how increasingly complex forms of communication alter the very perception of war's landscape, but for the fact that Bishop reminds us of the unalterable fact of war: soldiers who "lie heaped together [. . .] in hideously contorted positions, all dead." As Axelrod phrases it, "the television journalist's prose narration (on the right side of the page) turns desktop objects (indicated in italics on the left) into scenes from a televised war zone" (39). How savagely appropriate, then, that the corresponding object for the battlefield is the poet's "*ashtray*". This takes us back to the "ash-heap" in "Roosters," graveyard of the fighting cocks – the one thing about war that never changes, however reported.

Notes

1. Susan Schweik, *A Gulf So Deeply Cut: American Women Poets and the Second World War* (Madison: The University of Wisconsin Press, 1991), 213. The Bogan quotation also appears on this page.
2. Schweik, 216–17.
3. See Camille Roman, *Elizabeth Bishop's World War II—Cold War View* (Palgrave, 2001), 53–69.
4. Schweik, 216.
5. See Charles Berger, *Forms of Farewell: The Late Poetry of Wallace Stevens* (Madison: The University of Wisconsin Press, 1985); and Malcolm Woodland, *Wallace Stevens and the Apocalyptic Mode* (Iowa City: The University of Iowa Press, 2005).
6. Steven Gould Axelrod, "Bishop, History, and Politics," in *The Cambridge Companion to Elizabeth Bishop*, ed. Angus Cleghorn and Jonathan Ellis (Cambridge: Cambridge University Press, 2014), 35–48.

CHAPTER 19

The Cold War

Steven Gould Axelrod

Although Elizabeth Bishop typically sought to disengage from controversy, she remained very interested in public policy. Her poems recurrently registered the perspectives and issues of the Cold War, especially under the pressure of current events. Her language reflected her absorption into, and her resistance to, the political frameworks and vocabularies circulating during the period. She embedded her aesthetics, as Thomas Travisano has remarked, "in a detailed web of [. . .] cultural observation,"[1] so that her meditative poems often acquire unexpected layers of political significance. Subtle and ironic, they posit a sense, reinforced by her reading, that human beings are "a political animal."[2] As her acquaintance Hannah Arendt wrote, individuals pursuing creative and moral fulfillment must refuse an ideal of sheltered solitude and recognize instead the necessity of the "in-between" – a connection to others within "the public realm."[3]

Bishop's poem "View of the Capitol from the Library of Congress" (drafted in 1950, published in 1951) initiated her development of a Cold War poetics.[4] It employed the then-current vocabulary of containment culture for resistant ends. The poem brought together such Cold War staples as a two-valued orientation; a hyper-awareness of border (a transition line) and boundary (a limit); a fear of authoritarianism and violence arising from across (but also from within) any borderline; and a sense that "containment culture" (Nadel) reinforced the "epistemology of the closet" (Sedgwick).[5] In subsequent poems, Bishop deployed her entangled private and public poetics, and her mastery of both irony and pathos, to address imperialism and war, economic inequality, and the problematics of race, sexuality, and gender. The acuteness of her poems co-existed with, and undoubtedly grew out of, her ambivalent attachment to the very social conditions and discourses she critiqued.

The Cold War (1945–91), a period of political, economic, and military contestation between the Western Bloc led by the United States and the Eastern Bloc led by the Soviet Union, produced a lexicon so powerful that it injected its organization and compulsions into Bishop's awareness for most of her career. The Cold War represented a prolonged contest between "mighty opposites,"[6] as well as a series of crisis points. Moreover, it produced in its rival blocs certain features in common: a wish for territory; predictive narratives of victory shadowed and undermined by nuclear dread; a heightened degree of surveillance with the purpose of maintaining behavioral and ideational conformity within each sphere; a suppression of non-normativity; and a Gramscian or Kennanite common-sense framing of situations and issues as binaries, with an assumption that the two entities or values in question would naturally not simply contrast but require a moral choice. Associated with these features was an obsession with borders and frontiers, conceived not as liminal spaces but as dividing lines, paradigmatically marked by fences or walls, indicating geopolitical distinctions as differential as black and white. This two-valued orientation moved ghostlike and unnoted from the cartography of places like Korea and Germany to zones of thinking and feeling within each of the mighty blocs, whose mutual habit of seeing in dichotomies ironically bound them together.

Nevertheless, local conditions dictated that the commonalities of Cold War cultures – habits of dualism, surveillance, and social and sexual conformity; expectations of future victory or annihilation; and a fascination with the procedures of containing and closeting (often suggesting a prohibited fascination with the excluded element) – would play out in different ways. In the United States, State Department diplomat and intellectual George Kennan theorized the "containment" of communism in his landmark essay, "The Sources of Soviet Conduct" (1947).[7] This analysis had a profound impact on President Truman and most thinkers in or near Schlesinger's "vital center,"[8] and it soon transformed from a military and foreign policy strategy to an epistemology that influenced every aspect of American life. For example, it normalized the containment of any domestic group perceived as aberrant, including white women (through the process of suburbanization), racial minorities (through the effect of white flight), queers (through the mechanism of the closet), and dissidents (through the proliferation of carceral spaces). Yet even as hegemonic forces demanded that variant bodies and voices absent themselves if they could not worm their way into model citizenship, those same bodies and voices often discovered an alternative identity in resistance. These cultural complexities and conflicts, these circumambient habits of cognition and language, were the matrix out of which Bishop's poems emerged.

Bishop moved through the Cold War era within a circle of anti-communist liberals, though she did worry about "how certain red-capped liberal feelings can go with a sinister acceptance of the terrible" (*WIA* 452). She had a "horror of Communism" (*WIA* 362), and a horror of McCarthy. She read such political theorists as Reinhold Niebuhr, Arthur Schlesinger, Jr., Raymond Aron, and Hannah Arendt. She cited those theorists in her correspondence, and socialized with the latter three. When she wrote that Lowell's *Life Studies* raised her awareness of "those 'ironies of American History'" (*PPL* 707), it was Niebuhr's *The Ironies of American History* to which she was referring.[9] Her reference, however, is a backhanded compliment, since she implies that she prefers Lowell's actual ironies to Niebuhr's theorizing about irony. Beyond her reading, however, Bishop's political interests doubtless also flowed from her positioning as a queer person inhabiting homophobic environments and her empathic sensitivity to social abandonment rooted in her interrupted childhood.

Bishop employed binary thinking in the service of queer nonconformity in her early Cold War poem, "View of the Capitol from the Library of Congress" (*P* 67). It's worth remembering that she composed the poem when the Korean War, the US–Soviet arms race, and McCarthyism were all raging. The poem's vocabulary of borders and oppositions echoes such Cold War dividing lines as those bifurcating Korea and Germany, as well as the "Iron Curtain" dividing Europe and the American Defense Perimeter proposed for Asia in 1950. If Bishop's paradigmatic use of a dividing line between contrastive forces confirms that way of thinking as a lingua franca, it also converts it into a subversive epistemic tool. As Kirsten Hotelling Zona observes in another context, Bishop teases our habits of "seeing with familiar oppositions" in order to pull the rug out from under them.[10] Instead of the "final, all-out battle between communistic atheism and Christianity" that McCarthy envisioned,[11] "View of the Capitol" presents us with an ironized battle between military music and the quiet of a library. The anti-patriarchal, anti-war poem evades Cold War policing by mimicking the prevailing epistemic orientation, while at the same time destabilizing the very epistemology it evokes.

In the poem's binary, the Capitol is associated with nationalist forces, whereas the Library of Congress is associated with the life of the mind. Bishop's skepticism toward the Capitol building, which houses the legislative branch of government, reflects her repulsion against warlike rhetoric as well as McCarthyist attacks on political dissenters, intellectuals, artists, and queers, among whom was a somewhat camouflaged Bishop herself, then serving as Poetry Consultant to the Library of Congress (1949–50). Bishop's skepticism toward democracy here may seem out of step with the more optimistic scenarios of consensus historians, but it reflects queer alienation at mid-century as well as forecasting later strains of liberal unease.

The music in Bishop's poem, emanating from a performance of the Air Force Band (which in 1950 must have been all-male, white, and straight-seeming) is "coarse" and "loud." It is also "hard," in contrast to the McCarthyist notion that liberal intellectuals were "soft," or effeminate. The Capitol's music, however, can't quite permeate a line of "giant trees" standing between the hypermasculine Capitol and the effeminate Library. The failure of the Capitol's military music to be heard in the library's sphere signals queer resistance. In effect, communism and anti-communism both occupy the "hard" side of a hard–soft binary, whereas thoughtful and queer cultural practices, implicitly including poetry, inhabit the "soft" side. Bishop uses Cold War epistemology against itself, turning her habitual stance of ironic aloofness into a form of engagement.

Later in the Cold War era, Bishop preferred to challenge the era's binary mode (and its culture of paranoia) more directly. She developed a metonymic counter-style emphasizing profusion and multiplicity. In "Over 2,000 Illustrations and a Complete Concordance," for instance, the speaker's world travels (as Jeffrey Gray argues[12]) blunt her impulse to repeat master narratives, impelling her instead to see "Everything only connected by 'and' and 'and'" (*P* 57–58). In "Santarém," the "I" remembers visiting the site where the Tapajós and Amazon rivers meet and flow together, and muses that such binary oppositions as "life/death, right/wrong, male/female" would have "resolved" and "dissolved" in that "watery, dazzling dialectic" (*P* 207–09).

When Bishop wrote of war and violence, however, she tended to revert from her aesthetics of multiplicity to her earlier epistemic of contending opposites – or to pit these alternative perspectives against each other. This representational contest of two-valued versus multivalued orientations appears, for example, in "Brazil, January 1, 1502." The poem, composed in the 1950s and published in 1960, locates an analogue for US–Soviet imperialisms in Portugal's early modern conquest of Brazil. Bishop describes the Portuguese "Christians," glinting in "armor," ripping into the new world (*P* 89–90) – much as Niebuhr described Americans and Soviets, each in their "armor" of nuclear weapons, exercising their "lust for power" on the vast "uncommitted world."[13] Bishop portrays the

Portuguese invaders as being oblivious to the richly varied landscape, intent only on raping indigenous women, who flee their assault. Whereas colonial conquest enacts redundant aggressions, women's culture forms an intricate tapestry modeled on nature itself.

Christian believers generate another apocalypse in "The Armadillo," published in 1957. They launch fire balloons, which at first appear picturesque but suddenly turn "dangerous," like bombers overhead, raining down fire on the forest and its creatures (*P* 101–02). The "*dreamlike mimicry*" of the final conflagration may simulate the random cruelty of an inimical cosmos; or it may suggest the ecocidal tendencies of human beings, as manifested by the numerous great fires of the 1950s, such as the Capitan Gap, Chinchaga, Rattlesnake, and Cleveland National wildfires and the longstanding efforts to deforest the Amazon through fire. Given its horrific parting exclamation, "*O falling fire and piercing cry / and panic*," the poem may also figure the nuclear dread of the mid-century or the terror of civilians caught in the regional wars that combusted throughout the 1950s in such places as Korea, Indochina, Algeria, and Costa Rica. The final vision of nest burning and animals fleeing evokes the refugee migrations that inevitably result from such wars.

Bishop's later poems, "One Art" and "12 O'Clock News," layer an implicit critique of the Vietnam War into lines that also expose private anxieties. As a result, the polis and the oikia are mutually imbricated in a manner that troubles the Cold War commitment to binary oppositions. Although "One Art" (*P* 198), for example, certainly evokes Bishop's "distress over the risk of losing Alice [Methfessel],"[14] it also condenses Cold War thought and feeling at a particular historical moment: 1975, the year when Saigon fell (in April) and when "One Art" was published (in November in *The New Yorker*). The poem's anxiety about "disaster" and its references to lost cities, rivers, and a continent echo the language of military defeat that had been circulating through US political discourse since 1968.[15]

"12 O'Clock News" (*P* 194–95), which was begun during the Korean War and completed during the Vietnam War, similarly flows from Bishop's understanding that "we live in a horrible and terrifying world, and the worst moments of horrible and terrifying lives are an allegory of the world" (*PPL* 914). The prose poem on the right side of the page satirizes a newscast of the horrible and terrifying world. The broadcaster who speaks this part of the text describes a war scene in which "visibility is poor." His eyes cannot fathom the scene, and he therefore emphasizes its opacity and exoticism. Although he admits that the details of this "small, backward country" are "far from completely known to us," he nevertheless organizes his inherently baffled account into a master narrative told from "our superior vantage point." This is the "artifactuality" that Derrida speaks of, produced through a process of fictional fashioning, and reflecting the privilege of "the Western."[16] Viewing the "natives" compulsively from above, the narrator portrays them in stereotypical terms of inscrutability, childishness, and threat. Like other Vietnam broadcasters, he never uses the term "imperialism." He finally zeroes in on a scene of dead native soldiers in "hideously contorted positions," victims of Western technological superiority (which, however, was failing to carry the day in reality).

When we read the marginalia on the left, however, we are invited to understand the story in a different way. The marginalia resignifies the moon as a gooseneck lamp, the dead soldiers as cigarette stubs in an ashtray, and so on. From this angle, the poem is about writer's block and late-night despair. Yet this alternative rendering of the scene, however disorienting, is not entirely incompatible with the broadcaster's narrative we have been citing. The refiguring of the twisted bodies as snuffed-out cigarette butts hardly reduces the horror of the image. The insomnia and desperation implicit on the left must relate in some way to the cold war rhetoric on the right. Through its veils of misprision, the poem focuses our awareness on the suffering of indigenes who, like the indigenous women in "Brazil, January 1, 1502," evade the invader's understanding.

Beyond Bishop's critiques of war, she sought to illuminate economic inequality as well, especially while living in Brazil. Spurred by the poverty so apparent in Rio, she was perhaps also inspired by Latin American styles of public poetry, and by the growing global attention to economic issues arising out of the competition between Western and Eastern blocs. Brazil struggled in the post-WWII era to maintain and improve its economic conditions, but a gradually increasing gross domestic product did little to improve the lives of the middle class and poor. A UN World Economic Report published in 1952 observed that domestic consumer spending had stalled because "the large profits from exports [. . .] accrued mostly to the large-scale planters and traders."[17] The middle and later parts of the decade saw an emphasis on industrialization over exports and a resultant lessening of economic inequality, thanks in part to UN support and in part to initiatives of center-left President Joselino Kubitschek.[18] Beginning in 1961, the United States, seeking to counter Cuban influence in the hemisphere, sought to improve Brazilian living conditions through a package of grants and loans under the aegis of the Alliance for Progress, though Stephen Rabe argues that despite its ostensible aims, the program ended up bolstering "undemocratic, conservative, and frequently repressive regimes and groups."[19] In any event, the Brazilian military coup of 1964 slowed economic development, though it did not reverse it.

Despite the slightly positive turn in per capita income and life expectancy in 1950s Brazil, "A Baby Found in the Garbage" (*PPL* 239–40), which was drafted in the mid-1950s but never finished, calls attention to the continuing disparities in the lives of the urban rich and poor. The poem is an elegy for an unclothed, dying baby, wrapped in a newspaper, while the city's "white fumes" curl around her, as if polluted air were her blanket. The poem's passion must derive from Bishop's anguished identification with the baby, abandoned as she herself had once been abandoned. But the agitated and the perhaps purposeful repetitions and self-interruptions of the text may also signal the poet's guilty identification with the child's mother and especially the mother's employer, who lives in an "apartment house for the rich," much like the Rio apartment house Bishop occupied. The poem oscillates between downward motions (the baby "slipped down" a garbage "chute" – the noun deriving from the Latin *cadere*, to fall) and upward motions (the birds over a garbage dump "flap up" before settling back again). Jonathan Ellis has helpfully identified these movements with the upward trajectory of the Romantic sublime.[20] I would add that they also provide visual and kinesthetic images of the gaping social disparity between rich and poor, much as similar images would do a few years later in Akira Kurosawa's great urban film, *High and Low* (1963), or in Bong Joon-ho's contemporary classic, *Parasite* (2019). Fallen or pushed out of the house of the rich, the little homeless baby dies, before even having much chance to cry.

A similar fusion of speaker and protagonist occurs in "Pink Dog" (*P* 212–13). Reflecting Bishop's "increasingly involved dialogue with Brazilian politics,"[21] this poem (like "A Baby Found in the Garbage" and "The Burglar of Babylon") surveys the urban geography as a space that ejects the weak, the poor, and the different. The passion here is suggested not by self-interruptions but by an excess of form: propulsive iambic triplets that draw on various sources, including Dante, nursery rhymes, as well as Carnival samba as exhibited by Maria Lúcia Milléo Martins in a recent essay.[22] The poem's diseased dog evokes the poet herself, who also suffered from skin disease, and it also figures the city's dispossessed, especially its poor and infirm women. But the dog, impelled to leave her babies, also resembles the mother in "A Baby Found in the Garbage" and Bishop's own mother. Again, the poem refers to – and in a sense becomes – a newspaper, detailing the urban apocalypse. It's been in "all the papers" how the police deal with beggars: "They take and throw them in the tidal rivers." There they exist in the "sewage," much like the baby cast down a garbage chute.

It's worth noting that this poem was begun in 1962, when the execution-style killing of two beggars was in all the papers, and it was completed in 1964, a year before the opening of Flamengo Park, a gigantic modernist park planned and overseen by Bishop's partner Lota de Macedo Soares. The park was one of many redevelopment projects initiated by Rio's rightist governor Carlos Lacerda, a close friend of Macedo Soares and valued by Bishop as well. Lacerda, as Hicok explains, was implicated in the rise of "deadly policies concerning the poor"; when he took office as governor, "he reorganized the state's military police in order to fight crime, and one of the solutions to combatting crime in Rio was the death squads."[23] There is no evidence that Bishop knew about Lacerda's connection to the killing of the poor, but she may have revealed her suspicions when she called him "dangerous" in a letter to Lowell (*WIA* 436). Moreover, Lacerda, encouraged by the United States and the IMF, cleared many slums and working-class neighborhoods adjacent to Flamengo Park, and relocated the inhabitants to underfunded housing projects including the infamous "City of God." His tenure as governor witnessed "some of the largest and most brutal favela razings in Rio's history."[24] Bishop's critique of class iniquity in "Pink Dog" may reflect both her own abjection and her apprehensions about the dire effect Lacerda was having on the city's poor. Using mockery to stave off despair, "Pink Dog" evokes the deathly situation of the marginalized and sacrificial, and then recovers their dignity in the subversive space of masquerade. Oscar Wilde observed, "Man is least himself when he talks in his own person. Give him a mask, and he will tell you the truth."[25] Bishop, who revealed some of her deepest feelings within the artifice of poetry, might have agreed.

Bishop's most radical politics appeared in her recurrent evocations of queer embodiment, subjectivity, and sociality, which were often hidden in plain sight in her published poems. At the height of the Cold War, she was positioned between two disparate but intersecting cultural phenomena. One was "the lavender scare." McCarthyism made little distinction between anti-Communism and homophobia, as suggested by the term "pinko" and such pairings as "perverts and security risks."[26] By 1950, the Red Scare/Lavender Scare derived its affective force more from homophobia than from anti-Communism. The number of Communists to discover and punish was small and diminishing, whereas gay men and lesbians existed in much more robust numbers, and queer desire could be discovered, or suspected, everywhere. Bishop observed the persecution of gays and lesbians first-hand in Washington during her year as a government employee in 1949–50, the same period in which Senator Joseph McCarthy told the nation that the Federal government was infiltrated by Communists and that Communism was linked to homosexuality, thereby initiating an era of cultural paranoia. As Clay Poupart has written, "the issue of gays in government was coming to increased public and official attention just as Cold War alarm was reaching a new high."[27] According to Lillian Faderman, it was "as deadly to be soft on homosexuals as it was to be soft on Communists."[28] Containment and its specular double, the closet, mutually fortified themselves, and, as a result, many more gay people were forced to leave the government during the ensuing purge than were Communists.[29] Moreover, Bonnie J. Morris notes that lesbians and gay men "continued to be at risk for psychiatric lockup as well as jail" throughout the 1950s and 1960s.[30] Given Bishop's traumatic loss of her mother to the psychiatric-carceral complex, the possibility of something similar happening to her must have been terrifying.

Although Bishop famously told Frank Bidart that she wanted "closets, closets, and more closets,"[31] she also wanted to leave the closet door ajar. She wanted to disguise but also to reveal in a straight culture that didn't necessarily want to hear queer messaging. The poems newly published in *A Cold Spring* (1955) and *Questions of Travel* (1965) often evoke domestic pleasures experienced with female friends or lovers. These poems make plain the degree to which Bishop found interest, humor, relief, and joy in addressing same-sex intimacy, gender play, lesbian desire, the female body, and feminist language. She designed her confessions within a medium marked by pronominal and other types of ambiguity, metaphoric and metonymic description, and code words such as "gay," "queer," and "inverted," which allowed resistant meanings to hide as seemingly secondary or farfetched. The 1950s and 1960s were famously a period in which a dominant ideology of heteronormativity felt driven to punish and discipline difference. Nevertheless, as many historians have documented, a nascent queer rebellion gathered strength despite and because of heteronormative policing.[32] *A Cold Spring* emerged in a Cold War, bearing outlines of the era's policing in its strategies of evasion.

A Cold Spring now comes across as a "long gay book," to adopt one of Gertrude Stein's titles, even if that semantic thread was visible only to mid-century readers who wished to see it. Breaking from the era's theme of "manliness on trial,"[33] the sequence creates an alternative queer world of female relations and desires. When texts are dedicated, they are dedicated to women. When close friendships are revealed, they are between women. When love relationships appear, the gender of the beloved lacks explicit designation, which by itself becomes a code for queerness. In "A Summer Dream" (*P* 60–61), the speaker and her (presumably female) lover are "wakened in the dark" by a babbling brook. In "Insomnia" (*P* 68), which plays on the then-current psychiatric category of sexual "inversion," the speaker imagines a "world inverted," in which "you love me." The poem evokes the devastation of love-loss, as does the later "One Art." The sequence concludes on a happier note with "The Shampoo" (*P* 82), in which the speaker offers to wash her dear friend's sparkling black hair.

Motifs of queer identity and trans sensibility reappear in such later poems as "Crusoe in England" (*P* 182–86) and "Exchanging Hats" (*P* 230–31). "Crusoe in England" evokes Bishop's attachment and separation fears regarding Lota de Macedo Soares in terms of Daniel Defoe's male protagonists.[34] "Exchanging Hats" playfully recalls or imagines an uncle and aunt wearing each other's hats, much as Bishop enjoyed wearing men's shirts (*OA* 381; *WIA* 229). Her very last poem published in her lifetime, "Sonnet" (*P* 214), ends with the cathected if ambiguous word "gay." She tells some of her readers what they want to know, but at the same time hides what others need to stay hidden.

The posthumously published poems make Bishop's queer meanings clearest. These include such powerful and varied texts as "It is marvellous to wake up together ..." (*P* 283–84), "A Drunkard" (*P* 317–20), "Vague Poem (*Vaguely love poem*)" (*P* 323–26), and "Breakfast Song" (*P* 327–28). In "Vague Poem (*Vaguely love poem*)," for example, she wrote perhaps the most embodied and ecstatic evocation of sexual love in her canon:

> Clear pink breasts and darker, crystalline nipples,
> Rose-rock, rose-quartz, roses, roses, roses
> Exacting roses from the body,
> And the even darker, accurate, rose of sex –

Elizabeth Bishop's texts from the late 1940s onward were strongly shaped by Cold War epistemics and vocabularies. Fascinated by borders, and by what could happen if she crossed them, she was fully engaged with containment culture. Her poems were to a significant extent generated by it even as they subverted or opposed it, or blasted it away.

Notes

1. Thomas Travisano, *Love Unknown: The Life and Worlds of Elizabeth Bishop* (New York: Viking, 2019), 141.
2. Aristotle, *Politics* (Digireads.com Publishing, 2017), 3, 52; Hannah Arendt, *The Human Condition* (Chicago: University of Chicago Press, 1989), 22–23.
3. Hannah Arendt, *Men in Dark Times* (New York: Mariner, 1970), 4.
4. See Camille Roman, *Elizabeth Bishop's World War II–Cold War View* (New York: Palgrave, 2001), 120–21, 138–40; Steven Gould Axelrod, "Elizabeth Bishop and Containment Policy," *American Literature* 75.4 (2003), 843, 849–67.

5. Alan Nadel, *Containment Culture* (Durham, NC: Duke University Press, 1995); Eve Kosofsky Sedgwick, *Epistemology of the Closet* (Berkeley: University of California Press, 1990).
6. William Shakespeare, *Hamlet* 5.2.62 (England, 1603).
7. George Kennan (writing as "X"), "The Sources of Soviet Conduct," *Foreign Affairs* 25.4 (1947), 566–82.
8. Arthur Schlesinger, Jr. *The Vital Center: The Politics of Freedom* (New York: Riverside Press, 1949).
9. Reinhold Niebuhr, *The Irony of American History* (New York: Charles Scribner's Sons, 1952).
10. Kirsten Hotelling Zona, "Bishop, Race, Class, and Gender," in *The Cambridge Companion to Elizabeth Bishop*, ed. Angus Cleghorn and Jonathan Ellis (New York: Cambridge University Press, 2014), 53.
11. Joseph R. McCarthy, "Communists in Government Service," *Congressional Record* (81st Congress, 2nd session, 1955).
12. Jeffrey Gray, *Mastery's End: Travel and Postwar American Poetry* (Athens: University of Georgia Press, 2005).
13. Niebuhr, *The Irony of American History*, 16, 33.
14. Travisano, *Love Unknown*, 368.
15. Daniel C. Hallin, *The "Uncensored War": The Media and Vietnam* (Berkeley, University of California Press, 1989), 159–210.
16. Jacques Derrida, "Artifactualities," *Echographies of Television* (Cambridge, UK : Polity, 2002), 3–4.
17. *World Economic Report 1950–51* (New York: UN Department of Economic Affairs, 1952), 38.
18. Mauricio Cárdenas and Steven M. Helfand, "Latin American Economic Development," *The New Palgrave Dictionary of Economics* (Online Edition, 2011); Pedro Ferreira de Souza, "A History of Inequality: Top Incomes in Brazil, 1926/2015" (Working Paper #167, 2017, ipcig.org), 9–10.
19. Stephen C. Rabe. *The Most Dangerous Area in the World: John F. Kennedy Confronts Communist Revolution in Latin America* (Chapel Hill: University of North Carolina Press, 1999), 195–99.
20. Jonathan Ellis, *Art and Memory in the Work of Elizabeth Bishop* (Aldershot: Ashgate, 2006), 97–98.
21. Bethany Hicok, *Elizabeth Bishop's Brazil* (Charlottesville: University of Virginia Press, 2016), 99.
22. Maria Lúcia Milléo Martins, "Elizabeth Bishop and Brazilian Popular Music: From Anonymous Sambas to Contemporary Composers," *Elizabeth Bishop and the Music of Literature*, ed. Angus Cleghorn (Palgrave Macmillan, 2019), 89–99.
23. Hicok, *Elizabeth Bishop's Brazil*, 114.
24. Brodwyn M. Fischer, *A Poverty of Rights: Citizenship and Inequality in Twentieth-Century Rio de Janeiro* (Stanford: Stanford University Press, 2008), 60, 79.
25. Oscar Wilde, "The Critic as Artist," in *Intentions* (London: Forgotten Books, 2012), 167.

26. William C. Levin, "Cultural Commentary: What's in a Name, You Pinko?" *Bridgewater Review*, 20.1 (2001), 14; David K. Johnson, *The Lavender Scare: The Cold War Persecution of Gays and Lesbians in the Federal Government* (Chicago: University of Chicago Press, 2004), 80.
27. Clay Poupart, "'When will my turn come?' The Civil Service Purges and the Construction of a Gay Security Risk in the Cold War United States, 1945–55." MA Thesis, History Department, University of Saskatchewan, Saskatoon, 2005, 52. harvest.usask.ca.
28. Lillian Faderman, *The Gay Revolution: The Story of the Struggle* (New York, Simon and Schuster, 2015), 22.
29. Johnson, *The Lavendar* Scare, 76.
30. Bonnie J. Morris, "History of Lesbian, Gay, Bisexual and Transgender Social Movements," American Psychological Association, web article, apa.org.
31. Gary Fountain, ed. *Elizabeth Bishop: An Oral Biography* (Amherst: University of Massachusetts Press, 1994), 327.
32. See, e.g., Michael Bronski, *A Queer History of the United States* (Boston: Beacon Press, 2011); Faderman, *The Gay Revolution*; Susan Stryker, *Transgender History: The Roots of Today's Revolution*, rev. ed. (New York: Seal Press, 2017); and Jessica Toops, "The Lavender Scare: Persecution of Lesbianism During the Cold War," *Western Illinois Historical Review* 5 (2013), 91–107.
33. Suzanne Clark, *Cold Warriors: Manliness on Trial in the Rhetoric of the West* (Carbondale: Southern Illinois University Press, 2000).
34. Travisano, *Love Unknown*, 336–37.

CHAPTER 20

Music

Christopher Spaide

In some unrealized universe, not exactly parallel to ours but branching off partway through the 1930s, *Elizabeth Bishop in Context* is not a book about a poet. "I'd love to be a composer!" Bishop proclaimed in a 1966 interview: "I studied counterpoint and the piano for years, and I suppose I'm still 'musical.'"[1] Bishop, typically, was understating things. Of the alternate paths she often dusted off in conversations and letters – painting and medicine were two others – music touched her life first and left last. In a 1977 talk on her influences, Bishop declared herself "full of hymns," even "saturated with hymns," having been "brought up singing Protestant hymns" at home, church, and school; those same hymns, sung by friends and colleagues, would punctuate her memorial service in Harvard's Aggasiz Ballroom ("I'm not the slightest bit religious," she clarified in her talk: "I just like these hymns.").[2] In terms of formal education and practical training, music vied only with poetry. She started piano lessons soon after "being kidnapped" to Worcester, and later recounted her studies as a Carrollian endeavor, alluringly out-of-scale: "The staves were enormous and I wrote notes in them as large as watermelons. I couldn't touch the pedals, of course. But how I loved the sound of the wide yellow piano keys!" (*Pr* 87, 95). After Walnut Hill – where she studied piano and harmony and sang alto in the Glee Club – Bishop arrived at Vassar intending to major in music and specialize in composition, but stage fright in required recitals and an aversion to advanced music theory steered her toward the English Department. She resumed music studies after college, attending Ralph Kirkpatrick's New School seminar in Early Keyboard Music and studying clavichord with Kirkpatrick and at the Schola Cantorum in Paris. Bishop's clavichord, custom-made by Arnold Dolmetsch in 1935, trailed her on nearly every intercontinental move, for four decades her life's sole unlosable thing – until she found a buyer, finally, in Howard Moss. Bishop never stopped dreaming of writing her way back toward music, planning and leaving unfinished a Jonsonian masque, a libretto, lyrics, translations of Brazilian popular songs, and prose pieces on the blues, Brazilian folk, and San Francisco's psychedelic rock. The completed music writing, all told, amounts to a cursory overview in *Brazil* (1962) of the country's folk and "formal" musics (see *Pr* 214–17, 224–25) and a 1965 *New York Times* dispatch on Rio de Janeiro's quatercentenary, "On the Railroad Named Delight," with translations of four Carnival sambas – some acidly timely, others giddily timeless. So much for Elizabeth Bishop the composer, lyricist, and musicologist.

As for Elizabeth Bishop, poet? At the least, she cherished music as one of the profoundest, most thoroughly studied analogues for poetry. When "thinking in musical terms," as she wrote to Robert Lowell in 1958, she identified with the modernist Austrian composer Anton Webern, whose small-scale achievements epitomized "That strange kind of modesty that I think one feels in almost everything contemporary one really likes [. . .] Modesty, care, *space*, a sort of helplessness but determination at the same time" (*WIA* 250). She reprised her Webern comparison in appreciations of Marianne Moore and the artist Wesley Wehr – two critical appraisals so sympathetic they pass as self-reflections, obliquely angled – and extended musical analogies to other poets; Lowell's contrasting sonorities, for instance, were all *Sturm und Drang*, "heavy-beat rhythms and trumpet sounds" (*Pr* 338, 352, 334).

At most, music was not only poetry's analogue but poetry's closest cousin among the arts, perched right at its outer edge. In 1935, justifying her curious fascination with the clavichord to Frani Blough Muser, a lifelong friend and music scholar, Bishop paraphrased Ezra Pound's *ABC of Reading* (1934): "Pound says somewhere, 'The further poetry departs from music, the more decadent it gets,' etc., and I want to learn whatever I can about the periods when it hadn't yet departed – which is approximately up to the end of the clavichord days" (*OA* 31). Bishop never lost the sense that lyric borders lyrics, poetry approaches song – a thesis she casually, unprogrammatically reiterated, whether she was musing that "hymns are poetry of a kind,"[3] celebrating sambas as "the living poetry of poor Cariocans" (*Pr* 346), or singing Cole Porter's praises to Lowell: "He really was quite a poet – I don't think you'd agree – but sometimes in his endless frivolity and modish detail he out-does Auden" (*WIA* 736).

Generations of critics have given us frames for understanding Bishop as a visualist, a poet of preternatural optics and painterly detail. But the poets fondest of her often framed her differently. Moore, reviewing *North & South*, championed the young Bishop's "musicianly qualities"; a quarter-century later, James Merrill paid slantwise tribute to his favorite contemporary poet with an homage to "The Victor Dog," the dutiful terrier on the RCA Victor label, an encyclopedic listener who dreamily "Gives rise to harmonies beyond belief."[4] What might it mean to shift focus from Bishop's seeing to her hearing, a shift Bishop herself conducts across the cold-blooded, dysmorphic self-caricatures of "Rainy Season; Sub-Tropics"? In her croaking overture as a "Giant Toad," she protests the bodily burdens of abnormally discerning sight: "My eyes bulge and hurt. They are my one great beauty, even so." So for her final guise as a "Giant Snail" she chooses another sense-organ, ventriloquizing a creature whose very footing on earth demands around-the-clock listening: "All night I shall be like a sleeping ear" (*P* 163, 165).

When Bishop's "sleeping ear" heard music, what did it listen for? Five characteristics distinguish music as it appears in her mature poetry. First, music, like poetry and unlike painting, unfolds over time. With its rhythms and refrains, skips and starts, accelerandos and ritardandos, music occasions Bishop's mediations on the fleeting, the lasting, and the cyclical, in human behavior and the natural world alike. Second, music is unmistakably marked by place: it could be countryfied or urban, consolingly local or invigoratingly foreign, American or European or Brazilian, but it was never placeless. (For that reason, and not to periodize her development rigidly, I follow Bishop's career chronologically, as she encounters new musics in new settings.) Third, music is an aesthetic plane where culture and nature can both participate and possibly synchronize – where, at a filling station in "Questions of Travel," "the sad, two-noted, wooden tune / of disparate wooden clogs / carelessly clacking" can play off "the other, less primitive music of the fat brown bird / who sings above the broken gasoline pump." Fourth, with its invisible workings yet precisely emotive effects, music allows escape into fantasy, transgression, and unverifiable reverie. Take the parenthetical digression, *sotto voce*, interrupting the careful listening above: "(In another country the clogs would all be tested. / Each pair there would have identical pitch.)" (*P* 92). But Bishop is too severe a self-ironist to be transported utterly: where a Baudelaire might notice the gas-flame-blue seawater of "The Bight" and fancifully "hear it turning to marimba music," Bishop leaves her fantasy conditional, an *if* indulged-in, then discarded (*P* 59). So Bishop's mature poems, finally, rarely depict music as transcendent but instead ground it within identifiable sources – musical instruments, vocalists, and the playback technologies of portables, jukeboxes, and hi-fis. Bishop presents these five characteristics as inhering in music itself, but we might also construe them as five objects – manipulation of time, markings of place, culture and nature's equal participation, emotionally driven fantasy, this-worldly sources – that Bishop juggles with her acrobatic attention then embeds in her poetry for our own close listening.

Fine-tuning that musical attention, for the young Bishop, required virtuosic efforts of trial and error. Music enters her poetry first as subject matter, in juvenilia like 1928's "Sonnet": "I am in need of music that would flow." Yearning for "A song to fall like water on my head," "Sonnet" is at once a plea for overpowering, self-forgetful experience and an aesthetic testing of waters, as Bishop's metronomic pentameters describe music's fluency without daring to replicate it (*PPL* 186). (This early poem's yearning, and a triad of elemental adjectives – bitter, deep, clear – resurface in a decades-later poem of "total immersion," "At the Fishhouses.") At Vassar, musical and literary enthusiasm interfused in the classroom – Bishop's music studies culminated with the yearlong course Music as a Literature – and in extracurricular performances and publications; Bishop named *Con Spirito*, a literary magazine launched with uncredited co-conspirators, after a musical notation, "with zest." To tease out literary theories in her undergraduate essays, Bishop leant on quasi-musical terms: "tempo" and "time-pattern" in "Time's Andromedas," "timing" in "Gerard Manley Hopkins," a multimodal sense of "rhythm" in "Dimensions for a Novel" (*PPL* 642–63; *Pr* 468–74, 487). After graduation, as Bishop waded into professional culture and magazine publication, she foregrounded musical models in her poems' titles: "Hymn to the Virgin," "Song" ("Summer is over upon the sea"), "Little Exercise," and "Song: Letter to New York" (later retitled "Letter to N.Y.").

The musical attention captured in Bishop's first book *North & South* reaches in two directions, not geographical north and south but backward and forward in time to two traditions and their respective vocabularies and milieux. One was the European classical tradition, whose terminology Bishop repurposes for the ethnomusicological fieldwork of "Florida" (*P* 33–34). Opening with faux-naïf sonic appreciation for "The state with the prettiest name," Bishop listens more closely, picking up "unseen hysterical birds who rush up the scale," then a tropical variation on a Keatsian "wailful choir" of gnats: "The mosquitoes / go hunting to the tune of their ferocious obbligatos." (With her Ogden-Nash-grade rhyme of "mosquitoes" and "obbligatos" – instrumental parts that should not be omitted – Bishop grants her swarm a rarefied, Italianate air while protesting their "obligatory" nuisance.) Absurdly furthering the classification of animal sounds into quantized musical scales, an eerie finale enumerates the alligator's "five distinct calls: / friendliness, love, mating, war, and a warning." But when an alligator "whimpers and speaks in the throat / of the Indian Princess," human scales prove futile, animal sounds indecipherable. Incidentally, a contemporary poem, "Roosters," was written to rhythms no listener could imaginably hear. Drafting the poem, Bishop recollected in 1966, she felt "hopelessly stuck": "Then one day I was playing a record of Ralph Kirkpatrick performing Scarlatti: the rhythms of the sonata imposed themselves on me and I got the thing started again."[5] The musical structures of "Florida" are a human listener's superimpositions, efforts to tame a natural soundscape; in "Roosters," musical structure insinuates subverbally, a guiding rhythm incommunicable in words and all-but-undetectable in the completed work.[6]

North & South's other musical tradition is the current, electrified, multiethnic delta of American and Caribbean popular musics Bishop encountered on recordings, through Manhattan nightlife, and in the Key West "dance-halls" and "honkey-tonks" mentioned in "Edgar Allan Poe & The Juke-Box" (*EAP* 49).[7] Pop seeps into *North & South* over the radio, the first of several playback technologies Bishop fascinated over, staving off any passing wish for music's transcendence. In "Late Air," she listens incredulously as "radio-singers / distribute all their love-songs / over the dew-wet lawns," their too-vague lyrics meaningful only when read into: "their marrow-piercing guesses are whatever you believe." Pivoting from listening to looking, from late-night love-songs ("late airs") to the "Navy Yard aerial" in the night sky (another "late air"), Bishop spots presences more durable than any tear-jerking single: "Five remote red lights," metamorphosing into "Phoenixes / burning quietly, where the dew cannot climb" (*P* 45).

Bishop listens back to pop's verbal sleights and unanticipated emotional heft in "Songs for a Colored Singer," likely the most contested sequence of poems she ever wrote – if they *are* poems, simply poems, at all. Their earliest, most admiring readers thought so: the Houghton Mifflin editor Jean Pedrick, finding them in *Partisan Review*, encouraged Bishop to apply for the press's Poetry Prize Fellowship (she won); reviewing *North & South*, Randall Jarrell and Lowell praised the "Songs" and singled out the first, which Lowell deemed "serious light verse" as excellent as Louis MacNeice's "Bagpipe Music" and W. H. Auden's "Refugee Blues."[8] Later readers, whether defending or denouncing the "Songs," have framed them as dramatic monologues, and shifted attention from the European men preceding Bishop to the Black women she purportedly speaks as and for. For Bishop, these "Songs" were not simply "for" her archetype-like personae but "for" one performer, Billie Holiday: "I put in a couple of big words just because she sang big words well," she explained in 1966.[9] Holiday's definitive 1939 recording of "Strange Fruit" – originally a poem, "Bitter Fruit," by the Jewish American writer Abel Meeropol – may have assured Bishop that finished poems could live double lives as lyrics, or that white authors could compose words for lives not their own. By some category-blurring logic, Bishop wrote "Songs" whose tunes need not arrive anytime soon; even while projecting one celebrity's hypothetical performances, she saw nothing contradictory in printing those "Songs for a Colored Singer" under the name Elizabeth Bishop – making them publications by a white poet – or in reading and recording them in her voice.

The "Songs" themselves, with their adventurously hybridized forms, propose less tangled conclusions. An inveterate close-reader of pop prosody, Bishop taught iambic pentameter through blues refrains, her favorite coming from W. C. Handy's "St. Louis Blues": "I hate to see that evenin' sun go down."[10] In her unpublished lyrics, she hews effortlessly to strict patterns: the blues stanzas prospectively titled "Lullaby for a Dark Child," the crisply rhymed tetrameter quatrains of "Dream – " (the form of "Strange Fruit," treading lightly where Meeropol's feet drag funereally) (*EAP* 68, 282, 37). But the forms assumed by all four "Songs for a Colored Singer" are unrulier, prone to modulation. In the first, Bishop wields couplets as miniaturized calls and responses, with every assured first line undercut by a curter second line, slumping in register:

> A washing hangs upon the line,
>   but it's not mine. (*P* 47)

More than they adapt any contemporary hit, Bishop's tapering couplets echo the metrical maneuvers of her beloved George Herbert. Compare the stanza-capping rhymes of "Love (III)":

> Love took my hand, and smiling did reply,
>   Who made the eyes but I?

Whatever Bishop's titles advertise, her "Songs" prove far more baroque than most pop standards, suggesting less an extended effort at ventriloquism than four one-off experiments, conducted at a busy crossroads of genres and traditions.

In her next two collections, Bishop listens as waywardly as she travels, whether to "Ay, Jalisco!" on a Mexican jukebox or to an Air Force Band in Washington, DC (*P* 58, 67). But her listening largely falls under two rubrics, "Brazil" and "Elsewhere" (the section-titles of *Questions of Travel*, *North & South*'s originary poles renamed and reversed). In her counterintuitive lexicon, Elsewhere was synonymous with Home, a Northeast remembered in the key of childhood, and landscapes resonating with the indelible scream of "In the Village": "Flick the lightning rod on top of the church steeple with your fingernail and you will hear it" (*Pr* 62). A fitting tuning fork, that steeple rod: Elsewhere's national music was hymns, Bishop's earliest introduction to metrical verses and musical phrasings; even after hollowing out the Christianity, she treasured hymns as models for local, intergenerational community and cultural heritage preserved within words. In identifiable snippets and half-heard echoes, hymns run through Bishop's prose ("Gwendolyn") and poetry ("Salem Willows"), but she gives only one hymn's name in any published poem.[11] In "At the Fishhouses," a plunge into the sea's distilled elements ("Cold dark deep and absolutely clear") is interrupted by a seal, "who arrives," in Seamus Heaney's taxonomizing, "partly like a messenger from another world, partly like a dead-pan comedian of water":[12]

> He was curious about me. He was interested in music;
> like me a believer in total immersion,
> so I used to sing him Baptist hymns.
> I also sang "A Mighty Fortress Is Our God."

This interspecies musical interlude is abundantly comic – Bishop lifts the phrase "total immersion" from interdenominational debates over baptism, which she promptly dunks underwater, a slapstick kerplunk – but not simply comic. Martin Luther's "A Mighty Fortress Is Our God" is both a prelude to and a foil for her poem's secularized, melodically distinct ending, which recapitulates the hymn's congregation-gathering plural pronoun: "It is like what we imagine knowledge to be." Against any "Mighty," paternalistic God, Bishop devises an earthly mother of "rocky breasts"; against the unchanging truth, seen *sub specie aeternitatis*, of Luther's hymn ("God's truth abideth still, / His kingdom is forever"), she pledges herself to the moving waters of provisional knowledge, "historical, flowing, and flown" (*P* 63–64).

Where Elsewhere's hymns flowed from known, replenishable sources, Brazil's music offered a wholly unfamiliar ocean to wade in. But the earliest musics audible in *Questions of Travel* are not Brazilian but foreign imports, like Bishop herself. Making "Arrival at Santos" (*P* 87–88), Bishop confronts the distance between the foreign country before her and every tourist's "immodest demands for a different world." Bishop encodes that distance into her self-spoofing end-rhymes: her first pair, "scenery"/"greenery," is pilfered from Lorenz Hart's pastoral love song "Mountain Greenery" (1926): "In a mountain greenery / Where God paints the scenery – / Just two crazy people together."[13] For intercontinental crossings at their earliest and most rapacious, Bishop relistens to "Brazil, January 1, 1502" (*P* 89–90). There, then, the Portuguese landed in South America to find a New World "not unfamiliar," with "no lute music," no Edenic soundtrack. Blithely "humming," these Christians introduce their own martial dissonances:

> Directly after Mass, humming perhaps
> *L'Homme armé* or some such tune,
> they ripped away into the hanging fabric,
> each out to catch an Indian for himself –

In the Renaissance, no tune was used for more settings of the Mass than the French secular song *L'Homme armé* – "The Armed Man." The historical armed men Bishop reanimates have orchestrated something similar: mass, masculinist imperialism structuring a liturgical procedure that legitimates it. Their humming cannot drown out the Native women "calling to each other (or had the birds waked up?)." But already, with that haunting parenthetical, those women's voices have dispersed throughout the landscape, until human outcry at momentous injustice becomes indistinguishable from birdsong's ambient noise.

As these poems' outsiders drive into Brazil's interior – encountering cultural exteriors at every turn – Bishop develops her ear for Brazil's musics and for Latin American rhythms generally. In her house above Petrópolis, Bishop wrote her last "song," so titled: "Song for the Rainy Season." In a letter to Lowell she flaunted the poem's "*rumba* rhythm" (*WIA* 346), presumably associating its play of dimeters and trimeters with the rumba clave, a two-against-three rhythmic pattern. Like her "Songs for a Colored Singer," this song is shaped by its dedicatory "for," yet here Bishop composes for an occasion, for a temporal cycle, for water itself. (Or for H_2O: Just as J. S. Bach cryptogrammatically signed his compositions with the four-note motif B-A-C-H, Bishop imprints "Song" with water's chemical formula: "**H**idden, **o**h **h**idden," "**H**ouse, **o**pen **h**ouse" [*P* 99].) "I have always wanted – like many other poets, I think – to write some really 'popular' songs, not 'art' songs," Bishop admitted to Anne Stevenson, citing Brazil's encouraging models: the "superb spontaneous folk-music" of the yearly sambas, and *literatura de cordel*, the ballad chapbooks that inspired "The Burglar of Babylon" (*Pr* 395–96). Nearly set to music by the Scottish singer-songwriter Donovan, that ballad just narrowly evaded a Sixties confluence of pop-music trends: the British Invasion, a Western appetite for prepackaged Brazilianness, and an American folk revival tolerant of songs with indiscriminate numbers of verses.[14]

In the crystalline lyrics and roomier meditations of *Geography III*, music becomes Bishop's pliant figure for making and self-making, for her lifework's culmination and its impending inclusion into archives. These meanings, among others, are played upon the "home-made flute" of "Crusoe in England," her most flimsily makeshift instrument and her most traditional. Like many self-deprecating creators, Crusoe doubts the enduring worth of his creative efforts, but not even Crusoe could deny his art's superlatively unconventional sound: "(I think it had the weirdest scale on earth)" (*P* 184). Bishop refigures music in "Objects & Apparitions," her translation of Octavio Paz's ode to Joseph Cornell, and a chanced-upon *ars poetica* for her own sensibility. Preserving the quaintly antiquated "solos of Jenny Colonne and Jenny Lind" inside her verbal assemblage, Bishop reveals her aptest musical metaphor for poetic voice – a soprano not simply found but effortfully trained, not quite the inwardly harbored expression of one self's "solos" but an operatic staging for unseen listeners – then promptly boxes it in (*P* 201).

What music accompanied Bishop's last years? How might music stand alongside, or stand for, one's art, one's self, or the through-composition of a life? In Bishop's final three poems, these questions receive three glancing, undecided answers. Maybe music is encapsulated best in her elegy for Robert Lowell, "North Haven," where she contrasts Lowell's now-unrearrangeable poems with "the White-throated Sparrow's five-note song." An emblem for repeating, revising, always-evolving nature, Bishop's birdsong nevertheless carries our mournful meanings, in tones we perceive as "pleading and pleading," with aesthetic distinction to rival any modern composer (*P* 210–11). (In a letter to Octavio Paz, Bishop shared one Maine neighbor's nickname for the white-throated sparrow: the Bartók bird.)[15] Or maybe music is sociable, gaudy, histrionic, low camp, like the Carnival sambas of "Pink Dog" (titled, in one draft, "Rio Blues"). In a sinister twist on the sensuous spectatorship of "The Girl from Ipanema" – not tall, thin, young, or lovely, the addressed dog is "Naked and pink, without a single hair" – "Pink Dog" ends by directing its ailing addressee to join in the sambas, a dance of death: "Dress up! Dress up and dance at Carnival!" (*P* 212–13). Maybe music, finally, resembles the freedom flown toward in Bishop's valedictory self-portrait, "Sonnet." With winnowed lines recalling the waterfalling music of "Song for a Rainy Season," "Sonnet" toyingly fulfills the form's Italian etymology: *sonetto*, "little song." Paradoxically, that song is "Caught" inside instruments (spirit-level, compass, thermometer), and "Freed" only when "broken" out of human measures. In the 1928 "Sonnet," music aspired to outlast life, as "some song sung to rest the tired dead" (*PPL* 186). In the 1979 "Sonnet," once Bishop's silent "rainbow-bird" departs – "flying wherever / it feels like, gay!" (*P* 214) – the rest is silence.

First in 1957, increasingly since her death, Bishop's poems have been set to music by everyone from American composers Ned Rorem and Elliott Carter to Dutch post-punk band The Ex.[16] If every audience – readers, teachers, critics, biographers, writers, writers' writers – picks their Bishop, which Bishop is the musicians'? Not the Bishop of a prosy poetics (or a "prosaic," in Vidyan Ravinthiran's coinage),[17] but the Bishop drawn toward song verse and its devices of "redundancy," enumerated by Mark W. Booth: borrowing, repetition, rhyme, meter, antithesis, alliteration, punning.[18] The Bishop attuned to jingles, earworms, nonsensical euphonies, stock phrases revisited and redeemed. The Bishop who occasionally tabled truth for beauty's sake, letting her microscopic observations slip out of focus, indulging lightly in the escapism of fuzzy appearances.

To be cryptically exact, she may be the Bishop who wrote "Insomnia" (*P* 68). Dismissed by Moore as "a cheap love poem," "Insomnia" eventually suffered Bishop's own second-guessing; after hearing Carter's setting, she determined "it sounded much better as a song."[19] But "Insomnia" was song-like from the start, before Carter ever wrote its melody. Gossiping with May Swenson in 1955, Bishop revealed that Moore likened "Insomnia" to "a 'blues' song – which I wish it were, but I think she meant something rather different and not a bit complimentary! I'm afraid she never can face the tender passion" (*PPL* 807). Perhaps Bishop had popular song on her mind (or on her hi-fi) when she wrote "Insomnia" and its final, stanza-spanning sentence (starting "So wrap up care in a cobweb" – a witchy variation on "Wrap Your Troubles in Dreams," a hit for Bing Crosby in 1931). Popular-song idiom keeps her lines fortified within strophes (three six-line stanzas), structural anaphora (four parallel "where"s), tiptoeing trimeters, and fluent end-rhymes – some resonantly full, others slurred-over ("sleep, or"/"sleeper"). And pop broadens Bishop's diction into unprecedented demotic forwardness, by turns brusque ("go to hell") and effusive ("you love me"). When Carter read "Insomnia," perhaps he heard what Moore couldn't, tender passion masquerading as cheap love. In program notes for his 1975 song-cycle *A Mirror on Which to Dwell*, he appreciated the poems' "secondary layer of meaning, sometimes ironic, sometimes passionate, that gives a special ambiance, often contradictory, to what the words say."[20] Alongside that self-contradicting subtext, he heard seductive surfaces, images worth translating into sound. For an insomniac's restlessness, he scores nervy, caffeinated leaps for marimba and viola; for the unsmiling moon, he lofts up aimless shimmerings of piccolo and violin; for "that world inverted," he drops his fretful vocal line down a well, submerging voice beneath accompaniment. Bishop the pseudo-songwriter struck Moore, and may strike us, as the opposite of Bishop the poet. As Bishop's "Insomnia" reminds us, and as Carter's "Insomnia" makes musically memorable, some opposites are mirror images.

Notes

1. Elizabeth Bishop, *Conversations with Elizabeth Bishop*, ed. George Monteiro (Jackson: University Press of Mississippi, 1996), 24.
2. Elizabeth Bishop, "Influences," *American Poetry Review* 14.1 (January–February 1985), 13.
3. Elizabeth Bishop, "Poetry Editor," *Poetry Pilot* (October 1964), 9.
4. Marianne Moore, "A Modest Expert: *North & South*," in *Elizabeth Bishop and Her Art*, ed. Lloyd Schwartz and Sybil P. Estess (Ann Arbor: University of Michigan Press, 1983), 178; James Merrill, *Collected Poems*, ed. J. D. McClatchy and Stephen Yenser (New York: Knopf, 2001), 354.
5. Bishop, *Conversations*, 25.
6. On musical triplets in "Roosters," see Katrina Mayson, "Elizabeth Bishop and 'A Bad Case of the *Threes*,'" in *Reading Elizabeth Bishop: An Edinburgh Companion*, ed. Jonathan Ellis (Edinburgh: Edinburgh University Press, 2019), 168–69.
7. Pop and classical were not exclusive within Bishop's listening or her social scenes. She took pride in hosting *the* party where Ralph Kirkpatrick and Billie Holiday first met. See Gary Fountain and Peter Brazeau, *Remembering Elizabeth Bishop: An Oral Biography* (Amherst: University of Massachusetts Press, 1994), 104.
8. Robert Lowell, "From 'Thomas, Bishop, and Williams,'" in *Elizabeth Bishop and Her Art*, 188.
9. Bishop, *Conversations*, 25.
10. Lloyd Schwartz, "Elizabeth Bishop, 1911–1979," *Elizabeth Bishop and Her Art*, 254.
11. On borrowings from hymns throughout Bishop, see Eleanor Cook, *Elizabeth Bishop at Work* (Cambridge: Harvard University Press, 2016).
12. Seamus Heaney, *The Government of the Tongue: Selected Prose 1978–87* (New York: Farrar, Straus and Giroux, 1989), 105.
13. Lorenz Hart, *The Complete Lyrics of Lorenz Hart*, ed. Dorothy Hart and Robert Kimball (New York: Knopf, 1986), 71.
14. See Fountain and Brazeau, *Remembering Elizabeth Bishop*, 246.
15. Brett C. Millier, *Elizabeth Bishop: Life and the Memory of It* (Berkeley: University of California Press, 1993), 545.
16. For a closer listen to five composers' settings, see Lloyd Schwartz, "'In Need of Music': Musical Settings of Elizabeth Bishop," in *Elizabeth Bishop and the Music of Literature*, ed. Angus Cleghorn (Cham, Switzerland: Palgrave Pivot, 2019), 101–12.
17. Vidyan Ravinthiran, *Elizabeth Bishop's Prosaic* (Lewisburg: Bucknell University Press, 2015).

18. Mark W. Booth, *The Experience of Songs* (New Haven: Yale University Press, 1981), 9–14.
19. Bishop, *Conversations*, 122.
20. Elliott Carter, "Selected Program Notes," *Chicago Review* 58.3–4 (Summer 2014), 13.

CHAPTER 21

Psychoanalysis

Lorrie Goldensohn

Sigmund Freud (1856–1939) overlapped with Elizabeth Bishop (1911–79) for almost thirty years, the overlap marking the ascendency of psychoanalysis in America, before its decisive tapering after that period.[1] Freud's concerns with symbolization, condensation, displacement, and projection certainly shadowed Bishop's rooted preoccupations with memory, dreaming, mental process, and the incursions of the child into adult mental life. Her inveterate fondness for personification lay close to these signature processes of the Freudian unconscious. Throughout her near-parables ("The Monument," "The Weed," and "The Unbeliever"), she was deeply sensitive to what Freud called "The Uncanny" – which Bishop, writing to Anne Stevenson, preferred to call "the always-more-successful surrealism of everyday life" (*Pr* 414). One might think of how projection is used in "Rainy Season; Sub-Tropics," and in all of Bishop's vulnerable, neurasthenic birds ("The Sandpiper," "Florida," "Seascape," and so on) as well as in the "formal, melancholy soul" of the mechanical horse in "Cirque d'Hiver." Her surrealism, kin to the animism of "The Riverman," leaps to that swift inhabiting of person, animal, and object, where Bishop blurs the line between subjective and objective, between animal and human voicing. It also lends her poems their singular spatial perspectives: early work like "Sleeping on the Ceiling" and "Paris, 7 A.M." comes to mind, or late-career poems like "Five Flights Up" and "Night City."

Rather than treat her habits as evidence of Freudian thinking, I choose to see doctor and poet as roughly parallel cultural investigators, rather than as influencer and influenced. For actual technique Bishop draws far more directly from seventeenth-century metaphysical conceits, French *symbolisme*, and surrealism than from Freud. In this chapter, I dwell on Bishop's relationship with psychoanalyst Dr. Ruth Foster, and follow the poet's own words on this experience and on the general subject of psychoanalysis – in letters, in poems, and in the occasional notebook entry.

Bishop saw Foster off and on from 1946 through 1948, as she sought to cure asthma, alcoholism, and more marginally, crippling shyness. Over time, psychoanalysis opened Bishop to a provocative and enabling style of introspection. Although formal appointments with Foster ended at a relatively early stage in Bishop's career, just after she had published her first book, she never completely abandoned her interest in analysis, and for decades read and commented on, with tantalizing brevity, practitioners like Melanie Klein and Germaine Guex. She favored female psychoanalysts.

Classical psychoanalysis altered granularly in the mid-twentieth century, as American analysts re-positioned or shrank the Oedipus complex, crucially putting the mother more into play within the family orbit. Transference also became two-way, allowing the analyst a less authoritarian relationship to the analysand – a rejection of Freud's well-known description of the surgeon analyst "who puts aside all his own feelings, including that of human sympathy."[2] For Freud, as "[e]xpressed in a formula," the analyst must "be as the receiver of the telephone to the disc,"[3] Bishop was no stranger to either speculation or descriptive accuracy, but this kind of radical dissociation from the "patient," coupled to mechanistic insight, failed to attract her. The one Freudian term she ever adopted was that of "transference," but in her poems you may seek in vain for any discussion of *cathexis*, *abreactions*, or any naming of *complex*.

Freud and Bishop both loved a joke, and each believed in dreamwork – although Bishop's touch was lighter and funnier. Perhaps more interested in *Aunt Sally's Dream Book*[4] which gave advice on numbers than in Freud's *Interpretation of Dreams*, she mischievously sent an unwelcome copy of the former to Marianne Moore. She shared Freud's profound interest in the multidimensional flexing of words, loving puns, and what Freud's translators magisterially called *parapraxis*, but which his plain German called *Fehleistungen* (mis-speakings). Bishop remained fastidious about special vocabularies. She relished the craftsman's language in metaphor, saying of stones on the beach that they were "set in their *bezels* of sand" (*P* 200; italics mine) – but stayed conspicuously aloof from anything that smacked of orthodox terminology in religion, psychology, and art.

Other than an enthusiastic report on Ernest Jones's biography of Freud, Bishop's allusions to Freud's writing were cursory, although she owned many of his books.[5] But once in the Key West Notebooks, she wrote: "Freud the perfect interpreter of <u>touch</u> only, in all his (its) grammar and vocabulary for sight, sound, etc., draws false conclusions (politics; art, etc.)" (VC 75.4a, 6). Damning, and sketchy. In September of 1937, she writes to Marianne Moore about Bryher's attempt to get her to psychoanalysis, quoting Bryher skeptically: "'Psychoanalysis makes one write better and more easily' – and if that were true of course one would want to reap its benefits whether one had asthma or whooping cough – but everything I have read about it has made me think that psychologists misinterpret and very much underestimate all the workings of ART!" (*OA* 63).

Her first experiences with psychotherapy were ineffective. As an adolescent, when taken to a psychiatrist by a school principal, she was helplessly mute. In 1940, hospitalized in Miami for asthma, she saw a Dr. Jameson briefly for psychotherapy, but refused further appointments. In the same year, in despair over the turn relations with Louise Crane were taking, Bishop met with Karen Horney for only a few sessions[6] – even though Bishop recommended *The Neurotic Personality in Our Time* approvingly to Jane Shore in the 1970s.[7] Reading about psychoanalysis was one thing, getting into a room alone with a psychoanalyst always another.

Brett Millier hazards that in Miami in the 1940s Bishop was full of anxiety: "Marjorie [Stevens] worried that she and Key West might be 'psychoanalyzed out' of Elizabeth; no small part of the tension in Elizabeth's life was her growing uncertainty about her commitment to Marjorie, and perhaps to a lesbian identity, which Marjorie saw clearly."[8] This would not have been an unreasonable supposition on Stevens' part; most therapists of the time found same-sex love problematic. Not until 1973 did the DSM remove homosexuality as a psychic disorder from its pages; yet there is no indication that Bishop was ever interested in or had experience of having her love of women treated as pathology.

By the spring of 1946, however, Bishop's physical and psychological distress had reached such a pitch that she began treatment with Dr. Ruth Foster: this analysis terminated mysteriously in 1948. The experience hardly erased for Bishop any of the problems for which she sought a cure, but it probably eased other resistances impeding her development as an artist. She was starting psychoanalysis, she explained to Dr. Anny Baumann (*OA* 163), for two reasons: first, her increasing desperation in coping with asthma, which she was beginning to think might be psychosomatic in origin; and second – with more uncertainty about how psychoanalysis could cure it – the alcoholism subverting both her life and her work.

The sheaf of letters addressed to Ruth Foster reached Vassar in 2011 (VC 118.33), and provides an astonishing window into both life and art. She saw Dr. Foster, with frequent interruptions as she traveled north and south, living in borrowed or rented houses, apartments, and hotel rooms, for only weeks or months at a time. The letters – disarmingly open, fearlessly candid – took place against the backdrop of a trip to Nova Scotia to retrieve medical records from the hospital in Halifax where Bishop's mother had been confined. Opening a notebook of the time (VC 75.3, 152–53) the left-hand page shows a poem realizing that across the harbor Bishop now confronts the hospital where her mother died: "I see you far away, unhappy, small, / behind those horrible little green grilles / like an animal at Bronx Park"; the right side is marked "from Halifax." This text faces an early draft of "Dear Dr. Foster, / yes dreams come in color" about the bright particularity of memory and dream. Neither poem was ever completed – but mother/doctor remain a charged dyad in these letters.[9]

In the first letter, Bishop connects kicking a dental assistant in the chest after coming out of anesthesia to William James musing about the unique force of revelations initiated by both anesthesia and alcohol.[10] Bishop continues:

> Something really seemed to happen [. . .] and I felt all right about everything – I still do and I think I'm going to keep on. I thought well its [*sic*] taken three quarts of whiskey and Dr. Foster but something has really occurred I feel the way I used to long ago, honestly and I don't think I'm going to be scared of anything or anybody ever again.

She closes: "I feel that I can talk to you now. I don't believe I'll be embarrassed any more. This must all be routine to you. But . . . laying all transference aside which is not impossible no matter what you think, I really do love you very much in which sentiment I am doubtless joined by countless others . . ." (VC 118.33; ellipses in original letter).

"Transference": we might contemplate the aptness of the Freudian term Bishop singles out. Richard Flynn, looking at the bottom of the unpublished draft of "Blue Postman," identifies lines about Dr. Ruth Foster, that run teasingly: "(To the tune of – / I love you / for scientific reasons / the transference is perfect // I've given you my past." Flynn shows the lines to be a friendly parody of a popular ballad, sung by both Ella Fitzgerald and Nat King Cole, "I Love You for Sentimental Reasons."[11]

Her tongue, or rather typewriter, had surely been released: she offers early glimpses of her mother, analyzes her childhood abuse by George Shepherdson, the husband of her beloved Aunt Maud, and enumerates adolescent erotic encounters in summer camp. She muses about crucial friendships at Vassar, and in New York, and describes her affair with Marjorie Stevens. While conceding her affectionate feelings for her grandfather and John Dewey, she admits to fear and unease in her relations with men – biographer Thomas Travisano remarked to me that it is only after her analysis with Dr. Foster that Bishop begins the most significant male friendships of her life, starting with Robert Lowell.

Interactively, in these letters, drafts of poems, and notebook entries, the impact of Dr. Foster on Bishop's creative energies is clear. While all three letters present a unified utterance, each bearing its own distinctive topics, the second letter links most closely Bishop's experience as both analysand and poet. Each letter does dreamwork, but the second analyzes the emergence of two foundational poems, "At the Fishhouses" and "The Moose." A swirl of dream transcription and sexual association, also showing material taken up by Bishop decades later in "In the Waiting Room," precedes extended discussion of "At the Fishhouses," which Bishop wishes to dedicate to Dr. Foster, identified in the poem as the listening seal for whose benefit she sings hymns. In the earliest, handwritten drafts (VC 56.7), we find the old man scaling fish and the seal. In all successive versions, the old man who remembered her grandfather remains mythic and solemn, the neutered seal, skeptical and comic.

The poem originated when Bishop fell into drunken sleep on the bus from Keene, sleep that later provides a setting for "The Moose" – but here suffuses a dream "in which everything was very wild & dark and stormy and you were in it feeding me from your breast"; the dream holds an outsize Dr. Foster and a "baby-size" Bishop "calm inside the raging storm," fed not on milk but "some rather bitter dark gray liquid." In the finished poem, the bitter milk, "drawn from the cold hard mouth / of the world" (*P* 64) becomes historical knowledge. Bishop felt this to be "obviously" a reference to "the process of psychoanalysis": in the making of this work, the decisive role of the analyst is hard to miss.

Bishop goes even farther in interpreting that milk: "Heavens, do you suppose I've been thinking of alcohol as mother's milk all this time and that's why I pour it down my throat at regular intervals?" Excited, she reaches for other associations. The "big old seal" on the actual beach a week later in Nova Scotia, where she "saw" her poem take shape in a rush of happiness after a bout of crying, she knew to be a confluence of "the appearance of the water with my dream on the bus"; she names the double meaning of seal – "a sort of interchange between kissing & feeding" and supposes (Freudian parapraxis) that "a kiss is always a sort of seal."

She begins to doubt, and wakes the following morning, to catch herself saying: "The image falls gratefully (that was the most important word, gratefully)" then re-begins: "The image falls gratefully from light, turning a little, back to the levels no sunbeam ever reaches" (echoing Coleridge's "Kubla Khan"). The image becomes a piece of gold jewelry falling through water, "only the feeling about it was the reverse of its being lost – it was very happy." She considers analyzing more of her poems, then writes, "but maybe it would be a bad idea to get too self conscious about them." Analysis stops, but that image falling through deep water reappears in a notebook (VC 75.4, 159) with words identical to the letter, posed in varying lineation. The image, a simultaneous gift and loss, might be read as experience exposed and articulated – whose fertile gold Bishop gives herself permission to drop into deep storage, perhaps for later use.

No response to these letters yet exists in an archive. Three letters begin "Dear Ruth," and date through February 1947, re-living Bishop's life up to this time in a white-hot fusion of autobiography and aesthetics. The only other Bishop correspondence equaling their depth and breadth are the letters that Bishop wrote in the 1960s to Anne Stevenson, but where the Stevenson letters convey the public image which Bishop wished to set before us, the Foster letters give us a private self.

Who was Ruth Foster, who created the climate of deep trust that brought such letters from a poet famed for reticence? Archival records bring us maddeningly sparse information. Ruth Foster's obituary from *The New York Times*, reports her death at age 56, from pancreatic cancer, on September 28, 1950. A native of Boston, she received an M.D. degree from Johns Hopkins. Surviving relatives included her mother and three brothers, all of Boston. She had been a psychiatrist and psychoanalyst for the last fifteen years in New York.

Linda Anderson quotes Megan Marshall: "[Foster's] pioneering choice of profession [. . .] came at the cost of 'estrangement' from 'her proper Bostonian family.'"[12] Anderson corrects *The New York Times*: Foster's medical degree, given in 1931, was from the University of Maryland. In 1937 and 1939 Foster corresponded with Dr. Adolph Meyer, who established the Henry Phipps Psychiatric Clinic at Johns Hopkins, in which both Clara Thompson and Harry Stack Sullivan were trained, and by whom they were influenced in establishing the William Alanson White Institute, from which Ruth Foster graduated in 1947.[13] Of Adolph Meyer, Helen Swick Perry writes: "There is a clear and traceable continuum between Charles Peirce, William James, John Dewey and George Herbert Mead; and the philosophical concepts that dominated their thinking – radical empiricism, pluralism, instrumentalism, pragmatism – informed American psychiatry as exemplified by Adolf Meyer and then later by Harry Stack Sullivan."[14] Adolph Meyer is one more of the figures in a historical loop tying Bishop to an individualist American psychiatric tradition with a wider sociopolitical outlook.

In 1941, Ruth Foster became part of the breakaway group from the New York Psychiatric Association, initially including Erich Fromm, Karen Horney, Clara Thompson, and Harry Stack Sullivan. From that point her records largely disappear into the institutions and people with whom she worked. The new William Alanson White Institute resisted what they regarded as Freud's narrow emphasis on sex, and in 1943, declared itself to be "based broadly on an integrated program of psychoanalysis, biology, and the human sciences of anthropology." This would have been anathema to European psychoanalysts who feared the dilution of their mission by pseudo-social science.

In one footnote, Crowley and Green show Ruth Foster graduating from the Institute in 1947 – precisely the year that Dr. Ruth Foster is again footnoted as one of three volunteer staff psychiatrists in Gerald Markowitz and David Rosner's *Children, Race, and Power: Kenneth and Mamie Clark's Northside Center*. Her traces are always light – and in supporting roles. But her interaction with children at this inter-racial, mixed-cultural Center impressed Bishop, contributing to what she described to Marianne Moore years later as Foster's "almost saintly" (*PPL* 498) character. The Clarks' conceptions of community service crossed neatly with what the people at William Alanson White represented as the liberal/radical politics of New York in the 1940s. Both institutions believed that psychoanalysts must serve across class and racial lines, following themes later preoccupying Bishop in her life with Lota de Macedo Soares.

Harry Stack Sullivan and Ruth Foster might have been linked through Sullivan's dominating presence at the William Alanson White Institute. Foster cannot have been unaware of Sullivan's teaching methods and interests, although no evidence of contact exists. Lloyd Frankenberg and his wife, Loren MacIver, who in the Foster letters are part of Bishop's daily life in New York, partied with Sullivan and his ambiguously defined "adopted son," James Inscoe. But as Naoko Wake shows, Sullivan's practice evinced a sharp asymmetry, typical of the time, between his lowered intellectual expectations for lesbian women in relation to the spirited give-and-take he offered to gay men.[15]

Lloyd Frankenberg reviewed Sullivan's *Conceptions of Modern Psychiatry*.[16] Bishop has nothing much favorable to say about either Sullivan or Erich Fromm – whom she described in a letter to Robert Lowell in 1948 as "rather disappointing" (*OA* 56). Frankenberg's involvement with Harry Stack Sullivan occurred while Bishop was in analysis with

Dr. Foster. Many years later, in 1957, she writes to Lowell of his poems about his mother in *Life Studies*, saying: "Oh – your mother might read Harry Stack Sullivan – he's by far the most soporific stylistically" (*OA* 351). While her opinions on the whole matched the New York rebel analysts, their bad style paired with overt sexism never gained her allegiance.

Dr. Ruth Foster must have dealt sympathetically with Bishop's affairs with women: we see Bishop progressively more candid about her sexual history. In the recurring rhythm of each letter, Bishop backs into instances requiring consolation or acceptance, then circles into painful disclosure. While her first letter builds on the explosive memory of coming out of anesthesia and kicking the "extractionist," Bishop merges this resistance to a doctor's "hurting her" with "dear Ruth" who "has made me feel very happy." From the onset, Foster has given her an overwhelming, even if fleeting, release from fear and doubt.

Before she reaches her final letter, in which she braves the uncovering of memories of childhood sexual molestation, she is frisky enough to be a little flirtatiously combative and competitive:

> You know Ruth you once said that I wouldn't think you had once been shy would I and I said yes. I should have been more emphatic I think – I felt right away that you had once and probably for a very long time been frightfully shy and that was another reason I took to you. I have to go out [. . .] to get ready to have dinner with Jarrell and I realize I am not worried about it a bit. I may be quite wrong and just getting too awfully pleased with myself but I feel that in some ways I could bet you are shyer than I am right now. (VC 118.33)

The strength of this psychoanalysis lay not in its Freudian detachment, but in an exchange between analyst and analysand, in which even commentary on her poetry was accepted: "tight," Bishop quotes Foster as saying, ruminating over what "tight" might mean. "Kind," "nice," "almost saintly" are the words Bishop later applied to Foster – but when relating Foster's speaking about Bishop's drinking back to Dr. Baumann after Foster's death, she recalls Foster saying quite sharply, "Well, go ahead then – ruin your life – " and Bishop adds, "I almost have" (*OA* 210).

In 1978, Bishop casually described her psychoanalysis to Elizabeth Spires, saying: "I once went to an analyst for a couple of years on and off in the forties, a very nice woman. [. . .] She said it was amazing that I would remember things that happened to me when I was two."[17] By then, psychoanalysis had become part of her anecdotal repertoire, blending extraordinary memory and extraordinary childhood as seamlessly innocuous. In 1950, she was disturbed to hear of Ruth Foster's death; a year earlier, however, she wrote to Loren MacIver that at least psychiatry taught her that "one must be oneself" (*OA* 190–91). She added: "no more doctors. I'm going to get my repair work done at the doll hospital from now on." Nevertheless, to Dr. Anny Baumann on January 9, 1950, she pleads for help, adding, "but maybe you'll be able to think of something this side of going to a psychiatrist which I never want to do again" (*OA* 199).

By February 18, 1956, in an unpublished letter to May Swenson – inquiring about the psychoanalysis of her partner, Pearl Schwartz – Bishop had mellowed. In a postscript, Bishop acknowledges: "The best results of analysis, tell her, come with the years – I realize it more all the time – ."[18] Bishop never altered in unwavering respect and deep affection for Ruth Foster. But whether in psychoanalysis or other forms of talk therapy, alcoholism has had mediocre or dubious cure rates. Bishop herself supposed that a large part of her problem was hereditary. In a 1954 letter to Dr. Baumann, however, she had come upon a Swiss associate of Jean Piaget – Germaine Guex, whose *La Névrose d'Abandon* she was reading in French. Bishop finds Guex "extremely brilliant – maybe pushed a little too far – or certainly the thesis could be. [. . .] I think it has showed me exactly where Dr. Foster and I went wrong, and has made me feel a good deal better about that particular fiasco" (VC f. 23.2).

Bishop read Guex in French in the 1950s; the book became available in English in 2015 as *The Abandonment Neurosis*. Guex maintains that classical psychoanalysis misconstrues the situation of the abandoned child, thrusting the child's anxiety erroneously into the category of post-oedipal trauma. She pushes this basic problem of disrupted infantile attachment back before the formation of the Oedipus complex, and centres treatment more on re-routing maternal fixations. The child sufferer, given the barbaric French name of the "abandonique" (in English the equally jarring "abandonic"), is treated nonetheless with deep listening and an avoidance of shaming. Bishop's "too far" registers how Guex on the ravages of maternal abandonment may have personally stung, as she read Guex on abandonics: "their psychology remains entirely dominated by a quest to find love embodied in the maternal image." And: "it is rare that an abandonic patient [. . .] does not recount, if not a life of exclusive homosexuality, then one where it has been at least episodic [where] the search for the mother [. . .] frequently involves fixation on a same gender object for the satisfaction of erotic desire and the need for love." Did Bishop resist being pegged as "fixated" on "the need for love"? Or was she rankled by a brilliant Guex fixated on heteronormativity?[19]

To Robert Lowell, on March 5, 1959, she remarks: "(See a grim little book by Melanie Klein, *Envy and Gratitude* – superb in its horrid way.)"[20] But by the 1970s, Bishop had passed over Klein's muted disapproval of women's erotic attachments. Richard Flynn indicates the dog-eared page 99 in Bishop's copy of *Envy and Gratitude*, where Klein writes: "much love can be put into these relationships." She types out for Alice Methfessel paragraphs where Klein gives counsel on women's friendships, emphasizing a balance of love, independence, and mutual caring. She writes: "I am aware of all this, at least – & really trying, baby –, " but characteristically adds that the quotation "doesn't apply very exactly!" In a late-night, undated letter, Bishop writes of Klein and Freud: "I am rather off of Freud and Freudians (she was his best successor, who worked with children – her books are wonderful – and she looks wonderful – even if I'm not sure how much of all of it I now believe.)" (VC, f. 118.35).

Private reading, and, as Richard Flynn notes, a likely "unhealthy combination of prescribed medicines including tranquilizers, antidepressants and amphetamines," supplanted any form of talk therapy for the remainder of Bishop's life.[21] She shelved psychoanalysis, trotting out the occasional quotation, and came a little further out of the closet: over a lifetime, she never tagged herself as either "homosexual" or "lesbian," but writing to Dorothee Bowie on June 14, 1970, during great distress, she accepted "queer" with more than a little pride, "You needn't spare my unstable personality – queer, drunk, and all the rest, I am sane, & I've never felt saner" (VC 27.5, 3).

Notes

1. See John Burnham, *After Freud Left: A Century of Psychoanalysis in America* (Chicago: University of Chicago Press, 2012); Nathan G. Hale, Jr. *The Rise and Crisis of Psychoanalysis in the United States/ Freud and the Americans 1917–1985* (Oxford: Oxford University Press, 1995); Eli Zaretsky, *Secrets of the Soul: A Social and Cultural History of Psychoanalysis* (New York: Alfred Knopf, 2004).
2. Sigmund Freud, "Recommendations for Physicians on the Psychoanalytic Treatment," in *Collected Papers*, vol. 2, translators James Strachey and Joan Riviere. (New York: Basic Books, International Psychoanalytic Library, 1959), pp. 323–33.
3. Ibid., p. 327–28.
4. Besides Aunt Sally, Bishop owned *The World of Dreams: An Anthology of the Literature of Dreams from the Pharaohs to Freud*, edited and introduced by Ralph L. Woods (New York: Random House, 1947).

5. Vassar College holds a partial collection of Bishop's personal library. Her books by Sigmund Freud include *Delusion and Dream: And Other Essays*, *Freud: On War, Sex and Neurosis*, *The Problem of Anxiety*, *The Future of an Illusion*, and *Moses and Monotheism.* She also collected Melanie Klein, Erich Fromm, Erik Erikson, Karen Horney, Harry Stack Sullivan, William James and John Dewey.
6. Megan Marshall, *Elizabeth Bishop: A Miracle for Breakfast* (Boston: Houghton Mifflin Harcourt, 2017), 78.
7. Shore in conversation with author, 1 July 2019.
8. Brett Millier, *Elizabeth Bishop: Life and the Memory of It* (Berkeley: University of California Press, 1993), 174.
9. Heather Treseler, "Dreaming in Color: Bishop's Notebook-Letter Poems," *Elizabeth Bishop in the 21st Century: Reading the New Editions*, ed. Angus Cleghorn, Bethany Hicok and Thomas Travisano (Charlottesville: University Virginia Press, 2012), 88–103.
10. On the relation to William James, see Lorrie Goldensohn, "Approaching Elizabeth Bishop's Letters to Ruth Foster," *Yale Review* 103.1 (January 2015), 1–19. Further discussion of the Foster letters comes in two subsequent articles by Treseler, "One Long Poem," *Boston Review*, July–August 2016, and "'Too Shy to Stop': Elizabeth Bishop and the Scene of Reading," *Elizabeth Bishop and the Literary Archive*, ed. Bethany Hicok (Lever Press, 2020), 17–43.
11. Richard Flynn, "Elizabeth Bishop's Sanity: Childhood Trauma, Psychoanalysis, and Sentimentality," in *Elizabeth Bishop and the Literary Archive*, ed. Bethany Hicok (Lever Press, 2020), 45–63.
12. Cited by Linda Anderson, "Disturbances of the Archive: Repetition and Memory in Elizabeth Bishop's Poetry," in *Reading Elizabeth Bishop: An Edinburgh Companion*, ed. Jonathan Ellis (Edinburgh: Edinburgh University Press, 2019), 23.
13. See ibid., 19–32.
14. Helen Swick Perry, *Psychiatrist of America: The Life of Harry Stack Sullivan* (Cambridge: Belknap Press/Harvard University, 1982).
15. Naoko Wake, *Private Practices: Harry Stack Sullivan, the Science of Homosexuality, and American Liberalism* (Brunswick: Rutgers University Press, 2011).
16. Lloyd Frankenberg, "A Theory of 'Interpersonal Relations,'" *The New York Times*, 3 August 1947.
17. Elizabeth Bishop, *Conversations with Elizabeth Bishop*, ed. George Monteiro (Jackson: University of Mississippi Press, 1996), 126
18. May Swenson Papers, University of Washington Libraries, Dept of Special Collections, from Elizabeth Bishop to May Swenson, begun Saturday, Feb. 18, 1956, ending "Sunday morning—." David Hoak kindly directed me to this letter.
19. Germain Guex, *The Abandonment Neurosis*, trans. Peter D. Douglas (London: Karnac Books, 2015), 46–7, 86.
20. Bishop owned Melanie Klein's *Narrative of a Child Analysis* (New York: Basic Books, 1961).
21. Flynn, "Elizabeth Bishop's Sanity."

CHAPTER 22

Religion

Cheryl Walker

"internal difference – / Where the Meanings, are"

(Emily Dickinson)[1]

During the first half of the twentieth century, Christianity in America lost its power and centrality as an explanatory doctrine. Among intellectuals, socialism and psychoanalysis seemed for many to have far greater relevance to contemporary life. In modernist journals such as *Partisan Review*, which published several of Bishop's successful early works of prose and poetry, religion was not taken very seriously. She did have friends, such as Flannery O'Connor, Richard Wilbur, Marianne Moore, and Robert Lowell (some of whom were also part of the *Partisan* crowd) who were believers. But by and large, among Modernists and intellectuals to be contemporary and cosmopolitan meant leaving such foolishness behind.

Bishop absorbed this contemptuous view, without, however, losing any of her interest in religious writing. Her reading included some very challenging authors and texts: Simone Weil (*Waiting for God*), St. Ignatius' *Spiritual Exercises*, St. Teresa of Avila, and Augustine's *City of God*, a book about immortality she was immersed in shortly before her death. She wrote to a friend: "I want to believe this. It is one of the most exciting things I've ever read."[2] But wanting to do something is not the same thing as doing it, and Bishop always recoiled from religious commitment.

In this chapter, I will discuss the complexity of Bishop's relationship to Christianity, what I believe to be its sources, her various stances on religious belief, and the uses to which she put the faith she was exposed to by her grandparents. For the truth is her poetry does not espouse a unified view either for or against the idea of God. Richard Wilbur put it best, perhaps, when he wrote: "she had many Christian associations [from her upbringing], cared about many Christian things, and had got [them] into her poems here and there [. . .] that's what she was left with, the questions, if not the answers of a person with a religious temperament."[3]

In *Blasphemous Modernism*, Steve Pinkerton cites Ezra Pound's concise statement about the status of religion in the increasingly secular American twentieth century: "Religion in the person of its greatest organized European institution [Christianity] resigned. The average man now thinks of religion either as a left-over or an irrelevance."[4] Though an independent thinker in many respects, Bishop was also influenced by this view. She, too, was inclined to dismiss overt expressions of piety when she met with them among her Brazilian servants or her friends. In their oral biography, Fountain and Brazeau offer Wilbur's memory of a difficult encounter with Bishop of this sort. At a garden party, she had accosted him when he mentioned that he and his wife had just been to church, questioning the depth of his belief. "Do you believe all those things? You can't believe all those things." When he responded, "Like most people I have my days of believing nothing, and I have my days of believing much of it, and some days I believe it all," Elizabeth began to list things she thought it intolerable to believe. "No, no, no. You must be honest about this, Dick. You really don't believe all that stuff. You're just like me. Neither of us has any philosophy. It's all description, no philosophy."[5]

At times, Bishop has been nicknamed "The Unbeliever," after the title of one of her poems. But even this early poem is not entirely clear about the value (or lack of it) of Belief. Though the poem itself is preceded by an epigraph about the Unbeliever from John Bunyan's *Pilgrim's Progress* ("he sleeps on the top of a mast"), an epigraph that suggests the dangers of *dis*belief, Robert Dale Parker's exegesis favors doubt over the fatuous claims of the gull and the cloud who are the staunch "believers." Parker elevates the unbeliever to the top of the Modernist literary mast, insisting: "By not believing, he implicitly chooses his precarious masthead of imaginative risk."[6] Parker sees Bishop as a courageous writer who prefers the risks of skepticism, claiming that she "likes unbelief because it primes her vision."[7]

Yet this reading is at odds with the language Bishop chooses to describe the position, literal and figurative, of the Unbeliever himself. He is not *choosing* his perch atop the mast but has been "transported" there in his sleep. His situation is precarious, both because he *is* asleep and because, like Ishmael in *Moby Dick*, from the top of the mast he might easily fall, a loaded word, of course, in Christianity. Instinctively, it seems, he recoils from this danger, curling "in a *gilded* ball on the mast's top" or climbing inside "a *gilded* bird," or "*blindly*" seating himself "astride" (*P* 24; italics added). Knowing how careful Bishop was with her choice of words and their sound, one must pay attention to the repetitions of "i" in these lines and the implicit judgment of the repeated word "gilded," implying that skepticism or disbelief is only superficially attractive and perhaps egotistical. In the last stanza his eyes are "closed tight." He does not wish to see. He fears the "spangled sea" (onto which he projects his fears of wrongdoing, making it vengeful and the opposite of what it actually is by calling it "hard as diamonds"). Rather than choosing imaginative risk, the Unbeliever seems to lack the courage of his convictions.

In my 2005 study of the poet and religion,[8] I considered the evidence of Bishop's uncertainty regarding religious belief. She was by no means as settled in her opinions as her friend Frank Bidart, for example, and this I believe was due principally to the imprint of her childhood. Bidart belonged to a younger generation, more inclined to the view of Ezra Pound quoted earlier. As I have already mentioned, Bishop had several friends who were believers. For instance, though she never actually met Flannery O'Connor, she and O'Connor corresponded for years. O'Connor was deeply religious, though capable of writing stories that delighted people who weren't. She and Bishop shared an offbeat sense of humor, especially about religious practices.

When in May 1955 Lowell admitted to Bishop that he had "become an Episcopalian again (a high one)" (*WIA* 158), she wrote back a letter thanking him for this news but also expressing her own spiritual qualms, especially in the face of Roman Catholicism, which she generally disliked.[9]

> Although a couple of my best and brightest friends are very Catholic, and of course everyone [in Brazil] is by education, I wish I had the 39 articles [the essential beliefs of the Anglican Church] on hand. I also wish that I could go back to being a Baptist – not that I ever was one – but I believe now that complete agnosticism and straddling the fence on everything is my natural posture, although I wish it weren't. (*WIA* 161)

The allusion to "being a Baptist" (a reference to her grandparents who were) suggests the residue of religion in Bishop's mind. In "At the Fishhouses," we find the speaker singing Baptist hymns to the seal. Originally, she included "A Mighty Fortress is Our God," but then she remembered that it is *not* a Baptist hymn, so she added the line: "I also sang 'A Mighty Fortress is Our God,'" (*P* 63), a Presbyterian hymn. Bishop was always careful about such matters. (See *OA* 307.)

As is now widely known, after her father's death Elizabeth spent the early years of her childhood with her mother and maternal grandparents in Great Village, Nova Scotia. As her mother descended into madness (a form of insanity that apparently involved episodes of religious fanaticism), Bishop increasingly clung to her down-to-earth working-class grandparents who believed in God.[10] There were only two churches in Great Village – one Baptist, one Presbyterian – and they staggered their services on Sunday. Sometimes her grandfather, who was Bishop's favorite relative, went to both. Her grandmother sang Baptist and Presbyterian hymns which became, as Brett Millier puts it, "her granddaughter's introduction to poetry."[11] Every day, her grandfather read from the massive family Bible (still housed with the Bulmer-Hutchinson papers at Acadia University in Wolfville, Nova Scotia). For Elizabeth, life was given the semblance of coherence and meaning through words that had special value because they were validated by adults whom she trusted and whose faith was never in doubt.

As she grew older, she gravitated to religious poets such as George Herbert and Gerard Manley Hopkins. They struggled with their faith but never really questioned the *existence* of God. In 1954, she contacted Joseph Summers about his recently published book on Herbert, praising him for his willingness to address "all these insoluble and endless and nagging problems of man's relationship to God." The problem of faith might seem a bit old-fashioned but, Ezra Pound notwithstanding, she insisted: "It is *real*. – It was real and it has kept on being real and always will be, and Herbert just happened to be a person who managed to put a great deal of it into magnificent poetry, – it is still real for all of us, after all."[12] These do not seem to be the words of an out-and-out unbeliever.

It must be said, however, that Bishop had mixed feelings about the value of religious practices. She was capable of seeing religion, or at least some people's use of it, as ridiculous or even dangerous. In her memoir "In the Village," the child Elizabeth takes the cow to pasture every day and sometimes runs into a neighbor, "Mr. Chisolm, who wears a beard. One evening he had met me in the pasture and asked me how my soul was. Then he held me firmly by both hands while he said a prayer, with his head bowed, Nelly right beside us chewing her cud all the time. I had felt a soul, heavy in my chest, all the way home" (*Pr* 71). This episode is both amusing for the reader (the cow, like Mr. Chisolm, chewing its cud) and frightening for Elizabeth.

Another story, "The Baptism," recounts an incident in the village when one of three orphaned sisters, Lucy, has a conversion experience and decides to become a Baptist. "They were Presbyterians. The village was divided into two camps, armed with Bibles. Baptists and Presbyterians. The sisters had friends on both sides" (*Pr* 4). Becoming a Baptist means that Lucy must give up her own mind and be dipped into the icy water of the recently melted river. In her enthusiasm for her new faith she stays underwater far too long, contracts pneumonia, and eventually dies.

Though the story is written with Bishop's signature irony at points, it is a frightening exposé of not exactly religion but religiosity, which Bishop always passionately decried. Given her mother's madness and religious fanaticism (her mother's scream in "In the Village" hangs on top of the church steeple), one should not be surprised that this was a hot button issue for her.

In 1964, as Anne Stevenson set to work on Bishop's poetry, she sent the poet a list of questions, including one about a sense of loss, asking if it was connected to a loss of faith. Bishop wrote in answer:

> You are probably right about a "sense of loss" and it is probably obvious where it comes from – it is not religious. I have never been religious in any formal way and I am not a believer. I dislike the didacticism, not to say condescension, of the practicing Christians I know (but maybe I have had bad luck). They usually seem more or less on the way to being fascists. But I am interested in *religions*. I enjoy reading, say, St. Theresa [*sic*], very much. And Kierkegaard (whom I read in vast quantities long ago, before he was fashionable), Simone Weil, etc. (*Pr* 415)

Clearly, Bishop was hostile to religiosity, the kind of religion that she thought might be compared to fascism. But in her thoughtfulness about where the meanings are, she often became tangled up with religious language, religious images, and even religious thoughts.

The phrase "where the meanings are" comes from a poem by Emily Dickinson that begins with "a certain slant of light" and reflects upon various issues (death, immortality, nature, perception); issues that in Dickinson's work often suggest religious contexts. Examples of poems where Bishop ponders epistemological issues – where the meanings are – include some of her greatest works: "The Weed," "Over 2,000 Illustrations and a Complete Concordance," "At the Fishhouses," "The Armadillo," "Filling Station," "The Moose," and "The End of March."[13] Bishop and Dickinson shared a concern with epistemology and both poets were ambivalent about organized religion. Yet when they pondered meaningfulness, they often found themselves alluding to the faith of their forebears.

I ended my book with a fragment I found in the Vassar Archive which seemed to me to be saying that Creation is always open to the curious and reverent.

> After the rain the puddles are blue.
> As St. Theresa said of God:
> "There are little pools for children,
> There are pools for all,
> Some large, some small."[14]

In both published versions of the poem – in *The New Yorker* and *Edgar Allan Poe*, the word at the end of the second line is "grace." I have argued that this is a mis-transcription. I believe that instead of "grace" the word in the second line should be "God." It is smeared in both the Key West Notebook and Bishop's 1940s fair copy. Bishop is quoting St. Teresa's *Way of Perfection* chapter 20, where she says that the Lord has different roads by which people may come to Him. He does not force any to drink from his fountain of life. "For from this rich spring flow many streams – some large, others small, and also little pools for children, which they find quite enough, for the sight of a great deal of water would frighten them: by children I mean those who are in the early stages [of religious training]."[15] It is obvious that Teresa is speaking not of grace but of God here. Bishop was extremely precise about attributions.

This is a poem that exemplifies what I mean by choosing Dickinson's phrase "where the meanings are" to talk about Bishop's poetry. It presents a quotation, which in *The Way of Perfection* is specifically religious, but Bishop's interest in it seems broader than that, more broadly epistemological. Why do people interpret their experience so differently, one from another? What is the best way of making meaning? Is there a "best way"? Or are there just different ways, governed by the multiple factors that make us each unique? I agree with Wilbur that, because of her upbringing, Elizabeth Bishop instinctively connected epistemology with religion. But she also shrank from doing that because she felt so deeply betrayed by what she had experienced as the complacency and judgmentalism of religious people.

"A Cold Spring," though rarely discussed, provides an interesting example of both Bishop's withdrawal from her grandparents' faith and the residue of it.[16] It begins with an epigraph from Gerard Manley Hopkins: "Nothing is so beautiful as Spring."[17] According to Brett Millier, Bishop was working on this poem during a long period of depression and heavy drinking, finally finding something with which to finish it off, something she *saw*: the birth of a calf on the hills of the Maryland estate of her friend Jane Dewey, to whom the poem is dedicated. In "A Cold Spring" this event ends the first stanza: "the calf got up promptly / and seemed inclined to be gay" (*P* 55).

For the reader this poem provides certain challenges. What is it about? Is it simply a story about the rehabilitative powers of nature, its capacity for self-repair, something Bishop herself very much needed at this time in her life? The first stanza sets a tone, a mood, and, in sharp contrast to Hopkins' picture of spring, the mood is very dark indeed, for it has been a "cold spring." In addition to the disappointment of the season, Bishop mentioned in a letter to Robert Lowell (*WIA* 107) that Jane Dewey, a physicist, was performing ballistic exercises that caused the whole landscape to shake periodically. Some have seen these as contributing to the poem's dismal setting: the violet was flawed, the trees hesitated. And: "Finally a grave green dust / settled over your big and aimless hills." The "chill white *blast*" of light in which the calf is born and its mother stops lowing (feeling low?), might literally have been caused by the ballistics, but in my reading Bishop is using the white blast of light, a familiar religious image, to direct us elsewhere.

In our search for "where the meanings are," "A Cold Spring" becomes much more interesting if we think about it as in conversation with Hopkins, an analytic strategy no one has yet undertaken. In a journal entry from 1934 that also mentions Hopkins, Bishop ponders the essentially spiritual content of nature poetry, adding that: "genuine religious poetry seems about as far as poetry can go – and as good as it can be."[18] However, Hopkins' poem "Spring" has a structure virtually opposite to hers. It begins happily with flowers, birds and long, lush weeds epitomizing fecundity. "The racing lambs too have fair their fling" (42). It is a sonnet, so we might well expect that in the sestet things will look different and they do. "What is all this juice and all this joy?" From here Hopkins goes on to present spring as a time of *evanescent* beauty, like the Garden of Eden, to be followed inevitably by fall and the Fall, "sour with sinning." Like "A Cold Spring," this poem has an addressee, but here the person addressed is named, as Christ. The poet enjoins Him to latch on to the emblems of spring – "Mayday in girl and boy" – whose minds are still innocent and worthy of the Lord: "O maid's child," the sinless one.

If we go back to Bishop's poem, some things come into focus that could not do so before. At first it seems that her poem is a refutation of Hopkins. There is no sinning in it; there is no Lord. It moves from joylessness to "glowing tributes." After the calf is born, the next day is warmer. There is movement, flowers, color, and bird song. Instead of the "grave green dust," "the sleeper awoke, / stretching miles of green limbs from the south." But there is a strange echo in these words. "Awake, O Sleeper / Rise from Death" is a Christian hymn which ends: "Awake, arise, go forth in faith, / And Christ shall give thee life."

Just as we are about to interpret this poem as a refutation of Hopkins' religiosity, there is a Christian reference that might take us back to "your big and aimless hills." Why did she introduce Hopkins at all, one might ask, if only to refute him? Surely there are other quotations about the beauties of spring that would not take the reader into the realm of religion. His poem is addressed to Christ. In Bishop's poem the word "your" is used three times. To whom is it addressed? The most obvious addressee is Jane Dewey: your white door, your aimless hills, your shadowy pastures. Bishop was staying at Dewey's estate, but must she be the only one addressed? Perhaps not. We might sense that there is a *secondary* level of meaning that hearkens back to Bishop's upbringing and may be an unconscious residue, especially since she once believed that all nature poetry is essentially spiritual. In that case, the land belongs to God, and the glowing tributes when the fireflies rise "much higher" are a sign of reverence, an ascent, perhaps a prayer. The word "aimless" now makes more sense, as a charge against God, the *deus absconditus* that Hopkins addressed so powerfully in his "terrible sonnets." In these hills, God is not offering us the meaning and certainty that we so deeply desire.

If that is the case, this poem shares epistemological concerns with "Over 2,000 Illustrations and a Complete Concordance." "Aimless" and the line "Everything only connected by 'and' and 'and'" have a lot in common (*P* 58). In that poem, the speaker sounds irritated when she says: "Why couldn't we have seen / this old Nativity while we were at it?": "the dark ajar," "the rocks breathing with light," like the calf who is ushered in by a "chill white blast of sunshine." Then, because it is a spiritual emissary, suddenly everything changes for the better. Is it just an accident that Bishop placed this later poem about searching for meaning on the page right after "A Cold Spring"? If not, the white door might *not* be Jane Dewey's after all, but a door to a different realm of meaning.

So many things at the end of this poem – the moths, the fireflies, the bubbles in the champagne (a celebratory libation) – are lit on an "ascending flight." So many of Bishop's spiritual poems – one thinks immediately of "At the Fishhouses" – are poems of falling and rising or the reverse, a kind of Jacob's Ladder. Here the "grave green dust" settles *down* but when the calf is born, it gets *up* immediately. As the evening comes on, "the fireflies / begin to rise: / up, then down, then up again." I find myself thinking of "Anaphora" with its falling and rising and "endless, endless assent" (ascent). "Anaphora," the last poem in *North & South*, precedes "A Cold Spring" in *Poems*, which itself precedes "Over 2,000 Illustrations." In the second edition, *North & South* and *A Cold Spring* were published together.

Of course, Bishop herself may not have been conscious of all this. Apparently, she didn't think of the Mass when she wrote "A Miracle for Breakfast," but when two critics pointed out the reference, she was delighted. She claimed: "I'd never thought of it consciously" (*OA* 477). Was she being ironic or merely self-protective? It is difficult to imagine that the poet, who grew up with church-going and the sacrament of communion, would not think of the mass in a poem about desiring to receive a breakfast miracle of bread (the roll) and libation (coffee). In Bishop's poem, however, the "miracle" is not transubstantiation in the Christian sense but rather that of imagination, the poet's recourse. If anything, this poem underscores the fact that, although she was always drawn to religion and found religious poetry "as far as poetry can go – and as good as it can be," the residue of religion in her poetry does not prove that she was actually a believer at heart.

Notes

1. "There's a certain Slant of light," *The Poems of Emily Dickinson*, 3 vols., ed. R. W. Franklin (Cambridge: Harvard University Press, 1998), 338.
2. Gary Fountain and Peter Brazeau, ed. *Remembering Elizabeth Bishop: An Oral Biography* (Amherst: University of Massachusetts Press, 1994), 347.
3. See Fountain and Brazeau, 349. For a book-length study of Bishop's ongoing relationship with her grandparents' faith, see Laurel Snow Corelle's *A Poet's High Argument: Elizabeth Bishop and Christianity* (Columbia: University of South Carolina Press, 2008).
4. Steve Pinkerton, *Blasphemous Modernism: The 20th Century Word Made Flesh* (New York: Oxford University Press, 2017), 3.
5. Fountain and Brazeau, Remembering Elizabeth Bishop, 348.
6. Robert Dale Parker, *The Unbeliever: The Poetry of Elizabeth Bishop* (Urbana: University of Illinois Press, 1988), 33.
7. See Parker, 36. My own preference is for Thomas Travisano's reading of this poem in which both positions – belief and unbelief – are presented as having limitations. See Travisano, *Elizabeth Bishop: Her Artistic Development* (Charlottesville: University of Virginia Press, 1988), 46–48.
8. Cheryl Walker, *God and Elizabeth Bishop: Meditations on Religion and Poetry* (New York: Palgrave Macmillan, 2005).
9. See Corelle, A Poet's High Argument, 22–23.
10. For material about Gertrude Boomer Bishop's religious fanaticism as she descended into madness, see Walker, *God and Elizabeth Bishop*, 10–11; and Fountain and Brazeau, 4.
11. Brett Millier, *Elizabeth Bishop: Life and the Memory of It* (Berkeley: University of California Press, 1993), 14. At Bishop's memorial service, the music was mostly made up of the hymns that EB loved so much.
12. Walker, *God and Elizabeth Bishop*, 17–18. I found this letter in the Vassar Archive. As far as I know, it has never been reprinted except in my book for which I received the required permission.

13. For readings of these poems that interpret them in terms of their religious allusions, see Walker, *God and Elizabeth Bishop*.
14. Walker, 145.
15. Teresa of Avila, *The Way of Perfection*. Trans. E. Allison Peers (New York: Doubleday-Image Books, 1991), 146. Though I assume that Alice Quinn also examined the Key West Notebook and the 1940s fair copy, she claims that the draft she is using in *Edgar Allan Poe & The Juke-Box* is as she gives it there (*EAP* 277). Both copies I examined were smeared but for the reasons I give here, I find her use of the "grace" to be a mistake.
16. Two important exceptions to this lack of attention can be found in Bonnie Costello's *Elizabeth Bishop: Questions of Mastery* (Cambridge: Harvard University Press, 1991) and Eleanor Cook, *Elizabeth Bishop at Work* (Cambridge: Harvard University Press, 2016). Costello reads this poem as one about the tragedy of embodiment. She says that the poet finds in Nature a way to accept change and loss. Cook believes that in this poem Bishop refutes all possibilities of "teleology," i.e. religion.
17. Gerard Manley Hopkins, *Immortal Diamond* (New York: Doubleday-Image Books. 1995), 42–43.
18. Jeredith Merrin, *An Enabling Humility: Marianne Moore, Elizabeth Bishop, and the Uses of Tradition* (New Brunswick, NJ: Rutgers University Press, 1990), 57–58.

CHAPTER 23

Anthropology

Barbara Page

If the most basic definition of anthropology is the study of mankind, then Elizabeth Bishop, by her own account, was not of that school, though perhaps nearby. She once remarked, "When I travel my principal interest is not people," and pointed variously instead to geography, scenery, animals, even architecture.[1] One can discern in her range of interests and in certain of her characters, however, some disposition toward anthropological thinking. In her early story "The Sea and Its Shore," for instance, Edwin Boomer spends his evenings construing and classifying the paper detritus he has collected from the beach each day, until "the world, the whole world he saw, came before many years to seem printed too" (*Pr* 16). Her tale weirdly anticipates anthropologist Clifford Geertz's view that "Doing ethnography [a branch of anthropology] is like trying to read (in the sense of 'construct a reading of') a manuscript – foreign, faded, full of ellipses, incoherencies, suspicious emendations, and tendentious commentaries."[2] To an anthropologist like Geertz or a poet like Bishop, *because* the world is mysterious and elusive, it requires the closest attention. As her narrator in "The Monument" commands: "Watch it closely" (*P* 27).

Bishop had scant regard for the academy, cared little for fields of interpretation – "To hell with explainers" (*WIA* 465) – and distrusted theories. She often named Darwin as her favorite author; what she admired most, however, was not his theory of evolution but his practice of painstaking, patient observation. After a decade in Brazil, Bishop had learned a good deal about the country and wanted to write about it, but with this, somewhat disingenuous, disclaimer: "I have no theories about Brazil, unlike so many people. Immediately upon arriving I did have theories and they were sharp ones. Little by little those theories evaporated. Brazil became my home."[3] But she was certainly aware of cultural interpreters, whose writings sometimes seep into hers.

Well before Bishop's long residence in Brazil, she was a traveler, curious about the peculiarities of the cultures she encountered. She was also alert to the difference between direct experience of cultures and interpretations of them. Her poem "12 O'Clock News," published late in her career but begun decades earlier, ruefully assesses a stalled writer's desk, viewed as an alien culture through the eyes of a smug commentator. Peering at an ink bottle on the desk, he speculates on a "secret weapon," adding pompously,

> given what we [. . .] have learned from our anthropologists and sociologists about this people, it may well be nothing more than a *numen*, or a great altar recently erected to one of their gods, to which in their present historical state of superstition and helplessness, they attribute magical powers, and may even regard as a 'savior,' one last hope of rescue from their grave difficulties. (*P* 195)

This brings us to the points of greatest affinity between our poet and field workers in anthropology: the premium placed on cultural immersion and direct observation – being there. And secondly, the ethical position – quite unlike that of the commentator of "12 O'Clock News" – of respect for the particularity of another culture, especially, in her case, as expressed in arts and artifacts. But then, for Bishop, there is a downside to drawing near to the sheer reality of otherness, voiced most jarringly, perhaps, in "Over 2,000 Illustrations and a Complete Concordance," first published in 1948. Bishop's text is *The Seven Wonders of the World*, with a drift toward an illustrated Bible, whose subject is "the human figure / far gone in history or theology" (*P* 57). Her subject is the disparity between what has been written and what travel reveals. Venturing farther afield as the poem progresses, her narrator encounters, not illumination, but disconcertion and growing fear. What she brings home is nothing like an engravable text – or an anthropologist's ethnography – but a childlike regression from statements to questions. The lesson of the traveler's encounters with ever more inscrutable and frightening otherness is: "Everything only connected by 'and' and 'and'" (*P* 58), the weakest of conjunctions, the loosest of narratives – voicing the poet's bone-deep skepticism about mastery over our experience.

Eventually, Bishop's travels took her to Brazil, where she lived for most of two decades. She read widely in Brazilian literature and texts about Brazil's history and culture. Among these books were works by the nineteenth-century English polymath Richard Burton, Brazilian social thinker Gilberto Freyre, and anthropologists Claude Lévi-Strauss and Charles Wagley. Burton, an inexhaustible explorer, controversialist and writer, known most for his work in Africa and the Middle East, was a precursor to modern anthropology who co-founded the Anthropological Society of

London in 1863. Bishop came to him, however, through his two-volume *Explorations of the Highlands of the Brazil*, which included a voyage down the Rio São Francisco that Bishop herself would undertake in her time. In 1953, while Bishop was working on her translation of *Minha Vida de Menina* (*The Diary of "Helena Morley"*), she wrote to her English friends Ilse and Kit Barker of reading "Burton's travels here, which are absolutely *marvelous* [...]. His knowledge of languages is fantastic. Lota says she hasn't found one mistake yet in his Brazilian Portuguese [...] and he has explained a great many words to her that she never knew about before." *Explorations* "is an extraordinary & fair book to have been written 85 years ago" (*OA* 266).

During his travels through the interior of Minas Gerais, including Ouro Preto, where Bishop would later buy the last of her "three loved houses" of "One Art," Burton had stopped at Diamantina and met the father of *Minha Vida's* author, which Bishop mentions in her introduction to the translation. In it, she recounts her only visit to Diamantina (*PPL* 347). Here, Bishop positions herself as a cultural observer in Burton's vein, commenting on what she takes to be particularly "Brazilian" characteristics of the diary and its author, observing physical features of the region, the town's architecture, and economic history, ending with sections on "Food" and "Money." Inspired by Burton's book, which gave "an excellent account" of the mining site at nearby Boa Vista, Bishop made her own excursion to the place where Helena Morley's father pursued his futile hope of riches at the played-out diamond mine (*PPL* 355).

Among the books about Brazil that Bishop recommended to several friends was a translation of Gilberto Freyre's greatly influential *The Masters and the Slaves*, which, she said, "really gives one some idea what it's like" to live in Brazil (*OA* 307). Freyre explained that, as a young man studying in the USA, he worried about Brazil's future prospects, especially as its population was the consequence of early Portuguese settlers' intentional practice of miscegenation. At this moment, he came under the influence of the German-born American anthropologist Franz Boas, widely regarded as the most consequential figure in early twentieth-century American anthropology. Boas's research among native peoples of North America led him to conclude that theories of human evolution prevalent in nineteenth-century science incorrectly presumed the racial superiority of white Europeans. Boas stated plainly that "the evidence given by anthropology does not sustain the claim of superiority of any race over the others."[4] We must guard against any assumption that "divergence from the European type is synonymous with inferiority."[5] He argued that "the mental processes of man are the same everywhere, regardless of race and culture," and that differences among groups arise from differing physical conditions and historical experience.[6]

Under Boas's tutelage, Freyre said, "I learned to regard as fundamental the difference between *race* and *culture*, to discriminate between the effects of purely genetic relationships and those resulting from social influences, the cultural heritage and the milieu."[7] Freyre's argument in *Masters and Slaves* that racial mixing in Brazil had resulted in a distinct and beneficial cultural enrichment widely influenced Brazilians, although his ideas about race were, and remain, controversial. To critics, Freyre seemed to claim that racial democracy prevailed in Brazil, and also seemed to justify the institution of slavery, which persisted until 1888. He denied both claims, arguing in a later preface to *Masters and Slaves* that the sometimes contradictory features of the plantation feudalism of Brazil led in modern times to "a society that is democratic in its ethnic, social, and cultural composition and, at the same time, aristocratic in its cult of superior individuals and superior families, and in the tolerance that it accords to differing personalities."[8]

When Bishop began to write about Brazil, she, too, entered controversial ground. In "Brazil, January 1, 1502," Bishop clearly rejects Freyre's presumption that Indian women were compliant to the invaders' "sexual intoxication," depicting the Portuguese conquerors as "hard as nails, / tiny as nails," ripping through the jungle tapestry, "each out to catch an Indian for himself" (*P* 90). In fairness to Freyre, he also described the Indians as "withdrawing or shrinking back"[9] from the Europeans, as Bishop does in her poem too.

For the 400th anniversary of Brazil, Bishop wrote a piece about the celebration in Rio, published in the *New York Times Magazine*. It concluded with an anecdote of a billboard in Rio depicting a "Negro cook" leaning over a new stove to exchange a pleased kiss with her "white mistress" (*PPL* 448). She intended a simple effort of cross-cultural comparison that favored Brazil, but a local journalist, enraged, accused Bishop of "racist certainties," citing none other than Gilberto Freyre to support his opinion.[10] Bishop retorted in an angry letter to his newspaper *Correio da Manhã*, pointing out that her anecdote had been intended to show that racial relations in Brazil were *better* than in the segregated USA (VC 38.18).

Despite what she considered its "awful faults," what Bishop likely found "most informative and readable" in Freyre's work were his vivid physical details, as well as anecdotes and folk stories drawn from his sources and observations (*WIA* 392). For example, he cited folk poems about the popular Brazilian feast of St. John and noted African terms and storytelling embedded in modern Brazilian culture. She, in her turn, tried a poem about St. John's Day (*EAP* 109), and another, "Apartment in Leme," about the coming, on New Year's Eve, of the African-originated sea goddess Iemanjá to the beach outside Lota's Rio apartment (*EAP* 134–36).

In 1958, Bishop accompanied the visiting English writer Aldous Huxley on a trip into the interior, ending with a visit to several tribes of Indians living under the Indian Protection Service on a tributary to the Xingu River (*PPL* 365). There they met Claudio Villas Boas, one of three brothers who were living among and advocating for the indigenous peoples of Brazil, especially in the Xingu region. A book of Xingu myths by two of the brothers, published much later, remains in Bishop's library. Villas Boas spoke of his worry about diseases brought from outside, where one case of measles could wipe out an entire village (*PPL* 392). A guide warned the visitors not to expect too much of the Indians at the Post, who "were not like those who live completely isolated in their own villages," and, in writing about this trip, Bishop concentrated on their social interactions and simple descriptions of the Indians' appearance, from the men's plump, almost hairless bodies to the vaccination mark on "every round dusky behind." She seemed little concerned by the awkwardness and voyeurism of the Polaroid-snapping visitors, remarking only that the Indians loved the pictures (*PPL* 389, 390, 394, 396). Bishop enjoyed the "childlike charm of the Indians," but feared for their survival. Flying back to the unfinished new capital of Brasília while listening to Huxley describe his new novel, about Utopia, she remarked that, from 5,000 feet in the air, it seemed natural to be "deserting one of the most primitive societies left on earth, rushing towards still another attempt at 'the most modern city in the world'" (*PPL* 398–99).

After *The New Yorker* rejected Bishop's essay on her visit to the new capital and the Xingu Indians, she remarked that she would return to writing "something more my natural bent" (*OA* 369). One result was her remarkable poem "The Riverman," cast in the voice of an Amazonian Indian. Although Bishop often insisted her poems and stories arose from real experience, "The Riverman" was drawn entirely from a book, and written *before* her trip down the Amazon. That book was Charles Wagley's *Amazon Town*. A distinguished American anthropologist of Brazil, Wagley had studied with Franz Boas and several of Boas's students at Columbia University, married a Brazilian, and in the course of his field studies there encountered both Gilberto Freyre and Claude Lévi-Strauss. As a social anthropologist concentrating on modern Brazil, Wagley lived in and studied a town with a mixed population of Indian and European descendants. As a stop on the river shipping route, the town was not isolated from modern culture, though Wagley discovered there a persistence of native practices of magic and healing arts, and he dedicated a chapter to the folklore still filtering into the town. His account is sympathetic: "The traditional folk culture of the Amazon region [. . .] contains much of great beauty and value which will be necessary in the future and which must be retained."[11] Although writing from the intellectual distance required by his profession, he is not judgmental, reporting of Satiro, an apprentice *sacaca* (medicine man), simply: "Satiro is still learning his profession. Though he wanted a rattle very badly, he told us that first he must have the power to travel under water." Satiro was told that "he also needs a 'virgin mirror' – one into which no one has ever looked – so that he could see his spirit companions without danger to himself while traveling under water. He has tried unsuccessfully several times to buy such a mirror, but someone always looks over his shoulder as the box containing them is opened in the store."[12] While borrowing substantially from this account, Bishop made an extraordinary leap of imagination in her poem, one that bridged her customary distance from her subjects and gave voice to the riverman.

Bishop was at first uneasy about "The Riverman," which she said she didn't approve of, partly of course because it did not arise from direct experience and probably because Bishop's Brazilian lover Lota objected to Bishop's "interest in the primitive," as Lorrie Goldensohn observes in her fine account of the poem. In "The Riverman," Bethany Hicok sees Bishop writing in part as an amateur ethnographer of "a culture in transition."[13] Goldensohn, heading into more primal and mythic regions, writes that, "water, salty element of both birth and tears, provided the medium of release" for Bishop.[14] Or, for Satiro, rebirth. Robert Lowell lauded "The Riverman" as "the best fairy story in verse I know" (*WIA* 321), although it includes elements of modern daily culture, in the box of manufactured mirrors and mention of the cinema (*P* 105). The mood of "The Riverman," however, certainly arises from another source, Bishop's dreams. Lowell said that the poem put him in mind of a dream Bishop had reported to him of "a mermaid scraping barnacles off a wharf-pile" (*WIA* 321). In "The Riverman," the narrator says, "I waded into the river / and suddenly a door in the water opened inward," where they "gave me a shell of *cachaça* / and decorated cigars" (*P* 103–04). In "Current Dreams," from a notebook of the 1940s, Bishop writes of "air turning salt-water" as "we descend some creaking stairs / drawn by music of marimbas," where "impetalled fish / swim seriously," and "fresher tears, naturally, cannot fall" (*EAP* 70). Whether dream, myth or fairy tale, "The Riverman" gives poignant expression to Bishop's long preoccupation with the transformative power of water.

Bishop may be acting as an amateur ethnographer, as Hicok argues, but to understand this poem another, emerging branch of anthropology, neuroanthropology, may prove fruitful. An early influence in this field, anthropologist George Laughlin, studies shamanistic practice, like that of the riverman, which "transcends ego expectations"; it "calls a person's identity into question because of dissonance between what was once thought about oneself and one's well-ordered world and what one is actually experiencing."[15] In "The Riverman," in her dream reports, in "Over 2,000 Illustrations and a Complete Concordance," even in the shock of altered consciousness of "In the Waiting Room," Bishop approaches this territory. As a branch of neuroscience, neuroanthropology focuses on brain capacities and development, but the anthropological side of this field studies the way "we use the material world to think and act, even as that world shapes our cognitive capacities, sensory systems, and response patterns."[16] "Anthropology is often described as the most scientific of the humanities, and the most humanistic of the sciences. However, a deep split remains between biological and cultural anthropologists within the field. Neuroanthropology is an explicit effort to bridge that divide: to show that both neural processes and ethnographic insight matter in doing good research on human variation, whatever its shape and form."[17] Such studies may also shed light on the importance to our human capacities of encounters with the new and strange, and the shock to one's sense of self they cause, as Bishop's poems attest.

Among the anthropological works that mattered most to Bishop was Claude Lévi-Strauss's *Tristes Tropiques*.[18] Bishop and Lévi-Strauss were near contemporaries, born only three years apart. When *Tristes Tropiques* was published in 1955, Bishop was forty-four years old, and had published a number of her major poems. Both she and the anthropologist had been educated into the modernist movement, and, though Lévi-Strauss's education had been in philosophy, law and social science, he had tried his hand as a writer, composing poems, a novel and a play. Both were keen on geography, and Bishop read a number of nineteenth-century naturalists with admiration. As to the culture each grew up in, both were repelled by the tempo of modern industrial society and its mass production of goods. Lévi-Strauss deplored, for example, the reduction of farming to monocultures of sugar cane or corn. Bishop, for her part, decried homogenized and mediocre media broadcasts of music, fearing that these would corrupt the authentic folk music rising from Brazil's favelas each Carnival season. Reading Lévi-Strauss, as Angus Cleghorn notes in his examination of Bishop's Life World Library *Brazil*, focused Bishop's skepticism about the alleged benefits of spreading Western imperial culture in developing societies.[19] Facing overpopulation and massive industrial production, Lévi-Strauss believed that the human species was no longer "in proportion to the world." Worse, for his aspirations as an ethnographer, primitive cultures had been contaminated and sickened by modern intruders. Both found in modern cities not the epitome of civilization but cultural illness. Lévi-Strauss wrote of New World cities, "they are perpetually young, yet never healthy."[20] Bishop, less imperious in her judgment, knew mainly that, in cities, *she* did not feel healthy.

They had their differences. Lévi-Strauss famously disliked travel and travel writing. Bishop liked both. After his first anthropological explorations of Brazil's interior, Lévi-Strauss found himself demoralized by a sense that, "Journeys, those magic caskets full of dreamlike promises, will never again yield up their treasures untarnished."[21] But, for Bishop, her trip down the Amazon remained "dreamlike" in memory: material, in due course, for one of her finest poems of leave taking, "Santarém." But their travels inspired similarly profound self-scrutiny. Lévi-Strauss wrote that the anthropologist, above all, "asks himself questions. Why has he come here? With what hopes or what objectives?"[22] Jeffrey Gray argues that Bishop's "Questions of Travel" seems "to rise out of anthropological writing, particularly out of Claude Lévi-Strauss."[23] Ultimately, though, their inquiry leads them in different directions. Toward the end of *Tristes Tropiques*, Lévi-Strauss asks whether his choice to explore other cultures radically calls into question "the system in which he was born and brought up."[24] Bishop, instead, confronts an ethical dilemma in "Questions of Travel": do I have any right to be here, or am I transgressing where I don't belong? Her question is also implicit in anthropology, where the sheer presence of the "participant-observer" may change and undermine the integrity of the place into which he or she has intruded.

Susan Sontag argues that in our time it is mainly poets and novelists who have confronted the "intellectual homelessness" arising from "self-imposed exile and [. . .] compulsive travel" to "strange domains of experience." Her remarks might well describe Bishop, but they appear in her essay on Lévi-Strauss's *Tristes Tropiques*. Unlike other social scientists, Sontag writes, "The anthropologist [. . .] is an *eye-witness*."[25] As travelers, Lévi-Strauss and Bishop differ, however, in how they position themselves. Lévi-Strauss argues that those who go to study foreign cultures "are no longer agents but spectators." By definition, "Being human signifies, for each one of us, belonging to a class, a society, a country, a continent and a civilization." In his view, "each society has made a certain choice," and such choices "cannot be compared with each other."[26] The shift from "agent" to "spectator" calls into question a method fundamental to anthropology, cultural comparison. It also challenges the assumption that, by stepping outside one's culture into another, one can more truly understand and evaluate each.

Although Bishop positions herself in "Questions of Travel" as a spectator, "watching strangers in a play / in this strangest of theatres" (*P* 91), she learns from her travels that, finally, choice has its limits, even while echoing Lévi-Strauss's terms: "*Continent, city, country, society: / the choice is never wide and never free*" (*P* 92). With her next words, "*And here or there – No*" (*P* 92), Bishop rejects the notion, not only of having a choice, but of the way the question is posed, in terms of binary opposition. Her "No" rejects an entire structure of thought. As Gray observes, "The gesture of this poem is not to answer but to inhibit the questions posed by and to the traveler."[27] Lévi-Strauss found himself unseated by his field experience, writing that, after his travels, he had become rootless, at home nowhere.[28] Bishop's seat, however, was never secure, so that, for her, whether "here" or "there," the question of home was forever in doubt: "*Should we have stayed at home, / wherever that may be*" (*P* 92)?

In *Tristes Tropiques*, Lévi-Strauss includes a chapter titled "Robinson Crusoe," recounting his attempt "to find the extreme limits of the savage," which he thought he had discovered in the Mundé tribe deep in Brazil's western state of Mato Grosso. But his discovery brought, not the key to the roots of social organization, as he hoped, but rather despair that such discovery was even possible: "Alas! They were only too savage." Ignorant of their language, "I could touch them, but I could not understand them." He found himself on the horns of a dilemma: "I had only to succeed in guessing what they were like for them to be deprived of their strangeness [. . .]. Or if [. . .] they retained their strangeness, I could make no use of it, since I was incapable of even grasping what it consisted of."[29]

When Bishop came to write her own version of Crusoe, although it contains enough of strangeness and despair, it becomes a meditation on the meaning of home, or of what happens when one has lived both "here" and "there." Early drafts of the poem are titled "Crusoe at Home" (VC 58.16), but that would not do, because becoming at home on his island ("Home-made, home-made! But aren't we all?"), absorbing it into his being and shaping it to his needs, changed not only the place and himself but also his relation to the England that had been his home (*P* 184). In the poem, Crusoe voices the experience of being neither wholly agent nor spectator, but one who suffers, in the ordinary meaning of that word, but also in the biblical sense, of one who allows that place and those creatures to enter into his very being. Sadly, when he is taken off the island and brought to England, Crusoe feels his deepest sense of loss, an emptying of meaning from what had once been vital to him. Hence, his indifference to the museum collectors of his "home-made" artifacts from the island.

Crusoe's – Bishop's – sense of loss differs from the anthropologist's. Lévi-Strauss desired to know the ultimate strangeness of another culture in order to understand the presumed intrinsic meaning of culture itself. Back in England, Crusoe finds that the passionate feelings attached to the things of his life on the island are now lost. In this regard, Bishop meditates, as surely as Lévi-Strauss does, on what "being human" means. For him it means "belonging to a class, a society, a country, a continent and a civilization." For Bishop, being human means both attachment and inevitable loss. To overcome the binary state of mind requiring choice of one condition over another, she has one crucial resource: memory. Her great final poems of memory, "Poem" and "Santarém," bear witness to this shaky conviction. The differences that sometimes kill, as she predicts in "Song for a Rainy Season" (*P* 100), are swept away in the "watery, dazzling dialectic" of Santarém's great rivers (*P* 207).

Notes

1. George Monteiro, ed., *Conversations with Elizabeth Bishop* (Jackson: University Press of Mississippi, 1996), 51, 58.
2. Clifford Geertz, *The Interpretation of Cultures* (New York: Basic Books, 1973), 10.
3. Monteiro, *Conversations with Elizabeth Bishop*, 80.
4. Franz Boas, *The Shaping of American Anthropology 1883–1911*, ed. George W. Stocking (New York: Basic Books, 1974), 273.
5. Franz Boas, *Primitive Art* (Irvington-on-Hudson: Capitol Publishing, 1951), 1.
6. Ibid.
7. Gilberto Freyre, *The Masters and the Slaves: A Study in the Development of Brazilian Civilization* (New York: Knopf, 1946), xxi.
8. Ibid., 7.
9. Ibid., 12, 85, 82.
10. Ferdinand de Castro, "Paternalismo e Antiamericanismo," *Correia da Manhã*, 28 Março 1965, 2nd Notebook, 4. Web.

11. Charles Wagley, *Amazon Town: A Study of Man in the Tropics* (New York: Macmillan, 1953), 295.
12. Ibid., 232.
13. Bethany Hicok, *Elizabeth Bishop's Brazil* (Charlottesville: University of Virginia Press, 2016), 122.
14. Lorrie Goldensohn, *Elizabeth Bishop: The Biography of a Poetry* (New York: Columbia University Press, 1992), 209.
15. George D. Laughlin, "The Ethno-Epistemology of Transpersonal Experience: The View from Transpersonal Anthropology," *International Journal of Transpersonal Studies* 32.1 (2013), 46.
16. Daniel H. Lende and Greg Downey, *The Encultured Brain: An Introduction to Neuroanthropology* (Cambridge: MIT Press, 2012), 28.
17. Ibid., 391.
18. Bishop's only mention of Lévi-Strauss in a poem is inscribed in a gift copy of Fannie Farmer's cookbook, given to Frank Bidart (*PPL* 254).
19. Angus Cleghorn, "The Politics of Editing Elizabeth Bishop's 1962 *Brazil* Volume for Life World Library," *Berfrois*, 20 September 2011. Web.
20. Claude Lévi-Strauss, *Tristes Tropiques* (New York: Penguin Books, 1992), 150, 21–22.
21. Ibid., 37.
22. Ibid., 376.
23. Jeffrey Gray, *Mastery's End: Travel and Postwar American Poetry* (Athens: University of Georgia Press, 2005), 26.
24. Lévi-Strauss, *Tristes Tropiques*, 376.
25. Susan Sontag, "The Anthropologist as Hero," in *Essays of the 1960s and 70s*, ed. David Rieff (New York, Library of America, 2013), 71, 77.
26. Lévi-Strauss, *Tristes Tropiques*, 393, 384–85.
27. Gray, Mastery's End, 44.
28. Lévi-Strauss, *Tristes Tropiques*, 55.
29. Ibid., 332–33.

CHAPTER 24

Travel

Jeffrey Gray

While several of Elizabeth Bishop's poems certainly qualify as travel poems in the sense that thoughts and events are pinned to the timeline of a journey – as in "Arrival at Santos" and "Santarém," for example – many of her most important poems do not trace journeys so much as pose ethical, representational, or epistemological questions about them. These more philosophical excursions – for example, "Brazil, January 1, 1502," "Over 2,000 Illustrations and a Complete Concordance," and even some that *begin* with an account of journey, such as "Questions of Travel" – are broader meta-poetic meditations on travel, as well as, often, meta-ethnographies of the kind familiar from writers such as Clifford Geertz or James Clifford.

This tendency to turn more to the implications than to the narratives of travel appears in the first poem of Bishop's first book, "The Map," in which the young narrator, looking at a world atlas, puzzles over geographical formations and the boundaries of nations but also their graphic representations, which somehow supersede the physical and political worlds. Are the mapmaker's darkened contours at the shore "shadows" or "shallows"? "Are they assigned, or can the countries pick their colors?" (*P* 5). With such questions, Bishop set up the trope with which almost all her poems would be freighted, identifying her as the poet of inquiry, whose poems stand as efforts to grasp rather than to present realities.

The biggest question of travel for an American or European traveler – at once ethical, historical, and psychological – appears in the title poem of Bishop's third volume, *Questions of Travel*: "Should we have stayed at home and thought of here?" (*P* 91). Seen not merely personally but geopolitically, the question reflects an anxiety of Bishop's historical moment. It suggests the discomfort of being a tourist but, beyond that, of being a North American in Latin America during the Cold War, when the slogan "Yankee Go Home" was a battle cry in dozens of nations in which the United States supported military dictatorships. This sense of uneasiness is emphasized in the even more pointed question that follows:

> Is it right to be watching strangers in a play
> In this strangest of theaters? (*P* 91)

Bishop offers her own response to these questions, in the form of a catalogue, the longest part of the poem, of what would be missed had one not made the journey. Some of the reasons are aesthetic: glimpses along the road, such as the trees "like noble pantomimists, robed in pink" (*P* 92); others are anthropological, such as her pondering the connection that might exist between crude footwear and "the whittled fantasies of wooden cages" (*P* 92) – that is, the reversal of northern priorities, where the manufacture of footwear would be precise and that of bird-cages merely fanciful.

The poem is not conclusive, and indeed it ends with the same, central question, slightly re-worded, cited above: "*Should we have stayed at home, / wherever that may be?*" (*P* 92), now made complex, distanced from the narrator by the use of italics and quotation marks, in a brief philosophical passage purportedly taken from the traveler's "notebook."[1] Moreover, the addition ("*wherever that may be*") is crucial, since the poem, up until these words, has focused on the visited place; now, however, the misgivings about travel are turned upon the observer, who, unable to locate "home," becomes the estranged one.

Does the traveler or tourist have the right to observe others as if they were actors in a drama? As vexed as the question is, the reasons for travel nevertheless occupy the center of the poem and incidentally incorporate their own modest critique of capitalism: "(In another country the clogs would all be tested. / Each pair there would have identical pitch)"; Bishop clearly prefers the "two-noted, wooden tune / of disparate wooden clogs" she hears and sees at the filling station to the industrially "tested" ones of home (*P* 92).[2]

Geography III (1976), the book that followed *Questions of Travel*, includes Bishop's three great long poems: "In the Waiting Room," "Crusoe in England" (her longest), and "The Moose," as well as her most-quoted poem, "One Art." Neither "In the Waiting Room" nor "Crusoe in England" recounts voyages, but both poems pose questions of travel. Both, also, are text-based, with "In the Waiting Room" describing the trauma of a seven-year-old girl's perusal of a 1917 issue of *National Geographic*, and "Crusoe" representing Bishop's effort to write a sequel to Daniel Defoe's novel, a kind of postcolonial supplement depicting Crusoe's (imagined) life in England following his rescue.

If "Crusoe" reflects Bishop's late-life preoccupations, "In the Waiting Room" reflects those of her childhood and poses one of the most profound questions a human being can ask: "What similarities [. . .] held us all together / or made us all just one?" (*P* 181). The "us" in that question embraces the girl's family, the "strange" Massachusetts locals in the dentist's waiting room, the half-naked African women whom she sees in the photos in *National Geographic* (which apparently have prompted her question), and herself in the process of becoming unrecognizable. The poem crescendos in her experience of vertigo and nausea, the room "sliding / beneath a big black wave, / another and another" (*P* 181), until, like Dorothy in *The Wizard of Oz*, she falls back into the reassuring stability of home: a place ("Worcester, Massachusetts") and a time in history ("the fifth / of February, 1918" [*P* 181]). The "uneasy heightening of sensation" that Bishop described to Marianne Moore in 1942 may be an indispensable ingredient of travel (*OA* 108), but that does not mean Bishop was able to endure it easily.

The peculiarity of this poem is that it looks back to the writer's childhood, which in turn prefigures the travels and radical instability to come. The speaker in "Crusoe in England" is beyond such traumas (the trauma of his own shipwreck many years behind him). In important regards, as with other of the poet's narrators, Crusoe seems to stand in, temperamentally, for the mature poet: his concern with "[getting] it right" (*P* 182) which was Bishop's concern always; the dystopic island, "a sort of cloud dump," based on a brief impression Bishop once had of Aruba; even the homoerotic bond, as some readers have seen it, between the castaway and his "man" Friday, all bring him close to the poet herself.[3] Moreover, when Friday appears in the story, he is presented with the same flatness of affect ("Friday was nice, and we were friends" [*P* 185]) that frequently characterizes the tone of Bishop's other traveling narrators.

Bishop's narrators, like those in the travel prose of D. H. Lawrence, V. S. Naipaul, or Robert Byron, can in fact be querulous, disgruntled, sometimes narrow-minded, and yet they are open to wonder. This is especially true in the case of the tourist persona in poems such as "Arrival at Santos," "Questions of Travel," and "Travelling, A Love Poem." Perhaps Bishop was simply being candid – her narrators, as I have noted, strongly resemble herself – but, beyond that, she intuited that the repudiation of sentimentality would ring truer in the face of the unknown or the exotic, which are too likely to call up the kind of inflated rhetoric that she steered clear of. Thus, her poems often seem humble, diffident, like herself, a measure of the effort to contain sentiment while not losing sight of the wonder that elicits it. As I have commented elsewhere, the splendid sunsets of the late poem "Santarém," which took her twenty years to finish, were not possible for Bishop until her fear of sentiment (and sentimental language) surrendered to intimations of the transcendent and to a more expansive emotional register.[4] In that poem, the painterly palette resembles J. M. W. Turner's: the "golden evening" with its "gorgeous underlit clouds," the "golden sand," indeed with "everything gilded [. . .] everything bright" (*P* 207).

Nevertheless, in most of the poems, that register is subdued. In "Arrival at Santos," the opening observations sound like those of the most staid and blinkered kind of mid-century American tourist. After weeks at sea, a traveler might be expected to greet the sight of a South American port with something beyond this affectless language:

> Here is a coast; here is a harbor;
> here, after a meager diet of horizon, is some scenery:
> impractically shaped, and – who knows? – self-pitying mountains,
> sad and harsh beneath their frivolous greenery. (*P* 87)

One can accuse the language, spectacularly inauspicious for an arrival, merely of flatness, but the complaints become increasingly bizarre: is scenery supposed to be practical?[5] And at what extremes of the pathetic fallacy can mountains be "self-pitying," or, for that matter, "sad and harsh"? As for the greenery, it amounts to nothing less than bad taste for this traveler. She also complains, more conventionally, about the local postage stamps, glue, and soap, and worries whether the customs officials will speak English and leave them their bourbon and cigarettes. Bishop is of course satirizing tourists (and herself *as* tourist), as I will suggest later on. (Kim Fortuny notes that the prosaic language "contains a teasing, lyrical undercurrent that surfaces in waves of self-mockery in the poem."[6])

The complaints in "Questions of Travel" are similarly peevish, but now the grounds are reversed. Instead of the flat list of first impressions – "a coast," "a harbor," and "some scenery" – nature is charged with hyperbole: "There are too many waterfalls here; the crowded streams / hurry too rapidly down to the sea" (*P* 91), and, even when the speaker seems to love what she is seeing, "the trees along this road [are] really exaggerated in their beauty" (*P* 91). The reaction to excess here may remind one of the hypertrophied vegetation of "Brazil, January 1, 1502," a poem in which both tourists and conquistadors find "giant leaves," "monster ferns," and "giant water lilies" (*P* 89). Indeed, a similar superfluity irritates Bishop's Crusoe, who suffers from nightmares of endless repetition:

infinities
of islands, islands spawning
islands,
like frogs' eggs turning into polliwogs
of islands (*P* 185)

Without trying to psychoanalyze this horror at repletion, at least some of it can be seen as the visceral reaction of a far Northerner, accustomed to bleaker landscapes, in the face of the fertility of tropical flora, as well as the more elaborate manners, if not effusiveness, of Southerners, whether in Key West or Rio de Janeiro. ("Culture shock" may be an inadequate term for this reaction to both physical nature and culture.)

An element generic to travel writing, which may account for its consignment to the status of a poor relative of literary fiction, is the lack of the Aristotelian arc that we expect in fiction, an expectation happily surrendered when we turn from the novel to the notebook or the diary. For Lawrence, Norman Douglas, Byron, Freya Stark, or Graham Greene, to mention only the leading travel writers of Bishop's generation and just before, this arc was largely nonexistent. Bishop's account "A Trip to Vigia," similarly, has almost no arc. The insights, the anecdotes, the descriptions rest on their own merits. The same is true of "To the Botequim and Back," "A New Capital, Aldous Huxley, and Some Indians," "On the Railroad Named Delight," "A Warm and Reasonable People," and the unpublished "A Trip on the Rio São Francisco."[7]

I will cite one of these accounts as representative. "On the Railroad Named Delight" takes up a study of Rio de Janeiro, the festivities on the occasion of the city's 400th anniversary in 1965, the invocation of the Yoruba gods, and an extended treatment of the geography of Rio and its setting in Guanabara Bay. Bishop discusses the city's extremes of wealth and poverty and their political causes. She takes up the subject of sambas, which are often commentaries on local politics and scandals. She turns to the popular shows of the time and their implications, the coming elections, inflation, and the relatively free press. She introduces the classic Brazilian movie *Black Orpheus* (1959), the revived social conscience among Brazilian writers, and the influence of North American folk musicians such as Joan Baez and Pete Seeger. The essay closes with a description of a billboard showing a black cook, delighted with her new gas stove, leaning across it toward her white mistress, who leans from the other side so that they may kiss each other on the cheek. Bishop asks, "Could it have appeared on billboards, or in the newspapers, in Atlanta, Ga., or even in New York? In Rio, it went absolutely unremarked on, one way or the other" (*PPL* 448).

The rewards of the essay lie in the candor, the detail, the associative drift, and the vivid evocation of encounters and impressions. How disappointing it would be had these accounts been driven by a thesis. Thus, Bishop may have felt her essays were *essais* in the original sense – that is, efforts, meditations on or around a topic, not beholden to argument. But as regards the poems, Bishop was concerned about coherence and continuity. The best single example of this concern is the poem "Over 2,000 Illustrations and a Complete Concordance," in *A Cold Spring*, her second book, which begins with the speaker browsing an encyclopedia called, as we learn from her prose remarks, *The Wonders of the World*, and remarks in the first line, "Thus should have been our travels: / serious, engravable" (*P* 57). She is looking at pictures of famous Biblical stories and monumental Christian sites, at the same time that she is caught up in the textuality, the lay-out of the words and images on the page: the "scenes arranged in cattycornered rectangles" or, typographically, "a grim lunette / caught in the toils of an initial letter" (*P* 57). All that she sees is grandiose, hallowed, charismatic.

The next verse paragraph, by contrast, and without transition, consists of a catalogue of the poet's own, vivid travel experiences, which – perhaps incredibly, to us – she seems to see as disappointing or trivial. Intrinsically, they are full of interest:

> In Mexico the dead man lay
> in a blue arcade; the dead volcanoes
> glistened like Easter lilies.
> The jukebox went on playing "Ay, Jalisco!"
> And at Volubilis there were beautiful poppies
> splitting the mosaics; the fat old guide made eyes. (*P* 58)

These six lines, out of thirty, cannot convey the variety of the section, and only partially the surprising juxtapositions, but, at the end of the catalogue, we see that the speaker is disheartened by the fact that the events and images are not connected; rather, to be exact, they are "connected only by 'and' and 'and'" (*P* 58).

Arguably for the same reasons that Aristotle preferred fiction (for its connectedness, structure, and promise of moral improvement) to history (events told with no inherent coherence),[8] the mere connection of "and" appears unsatisfactory to Bishop, who longs for, and is intimidated by, the storied narratives with which the poem opens. This discontent can be expressed, grammatically, as a complaint against parataxis, a mode that, in her desire to translate experience into *sense*, seems inadequate or worse. The stories recounted in the canonical *Wonders* have codes and geometries; they are connected to large, even divine narratives: "The cobbled courtyard, where the Well is dry / is like a diagram," "the specks of birds / suspended on invisible threads above the Site, / or the smoke rising solemnly, pulled by threads." Moreover, the scenes taken together, several on a page, "when dwelt upon, [they] all resolve themselves" (*P* 57): a story is being told.

Although the middle catalogue of her travels outshines in its particularity the myths that begin and end the poem, she does not return to it. The poem ends, instead, with a reminder of the ancient and hallowed stories, and a brief meditation on the "heavy book," which includes a depiction of a Nativity she wishes she had seen, "the rocks breaking with light" (59), and its beholders struck with awe. The discontinuities that troubled Bishop do not trouble her readers, who, even before Bishop's time, had been raised on much more disjunctive modernist texts, and to whom events that seemed to demand expression but which resisted sense-making *made sense*, especially when filtered through this doubting and endearing sensibility. John Ashbery, in 1969, wrote that this particular poem, which had entranced him for years (his own poem "Soonest Mended" is based on it), represents the very best of Bishop's work; "one returns to it again and again, ravished and unsatisfied":

> After twenty years [. . .] I am unable to exhaust the meaning and mysteries of its concluding line: "And looked and looked our infant sight away," and I suspect that its secret has very much to do with the nature of Miss Bishop's poetry. Looking, or attention, will absorb the object with its meaning.[9]

This does not so much explain the line as confirm that Ashbery was as mystified as anyone else by the poem's ending. My sense of "looked our infant sight away" is not that the speaker turns away from that Nativity scene but the opposite. The entire last verse paragraph expresses the hunger to have seen more, the anxiety that something might have been missed. The last line should be read as one would say "And danced and danced the night away," that is, with all their hearts. "Infant sight" is, arguably, a Wordsworthian *primal* sight, oceanic, before language. *Infant = mute,* etymologically; the phrase is unusual enough that I suspect Bishop had the etymology in mind.[10] (Indeed, Bishop, in an earlier draft, had written "silent."[11])

The struggle – if there is one – between the storied sites in *Seven Wonders* and Bishop's own vivid encounters – cannot be weighed in any balance. In spite of the first line of the poet – "thus should have been *our* travels" (my emphasis), neither version of experience is satisfactory. She satirizes the first, perhaps, but returns to it at the end, without irony; as for the second, she seems unhappy with the mere paratactic recitation of her own accounts, yet they are the heart of the poem.

Bishop's longest and richest prose travel account is "A New Capital, Aldous Huxley, and Some Indians." Of the three topics in the title – the city of Brasília, still under construction when Bishop visited, to which she devotes eight small-print pages in the *Library of America* volume; the trip to the Amazon with Aldous and Laura Huxley; and the visit to the Uialipiti people of Mato Grosso – the latter, in spite of the bland, if not dismissive phrase "Some Indians," is by far the most interesting. (She commented to Lowell that it was "the best trip I've made here so far" [*OA* 362]). In her book, *Brazil*, Bishop had already written about the human contrasts in that country and referred to "the really timeless, prehistoric world of the Indians" (*Pr* 168). The depths of the interior of Brazil, promised in the last line of "Arrival at Santos" ("we are driving to the interior" [*P* 88]), may serve Western romantic fantasies, but they also materially exist, as Bishop saw on the trip with the Huxleys.[12] She describes the Indians carefully:

> The Uialapiti are short but well-built, the men almost plump, with smooth muscles, broad shoulders, and smooth broad chests. They are naked except for shell necklaces and strings of beads or shells around their hips; the women wear a symbolic *cache sexe* of palm leaf folded into a little rectangle about an inch and a half long, secured by a fine string woven from the same palm. (*PPL* 390)

For a similar mix of "objective" description and candid affection, compare Claude Lévi-Strauss, thirty years earlier, describing the Nambikwara people of the Amazon:

> The Nambikwara are small, the men about 1.6 metres and the women 1.5 metres, and although the latter, like so many South American Indian women, do not have a well-defined waist, their limbs are more slender, their hands and feet tinier and their joints smaller than is generally the case. [. . .] The sand in which they love to roll powders the body, giving it a beige-coloured bloom which, on the young women especially, is extremely attractive.[13]

Both of these descriptions continue for several paragraphs, illustrating how close Bishop was in her interests and sensibilities to her contemporaries in anthropology. Levi-Strauss's book *Tristes Tropiques* (which appears also in a Lowell poem, "Dropping South: Brazil," from Lowell's ill-fated trip to South America), seemed to strike a chord with Bishop, perhaps most of all in its fusion of science, travel, and elegy for the vanishing peoples of the Amazon. Levi-Strauss's strength was interpretation, not research, and Bishop's question from "In the Waiting Room," "What held us all together?" was Lévi-Strauss's as well.[14]

Bishop was affected and moved, as were many of the anthropologists of her time and slightly earlier – Lévi-Strauss, Franz Boas, and Margaret Mead, among them – by "primitive" or pre-literate cultures. Is her view of the Uialapiti romantic or naïve? Is it offensive? She was sometimes accused of a colonialist attitude,[15] although Fortuny suggests that Bishop "approached the subject [of travel] fully conscious of her position as a colonial writer."[16] This latter assessment may be less clear in the twenty-first century than it once seemed, but Fortuny also notes that "Bishop's travel writing anticipates concerns eventually taken up by postcolonial theorists."[17] This is certainly true of a poem such as "Brazil, January 1, 1502," in which the predations of the conquistadors are understood in relation to the twentieth-century tourists. More recently, some critics have made – perhaps too easily – the colonialist case *against* Bishop, and indeed against travel itself, which as Janet Wolf writes is too "*intrinsically* masculine."[18] Caren Kaplan takes her book's title, *Questions of Travel*, from Bishop, finding the poet guilty of the irresponsibility of modernist exile. The answer to Bishop's question "Should we have stayed at home?" is, for Kaplan, yes, you should have.[19]

But those critiques are already incorporated into Bishop's poems. In this regard, perhaps the most candid question of all of Bishop's is the one the narrator addresses to herself in "Arrival at Santos":

> Oh, tourist,
> is this how this country is going to answer you
> and your immodest demands for a different world,
> and a better life, and complete comprehension
> of both at last, and immediately,
> after eighteen days of suspension? (*P* 87)

That expectation – that the new place, the destination, is going to answer all your prayers – is the very target of Emerson's criticism of travel in "Self-Reliance," as it is also in this parodic poem.[20] However misguided the hope pinned on travel, and however unacknowledged by most travelers, it is a large part of the traveler's impetus.

Freud's insight about travel was that the traveler is not merely going somewhere but *leaving* somewhere, and that travel, necessarily, is a commentary on one's dissatisfaction with home.[21] As self-evident as this is, popular travel writers of our time usually ignore it. *New York Times* articles on "Why we travel?" by writers such as Pico Iyer or Paul

Theroux mention everything *but* this, what Baudelaire called "La Grande Maladie – horreur du domicile."[22] To leave is to turn your back on something. As Bishop writes in the last lines of "Questions of Travel," Pascal may not have been "*entirely right*" about staying in one's room. If Home is "Nature," the native world, then one leaves Nature in order to experience a freshening of one's own interiority, bringing a keener sense of loss (of history, possessions, relationships) and a keener sense of the self's constructedness, of the fiction of the self, than is offered at home.

Notes

1. While Bishop seems not to have read leading travel writers of her time, she may, given Aldous Huxley's fame and her acquaintance with him, have read his *Along the Road: Notes and Essays of a Tourist* (New York: Ecco, 1989), published in 1925 and again in 1952, the first chapter of which is titled "Why Not Stay at Home?"
2. Bishop devotes a section of *Brazil* (New York: Time-Life, 1962) to a discussion of these clogs and bird-cages. Kim Fortuny discusses them in her *Elizabeth Bishop: The Art of Travel* (Boulder: University Press of Colorado, 2003), 74–76.
3. With "getting it right," I refer to line 10 of "Crusoe," "None of the books has ever got it right" and line 145, "Accounts of that have everything all wrong." In a letter to Lowell, Bishop writes, "Aruba is a little hell-like island [. . .] nothing but cactus hedges and prickly trees and goats and one broken-off miniature dead volcano" (*WIA* 245).
4. See Gray, "Postcards and Sunsets: Bishop's Revisions and the Problem of Excess," in *Elizabeth Bishop in the Twenty-first Century*, ed. Thomas Travisano et al. (Charlottesville: University of Virginia, 2011), 26–40.
5. This odd remark appears, the terms switched around, also in a letter to Marianne Moore, in which Bishop mentions the "highly impractical mountains" (*OA* 236).
6. Fortuny, *Elizabeth Bishop: The Art of Travel*, 33.
7. Archives and Special Collections Lib., 55.4 (Vassar College Lib., Vassar College, Poughkeepsie, New York).
8. Aristotle, Book ix of the *Poetics*. www.authorama.com/the-poetics-10.html.
9. John Ashbery, "Throughout Is This Quality of Thingness." Rev. of Bishop, *The Complete Poems. New York Times,* June 1, 1969.
10. Infant, from L. unable to speak; from *in* (not) – *fant* (speaking), from the verb *fari.*
11. David Kalstone, *Becoming a Poet* (New York: Farrar, Straus and Giroux, 1989), 130.
12. The topic of geographic interiors is explored at greater length in Gray, *Mastery's End: Travel and Postwar American Poetry* (Athens: University of Georgia, 2006), particularly in the chapter on Elizabeth Bishop.

13. Claude Lévi-Strauss, *Tristes Tropiques*, trans. John and Doreen Weightman (New York: Atheneum, 1984), 276.
14. Lévi-Strauss makes a comic appearance in an occasional poem Bishop wrote for her friend Frank Bidart (*P* 320–21).
15. In 1967, Bishop writes, in a letter to U.T. and Joseph Summers, in response to a review they had seen of *Questions of Travel*: "I've been accused of that kind of thing a lot, particularly in the social-conscious days – 'Cootchie,' etc. were found 'condescending,' or I lived in a world (I was obviously VERY RICH) where people had SERVANTS, imagine, and so on" (*OA* 479).
16. Fortuny, 27.
17. Ibid., 28.
18. Janet Wolf, "On the Road Again: Metaphors of Travel in Cultural Criticism," in *Resident Alien: Feminist Cultural Criticism* (New Haven: Yale University Press, 1995), 229.
19. Caren Kaplan, *Questions of Travel: Postmodern Discourses of Displacement* (Duke University Press, 1996), 7.
20. Emerson writes, among several such comments, that "the soul is no traveler; the wise man stays at home," in ""Self-Reliance," in *Emerson's Prose and Poetry*, ed. Joel Porte and Saundra Morris (New York: Norton, 2001), 133.
21. Freud wrote that "a great part of the pleasure of travel [is] that it is rooted in dissatisfaction with home and family" in "A Disturbance of Memory on the Acropolis," in *The Standard Edition of the Complete Psychological Works of Sigmund Freud*, vol. 22, trans. James Strachey (London: Hogarth, 1964), 246–247.
22. Both Iyer and Theroux have written articles with this title. Pico Iyer, "Why We Travel," *Salon*, 18 March 2000 (http://picoiyerjourneys.com/index.php/2000/03/why-we-travel/). Paul Theroux, "Why We Travel," *New York Times*, 1 April 2011 (https://www.nytimes.com/2011/04/03/travel/03Cover.html). Baudelaire's remark comes from *Journaux intimes fusées: Mon Coeur mis à nu, 1887* (Create Space, 2011).

PART V

Identity

CHAPTER 25

Dreams

Bonnie Costello

Reviewing Elizabeth Bishop's 1969 *Complete Poems*, John Ashbery, recently returned from his expatriate life in Paris, remarked that a "special element" of Bishop's work was "the life of dreams. Always regarded with suspicion as too 'French' in American poetry."[1] Bishop's extensive French connections, cultivated during two winters in France, are deeply involved with dreams and dreaming. She read Baudelaire, who called Paris the "city of dreams." She read Proust, a recorder and theorizer of dreams. She tried translating Rimbaud, whose *Illuminations* has the character of dreams. Her library included Apollinaire, Char, Reverdy, Corbière – dreamers all. She translated several poems by Max Jacob, who, according to Peter Johnson, "tried to replicate the eerie calm of the dream, the other-worldly glow of its images, their fantastic metamorphoses, their irrational, apparently random sequences."[2] Bishop seems to have believed, with Valéry, that dreams give us access to the shadowy reality around us and within us.

Dreams provided Bishop with a creative resource, a motif, a model, and a literary device in her work, exceeding the contexts of surrealism, psychoanalysis, and autobiography in which they have been discussed. Bishop's titles are only the most obvious evidence of this preoccupation. Eleanor Cook has identified thirty-eight uses of the word "dream" in the *Complete Poems* and my count from the recent *Poems* edition adds another ten, not including translations.[3] But while the word "dream" and its variants turn up repeatedly in Bishop's work, her usage and attitude vary. I argue that dreams in Bishop might best be understood through a literary/aesthetic or cognitive/phenomenological lens. Furthermore, symbolist practices are as pertinent to Bishop's dream poetry as surrealist practices. I'd like to acknowledge that range here, and explore the nature of "dreaming" in Bishop as a poetic resource, a phenomenal experience, and paradigm of imaginative activity. And, quite differently, I'd like to acknowledge Bishop's ambivalence about dreams as a literary device and, more broadly, as a general pursuit of illusions with often precarious personal and social implications.

*

Bishop's 1964 letter to Anne Stevenson has been called "the Darwin letter," but it could also be called the "dreams" letter since for Bishop Darwin himself was a dreamer: "there is no 'split'" between conscious and unconscious awareness (*Pr* 414). She wrote this letter in the middle of her career; she invests more in the "split" in her earlier work, where dream life and waking life are often contrasted. What has not been emphasized enough, I think, is the way in her letter to Stevenson she puts dreams and works of art ("some") together in her list. "Dreams, works of art" have an affinity in the work they do, as forms that "catch a peripheral vision of whatever it is one can never really see full-face but that seems enormously important" (*Pr* 414). Furthermore, if dreams can be material for art, art can often feel dreamlike.

It is likely that, just as some of Bishop's poems were inspired by dreams, some "dreams" are inventions with thematic or formal cues, the dream frame inviting the reader to accept the poet's distortions and inversions. In one of her notebook entries, Bishop dreams *about* works of art, suggesting how powerfully paintings enter her mental life. "I dreamed last night of paintings that wouldn't sit still – the color moved inside the frames, the objects moved up closer then further back, the whole thing changed from portrait to scenery and back again – keeping the same 'lines' all the time."[4] And the quotation marks around the word "lines" suggest that she understands this dream as pertaining to poetry as well. Throughout Bishop's writing, we find both causal and metaphoric relations between dreams and works of art. She features not only dreams but also dreaming as an *activity* associated with the poetic imagination. As we evaluate the role of dreams in Bishop's poetry we might consider Donald Kuspit's distinction here, in his writing on the shift from symbolist to surrealist approaches to art: "What the artist and the psychoanalyst want from the unconscious are vastly different. For the artist, the dream it proffers is an aesthetic novelty, not a clue to psychic conflict."[5]

It is likely that many of Bishop's dreams are artistic fabrications, the dream frame allowing for distortion and invention. The relationship between dream and poetry is ancient, of course, long preceding Freudian ideas of *traumarbeit*, or the systematic use of dreams in surrealist work. Bishop clearly draws on an ancient literary tradition in her dream motifs. Her poem "Roosters" may have some connection to Chaucer's version of the "Chaunticleer and the Fox" fable, where the cock has a premonitory dream of a threatening figure in his yard. One finds dream-augury as well in the lullaby in "Songs for a Colored Singer," also written early in World War II. The dream images here suggest influences of Blake and Auden:

> Like an army in a dream
> The faces seem,
> darker, darker, like a dream
> They're too real to be a dream. (*P* 51)

*

"The Weed" owes something to the medieval dream vision or *visio*, and she would later absorb this device into her most descriptive poems. With "The Moose," for instance, Bishop echoes both Anglo-Saxon allegory (a deer appears to Saint Eustace with a crucifixion in his antlers) and Dante's dreamlike opening to the *Inferno* when he finds himself, midway in life, in an "impenetrable wood." Bishop's title "A Summer's Dream" evokes Shakespeare (*A Midsummer Night's Dream* and *The Tempest* – "we are such stuff / as dreams are made on and our little life / is rounded by a sleep"). Romantic dreaming pervades Bishop's poetry as well. She seems to be thinking of Coleridge's "Kubla Khan, or a Vision in a Dream: A Fragment" in "The Monument" with its "artist-prince" who wanted to build a "romantic scene." "The Man-Moth" has suggested to some readers the Kafkaesque nightmares of the urban subject. These models from dream-allegory traditions are not blindly imitated but adapted and complicated in her modern, skeptical perspective.

Bishop's own dreams were clearly also important source material for her. As a young writer she had heard that eating blue cheese late at night induced vivid dreams, so she tried that for a time. As she acknowledged to Anne Stevenson: "I use dream-material whenever I am lucky enough to have any," adding that "Varick Street" had its source in dream material (*Pr* 394). Barbara Page reflected that Bishop's accounts of her dreams in the Key West notebooks are "adumbrations of her mental territory and preoccupations."[6] But I would add that those preoccupations are phenomenological and artistic as much as they are autobiographical or psychological – she emphasizes heightened color and structure, distortions of perspective, scale, time, and motion. For example, before writing "The Fish" Bishop dreamt of a fish "about 3 ft. long, large scaled, metallic like a gold fish only beautiful rose color. I myself seemed slightly smaller than life-size."[7] Bishop's emphasis in Page's "mental territory" is not on her personal psychology but on image and event, and the strange alteration from everyday experience: "He led the way through the water, glancing around at me eerily now and then with his big eyes to see if I was following. I was swimming easily with scarcely any motion."[8] One thinks less of Freud, a doctor, than of Bishop's Riverman, a shaman. Dreams remained a source throughout her career. "I dream dreams every night," she writes to Lowell from Brazil (*WIA* 316). In a letter to Loren McIver she claims that "Five Flights Up" "began with a dream – a few of the first lines . . . " (*OA* 582–3). Bishop discusses a number of dreams in the recently discovered letters she wrote to her therapist, Ruth Foster. It is clear from her remarks to Foster that "At the Fishhouses" had its origin in a dream, and she identifies her therapist with the seal in that poem. The dream on the bus in her later poem "The Moose" seems to have been in Bishop's mind as early as 1947, when she is writing to Foster. It is also clear in these letters that Bishop has styled the representation of her poetic practice, and indeed her psychic makeup, to fit the psychoanalytical relationship. Dreams are foregrounded for her correspondent because they are, in the interpretive world of psychoanalysis, messages from her psyche. She also proposes to Foster that some of her earlier poems would be just as useful as material for analysis as any dreams could be, but then she withdraws the suggestion, worrying that she might become too self-conscious about them.[9] However, Bishop's poems are never transcriptions of her actual dreams, or relays to her unconscious; even when they present themselves as dream anecdotes they are largely invented, not dictated by the unconscious.

Dreams and dreaming are not just source but subject matter in Bishop's work. Many of her early poems are what we might call "meta-oneiric." Dreams for Bishop often allude to the dreamer's traumas or fears, or to desires that are unsanctioned by society or unsatisfied in life. But her poems tend to focus on the dream *state* and the affect of these unconscious experiences on waking life, rather than on specific personal struggles or revelations. In her Key West notebook she writes:

> I could never bear to go back there,
> Even in the armored cars of dreams
> That let us do so many dangerous things.[10]

*

Of course she *would* "go back there" in "In the Village" and by looking for strategies of screen memory and displacement we can identify images in Bishop's poems that relate to traumas of her past. But many poems are more interested in how dreams work for all of us in relation to waking consciousness, than in any specific personal content they retrieve. "Sleeping Standing Up" does not take us "back there," wherever "there" may be in the poet's past. Rather, the poem explores the pull of dream life and the dangers of that pull in a parable-like structure that connects the dream to the very public phenomenon of war. Bishop depicts these armored cars crossing a failing terrain of "crumbling shale" (perhaps the unconscious, but also the ruined ground of bombed and occupied Europe). But if these "armored cars" are defense mechanisms, they have a destructive potential as well, grinding "underneath" the very markers that might lead the dreamers to their desired home (*P* 31). (The same thing might be said of defensive war machinery; it often destroys or forgets the ideals or homes it is trying to protect.) Here, as in other early poems (such as "The Man-Moth"), Bishop is interested in the risk involved in dreams, as in works of art; they allow us to explore uncharted territory, but they also undermine the coherent structures that make conscious life possible.

The early sonnet "Some Dreams They Forgot" exemplifies Bishop's fascination with dreams in their structural relation to waking life, a relation she compares, rather darkly, to an organic process of germination (*P* 168). While the imagery of the poem is certainly dream-like, the dream itself is forgotten; the poem focuses instead on the dream's aftereffects before they are shaken off or repressed, and the dreamers resume their "endless assent" (a phrase from "Anaphora," the last poem in *North & South*) to the constraints of everyday social reality. The imagery of birds, flowers, and seeds charts this dynamic, but Bishop treats the images less as psychic symbols than as dream figures in themselves, imitating the quality of dream experience as well as symbolizing it. Bishop creates a Baudelairean atmosphere of evil and beauty. The "dead birds" falling suggest a nightmarish scenario (are the seeds poisonous?), but at the same time these "black" birds in a dreamlike scene are for the poet symbols of the dreamers themselves in their desiring, and perhaps poetic aspiration. Similarly, the "seeds," also black, signify the concentrated matter of the dreams, drawn from the center of the forbidden fruit of the dreamers' desires. The dream-flowers "shrink" to seeds, but will blossom again through the transmission of the birds if they revive in the night. The language of birds, flowers, and seeds is generic, but even in this early poem Bishop's description stands out from the allegorical mode. The flower is a "columbine," which does indeed produce miniscule black seeds. The syntax of "Some Dreams They Forgot" winds around its Shakespearean sonnet form, and snaps into place in its closing couplet, which marks the harsh break between dreams and waking life. The extended image of the three-syllable "columbine" is "shrunken" as the reality of time returns and dreams are made "inscrutable" with a morning alarm and the one syllable "nine."

The contemporary manner most closely connected to dreams is of course surrealism, which interested Bishop greatly in the 1930s. Bishop's relationship to this tradition has been both documented and debated. The direct and indirect presence of de Chirico, Ernst, Cornell, Jacob, Klee, and other artists in Bishop's canon and letters makes it hard to deny that some of the practitioners of this movement greatly impacted Bishop's work and her view of art even in her later years. Richard Mullen, the first to offer an extended examination of the topic in "Elizabeth Bishop's Surrealist Inheritance," identified Bishop with the oneiric rather than the automatic line of surrealism, and Ernesto Suarez-Toste has made a similar argument in several articles, emphasizing Bishop's connection to de Chirico and Magritte. Pushing back on these arguments, Zachariah Pickard in *Elizabeth Bishop's Poetics of Description* has insisted on distinguishing Bishop from the surrealists, even arguing that her practice is antithetical to theirs. The debate can be resolved somewhat if we acknowledge Bishop's discriminating taste in surrealism. We can also make a distinction between surrealist *works* and surrealist *theory* as it was propounded by Breton and others, who celebrated the liberating power of the unconscious. She did not appear to accept Breton's aesthetic premises.

Bishop's remarks on the relation of psychoanalysis and art further illuminate her ambivalence about surrealism, which is often tied to psychoanalysis and shares its confidence in the liberating authority of the unconscious. Of Winifred Bryher, Bishop writes, "she says: 'psychoanalysis makes one write better and more easily' – and if that were true of course one would want to reap its benefits [. . .] but everything I have read about it has made me think that psychologists misinterpret and very much misunderstand the workings of ART!" Bishop goes on to cite Christopher Caudwell, who complains that psychoanalytical criticism "finds its examples and material always either in third-rate artistic work or in accidental features of good work" (*OA* 63). Of course more recent psychoanalytical criticism has much to offer as we consider Bishop's approach to representation and to the construction of the self, but too often such criticism is reduced to autobiographical readings of the poet. The self is not always Bishop's central concern even in her account of dreams. In the fragments in the notebooks of a poem beginning "Dear Dr" it is "color," an aesthetic and phenomenological category, that excites Bishop, not trauma, a psychological category (*EAP* 77).

Dreams are, of course, a major source and theme in the aesthetics of surrealism, to the extent that Max Jacob, who claimed he had learned to "invent dreams," was considered "the first to introduce the systematic use of dreams in literature."[11] But Bishop abandoned dream frames in her later work. Bishop, instead, turned to "everyday life" and used elements of dream logic and color to actively re-see the world of waking life that is shrouded in a scrim of mimetic convention. She generally avoided the surrealist iconography of dreams, as well as the bizarre disjunctive elements that created a sense of the forced fantastic. Bishop might have agreed with Walter Benjamin who argued in "Dreams are Kitsch: A Gloss on Surrealism" that the surrealist import through dreams of a "common symbolic language" reflected not poetic agency but "the concerns of a particular historical age."[12] "Dreams are now a shortcut to banality," he writes in the essay, commenting on Louis Aragon's *Vague de rêves* (1924). Surrealist dreams are not creations of our thought, Benjamin protested, but furniture from an unconscious warehouse, rearranged but not transformed. In Bishop's metaphor, dreams are like jukebox tunes, mechanically replayed and ready for mechanical decoding. Benjamin, and Bishop, I would argue, are more interested in the *work* of art with choices made by the conscious individual; dreams are a transference and reordering of the forces and objects that already direct our inner lives. Bishop's project seems to have been to deploy not dream formulas but the formal properties of dreams (colors, inversions, illogical juxtapositions, synesthesia) in an active transformation of our habits of perception.

Bishop certainly admired and calls on Baudelaire's symbolist "Language of the dream" with its origins in "the furthest depths of the soul."[13] Bishop often does dramatize, as in "The Weed," disturbance and division. Still, the effort of her *art* is, as with the *symbolists*, toward unity. "Some surrealist poetry terrifies me because of the sense of irresponsibility & *danger* it gives the mind being 'broken down' – I want to produce the opposite effect" (*EAP* 272).

*

Dreams in Bishop are sometimes as vivid as experiences, and, conversely, actual experiences are often dreamlike. The perceptual aspect of dreams is as important as the iconographic and narrative aspects that tend to get emphasized in the psychoanalytic approach. In *The Visible and the Invisible*, philosopher Merleau-Ponty writes, "the difference between perception and dream not being absolute, one is justified in counting them both among 'our experiences'."[14] Throughout her career Bishop would explore the similarities, differences, and borders between these states of waking perception and dream awareness. The duration of dreams, their spatial arrangements, their point of view and construction of selfhood, their way of being both foggy and vivid, all of these qualities enter into her poems to unsettle our assumptions about objective reality. Merleau-Ponty's observations about the reciprocal interplay between these states resonates well with Bishop's poetry:

> The distinction between the real and the oneiric [dreamlike] cannot be identical with the simple distinction between consciousness filled with meaning and consciousness given up to its own void. The two modalities impinge on one another. Our waking relations with objects and others especially have an oneiric character as a matter of principle: others are present to us in the way that dreams are.[15]

Bishop's poetry, both in her dream frames and her surrealism of everyday life, seems to follow this principle, which would ultimately allow her to drop her reliance on the dream device and introduce the disorientations of the dream directly into her descriptions. The uncanny quality of objects in "Sestina" or "Going to the Bakery," for instance, and the strangeness of figures like "Faustina" or "Manuelzinho" suggest how the "modalities" of dream and waking are interfused.

Bishop seems especially interested in the way dreams create space/time coordinates that upset the structures that organize our waking life. In her poems we sleep standing up, or see the world inverted. Ceilings are floors and scale is enlarged or shrunken. Proximity and distance are ambiguous or collapsed, as I argued in my book *Planets on Tables.* Similarly, time becomes spatialized, with scenes "shut in its waters" rather than "floating / on momentary surfaces" (*P* 23). Spatial boundaries – between body and landscape, or mind and body, subject and object, or self and other – are transgressed. The early poem "The Weed," seems especially interested in dream phenomenology. "I dreamed" frames a highly detailed, descriptive account, despite the constant disturbance of empirical norms (*P* 22). As in dreams, the distinction between the experiential and the figurative is more difficult to establish in her narrative than in Herbert's coded one in "Love Unknown," which was a model for "The Weed." She repeatedly tells us what she has *seen* in this virtual world, that it counts as experience.

It's notable that several of the poems Bishop abandoned in crude draft have "dream" in their titles, suggesting her interest but also ambivalence about the reliance on this material. In some of her most successful poems dreams arise *within* the frame of description and narrative rather than defining the frame. The elements of inversion, heightened color, transitoriness, time and space skewing, the collapse of opposites, of near and far, the loosening of the boundaries of ego identity, features of concentration and displacement that are the characteristics of dreams: all these would become elements of her descriptions, unmooring positivist orderings of time and space, and lending the solid world a more ephemeral and fluid aspect. Dreamlike, anti-mimetic elements become a distinct aspect of her descriptive style, creating qualities of the uncanny, of reverie, of the numinous, within the ordinary.

Phenomenologists interested in dreams often note their depersonalized quality; the intentional self and identity fall away in dream experience to form a different subjectivity, what Gaston Bachelard called the "dream cogito."[16] This may account for Bishop's "impersonal" voice in some poems and her use of collective pronouns in dreams, her indeterminate "we," though critics have mostly seen the impersonal as a psychosocial strategy of masking, or as attempts to generalize from the personal. Dreams, like works of art, are "self-forgetful" to her, and they are also trans-personal. "Sleeping Standing Up" begins with what seems to be an impersonal, everyman "we" ("when we lie down to sleep the world turns half away"), but as the poem enters the "armored cars of dreams" a different "we" takes over, neither wholly impersonal or delimited within the narrative account: "we saw the crumbs or pebbles," "how stupidly we steered" (*P* 31). Who is this "we"? Is it simply the poet and another unnamed person within the narrative? Or has the dream collapsed the boundaries of the self? Similarly, the dream in "The Moose" is a collective one, both in terms of the dreamers and those they dream of, the grandparents talking in eternity; throughout, the poem is "self-forgetful."

Bishop creates hallucinatory and hypnogogic effects in her imagery even when the dream state is not explicit. Like her sandpiper, she was "a student of Blake," and also of Poe (*P* 129). This is particularly true in her second collection, *A Cold Spring*, where life itself seems "but a dream." "Cape Breton" dissolves the distinction of matter and spirit in its misty atmosphere of "rotting snow-ice sucked away / almost to spirit" (*P* 65). The dream-like quality of the scene conveys the sense of primordial time, punctuated now and then by abrupt event. As the sheep (often associated with going to sleep) stampede to the cliff, and as "The thin mist follows / the white mutations of its dream" (*P* 66), we may think of Valéry's aphorism that blends inner and outer worlds: "my soul is nothing now but the dream dreamt by matter struggling with itself."[17] The hallucinatory landscapes in "At the Fishhouses" and elsewhere connote the transitory nature of reality unanchored to any supernatural order.

Bishop's use of mystical rhymes and hypnotic rhythms, suddenly interrupted, also contributes at times to oneiric effects in her poetry. In her rhythms she is, to quote "A Summer's Dream," "dreaming audibly" (*P* 61).

The sudden shifts in rhythm may seem to jolt the reader awake, but on the other hand they introduce uncanny figures that seem to arise from the vividest sleep, the fourth or REM stage, rather than from a waking state. Thus, the seal in "At the Fishhouses" and the moose in "The Moose" have the uncanny quality of dream figures even though the soporific rhythms have been interrupted by the sudden appearance. It is hard to tell, when the seal or moose appear, whether we are wide awake or fast asleep.

Dreams in Bishop are not generally the pleasant ones of "food or love." They are sometimes nightmarish and sinister. Anxiety certainly builds up in "The Moose" with its rattling planks and trembling bridges, staccato rhythms suggesting a disturbed rest (*P* 189–93). But the dreamy divagation in "The Moose" offers an alternative to the "breaking down" of conscious orders that Bishop resisted in surrealism. Here the dream tells us "it's alright now / even to fall asleep" because the world is integrated, not broken apart. The bus is an armored car of dreams, the anthropomorphic imagery of "flanks" returning from the early dream poem "Sleeping Standing Up," but it does not crush the markers that lead the way home. Again, the poem leaves us in an uncompleted journey, but this time we are not lost in the impenetrable wood.

But there are real wake up calls in Bishop's poetry. She frequently uses the word "dream" in another sense from the one I have been exploring, a sense that is far less benign: "the old dream of wealth and luxury" destroys us (*P* 90). Dream in Bishop sometimes has the meaning of dangerously utopian ideals, illusions, and oblivion to the realities around us. Crypto-dream houses can become crypts. The dream life of culture has a sinister side, and many of Bishop's poems sound an alarm – "Get up! Stop dreaming!" (*P* 37). She jolts us out of the "dreamlike mimicry" (*P* 102) of cultural fantasy and its normative "tuning fork" (*P* 15) that enables denial and masks abuse of a fragile world.

Notes

1. John Ashbery, *Selected Prose* (Ann Arbor: University of Michigan Press, 2004), 120.
2. Peter Johnson, *Dreaming the Miracle: Three French Prose Poets*, trans. Beth Archer Brombert, Mary Feeney, Louise Guiney, William T. Kulik, and William Matthews (Buffalo, NY: White Pines Press, 2003), 23.
3. Eleanor Cook, *Elizabeth Bishop at Work* (Cambridge, MA: Harvard University Press, 2016), 51.
4. Quoted in Linda Anderson, *Elizabeth Bishop: Lines of Connection* (Edinburgh: Edinburgh University Press, 2015), 37.

5. Donald Kuspit, "From Vision to Dream: The Secularization of the Imagination," in *Dreams 1900–2000: Science, Art and the Unconscious Mind*, ed. Lynn Gamwell (Ithaca, NY: Cornell University Press, 1999), 77.
6. Barbara Page, "Off-Beat Claves, Oblique Realities: The Key West Notebooks of Elizabeth Bishop," in *Elizabeth Bishop: The Geography of Gender*, ed. Marilyn May Lombardi (Charlottesville: University Press of Virginia, 1993), 198.
7. Ibid., 198.
8. Ibid., 198.
9. Elizabeth Bishop to Dr. Ruth Foster, Elizabeth Bishop Papers, Special Collections, Vassar College Library.
10. Quoted in Page, "Off-beat Claves," 198.
11. Jacob Max, Francis Ponge, and Jean Follain, *Dreaming the Miracle: Three French Prose Poets*, trans. Beth Archer Brombert, Mary Feeney, Louise Guiney, William T. Kulik, and William Matthews (Buffalo, NY: White Pines Press, 2003), 23–24.
12. Walter Benjamin, *The Work of Art in the Age of Technical Reproducibility and Other Essays on Media* (Cambridge, MA: Harvard University Press, 2008), 236–39.
13. Quoted in Moshe Barasch, *Modern Theories of Art: From Winckelmann to Baudelaire*, vol. 1 (New York: New York University Press, 1990), 369.
14. Maurice Merleau-Ponty, *The Visible and the Invisible*, trans. Alphonso Lingis (Evanston, IL: Northwestern University Press, 1969), 6.
15. Ibid., 48.
16. Gaston Bachelard, *Poetics of Reverie: Childhood, Language, and the Cosmos*, trans. D. Russell (Boston: Beacon Press, 1969), 143.
17. Paul Valéry, *Paul Valéry: An Anthology*, selected by J. R. Lawler (Princeton, NJ: Princeton University Press, 1977), 291.

CHAPTER 26

Humor

Rachel Trousdale

Humor is frequently understood to create distance between the person who laughs and the object of laughter, especially when what we laugh at is another person. This is the case across many different models of humor, although the degree to which theorists believe that laughter increases the distance between us varies. Thomas Hobbes, in the most pessimistic model, describes humor as "sudden glory," which we experience when we notice that we are superior to someone else; for Hobbes, laughter is the province of the insecure bully, and those who are truly superior need not engage in it.[1] Sigmund Freud's account of tendentious jokes treats laughter as arising from active hostility towards its object. The hostility embedded in Freud's tendentious jokes may be more justified than in Hobbes' model, as when humor provides a way to safely critique those in a position of power. Freud also suggests that we may laugh to release tension, a model which, while less pointed than tendentious joking, still suggests that laughter is closely tied to negativity: an element of anxiety, effort, or distress is always built into Freud's laughter, and we laugh as a form of self-protection in a difficult world.[2] Henri Bergson's account of laughter arising from observing another person's "automatism" does not necessarily entail active dislike of its object, but requires that we see the object of our laughter as only partially human.[3] Much as they differ, Hobbes, Freud, and Bergson all agree that laughter significantly distinguishes the laugher from the object of laughter, generally at that object's expense.

Even the most morally neutral and benign theory of humor, incongruity theory, requires distance between laugher and object of laughter. Incongruity theory holds that we laugh when we first identify a pattern and then see that pattern broken or rearranged. Such a recognition requires that we view the object of laughter from an outside perspective, which is to say, at a critical distance.[4]

But while Elizabeth Bishop's humor is frequently wary, situated in physically threatening or emotionally difficult circumstances, it consistently bridges gaps between subjectivities – the opposite of the distanced models of humor discussed by Hobbes, Freud, and Bergson. As the following examination of “12 O’Clock News,” “One Art,” and “Filling Station” will show, the comic moments in her poems present simultaneous, apparently incompatible interpretations of the world and help us gain insight into the unfamiliar minds behind those interpretations. This is true even when those minds initially seem absurd or inimical. Essential to Bishop’s comic technique is a kind of Bakhtinian unfinishedness, in which irreconcilable or contradictory ideas are asserted simultaneously. Her humorous asides, wry ironies, and satirical critiques help her hold competing ideas in double exposure: her levity presents varying viewpoints without necessarily taking sides. Her humor fuses empathy with judgment, as her subjects’ and speakers’ frailties are to be both rejected and felt as our own.

As Jeredith Merrin, Susan Rosenbaum, Bonnie Costello, and Thomas Travisano have all noted,[5] humor – particularly ironic, sometimes “bleak” humor[6] – is threaded throughout Bishop’s work. She is clearly actively interested in the comic (rather than just entertained by it) as early as her undergraduate years: she was editor of the humor column in Vassar’s twice-weekly *Miscellany News*, to which she contributed light verse.[7] Shortly after her graduation, she began contributing funny items to the Talk of the Town column in *The New Yorker*.[8] While few of her mature poems are simply comic, many of them are based on playful ideas (“The Man-Moth,” “The Gentleman of Shalott”), constructed around amusing images (“Invitation to Miss Marianne Moore,” “Pink Dog,” “Exchanging Hats”), or studded with comical lines and asides (“Santarém,” “Rainy Season; Sub-Tropics”). I have argued elsewhere that humor in “Manuelzinho” constitutes both a form of self-revelation and an invitation to self-critique consonant with what Vidyan Ravinthiran describes as that poem’s “double-minded structure.”[9] That doubleness, the sustained, simultaneous presence of apparently incompatible ideas and images, is central to Bishop’s humor and to her poetics.

The prose poem “12 O’Clock News,” for example, purports to describe the landscape of a hostile country, which the broadcaster speaking in the poem regards from a “superior vantage point” (*P* 194). The broadcaster uses this phrase to describe the physical elevation of “aerial reconnaissance,” but it also implies the speaker’s condescending attitude towards the “small, backward country, one of the most backward left in the world today.” The poem gives “the lay of the land and the present situation” in a descending scale, moving from the astronomical (the “motionless” moon, which “may be dead”) to the geological (a terraced “escarpment”) to the man-made (a "field" which may be "an airstrip? A cemetery?"). The scene then becomes stranger with the addition of a mysterious dark object which may be either "some powerful and terrifying 'secret weapon'" or "nothing more than a *numen*," followed by the corpse of "one of the elusive natives" and at last "a 'nest' of soldiers [. . .] all dead," whose fate "gives further proof [. . .] either of the childishness and hopeless impracticality of [. . .] our opponents, or of the sad corruption of their leaders."

The description of the country, while grimly populated with a dead moon and dead soldiers, is already odd enough to be overtly playful if taken at face value: the "native" is "a unicyclist-courier," for example. More substantively, the voice of the news reporter is comically undercut by their own vocabulary. The poem highlights its use of the language of colonialism and militarism – "industrialization," "secret weapon," "battle dress," – by using scare quotes, thereby throwing the superior tone into question: the ideologies implied by these terms, and the reporter's willingness to echo them, may increase our sympathy with the "indigenes" (already provoked by the description of the soldiers' "contorted" bodies) and suggest a satirical critique of the reporter's attitude.

But the poem's major comic move is in the framing of the supposed landscape. In the wide margin next to the description of the landscape, each paragraph is identified as a household object: "*gooseneck lamp*," "*typewriter*," "*typed sheet*," "*ashtray*." This country is really a writer's desk, and the struggle described in it turns out to be the struggle to write. The battle suggested by the marginal text is not a war with "elusive natives" but with the act of writing.[10]

The comparison of the writer's desk to a country in wartime – worse, a country that seems to be in the process of losing a war against a stronger power – is amusing to anyone who has ever written anything, but it is also complex and revealing precisely because of the amusement it provokes. The description of the eight "hideously contorted" dead soldiers – which turn out to be cigarette butts – appeals to our sympathy for the imagined victims of battle; provides a measurement of the writer's struggle to compose (eight cigarettes is a lot); provokes our sympathy for the writer (writing is like a battle!); and undercuts the very sympathy it creates (no, honey, it isn't).

Our recognition that the newscast is "really" a report from the "front" of writing dramatizes and parodies the aims of poetry: identifying the "*typed sheet*" as either "an airstrip" or "a cemetery" suggests that a poem must fly or die, echoing Bishop's 1937 note that "Poetry = air transportation (in its present state)" (*EAP* 31). The ambiguous "*ink-bottle*" which may be either "secret weapon" or "*numen*" parodies a Romantic notion of poetry as a potential "savior" – a notion that the speaker connects to the "historical state of superstition and helplessness" of the believers. (This parody of Romantic poetic heroism is sustained throughout "12 O'Clock News": as Paul Muldoon points out, the poem's form echoes Samuel Taylor Coleridge's "Ancient Mariner.")[11] The incompetent leadership implied by the dead soldiers is, of course, the writer herself, whose doomed terrain we survey – but the speaker of the poem also provides a second writerly persona, exercising judgment and producing the text that we read. Both sides of the war, then, are aspects of the writer, and "12 O'Clock News" requires us to imagine several completely different things simultaneously: a war-damaged principality; a writer's desk; the perspective of an imperial power; a critique of that perspective; the struggle to compose; failed composition; successful composition; the high philosophical stakes of writing poetry; and a comparison of writing to the life-and-death struggle of war which both elevates and deflates those stakes. The poem's humor, and its point, comes from the fact that we both must and cannot take this equivalency seriously. Thomas Travisano suggests that Bishop seeks "to portray, not a thought, but the mind thinking";[12] in "12 O'Clock News," that technique helps her to encapsulate a dynamic argument about the difficulty and value of writing (and, perhaps, to believe six impossible things before breakfast). "12 O'Clock News" does not leave us with the position that writing is or is not important, is or is not like war, is or is not worth the struggle; rather, it grants us intimate insight into the writer's process, with its ambivalences intact.

"12 O'Clock News" provides an extended example of Bishop's double- or triple-exposure comic technique. This principle of humor arising from incommensurable simultaneous ideas is constant throughout her career. But "12 O'Clock News" is atypical of her humor in its focus on the process, and especially the frustrations, of writing (those eight cigarettes). The distanced-yet-intimate scrutiny of a mind's thought process Bishop applies to her own divided authorial self in "12 O'Clock News" is repeatedly directed outwards in the other poems, and humor becomes the vehicle of insight into another mind. This use of humor is continuous with Bishop's own overt linkage of laughter to friendship. In a letter to Anne Stevenson written in 1964, Bishop cites humor as an important shared quality among her loved ones:

> I have been very lucky in having had, most of my life, some witty friends, – and I mean real wit, quickness, wild fancies, remarks that make one cry with

> laughing.[. . .] The aunt I liked best was a very funny woman: most of my close friends have been funny people; Lota de Macedo Soares is funny. Pauline Hemingway (the 2nd Mrs. H.) a good friend until her death in 1951 was the wittiest person, man or woman, I've ever known. Marianne [Moore] was very funny – [E. E.] Cummings, too, of course. Perhaps I need such people to cheer me up." (*Pr* 412)

This letter suggests a deep-seated connection between humor and friendship. Laughter "cheers [Bishop] up" not just because it is pleasurable, but because it can forge intimacy, even between people far less similar than Bishop and her witty friends. In her poems, Bishop's laughter repeatedly appears to set up a Hobbesian superiority, but then transforms the initial distancing impulse into a fragile but meaningful insight into the object of laughter.

The connection between laughter and intimacy is made explicit at the end of "One Art," when the speaker of the poem addresses a lost beloved: "Even losing you (the joking voice, a gesture / I love) I shan't have lied" (*P* 198). The loss of the beloved is the climax of a catalogue of lesser losses – the speaker's keys, her mother's watch, houses, "rivers, a continent." The loss of the beloved is the final straw, and forces the speaker to admit for the first time that loss "may look like (*Write* it!) like disaster." In the context of such disaster, the apparently trivial details of the beloved's "joking voice" and "gesture" may initially be surprising choices as the only specifics we learn about her – why not her name, or, as in several early drafts of the poem, the color of her eyes (see *EAP* 225–40). But the parenthetical description places "joking" at the center of the loss: far from being distancing, laughter is part of what makes this intimate relationship important to the speaker, and is far more significant than even her beloved's "eyes of the Azure Aster" (*EAP* 234). The metonymic use of the "joking voice" to stand in for the beloved herself alerts us to the fact that the loss is also of merriment, of communication, and of the complex person with whom it is possible to share lighthearted understanding, rather than of the beloved as aesthetic or erotic object.

As Timothy Materer notes, Bishop frequently uses such parentheticals and asides, often to comic effect.[13] The parenthesis in "One Art" makes joking initially appear tangential or like an afterthought, but as we have just seen, that appearance is misleading. These asides do not simply insert extraneous or superfluous material; rather, they shift the frame of the poem to include additional perspectives, suggesting both the point of view of outsiders – the beloved's own amusement at the joke – and the speaker's mixed feelings. Something similar happens in, for example, the self-correction "(Cathedral, rather!)" in "Santarém" (*CP* 186), which conveys both the local people's repeated insistence that their church is a cathedral and the speaker's amusement at the idea. Such comic asides undercut the lyric poem's tendency to present a single, unified perspective, instead suggesting the coexistence of different subjectivities both within and beyond the speaker. The parentheses of "One Art" illuminate both the interiority of the beloved and – with "(*Write* it!)" – the conflicted viewpoint of the speaker, who has hitherto claimed to be indifferent to her own losses.

While such comic intimacy is most evident in the wit Bishop shared with likeminded friends and lovers – Marianne Moore, Lota de Macedo Soares – laughter can also reveal our commonality with people we take to be entirely unlike us, those whom we initially disdain or envy or ignore. "Filling Station" shows how Bishop's metaphysics of humor can make the unattractive, uncomfortable real world unexpectedly congenial by revealing commonalities among its inhabitants, as well as by skewering their flaws. The poem's mockery of a family running a filling station gives way to a recognition that the individual idiosyncrasies which produce laughter are also themselves the object of love. In "Filling Station," we find that the lover's comic "gestures" are necessary if the lover is to be understood not only by the beloved but by disinterested onlookers. Humor is required because humans are fallible; we are all inadequate in various ways, and only by treating our failures as comically constructive can we redeem them from tragedy.

Like "At the Fishhouses" with its coating of scales or the "awful but cheerful" activity in "The Bight," "Filling Station" foregrounds the ugliness of its setting:

> Oh, but it is dirty!
> – this little filling station
> oil-soaked, oil-permeated
> to a disturbing, over-all
> black translucency. (*P* 125)

The initial exclamation point suggests a lightness of tone which is echoed and undercut by a second, as the speaker warns us to "be careful with that match!" This is both a serious and a funny injunction: while the risk of fire is real at any gas station, this particular station's permeation with oil creates a hyperbolic threat of catastrophe, with the entire building and yard potentially going up in flames at a single spark. This danger is mentioned only in passing, however, giving way to a comic description of the proprietors: "Father" in his "dirty, / oil-soaked monkey suit," assisted by "several quick and saucy / and greasy sons." This portrait echoes the class snobbery of

"Manuelzinho," but, as Helen Vendler argues, the poem also suggests the attraction of the domestic world.[14] This attraction is hinted at by referring to "father" and his "sons" not by their professional identity as mechanics but in the terms of their family relationships, reinforced by yet another parenthetical: "(it's a family filling station)." As details accumulate (a "wicker sofa"; a "dirty dog, quite comfy"; a begonia; a porch full of oil-covered attempts at decoration), the speaker begins to speculate about their significance: "Why the taboret? / Why, oh why, the doily?" This comic speculation finally leads to something like what Siobhan Phillips, writing about "A Miracle for Breakfast," calls a "secular redemption"[15]: the inference that there is a "somebody" responsible for all these decorative touches leads to the more startling revelation that

> Somebody
> arranges the rows of cans
> so that they softly say:
> ESSO – SO – SO – SO
> to high-strung automobiles.
> Somebody loves us all. (*P* 126)

Vendler calls this description a "parody of metaphysical questioning."[16] The comedy of the scene comes from its contradictions: the grotesque decorations (the "big dim doily" "heavy with gray crochet"; the "big hirsute begonia") are an amusingly misguided attempt at beautifying the "disturbing" station. Bishop heightens the incongruity of the picture ("Somebody waters the plant, / or oils it, maybe"), but she also reads past the absurdity to the serious truths the comic details reveal. The porch and its furniture suggest a home; the "comic books" leisure time; the comfy dog its comfy owners. Most important, of course, is the absent personality implied by the accruing details. The floral crochet of the doily and the living begonia are feminine notes in this otherwise male-dominated scene – equivocally feminine, as the doily is "heavy" and the begonia "hirsute," but sufficient in conjunction with the presence of the "father" and his "sons" to suggest an invisible maternal figure. The attempts at beauty are comical not simply because they fail, but because they provide insight into the men we see and the woman whose existence we deduce. We learn to read grotesque physicality sympathetically in order to recognize the existence of maternal love. Bishop, placing herself and her readers in the masculine world of the father and sons, imagines an invisible but undeniable feminine presence which does not simply see past dirt but embraces it as an essential component of individuality – an unavoidable part of the bodies that let us move through the world as distinct, recognizable people. The final line of the poem, "Somebody loves us all," broadens the significance of this deduction to include not just the dirty father and sons, but the speaker, the reader, and the rest of "us," who are all laughable in our own ways. Our failings, which are obvious and even funny to observers, do not prevent us from being lovable.

Or so an optimistic reading of the poem's final line suggests. Bishop's biography may complicate that reading. Bishop's mother admitted herself to the Nova Scotia Hospital in Dartmouth in 1916 when the young Elizabeth was five, and they never saw each other again, although Gertrude Bulmer Bishop lived until 1934. Bishop's few recorded memories from before her mother's disappearance were mainly traumatic, and often involve failed communication: trying and failing to get her attention while watching the Great Salem Fire across the bay, or hearing her screaming.[17] Nor were the aunts and grandmothers who raised the child satisfactory maternal substitutes. Bishop's absent mother was significantly less present than the absent mother of "Filling Station." Treating maternal love as a stand-in for universal love, then, is far less sentimental coming from Bishop than it might appear, and we have little choice but to read "somebody loves us all" as partly ironic. Love does not commute; one mother's love for her sons does not guarantee another mother's love for her daughter. Why, then, does Bishop make the dirty filling station the scene of emotional fulfilment?

Not all critics agree that she does. Luke Carson reads "Filling Station" as evidence that "Bishop is [. . .] capable of exploring the affects of disgust and contempt characteristic of the urban snob." Certainly Bishop never abandons her amusement at the idea that anyone would find the monkey-suited father and his greasy sons loveable; the poem's humor, at least initially, is close to the Hobbesian model.[18] In this reading, the absent mother of Bishop's life is more important than the implied one of the filling station: "Somebody loves us all" is to be read as insincere, a platitude deliberately invoked to undercut the assertion it claims to make.

But however ironic the ending, the poem unarguably recognizes the organizing and life-sustaining hand of love at work, and we can no more read the poem as simple snobbery than we can read it as simple sentimentality. The "vulnerability" that Stephanie Burt notes in the poem is thus twofold: the danger of fire and the danger of reductive misreading.[19] We may try to dismiss the speaker's revelation of love as sappy, or as contaminated by her ironic disgust, just as she threatens to dismiss the filling station as too contaminated by oil. But by virtue of these opposed temptations, the oil which permeates the filling station and its occupants – father, sons, dog, begonia, and all – becomes an illuminating metaphor for love: it may sometimes be greasy, but it is everywhere and it is essential. The Esso cans demonstrate how love and oil interpenetrate: in a letter to a publisher, Bishop points out that "so-so-so was – perhaps still is in some places – the phrase people use to calm and soothe horses" (*OA* 638). In "Filling Station," love, which soothes and beautifies, entails an immersion in the elements of the beloved – especially those elements which are most idiosyncratic and even perilous. Love oils the begonia. From the outside, it is thus inevitably comic (you live with *that?*), but the comedy of love reveals its profundity precisely because it locates the transcendent in life's absurd details.

In the work of another poet, such a love might be read as divine. For Bishop, that reading must be taken at a slant; as Hugh Haughton argues, Bishop's humor "turn[s] on a sense of human comedy in a natural world without religious dispensation."[20] Instead, it is essential to the nature of comic revelation that the claim that "Somebody loves us all" is both mystical and mundane, sincere and ironic; the "love" of the poem, expressed through oil and Esso cans, is essentially earthly and manmade. The "somebody" cannot be a single person who loves all of us at once, any more than all mothers can be present and affectionate; instead, the poem suggests that each of us is loved by *someone*, although who that lover is must vary. Universal love, like mutual understanding, or the poem itself, is built out of accruing details, specific relationships, and individual actions, which by virtue of their idiosyncrasy are also all comic when viewed on the grand scale. The presence Bishop invokes in "Filling Station" is fundamentally human, and the humanity of that love is part of its comedy as well as of its depth: the "somebody" who loves us all is, in each case, a flawed individual – mother or lover or friend – who recognizes and accommodates our peculiarities and creates beauty from our dirt.

The humor of "Filling Station," then, holds in tension a series of oppositions: love/snobbery, self/other, absence/presence, epiphany/irony. We cannot select one side: to read "somebody loves us all" as entirely sincere is to miss the poem's very real disgust at its objects and to reduce it to sentimentality. To read it as entirely ironic is to miss out the poem's attraction to the idea of nurturing family love. Its humor and its larger philosophical claims about the nature of love are equally constructed out of its refusal to resolve these contradictions.

Taken together, the humorous simultaneity in "12 O'Clock News" and the ironized intimacy suggested by "Filling Station" provide a model from which to explore not just Bishop's humor, but the fundamental relationship between such humor and poetry. Like Bishop's comic contradictions, poems show us relationships among apparently incommensurable objects, and help us gain insight into the minds of others. They do this by valorizing ambiguity and flux, allowing us to juxtapose apparently incompatible ideas and thus gain access to other subjectivities without losing track of our own.

Notes

1. Thomas Hobbes, *Leviathan* (New York: Penguin, 1985), 125. Hobbes must have been in great demand at dinner parties.
2. Sigmund Freud, *The Joke and Its Relation to the Unconscious*, transl. Joyce Crick (New York: Penguin, 2002), 85.
3. Henri Bergson, "Laughter," in *Comedy*, ed. W. Sypher (Baltimore, MD: The Johns Hopkins University Press, 1956), 71.
4. For further discussion of theories of humor, particularly as they apply to twentieth-century poetry, see Rachel Trousdale, "Introduction," in *Humor in Modern American Poetry*, ed. Trousdale (London: Bloomsbury, 2017), 1–17.
5. Jeredith Merrin, "Elizabeth Bishop: Gaiety, Gayness, and Change," in *Elizabeth Bishop: The Geography of Gender*, ed. Marilyn May Lombardi (Charlottesville: University of Virginia Press, 1993), 153–72; Bonnie Costello, "Tragicomic Mode in Modern American Poetry: 'Awful but Cheerful,'" in *A Companion to Poetic Genre*, ed. Erik Martiny (New York: Wiley-Blackwell, 2011), 459–77; Susan Rosenbaum, "Elizabeth Bishop and the Miniature Museum," *Journal of Modern Literature* 28:2 (2005), 61–99; and Thomas Travisano, "'The Flicker of Impudence': Delicacy and Indelicacy in the Art of Elizabeth Bishop" *Elizabeth Bishop: The Geography of Gender*, 111–25.
6. Travisano, "Flicker of Impudence," 124.
7. Megan Marshall, *Elizabeth Bishop: A Miracle for Breakfast* (New York: Houghton Mifflin Harcourt, 2017), 32.
8. Joelle Biele, ed., *Elizabeth Bishop and The New Yorker: The Complete Correspondence* (New York: Farrar, Straus, and Giroux, 2011), 3.
9. Rachel Trousdale, "'I Take off My Hat': Elizabeth Bishop's Comedy of Self-Revelation," in *Reading Elizabeth Bishop: An Edinburgh Companion*, ed. Jonathan Ellis (Edinburgh: Edinburgh University Press, 2019), 77–89; Vidyan Ravinthiran, "'Manuelzinho,' Brazil and Identity Politics," in *Reading Elizabeth Bishop*, 33–47.
10. In *The End of the Poem*, Paul Muldoon examines this double exposure, showing how the literal and metaphorical wars coexist throughout the poem. Paul Muldoon, *The End of The Poem: Oxford Lectures* (New York: Farrar, Straus, and Giroux, 2007).
11. Ibid., 93.
12. Thomas Travisano, *Elizabeth Bishop: Her Artistic Development* (Charlottesville: University of Virginia Press, 1988), 71. The sentence is taken from M. W. Croll's

"The Baroque Style in Prose," quoted by Bishop in an essay she wrote as an undergraduate.

13. Timothy Materer, "Mirrored Lives: Elizabeth Bishop and James Merrill," *Twentieth-Century Literature* 51:2 (2005), 192.
14. Helen Vendler, "Domestication, Domesticity, and the Otherworldly," in *Elizabeth Bishop and Her Art*, ed. Lloyd Schwartz and Sybil P. Estess (Ann Arbor: University of Michigan Press, 1983), 34.
15. Siobhan Phillips, *The Poetics of the Everyday: Creative Repetition in Modern American Verse* (New York: Columbia University Press, 2010), 121.
16. Vendler, "Domestication," 35.
17. Brett Millier, *Elizabeth Bishop: Life and the Memory of It* (Berkeley: University of California Press, 1993), 4, 11.
18. Luke Carson, "James Merrill's Manners and Elizabeth Bishop's Dismay," *Twentieth-Century Literature* 50:2 (2004).
19. Stephanie Burt, "Elizabeth Bishop and the End of the Rainbow," *Reading Elizabeth Bishop*, 329.
20. Hugh Haughton, "Poetry and Good Humor: Marianne Moore and Elizabeth Bishop," in *Humor in Modern American Poetry*, 117. Bishop's skepticism of the supernatural can of course be overstated; as Anne Stevenson says, many of her poems contain "epiphanic showings forth." See Stevenson *Between the Iceberg and the Ship* (Ann Arbor: University of Michigan Press, 1998), 54. But readers like Cheryl Walker who try to place Bishop in the context of religious faith must do so in at best an impressionistic manner. See Walker, *God and Elizabeth Bishop: Meditations on Religion and Poetry* (New York: Palgrave Macmillan, 2005).

CHAPTER 27

Gender

Deryn Rees-Jones and Eira Murphy

How useful is bringing the lens of gender to a poet who herself showed little interest – or perhaps was less proportionately interested in gender – than she was in poetics? Bishop's famous and much quoted statements in relation to poetry, her dislike of the newly coined term "woman poet," and her refusal to be placed in women-only anthologies, are clear enough in their awareness of the impact of cultural norms on her writing. In a letter to Anne Stevenson in 1964, Bishop identifies an acute but perhaps revealing ambivalence that sees her navigating expectations of femininity, the literary tradition, and her own taste: "Because of my era, sex, situation, education, etc. I have written, so far, what I feel is a rather 'precious' kind of poetry" she writes, going on to add, "although I am very much opposed to the precious" (*PPL* 863).

Such a sense of needing to find a poetics that could respond to the complexities of the dynamic that runs between external cultural and literary constructions of gender and subjective and lived experience were not unique to Bishop as a woman poet. Throughout her life Bishop saw rapid changes in gender expectations and roles. From her days as a child in Nova Scotia where she spent her formative years, to her coming to adulthood in the USA during the Great Depression, she lived through a series of historical circumstances that became pressure points for gender constructions. While notions of gender were subject to degrees of flux and nuance, they frequently operated within a rigid binary that had as a core an idealisation of the feminine that translated into compulsory heterosexuality, maternal self-abnegation, and female sexual purity. As the century continued, the social and psychic frames that gender placed on self-consciousness and notions of gender and its relation to sexuality were being swept into a new domain of interrogation.[1] Such narratives as sexology, psychiatry, and hormone studies all sat alongside and sometimes interacted with the popularisation of psychoanalysis which sought to make clear the link between subjectivity and sexuality.[2] The relatively privileged white women with whom Bishop associated at Vassar in the early 1930s appear to have had a degree of freedom to explore their sexuality. Bishop's own sexual attraction to women, though unexplored in the poems published in her lifetime, was a constant in her life from her twenties onwards. While narratives of lesbianism were frequently framed negatively and censorship of openly lesbian literature was still in effect in the USA for most of her life – any depiction in film was banned for example until 1967 – communities of women did create spaces for open expression of their sexuality, most notably in Paris where Bishop spent time in the mid-1930s. Moving then as she did in 1951 to Brazil where she was to live with her partner Lota de Macedo Soares for fifteen years, Bishop's gendered expectations were again to run across a complex matrix of racial and intercultural frames.

Adrienne Rich, eighteen years Bishop's junior, in a review of *The Complete Poems* in the *Boston Review* in 1983, identifies what she sees as a rift between Bishop's lived experience as a woman, and her sexuality. "The price of 'external assimilation,'" writes Rich, is "internal division."[3] Instead of poems that examine intimate relationships, what takes their place, she continues, is "a series of poems examining relationships between people who are, for reasons of difference, distanced: rich and poor, landowner and tenant, white women and Black woman, invader and native."[4] Rich's comments are telling, not least because of the generational divide that sits between Bishop and Rich's own radical work as a lesbian poet. Early scholarship that addresses Bishop's approach to gender is exemplified by a generation of mostly feminist critics, many of whom were early pioneers in Bishop studies, who see Bishop's aesthetics less as a failure of personal testimony and political commitment than an attempt to navigate both social and literary worlds from a position of precarity. Lorrie Goldensohn, writing slightly later than Rich, has suggested that Bishop's apparent rejection of gender as a critical framework for reading and writing is a rejection of the personal which emerges from Modernism's rejection of a femininity closely allied with Romanticism.[5] Elsewhere, Joanna Feit Diehl takes care to describe what she sees as Bishop's own take on a masculine Modernism's repudiation of femininity, seeing her replace it with a "disengendered, highly-eroticized imagination."[6]

Bishop's letter from 1971 to May Swenson about the ghettoisation of women's poetry offers an interesting insight into her rationale about the lack of importance of gender to aesthetics, taking us on a journey through her thinking that allows for ideas of male and female differences, political activism, literature and literary history. Bishop writes:

> WHY "Women in Literature"? No – it's the WOMEN POETS IN ENGLISH, I see ... But, still, WHY? Why not MEN POETS IN ENGLISH? Don't you see how silly it is? [...] Literature is literature, no matter who produces it. Probably it's true that some of the earlier women poets have not been brought to people's attention enough – men's & women's attention – I have a student here who's preparing a paper on this for another class – in the history of women – or something [...] BUT I don't like things compartmentalized like that, and in this case I think it defeats the very purpose it's supposed to be for ... I like black & white, yellow & red, young & old, rich and poor, and male & female, all mixed up, socially – and see no reason for segregating them, for any reason at all, artistically, either. (*PPL* 883–84)

In this chapter, we approach Bishop as a poet engaged in an ongoing process of thinking through the relationship between poetry and gender. Bishop's complex use of gendered pronouns shows how, as her work develops, a self emerges in the poems at particular moments of embodiment within complex matrices of differences and relationality. Rosi Braidotti's notion of a subject as a "transversal assemblage"[7] is useful to us here in showing how Bishop's sense of the feminine evolves. We argue that for Bishop the poetic voice forms through moments of self-consciousness as it observes and genders itself within a gendered world and literary tradition, showing itself – in Braidotti's terms – not as given, but through "embodied and embedded, relational and affective perspectives."[8]

*

Bishop's first book, *North & South* (1946), is a book of sleepy disorientations; it is a book which creates a world in which bodies are not fully assembling or coming together, where attempts to locate the self within the geographical compass are also attempts to reorient that self. In the volume, sleeping and awakening become sites for an emerging consciousness. In these early poems, which date back to the 1930s in their genesis, it is not generally a female "I" who is evident but rather a "we" who speaks, often in relation to a "he."[9] By the last poem in the collection, "Anaphora," the "I" has moved from an identification with a ragged male body to one which has dissolved entirely.[10]

Such movements towards a complex gendering of a poem's subjects and speakers become manifest in "The Man-Moth" (1935), a poem which allows Bishop to enact and dramatise a shifting sense of gender through textual slippage and error. The single line – "*Newspaper misprint for 'mammoth'" (*P* 16) – that sits beneath the title offers what will become a common element of doubling and repetition in Bishop's poetics as the poem becomes an early vehicle for a set of intricate explorations of gender. Written when Bishop was just twenty-four, and not long after the death of her mother, the poem has at its centre a strange hybrid creation, part man, part moth, who negotiates his environment, disoriented but lured by the "queer light" of the moon (*P* 16). Perhaps in this hybrid creature Bishop had in mind the collages and hybrid creatures of Max Ernst. She certainly drew on them in another poem she completed during the same period, "The Monument." Whatever the nature of the visual collage that may have been in her mind, the poem seems to hold a melancholy sense of an observed creature reaching towards a relationality to the feminine moon, which is impossible and imbued with danger. Ostensibly Bishop's bringing to life of the misprint, the "m" that becomes an "n" through a performance of misreading that transforms into poetic process, is figured through two animals. Both animals, the mammoth and the man-moth, are "impossible" as living creatures. The man–moth hybrid is an object of imagined creation while the extinct mammoth can only exist within a historical record. Slippage of one into another allows a creature to unite within a poem as both a figure of the past and the imagination. This transformation is one which works in both temporal and biologically gendered ways and importantly the metamorphosis of animal into poem is one predicated on loss. For as "mam" becomes "man" in the typo, both loss and transformation also become intertwined with the idea of the maternal and the masculine. Here is sexual difference in both letter and in biology. In the miniscule shift, the curved stroke of the letter from m to n, rests the enormity of what is gone in their conflation and invention. The movement between the maternal and male – implied by "mam," and the embodied male "mistake" that is the man-moth – becomes both manifest and concealed. In the poem, the lost phoneme that recalls the mother is also present in a doubly mutilated way. "Mam" becomes "man," but in its new existence as a moth it also reminds us of another severance, the shift from "mother" to "moth," and perhaps even the vowel shift of "man" to "moon." It is in this set of absences and metamorphoses that we see a set of refractions, with mother becoming insect, and, in turn, the man becoming mother. Bishop's conception of gender in the poem depends on the introduction of a non-human element, using the moth as a place of differences through which to complicate what seems ostensibly to be an exploration of a male creature.

Bishop's acts of looking that foreground a hybrid gendered subject move towards an exploration of gender in the literary tradition in "The Gentleman of Shalott" (1936). Here Bishop uses Tennyson's poem, "The Lady of Shalott," a poem that exists in two versions, across a decade of two different publications, as an intertextual base from which to continue her interest in doubling and overlay across gender and time. The first version of Tennyson's poem was published in 1832; it was later revised in 1842. As in "The Man-Moth," we see that Bishop's "The Gentleman of Shalott" is a poem in which gender demarcations are again dependent on slippages. Written only a year after "The Man-Moth," this poem also sees Bishop using moments of gendering in relation to an engagement with the highly gendered literary tradition within which she was writing. The "gentleman" of the poem is another imagined and hybridised creation, whose existence also depends upon an interrelationship with a version of femininity. Here, however, the poem engages directly with the literary tradition as it self-consciously takes on the gendering of a poem as female and re-visions it as male.

The first version of Tennyson's poem ends with an image of a dead woman lying observed by "Knight, minstrel, abbot, squire, and guest" with a parchment on which is written "The web was woven curiously, / the charm is broken utterly, / Draw near and fear not, – this is I, / The Lady of Shalott." In Tennyson's later 1842 version, this ambiguous naming of the dead woman, which acts either as a conferred voice or suicide note, is replaced by Lancelot's "She has a lovely face, / God in his mercy lend her grace, / The Lady of Shalott." In Tennyson's second version, words are replaced by a voyeuristic, and necrophilic reading of a dead woman's body. This movement from text to body not only encodes an explicitly female body as something to be read and named by a male gazer and speaker – both Tennyson and Lancelot – but also lends Bishop the space of subjective slippage between these versions with which to play.

As Herbert Tucker has observed, in Tennyson's poem "Lancelot is no presence, but pure representation: a man of mirrors, a signifier as hollow as the song he sings."[11] Bishop, writing in the third person, makes this "man of mirrors" literal, adopting a new form of poetic seeing that focuses on the idea of identity, looking, and representation. It is not the Lady of Shalott, forced to see the world through a mirror, "half-sick with shadows," but Bishop's Gentleman, whose ability to exist as a "kind of half whole" is wholly dependent on the mirror. As Tennyson's Lady abandons the explicitly gendered artform of weaving for a new kind of artistry and a complete vision, away from the mirror, Bishop's Gentleman cannot escape his halved, incomplete gaze, based on reflection, by which the tenuous fallacy of the complete self might be upheld. Tennyson's curse of mirrored looking becomes the only way of looking in Bishop's poem. In declining to apply the necrophilic poetic gaze to a male corpse, as might be expected from the poem's title, however, Bishop shows the masculine gaze disoriented, glued to an act of narcissistic looking unable to escape or locate itself. The hierarchies of looking, so overt and problematic in Tennyson, become in Bishop's poem destabilised, dizzyingly self-reflexive and distorting. Her erasure of the image of the dead woman, the final enduring image of Tennyson's poem, from "The Gentleman of Shalott," consigns it to a half-cognition that plays at the peripheries of the reader's gaze; and like the slippage that occurs between the mammoth and the man-moth, the lady – femininity – is seen and not seen.

Bishop's interjection into the literary tradition as she swaps the image from Lady to Gentleman, opens up potential dialogue into gendered expectations and tropes that additionally extend to the male and female writer. But rather than being a poem in which these boundaries are rigidly set up, "The Gentleman of Shalott" is brilliant in its reversals and manoeuvres, rendering such fixed binaric distinctions impossible. Engaging with Tennyson's version of embodied female agency and speech, his morbid voyeurism allows Bishop to bring the male gaze under scrutiny. Instead of reversing that role and looking at the dead male body, she playfully shows the masculine gaze disoriented; there is a kind of cartoon hopelessness of a figure unable to locate the body from its image.[12]

Like the woman who looks into the mirror in Tennyson's poem, Bishop's poem is also a poem by a woman, looking into the mirror of its precursor. And yet it also asks us to sit in awareness that the gap between female author and the ungendered voice of the poem is a real one. The narratorial voice offers an engagement with this strange hybrid figure, an ethical positioning of the author/narrator that is not voyeurism but which also allows for identification. Here then is perhaps the first instance of a gender divide in Bishop that offers critique at the positioning of the female writer; and posits the alignment between self-reflection and self-knowledge.

As Bishop ages, female figures in the poems become increasingly present and embodied figures, resistant and powerful. In *A Cold Spring* (1955) and *Questions of Travel* (1965) relationships between genders are often figured generationally. We can think variously of the mother cow and her calf in "A Cold Spring"; in "Over 2,000 Illustrations and a Complete Concordance" the Englishwoman announces the pregnancy of a Duchess over tea; and, more problematically in terms of establishing hierarchies of gender and race, the "little pockmarked prostitutes" in the same poem, as well as the Indian Princess in "Florida" – nameless women who are simply itemised in a list and then returned to part of the landscape. Two of Bishop's most memorable character descriptions of people were women she knew well, her fellow poet Marianne Moore and Mary E. Breen, a retired police lieutenant she met on the long journey to Brazil. In "Invitation to Miss Marianne Moore" her friend and mentor arrives like a witch with black pointed shoes (*P* 80–81); and in "Arrival at Santos" Miss Breen is a scene-stealing "six feet tall / with beautiful bright blue eyes and a kind expression" (*P* 87).

Bishop moves in her later poems towards two key dramatic monologues which speak not just about men, but as a man: in "The Riverman" (1960), in which the speaker proclaims as he sees, "I glimpsed him – a man like myself" (*P* 103), and more complicatedly in "Crusoe in England" (1971), a poem begun ten years previously under the title "Crusoe at Home." In this poem Bishop uses the monologue and its triad of ironic displacements between author, reader, and writer, to create another kind of gender slippage, as she plays with gender, authorship, and sexuality, setting the by-now recognisable Bishop voice against a double narrative, of both Defoe's textual creation Robinson Crusoe, and his own male authorship. Notably, this dynamic is also complicated through the dynamic of race. First published in 1719, as if it were an autobiographical account, offering itself as the work of the eponymous Robinson Crusoe, early in Defoe's novel Crusoe, an English slave trader, sets off to Africa from Brazil. In Bishop's poem, the slippage between identifications of male and female become a space of code and irony: "If only he had been a woman! / I wanted to propagate my kind, / and so did he, I think, poor boy" (*P* 185). We hear when Bishop speaks both the voice of the lesbian writer, and simultaneously, her assuming of a male voice whose same-sex desire is also prohibited. Crusoe's relationship with the Black character Friday becomes, in Bishop's poem, a way of playing with codings of sexuality that seem to offer re-framings of difference while not wholly discarding longstanding racist narratives of otherness and hierarchy.

In the later poems, there is a marked movement towards an identification with the feminine through use of female pronouns and exploration of female experiences which culminate in "In the Waiting Room" and "The Moose." In "In the Waiting Room," Bishop returns to a prismatic identification of femininity which again invokes race: but in this instance it is the female Black body.

"In the Waiting Room" was first published in *The New Yorker* on 9 July 1971, and it is the first poem of *Geography III* (1976), her last collection. In the poem, Bishop narrates the story of a young girl visiting the dentist waiting room and during a moment of epiphany the speaker of the poem recognises and addresses herself as a child in terms of gender, as an "Elizabeth" comes into a state of coalescence. "You are an *Elizabeth*," Bishop writes, as shifts of identification occur again around pronoun use: "you are an *I*, / you are an *Elizabeth*, / you are one of *them*" (*P* 180).

Bishop sets herself in a place of difference from the Black women in the *National Geographic*, but also to a certain extent from her Aunt and the other "grown-up people" of the waiting room, and "Elizabeth" herself. Elizabeth becomes Elizabeth upon recognising her "family voice" at the same time making it distinct from her Aunt's cry of pain. The external voice is both separate and outside of her, and yet it works to externalise an internal moment of specifically painful realisation that assimilates the triad of experiences between young girl, older woman, and the photographs of the Black tribal women in the pages of the magazine. It is a process of identification reliant upon an oscillation between recognition and rejection, as a gendered self is constructed through the revelation of a seen if mediated Black female body and a heard if absent white older relative. Elizabeth emerges as "one of *them*" (*P* 180). The hierarchies created here in terms of race risk constructing a racist narrative of difference, a narrative which continues in Bishop's work.

In "In the Waiting Room," the realisation of femininity is also a realisation of pain, where self-knowledge and epiphany are directly connected to expressions of horror. The patterns and repetitions of emergence as signalled through pronouns – a trend towards what we will think of here as an ontological move towards "becoming an Elizabeth" – do not offer selfhood, or indeed gender, as an absolute, but become part of a series of patternings which may or may not be fixed to an embodied subject. Yet even in these latter poems of self-consciousness, Bishop's awareness of a female identity remains in a place of discomfort.

*

In a posthumously published poem of same-sex desire, we see Bishop continuing to set up the self as one built on provisionality and relationality. "Vague Poem (*Vaguely Love Poem*)" (1973) is spoken from her, by-now typical, disembodied voice. Nevertheless, here that voice owns an ungendered first-person pronoun, its identity constructed through its identification with a female other. This "other" in the poem also speaks as "I" to the "you," speaking the poem as the characters discuss, hesitantly, the science of crystallography:

> Later, as we drank tea from mugs, she found one,
> "a sort of one". "This one is just beginning. See –
> you can see here, it's beginning to look like a rose.
> It's – well, a crystal, crystals form –
> I don't know any geology myself . . ."
> (Neither did I.) (*P* 323)

The complex positioning of direct speech, pronouns, and brackets across the line breaks in this section visually, even literally, crystallise the dynamic between the poem's speaker and addressee: "'I don't know any geology myself. . . ' / (Neither did I.)" (*P* 323). Observation, examination, and understanding sit in parallel with the crystals coming into being. As the observers look, so then in their relationality and exchange, do they seem to be in a place where they are also coming into being. The two characters exist in a set of other relations: the dancing black dog, who is specifically female, the students, and even inanimate objects, the mugs and the rock rose itself, and even though we might want to assume the speaker like the poet, is female, the urge to gender the poem's "I" as female is never wholly allowed. In her use of crystallography as a metaphor for seeing/knowing, Bishop moves from the flat reflective plane of the mirror we have seen in "The Gentleman of Shalott" to the geometric structures, surfaces, and patterns that move her beyond outward surfaces to atomic structures. The material is reframed through an awareness of its mobility so that the emerging image of the mirror-like phrase "rose-rock, rock-rose," is grounded not simply in repetition but in a repetition which shifts words which double as things and movements, moving as they do from noun to verb, object to action. The "vagueness" of the poem, its errant, hesitant progression ends up by configuring the female genitals, the rose of sex, as a place to rest or conclude, yet that place is not one that proves essential or essentialist. Instead the feminine is something which, like the emerging crystal, is "Trying, working, to show itself / forming, folding over" (*P* 325).

*

Discussing the events which led to "In the Waiting Room" in a 1961 autobiographical essay, "The Country Mouse," Bishop writes:

> A feeling of absolute and utter desolation came over me. I felt . . . *myself.* In a few days it would be my seventh birthday. I felt *I, I, I,* and looked at the three strangers in panic. I was *one* of them too, inside my scabby body and wheezing lungs. 'You're in for it now,' something said. How had I got tricked into such a false position? I would be like that woman opposite who smiled at me so falsely every once in a while. The awful sensation passed, then it came back again. 'You are you,' something said. 'How strange you are, inside looking out. You are not Beppo, or the chestnut tree, or Emma, you are *you* and you are going to be *you* forever'. It was like coasting downhill, this thought, only much worse, and it quickly smashed into a tree. *Why* was I a human being? (*Pr* 99)

The repeated utterances of selfhood "*I, I, I*" seem here to be differentiated and estranged from the self as Bishop, smashing into the tree, metaphorically crashes into the "*I*" itself. Recent thinking about Bishop's poetics of displacement have read Bishop through ideas of the posthuman, seeing Bishop as a poet who, in Amy Waite's words, is both fascinated "with material entanglements" while at the same time being preoccupied with "opening up ontological borders" and "radical intra-relations."[13] What emerges reading Bishop across time is that a sense of gender is determined through sets of differences and a relationality which becomes increasingly able to address what femininity might be as a moment of emergence in the poem. Such framing of gender is potentially radical in its positioning of a subject in time and space, reaching as it does towards an aesthetic that would enable the articulation of an affirmative posthuman subjectivity. Yet even as she reaches towards something potentially radical, Bishop's emerging female subjects in the late poems of the 1970s are subtly intertwined with hierarchies that sit within culturally and historically racist narratives of difference.

Notes

1. See Bethany Hicok, *Degrees of Freedom: American Women Poets and the Women's College, 1905–1955* (Lewisburg: Bucknell University Press, 2008).
2. Freud's key essays on femininity include "On the Psychological Consequences of the Anatomical Distinction between the Sexes" (1925), "Female Sexuality" (1931), and "Femininity" (1933).
3. Adrienne Rich, "The Eye of the Outsider: Elizabeth Bishop's *Complete Poems*," in *Blood, Bread, and Poetry: Selected Prose, 1979–1985* (London: Virago Press, 1986), 128.
4. Ibid., 130–31.
5. See Lorrie Goldensohn, *Elizabeth Bishop: The Biography of a Poetry* (New York: Columbia University Press, 1992).
6. Joanne Feit Diehl, *Women Poets and the American Sublime* (Bloomington: Indiana University Press, 1990), 109. See also Susan Rosenbaum's excellent summary of Bishop's relationship with Romanticism in "Bishop and the Natural World," in *The Cambridge Companion to Elizabeth Bishop*, ed. Angus Cleghorn and Jonathan Ellis (New York: Cambridge University Press, 2014), 62–78.
7. See Rosi Braidotti, *Posthuman Knowledge* (Cambridge: Polity, 2019), 53.
8. See Stephanie Burt, "Elizabeth Bishop at the End of the Rainbow," in *Reading Elizabeth Bishop: An Edinburgh Companion*, ed. Jonathan Ellis (Edinburgh: Edinburgh University Press, 2019), 321–36.

9. This might be set against the fact that the book also seems populated by female characters through its many post-initial publication dedications to women friends. In a 1964 interview with Ashley Brown, Bishop spoke of writing "Songs for a Colored Singer" with Billie Holiday in mind.
10. See *Elizabeth Bishop and the Music of Literature*, ed. Angus Cleghorn (Cham, Switzerland: Palgrave Pivot, 2019).
11. Herbert Tucker, *Tennyson and the Doom of Romanticism* (Cambridge: Harvard University Press, 1988), 114.
12. We can think here too of the early love poem "Insomnia" (1951) which, with its mirroring, and surprise reversals, appeared in *A Cold Spring* (1955).
13. Amy Waite, "'The Color of the World All Together': Elizabeth Bishop's Diffraction Patterns," *Reading Elizabeth Bishop*, 59–60.

CHAPTER 28

Queerness

Michael D. Snediker

In her late essay, "Melanie Klein and the Difference Affect Makes," Eve Kosofsky Sedgwick muses on the speculative richness made possible by those books one knows about but hasn't actually read, "books that can therefore have a presence, or exert a pressure in our lives and thinking, that may have much or little to do with what's actually inside them."[1] This scene of imagined reading, of a textual archive whose envisioning sustenance depends on the closeness of an incapacity safe if not freed from the distorting seductions of appropriation, further complicates our sense of Sedgwick's shifting attention to what in an earlier essay she articulates as the "privilege of unknowing."[2] Our resistance to the "scornful, fearful, or patheticizing reification of 'ignorance'"[3] draws us closer to a range of intimacies, impasses, and affective situations irreducible to those narratives of apprehension and obstruction that our customary modes of engagement, no matter their spaciousness or sedulity, risk curtailing. As I've previously suggested,[4] this experiment in epistemological redistribution informs Sedgwick's eventual practice as a textile artist no less than it does her extant writings about texture and haptic variance. "I've written quite a lot elsewhere about texture," Sedgwick notes in *The Weather in Proust*:

> the base-line attraction of any textile art, and how the very fact of texture seems to confound any understanding of perception in terms of passive as opposed to active. 'To perceive texture is always, immediately, and de facto to be immersed in a field of active narrative hypothesizing, testing, and re-understanding of how physical properties act and are acted upon over time.'[5]

To a certain extent, Sedgwick's insistence on "the very fact of texture" and our "de facto" immersion in it may seem at odds with a hypothetical propensity largely beneficial for its autonomy from the pressures of facticity. Just as the passage's conjuring of "active narrative hypothesizing" leans uneasily against the preceding sentence's confounding of passivity and activity, I hear in Sedgwick's "always, immediately, and de facto" an echo of her earlier puzzling over Fredric Jameson's edict "Always historicize." "*Always* historicize? What could have less to do with historicizing than the commanding, atemporal adverb 'always'?"[6] What could have less, for that matter, to do with hypothesis? The conundrum of trying to formulate a sensibility less, or at least differently, susceptible to the foreclosing constraints of writing than what it writes against ultimately leads Sedgwick with no small relief to what she calls "the weaver's handshake," the "feel of any kind of fiber between my thumb and fingers – in a gesture I probably got from my grandmother, who also taught me to crochet and embroider," a gesture that posits less the fact than the "nub of reality."[7]

In a speculative spirit kindred to the "accumulated reverie"[8] afforded by those books one loves not despite but through their having not been read, these pages explore an imagined textual exchange between Sedgwick and Elizabeth Bishop. Notwithstanding the crochet and embroidery lessons of her grandmother, it seems at least possible that Sedgwick's appreciation of the weaver's handshake is prompted by Bishop's own figuration of this gesture in "The Map":

> The names of seashore towns run out to sea,
> the names of cities cross the neighboring mountains
> – the printer here experiencing the same excitement
> as when emotion too far exceeds its cause.
> These peninsulas take the water between thumb and finger
> like women feeling for the smoothness of yard-goods. (*P* 5)

These are wily lines, familiar though they may be. To what, for instance, can their deictic "here" definitively be said to refer? Even as it invokes the locative principle of cartography, Bishop's "here" only equivocally situates or otherwise identifies the excitement of a printer notionally responsible for the names of towns Byronically bleeding into sea or, for that matter, the excitement of a printer discovering the spill of names after the fact. The malfunctioning enthusiasm of the scene presses us to consider our own expectations when it comes to cartographic and poetic thresholds, the way we negotiate or tacitly correct such perceptual misprisions according to a benighted belief in textual transparency, which is to say, a mode of readerly openness capable of withstanding the vagaries of contingency that circulate through it. To a certain extent, the printer's suspensive occupation of these scenes of approximate writerly and readerly attachment repeats a more general orientational confusion unfolding from the difficulty of knowing where and how the poem's indication of cartographic exteriority cedes to or coincides with those elements of human interiority belied, however implicitly, as the text's purported stakes; or, at least, our own. And yet the question remains how best to conceptualize these purlieus of feeling in relation to the map-forms and suppositional derivations comprising the poem's manifest concern. The difficulty of parsing the circumstantial and figurative logic underlying "the same excitement," for example, insists we linger with the text's juxtaposition of emotion/excitement with the overflow of cartographic type. While the effects of this typographical extravagance give the impression of abandon or elation, their mechanical cause – such as can be inferred from a poem intent on scenic juxtaposition absent the finer mediating terms of relation – hews closer, I think, to the aleatoric smudge of Warhol's photo-silkscreens. When a blurt of ink invites us to register Marilyn Monroe's amassed mascara as a bruise or smear of tears, it's not that our response to the contingencies of reproduction wholly submits to the residua of naturalist emotion resembled, but that transformation moves in both directions at once.

It's along these lines that the previous excerpt from "The Map" conceptualizes anthropomorphosis and mechanical hypostasis as different sides of a single coin. I think in this context of Barbara Johnson's discussion of Wordsworth and Poe's deceptively convergent poetics in "Strange Fits: Poe and Wordsworth on the Nature of Poetic Language." "The operative opposition here," Johnson writes,

> is the opposition between the 'natural' and the 'mechanical.' Personifications, says Wordsworth, are not 'natural,' but rather 'a mechanical device of style.' But already there is an exception: they are sometimes naturally prompted by passion. If poetry is located at a point of vivid sensation, if it is defined as always being in some sense a strange fit of passion, then where does Wordsworth draw the line? Are personifications natural or mechanical? How natural is the natural language of passion?[9]

Johnson's tracing of Romantic poetry's mechanical and natural Möbius-involutions all the more pertains to an analysis of Bishop, given her complex captivation with Poe's work. Indeed, the resonance between Bishop's draft poem "Edgar Allan Poe and the Juke-Box" and Johnson's analysis is uncanny:

> Poe said that poetry was *exact*.
> But pleasures are mechanical
> and know beforehand what they want
> and know exactly what they want. (*EAP* 49)

Despite the echoes between the first line and the fourth, whole worlds stand between the predicate nominative of "poetry was *exact*" and the subsequent adverbial "know exactly what they want." That the text's entertainment of exactness as self-coincident sufficiency gives way to the non-equivalence of "exact" and "exactly" animates the strange syncope of Bishop's "[b]ut," imposing as it does a break between the severity of poetry's internal adequation and the non-fungible knowledge that refracts pleasure against itself. The Bartleby-like repletion of poetry's exaction, its nearly impervious grammar, calls our attention to the tribulation of knowledge alone. Pleasure's knowledge of what exactly it wants makes of it a sensorial despot remarkable less for its clarity than its punctiliousness. If pleasure could know its objects less exactly, less clairvoyantly, we might be less beholden to its demand; after all, that pleasures know "beforehand" and "exactly" what they want hardly guarantees their satisfaction. In this way, the passage's second citing of exactitude accedes to the personification of feeling's estrangement from itself, mechanically casting itself, like the printed names of "The Map's" litoral towns, beyond its own reach (*exigere,* to drive or force out).

Bishop's gloss of Poe thus conjures the exactness of poetry as prophylaxis against pleasure's correspondingly implacable inflexibility. Poe writes in "The Poetic Principle":

> the demands of Truth are severe. She has no sympathy with the myrtles. All *that* which is so indispensable in Song, is precisely all *that* with which *she* has nothing whatever to do. [. . .] We must be simple, precise, terse. We must be cool, calm, unimpassioned. In a word, we must be in that mood which, as nearly as possible, is the exact converse of the poetical.[10]

In Bishop's terms, the "exact converse" of the poetical – "con" as both argument against verse and verse's own perfidious swindle – amounts to an exactness whose whittling relation to the poetics it spurs recalls the double-bind of Marianne Moore's "Poetry," *I too dislike it.* As Jean-Luc Nancy writes of Hölderlin, such a poetry of exactness entails a "unified consciousness [. . .] compris[ing] less the moment of relation to the self, of re-presentation as such, than the unique moment of looking – not so much the intention but the opening, the gaze directed at or cast upon, before, outside the self."[11] Nancy's further remarks on a poem's unwavering quiddity – that it "is not the unsayable that would be said, fugitively or analogically and, consequently, hedged in a way. With respect to the calculation, there is neither unsayable nor sayable, there is only what is exactly said"[12] – model a form of poetic engagement whose attention to surface buoyancies[13] productively impede the penchant for interpretive narrativizing evidenced, for instance, in Victoria Harrison's account of "The Map's" erotic coordinates:

> Whether "The Map" suggests desired or actual love can only be conjectured, but in either case the sea lifting the land "unperturbed around itself" and the bays that we may stroke are sensual, even sexual [. . . .] Keeping her own same-sex love secret and separate from her public life, Bishop invented a language for lesbian love within a poem about a map, land, and water, a love that need not set containing and spilling in opposition.[14]

Counterintuitive though it may seem, it is the exactness of Bishop's text that cautions against Harrison's deliberation between "desired or actual love." In the quiet vigor of the poem's speculations, holding desired love and actual love apart grows all the more fraught an enterprise. From its opening lines, "The Map's" enactment of waver – "Shadows, or are they shallows" – invites us to conceptualize love in, as, the conjunctive no-man's land of "or," in relation to which the hypostases of "desired" and "actual" (irrespective of their denotative incongruences) prove equally sedimentary. The spacious irresolution of such assays unsteadies the poem's contrapuntal investment in discriminative refinement, registering the apparent confusability of poetic technique with the variously coarser and/or more spontaneous optics, so perceived, of nominally non-poetic experience. It's not that Bishop's poems impersonate experience so much as ventriloquize the intimacy through which experience attempts to communicate itself beyond itself, perfecting the impression of trying to make themselves understood.

Bishop's posthumously collected poem, "Vague Poem (*Vaguely love poem*)" affords a remarkable instance of this studied conversancy, proffering within its loosely chronicled demotic – "The trip west. / – I think I *dreamed that trip*. / They talked a lot of 'Rose Rocks' / or maybe 'Rock Roses'" (*P* 323) – the countervailing wonder occasioned by a prismatically Steinian object, "rose-rock, rose-quartz, roses, roses, roses" (*P* 325). Shuttling between explanatory idioms the poem colloquially references without understanding and a burgeoning erotic perceptibility that troubles where geological import gives way to allegorical substance, the narrative's petrified ravishment doesn't solve transformative mysteriousness by eventually naming it "the even darker, accurate, rose of sex" so much as articulates its clarity of desire as chance discernment inseparable from the text's non-crystalline source materials. If the text's penultimate appeal to "exacting roses from the body" reconceives poetic exaction as metonymic variant or distortion of excavation/extraction, the gerund form muddles the object-economy of roses by extending exacting acumen as the latter's own capacity (intimating the speaker herself, perhaps, as the object of their overdetermined discernment). No less keen a revision of pleasure's knowledge occurs in the preceding stanza's reflection on "Crystallography and its laws: / Something I I once wanted badly to study," the earnest avidity of "wanting badly" tacitly giving way to a queer counter-desire for miseducation, studying badly as its own object of desire.

It's not, then, that the "sea lifting the land" is "sensual, even sexual," whether or not the poem's amorous center of gravity were confirmable as actuated or intended, but that the text's sensuality – a word treated by Harrison's analysis as self-explanatory, even as Bishop's investigation of contact and contiguity across literal and figurative registers suggests the paucity of our understanding when it comes to its inflective interface – is inseparable from the aesthetics of its conjectural premise. If the poetry of exactness has a hand in "The Map's" peculiar meditativeness, the pleasure it generates recalls Roland Barthes's formulation of "[p]leasure's force of suspension" as a "veritable époché" that "can never be overstated,"[15] not least because no amount of recapitulation would bring it closer to the objects in the warp of its orbit.

Rather than too quickly returning Bishop's writing to those structures of intimacy we already (think we) know, it behooves us to inhabit their suspensive seduction on its own terms. While Thomas Travisano turns to "The Map's" peninsulas as evidence that "geography can be humanized,"[16] it's to the poem's credit that its conception of humanness will prove no less geographically or cartographically unmooring. That the peninsulas similetically aligned with the women "feeling for the smoothness of yard-goods" render the women as peninsular as the other way around all the more depends on the fricatively irresolvable tension – eddy and undertow – between the poem's landforms and the water that the latter takes in hand. Recalling Sedgwick's appreciation of the weaver's handshake for its troubling of active and passive dispositions, the water surrounding Bishop's peninsulas – or, to be more precise, the map's detemporalizing depiction of their concurrence – takes them in hand, too. At the same time that the poem's "thumb and finger" belong to the care of peninsular appraisal, this personification simultaneously extends a way of thinking about the vicissitudes of buoyancy and abrasion (at once more and less specific than the simile itself) to which a map only attests in shorthand. Bearing in mind the sartorial idiom of the stanza's yard-goods, land and water wear each other, and wear each other down. At their most distilled, the hypothetical modes of rapport illuminated in this encounter – whether between poet and reader, printer and publication, or lover and beloved, to postulate just three possible scenarios answering to Travisano's sense of humanization – inhabit the curious overdetermination of Bishop's "feeling for." Though it can't help but echo the language of emotion and excitement that it follows, Bishop's "feeling for" doesn't directly assert a relation between haptic and emotional phenomena so much as marks a space where the mystery of their affinity has been sighted. And yet at the same time, the formulation is remarkable for its departure from the optical inclinations of poem and map alike, turning as it does to a tactual responsiveness that the time of writing leaves unconfirmed; the difference between feeling for a key, and holding a key in hand.

An aside: the back-and-forth dynamism interlacing Bishop's peninsular entities with the water that surrounds them resembles in its constitutively kinetic incessancy a corresponding engrossment – on the part of Bishop and Sedgwick alike – with an aesthetics of rubbing friction. Bishop's interest in Max Ernst's surrealist practice of frottage surfaces in a letter she writes to Herbert scholar Joseph Summers and his wife, UT, just weeks following the death of her lover, Lota de Macedo Soares. As Bonnie Costello and others, however, have noted, Ernst's term also appears in one of Bishop's notebook entries associated with her 1938 poem, "The Monument." *Take a frottage of the sea,* Bishop exhorts, as though Ernst's process of rubbing were akin to taking a picture.[17] Even were one able to hold a sheet of paper against water without it being reduced to pulp, frottage would remain all but impossible insofar as we understand its commemorating surface in terms of lifting the texture of an object from the object. Whereas the grooves and whorls of a wooden plank might bear the accumulated affliction of brush-bristles or other forms of quotidian injury, the constant mode of an aquatic surface absorbs the contingencies it sustains. Just as the rubbing gesture of Ernst's practice repeats the movement of scrubbing that he fantasizes as having deepened the grooves in the planks, the traversing motion of the waves fleetingly comes to resemble not only the shapes in the wood, freed from stasis, but the energetics of frottage itself.[18]

In the parlance of queer theory, the tautology of reading for what one already recognizes and, in recognizing, understands, evokes Sedgwick's exasperated appraisal of paranoid reading, the most extensive formulation of which appears in her preface to *Novel Gazing,* "Paranoid Reading and Reparative Reading; or, You're so Paranoid, You Probably Think This Introduction is About You." One measure of the distance of Bishop's poetics from the blinkered fervour of paranoid reading practices may be gleaned in her abiding exercise of the conjunctive "or," its participation in what Sedgwick denominates the "additive and accretive" "desire of a reparative impulse."[19] Lee Edelman's reading of Bishop's late poem, "Santarém," appositely gravitates toward the alchemizing value of "or" in terms of its subtending disruption of a literariness that names "the logic of naming, of linguistic or rhetorical positing, responsible for instituting identities endowed with the self-evidence of the literal only insofar as they manage to repress their determining rhetoricity."[20] To the extent that queer remediations of Bishop's writing lead back to the irrefragable influence of Poe, I can't help but hear in Bishop's "or" Poe's own devotion to the word – or, rather, the sound of the word, hovering in the wings of perceptibility – in his rationale for choosing *nevermore* as the refrain of "The Raven." "The question now arose as to the *character* of the word [. . .]. That such a close, to have force, must be sonorous and susceptible of protracted emphasis, admitted no doubt: and these considerations inevitably led me to the long *o* as the most sonorous vowel, in connection with *r* as the most producible consonant."[21] The persistent vacillation of "or," its proliferative spooling of perceptual unity into further unfolding complexity, haunts Poe's disavowal of doubt, which troubles the variously erosive and accretive materiality of a language becoming, beside, itself.

Although his work on Bishop seems not to address queer theory,[22] Edelman's formulation of rhetoricity as that which institutionalizing literariness "repress[es]" provocatively illuminates the unremitting textuality of Bishop's "or" as performatively interceding hesitation.[23] In terms of both throat-clearing stammer and fabricative edge, the latter's hem speaks to the uncanny intrusion of the writerly appearance of extemporaneity onto the scene of lapidary perfectionism as which Bishop's poetic voice so frequently passes.[24] Hesitation and its unsettling constellation of appetites work against the fictions of self-evidence and demystifying exposure that have limited much of queer Bishop criticism. Invoking "One Art" as "one of his favorite poems," Jose Muñoz argues that "if you read [Bishop's] poems expecting to read about queerness, it is there throughout."[25] I worry, however, that finding in Bishop's oeuvre the queerness one tautologically expects to have found yields a queerness whose legibility-on-arrival disservices both the poetry and attendant theoretical animus. Indeed, Muñoz's takeaway that "One Art" "should be read as a primer for queer self-enactment or queer becoming"[26] illuminates, by contrast, a speculative mode in Bishop that undermines reading itself, whether as poetic subject or perceptual practice. And Sedgwick herself, oppositely turning to "One

Art" as "the one poem" of Bishop's she's "never liked," reduces that text to its "repeated refrain," *the art of losing isn't hard to master*, reducing the refrain in turn to what she designates its "insistence on a purgative aesthetic."[27] Treating the economy of their respective paraphrases as coextensive with the poem itself, both Muñoz and Sedgwick register our ongoing need not to take for granted what it is we take for granted when it comes not only to reading for queerness, but queerly feeling, in the manner of Bishop's figuratively peninsular women, for reading.[28]

Notes

1. Eve Kosofsky Sedgwick, *The Weather in Proust*, ed. Jonathan Goldberg (Durham: Duke University Press, 2011), 123.
2. Eve Kosofsky Sedgwick, *Tendencies* (Durham: Duke University Press, 1993), 23.
3. Ibid., 24.
4. Michael D. Snediker, "Weaver's Handshake: The Aesthetics of Chronic Objects," in *Reading Sedgwick*, ed. Lauren Berlant (Durham: Duke University Press, 2019), 203–36.
5. Sedgwick, *The Weather in Proust*, 84.
6. Eve Kosofsky Sedgwick, *Touching Feeling: Affect Pedagogy, Performance* (Durham: Duke University Press, 2003), 125. Italics in original.
7. Sedgwick, *The Weather in Proust*, 71, 90.
8. Ibid., 123.
9. *The Barbara Johnson Reader: The Surprise of Otherness* (Durham: Duke University Press, 2014), 47–8.
10. Edgar Allan Poe, *Essays and Reviews*, ed. Gary Richard Thompson (New York: Library of America, 1984), 76.
11. Jean-Luc Nancy, *Expectation: Philosophy, Literature*, trans. Robert Bononno (New York: Fordham University Press, 2018), 85.
12. Ibid., 87.
13. Gilles Deleuze, *The Fold: Leibniz and the Baroque*, trans. Tom Conley (New York: Continuum, 2006), 131.
14. Victoria Harrison, *Elizabeth Bishop's Poetics of Intimacy* (New York: Cambridge University Press, 1993), 46.
15. Roland Barthes, *The Pleasure of the Text*, trans. Richard Miller (New York: Hill and Wang, 1998), 65.
16. Thomas Travisano, *Elizabeth Bishop: Her Artistic Development* (Charlottesville: University of Virginia Press, 1988), 42.
17. The story goes that Ernst was in a hotel room on France's Atlantic coast, captivated by the old floorboards "upon which," Ernst writes, "a thousand scrubbings had deepened the grooves." Ernst proceeds to make "from the boards a series of drawings by placing on them, at random, sheets of paper which [he] undertakes to rub with black lead. [. . .] There my eyes

discovered human heads, animals, a battle that ended with a kiss (the bride of the wind), rocks, the sea and the rain" (*Max Ernst: A Career Retrospective*, 38). In other words, Ernst's practice short-circuits the pathos of mimetic distance by turning the hand's assemblage of pastel and paper into a rudimentary mode of mechanical reproduction yielding less an image than something like a negative reflection, footprint, or moulage. This trace of surface perseveration calls back to Erich Auerbach's account of *figurae*, imagined by Lucretius, so Auerbach writes, as "structures that peel off things like membranes and float round in the air" (*Scenes from the Drama of European Literature*, 17).

18. Consider also Bishop's frustration, recounted in a 1940 letter to Marianne Moore, regarding a "continuous [...] feeling of 'things' in the head, like icebergs or rocks or awkwardly placed pieces of furniture. It's as if all the nouns were there but the verbs were lacking – if you know what I mean. And I can't help having the theory that if they are joggled around hard enough and long enough some kind of electricity will occur, just by friction, that will arrange everything. But you remember how Mallarmé said that poetry was made of words, not ideas – and sometimes I'm terribly afraid I am approaching, or trying to approach it all, from the wrong track" (*OA* 94).
19. Sedgwick, Touching Feeling, 149.
20. Lee Edelman, "Aesthetic Value and Literary Language: Bishop and de Man," in *Never Again Would Birds' Songs Be the Same: Essays on Early Modern and Modern Poetry in Honor of John Hollander*, ed. Jennifer Lewin (New Haven: Beinecke Library, 2002), 222.
21. Poe, *Essays and Reviews*, 18.
22. At least not explicitly, as Corey McEleney notes. See "Reading to the Letter: *No Future* and the Question of Rhetoric," *GLQ* 25:3 (June 2019), 431–55.
23. With sufficient space, this analysis might examine not only Edelman's dexterous reading of conjunctions in the title of Sedgwick's aforementioned preface to *Novel Gazing*, but the conjunctive hinge at work in the title of Edelman's book-length collaboration with Lauren Berlant, *Sex, Or the Unbearable*, in which his parsing of Sedgwick's "or" appears.
24. As Elizabeth Hardwick writes in 1984, five years after Bishop's death, Bishop "was indeed a perfectionist. She was also a natural writer with an unusual patience; nothing appears to have been excavated with visible sweat and aching muscle. And yet perhaps it was that the great natural gifts seemed too easy, and she must wait to make everything just so in tone and rhythm, without insistence" (Hardwick, "The Perfectionist"). If there is truth in the auratic spin of Hardwick's appraisal, it is as incomplete as an earlier generation's myth of a retreating Dickinson. An insistence on Bishop's non-insistence likewise pervades Eleanor Cook's claim that the "love poem that attains simplicity shows Bishop's remarkable art at its best: 'The Shampoo.'" See *Elizabeth Bishop at Work* (Cambridge: Harvard University Press, 2016), 130.
25. Jose Muñoz, *Cruising Utopia: The Then and There of Queer Futurity* (Durham: Duke University Press, 2009), 72.

26. Ibid.
27. Sedgwick, *Touching Feeling*, 3. While Ravinthiran is right to suggest the influence of Gerard Manley Hopkins's "The Wreck of the Deutschland" on the "baroque ending" of "One Art," the presence of Poe's recursive spiraling is no less thrillingly palpable. Compare, for example:

    The art of losing isn't hard to master.
    Then practice losing farther, losing faster:

    [. . .] None of these will bring disaster

    to the following:

    Caught from some unhappy master whom unmerciful Disaster
    Followed fast and followed faster till his songs one burden bore—
    Till the dirges of his Hope that melancholy burden bore
    Of 'Never—nevermore'.
28. Sedgwick's observation that "what seems least settled is any predetermined idea about what makes the queerness of a queer reading" likewise intimates the need for querying the phenomenological, aesthetic, and epistemological errancies of reading itself, since the latter hardly represents an innocuous or transparent praxis to which queerness subsequently has been added. See *Novel Gazing: Queer Readings in Fiction* (Durham: Duke University Press, 1997), 2–3.

CHAPTER 29

Race

Sandeep Parmar

In December 1951, an allergic reaction curtailed Elizabeth Bishop's sea voyage from New York to circumnavigate South America. Intending to spend only a few days in Rio de Janeiro with friends, Bishop instead recuperated for months in Petrópolis, at the home of Mary Morse and her partner, the architect Lota de Macedo Soares, sixty miles inland from Rio.[1] As Bishop's readers will know, this unexpected hiatus in Brazil turned into a residency lasting nearly two decades, during which time she wrote not only about her unfamiliar surroundings but also made use of the distance between a nominal home and 'elsewhere' to reflect on her upbringing and life in North America. She and Soares quickly developed a relationship which gave Bishop entry into professional, aristocratic, political, and artistic social circles. As a white American middle-class lesbian woman, orphaned at an early age and raised by a succession of relatives in New England and, notably, Nova Scotia, Bishop exhibits what Adrienne Rich describes in a review of *The Complete Poems* as "the eye of the outsider." Sojourns in Florida and Paris also feature in her imagined mapping of an observant lyric self onto brief human dramas and their landscapes, remarkably alive in their exotic coloration, especially of Brazil and its people. It is perhaps fitting to think of Bishop as the inveterate outsider, even in her own birth country. Her self-consciously constructed scenarios in which the poem's speaker dissolves from sight save the tenor of her seeing, the oblique angle of her silent reserve, illustrate what Rich appreciates as "her lack of self-indulgence: and the marvellous flexibility and sturdiness of her writing."[2] Scholars of Bishop's work have pointed repeatedly to her extemporising of familial and other forms of loss – its biographical resonances both confirming and resisting a confessional poetics. But, as Rich points out especially with regards to Bishop's sexuality, "outsiderhood" as it appears in Bishop's writing demonstrates that the "price of external assimilation is internal division."[3]

Primarily, I am interested in the cost of outsiderhood not for Bishop, but for the racialised others onto whom this internal division is projected. Through reading her poems dealing with racial difference, it is evident that the enactment of lyric interiority produces violence in the poem's space. Mapping, an attention to concrete imagery and detail, the formal qualities of what, at times, appears simple or slight, often obscures what I regard as the problematic nature of Bishop's figuring of race and subjects of colour.

Although several scholars have engaged with race (and class and gender) in Bishop's writing about Brazil and African Americans, the following discussion attempts to bridge some of these interpretations with the figuration of what I have termed lyric violence, namely that which reproduces repressive systemic power unconsciously through a white literary imagination. Simply put, lyric violence occurs when the assumption of a lyric speaker's universality or neutrality goes unchecked. In this space of address, which historically and culturally objectifies anything other than white, male, heteronormative points of view, violence occurs when the disappearance of the speaker into the universal raises the prominence of the addressee who is meant to stand in as a projection of the speaker's interior life. This violence, a function of an unimplicated observer, removes agency from the addressee by instrumentalising their perceived otherness, effectively diminishing their voice within the lyric space to produce a fantasy for the reader. A tertiary form of violence might also be said to occur for readers who do not identify with the normative universal speaker, certainly if they themselves are implicated in the projection of race onto subjects in the poem.

A critical reading of Bishop and her legacy with regards to race should, for example, question assumptions about impersonality and fluxive poetic perspectives. Bonnie Costello's view that Bishop's lyric narrative "self is amorphous in an amorphous world" that uses "a variety of distancing techniques" without privileging a single perspective is the pervasive critical approach.[4] And while this is true, what remains uninterrogated by the critical stance of impersonality with regards to Bishop is the ethics of utilising particular identities externally in service of the fluxive, distant speaking subject.

Bishop's "Arrival at Santos" (*P* 87), published in *The New Yorker* in 1952 and later in *Questions of Travel*, shares notable similarities with poems written throughout her career in which racial difference, or otherness, specifically blackness, is thrown into sharp relief against a dominant American white imaginary. This whiteness polarises, in Bishop's work, around a dissembling lyric subject who sharply correlates an exterior world into categories of the seen and unseeable. "Arrival at Santos" describes seeing the first port of call on the speaker's journey at a distance with disappointment and apprehension, "Here is a coast; here is a harbor; / here, after a meager diet of horizon, is some scenery." The "uncertain" terrain with its flag, a "strange and brilliant rag," inverts the tourist's conquistador-like wish for a fertile and undiscovered landscape on which to make "your immodest demands for a different world, / and a better life." It might be possible to argue that the missionary's "little church," the surrender to commercial exploitation in the form of coffee beans and money, the "warehouses, / some of them painted a feeble pink, or blue," demonstrate the traveller's awareness of colonial degradation. However, it is also the case, as Costello claims, that "Bishop's travellers are driven by contradictory impulses. They want change, renewal, originality, but also mastery (whether aesthetic, intellectual or political) over the world they approach, in terms of the world they left behind."[5] I see this as less of a contradiction than a strategy in which the subject deflects the will towards power onto the failures of the powerless. This impulse towards mastery of an external world, in service of the lyric subject's desires, formulates the poem's closing judgements, rhyming "inferior" with "interior." In Bishop's real-life journey, the drive 'to the interior' is not as straightforwardly linear as departing the port (Santos, near São Paulo) and leaving the coast. What is interesting then is how this rewriting of the journey – Bishop's travelling companion on the boat was a Miss Breen, the retired police lieutenant of the poem, who drops out well before Bishop's drive to the mountains of Petrópolis – is the forthright motion from port to the unknowable, seeing the unseeable in order to remain unseen. The poem's closing lines are resolute but also apprehensive in the shift from the past to the present: "We leave Santos at once; / we are driving to the interior." The inferiority within is the traveller's ambivalence towards coherence, symbolised through the other. When the realisation of difference – what Rich describes as the price of assimilation – ruptures the lyric moment, what we find is an interiority that resists being known. Here, as with several of Bishop's writings, a cartography of racial otherness, resulting in lyric violence, offers a way of exploring the integrity – and fragility – of the self's outsiderhood.

Although Rich's review is primarily a call for new and complex ways to enter Bishop's work via feminist and lesbian traditions, Rich is an early, prominent reader of Bishop who is willing to consider the social and political risks of poems that appear to evade their historical moment. I am interested in the positioning of Bishop as a mannered lyric poet somewhere between what Robert Pinksy describes as the Wordsworthian "curious element of supremacy" of Nature's transformational visions and Helen Vendler's reading of domesticity via "the exquisitely noticed modulations of whiteness" in the articulation of "The Moose" and its landscape.[6] A contemporary reading of Bishop's writings about racialised subjects requires a cauterising of laudatory impersonality – an interrogation of the means by which white writers deploy black voices and bodies in the lyric space. And to do so is to also make room for readers who do not identify with the neutrality of the speaker's whiteness as a given, who experience differently the linguistic and formal dimensions of violence.[7]

For decades, scholars have puzzled over Bishop's engagement with race.[8] Margaret Dickie, Renée R. Curry, and Kirstin Hotelling Zona offer sometimes diverging viewpoints on Bishop's characterisations of people of colour in her poems about African Americans and dark-skinned (often servant-class) Brazilians. Dickie makes note of Bishop's varied experiences living in places marked by ethnic difference, both in the United States and in Brazil, arguing that Bishop had a "life-long need to speak through another, often ethnically-charged, voice."[9] While Dickie admits that the level of identification Bishop's speakers exhibit across a power dynamic marked by race and class is problematic, she explains it as a demonstration of intimacy:

> In some sense, they held her interest over a lifetime and in varying environments because she identified with them. So she writes too as an insider, knowledgeable about the marginal, the exiled, and the dispossessed because she was one herself. She knew the bonds, even chains, of affection between classes and races that linked lives which would be solitary and lonely without them. In taking up such subjects, Bishop was acknowledging a range of experience that she, as a solitary woman, even a lonely tourist, knew intimately.[10]

Rich is less forgiving of Bishop taking up such subject positions. For example, "Songs for a Colored Singer" (*P* 47–51) is, according to Rich, "a white woman's attempt [. . .] to speak through a Black woman's voice" that "betrays the failures and clumsiness of such a position." Rich is emphatic that such authority relies on racial stereotypes. The poem is comprised of four "songs," each with a slightly different rhyme scheme, relying on rhymes that mimic, if not the forms of blues poems, the tone of longing, loss, and themes of itinerancy and unrequited love associated loosely with the blues. Often, as others have noted, these rhymes are forced and unconvincing, "bus" and "monogamous" being perhaps the most obvious. Dickie references Lloyd Schwartz's claim that Bishop transcribed conversations with her black cleaner in Key West but argues that the female voice is largely unraced because of its lack of dialect and "speaks in more standard grammatical form."[11] Yet rather than engage with Rich's critique of appropriation, Dickie claims instead

> The melancholy that pervades them is quite different from the blues that a coloured singer might be imagined to sing. These are not songs that allow the singer to console herself, to hold off the sadness that is sure to overtake her, as blues would be. The first three are rather songs of social protest against relationships that are harmful, remediable, and rejected. They are poems about women who have been hurt by social rather than racial circumstances.[12]

What is most troubling about Dickie's reading is her underlying assumption about what is culturally specific to the African-American experience and what is universal, or, to put it another way, that whiteness is unmarked by race. It is interesting that Dickie sees these four voices as separate and unrelated. The individuality afforded to each denies the progression that is inherent in the poem, in spite of the plural "songs." I see them as connected by a wish towards the renunciation of heteronormative femininity, the "shadow of the crib" that "makes an enormous cage / upon the wall" (*P* 47–51). Relatable, yes, to a cross-section of female experience – but where this all-encompassing female voice becomes problematic in terms of race is in the speaker's ability to transcend their social and economic conditions.

The first two of Bishop's "songs" describe displacement and dispossession through a female voice who is effectively being abandoned by a philanderer.

> A washing hangs upon the line,
> but it's not mine.
> None of the things that I can see
> belong to me.
> The neighbors got a radio with an aerial;
> we got a little portable.
> They got a lot of closet space;
> we got a suitcase.

It would be difficult to argue that class alone divides women deprived of socioeconomic status in the pre-Civil Rights era. The racially specific history of disenfranchisement, applied unequally to African Americans, is, in effect, Bishop's projection onto a displacement that she herself takes up voluntarily in her adult life. The speaker here, dramatised and romanticised by the poet's white imagination, naively arrives at the fourth and final song by betraying the anxiety of her volition. This last song relies on call and response:

> What's that shining in the leaves,
> the shadowy leaves,
> like tears when somebody grieves,
> shining, shining in the leaves?
>
> Is it dew or is it tears,
> dew or tears,
> hanging there for years and years
> like a heavy dew of tears?

The falling "black seeds" plant themselves, take a "conspiring root" that ultimately flower into one and then many faces – an "army" of faces, dreamlike, that are "too real to be a dream." The shadowy unconscious, where dream and reality become indiscernible, imagines in the darkness what amounts to a rising resistance of faces "darker, darker" out of a grief that turns to action, resistance, to life from death.

In a letter written over two decades after the poem appeared in *North & South*, Bishop suggests that her "Songs" were written for Billie Holiday, whom she had apparently met in the 1930s, "very vaguely," and that she left New York before she was able to find music for them (*OA* 478).[13] One wonders if Bishop had "Strange Fruit" in mind by the Jewish-American writer Abel Meeropol. His poem-song, written in response to Lawrence Beitler's now well-known photograph of the lynching of Thomas Shipp and Abram Smith, was recorded and made famous by Holiday in 1939. Certainly, the imagery of roots, trees, and leaves in Bishop's poem is ominously familiar. In deliberating whether a "flower or fruit" will grow from this root, it may well be the case that Bishop is imagining the strange fruit of black brutalised bodies "taking root like weeds" in "that dark and dreary place." Bishop invoked this poem in her own defense against charges of racism much later by Fernando de Castro, a Brazilian journalist who criticised her essay on Rio's Carnival, which I'll discuss later. By her own account, she considered her fourth and final song "a prophecy, or a prayer, that justice will eventually triumph for the Negro in the USA."[14] While this may be the case, the poem's dark and conspiratorial imagery and the multiplying indistinct faces of a rising army conveys a sense of panic. The African Americans in this final song lack the (often clumsy) dialect of the previous three songs. This is far from Langston Hughes' 1951 poem, "Harlem," and the deferral of the American dream that inspired Martin

Luther King with its hope and anguish on behalf of a dispossessed population. This surreal dreaming, a prophecy of justice, is not delivered by Bishop with ambivalence or the wish for restitution. Rather, this is the projection of a fantasy that, taken alongside the stereotypical narratives of female loss and violence, as well as evidence of racism in her letters, rings entirely hollow. It puts one in mind more of the self-emancipatory acts of imagination precipitated by European surrealists through primitivist visions of blackness in the very same era that this poem was written.[15] These songs are not "for a colored singer"; they were written as a way for the lyric subject to transfer displacement and anxiety onto a readymade situation in which the poet is, by nature of her whiteness and privilege, implicated. "We went to the dark cave of the street-corner . . . " (*P* 265), also written in the 1930s but never published during Bishop's life, raises the prophecy of impending war from the "black mouths" of "white-faced angel-newsboys." The poem moves quickly into an African dream landscape, where an ominous fountain "filled with blood" stands in a Roman circus bathed in the light of a red sun. The ancient vision appears uncomfortably, dangerously close to civilisation, threatening impending violence.

A nightmarish vocabulary associating blackness, and specifically Africa, with the cataclysm of an arriving world war, is consistent with Bishop's binary logic of white and black, as Renée Curry details in her work on Bishop and whiteness. Elsewhere, in Bishop's autobiographical portrait, "Memories of Uncle Neddy," a nightmarish scene features a young Elizabeth mistaking Neddy dressed up as Santa Claus for a Negro. This "Black Christmas" layers the trauma of her absent grandparents and the meanness of the holiday with the abject fear of a terrifying stranger who is a blood relation. His black face and his beard – "a mass of frayed-out rope" – so affects her that it sparks further nightmares involving a feral horse, itself a stand-in for the bestial other.[16] The panic of separation, of loss, is transposed here as it is in another poem Bishop left unfinished during her lifetime, "Something I've Meant to Write about for 30 Years" (*EAP* 137–38). Yet another waking nightmare, this poem ends in a "crazy iconography" of "disconnected mad" mirrors decorating fences, the speaker waking to look "right into nigger town" on a train through Georgia at dawn. What disturbs the speaker is not the scene of downtrodden homes or its people – they are asleep and therefore absent – but the appearance of the light "reflecting, white / and bluish, sadly, over and over again." The title suggests a recurring fascination, putting one in mind of Virginia Woolf's scene in *Between the Acts* where an audience assembled for a play is forced to watch itself watching the action through a series of mirrors. The reflection of light, its whiteness, is no doubt the speaker's own fascination and revulsion at the deprivation before her. If Bishop's speakers regard blackness as a means to shore up whiteness, or to make visible their own outsiderness – an exteriority made interior/inferior – then this archival draft poem is an artefact testifying to an incomplete realisation of their failure.

Bishop was able to hold differing views on race, supporting the Civil Rights movement and the work of black poets while also expressing hope in a letter that Mary Morse's daughter would not turn out to be too "Negroid," as well as stating dissatisfaction with black hospital staff – "I had thought I liked Negroes, too."[17] Curry writes that

> A positionality steeped in the belief of essential difference informs our words about race. A white position in literature may often only be glimpsed by discerning a remote reflection from the language on the page. We must look into the mirror of the differentiation marker. To read white, we must reflect upon black, red, brown and yellow – the words marked *different*. We best know whether a writer is white by the naming of other races on the page. Whiteness is presumed by its absence in language.[18]

For Kirstin Hotelling Zona, "it is precisely Bishop's determination to expose the tension between her attempts to identify with those marked as radically different from herself and her own investment in maintaining those very distinctions that creates the opportunity for *us* to reexamine *our* own habits of identification while reading her poems"[19] (my emphasis). But the assumption underlying this statement – that "our own habits of identification" would take on similar racial dimensions to Bishop's – is based on a white critical readership, one that is in danger of mimicking the poet's own conscious or unconscious violence in the lyric space through uninterrogated forms of reading.

Bishop's writing about Brazil shifts the dynamics of race to a national context that she likely only understood through relations limited by her incomplete comprehension of the language and the relatively elite social circles she and her partner Lota inhabited. This is certainly evident from her book for Life World Library, *Brazil*, in which she misunderstands the racial harmony between servant and mistress through a mishearing of "*minha negrinha*" ("my little nigger") for *minha neguinha*, or "my little sweetie."[20] Whenever she seems to get it wrong, Bishop digs her heels in, even claiming libel, as with her response to criticism of her essay for *The New York Times Magazine* "On the Railroad Named Delight." Bishop's lyric speakers in "Faustina, or Rock Roses," "Manuelzinho," "Pink Dog,"

"Twelfth Morning; or What You Will," and "Santarém," take on a distance sometimes grounded in private employer–servant relations or observations of strangers in public. The level of intimacy demonstrated by the speakers across these poems varies little, presumably because familiarity – and even recorded speech – rarely affords raced subjects within these poems any substantial autonomy or access to empathy.

Responding in 1967, after she returned to the USA, to criticism about race in her poetry, Bishop wrote in a letter

> I wonder who the reviewer was who misunderstood "Manuelzinho" so – but then I've been accused of that kind of thing a lot, particularly in the social-conscious days – "Cootchie," etc., were found "condescending," or I lived in a world (I was obviously VERY RICH) where people had Servants, imagine, and so on. Actually, Brazilians like "Manuelzinho" very much. I've had several English-reading friends tell me, "My God (or Our Lady), it's *exactly* like that." And that's why Lota is supposed to be saying it . . . (*OA* 479).[21]

"Cootchie" (*P* 46) narrates the death of a servant in Key West whose life is "spent" – in both senses of the word – looking after her deaf employer Miss Lula. What is striking about the poem is that although the title commemorates the black servant, the poem focuses on Miss Lula's "losses" and we learn little of Cootchie herself beyond her sacrifices. The reader's empathy is pointed at Miss Lula while Cootchie's inexplicable death, possibly from suicide ("black into white she went / below the surface of the coral-reef") is dismissed "as trivial." Dickie's analysis suggests that the poem is a celebration of Cootchie's significance for the poet and Miss Lula by virtue of its unusual rhyme scheme. The poem, for her, is a comment on the artificiality of art, which still offers comfort in the poem's detail of melting cans of pink wax roses.[22] This reading fails to account for the power dynamic of race as Bishop exteriorises it onto an ambivalent landscape. From "black into white," to the "egg-white" skies, the moonlight, and the white of the lighthouse "searching for someone else," the imagery makes very clear that Cootchie is secondary to the whiteness pervading the poem and that ultimately the speaker's sympathy is reserved for Miss Lula who is left behind.

The figuration of a defenseless white woman and her black servant reappears in the poem "Faustina, or Rock Roses" (*P* 70–72). Several scholars have speculated about the "crazy house" where a nameless visitor finds herself amid racial hierarchies upended by a dependent, ill white woman who is being overpowered by her black "complaining" servant. Zona reads images of whiteness as jarring and juxtaposed to betray a failure of the white woman's power. She writes that the recurrence of whiteness is "hardly a trope of natural superiority in this poem," instead, "whiteness is the mark of vulnerability, failed illusions, and tenuous, decayed control."[23] And what of blackness? Faustina herself is described thus as she is complaining about "the terms of her employment":

> Her sinister kind face
> presents a cruel black
> coincident conundrum.
>   Oh, is it
>
> freedom at last, a lifelong
> dream of time and silence,
> dream of protection and rest?
> Or is it the very worst,
> the unimaginable nightmare
> that never before dared last
>   more than a second?

It would be difficult to argue that the lyric speaker operates outside of a clearly racialised dynamic of whiteness as good and blackness as evil. The enjambment between "cruel black" and "coincident conundrum" suggests that the question of Faustina's right to autonomy is both outside of her hands and dependent on the will and power of others who haven't the strength of body, mind, or will to release her from the cruelty of her situation. The white woman may be dying, but Faustina is suffering a slower death still through her lack of time, protection, silence, and freedom which she must devote to her employer on someone else's terms. "Oh, is it," followed by a caesura, shifts the poem, again, towards a nightmare, the origins of which are unclear but chime with other such expressions, even perhaps the scream of mortal reality that we hear coming from a young Elizabeth contemplating the "horrifying" black breasts of women in "In the Waiting Room" (*P* 179–81). Blackness as death or dissolution of self is formed by a terror of otherness in her most famous poem – from the poem's black volcano and the black naked women to, finally, the "blue-black space" of oblivion overwhelming the child-speaker in "big black" waves. Only the frames of the date, a location, the ordinariness of the room itself, and the familiar yellow borders of *The National Geographic* restrain the lyric panic and repel the threat of age and all it implies. "But I felt: you are an *I*, / you are an *Elizabeth*, / you are one of *them*." The contrast between the speaker's fascination with naked black bodies ("I read it right straight through. / I was too shy to stop") and her avoidance of the presumably white bodies in the waiting room ("I scarcely dared to look") is worth noting. Ultimately, being is "unlikely." Perhaps this anticipates how "unlikely" it is that selfhood be afforded to those fixed in the gaze of primitivism; perhaps it speaks to the unlikelihood of oneness which pervades Bishop's writing with such terror.

Blackness, and black bodies, either jar or invite horror in the lyric space throughout Bishop's work. We see repeatedly how the violences of colonialism, segregation, and racism, the effects of displacement, othering, and repression, become a vehicle for Bishop's lyric violence to create a place of rupture, a site of abjection, so that the dominant, detached, and universal lyric "I" can come to know and understand its own fragmented outsiderness but largely at a cost to others.

Notes

1. Brett C. Millier, *Elizabeth Bishop: Life and the Memory of It* (Berkeley: University of California Press, 1992), 243.
2. Adrienne Rich, *Essential Essays: Culture, Politics, and the Art of Poetry* (New York: Norton, 2018), 220.
3. Ibid., 221.
4. Bonnie Costello, "The Impersonal and the Interrogative in the Poetry of Elizabeth Bishop," in *Elizabeth Bishop and Her Art*, ed. Lloyd Schwartz and Sybil P. Estess (Ann Arbor: The University of Michigan Press, 1983), 117.
5. Bonnie Costello, *Elizabeth Bishop: Questions of Mastery* (Cambridge: Harvard University Press, 1993), 128.
6. Robert Pinksy and Helen Vendler in *Elizabeth Bishop and Her Art*, 44 and 51, respectively. I raise these examples (somewhat out of their contexts) to draw attention to their language in relation to Romantic lyricism.
7. Very few critics I found writing specifically on Bishop's poetry and race could be identified as people of colour besides Vidyan Ravinthiran and Marvin Campbell. If critical appraisals must also take into consideration the subjectivity of the critic, then this essay acts as a critique of normative attitudes towards otherness and the fetishising of black bodies and voices. I am deeply indebted to Ravinthiran for his guidance and feedback on this chapter.
8. For a further consideration of Bishop's writing and race, see Marvin Campbell, "Elizabeth Bishop and Audre Lorde: Two Views of 'Florida' in the Global South Atlantic," in *Reading Elizabeth Bishop: An Edinburgh Companion*, ed. Jonathan Ellis (Edinburgh: Edinburgh University Press, 2019), 280–93; and Steven Gould Axelrod, "Bishop, History, and Politics," in *The Cambridge Companion to Elizabeth Bishop*, ed. Angus Cleghorn and Jonathan Ellis (Cambridge: Cambridge University Press, 2014), 35–48.
9. Margaret Dickie, "Race and Class in Elizabeth Bishop's Poetry," *The Yearbook of English Studies* 24 (1994), 44–58 (45).

10. Ibid., 46.
11. Ibid., 49.
12. Ibid., 50.
13. See also Millier, *Elizabeth Bishop,* 364.
14. Ibid., 365.
15. See Renée R. Curry, *White Women Writing White: H.D., Elizabeth Bishop and Sylvia Plath and Whiteness* (Westport, CN: Greenwood Press, 2000), on Bishop's fascination with primitivism (81).
16. Elizabeth Bishop, *Prose,* ed. Lloyd Schwartz (New York: Farrar Straus & Giroux, 2011), 157.
17. Millier, 364.
18. Curry, *White Women Writing White,* 11.
19. Kirstin Hotelling Zona, "Bishop: Race, Class and Gender," in *The Cambridge Companion to Elizabeth Bishop*, 49.
20. For a fuller analysis, see Benjamin Moser's "Elizabeth Bishop's Misunderstood 'Brazil'" in *The New Yorker* (2012), www.newyorker.com/books/page-turner/elizabeth-bishops-misunderstood-brazil [date accessed 1/8/19] and Bethany Hicok's *Elizabeth Bishop's Brazil* (Charlottesville: University of Virginia Press, 2016).
21. Vidyan Ravinthiran's critical reading of "Manuelzinho" makes a persuasive argument about Bishop's use of the dramatic monologue as a form of social critique. See "'Manuelzinho', Brazil and Identity Politics" in *Reading Elizabeth Bishop*, 33–47.
22. Dickie, "Race and Class," 48.
23. Zona, "Bishop," 54.

CHAPTER 30

Nature

Angus Cleghorn

Since nature is "flowing, and flown" (*P* 64), it is active in the present participation of Bishop's poetry and in renderings of the past. Constantly happening natural process invigorates present living. Sensory experience is felt in Bishop's tactile language of touch, taste, smell, sound, and sight. As a poet, she activates the reader's senses through alliterative sounds that imprint natural images in the mind. As a prose writer, she uses synesthesia to compound senses into heightened artistic understandings.

"In the Village" is the centre of this action in her oeuvre. This memoir lays bare the natural elements – earth, air, fire, water – that sustain Bishop as a poet of survival. This autobiographical story demonstrates its young narrator's elemental discoveries through work – the human workmanship of nature exemplified by Nate the blacksmith's manufacturing of horseshoes: "Clang" is the sound that saves Bishop in the village as it annunciates her birth as a lifetime nature poet. And work nature she does in the mechanics of poems such as "The Fish," "Cape Breton," "At the Fishhouses," "Pleasure Seas," and "The Moose." While these poems activate present experience and extend it to human machines amidst natural resources, this recognition of living from land and sea also leads to a registration of history. As Bishop moves from what is flowing to what has flown before us, she travels upon historical sites of colonial abuse. This is evident in the indigenous populations of "Florida," "Cape Breton," and "Brazil, January 1, 1502." And while Bishop like Wordsworth in "The Tables Turned" agrees to "Let Nature be your teacher,"[1] she also recognizes its difference from us, and our representation of it as an erratic imposition. Writing itself, as well as painting, music, mapmaking, history, religion, and embroidery are all somewhat artificial in their rendering of the natural.

The technology of language shows up in letters on the page, sounds, jokes, ironies, and her constantly adjusting poetic lines and forms.[2] And since she is constantly attuned to the mediated sounds made of nature, Bishop is able to project our relationship with it as simultaneously unnatural (like grandmother's glass eye[3]) and intrinsic to perception. The reader feels the senses enliven through Bishop's innovative depiction of imagery in lines of poetry that display their written fabric. Their materiality is made evident in early *North & South* poems such as "Large Bad Picture," where over tall cliffs "hundreds of fine black birds / [are] hanging in *n*'s on the banks" (*P* 13). A different touch brings "The Map" to life in which "We can stroke these lovely bays," and "These peninsulas take the water between thumb and finger / like women feeling the smoothness of yard-goods" (*P* 5). Bishop uses textured similes in "The Fish" to observe "skin like ancient wallpaper with shapes like full-blown roses," and further in "a pink swim bladder like a big peony" (*P* 43). Readers feel, see, and then imagine the body and beyond: we transcend into the guts, and with "the terrible oxygen" in the gills we fear death, which is heightened by the epiphanic "rainbow" of victory in the oily pollution around the fish. Bishop's epiphany is sublime, for she does carry forward this Romanticism from Wordsworth, but it is also ironic as the fisher's traditionally victorious catch is sullied by the oil and her realization of culpability in this destructive ecology. The fish too reaches a noble height with his decorated "five haired beard of wisdom trailing from his aching jaw." The fish, fisher, and whole poem undergo inflation and updraft while all that is "tremendous" is let go as "homely," such as the fish's "lower lip / – if you could call it a lip" (*P* 44). Even the poet's job of using similes and personification is depicted as part of the bathetic joke of our species' superiority.

This early 1940 signature poem is the perfect introduction to teaching Bishop's poetry as it makes the familiar strange and strange familiar. Her constantly innovative depictions outshine her modest self-evaluation as "a minor female Wordsworth," "a Nature Lover" (*OA* 221–22). The sublime is evoked and undercut consistently through her career – all the way to her retrospective biographical Crusoe in the early 1970s who cannot quite remember the old books "full of blanks," from which the islander "tried / reciting to my iris-beds, / 'They flash upon that inward eye, / which is the bliss of . . . ' The bliss of what?" (*P* 184). Solitude is not the haven it was for Wordsworth although Bishop in Brazil uses her "inward eye" to recollect childhood. Before the late Bishop experienced "total recall" in Brazil she had to connect with her own nature and establish a durable poetic language.

The raw nature of Florida exuded a physicality that inspired Bishop to develop a more concrete style than she experimented with in *North & South*'s architectural dream-poems of Paris and New York. "Florida" is at once "The state with the prettiest name, / the state that floats in brackish water, / held together by mangrove roots" with "long S-shaped birds" and a long assortment of creatures trying to live in this dense environment (of nature and poem). Images stand out when alliteration makes us hear what we envision[4]: "The palm trees clatter in the stiff breeze / like the bills of pelicans" (*P* 33). Long vowels offer space to visualize the palm trees, then short vowels and consonants focus on the firm leaves clattering in the stiff breeze "like the bills of pelicans" – the simile brilliantly coalesces the shape and sound of palm leaves with pelican bills. Most of the imagery exists of its own accord without extrapolation, and yet humour – "mosquitoes / go hunting to the tune of their ferocious obbligatos" (*P* 34) – and despair creep into this "poorest / post-card of itself." Perhaps because the poet prioritizes concrete natural imagery without transcendence, when she allows human extrapolations they are not necessarily taken seriously, although they could be:

> The alligator: who has five distinct calls:
> friendliness, love, mating, war, and a warning –
> whimpers and speaks in the throat
> of the Indian Princess.

Earlier in the poem "the buried Indian Princess's skirt" was found along the coastline. Bishop's alligator warns of revenge coming from the speechless victim of Florida's colonial past. Here in this poem a concentrated depiction of nature gives it primacy, and then human intervention leads to troubled history. Colonial rape is later magnified similarly in "Brazil, January 1, 1502."

Bishop writes poems tracing indigenous genocide in the USA, Brazil, and Canada. She never develops these histories into extended critiques, preferring to let the suggestive images speak for themselves. In "Cape Breton" from *A Cold Spring* "The little white churches have been dropped into the matted hills / like lost quartz arrowheads" (*P* 65). This nexus of imagery follows a similar condensed style as in "Florida," and yet it zooms in with more concentrated historical power. On a quiet sabbath Sunday, the poet aesthetically observes the little churches dotting the landscape as in a painting (recall that Florida is like a postcard, and Brazil a tapestried landscape). Although "Cape Breton" is not a painting, it is depicted with the textured depths of one, and, as is the case with "Florida" and "Brazil, January 1, 1502," we are left wondering what's behind the scenes. In "Cape Breton" the "white churches" are placed, almost super-imposed upon the "lost quartz arrowheads" belonging to the aboriginal people they supplanted. In these two lines Bishop provides a long if understated view of colonial historical process.

Historical depth is presented by including numerous scenes with various tones. In "Cape Breton," Bishop sets the stage with a sense of humour – "silly-looking puffins all stand / with their backs to the mainland" and "the few sheep pastured there go 'Baa baa.' / (Sometimes, frightened by aeroplanes, they stampede / and fall over into the sea or onto the rocks.)" (*P* 65). Drawing comic-strip poetry lightens the tone before setting up the later troubled history, and the seriously sublime mode that moves through the poem. As always with Bishop, Romantic sublimity is tempered by other factors, and in so doing she updates what poetry can do. In "Cape Breton" there is consistent interplay between nature and man-made machinery. The whole poem depicts this part of Nova Scotia permeated by mist, which flows through the air to join the land and sea: "The silken water is weaving and weaving, / disappearing under the mist equally in all directions, / [. . .] and somewhere the mist incorporates the pulse, / rapid but unurgent, of a motorboat." The mist is the ghostly primary agent of the seascape that envelops all, including the rhythmic resonance of a motorboat. Alliteration enables this image to work maximally. While "mist" has a short sound, it "somewhere [. . .] incorporates the pulse" of these long vowel sounds enveloping the short staccato alliteration of "pulse, / rapid but unurgent, of a motorboat."

As sublime as this is, natural immanence is complemented by machinery. Just as the boat motors through the previous scene, in the following stanza "stand occasional small yellow bulldozers, / but without their drivers, because today is Sunday." The word "stand" was used at the start with the "silly-looking" birds, and so the personified humour continues to vary tone and agency, which become solemn with the churches, arrowheads, and then "burnt forests standing in gray scratches / like the admirable scriptures made on stones by stones – " (*P* 66). While the burnt forests may further the effects of human devastation, it is just as possible that natural forest fires scratched out these tracts. So when Bishop's simile has "scriptures made on stones by stones" we are free to imagine natural erosive markings, or early human inscriptions. This open-endedness in which "these regions now have little to say for themselves" continues the immanently ghostly motif while liberating the landscape to its own operation. It becomes a paradise on earth (rather like Stevens' "Sunday Morning") with "thousands of light song-sparrow songs floating upward / freely, dispassionately, through the mist, and meshing in brown-wet, fine, torn fishnets." Flocks of sparrows do look like fish-nets, yet it is the sparrow songs that mesh net-like (perhaps suggesting musical notes); again the mist unites elements of sky, land, and sea.

A bus with people, preachers, "spare automobile parts, and pump parts" continues to alliteratively meld machine, humanity, and nature. Bishop's unique vision includes "a man carrying a baby" who "goes down through a small steep meadow, / which establishes its poverty in a snowfall of daisies, / to his invisible house beside the water." Is this Bishop's first crypto-dream house? Not only has she brought in a nurturing father, she's transformed the previous imagery of white churches and arrowheads into, ironically, "poverty in a snowfall of daisies." Who wouldn't want to live in this hallowed place where in the end the "thin mist follows / the white mutations of its dream; / an ancient chill is rippling the dark brooks" (*P* 66). The spirit of the land holds powerful agency.

Sublime awe for the natural world, along with how humans work within it, returns in another Canadian maritime poem of *A Cold Spring*, "At the Fishhouses." This is no ideal world; "it is a cold evening" where "an old man sits netting" (*P* 62). "He was a friend of my grandfather. / We talk of the decline in the population / and of codfish and herring / while he waits for a herring boat to come in." This story of lost work due to depleted fish stocks has steadily intensified from the 1940s to the present. The poem's narrative and imagery give way to things themselves such as wheelbarrows, knives, ramps, and fish scales in tubs. "The air smells so strong of codfish / it makes one's nose run and one's eyes water." Grey mucous colour permeates and varies into "All is silver" in the surfaces of scales and sea; the language's materiality is performative, as Yuki Tanaka observes: "The sea threatens to spill over and asserts its presence with sibilant alliteration (' . . . *s*ilver: the heavy *s*urface of the *s*ea, / *s*welling *s*lowly as if con*s*idering *s*pilling over')."[5]

There is a small middle stanza of descent: "Down at the water's edge, at the place / where they haul up the boats, up the long ramp / descending into the water" (*P* 63). The meeting of land and sea, as is the case in many nature poems by Whitman, Frost, and Stevens, is where the transformations happen. For Bishop this entrance into the icy water does not lead to a myth of self, and yet the power of the poem toys with transcendence in its considerable respect for the primary element of our planetary existence. When *The New Yorker* editor was accepting the poem for publication in 1947, she wanted to insert commas between adjectives in the following lines: "Cold dark deep and absolutely clear, / element bearable to no mortal" (*P* 63).[6] However, Bishop needed the ocean water unified as the primary agent. The serious tone returns upon second mention of the same line, and yet she quickly varies it: the unbearable sea is home "to fish and to seals . . . One seal particularly / I have seen here evening after evening. / He was curious about me. He was interested in music; / like me a believer in total immersion, / so I used to sing him Baptist hymns." While the Atlantic Ocean is inhospitable to us, it naturally encases the seal – and a comedic interaction ensues complete with a joke to immerse them together yet separate. When the poet sang "A Mighty Fortress is our God," the seal disappeared "as if it were against his better judgment." The singer's Presbyterian hymn that could traditionally define this creation poem is rejected with the seal's head-tilting shrug, after which the lines resume: "Cold dark deep and absolutely clear, / the clear gray icy water . . . Back, behind us, / the dignified tall firs begin. / Bluish, associating with their shadows, / a million Christmas trees stand / waiting for Christmas" (*P* 63). The trees are likewise personified as associating with their environment, and again the tragicomedy envisions their future demise for the sake of Christmas. Bishop again uses comic-strip humour in a predominantly serious poem to criticize our history of religious dominion and natural sacrifice.

The alternative to false pretence and enforced superiority is honest experimentation that recognizes a powerful physical world: "If you should dip your hand in, / your wrist would ache immediately, / your bones would begin to ache and your hand would burn" – this simple immersion reveals the cold effects that cause pain and potential death. It is a plain observation of fact, and as such it gives no power to humanity and all to nature.[7] To extend the point, Bishop uses simile to lend apocalyptic force to the sea "as if the water were a transmutation of fire / that feeds on stones and burns with a dark gray flame." Then tasting the brine with a burning tongue realistically harnesses biblical transcendence in the senses before providing an accessible epiphany: "It is like what we imagine knowledge to be: / dark, salt, clear, moving, utterly free" (*P* 64). Knowledge is beyond us; we may be able to touch and taste it but we cannot possess its fluidity. Our dependence on nature despite its majestic indifference is then surprisingly embodied in the "rocky breasts forever" jutting out of the landscape. A somewhat Wordsworthian association between sublime nature and the lost thing (Kristeva's maternal bond) has acquired additional support in Bishop's letters to Dr. Ruth Foster revealing memories of her mother's body.[8] This personal connection with the elemental landscape deepens the effusive conclusion that "our knowledge is historical, flowing and flown." History is not a record of facts, but a condition of lost substance as the present flows and flies into the past.

Upon her arrival in Brazil, Bishop is cognizant of the way "Nature greets our eyes / exactly as it must have greeted theirs" (*P* 89), those being the

Portuguese colonial conquistadores of the 1500s. In "Brazil, January 1, 1502," "Arrival at Santos," and "Questions of Travel," Bishop uses the poetic voice of the tourist to register the overwhelming natural bounty and cultural differences of her new country. The ignorant and impatient tourist in "Arrival at Santos" finished that poem "driving to the interior" and dated it "January 1952" (*P* 88). On the next page we find "Brazil, January 1, 1502," in which her quest is compared with Portuguese colonial history. To get inside the country, she uses Sir Kenneth Clark's *Landscape into Art* for its " . . . embroidered nature . . . tapestried landscape" (*P* 89). Exotically colourful beauty and mythological maps lead to the brutal historical takeovers of "the Christians, hard as nails [. . .] in creaking armor," "humming perhaps / *L'Homme armé* or some such tune, / they ripped into the hanging fabric, / each trying to catch an Indian for himself – " (*P* 90). The next poem, "Questions of Travel," becomes self-doubting and inquisitive, as the guilty conscience asks, "Should we have stayed at home [. . .] Is it right to be watching strangers in a play / in this strangest of theatres?" (*P* 91) As Jeffrey Gray concludes in his "Travel" chapter in this volume, the accumulation of new experiences, fascinating observations, expanded cultural awareness, a broadened self, and wider earthly knowledge lead to affirmation. And yet, the poem ends with the traveller again questioning in her notebook, "*Should we have stayed at home, / wherever that may be?*" (*P* 92). For Bishop, unresolved home makes travel inevitable. Brazil, as is shown in the first three poems of *Questions of Travel*, offers abundant natural imagery in a newly evolved style of cascading rhythmic flow, even if there are "too many waterfalls here."

Bishop did not complain about the "soft slow-motion" (*P* 91) of water rushing outside the window of her writer's studio built for her by her lover, Lota de Macedo Soares, in the mountaintop property of Samambaia outside of Petrópolis. Bishop felt as though she had "died and gone to heaven" (*OA* 249). No wonder the 1950s were the happiest time of her life in which she was most prolific. "Song for the Rainy Season" registers the natural paradise of Samambaia: "Hidden, oh hidden / in the high fog / the house we live in, / beneath the magnetic rock, / rain-, rainbow-ridden, / [. . .] lichens, / owls, and the lint / of the waterfalls cling, / familiar, unbidden" (*P* 99). Somewhat like the natural dream house envisioned in "Cape Breton," the "inscrutable house" yearned for in the drawings of the young child in "Sestina," and the "crypto-dream house" of perfect impossibility that comes later in "The End of March," much is realized here. That unifying mist of "Cape Breton" holds "house and rock, / in a private cloud" that flows through the open glass doors of Samambaia.

This otherworldly natural home also enabled "total recall about Nova Scotia" (*OA* 249). In her studio Bishop composed "In the Village" for *The New Yorker* in 1953. The maternal presence that rose from dream to primordial life force at the end of "At the Fishhouses" continues, yet much more literally as "In the Village" begins with her mother's scream. Much of this autobiographical story details her mother's delicate mental state as she moves from her Great Village home into the Dartmouth hospital where she would stay for the rest of her life. The young narrator offsets her domestic stress by getting out of the house to run errands. As she roams around the village, she finds joy amidst the working environment of Nate the blacksmith clanging horseshoes.[9] These "beautiful sounds" (*Pr* 63) heard from the beginning to the end of the narrative "turn everything else to silence" (*Pr* 77). Nate's relieving work comes "from the blacksmith's shop at the end of the garden! Its gray roof, with patches of moss, could be seen above the lilac bushes" (*Pr* 63). This shop works with nature and provides an alternative peace to the unsettling screams of her mother in their anxious house from which the "child vanishes." The young narrator is drawn inside the workshop with Nate and two other men where "the horse is the real guest" (*Pr* 66). There may not be a more exalted passage in Bishop's literature than this one with the "improbable" horse whose "harness hangs loose like a man's suspenders": "He is enormous. His rump is like a brown, glossy globe of the whole brown world [. . .] the cloud of his odor is a chariot in itself" (*Pr* 66). Bishop's ability to register abject excrement beautifully, also found in "A Cold Spring," typifies her ability to dig up unsettling material that people prefer to repress. Bishop recalls "marching through the village with a big stick, directing" Nelly the cow with a "*Whack!*" who "looks up at me, drooling glass strings" and "makes cow flops. Smack. Smack. Smack. Smack. It is fascinating. I cannot take my eyes off her. Then I step around them: fine dark-green and lacy and watery at the edges" (*Pr* 68–70). Bishop unflinchingly appreciates the shit from which adults customarily turn away.

Whether hanging with the men in the blacksmith shop or marching around town like a general with the cow, Bishop displays her admiration of masculine types of labour. When she was nineteen, she expressed this appreciation to Rhoda Wheeler Sheehan:

> I've just been reading my friend, [Elizabeth Lincoln Otis'] "An 'If' for Girls." In closing, Rhoda, I want to leave you with this quotation from it:
>
> "If you can ply a saw and use a hammer,
> Can do a man's work when the need occurrs [*sic*],

> Can sing, when asked, without excuse or stammer
> Can rise above unfriendly snubs and slurs. . . ."

After the quotation, Bishop encourages her friend "to sing, be a man and [. . .] face the music."[10] "In the Village" is about doing that in difficult circumstances, and she learns from her grandfather. Leaving their house at night, the "men have to go to fight the fire" while "my grandmother is crying somewhere," and her aunts say "Sh! Don't let her . . .." The narrator says, "I am struggling to free myself [. . .]. I get up and dress by myself and go downstairs. My grandfather is in the kitchen alone, drinking tea. He has made the oatmeal himself, too. He gives me some and tells me about the fire very cheerfully" (*Pr* 75). Bishop admires the work done by men, even the simple domestic task of making oatmeal. Nate's "Clang" is the favoured "beautiful pure sound" that silences everything in a passage where "I go past the blacksmith's shop with the package under my arm, hiding the address of the sanitarium" (*Pr* 77). While she has been taught to repress her relationship with her mother inside a house with screaming, shushing, and slamming doors, when Bishop walks outside she is no longer caught but freed.

Nate's clang obliterates the pressures inside, "But still, once in a while, the river gives an unexpected gurgle. '*Slp*,' it says, out of glassy-ridged knots sliding along the surface. / *Clang.* / And everything except the river holds its breath. / Now there is no scream" (*Pr* 78). Nate's work fits the natural environment. "*Clang.* / It sounds like a bell buoy out at sea. / It is the elements speaking: earth, air, fire, water." These are the elemental materials of Bishop's poetry and this memoir is Bishop's "Out of the Cradle Endlessly Rocking." ("At the Fishhouses" is her cradle.) Her nature is formed by the outside world, which then informs her unique innerscape. The bell buoy clanging in the sea of "In the Village" was also depicted in "Pleasure Seas": "bells vibrate / [. . .] rhythmically / To shock after shock of electricity. / The sea is delight. The sea means *room.* / It is a dance-floor, a well-ventilated ball-room" (*P* 279). This poem, written in Florida during the late 1930s, expresses the invigorated poetic body charged by the pleasurable seas of the Keys, and the electric night life that created room for Bishop's liberation as also expressed in the erotic charges of "It is marvellous to wake up together."[11] Lightning strikes the lovers' house with a current that runs through their bedroom.

In 1976's *Geography III,* "The Moose" is the primary natural agent in that narrative poem telling the story of a bus ride through Nova Scotia's physical and human territory. As with "Cape Breton," "At the Fishhouses," "In the

Village," "Pleasure Seas," and "It is marvellous to wake up together . . ." sublime nature includes our mechanical involvement in it: "A moose has come out of / the impenetrable wood / and stands there, looms, rather, / in the middle of the road. / It approaches; it sniffs at / the bus's hot hood" (*P* 192). As with the seal in "At the Fishhouses," the moose is sublimely different and somewhat comical: "Towering, antlerless, / high as a church, / homely as a house / (or safe as houses), / A man's voice assures us / 'Perfectly harmless'" (*P* 193). Juxtaposition between high church and homely house makes both extremes slightly ridiculous, between which an effort at cozy domestication is made with "(safe as houses)" as if to settle the matter. As usual in Bishop's natural encounters (recall singing hymns to the seal), people are the silly ones, and this gentle satire is often heightened by religious context. Yet the poet still values the mysteries of "otherworldly" creation from "Curious creatures" – "Why, why do we feel / (we all feel) this sweet / sensation of joy?" This collective sublime experience is not a private sanctuary, and to "turn and face the strange"[12] repeatedly this poet gathers a bountiful life around her. Precious realizations are always qualified by self-awareness of human imposition; in this case the poem ends with "a dim / smell of moose, an acrid / smell of gasoline" as human effect upon the environment leaves its trace.

What we leave behind is the subject of "Poem," about "a minor family relic" in the form of a small painting by a great-uncle. The material representation of nature is envisaged through paint: "two brushstrokes each" for "tiny cows," "a wild iris, white and yellow, / fresh squiggled from the tube," a barn "titanium white, one dab" (*P* 196). Memory of this recognized place in Nova Scotia is "the little that we get for free, / the little of our earthly trust. Not much" (*P* 197). It is one art cherished because it is "life and the memory of it so compressed / they've turned into each other." At the end, this delicately painted nature gains value by the vulnerability of "the yet-to-be-dismantled elms, the geese." Flown and flowing at once is the power of fleeting life.

Notes

1. William Wordsworth, "The Tables Turned," in *Selected Poetry* (Oxford: Oxford University Press, 1998), 56–57.
2. See Bonnie Costello, "Bishop and the Poetic Tradition," in *The Cambridge Companion to Elizabeth Bishop*, ed. Angus Cleghorn and Jonathan Ellis (Cambridge: Cambridge University Press, 2014), 79–94.
3. See Bishop's "Writing poetry is an unnatural act . . . " (*EAP* 207–12) for her much-quoted section on "Grandmother's Glass Eye" and poetry's synthesis of the real and unreal (212). See Susan Rosenbaum, "Bishop and the Natural World," in *The Cambridge Companion to Elizabeth Bishop*, 62–78. Rosenbaum

begins with sections on "Nature through a Glass Eye" and the Romantic tradition while thoroughly progressing through scholarship of nature in Bishop's work, culminating in a brilliant section on "Natural History: Bishop and the Surrealism of Everyday Life."

4. Andrew Eastman describes "speech-soundscapes" in "'Hearing Things': Voice and Rhyme in the Poems of Elizabeth Bishop," in *Elizabeth Bishop and the Music of Literature*, ed. Cleghorn (Cham, Switzerland: Palgrave Macmillan, 2019), 41–50.
5. Yuki Tanaka, "The Rhythm of Syntax in 'At the Fishhouses,'" in *Elizabeth Bishop and the Music of Literature*, 31–40.
6. See letter in *One Art: Selected Letters* and *Elizabeth Bishop and The New Yorker.*
7. See Erica Dawson, "The Principal Beauty of 'At the Fishhouses,'" *Ecotone* 9.2 (Spring/Summer 2014), 33–37, for a powerful reading of the engulfing nature that leads Bishop to give way to it as an agent of knowledge.
8. See Lorrie Goldensohn, "Approaching Elizabeth Bishop's Letters to Ruth Foster," *Yale Review* 103.1 (January 2015), 1–19; and Heather Treseler, "One Long Poem," *Boston Review* (August 17, 2016). Web.
9. In a July 27, 2020, e-mail, Sandra Barry wrote to me about Nate in Great Village: "I read your 'Nature' chapter – lovely. I hadn't really thought about the masculine world that little EB saw in GV – but of course it was there and vital to her: Pa and Nate and also Angus Johnson the post master – and how her marching through the village was a 'doing' like that of the men around her. A very positive image for her, especially since she had no father. Uncle Arthur was a much more complex male image and then later on Uncle Jack and George Shepherdson were decidedly negative and damaging images. Well, EB had the gamut of forces from highly positive to highly negative – some lives are like that.

   I met Mayhew (Mate/Nate) Fisher's daughter some years ago – she was very elderly. She told me one of her most vivid memories of him was going into his forge (which by that time was in Bass River) after school and him stopping what he was doing to sit down and talk with her, ask her about her day. She said he loved to sing (came from a very musical family) and would sing and recite poetry while working – so, EB's description of him doing so is entirely factual. I was rather amazed to hear it – she is not 'idealizing' him – but reporting his actual nature. I can't remember his daughter's name at the moment . . ., but she was a wonderful person – and she had never read 'In the Village' – so I was happy to get her a copy, in which her father is so beautifully memorialized. The amazing thing is he lived to nearly 100, he was still alive in the 70s when Bishop returned to NS – he died right around the time she did . . . .

   He is almost mythic in 'In the Village' – but the fact of the matter is, he was really like that – few of us can say we have inspired such a poet by our very nature. I have also learned that Angus Johnson was equally like EB's evocation of him – accurate memory."

10. Fiona Sheehan, "'Affectionately Yours, Bishop': The Early Correspondence of Elizabeth Bishop and Rhoda Wheeler Sheehan," *Resources for American Literary Study* 40 (2018), 229–280.
11. See my essay, "Bishop's 'Wiring Fused': 'Bone Key' and 'Pleasure Seas,'" from *Elizabeth Bishop in the 21st-Century: Reading the New Editions*, ed. Cleghorn, Hicok and Travisano (Charlottesville: University of Virginia Press, 2012), 69–87.
12. David Bowie, "Changes," *Hunky Dory*, RCA Records, 1971.

CHAPTER 31

Animals

Marianne MacRae

In a 1951 letter to Robert Lowell, Elizabeth Bishop famously stated that "On reading over what I've got on hand I find I'm really a minor female Wordsworth. At least, I don't know anyone else who seems to be such a Nature Lover" (*WIA* 122). Her observations of nature frequently broaden into considerations of animal otherness, where the animal becomes a lens through which humanity can be viewed. Several of her poems, including some of her most renowned and often-anthologised works such as "The Fish" and "The Moose," ruminate on animal life, frequently suggesting a transformative, near-spiritual encounter with nature, while maintaining the truth of the animal's existence.

Guy Rotella suggests that Bishop's "concern with how the spiritual proceeds from the material has religious roots."[1] A self-proclaimed agnostic, Bishop was open in her scepticism of organised religion. However, her work suggests, at the very least, an inescapable attraction to the beliefs and practices that are elemental to religious faith and to the idea that there is "something bigger" that unites life on earth. Bonnie Costello states that "religious rhetoric of the soul and of divinity haunts Bishop's poems," and indeed it features heavily throughout her collected works.[2] Many of her considerations of animals see the animal function both as a well-executed portrait and a coded suggestion of something beyond earthly comprehension. However, while her animal poetry is often profuse with this "religious rhetoric," there is also a steady rejection of the anthropocentric and, in turn, androcentric outlooks that developed in part through the propagation of Judeo-Christian religious teachings. Lorrie Goldensohn notes that in the majority of her work, "Bishop says little about the world of female possibility, but if we look at what is enacted in animal terms there is a richer field of discourse."[3] Despite the term's rise to prominence happening only after her death, ecofeminism becomes relevant to Bishop's animal poetry and can be linked to her reimagining of religious traditions into a spiritual communion with nature.

Margo DeMello defines ecofeminism in basic terms as "a philosophy and a social movement which focuses on the links between the oppression of women and the destruction of nature."[4] By recognising the parallels between their position in a patriarchal society and that of a commodified nature, female writers can reclaim their connection to the natural world and embolden their readers to seek out their own ecological posture. In "Brazil, January 1, 1502" (*P* 89), Bishop depicts a feminised nature scene ("Nature greets our eyes / exactly as she must have greeted theirs") that is invaded by "the Christians" (Portuguese colonisers). These colonisers attempt to bring the landscape, which is in part representative of the native Brazilian people, under their control. By the poem's end, the colonisers are, ominously, "each out to catch an Indian for himself," specifically one of "those maddening little women." The lizards that feature towards the end of the second stanza become a metaphor for the dehumanisation and over-sexualisation of the women. Here, "all eyes / are on the smaller female one" with her "wicked tail," "red as a red-hot wire," so dangerously tempting for the male lizards who watch her. The blame for any resultant action taken by the male lizards seems to be placed on the female. She is, however, defiant in her display of femininity, refusing to reign herself in under the male gaze. The implication of the "red-hot" tail suggests the male lizards might find themselves injured should they go near her. Conversely, the "maddening little women" at the end of the poem, who also fall under this gaze from the male colonisers, are "retreating, always retreating" into the landscape in an attempt to escape it. The landscape, and the women who are so much a part of it, become nothing more than a commodity for the colonisers to abuse. The question of whether they survived unscathed is left to our imaginations, and history, to answer.

Bishop's animal poems rarely employ their animal subjects as proponents of anthropocentrism, instead highlighting and celebrating the congruence and contrast of life on earth, while hinting towards a more esoteric interpretation. There is a kinship with nature at work that undermines patriarchal systems and centralises the ways in which both nonhuman animals and women might be perceived as "other." In "The Moose," the narrator, travelling on a night bus to Boston, allows her mind to drift from the immediate, and largely human, imagery passing by outside the window, into a dreamlike state of memory that blurs the line between the real and the unreal. The appearance of the moose, the intrusion of the animal other into this human realm, serves to break these meditations and at the same time to solidify them, reawakening and reconfirming the self. The moose's femininity comes as a shock to the passengers ("Look! It's a she!"), who (if they've ever read Elizabeth Bishop) might have assumed something so "grand" and "otherworldly" to be male. However, the "sweet / sensation of joy" that they collectively find in this moment of alterity is perhaps thus *because* the moose is female, an unexpected break from the norm.

The dog in "Pink Dog," on the other hand, is from the outset very blatantly female ("[a] nursing mother, by those hanging teats"), though unlike the stunning spectacle of the moose, here femininity is something to be disguised ("[t]onight you simply cannot afford to be a- / n eyesore"). However, before the suggestion to dress up for Carnival, the dog is imbued with a dark power, drawn from her ability to startle and scare "the passersby" with her nudity and her unsightly skin conditions. This turns the dog from something wholly pathetic to a sort of antihero. Where the moose is able to inspire a "sweet / sensation of joy," the dog has the capacity to make people "mortally afraid," suggesting perhaps the potential power of the ecofeminist posture.

Rotella suggests that "Bishop worked at the boundary of the visible and the invisible, interrogating human claims to knowledge and questioning whether we discover or impose the meanings we [. . .] assert."[5] Her considerations of boundaries defy the rigidity of the anthropocentric "us versus them" division and can be seen throughout her animal poems. Often animal lives are explored along the physical lines of separation. For example, the titular animals in "The Fish" (*P* 43–44) and "Sandpiper" (*P* 129) both traverse the border between land and water, while the central character in "The Man-Moth" (*P* 16–17) switches between under- and over-ground worlds. At times, too, the borders become more abstract; the man-moth also straddles the taxonomy of species, while the dog of "Pink Dog" negotiates echelons of social class. "The Riverman" (*P* 103–07) examines ideas of magical transformation between human and animal worlds, and the animals in "Sleeping on the Ceiling" (*P* 30), "Roosters" (*P* 36–40), "Rainy Season; Sub-Tropics" (*P* 163–65) and "The Moose" bridge the gap between sleep and consciousness. By formulating meetings with animals this way, she distorts the lines of perception, pushing against the apparent constraints of what is human and what is animal, acknowledging both as part of the same scale of life on earth. Bishop's approach to animal life is one that relies on recognising the sense of similarity and difference in life beyond the self.

In "Rainy Season; Sub-Tropics," an uncollected poem first published in *The Kenyon Review* in 1967, she examines a boundary rare in her work, that of the anthropomorphised animal speaker. A prose poem, it is split into three sections, each voiced by a different animal, namely a giant toad, a crab, and a giant snail. The removal of the human poet-speaker turns these monologues into almost-cartoonish dramatisations of animal life, while at the same time closely aligning Bishop herself with the natural world. In order to formulate these speeches, she must first imagine herself into the mind of the animal.

Despite her tangential links to the movement (most likely stemming from her close friendship with Robert Lowell), Bishop was clear in her rejection of confessional poetry, which rose to prominence in the late 1950s and early 60s. Though there has been little critical exploration of this poem, Zhou Xiaojing has suggested that "[b]oth the form and content of these monologues are at once an assimilation of and a resistance to the confessional practice in American poetry."[6] While this poem is an unlikely contribution to the genre, she does toy with the idea of oversharing the innermost details of one's life. The irony of this, of course, is that she's imposing her opinions onto three animals who are unable to advocate for themselves. However, Scott Knickerbocker suggests that "personification can be employed ironically precisely to foreground the epistemological gap between the human and the nonhuman."[7] And Bishop does seem aware of her own irony, acknowledging that to attempt to force an experience onto another can become a violation. This is illustrated by the toad's cigarette anecdote, which can also be seen as a parable about humanity's domineering treatment of nature, and perhaps a reflection on the patriarchal suppression of women.

When the toad says, "pity me," it implies the presence of an outside observer, from whom it asks for compassion. The identity of this observer is open to interpretation, but in some ways recalls the speaker from "Cirque d'Hiver." While Bishop does not attempt to inhabit or personify the horse in this poem, through it, her human speaker achieves a moment of clarity, seeing aspects of herself in this animal counterpart. In the end, the horse's "eye is like a star," elevating the scene towards the heavens, suggesting the intangibility of nature, knowledge, and spirituality. The three animals featured in "Rainy Season; Sub-Tropics" all make reference to their eyes too, drawing attention to what can and cannot be seen. The toad, whose eyes, "bulge and hurt," despite being its "one great beauty," complains that "[t]hey see too much," suggesting a weariness with the world that supports the toad's opening request for pity. The crab, though an outsider here, speaks in a comparatively more cocksure voice, stating that its eyes are "small, but good." This implies perhaps a narrower worldview, which in turn heightens the sense of the crab's displacement; it is both self-assured and uncertain, speaking at length about its various means of armour and attack (a "tough and tight" shell, a "powerful right claw"). Finally, the snail referencing its "blind, white bull's head" draws attention to the fact it is roaming the terrain with no physical means of seeing where it is going, but asserts that is has "a goal, a certain rock," implying an innate knowledge of the landscape. By drawing attention to the animals' eyes, Bishop casts their gaze back on the observer, forcing them to try and see the world from these three different perspectives.

Working in contrast to this are the numerous references to that which is hidden or unseen. For example, the toad is "an angel in disguise," both not of this world, and concealed behind a façade. It threatens to release its poison of "blue-black fumes," which would obscure the situation and potentially prove fatal to anyone in the area. The crab describes the eyes of the fish as "opaque," suggesting an inability to see through the eyes of the other, before describing how it catches and eats them, perhaps referencing the anthropocentric destruction of nature and the human inclination to kill and consume animals. Finally, the snail describes the impenetrable "mountains of black rock" giving off "such clouds of steam" that leave a blurred impression of the scene. It also describes itself as "ghostlike," an otherworldly presence who seems to float, leaving behind only "a lovely opalescent ribbon" in its wake, an unreadable trace akin to a supernatural ectoplasm. The snail's shell too, becomes an emblem of the unknown, even to the snail ("I have not seen it"). Once the snail retreats into the shell, it is shielded from the outside world and the implied observer, suggesting there are parts of animal life that are eternally unknowable to humans.

These examples draw attention to the idea of a physical, observable nature, while at the same time, subtly signposting the unseen, unfathomable idea of what is beyond the self, the animal other, and nature as a whole. Through these animal speakers, Bishop highlights the importance of a close kinship with animals, while also insisting there are things we cannot, and should not, attempt to comprehend.

However, like the work of her friend and one-time mentor, Marianne Moore, Bishop's animal poems do not readily submit to a singular interpretation, instead offering multiple diverse readings that often feed into one another. This becomes particularly prevalent when considering religious and ecofeminist narratives. Her ruminations on nature tend towards a spiritual transcendentalism that challenges both traditional, organised religious practices, and the position of women and animals in society, with numerous points of crossover. At the same time, they maintain the essential spirit of the animal itself, carefully avoiding sustained anthropomorphism.

"Roosters," for example, oscillates primarily between the subjects of militarism, gender, marriage, and religion, while invoking an accurate depiction of roosters crowing at dawn. Written in 1940, it is an early example of Bishop's animal poetry, and unlike many of her later works, the use of animals-as-symbols is perhaps more overt. The poem explores the Christian symbol of the rooster as a vessel for both betrayal and forgiveness, before lifting its attention to the sky of a new day, suggesting a comparison with our small, human history and the expanse of the infinite. The nature/culture divide manifests distinctly in each of the poem's three sections with the roosters acting as the linking factor between them.

Though this is famously the poem that brought their mentor/mentee relationship to an end, in correspondence with Marianne Moore prior to its publication Bishop noted that "I want[ed] to emphasize the essential baseness of militarism. In the first part I was thinking of Key West, and also of those aerial views of dismal little towns in Finland and Norway, when the Germans took over, and their atmosphere of poverty" (*OA* 96). Critics offer several varied readings of this opening section, which depicts the morning crows of roosters in a domestic garden. Goldensohn suggests that while the invasion of Finland and Norway may have been Bishop's initial source of inspiration for the poem, its true meaning lies in the wider condemnation of militarism in general.[8] Alicia Ostriker ties the poem's militaristic implications to the idea of feminism, suggesting it as "a capsule representation of the invisible constraints inhibiting poets who would be ladies," describing the first two-thirds of the poem as "a strong and brilliant parody of male brutality and male aesthetics."[9] Victoria Harrison combines these sentiments, stating that it "relentlessly juxtaposes the dailiness of lovers in bed and the violence of war, undermining any myth of moral righteousness outside war."[10]

Conversely, Colm Tóibín disagrees with many critics, stating that "it is important to insist that 'Roosters' is about roosters," that this is a poem describing the real roosters of Key West and their natural arrogance.[11] He goes on to say that "if Bishop had wanted to write a poem about the war and maleness and militarism, she would, or might, have done so, although it would have been unlikely."[12] While the roosters never entirely lose their animality, it is difficult to agree that their otherness is explored with no duality of function. Each of these readings also tend to side-line the religious examination of the rooster in the second section, which occupies thirteen of the forty-four stanzas and undeniably alters the way in which the poem's opening is read. Setting the poem at the border of sleep and consciousness allows Bishop to play with ideas of what is real and what is unreal. She uses animal otherness here to suggest difficult themes of warfare, religion, gender roles, and love, highlighting the similarities between humans and animals and their shared inclinations towards brutality and sordidness. At the same time, she employs ambiguity and irony to demure from one straightforward reading. The poem's progressive turns from warfare to religion to nature endeavour to address the broader question of existential meaning.

The roosters begin as ruthless sirens waking the world with their cries. The clipped, three-line stanzas are relentless, pushing from one image to the next in quick succession, driven forward by their hard end-rhymes. The profusion of monosyllabic phrasing likens this onslaught to gunfire, supported by the repetition of "gun-metal blue," which immediately initiates the connotations of warfare. Roosters infiltrate every corner of the garden, depicted as jubilant in their invasion. This implies debased, animal nature, with an almost-sexual inclination, heightened by the alternating [æ], [ɔː] and [ɒ] sounds in stanza five.

In conversation with George Starbuck in 1977, when asked "which are your feminist tracts?" Bishop responded, "I don't think there are any. The first part of 'Roosters,' now, I suppose. But I hadn't thought of it that way."[13] Despite this assertion, it is difficult to deny the clear divisions between genders portrayed throughout the poem. The hens are reduced to no more than "rustling wives," reinforcing an underlying connotation of male primacy that is present throughout the poem's opening section. The personification of the hens here as "wives" parodies marriage, suggesting the birds as representations of human women. When the male birds are depicted as "stupid," "cruel," and "uncontrolled," it highlights their otherness, distancing them not only from the apparently civilised humans who want to carry on sleeping, but also the hens, who become comparatively innocent. However, while "Roosters" may appear at first as a condemnation of only the male aspects of a patriarchal society, it becomes apparent that Bishop is not necessarily siding with the hens over the militant roosters; the wife-hens are also being satirised. These stanzas become a comment on both genders; the "rustling wives" serve to facilitate the "cruel," "stupid" roosters and their aggression by submitting to "lives / of being courted and despised."

Here the narrator's contemplation of the birds seems to distance the human/animal contingents of the poem. However, their animal otherness draws attention to the apparent absurdity found in the traditional, gendered roles in relationships. The caricature of marital life continues in stanzas 10–12 where Bishop parodies the idyllic family home with a white picket fence, turning the scene into one of dilapidation, over which the rooster presides. The "tin rooster" sits on top of the church, suggesting himself as a pseudo-god, the emblem of nature standing in judgement over humanity.

The roosters then briefly become anthropomorphised parodies of human patriotism, with

> each one an active
> displacement in perspective:
> each screaming, "This is where I live!"
>
> Each screaming
> "Get up! Stop dreaming!"
> Roosters, what are you projecting? (*P* 37)

As previously stated, examples of lucid speech from animals are rare in Bishop's work, but it is used here to draw a direct comparison between humans and animals. Their voices progress from "uncontrolled, traditional cries" to intelligible "screaming" speech, which implies both madness and a tipping over into human faculties of communication. By turning them into "active / displacement[s] in perspective," Bishop acknowledges an intended multiplicity of meaning and at the same time suggests the impossibility of understanding the birds' otherness. However, when one rooster is killed and "flung / on the gray ash-heap, [and] lies in dung / /with his dead wives," it suggests that, whether rooster or hen, male or female, human or animal, all creatures are united under the inexplicable otherness of death.

At the end of the first section there is a focus on the idea of legacy and life after death. When paired with the cursory glance towards the "dead wives," the reference to "Magdalen" (assumedly Mary) in the opening stanza of the second section, becomes more significant than it first appears, drawing attention to the idea that female histories are less thoroughly explored than those of men. Kirsten Hotelling Zona states that the poem "interrogates our compulsion to selfishness and cruelty, our propensity for mistaken judgment and regret, and the process of forgiveness that is elemental to the transition between them."[14] It might also be added that the poem highlights the tendency to forget, as characterised by these brief mentions of the female chickens and Mary Magdalen, which suggest that females become background characters in stories that emphasise and extol their male counterparts.

Moving into the second section of the poem, Bishop toys with the Christian symbolism of the rooster as a signifier not only of Peter's denial of association with Christ, but also Christ's forgiveness of his apostle. At the same time, she addresses the popular (though unrecorded in any of the Gospels) characterisation of Mary Magdalen as a prostitute, referencing her "sin of the flesh." Bishop takes Christ's words to his disciples in the Garden of Gethsemane articulating that "the spirit indeed is willing, but the flesh is weak" (King James Bible, Matthew 26:41), reconfiguring them to emphasise an apparent weakness in Magdalen's character:

> St. Peter's sin
> was worse than that of Magdalen
> whose sin was of the flesh alone;
>
> of spirit, Peter's,
> falling, beneath the flares,
> among the "servants and officers." (*P* 38)

The females who feature in the poem are now reduced to little more than "sin[s] of the flesh," there to service and support the men they are surrounded by. "Peter's sin / was worse," but he is, as shown in the rest of the poem, remembered much more favourably overall. Though their parts within the poem are fleeting, the female characters become significant *because* of the brevity of examination given to them. When they are overridden by loud, arrogant roosters, Bishop creates a neatly observed parody of reality; the otherness of the hens recognises the supposed otherness of human women in a patriarchal society.

The animal rooster outshines even the human Magdalen, becoming the blessed symbol of forgiveness. Alongside this, Peter is not only pardoned, but resplendently immortalised in stone alongside Christ. Peter's remorseful tears turn "our chanticleer's" potentially violent spurs into sparkling artefacts that might garner admiration. Peter is raised to the position of "the Prince / of the Apostles" under the image of the rooster. The militant assault of the roosters that was explored in the first section is forgotten as they are reduced to just one rooster that becomes the "inescapable hope, the pivot," an emblem of absolution, for the poem's male characters at least. At the same time, however, it is difficult to imagine Bishop missing the irony of the "little cock" so pointedly positioned between Peter and Christ within this scene, perhaps satirising these men, extravagantly forgiving one another under the insignia of the "bronze cock."

Throughout the poem there is a prevalent attempt to solidify the roosters and turn them from real, living birds into iconographic renderings in metal and stone. There is a proliferation of metal that persists from the "gun-metal blue dark" of the opening stanza. The roosters are dressed in "green-gold medals," coloured in "oil-golds and copper greens"; the "tin rooster perches" over the church; the dead rooster's "metallic feathers oxidise." And later Peter's "dreadful rooster" is rendered in the "old holy sculpture [. . .] carved on a dim column in the travertine." It then becomes "a new weathervane [. . .] a bronze cock on a porphyry / pillar." Each example suggests an attempt to make the rooster into a palpable artistic object; to pin down their otherness into a human frame of reference that will outlast the mortality of the birds and their human counterparts.

However, as Siobhan Phillips suggests, with reference to W. B. Yeats's "Sailing to Byzantium," Bishop's "metallic cocks do not seem to provide that timeless place 'out of nature.'"[15] Instead, the constant shift of these emblematic statues implies the flux of an earthlier impression of nature, time, and history. Bishop highlights the ways in which the human cultural significance of an animal can alter with time, while simultaneously reinforcing the idea that the animal other can never be entirely taken "out of nature" or comprehended in human terms. There is a reassurance that real, living roosters will always crow, but that "'Deny, deny, deny' / is not all [they] cry" – that they cannot be assigned any one meaning except inconclusiveness. She uses the otherness of the roosters to represent the ways in which human behaviour can be read, suggesting that everything is dependent on the context, refusing to confirm that the birds represent any one thing in particular. Their animal instinct to crow at the break of each new day gives them the characteristics of both reliability and transformation. They demarcate the passage of time and in doing so can become the embodiment of multiplicity.

The final section of the poem turns to what Costello calls "the noniconic force of nature," and it is the "low light" that comes, "gilding // from underneath / [. . .] gilding the tiny / floating swallow's belly," that admits nature's changeability.[16] This gilding is transient, echoed in "the day's preamble / like wandering lines in marble," which suggests permanence, but also movement and unpredictability. By ending the poem back in the post-dawn morning where "[t]he cocks are now almost inaudible," Bishop implies that the "noniconic force of nature" can always undermine anthropomorphic symbolism, despite the multiple layers of artistic meaning that might be derived from an animal. This turn towards the dawn sky renders both human and animal, and their concerns, insignificant, suggesting once more the question of a spiritual otherness, which ultimately goes unanswered.

In "Roosters," as in several of Bishop's animal poetics, traditional religious teachings are transformed to encompass a broader sense of ecological spirituality. As demonstrated, within her work, animals often function to suggest a broader spiritual communion with nature. Their presences undermine traditional incarnations of religious practice in an attempt to equalise human/animal life. Though she maintains their absolute otherness, by suggesting animal life as emblematic of humanity, she creates a sense of recognition between human and animal.

Notes

1. Guy Rotella, *Reading and Writing Nature: The Poetry of Robert Frost, Wallace Stevens, Marianne Moore, and Elizabeth Bishop* (Boston: Northeastern University Press, 1991), 188–89.
2. Bonnie Costello, *Elizabeth Bishop: Questions of Mastery* (Cambridge: Harvard University Press, 1991), 91.
3. Lorrie Goldensohn, *Elizabeth Bishop: The Biography of a Poetry* (New York: Columbia University Press, 1992), 279.
4. Margo DeMello, *Animals and Society: An Introduction to Human-animal Studies* (New York: Columbia University Press, 2012), 390.
5. Rotella, *Reading and Writing Nature*, 189.
6. Zhou Xiaojing, "'The Oblique, the Indirect Approach': Elizabeth Bishop's 'Rainy Season; Sub-Tropics,'" *Chicago Review* 40.4 (1994), 75. See also Vidyan Ravinthiran's discussion of the poem in *Elizabeth Bishop's Prosaic* (Lewisburg: Bucknell University Press, 2015), 155–73; and Sarah Kennedy, "'Swerving as I Swerve': Elizabeth Bishop's Fugitive Empathy," *Reading Elizabeth Bishop: An Edinburgh Companion*, ed. Jonathan Ellis (Edinburgh: Edinburgh University Press, 2019), 117–31.
7. Scott Knickerbocker, *Ecopoetics: The Language of Nature, the Nature of Language* (Amherst: University of Massachusetts Press, 2012), 5.
8. Goldensohn, *Elizabeth Bishop*, 155–56.
9. Alicia Ostriker, *Stealing the Language: The Emergence of Women's Poetry in America* (London: The Women's Press, 1987), 54.
10. Victoria Harrison, *Elizabeth Bishop's Poetics of Intimacy* (Cambridge: Cambridge University Press, 1993), 89.
11. *On Elizabeth Bishop* (Princeton University Press, 2015), 66.
12. Colm Tóibín, *On Elizabeth Bishop* (Princeton: Princeton University Press, 2015), 67.
13. Bishop, *Conversations with Elizabeth Bishop*, 90.
14. Kirsten Hotelling Zona, *Marianne Moore, Elizabeth Bishop, and May Swenson: The Feminist Poetics of Self-Restraint* (Ann Arbor: University of Michigan Press, 2002), 65.
15. Siobhan Phillips, *The Poetics of the Everyday: Creative Repetition in Modern American Verse* (New York: Columbia University Press, 2010), 120.
16. Costello, *Elizabeth Bishop*, 67.

PART VI

Reception and Criticism

CHAPTER 32

Bishop Studies

Thomas Travisano

Jonathan Ellis's "Introduction: Incompatible Bishops?" serves to preface his 2019 essay collection *Reading Elizabeth Bishop: An Edinburgh Companion*, which grew out of the international conference "Elizabeth Bishop's Questions of Travel: 50 Years Later," organized by Ellis at the University of Sheffield, UK, in 2015. This introduction provides a recent and judicious accounting of important trends and publications in the field of Bishop studies. However, Ellis's otherwise comprehensive review moves somewhat briskly over the field's formative stages. By contrast, the present essay will begin by focusing attention on these dramatic formative stages, since the development of Elizabeth Bishop studies – so slow to find its footing, then so rapid and complete in its arrival – offers a singular and revealing case study of the emergence, establishment, and evolution of an impressive author-studies field. Such a case study should prove useful not only as a specimen of literary history, but as a roadmap for scholars seeking to foster the study and appreciation of other authors who are now unjustly neglected – as Bishop herself once was. The success of Bishop studies suggests that ground-building, scholarly interchange, teamwork, and the coordination of effort, often on an international scale, can have a significant impact not only on an author's reputation, but on the range, depth, quantity, and quality of scholarship in a particular field of author-studies.

My own observation of the growth of Bishop studies began with its first stirrings in the late 1970s and continues to the present day. Like many Bishop scholars, I have played the role of jack-of-all-trades, serving as the need arose as a critic, biographer, conference organizer, literary journalist and historian, newsletter editor, bibliographer, co-editor of essay collections, author-society president, and editor – in both book and periodical form – of examples from Bishop's own poetry, prose, and correspondence. My varied experience over the past four decades brings home to me that for a field of author-studies to flourish it must establish, at a functional level, all six of the following components: (1) access to a substantial and representative canon of the author's published work, in both primary and secondary genres; (2) an extensive body of critical literature, deploying diverse critical approaches and methodologies to illuminate the author's work; (3) access to a significant body of relevant archival materials; (4) regularly updated bibliographic studies to establish the chronology of the author's work and facilitate access both to primary writings and to the critical literature; (5) one or more sound and current biographical studies of the author; and (6) a compelling articulation of the author's role in literary and cultural history. Of course, any or all of these six components might never be achieved to perfection. For example, as Ellis observed with regard to Bishop in 2019: "We do not as yet have critical editions of the poems or stories, never mind a collected letters."[1] Yet the evolution of Bishop studies suggests that once each of these six components has been established on a working level, the study of an author is poised to come into its own, and the field may begin to thrive on its own momentum. If any of these components is missing, to address that lack becomes a matter of urgent concern to scholars in that field of author-studies. The emergence of Bishop studies required a coordinated global effort, and the first intimations of that effort occurred in the late 1970s, while Bishop was still alive, residing in Boston, and producing some of her very best work.

In David Kalstone's groundbreaking 1977 essay "Questions of Memory, Questions of Travel," published just two years before the poet's death, this imaginative and resourceful critic characterized Bishop as "the most honored yet most elusive of poets." He observed further that there was something about Bishop's work "for which elegantly standard literary analysis was not prepared." Kalstone felt that it was to Bishop's credit that she "has always been hard to place."[2] However, other critics of the time were not so receptive to Bishop's determined individuality. In 1984, James Breslin dismissed Bishop from literary history in *From Modern to Contemporary* with a single sentence, citing her as representative of the "apparent defeat" of "the middle generation of poets" and framing her as a poet who "worked steadily and independently, but the cost was isolation and critical neglect."[3] Despite such dismissals by influential literary historians, over the course of the 1980s, the incipient field of Bishop studies moved forward. Step by step, and almost entirely beneath the radar, the groundwork was being laid for the sudden explosion of Bishop studies in the 1990s.

Candace MacMahon's meticulous *Elizabeth Bishop: A Bibliography, 1927–1979*, a foundational work in Bishop studies, established the chronology of Bishop's published oeuvre and made accessible many important and then all-but-unknown writings tucked away in decades-old periodicals. MacMahon's bibliography, prepared in cooperation with the poet, was published in 1980, the year following Bishop death. In a "Foreword," Bishop expresses surprise at seeing "that I've written so much when I've always thought I'd written so little."[4] In 1981, the Archives and Special Collections Library at Vassar College, Bishop's alma mater, acquired from Alice Methfessel, Bishop's partner and literary executor, a substantial – though, as we later learned, not quite complete – collection of Bishop's unpublished manuscripts. This was a body of papers that Bishop had carefully maintained and curated throughout her own lifetime. This vast collection, including correspondence, diaries, notebooks, manuscripts, artwork, and drafts, was promptly catalogued by the library and made available to scholars in 1982. When this work became available, a new world began to open for Bishop scholars that took them well beyond the still-comparatively small published canon documented in MacMahon's bibliography. This Vassar collection, so central to the development of the Bishop studies, has been continuously expanded in the decades that followed. Its offerings are complemented by important caches of Bishop's letters and papers in other libraries, including the collection of papers related to Bishop's life and family in Nova Scotia, housed at the library of Acadia University.

Access to Bishop's published work made an important step forward with the appearance in 1983 of *The Complete Poems: 1927–1979*, followed in 1984 by her *Collected Prose*, edited by Bishop's publisher and friend Robert Giroux. Each of these Farrar, Straus and Giroux editions drew in significant ways on both MacMahon's bibliography and the Vassar archive. As these volumes were appearing, Lloyd Schwartz and Sybil Estess's *Elizabeth Bishop and Her Art* (1983) was making available, in a section titled "In Her Own Words," more than twenty important prose statements, interviews, and brief extracts from letters by Bishop not included in *Collected Prose*. Access to Bishop's published and unpublished writings – far more copious, it seemed, than anyone had previously imagined – was moving forward. Still, only at the end of the decade did published criticism begin to catch up with and take full advantage of these new resources. Yet when the change came, it came decisively. When my own *Elizabeth Bishop: Her Artistic Development* appeared in 1988, it could make the perhaps-surprising claim to be the first critical monograph devoted to Bishop's entire career. Just three weeks later, this effort was followed by Robert Dale Parker's *Elizabeth Bishop: The Unbeliever*, the second such critical monograph. This remarkable case of critical synchronicity was a portent of things to come. Each of these works was a chronological study stressing Bishop's literary development and her response to intellectual history – and each drew heavily on MacMahon's bibliography and on the resources of the Vassar archive.

The year 1989 was graced by Kalstone's posthumously published *Becoming a Poet: Elizabeth Bishop with Marianne Moore and Robert Lowell*, a volume that makes Bishop the pivotal figure in relationships with a pair of poets whose canonical status then ranked higher than her own. Kalstone's volume, too, was centered on archival resources – the letters (then-unpublished) between Bishop and Lowell and between Bishop and Moore. Kalstone's proved to be the first in a long series of group studies serving in concert to establish beyond doubt Bishop's crucial role in her era's literary and cultural history. Like Travisano and Parker, Kalstone centered attention on Bishop's process of "becoming" as a writer. Each of these studies brought out, in its distinctive way, a reading of Bishop's creative interplay with literary and cultural traditions. Questions of gender, issues of cultural studies, and views of Bishop as a transgressive artist had not yet come to the fore in these volumes, but within a few years, these too would establish themselves as central to any reading of Bishop's life and work.

In this decade's final year, Lorrie Goldensohn sounded a new note – the role of the scholar as traveler and adventurer – when she journeyed to Brazil and brought back a surprising discovery, that beautiful and till-then unpublished lesbian-erotic lyric "It is marvellous to wake up together . . .," a poem in typescript Bishop left some years before in Ouro Preto in the care of her friend Linda Nemer. This fine and intimate poem, published for the first time with Goldensohn's introduction in the *American Poetry Review*, was a harbinger of the posthumous publication of many future poems and prose pieces, discovered both inside and outside the Vassar archive, a series of posthumous publications that would culminate in the 2006 *Edgar Allan Poe & The Juke-Box: Uncollected Poems, Drafts and Fragments*, edited by Alice Quinn. Meanwhile, as the 1980s drew to a close, a remarkable array of talented scholars were quietly working away at books and articles that would, through the force of their innovative and compelling scholarship, change the face of Bishop studies and elevate her standing as poet, writer, and cultural figure.

The extraordinary growth and development of Bishop studies in the decisive decade of the 1990s is chronicled almost from its inception in the pages of the *Elizabeth Bishop Bulletin*, the newsletter of the Elizabeth Bishop Society. In its first issue in Spring 1992, the *Bulletin* recounted the formation of the Bishop Society at the December 1991 annual meeting of the Modern Language Association in San Francisco. The Society's formative meeting followed a conference session on Bishop chaired by Marilyn May Lombardi that was "so crammed with auditors that many had to sit in the aisles" while others "had to stand in the hallway and crane their necks for glimpses of the speakers."[5] The stated mission of the *Bulletin* – which continues to this day under Angus Cleghorn, its present editor – is to "facilitate the exchange of news and information about the study of Elizabeth Bishop," as well as to provide information on "upcoming conferences and events," to review recent publications, sponsor conference panels and symposiums, and to "provide a bridge between Bishop's readers inside and outside the academy."[6] That opening issue of the *Bulletin*, of which I was the founding editor, announced a series of upcoming Bishop-related events in Great Village, Nova Scotia, in Key West, Florida, in Costa Mesa, California, and at Vassar College. The second issue of the *Bulletin* provided a bibliography of recent Bishop scholarship, both published and forthcoming, including critical volumes by Bonnie Costello, Lorrie Goldensohn, Victoria Harrison, Marilyn May Lombardi, and a biography by Brett Millier, each of which has proved to be a germinal work in the field. Continuing its bibliographic mission, this issue of the *Bulletin* cited, as well, the posthumous publication of Bishop poems in manuscript introduced by Goldensohn (as noted), along with further poems uncovered by Schwartz and Travisano and the publication of previously unknown or inaccessible juvenile poetry and prose edited by Travisano.

The third issue of the *Bulletin* offered "Notes on a Landmark Elizabeth Bishop Year," including mention of an American Literature Association panel on "Radical Bishop" chaired by Jacqueline Vaught Brogan. The reading by Brogan and others of Bishop as an understatedly radical author – an author subversive of existing cultural, political, artistic, and gender norms, had begun in earnest at that December 1991 MLA session, and it would continue throughout the 1990s and beyond. The *Bulletin* also offered a detailed account of the first of a long series of international symposiums on Bishop, in this case hosted by the Key West Literary Seminar in January 1993, featuring a glittering array of Bishop's friends and fellow poets. One of the most memorable remarks arising from that conference was Frank Bidart's observation that Bishop's poems "are in the service of the illusion of directness. They use calculation and art very cunningly to that end." Bishop's former student Mary Jo Salter also recalled Bishop saying of one of her lines "That's *perfect*." Salter of course was thrilled, "And then [Bishop] said, 'So you're going to have to rough it up a bit.' That was a lesson to me."[7]

Over the course of the 1990s, the *Bulletin* chronicled what would prove to be an annual series of events: a sequence of conferences and symposiums centering on or featuring Bishop. These included a major scholarly conference at Vassar College in September 1994, a celebration of Bishop in Great Village, Nova Scotia, in June 1995, a conference on Bishop and John Ashbery at the University of Reading, UK, in July 1996, a major conference on Bishop in Worcester, Massachusetts, the city of Bishop's birth, in 1997, a symposium at Acadia University, in Wolfville, Nova Scotia, in September 1998, and an International Conference and Celebração in Ouro Preto, Brazil, in May 1999. These events of the 1990s were capped by the UK's first all-Bishop conference at the University of Newcastle in November 1999 and a conference and celebration of "Jarrell, Bishop, Lowell & Co." at Case Western Reserve University in Cleveland in May 2000. Five of these conferences – those held in Reading, Worcester, Acadia, Newcastle, and Cleveland – published their proceedings in the form of essay collections. These essays were composed by an international array of poets and scholars, including many from Brazil, Canada, and the UK, and they offered much deeply informed exploration of Bishop's life, art, worlds, and personal and cultural engagements in specific locales and the world at large. And these assemblages of essays formed just one part of the ever-growing critical literature surrounding Bishop, as did the essays in a 1995 special issue of the *Wallace Stevens Journal* that focused on Stevens and Elizabeth Bishop. As Margaret Dickie argued in that issue's introduction, although both Stevens and Bishop were once viewed as aloof figures, each emerged from this issue "as poets refreshed by the lively interchange that these critics have created."[8] It is impossible to summarize here both the dizzying and the eye-opening effects of this rapid succession of Bishop-related events and celebrations. A scholar who attended each of these events – and I believe I missed only one – could not help but come away with an enriched understanding of Bishop's personal and cultural geography and to be swept up, willy-nilly, into that vigorous ongoing dialogue about their beloved poet that would become one of the characteristic features of what Ellis has termed the "first generation" of Bishop scholars. For many of us, the process of total immersion had begun.

In the fourth issue of the *Bulletin*, which appeared in Spring 1994, one correspondent is cited as observing, perhaps a bit ruefully, that "The subject of EB is becoming tremendously massive (more so than I think anyone might have thought even a few years ago)."[9] In that same issue, Richard Flynn's review-essay "Bishop Studies Comes of Age: The Books of 1993," underlined that point and in the process delineated important features of this Bishop *annus mirabilis*. Flynn asserts that "Articles [on Bishop] have appeared at a dizzying rate, but the appearance in 1993 of five new book-length studies confirms Bishop's status as the major poet of her generation."[10] These five books included three critical monographs by Victoria Harrison, Joanne Feit Diehl, and Carole Doreski. Each of these monographs featured a strong biographical element, and each involved a deep dive into Bishop's manuscripts and an exploration in varied terms – with reference, for example, to Kleinian psychoanalysis or pragmatic philosophy – of Bishop's literary and cultural relations. The series of five 1993 volumes also included a groundbreaking collection of essays, *Elizabeth Bishop: Geography of Gender*, edited by Marilyn May Lombardi, and the poet's first full-dress biography, Brett C. Millier's *Elizabeth Bishop: Life and the Memory of It*. The landmark Lombardi collection, which grew in part out of that notable 1991 MLA session and featured in Flynn's words "most of the leading Bishop scholars" then writing, explored, as the title of one of the collection's three sections puts it, questions of "Body, Gender, and Race," along with, as Flynn observes, varied explorations of the "complexities of Bishop's famous 'restraint'" – complexities that revealed, according to Lombardi in the collection's Prologue, "the elements of subversion and gaiety in Bishop's verse."[11] In his recent review of Bishop studies, Ellis rightly calls attention to the continuing importance of Lee Edelman's essay, which urges us to attend to the "cry of female textuality" in Bishop's work. Both Ellis and Flynn draw attention to Barbara Page's germinal essay on Bishop's Key West notebooks, which explores, as Flynn puts it, "Bishop's rejection of 'finality and closure' in favor of 'unofficial and unstable positionings.'" According to Flynn, "Page's account of how Bishop made herself into a poet of 'interstitial situations' is worth the price of the volume alone."

Brett Millier's extremely sound, thorough, and well-researched 1993 biography of Bishop was followed a year later by Gary Fountain and Peter Brazeau's important 1994 *Remembering Elizabeth Bishop: An Oral Biography*. This work, as one blurb put it, "captured, just in time, the memories of people who knew Bishop." Another vital work of 1994 was Robert Giroux's edition *One Art: Letters*. This 650-page selection was a substantial and important contribution to Bishop scholarship, and it began to suggest the sheer amplitude, literary excellence, and self-revelatory quality of Bishop as a letter writer. As subsequent and forthcoming volumes would and will amply prove, Bishop's casual art as a correspondent may be seen as rivaling her perfect art as a poet. It is beyond the scope of this essay to summarize further the extraordinary richness and diversity of Bishop scholarship in the 1990s. By the middle of the decade, Bishop had been almost universally recognized as a great and major poet – and her reputation has only grown with the years. Also by the mid-1990s, Bishop scholarship had clearly met the criteria suggested earlier for a thriving field of author-studies. A substantial and representative (if by no means complete) canon of Bishop's work was now in print. An extensive body of critical literature, already bordering on "massive," was rapidly assembling. Archival access to Bishop's extensive body of manuscripts had been established. These manuscripts had become the basis for ongoing critical study and their importance and volume would continue to expand. A pair of important biographical studies had appeared in the course of the past two years, and had solidified our understand of the relationship between Bishop's life and art. Bibliographical updates were appearing twice-annually in the *Bishop Bulletin*. And a compelling case had been made for Bishop's wide-ranging importance in literary and cultural history. In all of these areas, the scope of Bishop studies would steadily expand with each passing year.

Limitations of space make it impossible for me to comment on the many important critical monographs, group studies, and essay collections featuring Bishop that have appeared from the mid-1990s to the present day. For these, I refer readers to Ellis's comprehensive review of said works in his 2019 introduction to *Reading Elizabeth Bishop*. Instead I will now mention briefly six important editions of Bishop's work that appeared between 2006 and 2011 and then go on to cite, with regrettable brevity, seven important essay collections on Bishop that have appeared or are now forthcoming in the years following Bishop's 2011 centennial. Each of the essays collections responds, in its own way, to these new editions and to our evolving understanding of Bishop as a writer and cultural figure.

The first of these six important editions of Bishop's is the aforementioned *Edgar Allan Poe & The Juke-Box: Uncollected Poems, Drafts and Fragments*, edited by Quinn and published in 2006. This collection offered ready access to about 100 poems and drafts that were, for the most part, unknown to the reading public. Current bibliographic work again proved its value when Quinn privately acknowledged to this author that his "Bishop's Uncollected Poems: A Bibliography," published in the Winter 2000 *Bulletin* with advice from Schwartz and Brazilian scholars Maria Lucia Milleo-Martins and Regina Przybycien, had proved extremely helpful as a source for her annotations.[12] Next to appear, in 2008, was the Library of America's *Elizabeth Bishop: Poems, Prose & Letters*, edited by Lloyd Schwartz with Giroux. This 980-page volume provides the most comprehensive compilation to date of Bishop's poetry and prose, and also provides an extensive selection of her letters, including many not appearing in *One Art*. It provides an excellent single-volume teaching text and a fine starting point for a study of this ever more prolific-seeming author. Also appearing in 2008 from Farrar, Straus and Giroux was *Words in Air: The Complete Correspondence between Elizabeth Bishop and Robert Lowell*, an 850-page volume edited by Travisano with Saskia Hamilton. These three volumes, appearing in such rapid succession, inspired the 2012 essay collection *Elizabeth Bishop in the 21st Century: Reading the New Editions* edited by Cleghorn, Bethany Hicok, and Travisano. This collection featured seventeen essays by leading and rising Bishop critics. It explored, as suggested by its section headings, "Textual Politics," "Self, Politics and Place," "The Poet and her Peers," and "The New Elizabeth Bishop and Her Art." Its "Introduction" argues that these essays make a case for Bishop as a poet "crucially engaged with such vital cultural and political issues as outsiderhood, gender, sexuality, national identity, social class, war, the environment, power relations, and family intimacy and conflict."[13]

After *Elizabeth Bishop in the 21st Century* went to press, but before it appeared in print, Farrar, Straus and Giroux published three new centennial volumes in December 2011: a not-altogether-satisfactory edition entitled *Poems*; a 500-page volume of *Prose* edited by Schwartz containing important new additions to the published canon, while curiously omitting some items that appeared in his excellent Library of America volume; and *Elizabeth Bishop* and *The New Yorker: The Complete Correspondence*, edited by Joelle Biele, a volume of letters that brings to life Bishop's relationship with her principal periodical venue over more than three decades. The appearance within three years of Bishop's complete correspondence with a friend and distinguished fellow poet and with a famous magazine began to establish as its own distinctive genre books of Bishop's complete correspondence in dialogue with an important other. Volumes of Bishop's correspondence with Marianne Moore and with May Swenson are now in preparation from Farrar, Straus and Giroux, and we may also expect her *Notebooks* edited by Alice Quinn, which establish yet another prolific Bishop genre and offer further insight into Bishop's process of "becoming." These new editions will no doubt excite further waves of critical response from the ever-growing community of Bishop scholars, while helping the published Bishop canon continue to burgeon, with no end in sight.

Two years after the appearance of *Elizabeth Bishop in the 21st Century*, a new and important essay collection arrived on the scene, the 2014 *Cambridge Companion to Elizabeth Bishop*, edited by Cleghorn and Ellis. This volume presents essays, once again by an assortment of established and rising scholars, that explore in well-judged but frequently provocative ways such issues, among others, as biography, politics, race, class and gender, the natural world, poetic tradition, the visual arts, and posthumous publications. Next to appear, in 2015, was an essay collection edited by Ellis titled *Letter Writing Among Poets: From William Wordsworth to Elizabeth Bishop*. This collection featured two essays centered specifically on *Words in Air*, along with many others that engage with Bishop as a pivotal figure. Overall, the volume makes the case that correspondence is not necessarily an ancillary genre. It may have major literary value in its own right. In any case, the fact that Bishop was one of the great letter writers of the twentieth century no longer remains in doubt.

As this piece on Bishop studies is in the editorial process of going to press, two additional collections of essays devoted to Bishop have appeared: *Elizabeth Bishop and the Literary Archive* is a book of essays edited by Hicok that grew out of a 2017 National Endowment for the Humanities Summer Seminar she directed at the Bishop archive in the Vassar College Library. This deeply researched and imaginative collection explores the complex significance of archival study for Bishop scholarship and illustrates again the attraction Bishop studies feels toward the creative possibilities of the trope of total immersion. The second essay collection that came out before this volume's publication is *Elizabeth Bishop and the Music of Literature*, edited by Cleghorn and published by Palgrave Pivot. This collection grew out of a pair of 2017 panels on Bishop at the American Literature Association Conference, and it explores the many ways in which music and poetry intertwine in Bishop's writing. Finally, there is the present volume, *Elizabeth Bishop in Context*, a title most apropos of my own essay, because it was precisely by learning to read Bishop's work *in context* that Bishop studies emerged as the steadily expanding and influential international field that we know today.

Notes

1. Jonathan Ellis, "Introduction: Incompatible Bishops?", in *Reading Elizabeth Bishop: An Edinburgh Companion*, ed. Jonathan Ellis (Edinburgh: Edinburgh University Press, 2019), 1.
2. David Kalstone, *Five Temperaments* (New York: Oxford University Press, 1977), 12.
3. James E. B. Breslin, *From Modern to Contemporary* (Chicago: University of Chicago Press, 1984), 3–4.
4. Elizabeth Bishop, "Foreword" to Candace MacMahon, *Elizabeth Bishop: A Bibliography, 1927–1979* (Charlottesville: University Press of Virginia, 1980), ix.

5. "Why an Elizabeth Bishop Society?" *Elizabeth Bishop Bulletin* (hereafter *EBB*) 1.1 (Spring 1992), 1. Web, accessed July 1, 2019.
6. Ibid.
7. "Key West Literary Seminar, January 7–10, 1993," *EBB* 2.1 (Summer 1993), 2.
8. Margaret Dickie, "Introduction," *Wallace Stevens Journal* 19.2 (Fall 1995), 114.
9. "The Growth of Bishop Studies," *EBB* 2.2 (Winter 1993), 1.
10. Richard Flynn, "Bishop Studies Comes of Age: The Books of 1993," *EBB* 2.2 (Winter 1993), 2.
11. Marilyn May Lombardi, "Prologue: Another Way of Seeing," in *Elizabeth Bishop: The Geography of Gender* (Charlottesville: University of Virginia Press, 1993), 7.
12. Thomas Travisano, "Bishop's Uncollected Poems: A Bibliography," *EBB* 8.2 (Winter 2000), 2–4.
13. "Introduction," in *Elizabeth Bishop in the 21st Century: Reading the New Editions* (Charlottesville: University of Virginia Press, 2012), 2.

CHAPTER 33

Criticism and Reviews

Jonathan Ellis

> "Most of my life I've been lucky with reviews. But at the very end they often say 'The best poetry by a woman in this decade, or year, or month.' Well, what's that worth?"
>
> (Elizabeth Bishop, 1977)[1]

A year before her death, Bishop asked Mildred Nash, a former student of hers at Harvard, to help her re-arrange her library in exchange for a "first crack" at Bishop's discards and duplicates.[2] In a short memoir, Nash provides a remarkably frank biographical study of Bishop via her bookshelves. Nash recalls beginning in the living room with Bishop's travel books, before moving on to art, philosophy, fiction, psychology, a section dedicated solely to Octavio Paz, and cookbooks. After lunch and coffee, they turned to the study where Bishop kept her best books: "dictionaries, rhyming dictionaries, George Herbert, [and] an annotated edition of the Opies' *Nursery Rhyme Book*."[3] Finally, they arrived at the bedroom, "the inner sanctum of her library. Here she kept some of her treasures: her field guides to birds, wallflowers, seashores, rocks, and the like. Almost all of Beatrix Potters' volumes [. . .] Here were biographies galore, a full shelf and a half from ceiling almost to floor. Lewis Carroll had two biographies, as did Edward Lear."[4] Nash is an equally astute observer of omissions: "Significantly missing among her library holdings were books of criticism, an area for which she seemed to have little use. The few such books she kept, written by friends, were tucked in among their authors' more respectable volumes of poetry and fiction."[5]

Nash makes assumptions about Bishop's attitude to literary criticism via her bookshelf choices, assumptions that are not necessarily incorrect if we cross-reference this essay with what we know from her letters in which she frequently complains to friends about being misread or misunderstood by reviewers. In a letter from 1975, in response to a mysteriously named correspondent called Miss Pierson, Bishop advised her not to read "too much *about* poetry [. . .] Prosody – metrics – etc. are fascinating – but they all came *afterwards*, obviously. And I always ask my writing class NOT to read criticism" (*OA* 596). Asking her writing class not to read criticism doesn't mean that she didn't read criticism herself. Dana Gioia, another student of Bishop's at Harvard, qualifies Nash's opinion with the statement that "Bishop did make a few exceptions: there were critics whom we were allowed to read without danger."[6] William Empson was one exception, Randall Jarrell a second, Helen Vendler a third. "When she liked a critic's work," Gioia points out, "she liked it as intensely as the poems it talked about."[7] References to Empson, for example, occur throughout her correspondence. In a 1963 letter to Lowell she writes of admiring "his prose-style as a critic more than anyone else's. He manages to say the hard-to-express in colloquial language with just the right idiosyncratic twist to it" (*WIA* 480). Jarrell was a friend who Bishop remembered after his death as "difficult, touchy and oversensitive to criticism," but also "the best and more generous critic of poetry I have known" (*Pr* 354). Vendler was another friend whose poetry criticism Bishop rated highly, perhaps because of their shared love of George Herbert.

As a student at Vassar, she was an avid reader of modernist critical prose, including essays by T. S. Eliot and Gertrude Stein. She refers to Stein's essay, "Composition as Explanation" (1925), in her own essay, "Time's Andromedas," and in 1934 returned to Vassar specifically to hear Stein's lecture, "Portraits I Have Written and What I Think of Repetition, Whether It Exists or No." In Paris a few years later, she heard Stein lecture again, this time on "Entity vs Identity." Later in life, Bishop also praised Virginia Woolf's critical prose, describing *Three Guineas* as "a wonderful little book."[8]

The fact that, to employ Nash's words, criticism had "little use" to Bishop does not necessarily mean that it was of no use at all, more that its use value was hidden, often in plain sight in her most well-known lines. Apparently useless objects, it is worth remembering, often become of use in Bishop's writing. This is particularly the case in her last book, *Geography III*, where she frequently ponders the value of old, overlooked or lost things, including her own earlier work. An uncle's painting might look "useless" to begin with – "a minor family relic" – before she realises what she is actually holding in her hands (*P* 196). Criticism in all its forms and genres performs the same function in Bishop's imagination, something that is consistently present but rarely admitted to being of use. It performs this function from the very beginning of her adult life, not just as a teacher of poetry, but also as a writer of poetry too.

M. W. Croll's essay, "The Baroque Style in Prose," was, for example, an important touchstone throughout her career (critics are fond, perhaps *too* fond, of citing Croll's phrase, "their purpose [. . .] was to portray, not a thought, but a mind thinking" (*OA* 12) in relation to Bishop), as more generally were the "resources of prose," as her friend Howard Moss pointed out in a short review of *Questions of Travel* in 1966[9] and Vidyan Ravinthiran demonstrates at length in his book, *Elizabeth Bishop's Prosaic*. Ravinthiran proposes several ways in which Bishop's poetry might be described as prosaic, including multiple allusions in her work to literary criticism. He suggests, for instance, that the phrase "dazzling dialectic" in "Santerém" (*P* 207) may owe something to M. H. Abrams's use of the same words in *The Mirror and the Lamp*.[10] Art criticism, as William Benton, Peggy Samuels, and Linda Anderson prove, informed her thinking about colour, line, perspective, and scale. Her reading of *The History of Impressionism* in 1947 affected her thinking about poetry, at least if her letters to Dr. Ruth Foster are anything to go by. In them, she admits to a fear of repetition that reading Edgar Degas's thoughts on art as recapitulation helped her overcome: "I feel that in poetry now there is no reason why I should make such an effort to make each poem an isolated event, that they go on into each other or overlap etc., and are really all one long poem anyway."[11] Did the experience of reading art criticism help her conceive of a poetry collection differently? Certainly, the books she published after this, especially *Questions of Travel* and *Geography III*, read less like individual poems artificially brought together in a book and more like carefully composed variations on an overall theme, what Thom Gunn, writing about "The Moose" though I think it applies equally to the whole volume, describes as "*connected units*" like "the houses in a friendly village."[12]

Bishop drew on other critical fields too, not least architecture and music. At least two of her "three loved houses" (Samambaia near Petrópolis and Casa Mariana in Ouro Preto) were architectural masterpieces. She lived with an architect for nearly two decades and in the mid-1950s helped Henrique Mindlin translate his book, *Modern Architecture in Brazil* (1956), into English. In 1958, she travelled to Brazil's new capital, Brasília, with several illustrious guests, including the author Aldous Huxley. Bishop's account of the trip, "A New Capital, Aldous Huxley, and Some Indians" (1958), is as much about the new city's architecture as her famous co-traveller. She particularly objected to architect Oscar Niemeyer's Palace of the Dawn in which the servants' quarters were hid underground: "Niemeyer's response to the flat empty spaces of Brasília has been this transparent, gracefully supported, but essentially severe, box [. . .] his solution of practical problems seems to have been the same: put them underneath, or underground, like a lazy housewife shoving household gear out of sight under a deceptively well-made bed" (*Pr* 304). It is a pity Bishop's essay is not better known. Three editors read it at *The New Yorker*. All of them thought the essay started well but disliked its architectural descriptions (*NYr* 208). I do not share this view though I accept the title is misleading: Aldous Huxley is hardly present at all. What is here, however, is a sophisticated account of Brazilian architecture that shows Bishop's intimate knowledge of the forms and structures of modern buildings and the extent to which they reflect the connections and disconnections between families, communities, and nations, a thought process that, like her reading of art criticism, finds its way into the poems she was drafting at the same time, poems like 'The Riverman" (1959), "Electrical Storm" (1959), and "Song for the Rainy Season" (1960). There is, in other words, a porousness between the criticism she was reading and sometimes writing, if not necessarily publishing, and the poems she was drafting, sending off for publication and largely seeing successfully into print.

Bishop's own poems might be seen as sly forms of literary criticism too, particularly when she misquotes or misremembers another author's work. We find, in order of their composition, a man in a mirror who appears to have swapped places with Tennyson's lady and as a consequence gone mad (*P* 11–12); an unnamed, possibly unhinged poet whose circumstances resemble those of Ezra Pound (*P* 131–3); a sandpiper who is a "student of Blake" but doesn't recall a single line of his writing (*P* 129); and a Crusoe who has absorbed Romantic thinking about nature but can't complete Wordsworth's most famous poem (*P* 184). In each of these poems Bishop evokes, revises, and sometimes parodies a canonical work by a male author, displaying little respect for respectable verse. Poems allow her a safe space – a space for irony, transformation, wit – in which to say things she could not write in conventional literary criticism.

When Bishop began her literary career properly at Vassar, she wrote almost as much criticism as poetry. Three long pieces of prose stand out from this period: "Time's Andromedas" (1933), "Gerard Manley Hopkins: Notes on Timing in His Poetry" (1934), and "Dimensions for a Novel" (1934). Reading them today, one is struck both by the precociousness of Bishop's choice of authors (a cast list of both the modernists we might expect – Proust, Woolf, Joyce, Eliot – *and* those often left out: Mann, Richardson, Stein) and by the perspicacity of her overall arguments, arguments she sustains confidently and persuasively in each long essay. In "Time's Andromedas," for example, she speculates not just on time patterns in Victorian and early twentieth-century novels but also on what the novel might do with the subject of time next:

> Is it possible that there may be a sort of *experience-time*, or the time pattern in which realities reach us, quite different from the hour after hour, day after day kind? [. . .] If you've seen boys dive after pennies you know how the coins sink shimmering to the bottom at unequal rates, and the diving boys sometimes pick them up halfway down, or even get there before the coins do. Why should the days retreat behind me systematically – Friday, Thursday, Wednesday, Tuesday – and not any other way? why not Wednesday, Friday, Tuesday, if they seem that way to me? (*PPL* 659)

There is much to admire here, above and beyond its prefiguration of the language of open-endedness we are familiar with from mid-career poems like "Over 2,000 Illustrations and a Complete Concordance," a language she is at least a decade away from perfecting in poetry at this point. Concluding her discussion of tempo and timing in Richardson and Stein's work and how the next generation of writers "will discover new beauty in breaking up this most ancient of patterns" (*PPL* 659), Bishop declares herself a prominent member of this new generation through the establishment of her own prose rhythms that advance and retreat across the page similar to the image of boys diving after pennies. Hers is a criticism content not just to observe what it sees but also to predict what might happen next. What a pity she rarely spoke in this voice again.

What we find instead are brief, curt, often irascible statements about the genre of literary criticism, written not from the perspective of a critic, or indeed poet-critic as she might have identified herself in 1933–4, but from the viewpoint of a poet. This is not to say she didn't try to write long form criticism again. In 1950 she struggled all summer to write an essay for John Ciardi who was assembling an anthology with commentary called *Mid-Century American Poets*. Ciardi had asked for a five-thousand-word essay; Bishop managed just two hundred words, including the following diatribe against poetry criticism: "The analysis of poetry is growing more and more pretentious and deadly. After a session with a few of the highbrow magazines one doesn't want to look at a poem for weeks, much less start writing one" (*PPL* 687). Reading comments like this, one might be forgiven for assuming Bishop had never attempted literary criticism herself or that it had been a failure, when, as we have seen, this was clearly not the case. Was she embarrassed by what she had already written or frustrated she couldn't do more?

It is difficult to tell when Bishop definitely began to turn against literary criticism, her own included. She continued to publish short book reviews throughout her career, albeit infrequently. In later years, she was also commissioned to write blurbs and memoir pieces. In a slightly out of character gesture, she asked *The New Yorker* about becoming their poetry reviewer at least twice, describing it in a letter to as the "one critical job I could do" (*NYr* 312). To Katherine White in 1956, she described *The New Yorker* as "the only publication I'd like to write a review for. For one thing, Miss Bogan's reviews only mention those books that really seem to be of some relevance; for another, they are brief reviews and don't attempt to write like Kenneth Burke every time, the way reviews in the little 'magazines' do, – Burke, or Empson, or imitation Jarrell – which I've always felt was unnecessary" (*NYr* 175). When Bogan died in 1969, Bishop offered her services again, this time to Howard Moss, welcoming the fact that "Louise didn't have to discuss a lot of books she *didn't* like, or make the kind of attack-in-general that I dislike so much" (*NYr* 312). Astonishingly, given her less than compelling curriculum vitae as a reviewer (she was fifty-nine years old at the time she sent the second letter), Bishop convinced Moss to appoint her but never filed a single review, a fact both parties decided it was best to forget.

In between these two letters, we find a less confident Bishop, here writing to Jarrell: "I am NOT an articulate critic [. . .] I don't really try to be, since I read for my own pleasure and comfort and curiosity only – so I just get intuitions here & there, and love this and am repelled by that, and let it go" (*OA* 434). Michael O'Neill, in an essay on Bishop's literary criticism, describes this sentence as "a mini-manifesto, as much in its manner as its matter,"[13] a gloss I agree with, though I wonder if it doesn't downplay the achievements Bishop had already made as a young essayist. O'Neill identifies Bishop's literary criticism not in these essays but in "her scattered observations about poetry, chiefly in letters and brief prose pieces."[14] The influence of criticism on her thinking is, as I have shown earlier in this chapter, almost everywhere.

Early introductions and reviews by friends who became critics or critics who became friends perhaps inevitably helped establish the terms by which Bishop's poetry was interpreted during her lifetime and how it is interpreted today as well. In one sense, as Bishop acknowledged, she was "lucky with reviews," lucky that poets like Moore and Lowell thought highly of her work and were willing to say so in print. In another sense, she was "unlucky," since this praise attracted envy and resentment. Assessing *Questions of Travel* in 1965, Sheridan Baker complained about "a world-wide reviewer's pact never to say anything bad about Elizabeth Bishop"[15] (before going on to do so!). The near universal praise of her peers identified Bishop as an establishment author, a safe choice to appoint as Poetry Consultant or award the Pulitzer Prize. Her politics and sexuality actually put Bishop's job at risk in Washington but this wasn't known at the time. To Bishop's evident discomfort and frustration, she was compared and contrasted with the same narrow range of poets: Moore at the beginning of her career, Lowell towards the middle and end. As David Kalstone proved in his subtle account of how Bishop became Bishop in part through her relationships with Moore and Lowell, there was obviously some truth to this narrative but it didn't tell the whole story or perhaps even the half of it.

Moore was almost certainly the first critic to call Bishop "modest," an epithet that most critics now rightly view as patronising. That occurred in her overwhelmingly positive review of *North & South* for *The Nation* in 1946 titled "A Modest Expert" in which she announced that "at last we have a prize book that has no creditable mannerisms."[16] Moore's first comments on Bishop's poetry in print (there were of course thousands of words exchanged between the two poets in private) came in 1935 in her introduction to a selection of early work. Much of what Moore says about Bishop's early poems is astonishingly perceptive, not least for twenty-first century readers of her animal poems. This is the opening line of her introduction: "In trying to reveal the clash of elements that we are – the intellectual, the animal; the blunt, the ingenious; the impudent, the imaginative – one dare not be dogmatic."[17] Moore identifies Bishop's influences accurately (Donne and Hopkins) as well as the precise combination of intimacy and secrecy that characterise her best work: "One asks a great deal of an author – that he should not be haphazard but considered in his mechanics, that he should not induce you to be interested in what is restrictedly private but that that there should be the self-portrait."[18] Bishop was lucky to have Moore on her side, unlucky to discover most critics skipping over the substance of her analysis. In mid-century America, especially for women poets, "modesty" (not "mechanics") was unfortunately the word that stuck.

Randall Jarrell's review of *North & South* in *Partisan Review* was more or less contemporary with Moore's. Jarrell praises, as Moore did, Bishop's moral attractiveness, a term of praise one rarely finds in contemporary reviews nowadays. His aphoristic statement – "all her poems have written underneath, *I have seen it*"[19] – remains one of the most repeated critical phrases about Bishop's writing, justifiably so in my opinion since it acknowledges the importance of observation in Bishop's poetry and of equal importance, the presence and signature of a lyric voice. If Moore was the first critic to call Bishop "modest," Jarrell was probably the first to consider her voice "calm." In her best work, he explained, "restraint, calm, and proportion are implicit in every detail of organization and workmanship. Instead of crying with justice, 'This is a world in which no one can get along,' Miss Bishop's poems show that it is barely but perfectly possible – has been, that is, for her."[20] Like "modesty," this was another false impression that stuck.

In 1963, when Anne Stevenson contacted Bishop to request information about her for the monograph she was about to begin writing, Bishop was fed up of being compared to Moore, fed up of what she saw as critics simply repeating each other:

> I am rather weary of always being compared to, or coupled with, Marianne – and I think she is utterly weary of it, too! We have been very good friends for thirty years now – but except for 1 or 2 early poems of mine and perhaps some early preferences in subject matter, neither she nor I can see why reviewers always drag her in with me. For one thing – I've always been an umpty-umpty poet with a traditional 'ear.' Perhaps it is just another proof that ~~critics and~~ reviewers really very rarely pay much attention to what they're reading *& just repeat each other* – (*Pr* 393)

Bishop's letters to Stevenson are not literary criticism or, if they are, they adopt a chatty tone more reminiscent of Romantic poets like Coleridge or Keats than the impersonal voice expected of reviewers in magazines of the time like *The New Yorker*. Bishop went through a self-confessed "Shelley period, around 16,"[21] as is clear from an early letter to Donald Stanford in which she joked that he was probably "the first person to call me Elizabeth – excepting a couple of aunts. I'm always just called Bishop or Bish or Bysshe" (*OA* 13). Whatever we call the genre of such interventions (*ars poetica*? epistolary criticism?), they were clearly attempts on Bishop's part to influence the way her work would come to be interpreted not just by Stevenson in the 1960s but by critics afterwards too. She was writing to Stevenson *and* to future critics. The same is, I think, true of many of her letter writing relationships, including those we know about (Moore and Lowell) and those we have only read in abridged form (May Swenson, Ilse Barker, James Merrill, Frank Bidart, her Aunt Grace).

By way of conclusion I'd like briefly to discuss Lowell's lengthy review of *North & South* in *Sewanee Review* in 1947, juxtaposing it with statements

Bishop made about literary criticism in general in the years afterwards. Lowell, like other reviewers before him, couldn't help comparing Bishop to a particular poet, declaring "Bishop [. . .] unimaginable without Moore."[22] Where Jarrell considered her "calm," Lowell considered her "cool".[23] The oddest moment in the review comes towards the end when Lowell offers the following teacher-like verdict on individual poems:

> About ten of its thirty poems are failures. Another ten are either satisfactory as wholes, or very slight. This leaves "Roosters" and "The Fish," large and perfect, and, outside of Marianne Moore, the best poems that I know of written by a woman in this century. The first of her "Songs for a Colored Singer" is serious light verse; it is of the same qualities as MacNeice's "Bagpipe Music" and Auden's wonderful "Refugee Blues." In roughly descending order, "The Monument," "The Man-Moth," "The Weed," "Cirque d'Hiver," "Large Bad Picture," "Sleeping on the Ceiling," the second "Song for a Colored Singer," "Jerónimo's House," "Florida," "Seascape," and "Quai d'Orléans" are all wonderfully successful and good.[24]

This is a very peculiar form of praise, if one considers it praise at all. To me, it seems gendered, patronising and, in places, plain rude. If Bishop considered it such, she did not say so at the time, at least not explicitly. On the contrary, in only her second-ever letter to Lowell, she admitted to being "quite overwhelmed" by the experience of reading it, praising his attempt to find "consistency in the individual poems [. . .]. I suppose for pride's sake I should take some sort of stand about the adverse criticisms, but I agreed with some of them only too well – I suppose no critic is ever really as harsh as oneself" (*WIA* 5). It is a matter of debate whether one is in fact one's own worst critic. Lowell doesn't hold much back here.

Although Lowell's review didn't affect their growing friendship – if anything it seems to have emboldened Bishop to be equally direct when she found something amiss in his poetry – it did affect her view of literary criticism, perhaps permanently. From this date onwards, she has hardly a single good word to say about criticism, particularly literary criticism. After initially praising Anne Stevenson's critical book on her writing, a book she had ghost-authored in some respects, at least in terms of identifying her influences, she spent the rest of her life bad-mouthing it to friends. In a letter to Anny Baumann, for example, she dismissed it as "badly written, out-of-date, and full of mistakes" (*OA* 601). She particularly objected to Stevenson's employment of Wittgenstein: "I've never ever read him. I don't know *anything* about his philosophy."[25] Interviews allowed her to correct what she believed to be critical mistakes. She hated being called anti-feminist for refusing to appear in anthologies of women poets. She objected, no doubt remembering Jarrell and Lowell's comments, to being thought a "calm person": "I'm not a calm person at all. [. . .] There are times when I really start to wonder what holds me together – awful times. But I feel a responsibility, while I'm here at least, to *appear* calm and collected."[26]

Lowell's words, above all others, stayed with Bishop, as perhaps did her own ambivalent reply thanking him for his "*attempt*" (my emphasis) to find "any general drift or consistency in the individual poems" (*WIA* 5). In an unfinished essay from the late 1950s/early 1960s, she announced the following: "I'm not a critic. Critics can't rest easy until they have put poets in descending orders of merit; they change the lists every night before they go to bed. The post doesn't have to be consistent" (*Pr* 329). Who but Lowell put poets (and of course poems) in (Lowell's own words) "roughly descending order"? In the famous "Darwin" letter to Stevenson, begun in January 1964, she is at it again, distinguishing her own practice explicitly from that of Lowell: "Criticism is important, 'weeding has to be done' (R. Lowell), but *I* don't want to do it. I feel that art would probably struggle along without it in very much the same way, probably. I trust my own taste and usually don't want to explain it – at the same time I occasionally wish I could explain it better" (*Pr* 412–13). This is probably Bishop's most nuanced statement on the purpose of criticism. Although she accepts it is an "important" job, one that friends like Lowell were happy to take on, she worries with good reason that it will interfere with her own writing. In its place, we find the expression of "taste," a word that acknowledges individual biases and preferences but doesn't promise to be objective.

Bishop finished relatively little long-form criticism after graduation from Vassar but what she did complete both there and afterwards is audacious, original, and witty. She engaged with and incorporated the ideas and words of literary critics into her poetry throughout her career, rebuffing reductive assessments of her writing as "calm" and "modest." If it is difficult to find her adopting a consistent position on criticism, we should not be surprised. Consistency was something she consistently avoided.

Notes

1. Elizabeth Bishop, "A Conversation with Elizabeth Bishop," in *Conversations with Elizabeth Bishop*, ed. George Monteiro (Jackson: University Press of Mississippi, 1996), 92.
2. Mildred J. Nash, "Studying with Miss Bishop," *Conversations*, 134.

3. Ibid., 137.
4. Ibid.
5. Ibid.
6. Dana Gioia, "Studying with Miss Bishop," *Conversations*, 147.
7. Ibid.
8. Bishop, "A Conversation," *Conversations*, 92.
9. Howard Moss, "All Praise," *Kenyon Review* 28.2 (March 1966), 259.
10. Vidyan Ravinthiran, *Elizabeth Bishop's Prosaic* (Lewisburg: Bucknell University Press, 2015), 186.
11. Elizabeth Bishop, Letters to Ruth Foster (1947), Vassar Archive, folder 118.33.
12. Thom Gunn, "Out of the Box," *Shelf Life* (London: Faber and Faber, 1994), 84.
13. Michael O'Neill, "'Thinking with One's Feelings': Elizabeth Bishop's Literary Criticism," in *Reading Elizabeth Bishop: An Edinburgh Companion*, ed. Jonathan Ellis (Edinburgh: Edinburgh University Press, 2019), 241.
14. Ibid., 237.
15. Cited by Brett C. Millier, *Elizabeth Bishop: Life and the Memory of It* (Berkeley: University of California Press, 1993), 372.
16. Marianne Moore, "A Modest Expert," in *Elizabeth Bishop and Her Art*, ed. Lloyd Schwartz and Sybil P. Estess (Ann Arbor: The University of Michigan Press, 1983), 179.
17. Moore, "Archaically New," *Elizabeth Bishop*, 175.
18. Ibid., 176.
19. Randall Jarrell, "On *North & South*," *Elizabeth Bishop*, 180.
20. Ibid., 181.
21. Bishop, "An Interview with Ashley Brown," *Conversations*, 21.
22. Robert Lowell, "Thomas, Bishop, and Williams," *Elizabeth Bishop*, 187.
23. Ibid., 186.
24. Ibid., 188.
25. Bishop, "Elizabeth Bishop: Conversations and Class Notes," *Conversations*, 43.
26. Ibid.

CHAPTER 34

"My Saving Grace": On Editing Elizabeth Bishop

Lloyd Schwartz

Between 1976, three years before Elizabeth Bishop died, and the centennial of her birth in 2011, I was directly involved with editing three books that included work by and about her and indirectly with the editing of two other editions. In the course of those years there was a tectonic shift from how difficult it was to get a publisher interested in a book about Bishop to the current flood of new publications.

My first work on Bishop was my Ph.D. thesis. I was not the first young scholar to write one, and Bishop was not my first topic. But by the time I started writing about her, we had already become close. And in at least one crucial way, she rescued me.

In 1968, I had begun a dissertation, and after seven years of arguing with an unsympathetic advisor, with only one chapter completed, I shelved the project. When the college where I was teaching was about to be shut down, teaching jobs were scarce, and it seemed as if my academic career was about to end. I couldn't bear ending this part of my life without a terminal degree. But how could I finish a Ph.D. without changing my advisor, which also meant having to change my topic. But to what? The only figure I could think of who really demanded further study was Bishop, especially since the only substantial critical work on her (a 1966 monograph by Anne Stevenson) was already a decade out of date. I knew I couldn't proceed without Bishop's approval, but knowing how much she disliked discussing her poems with her friends, I wasn't optimistic.

Her first response was classic Bishop. Did I really think there was enough to write about? Her second question was more pointed: Would I finish it? Why would anyone consent to a project all too likely to get abandoned (like my old thesis)? Later, I came to regard her question not as self-protective but of maternal concern. I gave her my word that if she agreed, I would finish it. Astonishingly, she then offered to meet regularly with me, specifically to answer any questions I might have. I knew her well enough to understand the generosity of her offer. I may not have been the first person to write a Ph.D. thesis on Bishop, but I was certainly the first one she ever volunteered to help.

The questions she was willing to answer were essentially factual. My bibliography would include pieces she had published under a pseudonym or anonymously – items few others could have known. She was also willing – even eager – to describe the circumstances behind various poems: where they took place or whom they were about. One of my favorite stories was about the comic rhyme in the second of the "Songs for a Colored Singer": "I'm going to go and take the bus / And find someone monogamous" (*P* 48). She was tempted, she confessed, to write "mo-NA-gamous," since that was how her cleaning woman had pronounced it, but she was afraid it sounded condescending. She told me about the rows of ESSO cans in "Filling Station," how "SO – SO – SO" was what one said to calm a horse. But any questions about interpretation she dismissed with a "But it's obvious!"

I completed my dissertation in 1976. Bishop was in the hospital when I presented her with a bound copy. She told me reading it cheered her up. *"That Sense of Constant Re-Adjustment": Elizabeth Bishop's North & South* (with the first comprehensive Bishop bibliography) was selected in 1987 for the Garland series of "outstanding dissertations in American and English language and literature."

The year 1976 was a watershed year in Bishop studies. Sybil Estess, who had recently completed her own Bishop dissertation at Syracuse University and was teaching at the University of Houston, was planning an ambitious Bishop celebration for the Modern Language Association convention at the Americana Hotel in New York. She invited me to give a paper, along with other young Bishop scholars including Edward Hirsch, Willard Spiegelman, and herself, on a morning panel. Later, Bishop herself would read, mostly from *Geography III*, just out. Following her would be another panel, this one with more established academics, and then a performance of Elliott Carter's recent Bishop song cycle, *A Mirror on Which to Dwell.* Bishop preferred to forego the panels. It was my job to retrieve her, in time for the music, from the Stage Deli, across Seventh Avenue from the hotel, where she was having her favorite corned-beef hash with her friends Arthur Gold and Robert Fizdale.

After the conference, Estess assembled a festschrift of all these MLA papers. Although there had never been a collection of essays on Bishop, no publisher was interested, even with several formidable scholars among the contributors. Discouraged, Estess asked me if I would take over the project. But I knew there had to be changes. Some of the papers had disappointed me. And since there had never been such a collection before, why should it be limited only to academic essays? Of course, I wanted the strongest selection of recent critical work: Octavio Paz, Helen Vendler, Robert Pinsky, Frank Bidart, David Kalstone, and Spiegelman, with strong new pieces by David Lehman, Bonnie Costello, Penelope Laurans, and Alan Williamson.

Then I organized a chronological miscellany of reviews (including Robert Lowell's long-forgotten review of *North & South*, which triggered his lifelong friendship with Bishop and remains one of the most prescient discussions of her poetry), blurbs, and other statements about Bishop, including "Invitation to Miss Elizabeth Bishop," the humorously pointed homage poet William Meredith read at the MLA. I requested contributions from Harold Bloom and James Merrill (both well-known Bishop admirers). Bloom responded with a foreword and James Merrill sent me a witty verse encomium he called "Her Craft." I also thought it would be crucial to include a section of Bishop's own writing, dazzling excerpts (I was sure these would all eventually appear complete in a volume of Bishop's collected prose) from essays dating back to her undergraduate days, along with reviews, an unpublished poem, and other documents – none ever collected and all virtually unknown; plus two recent interviews with Ashley Brown and George Starbuck (both from 1977).

I retitled the collection *Elizabeth Bishop and Her Art.*

Bishop was extremely helpful. She told me which early pieces she liked most and pointed me to pieces I hadn't known about. She not only gave me permission to include the teasing, self-knowing verse she inscribed in a book for Frank Bidart, she even gave it a "Wordsworthian" title ("Lines Written in a Copy of *Fannie Farmer's Boston Cooking School Cookbook,* given to Frank Bidart"). I wanted this collection to provide both serious new criticism and an illuminating context. I hoped it would reveal a more surprising and complex writer than the one most people knew.

I thought the perfect home for this volume would be Cornell University Press, which had recently published a critical collection on John Ashbery and was about to do one on James Merrill. One of the Cornell reviewers wrote an extremely favorable report expressing an urgent need for such a volume. But the other report was shockingly negative – and a complete fabrication, a total misrepresentation of the contents. Who would do such a thing? I replied to this slander with a three-page single-spaced refutation, but the editor at Cornell insisted that the press required two positive reports and refused to send it out to a third reviewer.

Then nothing.

And then Bishop died.

But the winds were beginning to shift. In 1982, I received a postcard from Donald Hall (whom I didn't know). He told me he was starting a new series for the University of Michigan Press called Under Discussion. He had heard about my Bishop collection and asked if it was still available. He knew it was what he wanted to begin his new series, sight unseen. Of course, he eventually read it and liked it. But by 1983, a volume on Bishop had become a literary necessity. In 1990, Harold Bloom published his own Bishop collection, but sadly most of what he included had already appeared in mine – even his own foreword!

Bishop's reputation kept growing. After her death, Farrar, Straus and Giroux planned a new edition of her poetry and the first collection of her prose. Robert Giroux asked me to be an "editorial advisor" for both *Complete Poems, 1927–1979* (1983) and *Collected Prose* (1984).

I had reservations about both of these.

Bishop herself had overseen her first *Complete Poems*, and won the 1970 National Book Award for Poetry. She made one significant departure from the way her collections first appeared. In her 1965 book *Questions of Travel*, perhaps following Robert Lowell's decision to include his autobiographical prose piece "91 Revere Street" in his landmark *Life Studies* six years earlier, she gave her own autobiographical story "In the Village" a pivotal position. But she omitted it in her *Complete Poems*. Was she too timid to include a prose work in a collection called *Complete Poems*? Or did she want to save it for a possible collection of her stories – an idea she always had at the back of her mind? She later confessed some regrets about this omission.

Giroux's *Complete Poems 1927–1979* essentially repeated Bishop's earlier format, adding the poems from *Geography III*, her final volume; the four major poems she published after that; and short sections of "uncollected" and "occasional" poems, "poems written in youth," and translations. I loved the new cover, which reproduced one of Bishop's own watercolors, but regretted that Giroux had not restored "In the Village" to its original place at the midpoint of *Questions of Travel*. And – even more damaging – he removed her translation of Octavio Paz's poem about Joseph Cornell, "Objects & Apparitions" (a translation Paz himself considered better than his own Spanish and the only translation Bishop ever included in any of her collections), from its strategic place near the end of *Geography III*, where it connected to and commented on the poems around it, and plunked it down among a group of unrelated and weaker Paz poems in the new section of translations – a posthumous change clearly not Bishop's intention.

A year later, I was even more frustrated with the new *Collected Prose*, in which Giroux essentially limited "prose" to only "fiction" or "memoir." I had mistakenly assumed this would include far more of Bishop's uncollected prose pieces.

Then in 2000 Robert Giroux asked me to be his co-editor for an extensive new Bishop volume for the Library of America, a publication he negotiated. This would be the first Library of America volume devoted to a woman poet – twenty-five years after *Elizabeth Bishop and Her Art* became the first critical anthology devoted to Bishop.

I immediately started working on *Elizabeth Bishop: Poems, Prose, and Letters*, which ultimately didn't appear until 2008 because of a contractual obligation with Farrar, Straus and Giroux to wait until after the publication of *Edgar Allan Poe & The Juke-Box*, Alice Quinn's edition of Bishop's "uncollected poems, drafts, and fragments," which everyone knew would be a major turning point in Bishop studies (though few predicted would arouse such controversy).

I felt strongly that I did not want this new collection simply to repeat old decisions – even if some of those decisions had been made by Bishop herself. Essentially, I wanted to show readers what none of the previous "complete" collections did: her volumes of poetry as she had first conceived them (although I would keep the small changes she made in later printings of individual poems). This meant restoring one poem, "The Mountain" (one of the first poems she wrote in Brazil, which she first published in *The New Yorker*), to its original place in *A Cold Spring*, though she had chosen not to reprint it. It meant keeping "In the Village" as the fulcrum between the "Brazil" and "Elsewhere" sections of *Questions of Travel.* And it meant restoring the Paz translation to its rightful place in *Geography III.*

It also meant repeating "Arrival at Santos" (her first poem about Brazil), which had come near the end of *A Cold Spring* before she placed it at the beginning of her next book, *Questions of Travel* (repeating a similar decision Lowell made with his poem "For the Union Dead").

The Library of America was reluctant to reprint the same poem twice, but ultimately acceded to my argument, to maintain the original structural integrity of these books. I was also tickled by a word change. In the first version of "Arrival at Santos," Bishop worries about Brazilian customs confiscating her "Scotch and cigarettes"; in the second version, it's "bourbon" she's worried about losing, which I felt was more truly autobiographical. I thought readers who noticed would find this fascinating.

The Library of America also offered an opportunity to include all of Bishop's shorter prose pieces, most of which had never been collected before in their complete form. Besides her published stories and undergraduate fiction, there were astonishing essays (some more impressive than her early poems), book reviews (several published anonymously), a selection of her incisive literary "statements," and the handful of eloquent blurbs she had written for poets she was close to. Several ambitious pieces had never appeared in print before, including her journal-like essays about her trip on the Rio São Francisco and her visit to Brasília and the Amazon with Aldous Huxley and his wife.

Bishop had also published two full-length prose books – her 1957 translation of a young Brazilian girl's diary, published in English as *The Diary of "Helena Morley,"* and the Life World Library *Brazil*, a volume she is credited as having written "with the editors of *Life*" – a book she practically disowned because she detested the changes those "editors" had made. These were deemed by the Library of America too long to be included, and we chose not to include excerpts.

There was also the question of her letters. Bishop was a great correspondent. Perhaps the major work of Robert Giroux's career was his landmark edition of Bishop's letters, which he titled *One Art* (1994). I believe he considered his selection a kind of Bishop autobiography, and so felt free to omit passages that didn't contribute to his linear narrative. He also left out the various ways Bishop signed her letters – different for practically every person she wrote to. So even though there are fewer letters in the Library of America *Bishop,* every letter is complete, down to each particular signature.

I lost several arguments with the Library of America. Instead of a variety of letters, I had originally suggested including Bishop's complete correspondence with poet Anne Stevenson from the 1960s, when Stevenson was working on her monograph. These letters are remarkable for Bishop's candid autobiographical answers to Stevenson's questions, almost her *ars poetica*, though they may not be among her most amusing letters. The Library of America thought a greater variety of correspondents would be more appropriate to its purposes, and I couldn't argue my way out of that.

Of course, I put "Objects & Apparitions" back where Bishop intended it to appear. I then repeated the rest of Giroux's section of translations. This included all of Bishop's eloquent versions of Brazilian poems from her Wesleyan *Anthology of Twentieth-Century Brazilian Poetry*, her other Paz translations, and her translations of Max Jacob. To these, I added her undergraduate excerpt from Aristophanes' *The Birds*, her translation of a Brazilian popular song by Chico Buarque, and her breathtaking translations of three very short stories by Clarice Lispector, which had never been reprinted after their first appearance in *Kenyon Review* in 1964.

I had also wanted to include Bishop's only known surviving poem in Portuguese, a bit of darkly humorous light verse that she wrote to her Brazilian friend Linda Nemer after her arrival at Harvard in the spring of 1970 – a little poem about the inextricable "mixture" of improvements and discomfort that greeted her in America ("The water is so hot / that I burned my hand. / All the lights work. / The bed is soft; the pillows / give me asthma."). One particularly unsettling new experience was the student "mixers." I had seen this poem in a poor English translation. The Vassar library had the original letter in Portuguese, but it had been misfiled and couldn't be located before my deadline. Eventually, the original was found, and Bishop scholar Barbara Page, with Brazilian author Carmen Oliveira, had written a translation that really sounded like Bishop.

> Tonight there is something
> called "a mixer."
> Students, male and female,
> are mixing, mixing
> in the large dead halls.

But it was too late. By the time the errors of earlier printings had been corrected in the third printing, the Library of America declined to add pages for both the original Portuguese and the translation of a poem of such modest literary value (any new pages would have created the costly domino effect of having to change and renumber all the pages that followed it).

I also considered changing one bit of punctuation in "One Art." Every one of Bishop's drafts of the now famous opening line – "The art of losing isn't hard to master" – ends with a colon. *The New Yorker* changed it to a semi-colon, which to me seems softer, less direct, and more academic, and not necessarily more correct. Bishop was always nervous about punctuation (she never regarded herself an academic), and she was easily intimidated by *The New Yorker*. But unlike *The New Yorker*'s disastrous changes to the unusual Shakespearean capitalization in her poem "North Haven," which she did everything possible to change back the second she saw it in print, she never restored her original punctuation to "One Art" when she included it in *Geography III*. I discussed this possibility with the Library of America, but no one felt that I was on completely solid ground.

Two more large decisions remained for the Library of America edition. One was how to treat the poems Bishop herself didn't choose for any of her books. Essentially, I wanted to include every poem Bishop had ever decided to publish, along with the unpublished poems that were beginning to appear posthumously in magazines. I felt it was important to have as many as possible of the poems from *Edgar Allan Poe & The Juke-Box*, and I chose the ones I considered most important and/or most finished. I considered doing some of my own re-editing, but the Library of America insisted that it was not its mandate to do a new edition. In the meantime, rare-book dealer David Stang discovered in an auction catalogue a revealing early poem Bishop wrote on the inside cover of one of her school books. It began "I am neither here nor there," a phrase presciently foreshadowing the "wobbling and wavering" compass needle of Bishop's late "Sonnet." It made its first print appearance in the Library of America.

The other large issue was how to organize – and categorize – the prose – many more pieces than appeared in Giroux's *Collected Prose.* I decided to label as an essay anything I didn't think was fiction. But I soon had another chance to reconsider these labels.

From the very beginning of this project, Robert Giroux had turned the work entirely over to me. By the time he saw the table of contents, despite all the departures I made from his previous editions, he accepted my work without argument – relieved, I suspect, to see his final effort completed. He died at the age of 94, only a few months after the publication of *Elizabeth Bishop: Poems, Prose, and Letters.*

Jonathan Galassi, president and publisher of Farrar, Straus and Giroux, was beginning to plan new editions of both Bishop's poetry and prose, using the centennial of her birth as an occasion to update the popular FSG Bishop volumes. He told me he liked my Library of America Bishop and invited me to edit the new volume of Bishop's prose for FSG.

This was an opportunity to both rethink and add to the prose that was in the Library of America edition. I first turned to the Life World Library *Brazil.* This slim coffee-table picture book was part of a series of popular histories of each different country. Bishop took the assignment seriously, along with perhaps her heftiest fee – probably the most she was ever paid for her writing. But she hated how the editors changed her prose and photo captions, sentimentalizing and propagandizing what she had originally written. The greatest damage was to the last chapter, dealing with what Americans could learn from Brazil, especially concerning issues of race. Much of Bishop's original version still exists, and I was determined to present the *Brazil* book as closely as possible to what Bishop had originally intended. Using drafts in the Vassar archives and her own annotated copy in Harvard's Houghton Library, I made a good stab at how Bishop herself might have preferred to see this work. I now hear more of her own distinctive voice than in the book as modified by the editors of *Life* – her sense of color and smell and taste, and, especially, her sense of irony.[1]

While the Library of America book includes Bishop's introductory essay to *The Diary of "Helena Morley,"* I was sorry to omit any of her actual translation, though it seemed wrong to make an arbitrary selection. But I discovered that Bishop herself had selected several excerpts to publish in *Harper's Bazaar,* so I added these to the translation section in the FSG *Prose.* And instead of the Library of America's selection of letters to various people, I included only the crucial Bishop/Stevenson correspondence (omitting only a handful of their later, thinner, unrelated follow-up letters).

The more I considered the genres of Bishop's prose, the harder it became to isolate them. In the Library of America edition, I divided the prose into sections called Personal Essays, Reminiscences, and Reporting; Stories; and Literary Statements and Reviews. In the FSG *Prose,* I reduced the number of sections to "Stories and Memoirs" and "Essays, Reviews, and Tributes" (and added a small selection of her earliest prose in an appendix). This change in nomenclature comes from my increased sense that Bishop's best stories are at least part memoir, and that it's more useful to see how she interweaves fiction and memoir than to try to make a distinction between them. I've come to regard these "memoirs-written-as-if-they-were-fiction" as Bishop's personal genre.

One of my happiest inspirations was to begin sections, where appropriate, with facsimiles of Bishop's typescripts and handwritten annotations. A possible table of contents for a collection of stories precedes the section of her stories and memoirs. Her original table of contents for the *Brazil* book introduces the restored version of *Brazil.* And the section of Bishop's essays is preceded by a 1975 handout to her students headed IF YOU WANT TO WRITE *WELL* ALWAYS AVOID THESE WORDS (among the verboten vocabulary are "creative, and even more, creativity," "most ivity-words," "meaningful," and "to have sex").

I've done at least one other bit of "editing" – on a smaller scale but perhaps even more important. Early in 1974, Bishop broke her shoulder. Remembering a conversation we had in which we were complaining about being stuck in Cambridge over the Christmas break, she phoned me from the Harvard infirmary and asked if I could bring her several items from her apartment, including a small notebook, a request I was happy to oblige. While she was out of the room, perhaps getting an X-ray, I – how can I put this? – I couldn't help glancing at her notebook. Inside was a draft of a short poem called "Breakfast Song" – a love poem, virtually finished except for a few small but thrilling changes. I'd never seen anything by Bishop so heartbreakingly naked, both in its expression of affection and fear of death. I assumed it was written to Bishop's partner, Alice Methfessel. But some bolt of apprehension shot through me that she might never publish anything so personal. I found the thought of never seeing "Breakfast Song" again unbearable. So I copied it, carefully transcribing her few final emendations. I hoped I would one day see this poem in print.

When Bishop died, suddenly, five and a half years later, it had still not been published. Immediately after her death, it seemed inappropriate to tell Alice Methfessel that I happened to have a copy of a love poem addressed to her. Surely someone would discover that notebook.

Some twenty years later, with the possibility of a new edition of Bishop's poems, I thought it was essential to include "Breakfast Song." I sent the poem, typed with what I believed were Bishop's final thoughts, to both Methfessel and Robert Giroux. "Oh, that poem!" Methfessel remarked with utter nonchalance. Had she seen it before? Did she have a copy of it? I couldn't ask. Robert Giroux sent a copy to Alice Quinn at the *New Yorker*, where it was finally published in 2002. Quinn included it in *Edgar Allan Poe & The Juke-Box,* and I of course included it in the Library of America edition.

For the new "centennial" edition of Bishop *Poems*, FSG decided to include a section of "unpublished manuscript poems," with facsimiles of the original manuscripts on facing pages. Yet even after much searching, the notebook from which I copied "Breakfast Song" had never turned up, only a fragment called "Simple-Minded Morning Song," with two lines beginning "My love, my saving grace" (the opening line of "Breakfast Song"). I couldn't imagine a new Bishop edition without "Breakfast Song," and both Frank Bidart, now Bishop's sole literary executor, and I argued for it. And so, while this edition of Bishop's *Poems* includes twenty-six facsimiles of her own typed or handwritten drafts, the facsimile of "Breakfast Song" is my own original handwritten copy. I regard my work on Bishop as an ongoing attempt to repay her kindness. She was in many ways *my* saving grace. Helping to get this poem out into the world is the most personally gratifying of all my efforts on her behalf – and surely the most enduring.

Notes

1. Daniel Bosch, "Poetry, Prose, and Politics—Elizabeth Bishop at 100," *The Arts Fuse*, March 3, 2011 (http://artsfuse.org/22446/fuse-review-poetry-prose-and-politics-elizabeth-bishop-at-100/), includes the most comprehensive analysis of the difference between the published *Brazil* book and what Bishop originally intended.

CHAPTER 35

Bishop's Influence

Stephanie Burt

"Now everyone likes Elizabeth Bishop except the ones who don't," quipped Maureen McLane in 2012.[1] Some well-known poets liked her, and imitated her, in the decades before that. James Merrill published a well-known tribute ("Overdue Pilgrimage to Nova Scotia") that doubles as an analysis of her style. Mark Doty's debts to Bishop during the 1990s went far enough that Helen Vendler called him out: in Doty's *Atlantis*, she remarked, "the tics of style we associate with Elizabeth Bishop are everywhere: the interpolated exclamations, the self-conscious queries, the corrections of perspective," and even "a lighthouse that is, like Bishop's, a preacher."[2] Vernon Shetley devoted a chapter from *After the Death of Poetry* (his 1994 study of the state of play in America) to the putative "MFA mainstream" who had taken Elizabeth Bishop as a role model. James Longenbach's important *Modern Poetry After Modernism* (1997) "was prompted by [Longenbach's] sense that the stories we usually tell about American poetry cannot account for Elizabeth Bishop's career."[3]

The stories we now tell have changed. Some make her central. She has also arrived in other media: consider the multiple biographies, the 2013 film *Reaching for the Moon*, or Liza Wieland's 2019 novel *Paris, 7 A. M.* Well-known poets still center her and her work. Willard Spiegelman has shown how, and how much, former US poet laureate Kay Ryan learned from Bishop, whom Ryan even addresses by name.[4] Sometimes it's even in the title, as well as in the stylistic goals: Paisley Rekdal's careful, knowing, melancholy "At the Fishhouses," for example, which begins with "black water under the boats with their pools / of bilge rainbowed out like rinds / of steak fat," "details / I still keep from Bishop's poem."[5] Another of Rekdal's poems takes off from "The Man-Moth," sketching an imaginary animal and ending with "real tears."[6] You can find Bishop's energies and Bishop's devices percolating through American poets who have made much of their influence from other directions. Kevin Young's "East Jesus," for example, echoes "Filling Station" and "The Moose":

SAW CHAIN on a sign somewhere
between Boonies & Sticks, pop.
10, now, 9, now 11.

Sleep it off
& tomorrow's another yesterday – AVOID
Sins Tragedy Learn Satans
STRATEGY our roadside church
announces[7]

One might conclude: Somebody loves us all.

And yet much of the energy in American poetry, and in other English-speaking countries, seems to have come from directions antithetical to Bishop's careful, lyrical concision. McLane organizes an essay around the supposed opposition between Bishop's achievements and a post-avant-garde: "Some people say you cannot like both Stein and Bishop they line up in little teams." McLane adds: "this is moronic."[8] Prose poems and verse essays, descendants of Stein and of continental avant-gardes, writers who rely on performance traditions and on a digital-native experience (the New Zealand critic Steven Toussaint calls them the "TMI generation") antithetical to Bishop's reserve: how can these writers continue to get much out of Bishop's particular slice of the twentieth century?[9]

And yet, sometimes, they do. I have argued elsewhere that Bishop's mix of epistemological skepticism and aesthetic closure – represented, in her own work, by the repeated figure of the rainbow – persists into the 2010s, in midcareer poets as otherwise dissimilar as Emily Berry, Lavinia Greenlaw, and Allan Peterson.[10] I want to show here how not only that outlook, but also other Bishopesque scenes, devices, and symbols, recur in other poets who seem stylistically far from her but who end up remarkably – more than coincidentally – close to Bishop's tropes and goals. These poets use external forms far from any that Bishop made her own: the lyric essay, the extended prose poem, the open-ended free verse sequence. Such forms both echo specific Bishop poems, and extend her practice of intense, focused observation, in ways that can help us read not only Bishop's gift to the future, but her own body of work.

Few recent books attest to that legacy more surprisingly, or more comprehensively, than Kate Colby's *Dream of the Trenches*. Her volume mixes one-page prose poems entitled "Dream of the Trenches" with one-page prose poems entitled "Driving to Margaret's Mother's Memorial Service." On her way to the service on Cape Cod, Colby meditates on friends' grief, on the vicissitudes of perception, and on attempts to represent those vicissitudes: "Description and narration are bound by a temporal standard that communication necessitates. So you become dependent on description for experience, and then the description compromises the experience."[11] As Bishop put it: "the target is a moving target and the marksman is also moving" (*PPL* 665). That nearly hallucinatory puddle-shape that Peggy Samuels, writing on Bishop, saw as a symbol for unreliable perception, appears in Colby too: "Mirages on a hot highway look more like water than that alongside which I'm driving. It's weird that water is the very thing you're most likely to need in the condition producing the illusion of it."[12]

Imagining herself installed permanently by the sea and its shore, the poet inhabits the grammar of "At the Fishhouses": "If you were to bury yourself alive and rub your eyes, glowing green floaters would still scroll by. Staticky screens on the backs of the lids recapitulate the night sky"[13] Colby's sequence, begun as a record of secondhand or empathetic grief, becomes a way to connect her prior experiences of inauthenticity, of trying while failing to know just what she sees and feels. Among these experiences is "a job as a copywriter at a gift catalog," reminiscent of "The U.S.A. School of Writing," producing copy whose mixed effects parallel the whispers and symbols in "Filling Station," conferring love and "significance for a piece of laminate junk mass-manufactured with cheap labor on the other side of the world."[14]

Half of Shane McCrae's much-noticed volume *In the Language of My Captor* comprises paragraphs, set as prose poems, remembering McCrae's suburban Oregon childhood, when the poet was serially abused, "passed around the neighborhood," "sometimes from child to teenager to child," living with "a white supremacist" grandfather.[15] McCrae's successive paragraphs describe uncanny scenes with an anxious child's eye. In an abandoned warehouse, when the poet was "six or seven,"

> A dusty toolbox, a small lamp with a flexible neck and a metal, cup-shaped head, and a Phillips screwdriver sat on the desk [. . .] I stared at the glowing lamp, terrified, feeling suddenly near, as children sometimes for imaginary reasons do, death, hoping the lamp was on.[16]

The mysteriously animated, populated desk looks back to Bishop's "12 O'Clock News." McCrae's holding off on the noun that "near" modified – he felt "near [. . .] death" – marks the sentence as other than straightforward expository prose: it is, perhaps, what Jeremy Noel-Tod identifies as "the banishment of lyric verse into its formal antithesis."[17] Verse stops and starts: prose keeps going, will not let itself stop, until it reaches a grammatical full stop, until the whole claim has been made. Verse represents either hesitation or confidence; prose, in this context, a dogged endurance, or stubborn persistence. And McCrae's sense of stubborn, sustained attention – looking for reference points, secure facts, and also alert for danger – becomes a constant throughout these paragraphs, or narrative units, or prose poems: "What I remember most distinctly is not any single act, but the sensation I felt, both empty and vast, as I watched what people did to me, and what I did to them, reluctantly, but I would if they asked me to, checking to make sure it looked right."[18]

The landscapes and interiors of McCrae's abusive childhood included (as Bishop's oevure does) portraits and landscapes and domestic interiors, frames within frames, and versions of other people's memories. McCrae writes:

> The first thing my grandfather did – that was the way my grandmother always told the story – the first thing he did after we moved into our new house was throw me into a wall, the living room wall, the stretch of wall, maybe four feet wide – in a few years he would hang a painting of a Native American crouching to touch the still surface of a lake, which he later replaced with a self-portrait, there.

He remembers other, outdoor landscapes too, among them a pond where "every morning, I might have been seeing new minnows swirling in the bright shallows – or they might have known to fight hardest there, at the mouths of the tunnels, where the water was still clear, against the darkness the element they lived in pushed and pulled them toward."[19] As often in McCrae (and in Bishop), the pellucid surface of the prose belies its intense allusiveness: the child-observer and the minnows, are almost submerged in their element, like Shakespeare's "dyer's hand"; the pond's false promise of clarity is like the metaphysical promise (almost never fulfilled) of the well in Robert Frost's "For Once, Then, Something"; and of course the child's experience, in which the world is a blur, and then minute and vast and clear, is the experience of Bishop's sandpiper, while the minnows recapitulate the sublimity of water from the famous conclusion to "At the Fishhouses."

Far from McCrae's influences, and also far from Bishop's, comes the West Coast poet and critic Lyn Hejinian, whose most widely admired works use a kind of non-sequential, post-Steinian, always-re-beginning prose: why would she sound like Bishop, ever? And yet she does: consider the beginning of Hejinian's recent *Positions*:

> Humans are forever creating new allegories out of things they find in the world. A feather, a paper flag on a stack, an ivory chopstick are stuck beside an upright tulip in a jar. Evidently someone has combed a rubbish heap,

> reevaluated some bits of debris [...] Aesthetic recontextualization brings things to a temporary halt, which is different from the false half to which decontextualization had brought them. Somewhere in the neighborhood a dog is barking, saying unmistakably, Hurt, *hurt* — hurt, *hurt* — hurt, *hurt* – hurt, *hurt* – hurt, *hurt* – hurt, *hurt*." It speaks in iambic pentameter.[20]

That last sentence, about canine prosody, is Hejinian's too. Her hurt dog enters the realm of poetry and poetics, the realm of figure, because it is hurt, like the dog in Bishop's "Pink Dog." Could it be that humans fly flags, or arrange "new allegories," because we too hurt, because we are hurting?

Positions, too, is a "self-portrait in observation," by a poet who is watching herself watching herself watching herself; and this kind of portrait, as Jonathan Farmer has written, "is at the hesitant, elegant heart of so much of Bishop's work."[21] You can even find this sort of "performance of revision," once you look for it – this way of "making connections," venturing interpretations, then "pushing [...] away into the factual" – in much more prominent work of the 2010s, such as Claudia Rankine's *Citizen*, where "your attachment seems fragile, tenuous, subject to any transgression of your historical self."[22]

Can we find those kinds of resistance to micro-aggressions, that sense of an "I" or a "you" who are just barely holding themselves together, in Bishop too? And are they, in Bishop, dependent for that minimal coherence on self-consciousness, the sense that you are watching yourself very carefully so as to keep yourself from collapsing or flying apart? Bishop's personae sometimes seem to think so: consider the Gentleman of Shalott, who "wishes to be quoted as saying/ 'Half is enough,'" or "The Unbeliever," who "sleeps on the top of a mast/ with his eyes half closed," or the "seamstress" – perhaps Lachesis, perhaps Atropos – of "House Guest" (*P* 11, 24, 170–71). Then consider the figures in other contemporary poems who seem to be, just barely, keeping together: the friend, or perhaps a house guest, or a shadow self, in Patrick Morrissey's "Figures":

> Agitated
> then matter
> of fact, he has
> a story to tell [...]
>   His
> hands curl and
> leap, crackling
> syllables, maybe
> a sentence.[23]

Like Bishop's sandpiper, like her observer in "Poem" – "About the size of an old-style dollar bill" (*P* 196) – like so many of her personae, Morrissey and his character fixate on details as ways to keep their bearings in an otherwise disorienting, unpredictable world, even though the details themselves remain in flux. Like Bishop, he finds himself drawn to the sea and its shore:

> Irregular bobbing gulls or recurrent whitecaps at this distance
> The passenger jet's slow, noiseless ascent, clouds plowing the horizon
> Accident assumes a form and repeats in what we say about it[24]

The double focus on the thing seen and on the work of seeing could scarcely be more Bishopesque, though the cadence lands far from hers: Morrissey, too, deploys what Jane Shore calls Bishop's wish to "call into question the accuracy of her images as she writes them."[25] There's even that trademark "or."

Morrissey does not write prose poems; he writes, instead, a kind of line and stanza deriving from William Carlos Williams, one that sometimes announces its independence from the pentameter-based tradition that lies behind even Bishop's most unruly free verse. Andy Stallings works out of the same post-Williams, anti-European free verse toolkit, and like Morrissey (and Williams, and Oppen, and Rankine) he writes long sequences whose individual segments bear no titles. Morrissey's sense of line and sound comes from Williams (it is his pattern of feeling that recalls Bishop). Stallings's series of anticlimaxes, re-beginnings and retreats, in his book-length sequence *Paradise*, seem derived from James Schuyler (UK readers may think of W. S. Graham). And yet the scenes may seem familiar to anyone who knows "Squatter's Children," or "Song for the Rainy Season," or "The End of March," or "The Bight":

> The afternoon passed, bugs
> on a screen. Can't make the
> sun more meaningful than
> the sun, as children at play
> in a gravel driveway accept
> without knowing the name [. . .]
>
> The world made small
> by my smallness grows in
> accordance, as I grow, distant
> supple whanging of a train.
> The children, by extension,
> warm the cabin that will
> one day be their own.[26]

What connects these instances of minute attention, some – but not all – of which might be founded in conscious, intentional, repeated reference to Elizabeth Bishop? Do they represent something significant in contemporary poetry, something that can also tell us what's special in Bishop? Or does their appearance say mostly that for Elizabeth Bishop scholars, Bishop is the proverbial hammer before which all poems become nails? The former seems more likely, in part because the claim is falsifiable: one could not go through contemporary poetry rapidly – much less through prose poems and free-verse sequences – and find echoes of Robert Lowell, or Wallace Stevens, or even Auden, in this way.

These poets' echoes of Bishop may be literary examples of what evolutionary biologists call homology, emerging separately from poets' readings of Bishop at different moments, serving various purposes despite their common source. But they may also be examples of what biologists call analogy, where similar adaptations (say, wings, or bright striped colors to signify poison) arise independently given similar environments and similar needs. In this case, the adaptations are sentences paying up-close, self-conscious, slowed-down attention to the process of paying attention, especially at sites and scenes – cluttered desks, empty homes, ponds, seashores – that may themselves stand for the borders of an uncertain world.

What, then, are these poets' similar needs? Other critics (Samuels and Shetley among them) have underlined Bishop's uncertain epistemologies, suited to a postmodern, uncertain world. But answers that confine themselves to perception and epistemology shortchange the feelings in these poems – feelings, often, of wariness, unsettlement, uncertainty, and in McCrae's case at least, of reaction to severe trauma. That trauma may provide another lens, not just on Bishop's heirs, but on Bishop herself.

The intense, self-conscious and above all unstoppable perception in these poets may resemble the perceptual phenomenon that clinical psychologists call hypervigilance. Hypervigilant persons pay unusual, excessive, repeated, or unstoppable attention to their immediate environment, scanning for signs of threat and things to avoid, making "a wide array of safety threats and related threat appraisals."[27] They may have a social anxiety disorder with no clear relation to their history; they may also be survivors of abuse or neglect, with systems developed early in life for "alerting and protecting the individual from harm."[28] This kind of hypervigilance overlaps, too, with other kinds of hyperalertness, like the kind that David Baker (himself a frequent user of Bishopesque detail) presents in "Hyper –," a poem about his daughter's diagnosis with ADHD:

In one sketch she finished, just before we
learned what was wrong – I mean, before we knew
what to call what was wrong, how to treat it,
how to treat *her* – she captured her favorite
cat with a skill that skips across my chest.
He's on a throw rug, asleep. The rug's fringe
ruffles just so. The measure of her love is
visible in each delicate stroke, from
his fetal repose, ears down, eyes sealed
softly, paws curled inward, to the tiger lines
of his coat depend by thick textures
where she's slightly rubbed away the contours
with her thumb to winter coat gray.[29]

The cadences belong more to Moore than to Bishop, but the attitudes towards this child's drawing, the attention paid to the way she has paid attention, is a mode we may recognize from "Large Bad Picture," or "Poem," or "Filling Station." Baker's daughter pays attention to everything, and flits from point to point, unless she's drawing it, because she has a treatable disorder that can be diagnosed in childhood; McCrae, and Colby, and (so the poems imply) Morrissey, pay obsessive, self-revising attention to the visible world because they have had to do so, for their own safety, in a childhood that feels like it may not be over yet. That kind of attention is not hyperactivity but hypervigilance: an ability – or a disability – in which you need to scan the world again and again and again, because danger could come from anywhere, and objects of fascination must be understood inside and out, to be sure they are safe.

My point is not to diagnose Bishop – though her early childhood seems relevant! – but to describe the personae in the poems, along with her choices about what and when to describe and redescribe. A world not obsessively processed, tagged and cataloged, for the hypervigilant person, is a world of "possible threat signals," "negative interpretation of ambiguous behaviors," and multiple scary unknowns.[30] It is, one might even say, a world of "controlled panic": the world of the sandpiper, and of "The Sea and Its Shore," and of the child who draws all those houses in "Sestina," and even the world of "At the Fishhouses," with its carefully sorted detail. It is certainly the world of McCrae's childhood, and maybe the world of Colby's driver too, always asking herself what she missed, what she needs to know next, what she could not get right. And it is the world of all three animals in "Rainy Season: Sub-Tropics," with their remembered threats and their drama of mutual misrecognition:

> Get down. Turn facing out, it's safer. Don't breathe until the snail gets by. [. . .] I live, I breathe, by swallowing. Once, some naughty children picked me up [. . .] and in our mouths they put lit cigarettes. We could not help but smoke them, to the end. I thought it was the death of me.
>
> [. . .]
>
> What is that big soft monster, like a yellow cloud, stifling and warm? What is it doing? It pats my back. Out, claw. There, I have frightened it away. [. . .] Out of my way, O monster. I own a pool, all the little fish that swim in it, and all the skittering waterbugs that smell like rotten apples.
>
> [. . .]
>
> The rain has stopped. The waterfall makes such a noise! (And what if I fall over it?) (*P* 163–4)

The beauty in all three animals' constant, and constantly re-figured, descriptions cannot be teased apart from their sense of constant threat.

And yet the same habitual attention that constitutes – when it's distressing – hypervigilance can also amount to a kind of self-care: recognizing harmless patterns in the world, colors, shapes, recurring sounds, harmless or trivial textures and shapes and similarities, becomes – for many sufferers from trauma, from complex PTSD, from hypervigilance – a way to calm down and avoid dissociation. Bishop's surrogates do this too, none more so than the three tropical animals in her own prose poems. So does the nonstop consciousness in Stallings's *Paradise*, forever processing new input. So do Colby and McCrae.

This kind of vigilance – this kind of hypertrophied attention to the external world – also deflects attention from the vulnerable interior self: the poem says "look over here, and here, and here, and here, and here! just don't look at me." And the same attention to detail that can feel like a symptom of anxiety, a habit developed in trauma, can also serve as a palliative, a way out. As it did in so many of Bishop's best poems, with their elements of attentive repetition; as it does, sometimes, in the living poets discussed here. The prose poem itself has served, in my argument, as a safe way to group together poets who do not imitate Bishop consistently; it may also fit her kind of existence as marginal, as threatened, since – as Steven Monte has explained – the prose poem in English has long functioned as a kind of generic evasion, known by what it avoids, by what it is not.[31] Bishop herself was once known by what she was not: she seemed, during her lifetime, unprepossessing, un-prolific, unforthcoming, physically absent from American literary scenes. Now she is – if not everywhere – in many places: not least in the scenes of hypervigilance – from Baker's house, to Hejinian's consciousness, to McCrae's memories – where less careful readers might think she had never been.

Notes

1. Maureen McLane, *My Poets* (New York: Farrar, Straus, and Giroux, 2012), 45.
2. Helen Vendler, "Comic and Elegiac," *The New Yorker*, April 8, 1996. 101.
3. James Longenbach, *Modern Poetry After Modernism* (New York: Oxford University Press, 1997), vii.
4. Willard Spiegelman, "Kay Ryan's Delicate Strength," *Virginia Quarterly Review* 88:3 (2012).
5. Paisley Rekdal, *Imaginary Vessels* (Port Townsend, WA: Copper Canyon, 2016), 14.
6. Ibid., 23.
7. Kevin Young, *For the Confederate Dead* (New York: Knopf, 2007), 65.
8. McLane, *My Poets*, 45.
9. Steven Toussaint, "TMI: An Essay on Contemporary Poetry in Aotearoa/New Zealand," *The Spinoff*, Apr. 27, 2019. https://thespinoff.co.nz/books/27–04-2019/tmi-an-essay-on-contemporary-poetry-in-aotearoa-new-zealand/.
10. Stephanie Burt, "Elizabeth Bishop at the End of the Rainbow," in *Reading Elizabeth Bishop: An Edinburgh Companion*, ed. Jonathan Ellis (Edinburgh: Edinburgh University Press, 2019), 321–36.
11. Kate Colby, *Dream of the Trenches* (Blacksburg, VA: Noemi, 2019), 34.
12. Peggy Samuels, *Deep Skin: Elizabeth Bishop and Visual Art* (Ithaca: Cornell University Press, 2010); Colby, *Dream of the Trenches*, 84.
13. Colby, *Dream of the Trenches*, 77.
14. Ibid., 91.
15. Shane McCrae, *In the Language of My Captor* (Middletown, CT: Wesleyan University Press, 2017), 28, 32.
16. Ibid, 22.
17. Jeremy Noel-Tod, "Logbook: Against Prose," *Critical Quarterly* 59:2 (2017), 56.
18. McCrae, *In the Language of My Captor*, 27.
19. Ibid., 36, 37.
20. Lyn Hejinian, *Positions of the Sun* (Brooklyn: Belladonna, 2017), 9.
21. Jonathan Farmer, *That Peculiar Affirmative: On the Social Life of Poems* (Nagodoches, TX: Stephen F. Austin State University Press, 2019.), 57.
22. Ibid., 67; Claudia Rankine, *Citizen: An American Lyric* (Minneapolis: Graywolf, 2014), 11.
23. Patrick Morrissey, *World Music* (Chicago: Verge, 2017), 12.
24. Ibid., 70.
25. Jane Shore, "Elizabeth Bishop: The Art of Changing Your Mind," *Ploughshares* 5.1 (1979), 182.
26. Andy Stallings, *Paradise* (Iowa City: Rescue, 2017), 52, 54.
27. Julian Ford and Christine Courtois. "Complex PTSD, affective dysregulation, and borderline personality disorder." *Borderline Personality Disorder and Emotional Dysregulation* 1:9 (2014). https://www.ncbi.nlm.nih.gov/pmc/articles/PMC4579513/

28. Wolf-Gero Lange, Mike Rinck and Eni S. Becker. "Behavioral Deviations: Surface Features of Social Anxiety and What They Reveal," in *The Wiley-Blackwell Handbook of Social Anxiety Disorder*, ed. Justin Weeks (Oxford: Blackwell, 2014), 355–64, 357.
29. David Baker, *Swift: New And Selected Poems* (New York: Norton, 2018), 95–96.
30. Lange, Rinck and Becker, "Behavioral Deviations," 357.
31. Steven Monte, *Invisible Fences: Prose Poetry as a Genre in French and American Literature* (Lincoln: University of Nebraska Press, 2000).

Works Cited

1 Nova Scotia

Barry, Sandra. *Elizabeth Bishop: An Archival Guide to Her Life in Nova Scotia* (Great Village, NS: Elizabeth Bishop Society of Nova Scotia, 1996).

Elizabeth Bishop: Nova Scotia's 'Home-Made' Poet (Halifax, NS: Nimbus Publishing, 2011).

Cleghorn, Angus, and Jonathan Ellis, eds. *The Cambridge Companion to Elizabeth Bishop* (Cambridge: Cambridge University Press, 2014).

Johnson, Alexandra. "Geography and Imagination," in *Conversations with Elizabeth Bishop*, ed. George Monteiro (Jackson: University Press of Mississippi, 1996), 98–104.

Schwartz, Lloyd, and Sybil P. Estess, eds. *Elizabeth Bishop and Her Art* (Ann Arbor: The University of Michigan Press, 1983).

2 New England

Logan, William. "Elizabeth Bishop at Summer Camp," *Virginia Quarterly Review* 88.2 (Spring 2012), 52–87.

Marshall, Megan. *Elizabeth Bishop: A Miracle for Breakfast* (Boston: Houghton Mifflin Harcourt, 2017).

Methfessel, Alice. Obituary, *San Francisco Chronicle*. 2009.

Moore, Marianne. *The Complete Poems of Marianne Moore* (New York: Macmillan Company, 1969).

Paton, Priscilla. *Abandoned New England: Landscape in the Works of Homer, Frost, Hopper, Wyeth, and Bishop* (Lebanon, NH: University Press of New England, 2003).

Sheehan, Fiona. "'Affectionately Yours, Bishop': The Early Correspondence of Elizabeth Bishop and Rhoda Wheeler Sheehan," *Resources for American Literary Study* 40 (2018), 229–75.

Travisano, Thomas. *Love Unknown: The Life and Worlds of Elizabeth Bishop* (New York: Viking, 2019).

Yeats, W. B., *The Collected Poems of W. B. Yeats* (New York: Macmillan Company, 1971).

3 New York

Anonymous. "Millions Watch Eclipse of Moon, the Longest Here in Fifty Years," *The New York Times* 16 July 1935, 1, 3.
Anonymous. "The City That Never Stops Slows in a Freeze," *The New York Times* 17 January 1994, 1, 23.
Barry, Sandra, Gwendolyn Davies, and Peter Sanger, eds. *Divisions of the Heart: Elizabeth Bishop and the Art of Memory and Place* (Kentville, NS: Gaspereau Press, 2001).
Cleghorn, Angus, and Jonathan Ellis, eds. *The Cambridge Companion to Elizabeth Bishop* (Cambridge: Cambridge University Press, 2014).
Cook, Eleanor. *Elizabeth Bishop at Work* (Cambridge, MA: Harvard University Press, 2016).
Corn, Wanda. "The Artist's New York: 1900–1930," in *Budapest and New York: Studies in Metropolitan Transformation, 1870–1930*, ed. Thomas Bender and Carl E. Schorske (New York: Russell Sage Foundation, 1994), 275–308.
Costello, Bonnie. "Bishop and the Poetic Tradition," in *The Cambridge Companion to Elizabeth Bishop*, ed. Angus Cleghorn and Jonathan Ellis (Cambridge: Cambridge University Press, 2014), 79–94.
Crane, Hart. *Hart Crane's "The Bridge": An Annotated Edition*, ed. Lawrence Kramer (New York: Fordham University Press, 2011).
Fountain, Gary, and Peter Brazeau. *Remembering Elizabeth Bishop: An Oral Biography* (Amherst: University of Massachusetts Press, 1994).
Hicok, Bethany. "Becoming a Poet: From North to South," in *The Cambridge Companion to Elizabeth Bishop*, ed. Angus Cleghorn and Jonathan Ellis (Cambridge: Cambridge University Press, 2014), 111–23.
Elizabeth Bishop's Brazil (Charlottesville: University of Virginia Press, 2016).
Johnson, Alexandra. "Geography of the Imagination," in *Conversations with Elizabeth Bishop*, ed. George Monteiro (Jackson: University of Mississippi Press, 1996), 98–104.
Koolhaas, Rem. *Delirious New York: A Retroactive Manifesto for Manhattan* (New York: The Monacelli Press, 1994).
Lombardi, Marilyn May, ed. *Elizabeth Bishop: The Geography of Gender* (Charlottesville: University of Virginia Press, 1993).
Moore, Marianne. *The Selected Letters of Marianne Moore*, ed. Bonnie Costello, Celeste Goodridge, and Cristanne Miller (London: Faber and Faber, 1998).
Morshed, Adnan. *Impossible Heights: Skyscrapers, Flight, and the Master Builder* (Minneapolis: University of Minnesota Press, 2015).
Scott Brown, Denise. *Having Words* (London: Architectural Association, 2009).
Yochelson, Bonnie. *Berenice Abbott: Changing New York* (New York: Museum of the City of New York, 1997).

4 Paris, France

Apollinaire, Guillaume. *Alcools* (Hanover, NH: Wesleyan University Press, 1995).

Baudelaire, Charles. *Flowers of Evil and Other Works*, ed. Wallace Fowlie (New York: Dover, 1992).

Cleghorn, Angus. "Bad Boy for Good: Baudelaire in Stevens and Bishop," in *Wallace Stevens, Poetry, and France: "Au pays de la métaphore,"* ed. Juliette Utard, Bart Eeckhout, and Lisa Goldfarb (Paris: Éditions rue d'Ulm ENS, 2017), 123–37.

Cook, Eleanor. *Against Coercion: Games Poets Play* (Stanford, CA: Stanford University Press, 1998).

Elizabeth Bishop at Work (Cambridge, MA: Harvard University Press, 2016).

Costello, Bonnie. *Elizabeth Bishop: Questions of Mastery* (Cambridge, MA: Harvard University Press, 1991).

"Bishop and the Poetic Tradition," in *The Cambridge Companion to Elizabeth Bishop*, ed. Angus Cleghorn and Jonathan Ellis (Cambridge: Cambridge University Press, 2014), 79–94.

Leviston, Frances. "Mothers and Marimbas in 'The Bight': Bishop's Danse Macabre," *Twentieth-Century Literature*, 61.4 (2015), 436–59.

Ravinthiran, Vidyan. *Elizabeth Bishop's Prosaic* (Lewisburg, PA: Bucknell University Press, 2015), 436–59.

Rimbaud, Arthur. *Complete Works, Selected Letters*, ed. Wallace Fowlie (Chicago: University of Chicago Press, 1966).

5 Florida

Bishop, Elizabeth. *Conversations with Elizabeth Bishop*, ed. George Monteiro (Jackson: University Press of Mississippi, 1996).

Browne, Jefferson B. *The Old and the New* (St Augustine, FL: The Record Company, 1912).

Cleghorn, Angus. "Bishop's 'wiring fused': 'Bone Key' and 'Pleasure Seas,'" in *Elizabeth Bishop in the 21st Century*, ed. Angus Cleghorn, Bethany Hicok, and Thomas Travisano (Charlottesville and London: University of Virginia Press, 2012), 69–87.

Covington, James W. *The Seminoles of Florida* (Gainesville, FL: LibraryPress@UF, 1993, 2017).

Dickie, Margaret. "Race and Class in Elizabeth Bishop's Poetry," *The Yearbook of English Studies* 24 (1994), 44–58.

Doreski, C. K. *Elizabeth Bishop: The Restraints of Language* (Oxford: Oxford University Press, 1993).

Ellis, Jonathan. *Art and Memory in the Work of Elizabeth Bishop* (Farnham: Ashgate, 2006).

"Elizabeth Bishop's Bone Key Poems," *PN Review* 34.3 (2008), 37–40.

Equal Justice Initiative. *Lynching in America: Confronting the Legacy of Racial Terror*, 3rd ed. (Montgomery, AL: Equal Justice Initiative, 2017).

Fountain, Gary, and Peter Brazeau. *Remembering Elizabeth Bishop* (Amherst: University of Massachusetts Press, 1994).

Gomez, Andrew. "Jim Crow and the Caribbean South: Cubans and Race in South Florida, 1885–1930s," *Journal of American Ethnic History* 36.4 (2017), 25–48.

Kalstone, David. *Becoming a Poet: Elizabeth Bishop with Marianne Moore and Robert Lowell* (New York: Farrar, Straus and Giroux, 1989).

Lombardi, Marilyn May. *The Body and the Song: Elizabeth Bishop's Poetics* (Carbondale, IL: Southern Illinois University Press, 1995).

Lowney, John. *History, Memory, and the Literary Left: Modern American Poetry, 1935–1968* (Iowa City: University of Iowa Press, 2006).

Lynskey, Dorian. *33 Revolutions per Minute: A History of Protest Songs* (London: Faber and Faber, 2011).

Millier, Brett C. *Elizabeth Bishop: Life and the Memory of It* (Berkeley: University of California Press, 1993).

Ogle, Maureen. *Key West: History of an Island of Dreams* (Gainesville: University Press of Florida, 2003).

Page, Barbara. "Off-Beat Claves, Oblique Realities: The Key West Notebooks of Elizabeth Bishop," in *Elizabeth Bishop: The Geography of Gender*, ed. Marilyn May Lombardi (Charlottesville and London: University Press of Virginia, 1993), 196–211.

Rich, Adrienne. "The Eye of the Outsider: Elizabeth Bishop's Complete Poems, 1927–1979," *Boston Review* (April 1983), 15–17.

Roman, Camille. *Elizabeth Bishop's World War II–Cold War View* (Basingstoke: Palgrave Macmillan, 2001).

Scandura, Jani. *Down in the Dumps, Place, Modernity, American Depression* (Durham, NC: Duke University Press, 2008).

Schmidt, Tyler T. *Desegregating Desire: Race and Sexuality in Cold War American Literature* (Jackson: University of Mississippi Press, 2013).

Xiaojing, Zhou. "Subject Positions in Elizabeth Bishop's Representations of Whiteness and the Other," in *White Women in Racialized Spaces: Imaginative Transformation and Ethical Action in Literature*, ed. Samina Najmi and Rajini Srikanth (Albany: State University of New York Press, 2002), 167–89.

6 Brazil

Almeida, Sandra Regina Goulart, Glaucia Renate Gonçalves, and Eliana Lourenço de Lima Reis, eds. *The Art of Elizabeth Bishop* (Belo Horizonte: Editora Universidade de Minas Gerais, 2002).

Besner, Neil K., trans. *Rare and Commonplace Flowers: The Story of Elizabeth Bishop and Lota de Macedo Soares* (New Brunswick, NJ: Rutgers University Press, 2002). Original in Portuguese: Oliveira, Carmen. *Flores Raras e Banalíssimas: A História de Lota de Macedo Soares e Elizabeth Bishop* (Rio de Janeiro: Rocco, 1995).

Bishop, Elizabeth. *The Diary of "Helena Morley"* (New York: The Ecco Press, 1957). Translation of Alice Brant's *Minha Vida de Menina* (1942).

Bishop, Elizabeth, and the Editors of Life. *Brazil* (New York: Time Incorporated, 1962).
Bosch, Daniel. "Poetry, Prose, and Politics: Elizabeth Bishop at 100," *The Arts Fuse*, March 3, 2011. Web.
Cleghorn, Angus. "The Politics of Editing Elizabeth Bishop's *Brazil*, Circa 1962," *Global Studies* 4.3 (Summer 2012), 47–59.
Cleghorn, Angus, and Jonathan Ellis, eds. *The Cambridge Companion to Elizabeth Bishop* (Cambridge: Cambridge University Press, 2014).
Elizabeth Bishop Bulletin 6.1 (Summer 1997) and 8.1 (Summer 1999). Web.
Ellis, Jonathan, ed. *Reading Elizabeth Bishop: An Edinburgh Companion* (Edinburgh: Edinburgh University Press, 2019).
Goldensohn, Lorrie. *Elizabeth Bishop: The Biography of a Poetry* (New York: Columbia University Press, 1992).
Hicok, Bethany. *Elizabeth Bishop's Brazil* (Charlottesville: University of Virginia Press, 2016).
Mello, Evelyn, and Maria Clara Paro. "Olhos de Elizabeth Bishop e Ana Cristina César: Paisagens em Deconstrução" ("The Gazes of Elizabeth Bishop and Ana Cristina César: Deconstructed Landscapes"), *Fólio: Revista de Letras* 7.2 (2015), 611–23.
Millier, Brett. *Elizabeth Bishop: Life and the Memory of It* (Berkeley: University of California Press, 1993).
Nogueira, Nadia. *Invenções de Si em Histórias de Amor: Lota Macedo Soares e Elizabeth Bishop* (Rio de Janeiro: Apicuri, 2008).
Przybycien, Regina. *Feijão-Preto e Diamantes: O Brasil na obra de Elizabeth Bishop* (Belo Horizonte, Minas Gerais: Editora UFMG, 2015).
Ravinthiran, Vidyan. "'Manuelzinho,' Brazil and Identity Politics," in *Reading Elizabeth Bishop: An Edinburgh Companion*, ed. Jonathan Ellis (Edinburgh: Edinburgh University Press, 2019), 33–47.
Travisano, Thomas. *Elizabeth Bishop: Her Artistic Development* (Charlottesville and London: University of Virginia Press, 1988).
Love Unknown: The Life and Worlds of Elizabeth Bishop (New York: Viking, 2019).

7 Lyric Poetry

Bogan, Louise. "The Situation in American Writing, 1939," *Partisan Review* 6.5 (Fall 1939) 105–08.
Chiasson, Dan. "Color codes: a poet examines race in America," *The New Yorker* (October 27, 2014), www.newyorker.com/magazine/2014/10/27/color-codes.
Cohen, Milton. *Beleaguered Poets and Leftist Critics: Stevens, Cummings, Frost, and Williams in the 1930s* (Tuscaloosa: University of Alabama Press, 2010).
Cook, Eleanor. *Elizabeth Bishop at Work* (Cambridge, MA: Harvard University Press, 2016).
Erkkila, Betsy. "Elizabeth Bishop, Modernism, and the Left," *American Literary History* 8.2 (1996), 284–310.

Filreis, Alan. *The Counter-Revolution of the Word: The Conservative Attack on Modern Poetry, 1945–1960* (Chapel Hill: University of North Carolina Press, 2012).
Genette, Gérard. "The Architext" (1979, trans. 1992), reprinted in *The Lyric Theory Reader: A Critical Anthology* (Baltimore, MD: Johns Hopkins University Press, 2014), 17–29.
Hirsch, Wendy. "Bogan, Louise (1897–1970), poet and critic," *American National Biography* (February 2000). Web.
Jeffreys, Mark. "Ideologies of Lyric: A Problem of Genre in Contemporary Anglophone Poetics," *PMLA* 110.2 (March 1995), 196–205.
Jackson, Virginia. "Lyric," in *Princeton Encyclopedia of Poetry and Poetics*, ed. Roland Greene and Stephen Cushman (Princeton, NJ: Princeton University Press, 2012), 826–34.
Lanier, Sidney. *The Science of English Verse* (New York: C. Scribner's Sons, 1880).
Longenbach, James. "Elizabeth Bishop's Social Conscience," *English Literary History* 62.2 (Summer 1995), 467–86.
Mill, John Stuart. "Thoughts on Poetry and Its Varieties" (1833), in *The Collected Works of John Stuart Mill, Volume I – Autobiography and Literary Essays*, ed. John M. Robson and Jack Stillinger (Toronto: University of Toronto Press, 1981), 343–66.
Perloff, Marjorie. *21st-Century Modernism: The 'New' Poetics* (Malden, MA: Blackwell, 2002).
"A Conversation with Marjorie Perloff," interview by Hélène Aji and Antoine Cazé (May 26, 2007), marjorieperloff.com/interviews/aji-caze-interview.
Sylvester, J.J. *The Laws of Verse, or, Principles of Versification* (London: Longmans, Green, and Co., 1870).
Thain, Marion, ed. *The Lyric Poem: Formations and Transformations* (Cambridge: Cambridge University Press, 2013).
Vendler, Helen. "Life Studies: The Collected Prose of Elizabeth Bishop," *The New York Review of Books* (February 16, 1984), www.nybooks.com/articles/archives/1984/feb/16/life-studies.
Voigt, Ellen Bryant, ed. *The Flexible Lyric* (Athens: University of Georgia Press, 1999).

8 Prose

Costello, Bonnie. *Elizabeth Bishop: Questions of Mastery* (Cambridge, MA: Harvard University Press, 1991).
Croll, Morris. "The Baroque Style in Prose" (1929); repr. in *Style, Rhetoric and Rhythm: Essays by Morris W. Croll*, ed. J. Max Patrick and Robert O. Evans, with John M. Wallace and R. J. Schoeck (Princeton, NJ: Princeton University Press, 1966), 207–36.
Kinzie, Mary. *The Cure of Poetry in an Age of Prose: Moral Essays on the Poet's Calling* (Chicago: University of Chicago Press, 1993).
Ravinthiran, Vidyan. *Elizabeth Bishop's Prosaic* (Lewisburg: Bucknell University Press, 2015).

Rich, Adrienne. *Culture, Politics, and the Art of Poetry: Essential Essays*, ed. Sandra M. Gilbert (New York: Norton, 2018).

Saintsbury, George. *A History of English Prose Rhythm* (London and Bloomington: Indiana University Press, 1965).

9 Letters

Altman, Janet Gurkin. *Epistolarity: Approaches to a Form* (Columbus: Ohio State University Press, 1982)

Bishop, Elizabeth. Letters to Louise Bradley. Louise Bradley and Elizabeth Bishop Correspondence Collection, Wylie House Museum, Indiana University Libraries, Bloomington.

Letters to Dr. Ruth Foster. Elizabeth Bishop Papers, Special Collections, Vassar College Library.

Carlyle, Thomas. *On Heroes, Hero-Worship, and the Heroic in History* (New York: Appleton, 1841).

Cleghorn, Angus, and Jonathan Ellis, eds. *The Cambridge Companion to Elizabeth Bishop* (Cambridge: Cambridge University Press, 2014).

Culler, Jonathan. *Theory of the Lyric* (Cambridge: Harvard UP, 2015).

Ellis, Jonathan. *Art and Memory in the Work of Elizabeth Bishop* (Aldershot: Ashgate, 2006).

"'Between Us': Letters and Poems of Stevenson and Bishop," in *Voyages over Voices: Critical Essays on Anne Stevenson*, ed. Angela Leighton (Liverpool: Liverpool University Press, 2010), 28–54.

Ellis, Jonathan, ed. *Letter-Writing Among Poets* (Edinburgh: Edinburgh University Press, 2015).

Goldensohn, Lorrie. "Approaching Elizabeth Bishop's Letters to Dr. Ruth Foster," *Yale Review* 103.1 (January 2015), 1–19.

Hamilton, Saskia. *The Dolphin Letters, 1970–1979: Elizabeth Hardwick, Robert Lowell, and Their Circle* (New York: Farrar, Straus and Giroux, 2019).

Hammer, Langdon. "The Art of Losing," *The New York Review of Books* 66.20 (December 2019), 52–56.

"Useless Concentration: Life and Work in Elizabeth Bishop's Letters and Poems," *American Literary History* 9.1 (1997), 162–80.

Logan, William. *Guilty Knowledge, Guilty Pleasure: The Dirty Art of Poetry* (New York: Columbia University Press, 2014).

Marshall, Megan. *Elizabeth Bishop. A Miracle for Breakfast* (New York: Houghton Mifflin Harcourt, 2017).

Millier, Brett C. *Elizabeth Bishop: Life and the Memory of It* (Berkeley: University of California Press, 1993).

Phillips, Siobhan. "Bishop's Correspondence," in *The Cambridge Companion to Elizabeth Bishop*, ed. Angus Cleghorn and Jonathan Ellis (Cambridge: Cambridge University Press, 2014), 155–68.

Ravinthiran, Vidyan. *Elizabeth Bishop's Prosaic* (Lewisburg, PA: Bucknell University Press, 2015).

Schwartz, Lloyd, and Sybil P. Estess, eds. *Elizabeth Bishop and Her Art* (Ann Arbor: University of Michigan Press, 1983).
Travisano, Thomas. *Love Unknown: The Life and Worlds of Elizabeth Bishop* (New York: Viking, 2019).

10 Translation

Bishop, Elizabeth, trans. *The Diary of "Helena Morley"* (New York: Farrar, Straus and Giroux, 1995).
Bishop, Elizabeth, and Emanuel Brasil, eds. *An Anthology of Twentieth-Century Brazilian Poetry* (Hanover and London: Wesleyan University Press, 1972).
Goldensohn, Lorrie. *Elizabeth Bishop: The Biography of a Poetry* (New York: Columbia University Press, 1992).
Harrison, Victoria. *Elizabeth Bishop's Poetics of Intimacy* (Cambridge: Cambridge University Press, 1993).
Henneberg, Sylvia. "Elizabeth Bishop's 'Brazil, January 1, 1502' and Max Jacob's 'Etablissement d'une communauté au Brésil': A Study of Transformative Interpretation and Influence," *Texas Studies in Literature and Language* 45.4 (2003), 337–51.
Hicok, Bethany. *Elizabeth Bishop's Brazil* (Charlottesville: University of Virginia Press, 2016).
Kalstone, David. *Becoming a Poet: Elizabeth Bishop with Marianne Moore and Robert Lowell* (New York: Farrar, Straus and Giroux, 1989).
Lombardi, Marilyn May. *The Body and the Song: Elizabeth Bishop's Poetics* (Carbondale: Southern Illinois University Press, 1995).
Machova, Mariana. *Elizabeth Bishop and Translation* (Lanham, MD: Lexington Books, 2017).
Monteiro, George, ed. *Conversations with Elizabeth Bishop* (Jackson: University Press of Mississippi, 1996).
Moser, Benjamin. *Why This World: A Biography of Clarice Lispector* (Oxford: Oxford University Press, 2009).
Fountain, Gary, and Peter Brazeau. *Remembering Elizabeth Bishop: An Oral Biography* (Amherst: University of Massachusetts Press, 1994).
Parker, Robert Dale. *The Unbeliever: The Poetry of Elizabeth Bishop* (Urbana: University of Illinois Press, 1988).
Paz, Octavio. *A Draft of Shadows and Other Poems*, ed. Eliot Weinberger (New York: New Directions, 1980).
"Translation: Literature and Letters," in *Theories of Translation*, ed. Rainer Schulte and John Biguenet (Chicago: University of Chicago Press, 1992), 152–62.
Robinson, Peter. *Poetry and Translation: The Art of the Impossible* (Liverpool: Liverpool University Press, 2010).
Vendler, Helen. "Domestication, Domesticity, and the Otherworldly," in *Elizabeth Bishop and Her Art*, ed. Lloyd Schwartz and Sybil P. Estess (Ann Arbor: University of Michigan Press, 1983), 32–48.

11 Visual Art

Altieri, Charles. *Painterly Abstraction in Modernist American Poetry: The Contemporaneity of Modernism* (Cambridge: Cambridge University Press, 1989)

Anderson, Linda. *Elizabeth Bishop: Lines of Connection* (Edinburgh: Edinburgh University Press, 2013)

"Disturbances of the Archive: Repetition and Memory in Elizabeth Bishop's Poetry," in *Reading Elizabeth Bishop: An Edinburgh Companion*, ed. Jonathan Ellis (Edinburgh: Edinburgh University Press, 2019), 19–32.

Caws, Mary Ann. *The Surrealist Look* (Cambridge, MA: The MIT Press, 1999)

Costello, Bonnie, *Elizabeth Bishop: Questions of Mastery* (Cambridge, MA: Harvard University Press, 1991).

Dijkstra, Bram. *Cubism, Stieglitz, and the Early Poetry of William Carlos Williams* (Princeton, NJ: Princeton University Press, 1969).

hattongallery.org.uk/collections/kurt-schwitters-merz-barn-wall.

Kantor, Sybil Gordon. *Alfred H. Barr, Jr. and the Intellectual Origins of the Museum of Modern Art* (Cambridge, MA: MIT Press, 2003).

Klee, Paul. *On Modern Art*, introduction by Herbert Read (London: Faber and Faber, 1966).

Leavell, Linda. *Marianne Moore and the Visual Arts* (Baton Rouge: Louisiana State University Press, 1995).

MacLeod, Glen. "Modernism and the Visual Arts," in *The Cambridge Companion to Modernism*, ed. Michael Levenson (Cambridge: Cambridge University Press, 2011), 245–67.

Wallace Stevens and Modern Art: From the Armory Show to Abstract Expressionism (New Haven and London: Yale University Press, 1993).

Miller, Margaret, ed. *Paul Klee* (New York: Museum of Modern Art, 1941).

Moore, Marianne. *Selected Letters*, ed. Bonnie Costello (Harmondsworth: Penguin Books, 1998).

Page, Barbara. "Off-Beat Claves, Oblique Realities: The Key-West Notebooks of Elizabeth Bishop," in *Elizabeth Bishop: The Geography of Gender*, ed. Marilyn May Lombardi (Charlottesville and London: University Press of Virginia, 1993), 196–211.

Rosenbaum, Susan. "Bishop and the Natural World," in *The Cambridge Companion to Elizabeth Bishop*, ed. Angus Cleghorn and Jonathan Ellis (Cambridge: Cambridge University Press, 2014), 62–78.

Samuels, Peggy. *Deep Skin: Elizabeth Bishop and Visual Art* (Ithaca: Cornell University Press, 2010)

Wolfflïn, Heinrich. *Principles of Art History: The Problem of the Development of Style in Later Art*, trans. M. D. Hottinger (New York: Dover Publications, 1932).

12 Archives

Anderson, Linda R. *Elizabeth Bishop: Lines of Connection* (Edinburgh: Edinburgh University Press, 2015).

Bailey, Iain. "Allusion and Exogenesis: The Labouring Heart of Samuel Beckett's *Ill Seen Ill Said*," in *The Boundaries of the Literary Archive: Reclamation and Representation*, ed. Carrie Smith and Lisa Stead (New York: Routledge, 2016), 31–44.

Barry, Sandra. *Elizabeth Bishop: An Archival Guide to Her Life in Nova Scotia* (Hantsport, NS: Lancelot Press, 1996).

Cleghorn, Angus, Bethany Hicok, and Thomas Travisano, eds. *Elizabeth Bishop in the 21st Century: Reading the New Editions* (Charlottesville and London: University of Virginia Press, 2012).

Colbrook, Claire. "The Anthropocene and the Archive," *Durham University Memory Network*, thememorynetwork.net/the-anthropocene-and-the-archive.

Cook, Eleanor. *Elizabeth Bishop at Work* (Cambridge, MA: Harvard University Press, 2016).

Craven, Louise. "From the Archivist's Cardigan to the Very Dead Sheep: What Are Archives? What Are Archivists? What Do They Do?" in *What Are Archives?: Cultural and Theoretical Perspectives: A Reader*, ed. Louise Craven (New York: Routledge, 2008), 7–30.

Derrida, Jacques. "Archive Fever: A Freudian Impression," *Diacritics* 25.2 (Summer 1995), 9–63.

Ellis, Jonathan. *Art and Memory in the Work of Elizabeth Bishop* (Burlington, VT: Ashgate, 2006).

Goldensohn, Lorrie. "Approaching Elizabeth Bishop's Letters to Ruth Foster," *Yale Review* 103.1 (January 2015), 1–19.

"Elizabeth Bishop: An Unpublished, Untitled Poem," *American Poetry Review* (January/February 1988), 35–36.

Elizabeth Bishop: The Biography of a Poetry (New York: Columbia University Press, 1992).

"Elizabeth Bishop's Drafts: 'That Sense of Constant Readjustment,'" in *Elizabeth Bishop in the 21st Century*, ed. Angus Cleghorn, Bethany Hicok and Thomas Travisano (Charlottesville and London: University of Virginia Press, 2012), 104–16.

Gray, Jeffrey. "Postcards and Sunsets: Bishop's Revision and the Problem of Excess," in *Elizabeth Bishop in the 21st Century: Reading the New Editions*, ed. Angus Cleghorn, Bethany Hicok, and Thomas Travisano (Charlottesville and London: University of Virginia Press, 2012), 26–40.

Harrison, Victoria. *Elizabeth Bishop's Poetics of Intimacy* (Cambridge: Cambridge University Press, 1993).

Helle, Anita. "Lessons from the Archive: Sylvia Plath and the Politics of Memory," *Feminist Studies* 31.3 (Fall 2005), 631–52.

Helle, Anita, ed. *The Unraveling Archive: Essays on Sylvia Plath* (Ann Arbor: University of Michigan Press, 2007).

Hicok, Bethany. *Degrees of Freedom: American Women Poets and the Women's College, 1905–1955* (Lewisburg: Bucknell University Press, 2008).

Elizabeth Bishop's Brazil (Charlottesville and London: University of Virginia Press, 2016).

ed. *Elizabeth Bishop and the Literary Archive* (Lever Press, 2020).

Knorr, Alyse. "'Keeping Up a Silent Conversation': Recovering a Queer Bishop through Her Intimate Correspondence with Alice Methfessel," in *Elizabeth Bishop and the Literary Archive*, ed. Bethany Hicok (Lever Press, 2020). Web.

Logan, William. "Elizabeth Bishop at Summer Camp," in *Guilty Knowledge, Guilty Pleasure: The Dirty Art of Poetry* (New York: Columbia University Press, 2014), 250–302.

Lombardi, Marilyn May, ed. *Elizabeth Bishop: The Geography of Gender* (Charlottesville and London: University Virginia Press, 1993).

Marshall, Megan. *Elizabeth Bishop: A Miracle for Breakfast* (New York: Houghton Mifflin Harcourt, 2017).

Millier, Brett C. *Elizabeth Bishop: Life and the Memory of It* (Berkeley: University of California Press, 1993).

Morra, Linda. *Unarrested Archives: Case Studies in Twentieth-Century Canadian Women's Authorship* (Toronto: University of Toronto Press, 2014).

Page, Barbara. "Off-Beat Claves, Oblique Realities: The Key West Notebooks of Elizabeth Bishop," in *Elizabeth Bishop: The Geography of Gender*, ed. Marilyn May Lombardi (Charlottesville and London: University of Virginia Press, 1993), 196–211.

Rich, Adrienne. "The Eye of the Outsider: Elizabeth Bishop's *Complete Poems, 1927–1979* (1983)," in *Blood, Bread, and Poetry: Selected Prose, 1979–1985* (New York: Norton, 1986), 125–35.

Roman, Camille. *Elizabeth Bishop's World War II–Cold War View* (New York: Palgrave, 2001).

Rosenbaum, Susan. "Elizabeth Bishop and the Miniature Museum," *Journal of Modern Literature* 28.2 (2005), 61–99.

Samuels, Peggy. *Deep Skin: Elizabeth Bishop and Visual Art* (Ithaca: Cornell University Press, 2010).

Smith, Carrie, and Lisa Stead, eds. *The Boundaries of the Literary Archive: Reclamation and Representation* (New York: Routledge, 2016).

Steedman, Carolyn. *Dust: The Archive and Cultural Memory* (New Brunswick, NJ: Rutgers University Press, 2002).

Travisano, Thomas. *Elizabeth Bishop: Her Artistic Development* (Charlottesville and London: University of Virginia Press, 1988).

Love Unknown: The Life and Worlds of Elizabeth Bishop (New York: Viking, 2019).

Treseler, Heather. "'Too Shy to Stop': Elizabeth Bishop and the Scene of Reading," in *Elizabeth Bishop and the Literary Archive*, ed. Bethany Hicok (Lever Press, 2020). Web.

Vincent, John Emil. "Odd Job: Bishop's 'The Fairy Toll-Taker,'" in *Elizabeth Bishop and the Literary Archive*, ed. Bethany Hicok (Lever Press, 2020). Web.

13 Romantic and Victorian Poetry

Baudelaire, Charles. *Oeuvres complètes* (2 vols) (Paris: Editions de la Pléiade, 1975–76).

Baudelaire: Selected Writings on Art and Artists, trans. P. E. Charvet (Cambridge: Cambridge University Press, 1972).

Blake, William. *The Complete Poems*, ed. Alicia Ostriker (Harmondsworth: Penguin Books, 1977).

Coleridge, Sara. *Collected Poems*, ed. Peter Swaab (Manchester: Carcanet Press, 2007).

Costello, Bonnie. "Bishop and the Poetic Tradition," in *The Cambridge Companion to Elizabeth Bishop*, ed. Angus Cleghorn and Jonathan Ellis (Cambridge: Cambridge University Press, 2013), 79–94.

Edelman, Lee. "Elizabeth Bishop's 'In the Waiting Room,'" in *The Geography of Gender*, ed. Marilyn May Lombardi (Charlottesville: University Press of Virginia, 1993), 91–110.

Eliot, T. S. *The Use of Poetry and the Use of Criticism* (London: Faber and Faber, 1933).

Hazlitt, William (1817). *Characters of Shakespeare's Plays* (London: Printed by C.H. Reynell for R. Hunter and C. and J. Ollier).

Hopkins, Gerard Manley. *Gerard Manley Hopkins: The Major Works*, ed. Catherine Phillips (Oxford: Oxford University Press, 2002).

The Journals and Papers of Gerard Manley Hopkins, ed. Humphrey House and Graham Storey (Oxford: Oxford University Press, 1959).

Lahey, G.F. *Gerard Manley Hopkins* (2nd ed., New York: Haskell House, 1969, first published 1930).

Lear, Edward. *A Book of Nonsense* ([1846]; 18th ed., London: T. McLean, 1866).

The Complete Verse and Other Nonsense, ed. Vivien Noakes (London: Penguin Books, 2001).

Millier, Brett C. *Elizabeth Bishop: Life and the Memory of It* (Berkeley: University of California Press, 1993).

Monteiro, George, ed. *Conversations with Elizabeth Bishop* (Jackson: University of Mississippi Press, 1996).

Moss, Howard. *Writing against Time: Critical Essays and Reviews* (New York: William Morrow and Co., 1969).

O'Neill, Michael. *The All-Sustaining Air: Romantic Legacies and Renewals in British, American, and Irish Poetry since 1900* (Oxford: Oxford University Press, 2007).

Ricks, Christopher. *Eliot and Prejudice* (London: Faber and Faber, 1988).

Wordsworth, William. *William Wordsworth: The Major Works*, ed. Stephen Gill (Oxford: Oxford University Press, 1984).

14 Surrealism and the Avant-Garde

Ashbery, John. "Second Presentation of Elizabeth Bishop," *World Literature Today* 51.1 (1977), 8–11.

Brown, Ashley. "An Interview with Elizabeth Bishop," *Shenandoah* 17.2 (1966), 3–19.

Carson, Luke. "John Ashbery's Elizabeth Bishop," *Twentieth Century Literature* 54.4 (2008), 448–471.

Cavell, Stanley. *In Quest of the Ordinary: Lines of Skepticism and Romanticism* (Chicago: University of Chicago Press, 1988).

Cleghorn, Angus, and Jonathan Ellis, ed. *The Cambridge Companion to Elizabeth Bishop* (New York: Cambridge University Press, 2014).

Costello, Bonnie. "Bishop and the Poetic Tradition," in *The Cambridge Companion to Elizabeth Bishop*, ed. Angus Cleghorn and Jonathan Ellis (New York: Cambridge University Press, 2014), 79–96.

Elizabeth Bishop: Questions of Mastery (Cambridge, MA: Harvard University Press, 1991).

Diehl, Joanne. *Elizabeth Bishop and Marianne Moore: The Psychodynamics of Creativity* (Princeton, NJ: Princeton University Press, 1993).

Ellis, Jonathan. *Art and Memory in the Work of Elizabeth Bishop* (Burlington, VT: Ashgate, 2006).

Goldensohn, Lorrie. *Elizabeth Bishop: The Biography of a Poetry* (New York: Columbia University Press, 1992).

Keller, Lynn. *Remaking It New: Contemporary American Poetry and the Modernist Tradition* (Cambridge; New York: Cambridge University Press, 1987).

Kornhiser, Laurel. "North and South: The Bishop-Neruda Connection," in *Jarrell, Bishop, Lowell, & Co.*, ed. Suzanne Ferguson (Knoxville: University of Tennessee Press, 2003), 217–38.

Marshall, Megan. *Elizabeth Bishop: A Miracle for Breakfast* (Boston: Mariner Books, 2017).

McCabe, Susan. "Stevens, Bishop, and Ashbery: A Surrealist Lineage," *Wallace Stevens Journal* 22.2 (1998), 148–68.

Millier, Brett C. *Elizabeth Bishop: Life and the Memory of It* (Berkeley: University of California Press, 1993).

Muldoon, Paul. *The End of the Poem* (New York: Farrar, Straus and Giroux, 2006).

Mullen, Richard. "Elizabeth Bishop's Surrealist Inheritance," *American Literature* 54.1 (1982), 63–80.

Pickard, Zachariah. "The Attack on Surrealism in Elizabeth Bishop's Darwin Letter," *Studies in the Humanities* 31.2 (2004), 121–37.

Rosenbaum, Susan. "Bishop and the Natural World," in *The Cambridge Companion to Elizabeth Bishop*, ed. Angus Cleghorn and Jonathan Ellis (Cambridge: Cambridge University Press, 2014), 62–78.

Samuels, Peggy. *Deep Skin: Elizabeth Bishop and Visual Art* (Ithaca: Cornell University Press, 2010).

"Bishop and Visual Art," in *The Cambridge Companion to Elizabeth Bishop*, ed. Angus Cleghorn and Jonathan Ellis (Cambridge: Cambridge University Press, 2014), 169–82.

Sheringham, Michael. *Everyday Life: Theories and Practices from Surrealism to the Present* (Oxford; New York: Oxford University Press, 2006).
Spires, Elizabeth. "Elizabeth Bishop: The Art of Poetry," *Paris Review* 80 (1981). Web.
Stevens, Wallace. *Collected Poetry and Prose* (New York: Library of America, 1997).
Suárez-Toste, Ernesto. "Une Machine À Coudre Manuelle: Elizabeth Bishop's 'Everyday Surrealism,'" *Mosaic* 33.2 (2000), 143–60.
Travisano, Thomas. *Elizabeth Bishop: Her Artistic Development* (Charlottesville and London: University of Virginia Press, 1988).

15 Modernism

Anderson, Linda. *Elizabeth Bishop: Lines of Connection* (Edinburgh: Edinburgh University Press, 2013).
Ashbery, John. *Self-Portrait in a Convex Mirror: Poems* (Harmondsworth: Penguin, 1976).
Axelrod, Steven Gould. "Between Modernism and Postmodernism: The Cold War Poetics of Bishop, Lowell, and Ginsberg," *Pacific Coast Philology*. 42.1 (2007), 1–23.
Bishop, Elizabeth. "It All Depends," in *Mid-Century American Poets*, ed. John Ciardi (New York: Twayne, 1950), 267.
Brown, Ashley. "An Interview with Elizabeth Bishop," in *Conversations with Elizabeth Bishop*, George Monteiro, ed. (Jackson: University of Mississippi Press, 1996), 18–29.
Ciardi, John, ed. *Mid-Century American Poets* (New York: Twayne, 1950).
Cleghorn, Angus, and Jonathan Ellis, ed. *The Cambridge Companion to Elizabeth Bishop* (New York: Cambridge University Press, 2014).
Cleghorn, Angus, Bethany Hicok, and Thomas Travisano, eds. *Elizabeth Bishop in the 21st Century: Reading the New Editions* (Charlottesville and London: University of Virginia Press, 2012).
Colônia, Regina. "Poetry as a Way of Life," in *Conversations with Elizabeth Bishop*, ed. George Monteiro (Jackson: University Press of Mississippi, 1996), 50–53.
Costello, Bonnie. *Elizabeth Bishop: Questions of Mastery* (Cambridge, MA: Harvard University Press, 1991).
Eliot, T. S. *The Complete Poems and Plays* (London: Faber and Faber, 1989).
Ellis, Jonathan, ed. *Reading Elizabeth Bishop: An Edinburgh Companion* (Edinburgh: Edinburgh University Press, 2019).
Jarrell, Randall. "A Note on Poetry," in *Kipling, Auden & Co.: Essays and Reviews 1935–1964* (New York: Farrar, Straus and Giroux, 1980), 47–51.
Kalstone, David. *Becoming a Poet: Elizabeth Bishop with Marianne Moore and Robert Lowell* (New York: Farrar, Straus and Giroux, 1989).
Longenbach, James. *Modern Poetry after Modernism* (New York and Oxford: Oxford University Press, 1995).
Mariani, Paul L. "Hopkins' 'Andromeda' and the New Aestheticism," *Victorian Poetry* 11.1 (1973), 39–54.

McGowan, Philip. "Reading Elizabeth Bishop's 'Artifact of [Words],'" *Maintaining a Place: Conditions of Metaphor in Modern American Literature*, ed. Maria Stuart, Fionnghuala Sweeney, and Fionnuala Dillane (Dublin: University College Dublin Press, 2014), 130–43.

Monteiro, George, ed. *Conversations with Elizabeth Bishop* (Jackson: University of Mississippi Press, 1996).

Page, Barbara. "Off-Beat Claves, Oblique Realities: The Key West Notebooks of Elizabeth Bishop," in *Elizabeth Bishop: The Geography of Gender*, ed. Marilyn May Lombardi (Charlottesville and London: University Press of Virginia, 1993), 196–211.

Perloff, Marjorie. *21st-Century Modernism: The "New Poetic"* (Oxford: Blackwell, 2002).

"'Pound/Stevens: Whose Era?' Revisited," *Wallace Stevens Journal* 26. 2 (Fall 2002), 135–42.

Stevens, Wallace. "The Noble Rider and The Sound of Words," in *The Necessary Angel* (New York: Vintage Books, 1951), 1–36.

Travisano, Thomas. *Midcentury Quartet: Bishop, Lowell, Jarrell, Berryman and the Making of a Postmodern Aesthetic* (Charlottesville: University of Virginia Press, 1999).

16 Mid-Century Poetics

Ashbery, John. "Throughout is This Quality of Thingness," Review of Elizabeth Bishop's *The Complete Poems*, *The New York Times*, 1 June 1969, BR8.

Bishop, Elizabeth. "Song for a Rainy Season," *The New Yorker* (October 8, 1960), 40.

"Elizabeth Bishop to Anne Sexton." October 18, 1962. Anne Sexton Papers, Harry Ransom Center, Box 18, Folder 1.

"Elizabeth Bishop to Grace Bowers." June 10, 1963 and August 3, 1963. Elizabeth Bishop Collection, Vassar College Library, Poughkeepsie, New York.

Eliot, T. S. *The Waste Land, The Poems of T. S. Eliot: Volume I: Collected and Uncollected Poems*, ed. Christopher Ricks and Jim McCue (London: Faber and Faber, 2015).

Green, Fiona. "Elizabeth Bishop in Brazil and the 'New Yorker,'" *Journal of American Studies* 46.4 (November 2012), 803–29.

Grobe, Christopher. *The Art of Confession: The Performance of Self from Robert Lowell to Reality TV* (New York: New York University Press, 2017).

Hammer, Langdon. "Useless Concentration: Life and Work in Elizabeth Bishop's Letters and Poems," *American Literary History* 9.1 (Spring, 1997), 162–80.

Lindstrom, Eric. "Money, Painting, and the Generic Abidance of Elizabeth Bishop's 'Poem,'" *Modernism/modernity* 25.2 (April 2018), 349–67.

Lowell, Robert. "Memories of West Street and Lepke," in *Collected Poems*, ed. Frank Bidart and David Gewanter (New York: Farrar, Straus and Giroux, 2003), 187–88.

Lowell, Robert. "Robert Lowell accepts the 1960 National Book Award in Poetry for *Life Studies*," www.nationalbook.org/robert-lowells-accepts-the-1960-national-bookawards-in-poetry-for-life-studies.
Martin, Meredith. *The Rise and Fall of Meter: Poetry and English National Culture, 1860–1930* (Princeton, NJ: Princeton University Press, 2012).
Merrill, James. "Elizabeth Bishop (1911–1979)," in *Collected Prose*, ed. J. D. McClatchy and Stephen Yenser (New York: Knopf, 2004), 231–33.
Millier, Brett C. *Elizabeth Bishop: Life and the Memory of It* (Berkeley: University of California Press, 1993).
Phillips, Siobhan. "Bishop's Correspondence," in *The Cambridge Companion to Elizabeth Bishop*, ed. Angus Cleghorn and Jonathan Ellis (Cambridge: Cambridge University Press, 2014), 155–68.
Pound, Ezra. *Pavannes and Divisions* (New York: Knopf, 1918).
The Cantos (New York: New Directions, 1996).
Sexton, Anne. "Anne Sexton to Elizabeth Bishop," September 26, 1962. Elizabeth Bishop Collection, Vassar College Library, Poughkeepsie, New York.
Vendler, Helen. "Domestication, Domesticity, and the Otherworldly," in *Elizabeth Bishop and Her Art*, ed. Lloyd Schwartz and Sybil P. Estess (Ann Arbor: University of Michigan Press, 1983), 32–48.
White, Gillian. *Lyric Shame: The "Lyric" Subject of Contemporary American Poetry* (Cambridge, MA: Harvard University Press, 2014).
Winnicott, D. W. *Playing and Reality* (London and New York: Routledge, 1971).

17 Brazilian Literature

Andrade, Carlos Drummond de. *Farewell* (Rio de Janeiro: Editora Record, 1996).
Carlos Drummond de Andrade: Poesia e Prosa (Rio de Janeiro: Editora Nova Aguilar, 1992).
Bakhtin, Mikhail M. *Speech Genres and Other Late Essays*, ed. Caryl Emerson and Michael Holquist (Austin: University of Texas Press, 1986).
Bandeira, Manuel. *Poesia Completa e Prosa* (Rio de Janeiro: Editora Nova Aguilar S. A., 1996).
Bishop, Elizabeth. "A Conversation with Elizabeth Bishop," in *Conversations with Elizabeth Bishop*, ed. George Monteiro (Jackson: University Press of Mississippi, 1996), 82–97.
Bishop, Elizabeth, and Emanuel Brasil, eds. *An Anthology of Twentieth-Century Brazilian Poetry* (Hanover and London: Wesleyan University Press, 1972).
Britto, Paulo Henriques. "Bishop no Brasil," in *Elizabeth Bishop: Poemas do Brasil* (São Paulo: Companhia das Letras, 1999), 9–54.
Gledson, John. *Poesia e Poética de Carlos Drummond de Andrade* (São Paulo: Livraria Duas Cidades, 1981).
Harrison, Victoria. *Elizabeth Bishop's Poetics of Intimacy* (Cambridge: Cambridge University Press, 1993).

Hicok, Bethany. *Elizabeth Bishop's Brazil* (Charlottesville: University of Virginia Press, 2016).
Lispector, Clarice. "The Smallest Woman in the World," trans. Elizabeth Bishop, *Kenyon Review* 26.3 (Summer 1964), 501–06.
Przybycien, Regina. *Feijão-Preto e Diamantes: O Brasil na obra de Elizabeth Bishop* (Belo Horizonte, Minas Gerais: Editora UFMG, 2015).
Sant'Anna, Affonso Romano. *Drummond: o gauche no tempo* (Rio de Janeiro: Lia, Editor S. A., 1972).
Schwartz, Lloyd. "Annals of Poetry: Elizabeth Bishop and Brazil," *The New Yorker* (September 30, 1991), 85–97.
Süssekind, Flora. "A Geleia & o Engenho: em torno de uma carta poema de Elizabeth Bishop a Manuel Bandeira," in *Papéis Colados* (Rio de Janeiro: Editora UFRJ, 1993), 331–36.
Travisano, Thomas, and Saskia Hamilton, eds. *Words in the Air: The Complete Correspondence of Elizabeth Bishop and Robert Lowell* (New York: Farrar, Straus and Giroux, 2008).

18 War

Axelrod, Steven Gould. "Bishop, History, and Politics," in *The Cambridge Companion to Elizabeth Bishop*, ed. Angus Cleghorn and Jonathan Ellis (Cambridge: Cambridge University Press, 2014), 35–48.
Berger, Charles S. *Forms of Farewell: The Late Poetry of Wallace Stevens* (Madison: The University of Wisconsin Press, 1985).
Roman, Camille. *Elizabeth Bishop's World War II–Cold War View* (Basingstoke: Palgrave, 2001).
Schweik, Susan. *A Gulf So Deeply Cut: American Women Poets and the Second World War* (Madison: The University of Wisconsin Press, 1991).
Woodland, Malcom. *Wallace Stevens and the Apocalyptic Mode* (Iowa City: The University of Iowa Press, 2005).

19 The Cold War

Arendt, Hannah. *The Human Condition* (Chicago: University of Chicago Press, 1958, rpt. 1989).
Men in Dark Times (New York: Harcourt Brace, 1968, rpt. Mariner, 1970).
Aristotle. *Politics*, trans. Benjamin Jowett (Digireads.com Publishing, 2017).
Axelrod, Steven Gould. "Elizabeth Bishop and Containment Policy," *American Literature* 75.4 (December 2003), 843–67.
Bronski, Michael. *A Queer History of the United States* (Boston: Beacon Press, 2011).
Cárdenas, Mauricio, and Steven M. Helfand. "Latin American Economic Development," *The New Palgrave Dictionary of Economics* (Online Edition, 2011), www.dictionaryofeconomics.com.

Clark, Suzanne. *Cold Warriors: Manliness on Trial in the Rhetoric of the West* (Carbondale: Southern Illinois University Press, 2000).
Derrida, Jacques. *Echographies of Television* (Cambridge: Polity, 2002).
Ellis, Jonathan. *Art and Memory in the Work of Elizabeth Bishop* (Aldershot: Ashgate, 2006).
Faderman, Lillian. *The Gay Revolution: The Story of the Struggle* (New York: Simon and Schuster, 2015).
Ferreira de Souza, Pedro. "A History of Inequality: Top Incomes in Brazil, 1926/2015," *Working Paper #167* (2017), ipcig.org.
Fischer, Brodwyn M. *A Poverty of Rights: Citizenship and Inequality in Twentieth-Century Rio de Janeiro* (Stanford: Stanford University Press, 2008).
Fountain, Gary, and Peter Brazeau. *Remembering Elizabeth Bishop: An Oral Biography* (Amherst: University of Massachusetts Press, 1994).
Gramsci, Antonio. *Prison Notebooks* ([1971], revised and rpt. New York: Columbia University Press, 2011).
Gray, Jeffrey. *Mastery's End: Travel and Postwar American Poetry* (Athens: University of Georgia Press, 2005).
Hallin, Daniel C. *The "Uncensored War": The Media and Vietnam* (Berkeley: University of California Press, 1989).
Hicok, Bethany. *Elizabeth Bishop's Brazil* (Charlottesville: University of Virginia Press, 2016).
Johnson, David K. *The Lavender Scare: The Cold War Persecution of Gays and Lesbians in the Federal Government* (Chicago: University of Chicago Press, 2004).
Joon Ho, Bong, director. *Parasite* (film, Neon, 2019).
Kennan, George, writing as "X." "The Sources of Soviet Conduct," *Foreign Affairs* 25.4 (July 1947), 566–82.
Kurosawa, Akira, director. *High and Low* (film, Japan, 1963).
Levin, William C. "Cultural Commentary: What's in a Name, You Pinko?" *Bridgewater Review* 20.1 (2001), 14–15.
Martins, Maria Lúcia Milléo, "Elizabeth Bishop and Brazilian Popular Music: From Anonymous Sambas to Contemporary Composers," in *Elizabeth Bishop and the Music of Literature*, ed. Angus Cleghorn (Cham, Switzerland: Palgrave Pivot, 2019), 89–99.
McCarthy, Joseph R. Senate Speech, "Communists in Government Service," 20 February 1950 (*Congressional Record*, 81st Congress, 2nd session, 1955).
Morris, Bonnie J. "History of Lesbian, Gay, Bisexual and Transgender Social Movements," *American Psychological Association*, web article, apa.org.
Niebuhr, Reinhold. *The Irony of American History* (New York: Charles Scribner's Sons, 1952).
Nadel, Alan. *Containment Culture: American Narratives, Postmodernism, and the Atomic Age* (Durham, NC: Duke University Press, 1995).
Poupart, Clay. "'When Will My Turn Come?' The Civil Service Purges and the Construction of a Gay Security Risk in the Cold War United States, 1945–55." MA thesis, History Department, University of Saskatchewan, Saskatoon (2005), harvest.usask.ca.

Rabe, Stephen C. *The Most Dangerous Area in the World: John F. Kennedy Confronts Communist Revolution in Latin America* (Chapel Hill: University of North Carolina Press, 1999).
Roman, Camille. *Elizabeth Bishop's World War II–Cold War View* (New York: Palgrave, 2001).
Schlesinger, Arthur. *The Vital Center: The Politics of Freedom* (New York: Riverside Press, 1949).
Sedgwick, Eve Kosofsky. *Epistemology of the Closet* (Berkeley: University of California Press, 1990).
Shakespeare, William. *Hamlet* (England, 1603).
Stryker, Susan. *Transgender History: The Roots of Today's Revolution*, rev. ed. (New York: Seal Press, 2017).
Toops, Jessica. "The Lavender Scare: Persecution of Lesbianism During the Cold War," *Western Illinois Historical Review* 5 (Spring 2013), 91–107.
Travisano, Thomas. *Love Unknown: The Life and Worlds of Elizabeth Bishop* (New York: Viking, 2019).
Wilde, Oscar. *Intentions: The Decay of Lying, Pen, Pencil and Poison, The Critic as Artist, the Truth of Masks* (London: Forgotten Books, 2012).
World Economic Report 1950–51 (New York: UN Department of Economic Affairs, 1952).
Zona, Kirsten Hotelling. "Bishop, Race, Class, and Gender," in *The Cambridge Companion to Elizabeth Bishop*, ed. Angus Cleghorn and Jonathan Ellis (New York: Cambridge University Press, 2014), 49–61.

20 Music

Bishop, Elizabeth. *Conversations with Elizabeth Bishop*, ed. George Monteiro. Jackson: University Press of Mississippi, 1996.
"Influences." *American Poetry Review* 14.1 (January–February 1985), 11–16.
Poetry Pilot (October 1964), 9.
Booth, Mark W. *The Experience of Songs* (New Haven: Yale University Press, 1981).
Carter, Elliott. *A Mirror on Which to Dwell (Six Poems of Elizabeth Bishop) for Soprano and Chamber Orchestra*, corrected ed. (New York: Associated Music Publishers, 2003).
"Selected Program Notes," *Chicago Review* 58.3–4 (Summer 2014), 13–45.
Cleghorn, Angus, ed. *Elizabeth Bishop and the Music of Literature* (Cham, Switzerland: Palgrave Pivot, 2019).
Cook, Eleanor. *Elizabeth Bishop at Work* (Cambridge, MA: Harvard University Press, 2016).
Fountain, Gary, and Peter Brazeau. *Remembering Elizabeth Bishop: An Oral Biography* (Amherst: University of Massachusetts Press, 1994).
Hart, Lorenz. *The Complete Lyrics of Lorenz Hart*, ed. Dorothy Hart and Robert Kimball (New York: Knopf, 1986).

Heaney, Seamus. *The Government of the Tongue: Selected Prose 1978–87* (New York: Farrar, Straus and Giroux, 1989).
Lowell, Robert. "From 'Thomas, Bishop, and Williams,'" in *Elizabeth Bishop and Her Art*, ed. Lloyd Schwartz and Sybil P. Estess (Ann Arbor: University of Michigan Press, 1983), 186–89.
Mayson, Katrina. "Elizabeth Bishop and 'A Bad Case of the *Threes*,'" in *Reading Elizabeth Bishop: An Edinburgh Companion*, ed. Jonathan Ellis (Edinburgh: Edinburgh University Press, 2019), 164–76.
Merrill, James. *Collected Poems*, ed. J. D. McClatchy and Stephen Yenser (New York: Knopf, 2001).
Millier, Brett C. *Elizabeth Bishop: Life and the Memory of It* (Berkeley: University of California Press, 1993).
Moore, Marianne. "A Modest Expert: *North & South*," in *Elizabeth Bishop and Her Art*, ed. Lloyd Schwartz and Sybil P. Estess (Ann Arbor: University of Michigan Press, 1983), 177–79.
Ravinthiran, Vidyan. *Elizabeth Bishop's Prosaic* (Lewisburg: Bucknell University Press, 2015).
Schwartz, Lloyd. "Elizabeth Bishop, 1911–1979," in *Elizabeth Bishop and Her Art*, ed. Lloyd Schwartz and Sybil P. Estess (Ann Arbor: University of Michigan Press, 1983), 252–54.
"'In Need of Music': Musical Settings of Elizabeth Bishop," in *Elizabeth Bishop and the Music of Literature*, ed. Angus Cleghorn (Cham, Switzerland: Palgrave Pivot, 2019), 101–12.
Schwartz, Lloyd, and Sybil P. Estess, eds. *Elizabeth Bishop and Her Art* (Ann Arbor: University of Michigan Press, 1983).

21 Psychoanalysis

Anderson, Linda. "Disturbances of the Archive: Repetition and Memory in Elizabeth Bishop's Poetry," in *Reading Elizabeth Bishop: An Edinburgh Companion*, ed. Jonathan Ellis (Edinburgh: Edinburgh University Press, 2019), 19–32.
Bishop, Elizabeth. Unpublished letter to May Swenson. May Swenson Papers, University of Washington Libraries, Dept. of Special Collections.
Burnham, John, ed. *After Freud Left: A Century of Psychoanalysis in America* (Chicago: University of Chicago Press, 2012).
Crowley, Ralph M., and Maurice R. Green. "Revolution within Psychoanalysis: A History of the William Alanson White Institute." Unpublished typescript. Erich Fromm Online.
Flynn, Richard. "Elizabeth Bishop's Sanity: Childhood Trauma, Psychoanalysis, and Sentimentality," in *Elizabeth Bishop and the Literary Archive*, ed. Bethany Hicok (Lever Press, 2020). Web.
Frankenberg, Lloyd. "A Theory of 'Interpersonal Relations,'" *The New York Times*, 3 August 1947, BR4.

Freud, Sigmund. "Recommendations for Physicians on the Psychoanalytic Treatment," in *Collected Papers*, vol. 2., trans. James Strachey and Joan Riviere (New York: Basic Books, 1959), 327–28.
Goldensohn, Lorrie. "Approaching Elizabeth Bishop's Letters to Ruth Foster," *Yale Review* 103.1 (January 2015), 1–19.
Guex, Germaine. *The Abandonment Neurosis*, trans. Peter D. Douglas (London: Karnac Books, 2015).
Hale, Jr., Nathan G. *The Rise and Crisis of Psychoanalysis in the United States: Freud and the Americans 1917–1985* (Oxford: Oxford University Press, 1995).
Klein, Melanie. *Narrative of A Child Analysis* (New York: Basic Books, 1961).
Envy and Gratitude & Other Essays (London: Hogarth Press and The Institute of Psychoanalysis, 1975).
Marshall, Megan. *Elizabeth Bishop: A Miracle for Breakfast* (Boston: Houghton Mifflin Harcourt, 2017).
Millier, Brett. *Elizabeth Bishop: Life and the Memory of It* (Berkeley: University of California Press, 1993).
Monteiro, George, ed. *Conversations with Elizabeth Bishop* (Jackson: University of Mississippi Press, 1996).
Swick Perry, Helen. *Psychiatrist of America: The Life of Harry Stack Sullivan* (Cambridge: Belknap Press/Harvard University, 1982).
Treseler, Heather. "Dreaming in Color: Bishop's Notebook-Letter Poems," in *Elizabeth Bishop in the 21st Century: Reading the New Editions*, ed. Angus Cleghorn, Bethany Hicok, and Thomas Travisano (Charlottesville and London: University Virginia Press, 2012), 88–103.
"One Long Poem," *Boston Review* (July–August 2016). Web.
"'Too Shy to Stop': Elizabeth Bishop and the Scene of Reading," in *Elizabeth Bishop and the Literary Archive*, ed. Bethany Hicok (Lever Press, 2020). Web.
Wake, Naoko. *Private Practices: Harry Stack Sullivan, the Science of Homosexuality, and American Liberalism* (Brunswick: Rutgers University Press, 2011).
Woods, Ralph L., ed. *The World of Dreams: An Anthology of the Literature of Dreams from the Pharaohs to Freud* (New York: Random House, 1947).
Zaretsky, Eli. *Secrets of the Soul: A Social and Cultural History of Psychoanalysis* (New York: Alfred Knopf, 2004).

22 Religion

Cook, Eleanor. *Elizabeth Bishop at Work* (Cambridge, MA: Harvard University Press, 2016).
Corelle, Laurel Snow. *A Poet's High Argument: Elizabeth Bishop and Christianity* (Columbia: University of South Carolina Press, 2008).
Costello, Bonnie. *Elizabeth Bishop: Questions of Mastery* (Cambridge, MA: Harvard University Press, 1991).
Dickinson, Emily. *The Poems of Emily Dickinson*, 3 vols., ed. R. W. Franklin (Cambridge, MA: Harvard University Press, 1998).

Fountain, Gary, and Peter Brazeau. *Remembering Elizabeth Bishop: An Oral Biography* (Amherst: University of Massachusetts Press, 1994).
Hopkins, Gerard Manley. *Immortal Diamond: The Spiritual Vision of Gerard Manley Hopkins* (New York: Doubleday-Image Books, 1995).
Merrin, Jeredith. *An Enabling Humility: Marianne Moore, Elizabeth Bishop, and the Uses of Tradition* (New Brunswick: Rutgers University Press, 1990).
Millier, Brett. *Elizabeth Bishop: Life and the Memory of It* (Berkeley: University of California Press, 1993).
Parker, Robert Dale. *The Unbeliever: The Poetry of Elizabeth Bishop* (Urbana: University of Illinois Press, 1988).
Pinkerton, Steve. *Blasphemous Modernism: The 20th-Century Word Made Flesh* (New York: Oxford University Press, 2017).
Teresa of Avila. *The Way of Perfection*, trans. E. Allison Peers (New York: Doubleday-Image Books, 1991).
Travisano, Thomas. *Elizabeth Bishop: Her Artistic Development* (Charlottesville and London: University Press of Virginia, 1988).
Walker, Cheryl. *God and Elizabeth Bishop: Meditations on Religion and Poetry* (New York: Palgrave Macmillan, 2005).

23 Anthropology

Boas, Franz. *The Shaping of American Anthropology 1883–1911*, ed. George W. Stocking, Jr. (New York: Basic Books, 1974).
Primitive Art (Irvington-on-Hudson: Capitol Publishing, 1951. First published 1927).
Castro, Ferdinand de. “Paternalismo e Antiamericanismo,” *Correia da Manhã* (28 Março 1965), 2nd Notebook p. 4., Web.
Cleghorn, Angus. “The Politics of Editing Bishop’s 1962 *Brazil* Volume for Life World Library,” *Berfrois* (20 September 2011), Web.
Freyre, Gilberto. *The Masters and the Slaves: A Study in the Development of Brazilian Civilization* (New York: Knopf, 1946).
Geertz, Clifford. *The Interpretation of Cultures* (New York: Basic Books, 1973).
Goldensohn, Lorrie. *Elizabeth Bishop: The Biography of a Poetry* (New York: Columbia University Press, 1992).
Gray, Jeffrey. *Mastery’s End: Travel and Postwar American Poetry* (Athens: University of Georgia Press, 2005).
Hicok, Bethany. *Elizabeth Bishop’s Brazil* (Charlottesville: University of Virginia Press, 2016).
Laughlin, George D. “The Ethno-Epistemology of Transpersonal Experience: The View from Transpersonal Anthropology,” *International Journal of Transpersonal Studies* 32.1 (2013), 43–50.
Lende, Daniel H., and Greg Downey. *The Encultured Brain: An Introduction to Neuroanthropology* (Cambridge: MIT Press, 2012). Web.
Lévi-Strauss, Claude. *Tristes Tropiques* (New York: Penguin Books, 1992).

Monteiro, George, ed. *Conversations with Elizabeth Bishop* (Jackson: University Press of Mississippi, 1996).
Sontag, Susan. "The Anthropologist as Hero," in *Essays of the 1960s and 70s*, ed. David Rieff (New York: Library of America, 2013).
Villas Boas, Orlando, and Claudio Villas Boas. *Xingu: The Indians, Their Myths* (Farrar, Straus and Giroux, 1973).
Wagley, Charles. *Amazon Town: A Study of Man in the Tropics* (New York: Macmillan, 1953).

24 Travel

Ashbery, John. "Throughout Is This Quality of Thingness," Review of Elizabeth Bishop's *The Complete Poems*, *The New York Times*, 1 June 1969, BR8.
Baudelaire, Charles. *Journaux intimes fusées: Mon Coeur mis à nu* (Create Space, 2011).
Bishop, Elizabeth. "A Trip on the Rio São Francisco," Elizabeth Bishop Papers, Special Collections, Vassar College Library.
Bishop, Elizabeth, and the Editors of Life. *Brazil* (New York: Time Incorporated, 1962).
Cleghorn, Angus, Bethany Hicok, and Thomas Travisano, eds. *Elizabeth Bishop in the 21st Century: Reading the New Editions* (Charlottesville and London: University of Virginia Press, 2012).
Emerson, Ralph Waldo. "Self-Reliance," in *Emerson's Prose and Poetry*, ed. Joel Porte and Saundra Morris (New York: Norton, 2001), 120–36.
Fortuny, Kim. *Elizabeth Bishop: The Art of Travel* (Boulder: University Press of Colorado, 2003).
Freud, Sigmund. "A Disturbance of Memory on the Acropolis," in *The Standard Edition of the Complete Psychological Works of Sigmund Freud*, vol. 22, trans. James Strachey (London: Hogarth, 1964), 239–248.
Gray, Jeffrey. *Mastery's End: Travel and Postwar American Poetry* (Athens: University of Georgia Press, 2006).
"Postcards and Sunsets: Bishop's Revisions and the Problem of Excess," in *Elizabeth Bishop in the 21st Century: Reading the New Editions*, ed. Angus Cleghorn, Bethany Hicok, and Thomas Travisano (Charlottesville and London: University of Virginia, 2011), 26–40.
Hallberg, Robert von. *American Poetry and Culture: 1945–1980* (Cambridge, MA: Harvard University Press, 1985).
Huxley, Aldous. *Along the Road: Notes and Essays of a Tourist* (New York: Ecco, 1989).
Iyer, Pico. "Why We Travel," *Salon* 18 (March 2000), picoiyerjourneys.com/index.php/2000/03/why-we-travel.
Kalstone, David. *Becoming a Poet* (New York: Farrar, Straus and Giroux, 1989).
Kaplan, Caren. *Questions of Travel: Postmodern Discourses of Displacement* (Durham, NC: Duke University Press, 1996).
Lévi-Strauss, Claude. *Tristes Tropiques*, trans. John and Doreen Weightman (New York: Atheneum, 1984).

Montaigne, Michel de. "On the Cannibals," web2.qatar.cmu.edu/~breilly2/odyssey/Montaigne.pdf.
Theroux, Paul. "Why We Travel," *The New York Times*, 18 March 2000, www.nytimes.com/2011/04/03/travel/03Cover.html.
Wolff, Janet. "On the Road Again: Metaphors of Travel in Cultural Criticism," in *Resident Alien: Feminist Cultural Criticism* (New Haven: Yale University Press, 1995), 115–34.

25 Dreams

Anderson, Linda. *Elizabeth Bishop: Lines of Connection* (Edinburgh: Edinburgh University Press, 2015).
Ashbery, John. *Selected Prose* (Ann Arbor: University of Michigan Press, 2004).
Bachelard, Gaston. *Poetics of Reverie: Childhood, Language, and the Cosmos*, trans. D. Russell (Boston: Beacon Press, 1969).
Barasch, Moshe. *Modern Theories of Art: From Winckelmann to Baudelaire*, vol. 1 (New York: New York University Press, 1990).
Benjamin, Walter. *The Work of Art in the Age of Technical Reproducibility and Other Essays on Media* (Cambridge, MA: Harvard University Press, 2008).
Bidney, Martin. "'Controlled Panic': Mastering the Terrors of Dissolution and Isolation in Elizabeth Bishop's Epiphanies," *Style* 34.3 (2000), 487–510.
Bishop, Elizabeth, and Alice Quinn. "Selections from Edgar Allan Poe & The Juke-Box: A Special APR Supplement," *The American Poetry Review* 34.6 (November–December 2005), 35–44.
Cook, Eleanor. *Elizabeth Bishop at Work* (Cambridge, MA: Harvard University Press, 2016).
Costello, Bonnie. *Planets on Tables: Poetry, Still Life, and the Turning World* (Ithaca, NY: Cornell University Press, 2008).
Curry, Renée R. "A Thirst for Reverie: Alcohol, Despair, and Dream Space in Elizabeth Bishop's Poetry," *Literature and Medicine* 18.1 (Spring 1999) 100–13.
Dickey, Frances. "Opening the Box," *Essays in Criticism* 57.1 (January 2007), 73–81.
Ellis, Jonathan. "'A Curious Cat': Elizabeth Bishop and the Spanish Civil War," *Journal of Modern Literature* 27.1/2 (Fall 2003), 137–48.
Frost, Carol. "Elizabeth Bishop's Inner Eye," *New England Review* 25.1–2 (2004), 250–57.
Gray, Jeffrey. "Resting Places," *Contemporary Literature* 51.4 (Winter 2010), 874–82.
Hudock, Sandra L. "Uneven Terrain, Engravable Journeys, and Dark-Gold Sand: Elizabeth Bishop's Inverted Portable Aesthetic," in *The Image of Power in Literature, Media, and Society: Selected Papers, 2006 Conference, Society for the Interdisciplinary Study of Social Imagery*, ed. Will Wright and Steven Kaplan (Pueblo: Colorado State University Press, 2006), 125–31.
Jacob, Max, Francis Ponge, and Jean Follain. *Dreaming the Miracle: Three French Prose Poets*, trans. Beth Archer Brombert, Mary Feeney, Louise Guiney, William T. Kulik, and William Matthews (Buffalo, NY: White Pines Press, 2003).

Kuspit, Donald. "From Vision to Dream: The Secularization of the Imagination," in *Dreams 1900–2000: Science, Art and the Unconscious Mind*, ed. Lynn Gamwell (Ithaca, NY: Cornell University Press, 1999), pp. 77–88.

Leviston, Frances. "Mothers and Marimbas in 'The Bight': Bishop's Danse Macabre," *Twentieth-Century Literature* 6.41 (December 2015), 436–59.

MacArthur, Marit J. "'In a Room': Elizabeth Bishop in Europe, 1935–1937," *Texas Studies in Literature and Language* 50.4 (Winter 2008), 408–42.

Merleau-Ponty, Maurice. *The Visible and the Invisible*, trans. Alphonso Lingis (Evanston, IL: Northwestern University Press, 1969).

Millier, Brett C. "The Prodigal: Elizabeth Bishop and Alcohol," *Contemporary Literature* 39.1 (Spring 1998), 54–76.

Mullen, Richard. "Elizabeth Bishop's Surrealist Inheritance," *American Literature* 54.1 (March 1982), 63–80.

Munson, Barbara Faye. "Gates of horn, gates of ivory: the dream motif in the works of Elizabeth Bishop and Flannery O'Connor," unpublished PhD thesis, University of Southwestern Louisiana (1996).

Page, Barbara. "Off-Beat Claves, Oblique Realities: The Key West Notebooks of Elizabeth Bishop," in *Elizabeth Bishop: The Geography of Gender*, ed. Marilyn May Lombardi (Charlottesville: University Press of Virginia, 1993), 196–211.

Pickard, Zachariah. *Elizabeth Bishop's Poetics of Description* (Montreal: McGill-Queens University Press, 2009).

Procopiow, Norma. "Survival Kit: The Poetry of Elizabeth Bishop," *The Centennial Review* 25.1 (Winter 1981), 1–19.

Powers-Beck, Jeffrey. "'Time to Plant Tears': Elizabeth Bishop's Seminary of Tears," *South Atlantic Review* 60.4 (November 1995), 69–87.

Samuels, Peggy. "Elizabeth Bishop and Paul Klee," *Modernism/modernity* 14.3 (September 2007), 543–568.

Schwartz, Lloyd, and Sybil P. Estess. *Elizabeth Bishop and Her Art* (Ann Arbor: University of Michigan Press, 1983).

Schwenger, Peter. "The Dream Narratives of Debris," *SubStance* 32.1 (2003), 75–89.

Shakespeare, William. *The Tempest*, ed. Virginia Mason Vaughan and Alden T. Vaughan (London: Arden Shakespeare, 1999).

Suárez-Toste, Ernesto. "Dream Logic and Multiple Metamorphoses in Elizabeth Bishop's Early Poetry," *Revista de Estudios Norteamericanos* 9 (2003), 111–21.

"'Straight from Chirico': Pictorial Surrealism and the Early Elizabeth Bishop," *Studies in the Humanities* 23.2 (1996), 185–201.

"*Une Machine À Coudre Manuelle*: Elizabeth Bishop's 'Everyday Surrealism,'" *Mosaic: An Interdisciplinary Critical Journal* 33.2 (June 2000), 143–60.

Treseler, Heather. "Dreaming in Color: Bishop's Notebook Letter-Poems," in *Elizabeth Bishop in the 21st Century: Reading the New Editions*, ed. Angus Cleghorn, Bethany Hicok, and Thomas Travisano (Charlottesville and London: University of Virginia Press, 2012), 88–103.

Valéry, Paul. *Paul Valéry: An Anthology*, selected and introduced by J. R. Lawler (Princeton, NJ: Princeton University Press, 1977).

Walker, Cheryl. "Metaphysical Surrealism in the Poetry of Elizabeth Bishop," *Christianity & Literature* 48.1 (December 1998), 45–60.
Wallace, Nathaniel. "Vertical Slumber, the Hypnoglyph, and the Outs and Ins of the Postmodern," *Comparative Literature* 53.3 (June 2001), 233–61.

26 Humor

Bergson, Henri. "Laughter," *Comedy*, ed. W. Sypher (Baltimore, MD: The Johns Hopkins University Press, 1956), 61–190.
Burt, Stephanie. "Elizabeth Bishop and the End of the Rainbow," in *Reading Elizabeth Bishop: An Edinburgh Companion*, ed. Jonathan Ellis (Edinburgh: Edinburgh University Press, 2019), 321–36.
Carson, Luke. "James Merrill's Manners and Elizabeth Bishop's Dismay," *Twentieth-Century Literature* 50.2 (2004), 167–91.
Costello, Bonnie. "Tragicomic Mode in Modern American Poetry: 'Awful but Cheerful,'" in *A Companion to Poetic Genre*, ed. E. Martiny (New York: Wiley-Blackwell, 2011), 459–77.
Freud, Sigmund. *The Joke and Its Relation to the Unconscious*, trans. Joyce Crick (New York: Penguin, 2002).
Haughton, Hugh. "Poetry and Good Humor: Marianne Moore and Elizabeth Bishop," in *Humor in Modern American Poetry*, ed. R. Trousdale (London: Bloomsbury, 2017), 97–119.
Hobbes, Thomas. *Leviathan* (New York: Penguin, 1985).
Marshall, Megan. *Elizabeth Bishop: A Miracle for Breakfast* (New York: Houghton Mifflin Harcourt, 2017).
Materer, Timothy. "Mirrored Lives: Elizabeth Bishop and James Merrill," *Twentieth-Century Literature*, 51.2 (2005), 179–209.
Merrin, Jeredith. "Elizabeth Bishop: Gaiety, Gayness, and Change," in *Elizabeth Bishop: The Geography of Gender*, ed. M. M. Lombardi (Charlottesville: University of Virginia Press, 1993), 153–72.
Millier, Brett C. *Elizabeth Bishop: Life and the Memory of It* (Berkeley: University of California Press, 1993).
Muldoon, Paul. *The End of The Poem: Oxford Lectures* (New York: Farrar, Straus and Giroux, 2007).
Phillips, Siobhan. *The Poetics of the Everyday: Creative Repetition in Modern American Verse* (New York: Columbia University Press, 2010).
Ravinthiran, Vidyan. "'Manuelzinho,' Brazil and Identity Politics," in *Reading Elizabeth Bishop: An Edinburgh Companion*, ed. Jonathan Ellis (Edinburgh: Edinburgh University Press, 2019), 33–47.
Rosenbaum, Susan. "Elizabeth Bishop and the Miniature Museum," *Journal of Modern Literature* 28.2 (2005), 61–99.
Stevenson, Anne. *Between the Iceberg and the Ship* (Ann Arbor: University of Michigan Press, 1998).

Travisano, Thomas. *Elizabeth Bishop: Her Artistic Development* (Charlottesville and London: University of Virginia Press, 1988).
"'The Flicker of Impudence': Delicacy and Indelicacy in the Art of Elizabeth Bishop," in *Elizabeth* Bishop : *The Geography of Gender*, ed. M. M. Lombardi (Charlottesville: University of Virginia Press, 1993), 111–25.
Trousdale, Rachel. "'I Take off my Hat': Elizabeth Bishop's Comedy of Self-Revelation," in *Reading Elizabeth Bishop: An Edinburgh Companion*, ed. Jonathan Ellis (Edinburgh: Edinburgh University Press, 2019), 77–89.
"Introduction," *Humor in Modern American Poetry*, ed. R. Trousdale (London: Bloomsbury, 2017), 1–17.
Vendler, Helen. "Domestication, Domesticity, and the Otherworldly," in *Elizabeth Bishop and Her Art*, ed. Lloyd Schwartz and Sybil P. Estess (Ann Arbor: University of Michigan Press, 1983), 32–48.
Walker, Cheryl. *God and Elizabeth Bishop: Meditations on Religion and Poetry* (New York: Palgrave Macmillan, 2005).

27 Gender

Braidotti, Rosi. *Posthuman Knowledge* (Cambridge: Polity, 2019).
Burt, Stephanie. "Elizabeth Bishop at the End of the Rainbow," in *Reading Elizabeth Bishop: An Edinburgh Companion*, ed. Jonathan Ellis (Edinburgh: Edinburgh University Press, 2019), 321–36.
Cleghorn, Angus, ed. *Elizabeth Bishop and the Music of Literature* (Cham, Switzerland: Palgrave Pivot, 2019).
Diehl, Joanne Feit. *Women Poets and the American Sublime* (Bloomington: Indiana University Press, 1990).
Goldensohn, Lorrie. *Elizabeth Bishop: The Biography of a Poetry* (New York: Columbia University Press, 1992).
Hicok, Bethany. *Degrees of Freedom: American Women Poets and the Women's College, 1905–1955* (Lewisburg: Bucknell University Press, 2008).
Lombardi, Marilyn May, ed. *Elizabeth Bishop: Geography of Gender* (Charlottesville: University Press of Virginia, 1993).
Rich, Adrienne. "The Eye of the Outsider: Elizabeth Bishop's *Complete Poems*," in *Blood, Bread, and Poetry: Selected Prose, 1979–1985* (London: Virago Press, 1986), 124–35.
Rosenbaum, Susan. "Bishop and the Natural World," in *The Cambridge Companion to Elizabeth Bishop*, ed. Angus Cleghorn and Jonathan Ellis (Cambridge: Cambridge University Press, 2014), 62–78.
Tucker, Herbert. *Tennyson and the Doom of Romanticism* (Cambridge: Harvard University Press, 1988).
Waite, Amy. "'The color of the world all together': Elizabeth Bishop's Diffraction Patterns," in *Reading Elizabeth Bishop: An Edinburgh Companion*, ed. Jonathan Ellis (Edinburgh: Edinburgh University Press, 2019), 59–60.

28 Queerness

Auerbach, Erich. *Scenes from the Drama of European Literature* (Minneapolis: University of Minnesota Press, 1984).

Barthes, Roland. *The Pleasure of the Text*, trans. Richard Miller (New York: Hill and Wang, 1998).

Berlant, Lauren, and Lee Edelman. *Sex, or the Unbearable* (Durham, NC: Duke University Press, 2013).

Cook, Eleanor. *Elizabeth Bishop at Work* (Cambridge, MA: Harvard University Press, 2016).

Deleuze, Gilles. *The Fold: Leibniz and the Baroque*, trans. Tom Conley (New York: Continuum, 2006).

Edelman, Lee. "Aesthetic Value and Literary Language: Bishop and de Man," in *Never Again Would Birds' Song Be the Same: Essays on Early Modern and Modern Poetry in Honor of John Hollander*, ed. Jennifer Lewin (New Haven: Beinecke Library, 2002).

Ernst, Max. *Max Ernst: A Retrospective* (New York: The Solomon R. Guggenheim Museum, 1975).

Hardwick, Elizabeth. "The Perfectionist," *The New Republic* 190.11 (March 19, 1984), 32.

Harrison, Victoria. *Elizabeth Bishop's Poetics of Intimacy* (New York: Cambridge University Press, 1993).

Jarraway, David. "'O Canada!': The Spectral Lesbian Poetics of Elizabeth Bishop," *PMLA* 113.2 (March 1998), 243–57.

Johnson, Barbara. *The Barbara Johnson Reader: The Surprise of Otherness*, ed. Melissa Feuerstein, Bill Johnson González, Lili Porten, and Keja L. Valens (Durham, NC: Duke University Press, 2014).

McEleney, Corey. "Reading to the Letter: *No Future* and the Question of Rhetoric," *GLQ* 25.3 (June 2019), 431–55.

Muñoz, José Esteban. *Cruising Utopia: The Then and There of Queer Futurity* (Durham, NC: Duke University Press, 2009).

Nancy, Jean-Luc. *Expectation: Philosophy, Literature*, trans. Robert Bononno (New York: Fordham University Press, 2018).

Poe, Edgar Allan. *Essays and Reviews*, ed. Gary Richard Thompson (New York: Library of America, 1984).

Poetry and Tales, ed. Patrick Quinn (New York: Library of America, 1984).

Ravinthiran, Vidyan. *Elizabeth Bishop's Prosaic* (Lewisburg: Bucknell University Press, 2015).

Sedgwick, Eve Kosofsky, ed. *Novel Gazing: Queer Readings in Fiction* (Durham, NC: Duke University Press, 1997).

Tendencies (Durham, NC: Duke University Press, 1993).

Touching Feeling: Affect, Pedagogy, Performance (Durham, NC: Duke University Press, 2003).

The Weather in Proust, ed. Jonathan Goldberg (Durham, NC: Duke University Press, 2011).

Snediker, Michael D. "Weaver's Handshake: The Aesthetics of Chronic Objects," in *Reading Sedgwick*, ed. Lauren Berlant (Durham, NC: Duke University Press, 2019), 203–235.

Travisano, Thomas J. *Elizabeth Bishop: Her Artistic Development* (Charlottesville and London: University of Virginia Press, 1988).

29 Race

Axelrod, Steven Gould. "Bishop, History, and Politics," in *The Cambridge Companion to Elizabeth Bishop*, ed. Angus Cleghorn and Jonathan Ellis (Cambridge: Cambridge University Press, 2014), 35–48.

Campbell, Marvin. "Elizabeth Bishop and Audre Lorde: Two Views of 'Florida' in the Global South Atlantic," in *Reading Elizabeth Bishop*, ed. Jonathan Ellis (Edinburgh: Edinburgh University Press, 2019), 280–93.

Costello, Bonnie. *Elizabeth Bishop: Questions of Mastery* (Cambridge, MA: Harvard University Press, 1993).

"The Impersonal and the Interrogative in the Poetry of Elizabeth Bishop," in *Elizabeth Bishop and Her Art*, ed. Lloyd Schwartz and Sybil P. Estess (Ann Arbor: The University of Michigan Press, 1983), 109–32.

Curry, Renée R. *White Women Writing White: H.D., Elizabeth Bishop and Sylvia Plath and Whiteness* (Westport, CN: Greenwood Press, 2000).

Dickie, Margaret. "Race and Class in Elizabeth Bishop's Poetry," *The Yearbook of English Studies* 24 (1994), 44–58.

Hicok, Bethany. *Elizabeth Bishop's Brazil* (Charlottesville: University of Virginia Press, 2016).

Millier, Brett C. *Elizabeth Bishop: Life and the Memory of It* (Berkeley: University of California Press, 1993).

Moser, Benjamin. "Elizabeth Bishop's Misunderstood 'Brazil,'" *The New Yorker* (December 5, 2012). Web.

Pinsky, Robert. "The Idiom of a Self: Elizabeth Bishop and Wordsworth," in *Elizabeth Bishop and Her Art*, ed. Lloyd Schwartz and Sybil P. Estess (Ann Arbor: The University of Michigan Press, 1983), 49–60.

Ravinthiran, Vidyan. "'Manuelzinho', Brazil and Identity Politics," in *Reading Elizabeth Bishop*, ed. Jonathan Ellis (Edinburgh: Edinburgh University Press, 2019), 33–47.

Rich, Adrienne. *Essential Essays: Culture, Politics, and the Art of Poetry* (New York: Norton, 2018).

Vendler, Helen. "Domestication, Domesticity, and the Otherworldly," in *Elizabeth Bishop and Her Art*, ed. Lloyd Schwartz and Sybil P. Estess (Ann Arbor: The University of Michigan Press, 1983), 32–48.

Zona, Kirstin Hotelling. "Bishop: Race, Class and Gender," in *The Cambridge Companion to Elizabeth Bishop*, ed. Angus Cleghorn and Jonathan Ellis (Cambridge: Cambridge University Press, 2014), 49–61.

30 Nature

Bowie, David. "Changes," *Hunky Dory*, RCA Records, 1971.
Cleghorn, Angus. "Bishop's Wiring Fused: 'Bone Key' and 'Pleasure Seas,'" in *Elizabeth Bishop in the 21st Century: Reading the New Editions*, ed. Angus Cleghorn, Bethany Hicok, and Thomas Travisano (Charlottesville and London: University of Virginia Press, 2012), 69–87.
Costello, Bonnie. "Bishop and the Poetic Tradition," in *The Cambridge Companion to Elizabeth Bishop*, ed. Angus Cleghorn and Jonathan Ellis (Cambridge: Cambridge University Press, 2014), 79–94.
Dawson, Erica. "The Principal Beauty of 'At the Fishhouses,'" *Ecotone* 9.2 (Spring/Summer 2014), 33–37.
Eastman, Andrew. "'Hearing Things': Voice and Rhyme in the Poems of Elizabeth Bishop," in *Elizabeth Bishop and the Music of Literature* (London: Palgrave Macmillan, 2019), 41–50.
Goldensohn, Lorrie. "Approaching Elizabeth Bishop's Letters to Ruth Foster," *Yale Review* 103.1 (January 2015), 1–19.
Rosenbaum, Susan. "Bishop and the Natural World," in *The Cambridge Companion to Elizabeth Bishop*, ed. Angus Cleghorn and Jonathan Ellis (Cambridge: Cambridge University Press, 2014), 62–78.
Sheehan, Fiona. "'Affectionately Yours, Bishop': The Early Correspondence of Elizabeth Bishop and Rhoda Wheeler Sheehan," *Resources for American Literary Study* 40 (2018), 242.
Tanaka, Yuki. "The Rhythm of Syntax in 'At the Fishhouses,'" in *Elizabeth Bishop and the Music of Literature* (Cham, Switzerland: Palgrave Macmillan, 2019) 31–40.
Treseler, Heather. "One Long Poem," Boston Review (August 17, 2016). Web.
Wordsworth, William. *"The Tables Turned," Selected Poetry* (Oxford: Oxford University Press, 1998).

31 Animals

Bishop, Elizabeth. *Conversations with Elizabeth Bishop*, ed. George Monteiro (Jackson: University Press of Mississippi, 1996).
Costello, Bonnie. *Elizabeth Bishop: Questions of Mastery* (Cambridge, MA: Harvard University Press, 1993).
DeMello, Margo. *Animals and Society: An Introduction to Human-Animal Studies* (New York: Columbia University Press, 2012).
Goldensohn, Lorrie. *Elizabeth Bishop: The Biography of a Poetry* (New York: Columbia University Press, 1992).
Harrison, Victoria. *Elizabeth Bishop's Poetics of Intimacy* (Cambridge: Cambridge University Press, 1993).
Kennedy, Sarah. "'Swerving as I Swerve': Elizabeth Bishop's Fugitive Empathy," in *Reading Elizabeth Bishop: An Edinburgh Companion*, ed. Jonathan Ellis (Edinburgh: Edinburgh University Press, 2019), 117–31.

Knickerbocker, Scott. *Ecopoetics: The Language of Nature, the Nature of Language* (Amherst: University of Massachusetts Press, 2012).
Ostriker, Alicia. *Stealing the Language: The Emergence of Women's Poetry in America* (London: The Women's Press, 1987).
Phillips, Siobhan. *The Poetics of the Everyday: Creative Repetition in Modern American Verse* (New York: Columbia University Press, 2010).
Ravinthiran, Vidyan. *Elizabeth Bishop's Prosaic* (Lewisburg: Bucknell University Press, 2015).
Rotella, Guy. *Reading and Writing Nature: The Poetry of Robert Frost, Wallace Stevens, Marianne Moore, and Elizabeth Bishop* (Boston: Northeastern University Press, 1991).
Stevenson, Anne. *Five Looks at Elizabeth Bishop* (Tarset: Bloodaxe Books, 2006).
Tóibín, Colm. *On Elizabeth Bishop* (Princeton: Princeton University Press, 2015).
Xiaojing, Zhou. "'The oblique, the indirect approach': Elizabeth Bishop's 'Rainy Season; Sub-Tropics,'" *Chicago Review* 40.4 (1994), 75–92.
Zona, Kirsten Hotelling. *Marianne Moore, Elizabeth Bishop, and May Swenson: The Feminist Poetics of Self-Restraint* (Ann Arbor: University of Michigan Press, 2002)

32 Bishop Studies

Anderson, Linda, and Jo Shapcott, eds. *Elizabeth Bishop: Poet of the Periphery* (Hexham: Bloodaxe Books, 2002).
Barry, Sandra, Gwendolyn Davies, and Peter Sanger, eds. *Divisions of the Heart: Elizabeth Bishop and the Art of Memory and Place* (Kentville: Gaspereau Press, 2001).
Cleghorn, Angus, and Jonathan Ellis, eds. *The Cambridge Companion to Elizabeth Bishop* (New York: Cambridge University Press, 2014).
Cleghorn, Angus, Bethany Hicok, and Thomas Travisano, *Elizabeth Bishop in the 21st Century: Reading the New Editions* (Charlottesville and London: University Press of Virginia, 2012).
Costello, Bonnie. *Elizabeth Bishop: Questions of Mastery* (Cambridge, MA: Harvard University Press, 1991).
Diehl, Joanne Feit. *Elizabeth Bishop and Marianne Moore: The Psychodynamics of Creativity* (Princeton, NJ: Princeton University Press, 1993).
Doreski, Carole. *Elizabeth Bishop: The Restraints of Language* (Oxford: Oxford University Press, 1993).
Elizabeth Bishop Bulletin. Web.
Ellis, Jonathan, *Letter Writing Among Poets: From William Wordsworth to Elizabeth Bishop* (Edinburgh, Edinburgh University Press, 2015).
ed. *Reading Elizabeth Bishop: An Edinburgh Companion* (Edinburgh: Edinburgh University Press, 2019).
Fountain, Gary, and Peter Brazeau. *Remembering Elizabeth Bishop: An Oral Biography* (University of Massachusetts Press, 1994).

Ferguson, Suzanne, ed. *Jarrell, Bishop, Lowell & Co.* (University of Tennessee Press, 2003).
Goldensohn, Lorrie. *Elizabeth Bishop: The Biography of a Poetry* (New York: Columbia University Press, 1992).
"Elizabeth Bishop: An Unpublished, Untitled Poem." *American Poetry Review* (January/February 1988), 35–36.
Harrison, Victoria. *Elizabeth Bishop's Poetics of Intimacy* (New York: Cambridge University Press, 1992).
Hicok, Bethany, ed. *Elizabeth Bishop and the Literary Archive* (Lever Press, 2020).
Kelly, Lionel, ed. *Poetry and the Sense of Panic: Critical Essays on Elizabeth Bishop and John Ashbery* (Amsterdam; Atlanta, GA: Rodopi, 2000).
Lombardi, Marilyn May, ed. *Elizabeth Bishop: Geography of Gender* (Charlottesville: University Press of Virginia, 1993).
Kalstone, David. *Five Temperaments: Elizabeth Bishop, Robert Lowell, James Merrill, Adrienne Rich, John Ashbery* (Oxford: Oxford University Press, 1977).
MacMahon, Candace. *Elizabeth Bishop: A Bibliography, 1927–1979* (Charlottesville: University Press of Virginia, 1980).
Millier, Brett C. *Elizabeth Bishop: Life and the Memory of It* (Berkeley: University of California Press, 1993).
Menides, Laura Jehn, and Angela Dorenkamp, eds. "*In Worcester, Massachusetts*": *Essays from the 1997 Elizabeth Bishop Conference* (Worcester: WPI Studies, 1999).
Parker, Robert Dale. *Elizabeth Bishop: The Unbeliever* (Champaign: University of Illinois Press, 1988).
Schwartz, Lloyd. "Annals of Poetry: Elizabeth Bishop and Brazil," *The New Yorker* (September 30, 1991), 85–97.
Schwartz, Lloyd, and Sybil P. Estess, eds. *Elizabeth Bishop and Her Art* (Ann Arbor: University of Michigan Press, 1983).
Travisano, Thomas. *Elizabeth Bishop: Her Artistic Development* (Charlottesville and London: University Press of Virginia, 1988).
"Emerging Genius: Elizabeth Bishop and *The Blue Pencil*, 1927–1930," *Gettysburg Review* 5.1 (Winter 1992), 32–47.
"'With an Eye of Flemish Accuracy': An Afterword," *Georgia Review* 46.4 (Winter 1992), 612–16.

33 Criticism and Reviews

Anderson, Linda. *Elizabeth Bishop: Lines of Connection* (Edinburgh: Edinburgh University Press, 2013).
Gunn, Thom. "Out of the Box," in *Shelf Life* (London: Faber and Faber, 1994), 77–86.
Millier, Brett C. *Elizabeth Bishop: Life and the Memory of It* (Berkeley: University of California Press, 1993).
Monteiro, George, ed. *Conversations with Elizabeth Bishop* (Jackson: University Press of Mississippi, 1996), 92.

O'Neill, Michael. "'Thinking with One's Feelings': Elizabeth Bishop's Literary Criticism," in *Reading Elizabeth Bishop: An Edinburgh Companion*, ed. Jonathan Ellis (Edinburgh: Edinburgh University Press, 2019), 237–49.

Ravinthiran, Vidyan. *Elizabeth Bishop's Prosaic* (Lewisburg: Bucknell University Press, 2015).

Samuels, Peggy. *Deep Skin: Elizabeth Bishop and Visual Art* (Ithaca: Cornell University Press, 2010).

Schwartz, Lloyd, and Sybil P. Estess, eds. *Elizabeth Bishop and Her Art* (Ann Arbor: The University of Michigan Press, 1983).

34 Publishing Bishop

Bishop, Elizabeth. *Poems, Prose, and Letters*, ed. Robert Giroux and Lloyd Schwartz (New York: Library of America, 2008).

Prose, ed. Lloyd Schwartz (London: Chatto & Windus; New York: Farrar, Straus and Giroux, 2011).

Bosch, Daniel. "Poetry, Prose, and Politics—Elizabeth Bishop at 100," *The Arts Fuse*, March 3, 2011. Web.

Schwartz, Lloyd. "Annals of Poetry: Elizabeth Bishop and Brazil," *The New Yorker* (September 30, 1991), 85–97.

Schwartz, Lloyd, and Sybil P. Estess, eds. *Elizabeth Bishop and Her Art* (Ann Arbor: The University of Michigan Press, 1983).

35 Bishop's Influence

Baker, David. *Swift: New and Selected Poems* (New York: Norton, 2018).

Burt, Stephanie. "Elizabeth Bishop at the End of the Rainbow," in *Reading Elizabeth Bishop: An Edinburgh Companion*, ed. Jonathan Ellis (Edinburgh: Edinburgh University Press, 2019), 321–36.

Colby, Kate. *Dream of the Trenches* (Blacksburg, VA: Noemi, 2019).

Farmer, Jonathan. *That Peculiar Affirmative: On the Social Life of Poems* (Nacogdoches, TX: Stephen F. Austin State University Press, 2019).

Ford, Julian, and Christine Courtois. "Complex PTSD, affective dysregulation, and borderline personality disorder," *Borderline Personality Disorder and Emotional Dysregulation* 1.9 (2014), www.ncbi.nlm.nih.gov/pmc/articles/PMC4579513.

Hejinian, Lyn. *Positions of the Sun* (Brooklyn: Belladonna, 2017).

Longenbach, James. *Modern Poetry after Modernism* (New York and Oxford: Oxford University Press, 1997).

McCrae, Shane. *In the Language of My Captor* (Middletown, CT: Wesleyan University Press, 2017).

McLane, Maureen. *My Poets* (New York: Farrar, Straus and Giroux, 2012).

Monte, Steven. *Invisible Fences: Prose Poetry as a Genre in French and American Literature* (Lincoln, NE: University of Nebraska Press, 2000).

Morrissey, Patrick. *World Music* (Chicago: Verge, 2017).

Noel-Tod, Jeremy. "Logbook: Against Prose," *Critical Quarterly* 59.2 (2017), 55–64.

Rankine, Claudia. *Citizen: An American Lyric* (Minneapolis: Graywolf, 2014).

Rekdal, Paisley. *Imaginary Vessels* (Port Townsend, WA: Copper Canyon, 2016).

Samuels, Peggy. *Deep Skin: Elizabeth Bishop and Visual Art* (Ithaca: Cornell University Press, 2010).

Shore, Jane. "Elizabeth Bishop: The Art of Changing Your Mind," *Ploughshares* 5.1 (1979), 178–91.

Spiegelman, Willard. "Kay Ryan's Delicate Strength," *Virginia Quarterly Review* 88.3 (2012), 159–68.

Stallings, Andy. *Paradise* (Iowa City: Rescue, 2017).

Toussaint, Steven. "TMI: An Essay on Contemporary Poetry in Aotearoa/New Zealand," *The Spinoff* (April 27, 2019) thespinoff.co.nz/books/27–04-2019/tmi-an-essay-on-contemporary-poetry-in-aotearoa-new-zealand.

Vendler, Helen. "Comic and Elegiac," *The New Yorker* (April 8, 1996), 101–103.

Lange, Wolf-Gero, Mike Rinck, and Eni S. Becker. "Behavioral Deviations: Surface Features of Social Anxiety and What They Reveal," in *The Wiley-Blackwell Handbook of Social Anxiety Disorder*, ed. Justin Weeks (Oxford: Blackwell, 2014), 355–64.

Young, Kevin. *For the Confederate Dead* (New York: Knopf, 2007).

Index

Lightning Source UK Ltd.
Milton Keynes UK
UKHW022221140921
390601UK00005B/95

9 781108 495974